Records and Information Management

Records and Information Management

SECOND EDITION

Patricia C. Franks

ALA Neal-Schuman

CHICAGO :: 2018

© 2018 by the American Library Association

Extensive effort has gone into ensuring the reliability of the information in this book; however, the publisher makes no warranty, express or implied, with respect to the material contained herein.

ISBNs
978-0-8389-1716-9 (paper)
978-0-8389-1757-2 (PDF)
978-0-8389-1756-5 (ePub)
978-0-8389-1758-9 (Kindle)

Library of Congress Cataloging in Publication Control Number: 2018010393

Cover design by Alejandra Diaz; imagery © Adobe Stock. Text design and composition by Karen Sheets de Gracia in the Cardea and Acumin Pro typefaces.

♾ This paper meets the requirements of ANSI/NISO Z39.48–1992 (Permanence of Paper).

Printed in the United States of America
22 21 20 19 18   5 4 3 2 1

ALA Neal-Schuman purchases fund advocacy, awareness, and accreditation programs for library professionals worldwide.

To Jerry, my husband and best friend.

CONTENTS

ILLUSTRATIONS

FIGURES

TABLES

ACKNOWLEDGMENTS

Writing the first edition of *Records and Information Management* was a joy and a challenge. Writing the second edition was as rewarding but even more challenging due to the expanding information landscape, the advances in technology, and the growing expectations that records and information professionals be both specialists in their fields and generalists when it comes to related fields.

I am sincerely grateful for the number of individuals who responded to my request for comments on the first edition and suggestions for the second. Although it was not possible to include every topic suggested in this one work, those suggestions did result in the inclusion of two additional chapters and numerous other changes.

Any errors in this book are mine alone, but any of the improvements you find useful are the result of the many individuals who shared their time and expertise. These individuals include but are not limited to:

- Mark Driskill, Freelance Writer/Researcher and MARA graduate. Mark provided invaluable assistance by editing each of the chapters, formatting the notes sections, and developing the bibliography and glossary of terms.

- Anna Maloney, a MARA graduate currently working in Records and Information Management in the financial services industry. Anna took the time to critique each chapter of the first edition and provide suggestions from a student's perspective.

- James Tammaro, Adjunct Professor, State University of New York at Buffalo. Jim not only provided suggestions for improvement but also expressed his desire for teaching materials. In response to his request, PowerPoint slides are available for this edition.

- In addition, special thanks go to a number of faculty from various universities who are familiar with the first edition and took the time to respond to a questionnaire about the usefulness of the content, including:

  ○ Alexis Antracoli, Drexel University
  ○ Jason Kaltenbacher, San José State University
  ○ Janice M. Krueger, Clarion University of Pennsylvania
  ○ Eun Park, McGill University
  ○ Catherine Stollar Peters, University at Albany, State University of New York
  ○ Christina Reedy, University of North Texas.

INTRODUCTION

In introducing the first edition of *Records and Information Management,* I asked,

> With all of the hype about social media, cloud computing, digital preservation, electronic records, big data, and the concept of information governance to tame the resulting chaos, why would anyone publish another book with a title as unpretentious as *Records and Information Management?*

Again, the answer is that the discipline of records management, which includes a responsibility to manage all information, is fundamental to every information governance program.

Since the first edition was published in 2013, much has changed—but much remains the same. Among the changes are the growth of the Internet of Things; the extreme volume and variety of data produced at a velocity hereto unmatched; the increased necessity of employing technology to categorize, analyze, and make use of the data; the recognition of the value of information assets; and the emergence of new business models that leverage the power of algorithms to manipulate data.

What has not changed since prehistoric times is our desire and need to create, capture, control, make use of, preserve—and at times destroy—records that document our personal and work lives. Advances in technology to facilitate the creation and management of records continue to introduce challenges that require technological solutions to resolve. Increasingly those solutions are offered by third-party cloud providers. In addition to employing machine learning and artificial intelligence to analyze data, vendors are offering blockchain technology to generate proof that records are authentic, verifiable, and possess integrity.

The terms *recordkeeper, records manager, records and information manager,* and *records professional* are used interchangeably in this edition to describe those who have recordkeeping responsibilities, including archivists, records managers, and information managers, regardless of their job title (e.g., digital archivist, knowledge management advisor, information governance specialist).

The breadth of knowledge expected of the successful records professional continues to expand. It now includes the need to better understand not only the business process but also the goals of the organization from a business perspective. In addition to the domain of records and information management, records professionals must master the fundamentals from related fields, including compliance, data governance, risk management, change management, and project management. This book, therefore, differs from traditional records management works by placing equal emphasis on the business operations from which records arise and the ways in which the records professional can contribute to the core mission of the enterprise beyond the lifecycle management of records.

ABOUT THIS BOOK

Seventeen individuals contributed their expertise to the conversation in the form of either perspectives (reflections) or paradigms (case studies) that are provided at the end of each chapter. The guest authors include archivists, records managers, and information gover-nance professionals from the United States, Canada, and the United Kingdom.

Chapter 1 provides the reader with a glimpse of the path recordkeeping and record-keepers have taken from prehistoric times to the present. Barclay Blair, founder and exec-utive director of the *Information Governance Initiative*, reflects on the evolution of records and information management and its role in information governance. He emphasizes the pressing need to manage information as you would manage a business.

Chapter 2 expands upon the topic of building an information governance framework of policies, processes, and compliance upon strong records and information management principles. This chapter introduces laws, regulations, and standards that impact records and information management programs for both government and private organizations in the United States and abroad. Robert Smallwood, Managing Director of the *Institute for Information Governance*, discusses the consequences of carelessness with records and infor-mation in the healthcare industry and the imperative for information governance initia-tives to drastically reduce medical mistakes.

Chapter 3 introduces the reader to records creation, capture, classification, and file plan development that result from business activities conducted using some of the many systems, components, networks, and applications employed by users at home and at work. Peg Eusch, University Records Officer for the University of Wisconsin–Madison, describes how a presentation she attended on File Plan Development provided the impetus for re-vamping the university's records management training program around the integration of records management file plan elements with the Generally Accepted Recordkeeping Prin-ciples framework.

Chapter 4 presents records retention strategies useful to those organizations that stress the role of retention and disposition in the overall information governance approach. In her contribution to this chapter, Susan Cisco, information governance subject matter expert and educator, describes how a new retention schedule was used to launch an information governance program for a consolidated entity that emerged as the result of the merger of two firms.

Chapter 5 describes ways in which records and information managers can contribute their expertise during the active phase of the information lifecycle to decisions being made about workflow processes, access controls, storage systems, metadata, and the search and retrieval processes. In her contribution to chapter 5, Charlene Cunniffe, Associate Direc-tor, Information and Records Management, uses a case study approach to illustrate the application of Lean Continuous Improvement practices to a real-world situation: records management programs and practices.

Chapter 6 describes systems of record and systems of engagement as well as the vi-tal role records professionals play in identifying records in both types of systems and in providing guidance to those responsible for capturing and managing them. Morgan King, Director and Head of Records and Information Management, and Stephen Aaronson, Di-rector and Head of IT Legal, explain how they work as a team to implement a full-service ERMS (electric records management system) at a leading global biotechnology company.

Chapter 7 explores the ways in which records and information managers are managing social media records, including those of the first social media president, Barack Obama. It introduces emerging technologies such as autonomous vehicles, Internet of Things plat-forms, and augmented reality and considers the impact they will have on recordkeeping in the future. The chapter presents two methods that can be used to prepare for the inevitable changes to take place: diffusion of innovation and trend spotting. In her paradigm, Vicki L.

Lemieux, Associate Professor of Archival Science at the University of British Columbia, describes blockchain technology and the ways in which it is beginning to impact recordkeeping. She presents a series of questions for consideration when determining if blockchain technology is the right direction for the organization to take.

Chapter 8 covers business resumption, which depends upon vital (essential) records protection, disaster preparedness and recovery programs, and business continuity plans. It also introduces two cloud-based options to assist an organization's recovery after a natural or man-made disaster—Backup as a Service (BaaS) and Disaster Recovery as a Service (DRaaS). In her contribution to this chapter, Helen Nelson of the Wirral Teaching Hospital, NHS Foundation Trust, reminds us that not all incidents are catastrophic or long-lived but need to be managed regardless. Readers will be reminded that there are times when our electronic devices fail and we must resort to paper-based solutions for at least some of our work.

Chapter 9 presents several methods of monitoring and auditing records and information management programs. Risk assessment—which includes risk identification, risk analysis, and risk evaluation—is explored. Lisa Daulby, Lecturer, School of Information at San José University, describes a unique approach to identifying, assessing, and controlling records and information management risks by combining risk management methodologies, the Generally Accepted Recordkeeping Principles and the five levels of the Information Governance Maturity Model.

Chapter 10, "Information Economics, Privacy and Security," is introduced in this edition of *Records and Information Management* in response to the growing recognition that information assets have economic significance. As with physical assets and other intangible assets already recognized by the Generally Accepted Accounting Principles (e.g., patents and goodwill), information assets should be appraised, protected, and utilized to assist the organization to achieve its goals. Ilona Koti, ARMA International President 2017–2018, provides her views on the integration of information governance into the privacy and security landscape.

Chapter 11 covers the topic of inactive records management within records centers and archives, with a heavy emphasis on physical holdings. In her contribution to this chapter, Lori Lindberg, Archivist and Consultant, provides an archivist's view of the relationship between sound records management principles and practices and the archival work involved to create a company archives for the Jelly Belly Candy Company.

Chapter 12, "Long-Term Digital Preservation and Trusted Digital Repositories," is the second new chapter in this work. It was created by combining information on long-term digital preservation from the first edition's chapter on inactive records management with an overview of trusted digital repositories. Two case studies complete this chapter. The first, by Lori Ashley, Principal, Tournesol Consulting, LLC, and Patricia Morris, President and Chief Process Consultant, eArchive Science, LLC, introduces us to the approach taken to use a popular commercial service to establish an eArchive for Pharmaceutical Pre-Clinical Research Study Information. The second, by Amber D'Ambrosio, Processing Archivist and Records Manager, Willamette University Archives and Special Collections, documents a practical open-source solution for institutions with limited financial resources.

Chapter 13 presents the reader with a variety of options for records and information management education and training, including degree programs, professional development opportunities, and in-house training programs. In the United States, there is often a divide between archives and records management both in the workplace and when it comes to professional associations and certifications. In recognition of the value archival studies programs offer the records and information management profession, the ARMA International Education Foundation (AIEF) presented its first Award for Excellence in Education to the Master of Archival Studies (MAS) program at the University of British Columbia (UBC), Canada. In her contribution to this chapter Luciana Duranti, Professor, School of Library, Archival and Information Studies at UBC, describes the MAS curriculum.

Chapter 14 explains how the information shared in chapters 2 through 13 can be used to develop a legally defensible records management program and an effective information governance strategy. In her contribution to this chapter, Diane Carlisle, Director of Professional Development for ARMA International, provides her perspective on information governance and tools available to help the organization more effectively manage its information assets.

This book is suitable for records professionals at any stage of their careers. Those wishing to learn all they can about records and information management would profit from reading all of the chapters. However, the book is also intended for experienced professionals who would benefit from a reference book that brings together a variety of topics—including archives, records and information management, information governance, information economics, privacy and security, digital preservation, and more. When necessary, important ideas or definitions are included in more than one chapter so that the chapters can be read independently.

Increasingly, organizations are forming information governance committees comprised of stakeholders from records management, information technology, legal, compliance, and business units, among others. Their task is to develop strategic information governance policies and programs. The glossary included at the end of this book will provide a basic vocabulary that should prove useful to members of these new information governance teams.

CHAPTER 1

The Origins and Development of Records and Information Management

INTRODUCTION

From the days of the early cave dwellers who painted symbols onto stone walls through today when social media-savvy citizens post their own digital messages on Facebook time lines, three factors remain constant: human beings are compelled to record their experiences, using the tools and technologies available to them, with the intent to share that information with others. Before we can develop a strategic approach to records and information management for today and tomorrow, we should look to the past at the custom of recordkeeping and the conventions that developed around it. As Shakespeare wrote in *The Tempest* and the US government has carved on the National Archives Building in Washington, DC, "What's past is prologue."[1]

RECORDS AND RECORDKEEPING IN SOCIETY

Long before the invention of the alphabet and the written word, stories and sagas were shared by those who mastered the skill of rote memorization. Memory aids were used, especially as evidence of an activity. A brief glimpse at recordkeeping practices from 15,000 BCE to the present day demonstrates that no matter how much civilization develops, our desire to remember and document remains the same.

Recordkeeping and Ancient Civilizations

Between 15,000 and 13,000 BCE, human beings documented the animals involved in their hunt for food through mural paintings on the walls of caves found in the "sole region of Paleolithic mural paintings" in Europe.[2] Abbe Breuil, an explorer and scientist who studied the paintings on the walls of the caverns of Lascaux, describes the caves not as dwellings for humans but as "places [that] could have served only as specially chosen repositories for the secrets of a civilization."[3]

Tangible and portable memory aids were needed to document transactions. In Mesopotamia as far back as 8000 BCE, plain clay tokens were utilized for recordkeeping, probably to count agricultural items such as grain or cereal. By 4000 BCE, tokens decorated with markings thought to record manufactured goods appeared in settlements in southern Mesopotamia. Similar tokens were used to record animals, with wedge-like shapes engraved into the clay to represent quantity followed by a sign that indicated the type of animal.[4] This method of recordkeeping is considered the precursor to the cuneiform writing system created by the Sumerians. The evolution of recordkeeping from tokens to the written word is illustrated in figure 1.1.

By 3200 BCE, hieroglyphics were developed in Egypt by a people who saw literacy as the most valued skill. Recordkeeping was used for commercial and religious purposes. Records of land holdings, crop yields, and taxes were made. Religious texts were written and copied by scribes in temples and were inscribed on funerary equipment and papyrus.

As writing skills became more widespread, the volume of information to be organized and stored grew. The archives of Ebla (modern Tell Mardikh, Syria) ultimately contained an estimated 20,000 clay tablets written in Sumerian script that dated from approximately 2250 BCE.[5] The archives are believed to have been a repository for records about economic matters, such as accounts of the state revenues, but they also contained royal letters, law cases, and diplomatic and trade contracts—all organized on shelves according to subject. The information contained in these tablets provided a glimpse into the everyday lives of the citizens of Ebla.

Papyrus scrolls were used as a recording medium throughout the known world until circa 170 BCE when Egypt cut off its supply of papyrus to Pergamum, an ancient Greek city located in Anatolia (now modern Turkish town of Bergama). In response, the people of Pergamum produced parchment made out of a thin sheet of sheepskin or goatskin. This innovative recording medium allowed for increased information to be recorded and its use spread throughout Europe and Asia.[6]

Recordkeeping: First Millennium through the Early Twentieth Century

The second century CE brought with it the development of a papermaking process in China by Ts'ai Lun, known to the Chinese as the patron saint of papermaking.[7] The paper was thin, strong, and flexible. In the third century, the secret art of papermaking made its way to Vietnam and Tibet. Over the next several centuries, it spread to the rest of the civilized world. By the ninth century, papyrus had been replaced by parchment in Europe. Paper was not used as a practical medium in Europe until Johann Gutenberg perfected moveable type and printed the Gutenberg Bible in 1456. This sparked a revolution in mass communication and ushered in the age of modern paper and the printing industry.

Just as we're experiencing today, past advancements in technologies and tools required new, often bureaucratic, solutions to managing records, such as:

- The fourteenth century saw the first office of the clerk of the rolls, register, and council, later known as the Lord Clerk Register, appear in Scotland. This office assumed responsibility for keeping the national archives.[8]
- The town clerk of the city of London was made responsible for the safekeeping of the city corporation's records in 1462.[9]
- In 1540, the Emperor Charles V transferred his most important records to a tower in the castle of Simancas in Spain, and Jacob von Rammingen, considered the father of archival science, wrote the manuscript of the

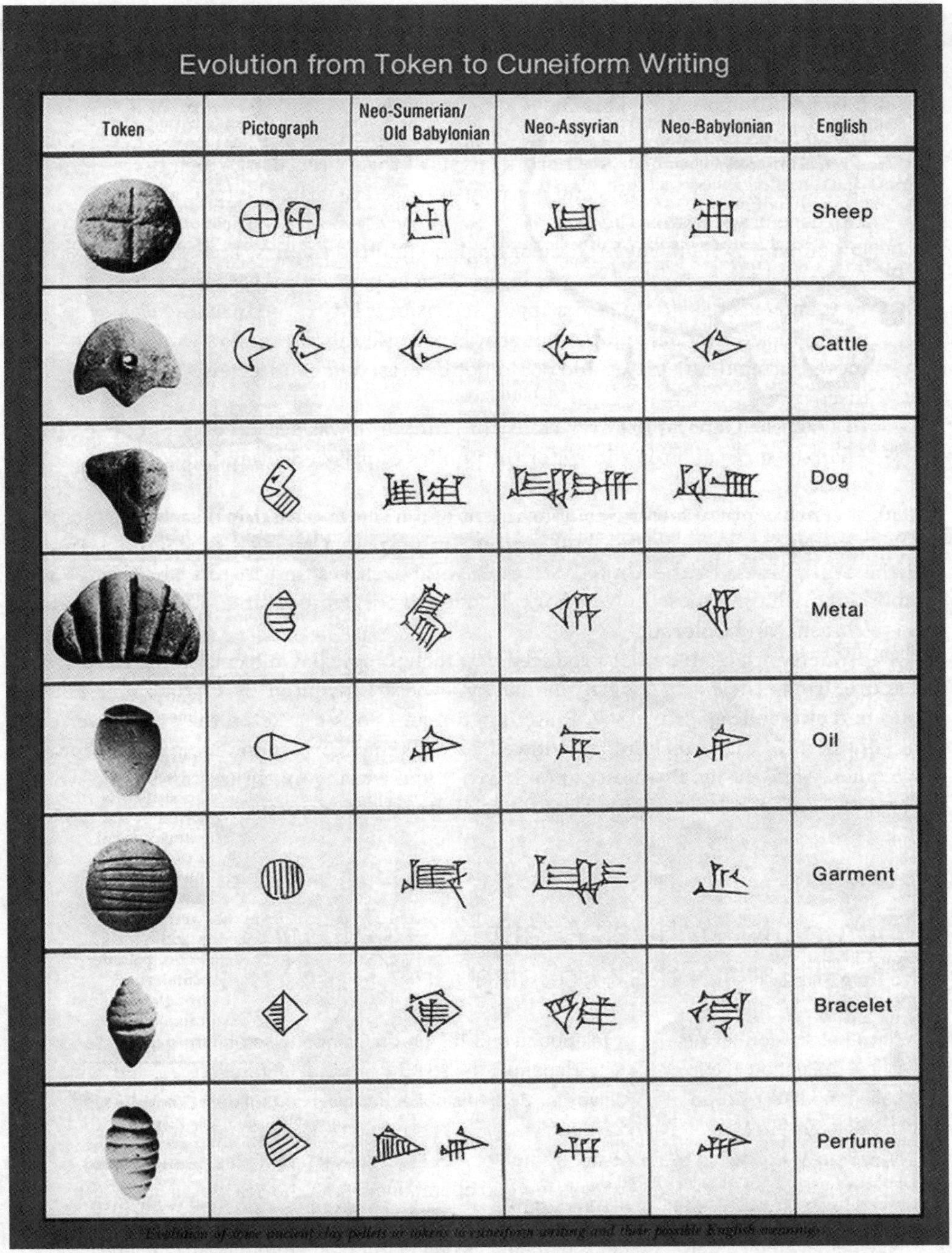
Evolution from Token to Cuneiform Writing
Token
Pictograph
Neo-Sumerian/ Old Babylonian
Neo-Assyrian
Neo-Babylonian
English
Sheep
Cattle
Dog
Metal
Oil
Garment
Bracelet
Perfume

FIGURE 1.1 Engraved clay tokens, evolution to cuneiform writing, and English equivalent.

SOURCE: Denise Schmandt-Besserat, "Reckoning Before Writing," Escola Finalay, accessed September 27, 2017, http://en.finaly.org/index.php/Reckoning_before_writing. ©Denise Schmandt-Besserat, licensed under the Creative Commons Attribution-ShareAlike 3.0 Unported License.

earliest known archival manual. Rammingen's archival manual was printed in Germany along with a more detailed book on the same subject in 1571.[10]

- In 1681, Jean Mabillon, a Benedictine monk, published De Re Diplomatica (Study of Documents). This six-volume treatise produced the name of a new science—diplomatics—that attempts to establish the provenance of a written text through systematic analysis of the material on which the text is written, the scripts and penmanship used to write the text, and the language usage within the text.[11]
- On January 7, 1714, Queen Anne of England granted the first known patent for a machine or method for the impressing or transcribing of letters "so neat and exact as not to be distinguished from print."[12] The machine was useful in settlements and public records because the impression would be more lasting than writing and could not be erased or counterfeited without discovery.
- In 1772, the General Register House in Edinburgh was designed by Robert Adam to serve as a repository for the public records of Scotland.[13]

The nineteenth century saw the establishment of a number of national archives, including those in the Netherlands, Portugal, Argentina, Italy, Spain, Canada, France, India, Ireland, and the Philippines. In the United States, several archives and historical societies were established, including those in New York, Rhode Island, Pennsylvania, Indiana, Maryland, Iowa, Nebraska, and Colorado.

The nineteenth century also produced new technology that automated the task of writing and editing—the first modern manual typewriter, invented by Christopher Latham Sholes and two colleagues in 1867. E. Remington and Sons marketed the typewriter commercially in 1874. This technology allowed records and correspondence to be produced more quickly and easily. Businesses purchased "type writing machines" and hired women as "typewriters" at salaries higher than for schoolteachers or nurses.

Corporate Archives Adapt to Capture and Preserve the History of the Organization

In 1922, the former American Telephone and Telegraph Company established its Historical Collection in New York City. Renamed the AT&T Historical Library in 1933, and later called the AT&T Corporate Archives in 1982, this collection was consolidated in 1987 with the Bell System Museum and the archives of Bell Labs and Western Electric, in Warren, New Jersey. Following the 2005 acquisition of AT&T Corporation by Texas-based SBC Communications, the AT&T Archives merged operationally with the SBC Archives to form the AT&T Archives and History Center with two locations: San Antonio, Texas, and Warren, New Jersey. Total archival holdings of materials dating from 1869 through 2017 include 45,000 cubic feet of books, periodicals, photographs, moving images, sound recordings, and microforms as well as 15,000 three-dimensional objects.

SOURCE: Courtesy of the AT&T Archives and History Center.

The population grew so rapidly in the United States that the 1880 census took seven and one-half years to complete. In a search for a method to streamline the process, the US Census Bureau offered a prize for an inventor to help with the 1890 census. The winner, Herman Hollerith, used Joseph Marie Jacquard's punched cards for the computation. The 1890 census was completed in three years and saved the government five million dollars. Hollerith built a company that would eventually become International Business Machines (IBM).

In 1893, an invention to organize and store the increasing volume of paperwork was unveiled at the Columbian Exposition in Chicago, Illinois—the filing cabinet. In 1897, the Library of Congress established its Manuscript Division with a staff of four and a collection of 25,000 items.

The first decades of the twentieth century ushered in additional state and national archives, along with the first of many laws and regulations designed to protect official records. In 1903, the State Library of Western Australia was authorized to accept official records, and the Archives of Ontario, Canada, was founded. On December 15, 1909, H.R. 15428 was introduced to create a Commission on National Historic Publications in the United States. In 1911, the British Royal Archives was established in Windsor Castle in England. In 1922, Sir Hilary Jenkinson's book, *A Manual of Archive Administration,* was published. Also in 1922, the former American Telephone and Telegraph Company established its Historical Collection in New York City. In 1925, South Australia passed an act to regulate the disposal of government records.

RECORDKEEPING IN THE UNITED STATES IN THE TWENTIETH CENTURY

The federal government was the primary driver for records management in the United States. Major technological innovations and unforeseen challenges emerged to which government and industry were required to respond.

Ground was broken for the US National Archives building in 1931; its cornerstone was laid in February 1933. In 1934, Congress established the National Archives to centralize federal recordkeeping, President Franklin D. Roosevelt signed the legislation creating the National Archives, and Robert D. W. Connor was appointed first Archivist of the United States.

In 1935, Emmett Leahy joined the staff of the National Archives. His first assignment was to form a committee of special examiners to analyze the records presented to the Archivist that were without "permanent value or historical interest" and to decide whether the records should be destroyed or otherwise disposed of.[14]

By 1937, as the initial survey of federal government records neared completion, the committee realized the enormity of the records problem it was facing due to a lack of conformity in procedures, unprecedented growth in volume of documents requiring management and storage, and the number of duplicate records retained across all agencies.

The National Archives initiated a records management program to segregate records of temporary value from those that had archival value. A key component of the program was the records lifecycle model developed by Leahy that controlled the creation, use, and disposition of records either by destruction or transfer to the National Archives.

The Society of American Archivists (SAA) was founded in 1936 with A. R. Newsome, a North Carolina historian, as its first president. Theodore C. Pease was appointed the first editor of the SAA journal, *The American Archivist,* in 1939.

During the summer of 1940, tired of being misquoted, President Roosevelt had a recording machine installed under the Oval Office, which he sometimes turned on before press conferences and turned off after capturing conversations. The device was also connected to his telephone. Digital copies of these original recordings reside alongside images, movies, and other radio addresses in the FDR Presidential Library and Museum in Hyde Park, New York.

New US agencies and departments were established during World War II, and, not surprisingly, the volume of documents grew as well. The scheduling of records for disposition was given legal status by the Records Disposal Act of 1943, which defined records and authorized the National Archives Council to develop procedures to dispose of records no longer needed as well as to reproduce permanent records on microfilm so that the originals could be disposed of. The Act was amended in 1945 to include the government-wide General Schedule (GS), which authorized the systematic disposal of government records.

In 1950, the Federal Records Act codified a series of laws—including prior legislation from the late 1930s and 1940s—in 44 United States Code (U.S.C.) sections 21, 23, 25, 27, 29, 31, and 33. The Federal Records Act set forth records management policies and practices of agencies within the federal government and established the National Archives and Records Administration (NARA) with the mandate and the responsibility to preserve records of permanent historical value to the United States.[15] In 1955, the first *Guide to Records Retention Requirements* was published.[16]

In addition to contributions to the National Archives, Emmett J. Leahy was central to the emergence of the commercial records center (CRC) industry. In 1948, he became the first executive director of the National Records Management Council and formed the Business Archives Center, thought to be the first CRC in the United States. During the 1950s and 1960s, CRCs continued to emerge in large metropolitan areas, including New York and Philadelphia, primarily to store inactive records for large corporations and organizations.

By the 1960s, the original US National Archives building on Constitution Avenue in Washington, DC, was out of room, forcing expansion to a new site. Most of the federal documents are now housed in Archives II, a 2-million-cubic-foot building in College Park, Maryland, dedicated in 1994 that can accommodate 400 researchers.

Like President Roosevelt, Presidents Harry S. Truman and Dwight D. Eisenhower recorded conversations, but President John F. Kennedy installed the White House's first secret recording network to protect himself against officials who told him one thing in private and said something different in public. A pen and pencil set on his desk turned the network of microphones on and off.

President Richard M. Nixon also employed a secret recording system that was discovered in 1973 as a result of the Watergate scandal. During the 1972 presidential campaign, five men connected to the Committee for the Re-Election of the President broke into the Democratic National Committee headquarters at the Watergate complex in Washington, DC. During the investigation, it was revealed that President Nixon had a tape-recording system in his office that recorded conversations that implicated the president in a cover-up of the break-in. The president's secretary, Rose Mary Woods, tried to take the blame for an eighteen-minute gap in the tapes that provided evidence that the president was involved in the Watergate break-in (see figure 1.2). The Watergate break-in and subsequent attempts to cover it up resulted in President Nixon's resignation from office in 1974.[17]

After archivists at presidential libraries confirmed that other presidents had secret tapes as well, the US Congress passed the Presidential Records Act in 1978, which established public ownership of records generated by subsequent presidents and their staffs.

FIGURE 1.2 Known as the Rose Mary Stretch, President Richard Nixon's secretary demonstrated how she accidentally hit the pedal beneath her desk that activated the machine that erased eighteen minutes of a taped conversation while talking on the telephone.

SOURCE: *Wikipedia*, accessed September 27, 2017, https://en.wikipedia.org/wiki/Rose_Mary_Woods.

INFORMATION TECHNOLOGY, RECORDS, AND THE INFORMATION AGE

In the United States, records management policies and procedures were implemented and modified over time as a result of an increasing volume of information generated by a growing population using emerging technology. This technology, which would eventually converge, initially followed two discrete paths: (1) computers for data processing and (2) electronic typewriters and word processing equipment for text processing.

Computers for Data Processing

Between 1943 and 1945, two University of Pennsylvania professors, John W. Mauchly and J. Presper Eckert, received funding from the US Department of War to build the first all-electronic digital computer, ENIAC (Electronic Numerical Integrator and Computer). ENIAC was expected to replace all the women who were employed calculating firing tables for the army's artillery guns. ENIAC filled a 20- by 40-foot room, weighed 30 tons, and used more than 18,000 vacuum tubes, which generated so much heat that it had to be housed in a specially designed room with a heavy-duty air conditioning system. The first task assigned by the war department was to determine the feasibility of building a hydrogen bomb.

Later, the US National Bureau of Standards won a contract to build the Universal Automatic Computer (UNIVAC) (see figure 1.3). One of the significant technical features of

FIGURE 1.3 The Remington Rand UNIVAC, 1951. Shown are the operator control board, central processor, and magnetic tape drive units.

SOURCE: Getty Images. Photo by Underwood Archives.

UNIVAC was the use of magnetic tape for mass storage. Due to the high cost, control remained in the hands of the few employees within the agencies using the technology. Reports were printed out to provide information and filed for the record.

Although the term *digital* was first used in 1938 to describe a computer that operates on data in the form of digits, the federal government did not introduce legislation concerning machine-readable materials until 1950 when the US Federal Records Act was expanded to establish the framework for records management in federal agencies.

In 1956, IBM launched the RAMAC 305, the first computer with a hard disk drive (HDD). It weighed over a ton but could store only about 4.4 MB (megabytes) of data. In 1962, the IBM 1311, the first storage unit with removable disks in disk packs, was released. Users could easily switch files for different applications.

In 1975, IBM announced the 5100 Portable Computer for the use of engineers, analysts, statisticians, and other problem solvers. It weighed 50 pounds, was available in twelve models with between 16 K (kilobytes) and 64 K of main storage and offered magnetic tape cartridges that provided more than one hundred routines applicable to math problems, statistical techniques, and financial analyses. This model was withdrawn from the market in March 1982 as more efficient models took its place.

The 5.25-inch floppy disk became the standard removable storage medium in 1978 and remained in use until the early 1990s. Three different options were available that provided from 160 KB to 1.2 MB of storage. In 1984, IBM again changed the way information was

Bits, Bytes, and Other Units of Information

A *bit* is the smallest unit of information stored on a computer in the form of either a 1 or a 0 (meaning on or off). A *byte* is made up of 8 bits and has the ability to represent 256 characters, either numbers or letters.

Computers use binary math (base 2), but the common units used to measure digital information are often simplified by using a digital numbering system. For example, you may see this representation: 1 KB (kilobyte) = 1,000 bytes.

UNIT	EQUIVALENT
1 kilobyte	1,024 bytes
1 megabyte	1,024 kilobytes
1 gigabyte	1,024 megabytes
1 terabyte	1,024 gigabytes
1 petabyte	1,024 terabytes
1 exabyte	1,024 petabytes
1 zettabyte	1,024 exabytes
1 yottabyte	1,024 zettabytes
1 brontobyte	1,024 yottabytes
1 geopbyte	1,024 brontobytes

stored by introducing 3.5-inch floppy disks that provided three options ranging from 720 KB to 2.88 MB of storage. The 3.5-inch disks were widely used in the 1990s but seldom used by the year 2000.

Electronic Typewriters and Word Processors for Text Processing

The first model of the Electromatic typewriter was completed in March 1930, and a new division of IBM, Electromatic Typewriters, was formed in 1933. This product greatly increased typing speeds and the ease with which documents could be created, resulting in the growth of paper records.

In 1961, IBM introduced the Selectric typewriter, which could print faster than previous typewriters because the moveable carriage had been replaced with a revolving type element (ball). The removable element also allowed the operator to select among different type fonts (see figure 1.4).

This was followed in 1964 by IBM's MT/ST (Magnetic Tape/Selectric Typewriter), which combined the features of the Selectric with a magnetic tape drive that could hold one to two pages of text. The text on the magnetic tape could be corrected and reprinted to produce as many copies as desired, and then the tape could be reused for other projects. This was the beginning of word processing technology that eventually would offer additional features at lower costs as more manufacturers entered the market.

IBM introduced the first 8-inch floppy disk in 1971 as an alternative to storage on a hard drive or magnetic tape. The floppy was reusable, portable, and inexpensive, but each disk could store only 80 KB of data initially. In 1973, Vydec was the first manufacturer to produce a word processing system using floppy disks for storage that could hold eighty to one hundred pages of text. These floppy disks were also used to store programs, separating programs from the equipment and encouraging the development of word processing and other programs independent of the hardware. The separation of the program from the

FIGURE 1.4 Removable type element on the Selectric typewriter allowed operators to select among a number of different fonts.

SOURCE: Flickr, accessed September 27, 2017, https://www.flickr.com/photos/teezeh/6089374659/sizes/z/in/
photostream. Courtesy of Thomas Cloer.

hardware marked the beginning of the convergence of word and data processing functions that could be performed by the increasingly popular personal computer introduced by IBM in 1981.

Word processors served as stand-alone office machines through the 1970s and 1980s, in most instances to replace the electric typewriter. As features including display screens and the ability to print to a dot matrix printer were added to personal computers, most business machine companies stopped manufacturing dedicated word processors.[18]

Some scholars assert that the information age, which arguably began with the advent of personal computers in the late 1970s, brought about a transition from a paper-based records environment to a hybrid environment that includes digital records. In spite of claims that we would soon see the paperless office, the ease with which documents could be created, edited, stored, retrieved, and printed resulted in a growth in the volume of paper records.

Electronic Records Bring Additional Challenges

In 1976, Ethernet (a computer network architecture) was developed to provide distributed packet switching for local area networks (LANs). The LANs provided a means for organizations to encourage employees to file documents, spreadsheets, and other work-related files to their private folders or to department folders, where the records could be subject to records management policies. During much of this time, though, printing copies of documents and storing them in file cabinets were standard practice.

As the volume of records grew throughout the 1980s, organizations searching for more efficient means to store and manage information turned to electronic document management systems (EDMSs). In addition to increasing accountability for the organization, EDMSs helped to enforce records management policies and procedures. A major problem with the use of EDMSs was the inability to access information when away from the office, which was increasingly the circumstance encountered by a more mobile workforce. Staff copied information to their laptops for use when out of the office and then uploaded files to the EDMSs when they returned.

Larger organizations that saw a need for connectivity between LANs at different geographic locations developed wide area networks (WANs), often using leased lines, which were quite expensive. By the early 1990s, the internet and the World Wide Web made connectivity possible, and businesses began to expand their own networks using virtual connections instead of leased lines. The demand for solutions to allow access from outside of the organization walls also resulted in virtual private networks (VPNs) provided by Cisco, Check Point, and Microsoft. In reality, VPNs were difficult to use with an EDMS and collaboration was challenging. Enterprising workers used email with file attachments to avoid the use of VPNs when necessary.

In 1990, Tim Berners-Lee created the World Wide Web in order to facilitate sharing and updating information among researchers.[19] By 1994, Jeff Bezos wrote a business plan for Amazon.com, and a new business model was born. Governments, businesses, and individuals came to realize the potential of the Web. Records were created through transactions taking place on websites. Web technology was also used to create intranets to facilitate access to information within the organization and extranets to allow business partners and customers to access information from outside the organization.

Communication Technologies

To this point we've discussed technologies used to record events and transactions, either for use in daily operations or to share information with future generations. However, in 1965 a method was developed for the primary purpose of facilitating communication among colleagues. Communications technologies would eventually be used to produce records that also had to be identified and managed.

Email

Email was introduced at the Massachusetts Institute of Technology (MIT) in 1965. The system called MAILBOX began with the concept of leaving an electronic note in people's directories so they could see it when they logged in.[20] Soon after, Ray Tomlinson, an ARPANET (Advanced Research Projects Agency Network) subcontractor to the US Department of Defense, wrote a program to alert users that they had a message in their directory if they were using dumb terminals to access the same mainframe computer.

When computers became networked, a better system was needed to exchange messages. Tomlinson is also credited with inventing internet-based email in 1971. His contributions included a file transfer protocol to adapt the local SNDMSG mail program to send electronic messages to any computer on the ARPANET network and the use of the @ symbol to tell which user was at which computer.[21] Those early addresses would be written as *sender-name@computer-name* to *recipient-name@computer-name*. By 1974, there were hundreds of military users of email; by the end of the 1970s, 75 percent of all ARPANET traffic was email.[22]

In all of 1978, 5,000 email messages were sent; by the end of 2021, the total number of business and consumer emails sent and received each day is expected to reach 319.6 billion.[23]

Records and information managers understand that although storage may not be a major factor due to declining costs, time wasted searching through and reading irrelevant communications, or even more time-consuming, retrieving and redacting information to present email for e-discovery, can be substantial. Today organizations have the option of outsourcing their email systems to take advantage of potential benefits, including:

- **Ease of management:** IT staff are not required to manage on-premise email systems, and hosted services can offer customer support 24 hours a day, 7 days a week.
- **Cost-effectiveness:** Email that lives in the cloud often costs less than in-house, server-based email platforms.
- **Productivity enhancement:** Hosted communication solutions can offer more functionality than email, for example, scheduling and information-sharing tools.
- **Flexibility:** Employees can access outsourced email from any location using a variety of devices, such as smartphones and tablets.
- **Data protection:** Outsourced email resides outside of the organization's data center and server, so email messages will not be destroyed by a natural or man-made disaster that strikes the organization. Hosted services offer their own data protection (e.g., daily backups) and security features (e.g., protection to reduce spam and detect intrusions).

Email systems are communication systems, not management systems. However, a number of email management systems exist that provide records management and retention functionality.

Instant Messaging (IM) and Online Chats

In the early 1990s, software was designed to set up chat rooms on web servers. People typed in messages that could be seen by everyone in the room. Early chat rooms allowed the equivalent of instant messages for everyone within the room. Early instant messaging became a chat for two. Today, instant messaging (IM) provided by services such as Skype allow more than one contact to be created, resulting in a group instant message.

In 1996, an Israeli company, Mirabilis, introduced a free IM utility called ICQ, a homophone for *I seek you*. It used a client residing on the user's computer to communicate with an ICQ server whenever the user was online and the client was running. AOL acquired Mirabilis in 1998 and named the IM utility AIM (AOL Instant Messenger). When AOL sold AIM in 2010 to Digital Sky Technologies, a Russian internet company later renamed Mail .ru Group, it had over 100 million registered accounts and had been updated to allow for integration with Facebook and other websites.[24] Today ICQ versions include ICQ Online, ICQ8 for Windows, and ICQ for Android, IOS, and Windows Phones.

Records and information managers may wonder about the implications of using this service on multiple devices and how ownership by a foreign entity impacts their ability to comply with their home countries' laws and regulations.

Today there are many instant messaging services available—WhatsApp, Facebook Messenger, QQ Mobile, WeChat, Skype, Snapchat, Viber, and Line to name a few.[25] To alleviate the inconvenience of having to switch IM services when communicating with users of different applications, users can employ an aggregator such as All-in-One Messenger or Franz.

Despite the introduction and growth of social media, according to BI Intelligence, the number of monthly active users for the top four messaging apps has surpassed the number of active users for the top four social networks.[26] Employees used to the convenience of using IM in their daily lives will find a way to incorporate IM into their work lives. Organizations that understand the benefits and risks related to IM have an alternative to prohibiting its use: they can offer an enterprise solution. For example, IBM employs and offers Sametime to replace voicemail in order to see when contacts are online and communicate with them effortlessly in real time. IBM Sametime provides instant messaging with online presence indicators and community collaboration in the form of integration with voice and video conversations, group chats, online meetings, and instant polls. Records managers will appreciate the documentation of online messages using time and date stamps and a log of sent files and links.[27]

Although not as popular as they once were, online chat rooms offered by platforms such as Twitch, Migme, and Nimbuzz provide individuals the opportunity to chat with others anonymously based on specific topics, such as Autism Spectrum Disorder.[28] Businesses increasingly offer chat services for customer support, such as LifeChat, that allow firms to interact with customers surfing their websites and provide customer service 24/7 through the use of a ticketing system.[29]

Although some of the previous events occurred after the year 2000, they seem conservative in nature compared to the technologies to be described in the next section. This is where the disruptive change brought about by new technology and evolving societal views and expectations can be most strongly felt.

WEB 2.0, SOCIAL MEDIA, AND SOCIETY

Until the end of the twentieth century, electronic systems were used mainly to conduct and record business transactions. But early in the twenty-first century, these *systems of record* were augmented by *systems of engagement*. By 2004, Facebook was founded, followed by YouTube one year later; it became easy to publish content on these websites. The authoritarian, closed, passive, static, one-way communications medium offered by early webmasters became democratic, collaborative, active, dynamic, and interactive. The organization no longer had complete control of the message or the record.

In the past, organizations introduced technology to employees in a top-down fashion, but the introduction of social media into the workplace was often bottom-up. As a battle between email and social networks for users' time and attention gained momentum, consumers increasingly turned to mobile devices for social activities. Employees, comfortable using social media in their personal lives, found ways to introduce Web 2.0 tools into the workplace, and the acronym BYOD (bring your own device) was coined to describe business acceptance of the use of personal devices to conduct business.

Records managers must be familiar with Web 2.0 tools and technologies, be aware of current implementation strategies within the organization, and be able to identify and manage the records created as a result of such implementation.

Web 2.0 Tools

Web 2.0 tools are used for communication, social networking, and web publishing, as well as to provide and acquire web services (see figure 1.5). A Pew Research Fact Sheet revealed that by the beginning of 2017, 69 percent of the US population used some type of social media.[30]

Social media tools continue to evolve; the lines between blogs, microblogs, and social networks have all but disappeared. The convergence of functions continues as successful social media platforms add new features to attract additional subscribers. For our purposes, though, we'll review the tools and categories as they are represented in each of the four spheres of activity of the Web 2.0 model.

Tools That Facilitate Communication

Communication tools have blurred the lines between journalist and reader, publisher and user, and communicator and broadcaster. It's simple and inexpensive to develop content and share it with the world.

RSS (Really Simple Syndication)

RSS is a form of web coding for delivering regularly changing web content directly to the subscriber.[31] Many news-related sites, personal blogs, and other online publishers use RSS feeds to syndicate their content, which can include text, music, and images. To enjoy the content, you must subscribe to a feed using a program called an *aggregator* or *feed reader*. Programs and add-ons can provide RSS functionality to email clients and browsers. Feedly is a popular, easy to use web-based RSS reader. Apps for the iPhone, iPad, and Android devices will synchronize read status with Feedly on multiple devices.

Text and Photo Messaging Tools

Most cell phones support Short Message Service (SMS), commonly known as *text messaging*. SMS allows one device to send and receive short messages of up to 160 characters to another device. Today, most cell phones also allow the transmission of pictures, video, or audio content to another device using Multimedia Messaging Service (MMS), an evolution of SMS.[32]

The ease with which smartphone users can take and share photos gave rise to the popularity of apps like Instagram and Snapchat. Those who did not want to keep a record of the exchanges applauded the fact that the photos shared through Snapchat were ephemeral (self-destructive after only a few seconds). There are ways to get around this, of course; for example, screenshots can be taken of photos in Snapchat. Although Snapchat alerts the sender when this occurs, it cannot delete the copy. Snapchat users can capture disappearing photos or videos, add overlaid text and imagery, and send them privately to friends or broadcast them as a Snapchat Story. Snapchat also provides a limited data storage service called Memories that users can turn on or off. Instagram, a Facebook-owned app, launched its own version of "stories" in 2016, resulting in a decrease of views of stories on Snapchat.[33] Because marketing dollars follow views, marketing campaigns devoted more resources to Instagram and fewer resources to Snapchat. Records managers should keep abreast of these types of events that impact business decisions and result in changes in the social media tools used.

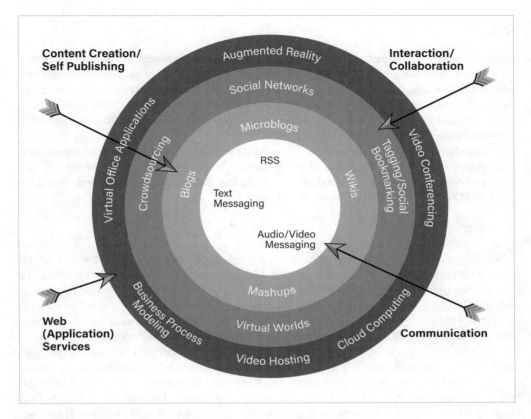

FIGURE 1.5. Web 2.0 model illustrating levels of activities organized into four categories.

Audio and Video Messaging Tools

Podcasting is a way to receive audio and video files over the internet on a mobile device or desktop. Companies like eBay, GE, Netflix and State Farm employ podcast companies to develop creative content for them, but tools are available to allow individuals to create their own podcasts.[34] eBay's successful podcast series, *Open for Business,* explores key issues businesses face, such as "Hiring, Firing and Scaling: Creating a Workplace Culture."[35]

Video files (vodcasts) can be used to create a diary, journal, or blog. Twitch, a social video platform and community for video gamers, recommends using vodcasts to entertain followers while interacting using chat.[36] Vodcasts can be created to share knowledge, document meetings, and more.

Tools That Facilitate Content Creation and Self-Publishing

Blogs and microblogs can be used to establish communities of interest by promoting interaction between and among publishers and readers. Additional tools in this sphere are wikis and mashups.

Blogs

Blogs (web logs) began as a form of personal online journal intended for public consumption. More than one person is often authorized to post on behalf of an organization. Posts are added to a single webpage in reverse-chronological order and may allow reader comments. Organizations can delete unacceptable comments. Such control, though, could damage the trust established within the blog community unless rules describing unacceptable comments are clearly explained on the blog.

Blogs are easy and inexpensive to create using a blogging platform such as WordPress. Blog search engines (e.g., BlogSearchEngine.org) can help you find posts of interest. By far the most visited site in 2017 based on the eBIZMBA Ranking was Huffington Post with 110,000,000 estimated unique monthly visitors.[37]

Microblogs

Microblogs allow individuals to communicate by exchanging short messages. Twitter, which since 2017 allows 280-character messages (double the original 140 characters allowed) called tweets, has played an important role in reporting natural disasters and political uprisings around the globe. As of January 1, 2018, Twitter had 330 million active monthly users, 80 percent of them using mobile devices.[38] The Twitter account with the most followers (more than 100 million) mid-2018 belonged to singer Katy Perry (@katyperry).[39]

One of the first examples of return on investment from microblogging came from @ Dell Outlet. Dell made over $2 million in sales of its refurbished products and another $1 million in sales of new products purchased by those who moved from the outlet site to the main site between 2007 and 2009.[40] By the end of 2016, Dell had trained more than 16,000 employees in forty-six countries through Dell's Social Media University to advocate on behalf of the company. Dell's employees "listen in" on 25,000 conversations in English every day as part of their jobs.[41]

In January 2012, Tumblr surpassed WordPress.com in the number of blogs hosted. Tumblr allows users to post short blogs in various formats—text, photos, links, music, and video—from their phones or desktops using email or a browser. Users can reblog a Tumblr post from another user's Tumblelog. By early 2017, there were 357.7 million Tumblr blog accounts compared to 75 million websites (27.5 percent of all websites globally) powered by WordPress.[42] A comparison of the features of both Tumblr and WordPress indicate that Tumblr could be a good vehicle for driving traffic to the main WordPress site.

Wikis

A wiki is a combination website and text document that allows groups to work collaboratively using only a browser. The best-known wiki is *Wikipedia,* an encyclopedia written by volunteers from around the world. It exhibits the qualities of "openness, sharing, and acting globally" identified by Tapscott and Williams as the principles of *wikinomics.*[43] Enterprise wikis are available as hosted options or for use on enterprise servers and are employed for everything from product development to knowledge management.

One of the earliest government wikis was *Intellipedia,* an online, collaborative system established in late 2005 for information sharing within the US intelligence community. Don Burke, *Intellipedia* doyen, and Sean P. Dennehy, *Intellipedia* and Enterprise 2.0 evangelist, were awarded 2009 Homeland Security Medals for their contributions to the nation. In

January 2011, Chris Rasmussen proposed to use the same wiki software to create *The Living Intelligence System.* In practice, neither *Intellipedia* nor *The Living Intelligence System* earned widespread acceptance.[44] Not one to acknowledge defeat, in 2017 Rasmussen announced *Tearline,* an app for senior US intelligence officers that is a wiki-style collaborative platform for reading and writing unclassified intelligence reports complete with charts, comments, and updates.[45]

Mashups

Mashups are webpages or applications that combine data from two or more online sources, such as application programming interfaces (APIs), other web services, and data feeds (e.g., RSS). The results are different from the original intent when the raw data was produced. Three distinct types of mashups are consumer mashups, business (enterprise) mashups, and data mashups.

A *consumer mashup* combines different data types from multiple sources and organizes the information through the browser interface. Craigslist provides an example of a consumer mashup that combines rental listings from Craigslist with mapping data from Google Maps' API.

Business (or enterprise) mashups combine the organization's own resources, applications, and data with other external web services and publish the results to enterprise portals, application development tools, or in a service-oriented architecture. Business mashups can help a company improve customer service. For example, a mashup of the organization's order management system with logistics information from UPS or FedEx will give call center representatives immediate access to order status and package tracking in one view.

Data mashups combine similar types of media and information from disparate data sources, or different tables within a single data source, into a single representation. For example, Havaria Information Services' Alert Map continuously combines data from over 200 sources related to severe weather conditions, biohazard threats, and seismic information.[46] Data sources can be combined to create reports or dashboards for business analysts to examine. One example, InetSoft's business intelligence (BI) platform, offers users the option to create and define their own data mashups.[47]

For records managers, two questions arise: (1) have new records been created as a result? (2) if so, where are they stored and how are they managed?

Tools That Facilitate Interaction through Social Networking

Social Networks

Social networking sites allow users to share content, interact, and develop communities of interest. Facebook's features include instant messaging, groups, forums, email, games, music, and videos. As of March 31, 2018, there were over 2.20 billion monthly active Facebook users worldwide.[48] LinkedIn is a professional networking site with 546 million users in over 200 countries and territories as of March 24, 2018; acquired by Microsoft in 2016, it is one of the two most popular social media platforms for CEOs (Twitter is the other).[49]

A different type of social networking site began in 2010 as a service for individual users to send email with an image attached for "pinning" to an online board. As of January 2018, Pinterest had 175 million monthly active users, 75 million of them from the United States;

by the end of 2016, more than one million businesses used Pinterest to share content, engage consumers, increase customer reach, and drive traffic to their websites and other social networking sites.[50] Examples include Lowes' use of Pinterest to promote its style expertise related to home improvements and Allrecipes' efforts to establish a community of home cooks that go to Allrecipes first when planning a meal.[51]

Virtual Worlds (Multiuser Virtual Environments)

Sometimes called *virtual worlds*, multiuser virtual environments share certain characteristics: 3-D graphics, web-based access, simultaneous interaction among users, and representation of a persistent virtual world. Users, called *residents,* interact with one another through avatars. The most successful virtual world for adults is Second Life, with about 800,000 monthly users in 2017.[52]

Early evidence of cost-savings potential was provided by the IBM Academy of Technology in the fall of 2008 when the company hosted a Virtual World Conference for over 200 members, which resulted in a savings of $320,000 compared to the potential cost of conducting the conference in the physical world.[53] The initial hype about virtual worlds, however, has not resulted in widespread adoption. By 2017, attention shifted to virtual reality, augmented reality, and mixed reality experiences.

Tagging and Social Bookmarking

The explosion of information posted to the Web has prompted the creation of author-created and user-created metadata used for social tagging, social bookmarking, tagging of photos, and tag clouds/word clouds.

Tagging, or *folksonomy,* a user-generated taxonomy, is substantially different from traditional taxonomies, which are classification systems arranged in a hierarchical structure. A folksonomy is comprised of terms in a flat namespace (no hierarchy and no parent-child or sibling relationships). Folksonomies are sets of terms used to tag content—not a predetermined set of classification terms or labels.[54]

Flickr, the photosharing site, encourages users to tag their photos with freely chosen index terms. These tags, however, may or may not make sense to others. Someone searching a simple term such as *apple* may have the fruit in mind but find the image returned to him is of the Apple Newton MessagePad or an apple cake. *Geotagging* is another form of social tagging that adds a geographic location to images based on a Google map. *Word clouds* (also known as *tag clouds*) are visual representations of terms found in text. A graphic of terms is created with each term presented in a size relative to the number of times it appears in selected text. Users of SurveyMonkey's premium account can generate word clouds as a way of visualizing responses to specific survey questions.

Crowdsourcing

Crowdsourcing involves using the general public to do paid or unpaid research or other work.[55] The Smithsonian Institution saves staff time by using the crowd to identify photographs placed on Flickr and provide additional descriptive information that is integrated with the Smithsonian's catalog entries. Crowdfunding is a variation that allows donors to contribute to pleas for monetary assistance. Go-Fund-Me is an example of this use of the technology.

Tools That Facilitate Web Services (Applications)

Web services rely on the technical requirements needed to allow different software applications to interoperate. In this category are augmented reality, videoconferencing, virtual office applications, cloud computing, video sharing, and business process modeling.

Augmented Reality

Between the real world and the virtual world lies augmented reality (AR), technology that blurs the lines by enhancing what we see, hear, feel, and even smell. Both video games and cell phones are driving the development of augmented reality, but commercial applications exist. In September 2017, IKEA launched IKEA Place, an augmented reality app that allows customers with iOS 11 on their smartphones to not only browse through approximately 2,000 products in the AR catalog but also see how they would look in their own homes. All products are 3-D and true to scale, making it easy to reposition and resize the images. Because we were at the beach, I wanted to see how a comfy sofa would look on the sand (see figure 1.6). What you're seeing in the background is what I'm viewing through my iPhone.

FIGURE 1.6 What fun—a comfy sofa on the sand—too bad it is just augmented reality! Learn more about IKEA's Augmented Reality app at www.ikea.com/us/en/about_ikea/newsitem/091217_IKEA_Launches_IKEA_Place.

Photo courtesy of G. J. Franks.

Video Hosting

YouTube, the largest video hosting service with over 1.8 billion logged-in users visiting the site each month, has become synonymous with video hosting.[56] But other options are available, including Vimeo (the second largest service), Google, Vidyard, and Wistia.[57] When selecting a hosting service as part of marketing and sales campaigns, consideration should be given to one that not only reaches out to the target audience but also provides deep analytics and integrates smoothly with marketing automation software. Businesses seeking to control its content should consider options that prevent unauthorized downloads.

Videoconferencing Services

Videoconferencing brings people together from different geographic areas in real time for online meetings, training sessions, and product demonstrations. GoToMeeting and WebEx are two popular web-conferencing platforms. Key features include the ability to share presentations and speak using a computer microphone or phone conferencing. Additional features vary but can include the ability to conduct web tours, share the desktop among multiple participants, use a chat feature, and record the session for later use—potentially creating new records that must be managed. In 2016, Gartner added Zoom as a new leader to its Magic Quadrant for web conferencing. Zoom can be deployed as SaaS (software as a service), on premises or in the cloud (hybrid and dedicated).[58]

Virtual Office Applications

Virtual office applications allow employees to access information they need to conduct their jobs from home or while traveling. Office applications are hosted on third-party servers to create virtual office environments.

Google's G Suite provides Gmail, Google Calendar, Google Docs, Google Drive, and more to over a million businesses and government agencies. Companies are attracted by offers of unlimited email storage for every employee and a guarantee to be available at least 99.9 percent of the time.

Cloud Computing

Cloud computing is a general term for delivering hosted services—for example, software, storage, backup, web hosting, and spam and malware filters—over the internet. Cloud computing services include social networking sites, photography websites, video sites, and tax preparation sites. Tim O'Reilly, credited with coining the term *Web 2.0,* viewed cloud computing as using the internet as a platform for all computing. The National Institute for Standards and Technology (NIST) defines cloud computing as "a model for enabling ubiquitous, convenient, on-demand network access to a shared pool of configurable computing resources (e.g., networks, servers, storage, applications, and services) that can be rapidly provisioned and released with minimal management effort or service provider interaction."[59]

Records managers should be included in discussions about cloud computing to ensure that records stored in the cloud receive the same level of protection as records stored on premise.

Cloud Computing

PRIVATE: Services and infrastructure are maintained on a private network.

PUBLIC: Services and infrastructure are provided off-site over the internet.

HYBRID: Includes a variety of public and private options with multiple providers.

GOVERNMENT: Products and solutions developed specifically for government organizations and institutions.

Business Process Modeling

A *business process* is a collection of activities designed to produce a well-defined goal. Business analysts and managers perform business process modeling (BPM) in order to improve efficiency and quality. Classic tools include flowcharts, data flow diagrams, Gantt charts, and program evaluation and review technique (PERT) diagrams. New tools are based upon a widely used standard called business process modeling notation (BPMN). These tools can be used to document, simulate, and improve business processes.

SmartDraw is business process management software that enables the creation of flowcharts and other process diagrams. Templates are provided to add professional design themes, and teams can collaborate on the same flowchart using SmartDraw Cloud or on another file using a file sharing app like Dropbox or OneDrive.[60]

Web 3.0 and the Semantic Web

Web 2.0 factors in the human element. Although it enables authors and users to tag objects in ways meaningful to them, many of the tools create their own silos of information. Web 3.0 places the focus on technology that will allow the user to search for information across silos using a common language related to real-world objects. It emphasizes a dependence on technology, not humans, to construct meaning and accomplish tasks. We're already seeing virtual assistants (like Alexa, Amazon's virtual assistant) analyzing speech and performing tasks (e.g., gathering and presenting information, dialing a phone number, ordering products, marking an appointment on a calendar). The successful completion of such tasks depends upon the ability of the disparate technologies to share data.

The *Semantic Web* is a web of data that "provides a common framework that allows data to be shared and reused across application, enterprise, and community boundaries."[61] It is an extension of the World Wide Web, sometimes described as *linked data*.

In 2007, Nova Spivack described Web 3.0 as "a set of standards that turns the web into one big database" (Metz).[62] By 2030, according to Spivack, artificial analysts that combine natural language understanding and conversation technology with advanced analytics could advise decision-makers "with actionable insights from their data, using natural language conversation, visualization, simulation, data storytelling, and eventually even mixed reality interfaces that illustrate insights in a more immersive way."[63]

Today, records managers are concerned with identifying and managing records created by employees across the enterprise and in the cloud. However, they must also be prepared to identify and manage records created by artificial agents regardless of where those records reside.

SUMMARY

From prehistoric times to the present day, human beings have recorded their experiences using tools and technologies to share that information with others. These records have served two purposes: primary (administrative, legal, and regulatory) and secondary (historic and research). The methods used to create and store the content of these records have changed over time based on a number of factors, including tools available to record the content and the medium on which the content could be recorded and stored. In the past, recording tools and storage media included clay coins, parchment, papyrus, and the Gutenberg printing press. Today, they include handheld devices and social media. Responsibility for records evolved from our early ancestors who memorized stories to pass along or painted drawings inside caves to today's information governance (IG) teams comprised of representatives from records management, information technology, business units, the legal department, human resources, and more.

During the late nineteenth and early part of the twentieth century, public and private organizations took steps to formalize the management of records, mainly in paper form. Toward the end of the twentieth century and the first decades of the twenty-first century, born-digital records outpaced the growth of physical records and organizations began to explore ways to manage records that were never meant to have a physical form, including those created using social media and mobile devices.

Efficiency and ease of use have always been the goals of the introduction of new technology, in spite of unintended outcomes (e.g., the growth in the volume of paper and digital files to be managed). Since the dawn of the twenty-first century, users have become more vocal in making their wants and needs known. This has resulted in the development of tools such as social networking sites and mobile devices that make it easier to create records but more difficult to manage them.

For those using the new technologies to conduct business, records creation is secondary and a result of their efforts to pursue their core mission. Records and information managers who understand the way work is conducted in their organizations have a better chance of identifying and providing intellectual and/or physical control over the information created.

In 2008, Steve Bailey tackled the topic of records management and Web 2.0 in his book *Managing the Crowd: Rethinking Records Management for the Web 2.0 World.*[64] He challenged records and information managers to find time amid their daily operational pressures to debate the larger issues presented by the new technological paradigm and the threat it poses to established theory and practice. Today, records and information managers are embracing this advice to think more broadly about the contributions they can make not only through records management but also information governance. In his contribution to this chapter, Barclay Blair, founder and executive director of the Information Governance Initiative, provides his perspective on records management and the role it plays in information governance.

PERSPECTIVE

Information Governance: We Are Finally Asking the Right Questions

Barclay T. Blair
Founder and Executive Director, Information Governance Initiative

Why do we keep information? Why do we throw it away? How do we decide between the two? Humans have presumably asked these questions since "information" meant a stone tablet that some poor soul had to lug around the desert.

The answer was easy when we could feel the weight of information in our hands and stub our toes on it when it piled up around us. We claim to be diligent, but the truth is that most of us still act as if we can still answer these questions this way: *we keep it all until we don't have room to keep it any more.*

However, this simple and imperfect human response is now as anachronistic as using an abacus for quantum physics. But it's not only outdated—it's dangerous. Our inattention to information is a creeping disaster in an age where we can no longer feel the weight of information, but we completely rely on it for our success and even our survival. Silicon Valley is an enabler, with business models that allow—and even depend upon—our atavistic fear of throwing things away by making information storage (and its costs, both economic and human) all but invisible.

The costs can be seen every day, all around us. Millions wasted on finding, reviewing, and producing the haystack in litigation because they could not locate the needle. Entire organizations brought to their knees because of their almost complete failure to understand, manage, and protect their shareholders' information assets, which criminals certainly understand how to value, even if CEOs and board somehow, incredibly, do not. Identities are stolen, lives damaged because managers can't be bothered to put even the most basic policies and technologies in place to manage, control, and protect that information.

The world is waking up to this fact. Questions now swirl on Wall Street and in financial hubs around the world about how investors can protect their investments when the companies they invest in treat information not as an asset that needs their attention, funding, and governance, but as a technology problem that can be solved by writing more checks. Citizens around the world are asking hard questions of their governments about how they use their personal data and why. Governments are responding, grappling with a plethora of new laws that impose onerous regulations and contending with the complexity of ever-changing technologies and societal expectations.

Another world is also coming into view—a world where a new wave of dedicated professionals is doing brilliant, exciting work based on a deeper and more profound understanding of information, that is, that information is *both* good and bad. They understand that some information is ore that we should spend tremendous amounts of time and money refining and exploiting. They also understand that some information (some would say most) is just an industrial by-product that we must remediate because it represents potential cost, risk, and pain. Telling the difference between the two is complicated and shifts based on context and time.

The research we conduct at the Information Governance Initiative each year shows that information governance (IG)—the holistic, coordinated approach to information—is shaping management practices across multiple sectors. In fact, the average large organization undertaking information governance has seven projects under way, each costing an average of $750,000 USD. At the same time, organizations are experiencing an unprecedented disruption in enterprise IT, driven by the cloud, consumerization, mobile, Big Data, and myriad other factors.

The science and discipline of records and information management (RIM) provides a critical foundation for IG. In fact, year after year, when we survey our community of information professionals about which disciplines they see as being part of (or coordinated by) IG, RIM is always at the top of the list (see figure 1.7).

As part of this transition, we see more and more organizations chartering new IG departments and giving them a mandate to steer and coordinate multiple activities from information protection to data remediation to technology decommissioning. In many cases, in addition to playing a coordinating role, these IG functions and their managers have direct responsibility for and authority over these activities.

We see plenty of evidence that we are on the threshold of rapid change around IG. We see it in the stories that practitioners in our community tell us. We see it in research data showing first movers and fast followers increasing investment in IG, deepening IG maturity, and assigning senior managers to the IG portfolio.

RIM is a critical component of IG. RIM is not going anywhere. However, as Pat describes in this book, it needs to evolve, and she has provided an excellent road map for that evolution. The inherent wisdom and philosophies that have underpinned RIM for decades are the same ones that underpin IG.

The Evolution of RIM and IG

Although there are many complex and fascinating evolutionary and revolutionary changes happening in the worlds RIM and IG inhabit, the biggest and most important change is quite simple.

Humans will not classify information.

This has always been true.

In a world of mail rooms, typing pools, interoffice mail, and records clerks, this didn't matter. Our ability to govern information did not depend upon every single employee acting like a records clerk.

But it matters now more than ever.

RIM (and its practitioners, including me!) has suffered from a delusion, a delusion that has affected every aspect of this discipline, from assumed best practices to the design of technology and tool.

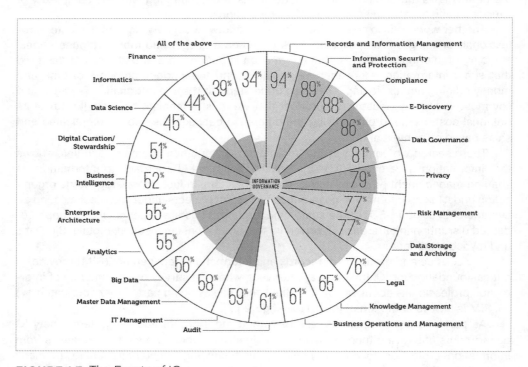

FIGURE 1.7 The Facets of IG.

SOURCE: Information Governance Initiative, https://iginitiative.com.

The delusion was that humans will classify information. The delusion was that we can create digital versions of those old office practices and file rooms, and voila, we are now managing our electronic records.

It never worked, and it never will work.

So, what will?

The bad news is that there is no push-button solution. The good news is that there *are* solutions, and we are now past the threshold where many of the same technologies that got us into this mess in the first place will help get us out of it. Cars that drive themselves are already on the road. Your phone can use your face as a key. Applying some of the same machine learning and artificial intelligence to the identification, classification, and governance of information is already here, and you will be using it at your organization sooner than you think.

But aside from the apparent magic of these algorithms and black boxes, the path forward is much more pedestrian. It looks something like this:

Concept 1. A significant percentage of all of your *unstructured* information is clearly the by-product of a *structured* business process. As such, the governance of that information should be built into that business process in a "silent" way that requires little human intervention beyond the initial design. The beauty of this approach is that it does not require data "classification" (automated or not) in the traditional sense, because the purpose, meaning, and nature of the information are deduced from the business process that generates it.

Concept 2. A significant percentage of your *unstructured* information is not the by-product of a *structured* business process and, thus, cannot be governed this way. Our 25-year experiment to manage unstructured information using concepts that worked well for paper (e.g., centralized capture and control, human records clerks for classification) has failed. All unstructured information does not require the same level of governance. In fact, a clear-eyed cost-benefit analysis at most organizations would reveal that the cost of attempting to do so (and the loss of employee productivity, creativity, and collaboration that usually follows) does not justify even the theoretical, much less actual, benefit.

Instead, we should:

1. Identify as many opportunities as possible to govern information as part of the business process (as described in Concept 1, above).
2. Identify use cases where automated or machine-assisted human classification makes sense as a tool for moving content into a managed state and maintaining it there.
3. Identify information that requires a level of document-by-document, content-based classification and governance that can only be practically accomplished by humans and invest in the best processes for doing this.
4. Manage the rest using broad rules targeting systems, roles, business functions, work groups, geographic areas, and other factors that reveal business function and thus are instructive regarding the governance rules that must apply.

Focus on progress and pragmatism. Perfection is not the goal.

This approach enables us to take care of the big risks, deliver business value, and move on from our fundamentally unworkable reliance upon human governance and classification for unstructured information.

Quantification of IG: Managing Information Like a Business

Life, business, and government are increasingly quantified by data—data that is driving critical decision-making. The demand for devices that track and analyze the data we generate just by living demonstrates the rise of the "quantified self."[65] Analysts predict that by 2020, the market for "fitness wearables" will grow to $10B USD (from $3.3B USD), with over 100 million people using the devices to enable data-driven decisions about health, sleep, and exercise.[66]

The promise of data-driven decision-making is this: processing and analyzing data at a scale far exceeding the capabilities of the human brain will transform our ability to understand and predict reality. The Information Governance Initiative believes that ability to govern information in a way that enables these deeper insights, unforeseen efficiencies, and new business models is what will separate the winners from the losers in this new era.

But we still have a long way to go. Although we invest in technology that can beat a human at Jeopardy in one part of our organization, we are stuck with the technology that prints Trebek's cue cards in another. For all the Big Data sexiness, "up to 80% of the total development cost of an analytics project" is spent on "data discovery and wrangling . . . the most tedious and time-consuming aspects of an analysis."[67]

Why does it take so long? Because most organizations quite simply have very little idea what data they have, where that data lives, what the data means, what rules must attach to the data, and whether or not the data represents measurable value or risk. Consequently, our data are messy, incomplete, difficult to find and access, duplicative, and missing context essential to enable its analysis and use. In short, it is the inevitable outcome of a generation of attempting to force analog practices to work in a digital world. It has failed.

Most organizations continue to make management decisions about their information based on *tradition, superstition,* and *supposition* instead of *innovation, evidence,* and *analysis.*

It's time that our approach to governing our information caught up to the information age. Quantified IG is the application of smart technology and evidence-based practices to the governance of information. It ensures that we have essential *facts* about our information and our operating environment so we can make *evidence-based decisions.*

The idea that we should make decisions based on facts or evidence of course derives from the Enlightenment and the scientific method itself. But even in areas where you might expect that this approach is already baked in, it is still challenging.

Why do we have 1,000 categories in our records retention schedule? Because that's the way the last guy did it. Or, because we inherited the schedule from a company we acquired. Because Janice liked it that way. Because that's what makes the most sense to me. Because that's what my old boss told us to do. Because that is what the consulting company sold us.

But is it right? Is it true? Is it the best way? Are these justifications based on anything more than tradition, superstition, or office politics?

Without quantification, it is impossible to know.

There is a generational movement to use quantification (evidence analyzed for insight) to inform a growing spectrum of decisions in our world. At its heart, this movement continues the intellectual evolution that began in the Enlightenment. The promise is better decisions: decisions based on better information and evidence; decisions that are more likely to be correct; decisions that are more likely to result in the planned outcome.

However, most organizations are only beginning to adopt this approach for the governance of their information. Many decisions in IG are made based on nothing more than a cognitively suspect human calculation of risk. Or, very commonly, decisions are effectively not made, evidencing the bias towards inaction that plagues organizational decision-making regarding information.

There is no excuse for this to continue. The techniques of data-driven decision-making and quantification are well understood. We now have exciting new technologies that finally empower us to collect facts, conduct deep analysis, and, at last, to take action on our data. In a world where most organizations are experiencing exponential growth of data generally, and pools of dark and potentially dangerous data specifically, a commitment to action, driven by powerful emerging IG best practices and technologies, is the only way forward.

NOTES

1. William Shakespeare, *The Tempest,* in *The Complete Pelican Shakespeare,* ed. Alfred Harbage (New York: Penguin Group, 1969), 2.1.247. References are to act, scene, and line.
2. P. M. Grand, *Prehistoric Art: Paleolithic Painting and Sculpture* (Greenwich, CT: New York Graphic Society, 1967), 34.
3. Ibid., 24.
4. AncientScripts.com, "Cuneiform," accessed August 13, 2017, www.ancientscripts.com/cuneiform.html.
5. C. H. Gordon, *Forgotten Scripts: Their Ongoing Discovery and Decipherment* (New York: Basic Books, 1982), 155.
6. *Encyclopaedia Britannica Online,* s.v. "parchment," accessed August 13, 2017, www.britannica.com/EBchecked/topic/443382/parchment.
7. HQ PaperMaker, "All about Paper," accessed August 13, 2017, www.hqpapermaker.com/paper-history/.
8. Athol L. Murray, "The Lord Clerk Register," *The Scottish Historical Review,* 53, no. 156, 124–56, Edinburg, Scotland: Edinburgh University Press, October 1974, www.jstor.org/stable/25529087.
9. Reginald R. Sharpe, D.C.L., ed., *Calendar of Letter Books Preserved among the Archives of the Corporation of the City of London, Introduction* (London, United Kingdom: John Edward Francis, BreaiM's Buildings, E.C., 1912), www.archive.org/details/cu31924103071134.
10. Ministry of Education, Culture, and Sport, "History of the General Archive of Simancas," General Archive of Simancas, accessed on August 13, 2017, www.mecd.gob.es/cultura-mecd/en/areas-cultura/archivos/mc/archivos/ags/presentacion/historia.html; "The History of European Archival Literature," *The American Archivist* 2, no. 2, (April 1939): 269–70, accessed http://americanarchivist.org/doi/pdf/10.17723/aarc.2.2.d7821153t468kr64?code=same-site.
11. Richard Pearce-Moses, s.v. "diplomatics," *Glossary of Archival and Records Terminology (GART),* Society of American Archivists, accessed August 13, 2017, www2.archivists.org/glossary/terms/d/diplomatics.
12. Great Britain Patent Office, *Patents for Inventions Abridgments of Specifications Relating to Printing, Including Therein the Production of Copies on All Kinds of Materials* (London: George E. Eyre and William Spottiswoode, 1859), 84.
13. "The Register House: The Adams Building," *The Scottish Historical Review* 53, no. 156 (October 1974): 117, Edinburgh, Scotland: Edinburgh University Press, www.jstor.org/stable/25529087.
14. Emmett Leahy Award, "Emmett J. Leahy (1910–1964)," accessed August 13, 2017, https://www.emmettleahyaward.org/leahy-bio.html.
15. Pearce-Moses, s.v. "Federal Records Act," www2.archivists.org/glossary/terms/f/federal-records-act.
16. Richard J. Cox, *Closing an Era: Historical Perspectives on Modern Archives and Records Management* (Westport, CT: Greenwood Press), 3.

17. *Encyclopaedia Britannica Online*, s.v. "Watergate scandal," by Rick Perlstein, accessed August 13, 2017, https://www.britannica.com/event/Watergate-Scandal.

18. *PC Encyclopedia,* s.v. "word processing machine," accessed August 13, 2017, https://www.pcmag.com/encyclopedia/term/54834/word-processing-machine.

19. Cover pages, "W3C Director Tim Berners-Lee Awarded Millennium Technology Prize," accessed August 13, 2017, http://xml.coverpages.org/ni2004-04-23-b.html.

20. Ian Peter, "The History of Email," *Net History*, accessed August 13, 2017, www.nethistory.info/History%200f%20the%20Internet/email.html.

21. Mary Bellis, "History of Email & Ray Tomlinson," *About.com Guide,* accessed August 13, 2017, http://inventors.about.com/od/estartinventions/a/email.htm.

22. Peter, *History of Email,* p. 21.

23. The Radicati Group, Inc., "Email Statistics Report, 2017–2021" (London, United Kingdom), accessed August 13, 2017, www.radicati.com/wp/wp-content/uploads/2017/01/Email-Statistics-Report-2017-2021-Executive-Summary.pdf.

24. "AOL to Sell ICQ Service to D.S.T. for $187.5 Million," DealBook, *The New York Times*, accessed August 13, 2017, https://dealbook.nytimes.com/2010/04/28/aol-to-sell-icq-service-to-d-s-t-for-187-5-million/.

25. Statista, "Most Popular Mobile Messaging Apps Worldwide as of January 2017, Based on Number of Monthly Active Users (In Millions)," accessed August 13, 2017, https://www.statista.com/statistics/258749/most-popular-global-mobile-messenger-apps/.

26. "Messaging Apps Are Now Bigger than Social Networks," *Business Insider* (September 20, 2016), accessed August 13, 2017, www.businessinsider.com/the-messaging-app-report-2015-11.

27. IBM, "IBM Sametime," accessed August 13, 2017, https://www-03.ibm.com/software/products/en/ibmsame.

28. "What Happened to AIM Chat Rooms?" *Lifewire*, accessed August 13, 2017, https://www.lifewire.com/what-happened-to-aim-chat-rooms-3969418.

29. Capterra, "Top Live Chat Software Products," accessed August 13, 2017, www.capterra.com/live-chat-software/.

30. Pew Research Center, "Social Media Fact Sheet," January 12, 2017, www.pewinternet.org/fact-sheet/social-media/.

31. *BusinessDictionary,* s.v. "Really Simple Syndication (RSS)," accessed July 23, 2017, www.businessdictionary.com/definition/Really-Simple-Syndication-RSS.html.

32. "Everything You Need to Know about SMS & MMS," *Lifewire,* accessed August 13, 2017, https://www.lifewire.com/what-is-sms-mms-iphone-2000247.

33. "Instagram Stories Is Stealing Snapchat Users," *Tech Crunch,* January 30, 2017, https://techcrunch.com/2017/01/30/attack-of-the-clone/.

34. Laurie Johnson, "Major Brands Are Betting Big on Podcasts and It Seems To Be Paying Off," *Adweek,* August 28, 2016, www.adweek.com/digital/major-brands-are-betting-big-podcasts-and-it-seems-be-paying-173035/.

35. eBay, "Open for Business," accessed July 24, 2017, https://www.ebayinc.com/stories/podcast/.

36. Justin Oh, "Vodcast Brings the Twitch Community Experience to Uploads," Twitch, May 31, 2017, https://blog.twitch.tv/vodcast-brings-the-twitch-community-experience-to-uploads-54098498715.

37. "Top 15 Most Popular Blogs, July 2017," *eBizMBA Guide,* accessed August 13, 2017, www.ebizmba.com/articles/blogs.

38. Salam Aslam, "Twitter by the Numbers: Stats, Demographics and Fun Facts," Omnicore, January 1, 2018, https://www.omnicoreagency.com/twitter-statistics/.

39. Twitter Counter, "Twitter Top 100 Most Followers," accessed August 13, 2017, https://twittercounter.com/pages/100.

40. DELL-Stephanie N. "@DellOutlet Surpasses $2 Million on Twitter," *Direct2Dell: The Official Dell Corporate Blog,* June 2009, accessed August 13, 2017, http://en.community.dell.com/dell-blogs/direct2dell/b/direct2dell/archive/2009/06/11/delloutlet-surpasses-2-million-on-twitter.aspx.

41. Russell Working, "6 Lessons from Dell's 'Social Media University'," Ragan.com, December 2, 2016, https://www.ragan.com/Main/Articles/6_lessons_from_Dells_Social_Media_University_52028.aspx.

42. Statica, "Cumulative Total Number of Tumblr Blogs from May 2011 to July 2017," accessed August 13, 2017, https://www.statista.com/statistics/256235/total-cumulative-number-of-tumblr-blogs/; Craig Smith, "42 Amazing Wordpress Statistics and Facts (April 2017)," accessed August 13, 2017, http://expandedramblings.com/index.php/wordpress-statistics/.

43. Don Tapscott, "Macrowikinomics: New Solutions for a Connected Planet," accessed January 27, 2013, http://dontapscott.com/books/macrowikinomics/.

44. Emily Dreyfuss, "The Wikipedia for Spies—and Where It Goes from Here," *Wired*, March 10, 2017, https://www.wired.com/2017/03/intellipedia-wikipedia-spies-much/.

45. Emily Dreyfuss, "American Spies Now Have Their Very Own Smartphone App," *Wired*, April 4, 2017, https://www.wired.com/2017/04/american-spies-now-smartphone-app/.

46. RSOE—Emergency and Disaster Information Service Alert Map, accessed August 13, 2017, http://hisz.rsoe.hu/alertmap/index2.php.

47. InetSoft, "Enterprise Data Mashups," accessed August 12, 2017, https://www.inetsoft.com/solutions/enterprise_data_mashup/.

48. Facebook Newsroom, "Stats," accessed May 11, 2018, https://newsroom.fb.com/company-info/.

49. LinkedIn, "The Top 100 CEOs on Social Media," March 17, 2016, https://www.linkedin.com/pulse/top-100-ceos-social-media-steve-tappin; Craig Smith, "220 Amazing LinkedIn Statistics and Facts (March 2018), March 4, 2018, https://expandedramblings.com/index.php/by-the-numbers-a-few-important-linkedin-stats/.

50. David Cohen, "New Look for Pinterest Business Profiles," *Adweek,* November 30, 2016, www.adweek.com/digital/pinterest-business-profiles-update/; Salam Aslam, "Pinterest by the Numbers: Stats, Demographics & Fun Facts," January 1, 2018, https://www.omnicoreagency.com/pinterest-statistics/.

51. Pinterest, "Success Stories," accessed August 13, 2017, https://business.pinterest.com/en/success-stories.

52. Rachel Metz "Second Life is Back for a Third Life, This Time in Virtual Reality," *MIT Technology Review,* January 27, 2017, https://www.technologyreview.com/s/603422/second-life-is-back-for-a-third-life-this-time-in-virtual-reality/.

53. *Engage Digital* (blog), "IBM saves $320,000 with Second Life," accessed August 13, 2017, www.engagedigital.com/blog/2009/02/27/ibm-saves-320000-with-second-life-meeting/.

54. Isabella Peters, *Folksonomies: Indexing and Retrieval in Web 2.0* (Berlin: Walter de Gruyter GmbH, 2009), 223.

55. *YourDictionary,* s.v. "crowdsourcing," accessed August 13, 2017, http://computer.yourdictionary.com/crowdsourcing.

56. Adi Robertson, "YouTube Has 1.8 Billion Logged-In Viewers Each Month," *The Verge,* May 3, 2018, https://www.theverge.com/2018/5/3/17317274/youtube-1-8-billion-logged-in-monthly-users-brandcast-2018.

57. G2 Crowd, "Best Video Hosting Software," accessed August 14, 2017, https://www.g2crowd.com/categories/video-hosting.

58. Gartner, "Magic Quadrant for Web Conferencing," November 10, 2016, https://www.gartner.com/doc/reprints?id=1-3LPJBEI&ct=161110&st=sb.

59. Peter Mell and Timothy Grance, "The NIST Definition of Cloud Computing," National Institute of Science and Technology, September 2011, http://nvlpubs.nist.gov/nistpubs/Legacy/SP/nistspecialpublication800-145.pdf.

60. SmartDraw, "Easy and Powerful Business Process Management Software," accessed August 13, 2017, https://www.smartdraw.com/business-process-mapping/business-process-management-software.htm?id=62200.

61. W3C, "W3C Semantic Web Frequently Asked Questions," accessed August 13, 2017, www.w3.0rg/RDF/FAQ.

62. Cade Metz, "Web 3.0," *PC Magazine,* March 14, 2007, https://www.pcmag.com/article2/0,2817,2102852,00.asp.

63. Nova Spivack, "AI, BI, and the Necessity of Automating the Analyst—It's Time to Automate the Analyst," September 8, 2016, www.novaspivack.com/science/ai-bi-and-the-necessity-of-automating-the-analyst.

64. Steve Bailey, *Managing the Crowd: Rethinking Records Management for the Web 2.0 World* (London, United Kingdom: Facet Publishing, 2008), 31.

65. "Quantified Self (QS)" was developed into a "movement" largely by two editors from *Wired Magazine.* See Deborah Lupton, "The Quantified Self Movement: Some Sociological Perspectives," *This Sociological Life* (blog), November 4, 2012, https://simplysociology.wordpress.com/2012/11/04/the-quantitative-self-movement-some-sociological-perspectives/

66. James Moar, *Wearables—The Heartbeat on Your Sleeve* (Juniper Research, November 2015), 4; James Moar, *Fitness Wearables—Time to Step Up* (Juniper Research, January 2016), 4.

67. Victoria Louise Lemieux, Brianna Gormly, and Lyse Rowledge, "Meeting Big Data Challenges with Visual Analytics," *Records Management Journal,* July 2014.

CHAPTER 2

Building an Information Governance Program on a Solid RIM Foundation

INTRODUCTION

The unprecedented growth of digital information, the diversity of file formats, and the accompanying challenges in determining what to trust, keep, secure, discard, and preserve have resulted in a renewed interest in and appreciation for the value of records and information management (RIM) to the organization.

During the first decade of the twenty-first century, organizations aspiring to manage records and information assets across the enterprise embraced the concept of information governance (IG). During the second decade of the twenty-first century, a focus on data governance reemerged, as raw digital data are recognized as a strategic business asset that can be analyzed (data analytics) to extract value in the form of patterns, predictions, and other insights. In this chapter, you'll be introduced to information governance and the role records and information management plays within that structure. Data governance (DG) will be addressed in chapter 10.

IG requires more than one point of view. Representatives from legal, human resources, information technology, and business units must participate in developing the information governance strategy. But because of their understanding of the flow of information across the enterprise, records professionals are in a unique position to contribute their knowledge and skills to this initiative.

The major element of IG is accountability—accountability with the laws, regulations, and standards governing records and information. Therefore, in this chapter, you will also be introduced to the major laws, regulations, and standards to which RIM programs (and IG initiatives) must comply.

INFORMATION GOVERNANCE

A renewed interest in RIM has resulted in a call by many to use fundamental records management principles as the foundation for sound IG.

Information is a vital organizational asset, and information governance is an integrated, strategic approach to managing, processing, controlling, archiving, and retrieving information as evidence of all transactions of the organization. Writing in the *eDiscovery Journal*

> **A**ccording to Gartner, *information governance* is viewed as "the specification of decision rights and an accountability framework to ensure appropriate behavior in the evaluation, creation, storage, use, archiving and deletion of information. It includes the processes, roles and policies, standards, and metrics that ensure the effective and efficient use of information in enabling an organization to achieve its goals."*
>
> *"Gartner, s.v. "information governance," IT Glossary, accessed August 20, 2017, www.gartner.com/it-glossary/information-governance/.

blog, Barry Murphy explained that IG provides a framework for the "conservative side of information management."[1]

Every organization must consider its legal and regulatory environment along with its tolerance for risk when designing its IG framework. Questions to be asked include:

- What records and information are needed to support business processes?
- What steps must be taken to be in compliance with governing laws and regulations?
- What records and information could/should be destroyed, when, and how?

Although the Gartner definition of IG, which describes the need for an accountability framework, is the most widely accepted, a recently released definition from the IG Initiative reads: "Information Governance is the activities and technologies that organizations employ to maximize the value of their information while minimizing associated risks and costs."[2] Although technologies and activities are basic to IG, on a higher level there are three core elements to an IG governance framework as shown in figure 2.1: policies, processes, and compliance. Accountability measures in the form of audits and metrics must be used to monitor the components of these elements. Records management must be integrated throughout the process.

An information governance model can be used to provide context to discussions of the integration of information management, risk management, and records management. This framework should address all types of information, whether meeting the criteria established for a record or not.

Records and Information Defined

Although an IG program manages both records and information, it is important to understand the difference between the two for legal and compliance purposes. A *record* is "any recorded information, regardless of medium or characteristics, made or received by an organization in pursuance of legal obligations or in the transaction of business" according to ARMA International.[3] The definition of *record* provided by the International Standard Organization (ISO) is slightly different: "information created, received, and maintained as evidence and as an asset by an organization or person, in pursuance of legal obligations or in the transaction of business."[4]

Information is a "collection of data, ideas, thoughts, or memories."[5] Information is also defined as "facts provided or learned about something or someone" and that which is "conveyed or represented by a particular arrangement or sequence of things;" for example, "data as processed, stored, or transmitted by a computer."[6]

Because no two organizations are the same, each IG program and IG framework will be unique. Ideally, the business will take a *holistic approach* as recommended by Robert Smallwood, Managing Director at the Institute for Information Governance. According to Smallwood:

> Information Governance is used as a means of improving the quality and security of information throughout its lifecycle. In essence, almost all of management must be involved in supporting an Information Governance program, and the business is adjusted as a whole . . . all departments must be involved in managing data to meet the regulatory, legal, and business demands of the modern business world, to maximize the data's value, while minimizing the risks and costs.[7]

Policies

An IG framework relies foremost upon a comprehensive RIM policy that draws on best practices and can be adapted for almost any circumstance. It must address roles and responsibilities, communications and training, and metrics and monitoring. The RIM policy must refer to the requirements for managing records resulting from all business activities. And the RIM policy must acknowledge additional considerations for managing records created by or residing in social media and the cloud.

Policy teams must include representatives from the appropriate functional areas, such as records management, information technology, business units, compliance, human

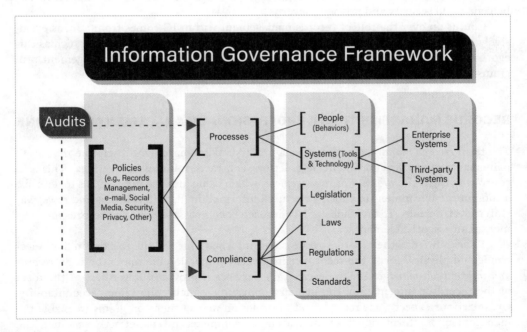

FIGURE 2.1 Information governance framework.

resources, sales and marketing, and communications and public relations. The advent of Web 2.0 and collaborative, web-based technologies has resulted in the formation of social media teams in many organizations. Input from this team should be included as well. Most organizations have a number of policies governing communications, security, privacy, compliance, and social media that must be harmonized.

Compliance

Organizations must adhere to applicable laws, regulations, and standards. To be in compliance, organizations understand that a records retention schedule should be media-neutral and that retention requirements must be met. At the same time, all new initiatives, such as wearable cameras for police officers, must be reviewed to determine if new records—and, therefore, records series—will result. Automated processes should be utilized as much as possible when capturing and managing information, including placing a hold on the disposition process when a legal action is pending. Guidance should be provided to all individuals involved, including employees and consultants.

Processes

Processes are implemented to ensure compliance at an acceptable level of risk for the organization. Operational guidelines govern the selection of appropriate technology and services to accomplish the core mission of the organization. Best practice should be established for all parties involved with managing information. These include guidelines for the use of personal and enterprise information technology, participation on social media sites, ethical behavior, and security and privacy concerns.

Confusion over the role of records management within IG comes from a focus exclusively on technology that can automate some records management functions, such as categorization, retention, and legal holds. There is much more to records management programs than automating technology to handle records management tasks.

RECORDS MANAGEMENT AS A PROFESSIONAL MANAGEMENT DISCIPLINE

The term *records management* describes a professional management discipline that originally managed physical documents (e.g., letters, contracts, minutes of meetings). This is in contrast to the term *information management,* which came into use in the 1970s to describe a computer environment in which structured information (data in columns and rows) was stored electronically. Today's holistic IG approach encompasses both—and records management is an essential element.

To acknowledge the fact that records and information continue to exist in both electronic and physical form, the records management profession embraces the term *records and information management* to describe the services it provides. Regardless of the form of the record or information, the primary obligation remains the same—accountability. Organizations expect their records and information management programs to enable the management of information in a timely, accurate, complete, and cost-effective manner. The information managed must be accessible and usable.

ISO 15489-1:2016 defines *records management* as the "field of management responsible for the efficient and systematic control of the creation, receipt, maintenance, use and disposition of records, including processes for capturing and maintaining evidence of and information about business activities and transactions in the form of records."[8]

Record and Information Management Objectives

The activities of a records and information management program are undertaken with specific objectives in mind. They are to:

- develop and/or identify standards or procedures for the effective, efficient, and secure management of records and information throughout the organization;
- provide effective control, appropriate security, and management over the creation, maintenance, use, and disposition of all records within the organization;
- ensure that the records accurately reflect the business practices, policies, and transactions of the organization;
- simplify the activities, systems, and processes of records creation, maintenance, and use;
- preserve and dispose of records in accordance with business needs, statutes, and regulations;
- protect vital records;
- provide business continuity in the event of a disaster;
- protect records of historical importance;
- provide evidence of business, personal, and cultural activity; and
- maintain corporate, personal, and collective memory.

Records and Information Management Risks

Organizations often look to RIM programs to mitigate risks. The risk management approach looks at the other side of the coin to describe what will happen if the organization does not have a comprehensive records management program in place. Major concerns are:

- damage to the organization's reputation;
- high costs for information management and storage;
- lost files and risk of spoliation;
- legal discovery penalties or sanctions; and
- audit and compliance violations.

An effective RIM program comprised of records management policy and procedures, well-trained personnel, and advanced information systems will reduce risks to the organization.

More recently, organizations have turned to its information assets (records included) as a source of business intelligence (BI). This value must also be considered when developing the organization's risk profile (risk will be discussed further in chapter 9).

RECORDS AND INFORMATION MANAGEMENT LIFECYCLE

An essential characteristic of information is its value, which may decline as time passes and eventually reaches zero. The value of information contained in records must be considered at each stage of the RIM lifecycle. But models change over time, influenced by current practices and the technology available.

Document-Centric Records and Information Lifecycle

Throughout the twentieth century, records were controlled in the form of documents. *Document* is defined as (1) any written or printed work (a writing); (2) information or data fixed in some media; (3) information or data fixed in some media, but which is not part of a record (a non-record); or (4) a written or printed work of a legal or official nature that may be used as evidence or proof; (a record.)[9]

A document was traditionally considered to be text fixed on paper, but today drawings, word processing files, web pages, and database reports are also considered documents. Like records, they have content, context, and structure, but the nature of these attributes may change in an electronic environment (e.g., a hypertext document on the web may be formed by combining different sections housed on different servers in different countries through the use of links).

The lifecycle model shown in figure 2.2 portrays a closed system that begins with the birth of a document (capture/creation) and ends with its death (destruction) or movement to an archive for permanent preservation. This model is useful when describing the management of paper-based records. In order to save storage space, retention schedules are developed to document the method of disposition and to establish destruction dates. Records that are no longer in active use but that have not yet met their retention requirements may be transferred to a records center for storage and eventual destruction. Records that have permanent value are most often transferred to an archive for preservation and use.

By 2011, the concept of document-centric records and information management lifecycle had evolved to reflect the electronic environment that allows for storage in a document library and to emphasize the continuing value of the information contained—the document management system. New electronic documents enter the system and those that no longer have value to daily operations

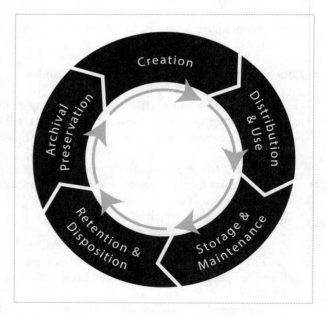

FIGURE 2.2 Document-centric records and information lifecycle model.

exit the system. Records management functionality—such as retention, disposition, and legal holds—is integrated into most document management systems.

Documents not born digital are also brought into document management systems through digitization (scanning). The document management system automates storage and retention through indexing, search, and disposal capabilities that allow users to store and retrieve records within the electronic library. Document management systems are available as self-hosted or cloud-based options. Today's systems feature integrations for Microsoft Office, Salesforce, DocuSign, QuickBooks, and other programs, and some offer an application programming interface (API) for customized integrations.[10]

Information Lifecycle Management

Not all information is created equal. Some will be classified as records, but other useful information may never be designated a formal record (e.g., work in progress). Therefore, organizations are justifiably concerned about managing all information and not just *official records* (those possessing legally recognized and enforceable qualities necessary to establish a fact). Some of the information will be structured and other information unstructured. *Structured data* is organized in a way that makes it identifiable. An Access or SQL database is structured in columns and rows, which makes searching for the data type within the content possible. All other electronic information that has the potential to be records is stored as unstructured data. *Unstructured data* is anything not in a database. Images, word documents, and even tweets are examples of unstructured data.[11] Unstructured data are more difficult to classify, maintain, archive, and dispose of than structured data.

Information, whether structured or unstructured, can be thought of as "the communication or reception of knowledge or intelligence" that must be managed.[12] *Information lifecycle management* (ILM) is a comprehensive approach to managing the flow of an information system's data and associated metadata from creation and initial storage to the time when it becomes obsolete and is deleted.[13]

There are many variations on the ILM model, from simple to complex. Like the records and information lifecycle model, it can take a *cradle to grave perspective,* as shown in figure 2.3.

This simplified diagram can be used to understand the controls that must be applied to information during each stage of its lifecycle, regardless of the technology employed.

- **Creation (including capture):** Planning is an essential part of the creation phase. Planning before creation can help ensure that the right information is created and by the right people, that it is reliable and in the most

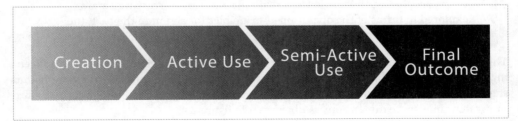

FIGURE 2.3 Information lifecycle model.

appropriate format, and that the necessary metadata are created and captured.

- **Active use:** During this phase, information and records are in constant or frequent use, primarily to conduct business. During this stage, the purpose(s) for which the information can be used must be defined, the information must be findable and accessible, the individuals who need access must be granted such access, and the integrity of the information must be secured.
- **Semi-active use:** These are the most vulnerable records and information because they have declined in value and controls tend to be less stringent. During this phase information may be held to satisfy retention requirements, referred to on occasion for reference purposes, or retrieved for evidential purposes.
- **Final outcome:** Information that is no longer useful to the organization and that has met its retention requirements is destroyed. Information that has enduring value for historic reference or research or that must be retained due to regulatory obligations is preserved. Disposal of information that has met its retention requirements and no longer has value must be controlled. Even more challenging, preservation of and access to information of enduring value must be ensured.

Records Continuum

Although most records and information managers in the United States embrace the records and information lifecycle model, many experts outside of the United States advocate the *records continuum* as an alternative. Australian archival theorist Frank Upward formulated the records continuum concept based upon four principles:

1. A concept of record inclusive of records of continuing value (archives) stresses their use for transactional, evidentiary, and memory purposes, and unifies approaches to archives/recordkeeping, whether records are kept for a split second or a millennium.
2. The focus on records as logical rather than physical entities, regardless of whether they are in paper or electronic form.
3. Institutionalization of the recordkeeping profession's role requires a particular emphasis on the need to integrate recordkeeping into business and societal processes and purposes.
4. Archival science is the foundation for organizing knowledge about recordkeeping. Such knowledge is revisable but can be structured and explored in terms of the operation of principles for action in the past, the present, and the future.[14]

The records continuum model emphasizes the overlapping characteristics of recordkeeping—evidence, transaction, and the identity of the creator. It deemphasizes the time-bound stages of the lifecycle model and combines the recordkeeping and archiving processes into integrated time-space dimensions as illustrated in figure 2.4.

In the United States, archives and records management are often viewed as two separate responsibilities managed by two different types of professionals, the archivist and the records manager. The Australian model's integrated approach, however, underscores the importance of managing records and archives seamlessly to fulfill both managerial and cultural responsibilities. Recordkeepers, whether they consider themselves archivists or records managers, must understand the uses and values of records from creation through long-term preservation.

The records continuum model illustrates a convergence of the functions of the archivist with those of the records and information manager by placing equal emphasis on the preservation of information to ensure societal memory.

Enterprise Content Management (ECM)

Enterprise content management (ECM) is an appropriate example of how quickly the technology landscape is changing. A search for document management systems in 2017 revealed Gartner Inc.'s 2016 magic quadrant for enterprise content management systems instead, underscoring the fact that, for many, document management has been subsumed into enterprise content management. The four leaders for 2016 were IBM, Dell EMC, OpenText, and Hyland. M-Files was considered the only visionary, and Oracle, Microsoft, Alfresco, and Lexmark were considered challengers. The six niche players were Newgen Software,

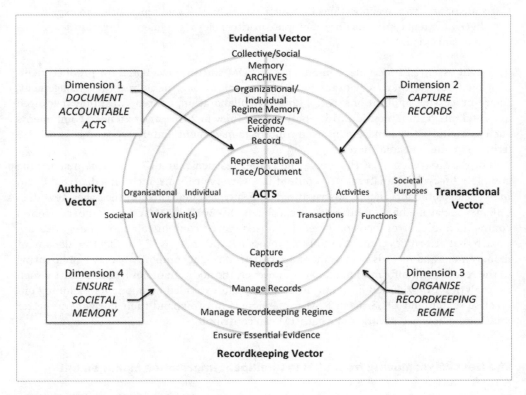

FIGURE 2.4 Records continuum model.

SOURCE: Understanding Society through its Records, "Australian Contributions to Recordkeeping." Courtesy of Frank Upward, Monash University, Australia.

Objective, Xerox, Laserfiche, SER Group, and Everteam.[15] By 2017, the landscape changed and a number of ECM companies had either split up or were acquired. Hyland (a leader in this sphere), for example, acquired Lexmark (a challenger).[16]

So what is ECM? First defined by AIIM (Association for Information and Image Management) in 2000, the definition has been modified several times since then. In 2005, the definition stressed the technologies used. By 2010, the definition was expanded to stress the strategies, methods, and tools used. Today, AIIM includes the users and the use of the content in this definition:

> Enterprise Content Management is the systematic collection and organization of information that is to be used by a designated audience—business executives, customers, etc. Neither a single technology nor a methodology nor a process, it is a dynamic combination of strategies, methods, and tools used to capture, manage, store, preserve, and deliver information supporting key organizational processes through its entire lifecycle.[17]

Gartner also revised its definition of ECM based on shifting business requirements and new technologies. The most recent definition is:

> ECM is a set of services and microservices, embodied either as an integrated product suite or as separate applications that share common APIs and repositories, to exploit diverse content types, and serve multiple constituencies and numerous use cases across an organization.[18]

The eight essential functional components of ECM software evaluated for product inclusion on 2016 Gartner's Quadrant were: document management, records management, image-processing applications, social content/collaboration, content workflow, packaged apps and integration (new in 2016), analytics /BI (new in 2016), and extended components such as digital asset management, web content management, enterprise search, and EFSS (enterprise file sync and share).

In the first version of this book, the reader learned that ECM systems manage the complete lifecycle of unstructured content in a variety of forms, including digitized documents, electronic forms, and unstructured data such as email, instant messages, text documents, social media content, and spreadsheets. By 2017, ECM systems "moved from a command-and-control focus on managing unstructured content to a more integrated approach that prioritizes content usability, processing, and analysis."[19] The fact that document management and records management are two of the eight components may be reassuring to the records and information manager; however, the addition of new functionalities such as Analytics/BI, packaged apps and integration, and extended components including enterprise search and EFSS mean RIM professionals must expand their horizons to better understand how users work and what RIM can contribute.

The Next Wave: Moving from ECM to Intelligent Information Management

The title for this section was irresistible. John Mancini, Chief Evangelist, AIIM, used the term intelligent information management to call attention to the changes occurring in the enterprise content management environment in a report published jointly with OnBase by

Hyland.[20] RIM professionals who now feel confident they understand ECM will need to be prepared for the "next wave" since ECM is dead (or so reported Gartner analyst Michael Woodbridge in a January 2017 blog post).[21]

I think most practitioners understood what those promoting ECM as a panacea knew all along: A single enterprise content management system did not/could not really manage all content within the Enterprise. What will be in place by the time this work is published is anyone's guess. Both Mancini (AIIM) and Woodbridge (Gartner) express slightly different views—and employ different terminology.

According to Woodbridge, ECM systems are only successful at one of four main goals associated with the utilization of content: regulatory compliance and risk management. One of the three remaining goals, retention and dissemination of knowledge could only be accomplished by complex integration of the ECM with other systems. And the remaining two goals: cost and process efficiencies and innovation and new ways of working were illusive.[22]

The solution proposed by Gartner is *Content Services,* which is comprised of Content Services Applications, Platforms, and Components. This is a new way of thinking about utilizing information regardless of where it resides. Using a Content Services approach, content services will be "delivered quickly, cost effectively and to meet emerging business innovations whilst maintaining the appropriate level of governance and compliance."[23]

Mancini, on the other hand, suggests a move to *intelligent information management.* He recognizes the reality that different species of technologies are currently employed, regardless of when they were introduced: Document management and workflow circa 1995, enterprise content management circa 2005, and mobile and cloud content management circa 2015. All provide different solutions to manage the interaction between people, processes, and technology. That means the systems introduced earlier in this chapter are likely still in use, sometimes all within the same enterprise. However, he also recognizes trends that will "mold and shape" content management going forward, including the rise of data-centric technologies such as Hadoop, NoSQL, blockchain, the Internet of Things, and the shift among solution providers to a cloud-first strategy.[24]

In Mancini's vision of the future, both data and content must be managed. To help us visualize this new world, we could use an Intelligent Information Management Roadmap comprised of six components Create, Capture, Automate, Deliver, Secure, and Analyze.[25]

RECORDS MANAGEMENT PROGRAM ELEMENTS, FUNCTIONS, AND ACTIVITIES

Although records management programs can and do vary depending on the size and culture of organization, the industrial sector to which they belong, and the applicable laws and regulations, common functions must be performed.

Records Management Program Elements

The elements of a comprehensive records management program listed here will be addressed further in future chapters:

- policy and procedure development
- records inventory, appraisal, retention, and disposition

- active files management (paper and electronic)
- inactive files management and control (records center and digital archive)
- preservation and access (digital and physical)
- vital records protection, disaster recovery and business continuity planning
- training and outreach programs

Through all of the stages of the RIM lifecycle, security, privacy, and risk management must be addressed.

Records Management Activities

In order to ensure that those functions listed previously are performed, the records and information manager is responsible for specific activities. The National Archives and Records Administration (NARA) defines the following typical records management (RM) program activities that are also applicable to records managers in the private sector:

- **Identifying records and records sources:** This involves distinguishing records from non-records for retention purposes; determining how, how many (in terms of volume) and by whom the records are being created and received; and identifying the relationship of the record to the agencies'/ organization's business operations or functions.
- **Developing a file plan:** Specify how records will be organized by identifying the classes of records (records series) the organization produces and establishing how to associate records within a class to other records in the same class.
- **Developing records schedules:** The schedules will document how long the records must be retained and their final disposition (destruction or transfer of legal and/or physical custody to an archives) based on time, event, or a combination of the two.
- **Providing records management guidance:** This involves developing policies and procedures for implementing records management activities, as well as recordkeeping practices establishing the records that are created to conduct agency/organization business and identifying parties within the agency/ organization with RM responsibilities, such as records officers of liaisons.[26]

When determining the specific activities mentioned here, such as developing a records schedule, the records professional must refer to governing laws, regulations, and standards. Prevailing trends in case law must also be monitored and taken into consideration when evaluating risk. The next section of this chapter is developed to standards, laws, regulations, and the legal environment.

STANDARDS, LAWS, REGULATIONS, AND THE LEGAL ENVIRONMENT

Regulatory compliance is required to safeguard physical and electronic records, shield the organization from unnecessary risk, and help control costs. Standards, technical reports, and guidelines create a professional environment of best-practice procedures that enable organizations to develop compliant records/information systems, policies, and procedures.

Standards

Standards provide us with codification of practice, explicit rules from implicit methodologies, development of a body of common knowledge, consistency in practice and quality, interoperability and interconnectivity, and efficiency. Many of the standards overlap and one standard cannot be used for everything; instead, several standards may work together to achieve standard practice.[27]

The appropriate mix of standards will be unique to each organization. Several of the standards often referred to by records/information managers are introduced in this chapter.[28]

De Facto Standards

Some programs and practices are used so often and widely that they are considered *de facto* standards. One example is the US Department of Defense standard *DoD 5015.2-STD Electronic Records Management Software Applications Design Criteria Standard*. This standard was originally developed to provide implementation and procedural guidance on the management of records in the US Department of Defense. The Joint Interoperability Test Command (JITC) tests the products and makes a product register available online to provide information about certified records management application (RMA) products. Currently all products listed on this project register are valid in perpetuity.[29]

NARA subsequently endorsed this standard for use by all government agencies. Eventually so many private firms turned to this standard when developing or evaluating enterprise records management system (ERMS) products that ARMA International published a technical report, *Using DoD 5015.02-STD outside the Federal Government Sector*, to help those outside of the federal government better understand how to apply the de facto standard for their own needs.

Outside of the United States, guidance is provided in the form of a similar de facto standard, *Model Requirements for the Management of Electronic Records (MoReq)*. MoReq2010 is the latest specification published by the *DLM Forum* intended for use throughout the European Union by public and private sector organizations. Like *DoD 5015.02-STD*, MoReq outlines the essential elements a records system requires to ensure that records are properly managed, accessible, and available as long as they are needed and are properly disposed of once the retention period has expired. MoReq test centers can test and certify software, systems, and site installations against the specifications.[30]

De Jure Standards

De Jure Standards are those adopted by an official standards-setting body, such as the International Organization for Standardization (ISO) and the American National Standards Institute (ANSI). Standards development is a complex task. Some standards are accompanied by a technical report to provide guidance for implementation.

ISO, the largest developer and publisher of international standards, is a network of the national standards institutes of 160 countries. In the United States, ANSI is the official representative to ISO. ISO has adopted a number of records management standards that belong on every manager's resource list.

The standards important to records managers are not just those that are considered records management standards. Records managers will identify other standards based on the needs of the organization and the task at hand. For example, three additional ISO standards that may provide useful are ISO/TR 15801:2017 *Document management—Electronically stored information—Recommendations for trustworthiness and reliability;* ISO/IEC 27000 family of standards, *Information security management systems;* and *ISO 31000:2009 Risk Management—Principles and Guidelines.*

Professional associations are active in developing standards, guidelines, best practices, and technical reports to assist their members.[31] These associations must work with a national standards development body if they wish to develop a standard.

AIIM, for example, was instrumental in moving the PDF file format forward from a popular de facto standard to an ANSI- and then ISO-approved standard, ISO 32000-1. Based upon the PDF 1.4 version of that standard, the first *PDF/A standard for long-term preservation* was approved, *ISO 19005-1:2005 Document Management—Electronic Document File Formation for Long-Term Preservation—Part 1 Use of PDF 1.4 (PDF/A-1).* Part 2 of ISO 19005 was approved as a final draft in 2011 based on version 1.7 of the PDF standard. Part 3, published in 2012, specifies the use of PDF 1.7 for preserving the static visual representation of page-based electronic documents over time, but it also allows any type of other content to be included as an embedded file or attachment.

In 2017, PDF 2.0 was released. *ISO 32000-02:2017 Document management—Portable document format—Part 2: PDF 2.0* is primarily intended for developers of software that creates PDF files (PDF writers), software that reads existing PDF files and (usually) interprets their contents for display (PDF readers), software that reads and displays PDF content and interacts with the computer users to possibly modify and save the PDF file (interactive PDF processors), and PDF products that read and/or write PDF files for a variety of other purposes (PDF processors). The new format, PDF 2.0, has not yet resulted in changes to the 19005 standards for long-term preservation, but it is important to keep abreast of the latest changes in the PDF/A format that might emerge.

In 2011, ANSI endorsed a standard developed by a consensus group formed by ARMA International. The standard *Implications of Web-Based, Collaborative Technologies in Records Management (ANSI/ARMA 18-2011)* provides requirements and best practice recommendations related to policies, procedures, and processes for an organization's use of internally facing or externally directed (public or private) social media technologies such as wikis, blogs, mashups, and classification (tagging) sites.

Laws and Regulations

How many articles have you read that included the phrase *exponential growth of information*? I know I've used those words myself. But what does this mean? There is broad consensus that the digital universe will double every two years (a fifty-fold increase between 2010 and 2020), with human- and machine-generated data growing ten times faster than business data.[32]

It is difficult to imagine traditional records management approaches being applied to all human- and machine-generated data. Records and information managers must become part of the solution to these challenges. However, records retention and disposition

Sampling of ISO Records/Information Management Standards and Technical Reports.

ISO 15489-1:2016 Information and documentation—Records management—Part 1 Concepts and principles. ISO 15489-1:2016 is a replacement for ISO 15489-1:2001. It establishes the core concepts and principles for the creation, capture, and management of records. Although it is self-contained, this standard is central to a number of ISO standards and technical reports that provide records management guidance and instruction.

ISO/TR 18128:2014 Information and documentation—Risk assessment for records processes and systems. This technical report provides assistance to organizations in assessing risks to records processes and systems so they can ensure records continue to meet identified business needs as long as required.

ISO 16175-1:2010—Information and documentation—Principles and functional requirements for records in electronic office environments. This standard establishes fundamental principles and functional requirements for software used to create and manage digital records in office environments. This standard should be used with *ISO 16175-2 Guidelines and functional requirements for digital records management systems* and *ISO 16175-3 Guidelines and functional requirements for records in business systems.*

ISO 23081-1:2017 Information and documentation—Records management processes—Metadata for Records—Part 1: Principles. This part of ISO 23081 covers the principles that underpin and govern records management metadata. It is applicable to records and their metadata, all processes that affect them, any system in which they reside, and any organization that is responsible for their management. This update to the 2006 version is supported by *ISO 23018-2:2009—Part 2: Conceptual and implementation issues* and *ISO 23018-3:2011—Part 3: Self-Assessment Method.*

decisions will still be made with regard to many high-value business records due to four different types of official actions: executive orders, legislation (statutes that become laws), administrative actions (regulations), and judicial decisions (case law).

Executive Orders

Executive orders are issued by the incumbent president, who can revoke orders of previous presidents, changing the way in which presidential records are to be managed. The Presidential Records Act (PRA) of 1979 changed the legal ownership of the official records of the president from private to public and established a new statutory structure under which presidents must manage their records. In January 1989, President Ronald Reagan issued Executive Order 12677 to establish procedures for NARA and former and incumbent presidents to implement the PRA. Shortly after the attacks of 9/11, President George W. Bush issued Executive Order 13233 revoking President Reagan's Executive Order 12677 and restricting access to the records of former presidents. This new executive order applied to the records of the Vice President as well. President Barack Obama's first act as president in 2009 was Executive Order 13489 revoking President Bush's Executive Order 13233 and limiting the authority of the president and former presidents to block the release of presidential records. Although President Donald J. Trump has not issued an executive order on this issue at the time of this writing, there has been much speculation over the status of his tweets on his private Twitter account, @realDonaldTrump, as presidential records and whether removal of any of the tweets would violate the PRA.

Legislation and Regulations

Laws are created by statutes that originate from legislative bills. Laws can be enacted on the federal, state, and local levels of government. On the federal level, the US Congress votes to adopt legislation, the president signs the legislation making it a law, and various agencies are charged with publishing regulations to provide guidance to implement the law. *Regulation* is defined as "a rule or order issued by an executive authority or regulatory agency of a government and having the force of law."[33] Regulations are applicable only within the jurisdiction or purpose for which such regulations are made.

Noncompliance with laws or regulations can result in fines, sanctions, litigation, and personal liability for corporate officers. Managing records in a prudent and defensible manner is essential to minimizing risk and establishing proof of compliance. But the question is, compliance with which laws and regulations? Responsibility for answering that question varies across organizations. There is an increased appreciation for the role of records management in reducing risk exhibited by the fact that records management is typically housed within governance and/or compliance areas.

The individual responsible for identifying applicable laws and regulations will need to consider those laws and regulations specific to his or her organization's situation. Regulations provide more detail than the laws from which they arise and will, in some cases, specify the length of time certain records must be available for audit. This information is essential to determining the retention period for records that result from a similar activity or that document a specific type of transaction.

In the United States, the Office of the Federal Register provides access to the official text of federal laws, presidential documents, administrative regulations and notices, and descriptions of federal organizations, programs, and activities. Of particular significance to records managers is the *Code of Federal Regulations* (CFR) that codifies the general and permanent rules published in the *Federal Register* by the departments and agencies of the federal government.

Records management issues are addressed in Title 44 of the United States Code (USC). The basis of records management in the federal government is the Federal Records Act of 1950 (44 US § 2901) , which states: "The law establishes the basis for records management programs in Federal Agencies."[34]

NARA regulations can be found in Title 36 of the *United States Code* and in the *Code of Federal Regulation*s, 36 CFR 1220, subchapter B—Records Management. Subchapter B specifies policies for federal agencies' records management programs relating to proper records creation and maintenance, adequate documentation, and records disposition.

Congress can also regulate the actions of private firms. The Sarbanes-Oxley Act of 2002 (SOX) is legislation enacted by the US Congress and signed by President Bush in response to the high profile Enron and WorldCom financial scandals. Administered by the Securities and Exchange Commission (SEC), it is designed to protect shareholders and the general public from accounting errors and fraudulent practices. It applies to all public companies

Key US Federal Statutes Related to Records Management

National Archives Act of 1934. Signed by Franklin D. Roosevelt, this act established the National Archives to centralize federal recordkeeping, with the Archivist of the United States as its chief administrator.

Federal Records Act of 1950. This act, as amended, establishes the framework for records management programs in federal agencies. As the primary agency for records management oversight, the NARA is responsible for assisting federal agencies in maintaining adequate and proper documentation of policies and transactions of the federal government. This is done by appraising records, regulating and approving the disposition of federal records, operating Federal Records Centers and preserving permanent records. President Obama signed into law H.R. 1233, the Presidential and Federal Records Act Amendments of 2014 that strengthened the Federal Records Act by expanding the definition of federal records to clearly include electronic records and granting to the Archivist of the United States final determination as to what constitutes a federal record.

Freedom of Information Act (FOIA) of 1966. This act, as amended, ensures public access to US government records. FOIA carries a presumption of disclosure. The burden is on the government to demonstrate why information may not be released. Upon written request, US government agencies are required to disclose their records, unless they can be lawfully withheld from disclosure under one of nine specific exemptions in the FOIA. This law was most recently amended by the FOIA Improvement Act of 2016.

Privacy Act of 1974. This act establishes safeguards for the protection of records that the federal government collects and maintains on US citizens and permanent records. The act mandates that the government must disclose what information is being collected and how it will be used. It also bars agencies from maintaining information not directly related to their mission. This act allows individuals to seek access to records retrieved by their name and personal identifier and to seek amendment of any inaccurate information. The Privacy Act of 1974, 5 U.S.C. § 552a establishes a code of fair information practices that governs the collection, maintenance, use, and dissemination of information maintained in the systems of records by federal agencies.

Presidential Records Act (PRA) of 1978. This act governs the official records of presidents and vice presidents created or received for all presidents who come into office after January 20, 1981. This Act changed the legal ownership of the official records of the president from private to public, and established a new statutory structure under which presidents must manage the records while in office, and the records automatically transfer into the legal custody of the National Archives when the president leaves office. Responsibility for the control, preservation of, and access to presidential records of past presidents lies with the archivist. H.R.1233, the Presidential and Federal Records Act Amendments of 2014 modernized the PRA of 1978. It codified procedures by which former and incumbent presidents review

[CONTINUED ON FOLLOWING PAGE]

[CONTINUED]

presidential records for constitutional privileges. Formerly, this process was controlled by an executive order subject to change by different administrations.

Paperwork Reduction Act of 1995. This act requires that agencies obtain the approval of Office of Management and Budget (OMB) before requesting most types of information from the public. It requires the head of each agency to designate a chief information officer to carry out the responsibilities outlined.

E-Government Act of 2002. This act promotes the use of the internet and electronic government services to make the federal government more transparent and accountable. In addition, it provides enhanced access to government information and services in a manner consistent with laws regarding protection of personal privacy, national security, records retention, access for persons with disabilities, and other relevant laws.

The US Government Publishing Office's Federal Digital System provides access to a dataset of publications, including acts signed by the President, at https://www.gpo.gov/fdsys/search/home.action. FDS will be replaced by govinfo in December 2018 (https://www.govinfo.gov/).

in the United States, international companies that have registered equity or debt securities with the SEC, and the accounting firms that provide auditing services to them. SOX contains three rules that affect the management of business records. The first rule deals with destruction, alteration, or falsification of records. The second defines the retention period for records storage at not less than five years. The third refers to the types of business records that need to be stored—all business records and communications, including electronic communications. Consequences for noncompliance include fines, imprisonment, or both.[35]

The Financial Industry Regulatory Authority (FINRA) regulates the financial industry and requires brokerage firms and their registered representatives to retain records of all communications related to the broker-dealer's business, including those that are made through public blogs and social media sites such as Facebook, LinkedIn, and Twitter. Regulatory Notice 10-06 (2010) provided guidance regarding the issues that arise from such use. Specifically, FINRA requires that any firm that "intends to communicate, or permit its associated persons to communicate, through social media sites must first ensure that it can retain and retrieve records of those communications as required by Rules 17a-3 and 17a-4 under the Securities Exchange Act of 1934 and NASD Rule 3110. In 2011, Regulatory Notice 11-39 was released to provide additional guidance. In 2013, Amendments to Rule 2210 codified the guidance provided in both Notices with respect to the supervision of interactive social media posts by member firms. Regulatory Notice 17-18 (2017) specifies that records of communications using text message applications (apps) and chats are also covered and reiterates that for records retention purposes, it is the *content of the communication* that determines what must be retained.[36]

Another heavily regulated industry is the healthcare industry. The Health Insurance Portability and Accountability Act of 1996 (HIPAA) is a federal statute to help consumers maintain their insurance coverage by standardizing the electronic exchange of information (transactions) between trading partners.[37] HIPAA regulations also established privacy and security standards to protect individually identifiable health information. Records and

Key US Provisions Governing Records Management by the Federal Government

***The Code of Federal Regulations* (CFR)** is the codification of the general and permanent rules published in the *Federal Register* by executive offices and agencies of the federal government. The CFR is divided into fifty sections called "Titles." Of most interest to records and information managers is Title 36.

36 CFR 1220–1239: Parts 1220–1239 are specific to the National Archives and Records Administration. Topics include Creation and Maintenance of Federal Records (1222), Records Disposition Programs (1224), Transfer of Records to Records Storage Facilities (1232), Electronic Records Management (1236), and Microforms Records Management (1238). [1]

The United States Code (USC) is the consolidation and codification of the general and permanent laws of the United States. The USC is comprised of fifty-three Titles. Of most interest to records and information managers is Title 44, Public Printing and Documents. [2]

44 USC Chapters 21, 22, 29, 31, and 33 are especially relevant to records management on the federal level. Topics include: NARA (chapter 21), Presidential Records (chapter 22), Records Management by the Archivist of the United States and by the Administrator of General Services (chapter 29), Records Management by Federal Agencies (chapter 31), and Disposal of Records, which includes a definition of *records* (chapter 33).

SOURCE: https://bookstore.gpo.gov/catalog/code-federal-regulations-cfrs-print;
https://www.law.cornell.edu/uscode/text/44.

information management professionals in healthcare-related organizations must understand and be prepared to comply with HIPAA rules and regulations. Employers outside of the health sector who store records regarding employee health, such as employee absences, must also understand and comply with HIPAA regulations.

A law that has far-reaching implications for organizations engaged in interstate and foreign commerce is the Electronic Signatures in Global and National Commerce Act (E-SIGN). E-SIGN was enacted by Congress and signed into law by President William J. Clinton using his electronic ID on June 30, 2000. The purpose of this law was to facilitate the use of electronic records and signatures by ensuring the validity and legal effect of contracts entered into electronically. Section 101 (1)(C)(ii) of the act requires businesses to obtain the consumers' electronic consent or confirmation to receive information electronically that a law requires to be in writing.[38] Almost two decades after this law was enacted, professionals within a number of industries, including insurance, real estate, legal services, and finance have adopted this technology to speed business transactions without increasing risk. However, a record of the transaction in the form of an audit trail is recommended. For example, "Insurance professionals are advised to use electronic signatures and electronic records for 'special consumer disclosures' and to create an audit trail documenting the date and time the document was sent, received and read, along with the recipient and sender IP addresses and a digital image of the signed document."[39]

Caution is advised when identifying applicable laws and regulations. To be compliant with these regulations, additional research is required. As illustrated by the number of executive orders repealing previous presidential executive orders, present, and future actions can modify or negate previous decisions.

Rule 26 and Other Amendments of the Federal Rules of Civil Procedure

Organizations must not only be prepared to demonstrate compliance with laws and regulations, but they must also be prepared to defend themselves in court. The *Federal Rules of Civil Procedure* (FRCP) govern the conduct of civil actions brought into federal district courts.[40] Many states have used the FRCP as a model for their own rules of civil procedure. Rules 26 and 27 govern the production of evidence in most federal court cases and make the efficient management of electronic records more important than ever. Implications for records management programs cannot be ignored.

On December 1, 2015, amendments to the FRCP were released that mainly impact e-discovery procedures. Rule 26(b)(1) introduces the concept of *proportionality* including whether the burden or expense of the discovery outweighs its likely benefit. Rule 37(e)now focuses on "failure to preserve Electronically Stored Information" as opposed to "failure to provide Electronically Stored Information." Consequences (e.g., dismissal of the action, default judgment, instructions to the jury that it may or must presume the information was unfavorable to the party) could result if reasonable steps (as per the *reasonableness standard*) are not taken to preserve information in anticipation or conduct of litigation.[41]

The Legal Environment

Court rulings on cases similar to those in which an organization may find itself is part of the risk assessment process used to determine which records and information demand additional protection.

One example that supports the concept of both proportionality and reasonableness is *Duffy v. Lawrence Memorial Hospital, No. 14-2256 (D. Kansas, Mar. 31, 2017)*.

A request to produce a random sampling of patient files was granted after the defendant demonstrated that in order to comply with the original request, 15,574 unique patient records would have to be located and gathered and that it would take thirty minutes to process and review each record for a total cost of $196,933.23. In addition, redaction of patient confidential information under the direction of one qualified attorney would cost another $37,259.50. The total cost to produce would be over $230,000.

Kansas Magistrate Judge Teresa J. James granted the Motion to Modify Discovery Order from the defendant (and counterclaimant), and directed the defendant to produce a random sampling of 252 patient records, along with five spares, in order to respond to the plaintiff/relator's document requests. The defendant was further ordered to have the patient's personal confidential information redacted.[42]

The Sedona Conference is a nonprofit research and educational institute dedicated to the study of law and policy related to antitrust law, complex litigation, and intellectual property rights. Among its research products are a number of articles on the topic of eDiscovery, such as the "Commentary on Proportionality in Electronic Discovery 2017," published in volume 18 (2017) of the *The Sedona Conference Journal,* which can be downloaded from The Sedona Conference website.[43]

Federal Rules of Civil Procedure (FRCP) and Implications for Records Management

The *Federal Rules of Civil Procedure* govern civil proceedings in the United States district courts. These rules impact records management programs: Rule 26(a), Rule 26(b)(1), Rule 26(b)(2), Rule 26(b)(5), Rule 34(b)(2), Rule 37(e), and Rule 37(f).

Rule 26(a): This rule defines electronically stored information as a specific category to be disclosed. Businesses (whether plaintiff or defendant) have a responsibility to produce e-records. The requesting party may ask that it be produced in a specific format. If the parties do not agree, the court may specify the format.

Rule 26(b)(1): This rule changes the scope of discovery. Parties may obtain evidence regarding any non-privileged matter that is *relevant* and *proportional* to the needs of the case [italics are the author's].

Rule 26(b)(2): This rule acknowledges that some electronically stored information (ESI} may be unduly burdensome to produce due to issues such as hardware or software obsolescence or damaged media. In such cases the party need not produce e-records it regards as "not reasonably accessible because of the undue burden of the cost." The court can order production in spite of the assertion.

Rule 26(b)(5): This rule relates to claiming privilege or protecting trial-preparation materials. It states that if information is produced in discovery that is subject to a claim of privilege or of protection as trial-preparation material, the party making the claim may notify any party that received the information of the claim and the basis for it. The notified party must promptly return, sequester, or destroy the specified information and any copies of it. The producing party, however, must preserve the information until the claim is resolved.

Rule 34(b)(2): This rule specifies the need for greater specificity in objections to requests for production. A "reasonable" time period applies to producing responsive information, and responding parties must explicitly state in their production response if documents are being withheld.

Rule 37(e): This rule authorizes courts to issue sanctions where four conditions are met: (1) the ESI should have been preserved in anticipation or conduct of litigation; (2) the ESI is lost; (3) the loss is due to a party's failure to take reasonable steps to preserve it; and (4) the ESI cannot be restored or replaced through additional discovery.

Rule 37(f): This rule recognizes that companies cannot preserve all of the data they produce. It states that "absent exceptional circumstances, a court may not impose sanctions as the result of the routine, good-faith operation of an electronic information system."

NOTE: The Federal Rules of Civil Procedure as amended to December 1, 2016 can be viewed at https://www.law.cornell.edu/rules/frcp.

If you are employed by an international firm, you must become familiar with legal requirements and codes of practice in the countries in which business is conducted. This can become complicated. For example, the Data Protection Act of 1998 (DPA 1998) is an act of the Parliament of the United Kingdom (UK) defining the ways in which information about living people may be legally used and handled.[44] DPA 1998 was enacted to bring the UK law up-to-date to reflect the European Parliament Directive 95/45/EC, which required member states of the European Union (EU) to protect individuals' fundamental rights and freedoms, including the right to privacy with respect to the processing of personal data.[45] In 2016, the EU Parliament approved a replacement for the DPA, the General Data Protection Regulation (GDPR). The GDPR is a framework with greater scope and tougher punishments for those who fail to comply with the new rules around the storage and handling of personal data as of May 25, 2018.

The goal of the European Commission, the European Union's governing body, is harmonizing the laws of its member states to promote standardization and facilitate compliance. However, not all countries belong to the European Union and not all that do are in compliance with the directives of the European Commission. Although in 2016 the people of the United Kingdom voted to withdraw from the EU, the GDPR is likely to become British law. A sampling of laws and regulations outside of the United States is included in the appendix.

Unlike the EU countries and a number of others, the United States does not have a blanket federal level privacy act or law in place to cover all privacy issues. The right to privacy is considered protected by the fourth amendment of the US Constitution (although the Supreme Court has determined that freedom from unreasonable search and seizure is different from other privacy rights). Several states have privacy protection explicitly written into their constitutions. Individual laws, such as HIPAA for healthcare, address privacy related to records of specific industries.

It is easy to see how complex this is becoming, which explains why large organizations employ chief compliance officers (CCOs) to ensure that their organizations are complying with regulatory requirements and that the company and its employees are complying with internal policies and procedures. Records and information managers must be aware of these complex issues in order to develop compliant retention and disposition policies on their own or in collaboration with the corporate compliance officer.

SUMMARY

The volume, velocity, and variety of data created today present enormous challenges to the organization. Constantly evolving laws, regulations, and case law, along with the fact that much of the data are being created outside of the organization's firewalls, add to the complexity of the situation. An accountability framework that includes policies, processes, roles, standards, and metrics is necessary for the organization to effectively govern its records and information.

An information governance program built upon a solid records and information management foundation can produce benefits and mitigate risks to the organization. Benefits include the protection of essential records and those of historical importance; the preservation of corporate, personal, and collective memory; and effective control, appropriate security and management over the creation, maintenance, use, and disposition of all records within the organization. Risks that can be minimized include those that arise from lost files and potential charges of spoliation; high costs for information management and storage; and audits and compliance violations.

A number of models have been developed to describe the various stages in the life of records and information, including the document management lifecycle model, the information lifecycle model, the records management lifecycle model, and the records continuum. The goal of each of these is to ensure that the right information is available to the right person at the right time in compliance with all governing laws and regulations.

Records management programs vary across organizations and industries, but they all possess certain core elements (e.g., retention, disposition, preservation) and activities (e.g., records identification, disaster preparedness, and business continuity planning).

Laws, regulations, and standards impact records and information management programs for both government and private organizations. Industry-specific laws and regulations must be taken into account. Organizations involved in international business must understand the laws and regulations of the countries in which they operate.

In the United States, we see a system struggling to provide adequate healthcare to its most important stakeholders, its patients. Robert Smallwood—an industry-leading author, keynote speaker, consultant, and educator on Information Governance and Electronic Records—provides an analysis of the problem and possible solutions. This paradigm is unique in that it is placed not in the context of one specific organization but of an entire industry—the healthcare industry.

PARADIGM

The Information Governance Imperative in Healthcare

Robert Smallwood
Managing Director, Institute for Information Governance

Introduction

Information governance (IG) is about minimizing information risks and costs while maximizing its value. More specifically, the American Health Information Management Association (AHIMA) defines IG as "an organization-wide framework for managing information throughout its lifecycle and supporting the organization's strategy, operations, regulatory, legal, risk, and environmental requirements."[46]

Healthcare has major IG issues and it is imperative to address them.

The healthcare industry is uniquely challenged in that information accuracy, security, and privacy are absolutely paramount. Failing to safeguard sensitive patient information, especially protected health information (PHI), can have catastrophic consequences. Bad actors can steal a person's healthcare insurance credentials and identity and then undergo expensive medical procedures, leaving the victim with an inaccurate health history to untangle and perhaps major financial liabilities.

Moreover, when caregivers are provided inaccurate or out-of-date information, people can die. And bad information is killing Americans at record rates: medical mistakes kill over 250,000 people each year in the United States and are the third leading cause of death overall, behind heart disease and cancer, according to a study by doctors at Johns Hopkins. (These numbers are certainly low, because they do not include deaths at nursing homes and in-home care settings).[47]

Problem Statement

The United States has the most expensive healthcare in the world, the most advanced equipment, the most advanced medicines, the best-trained doctors—yet in a recent study of healthcare quality the United States came in dead last out of eleven civilized nations.[48] The United Kingdom, Switzerland, and Sweden topped the list.

The United States' problem is not medical training, advanced equipment, medicines, or financial resources, the problem is mostly a failure to get the right information to the right people at the right time; that is, caregivers must have accurate, current clinical information to do their jobs properly.

The consequences of this carelessness with information are colossal IG failures that almost daily expose major corporations to reputational and financial risk; for instance, the Premera BlueCross, Excellus BlueCross BlueShield and Anthem Health breaches in 2015, and the 21st Century Oncology breach in 2016 that exposed 2,213,597 patients' records.[49] These organizations obviously did not know where all their PHI, personally identifiable information (PII), and confidential electronic documents were located and took inadequate measures to secure that valuable information.

They—and most healthcare organizations—are not managing information as an asset and do not have a current accounting of their information assets, particularly sensitive or confidential ones. That is, there is no information inventory or "data map" showing where different types of information are stored, and they would have difficulty finding all incidences of it so that it may be secured.

Most organizations are not paying attention: they leave sensitive information out there floating around on their servers unsecured, unencrypted. When it comes time to attend to the problem, most often they "kick the can down the road" and do nothing.

The impact only becomes clear after a major event like a data breach, which can severely damage an organization's reputation—especially healthcare institutions where people's health and lives are at stake—and can result in thousands of patients and or customers being dragged into a "lifelong battle" to control their personal information.

Sometimes, the realization may come when a major lawsuit causes runaway legal costs or a significant fine or sanction is levied.

Recommended Solutions

IG challenges in healthcare have life-or-death consequences. However, with focused analysis, planning, and dedicated effort, they can be fixed. But to do so healthcare professionals must gain the necessary education and tools, collaborate with IG experts and each other, and gain executive management support for IG initiatives.

Although still in the early stages of adoption, healthcare organizations are beginning to understand that IG is an important strategic tool for addressing compliance and legal demand, as well as capitalizing on major trends like the onslaught of Big Data and the emerging Internet of Things (IoT). IG also addresses related issues such as data quality and integrity, information lifecycle management (ILM), patient privacy, and regulatory compliance.

Legal, regulatory, and information security demands are often key drivers for establishing IG programs in all industries, but in healthcare, information quality and control demands are more extreme and consequential.

The US government mandate requiring all public and private healthcare providers and other eligible professionals to automate medical records by January 1, 2014, and the ensuing mad rush to install electronic health record (EHR) systems and to prove "meaningful use" of these systems has had consequences. It has resulted in a number of sloppy, haphazard implementations that are generating inaccurate information. What has been mostly missing in these slapdash implementations are redesigned business processes with a built-in focus on not only information privacy and security but also on data governance and quality. When approached in this way, resultant reports and analyses are more accurate and trustworthy.

Anticipated Results

With accurate and trusted information, healthcare professionals can do the job they were trained to do, and drastically reduce medical mistakes. This is an IG effort with the highest purpose: to save lives.

On top of this noble pursuit to save lives by improving information and its delivery are the layers upon layers of regulatory compliance requirements and increased litigation demands, all of which add cost to healthcare operations. These forces are adding increased cost pressures to healthcare organizations, especially in the United States, where they are already under pressure to cut costs and increase their financial performance. IG programs can reduce the ongoing costs of compliance and litigation by streamlining and standardizing business processes that manage and control information and building in information security and privacy requirements that can be accommodated routinely.

IG is not all about risk and cost reduction. IG programs also can improve patient care and outcomes. IG efforts in healthcare have the opportunity to greatly improve clinical insights by leveraging data science and analytics, which has the potential to improve healing, recovery rates, and patient satisfaction. Further, financial and service innovations can arise from new insights gained by leveraging business analytics and other tools.

Healthcare, particularly in the United States, is at a crisis point, because the industry has invested so much in automation, training, and advanced equipment and medicines—but are still yielding troubling results in healthcare quality and outcomes.

Strong, ongoing IG programs in healthcare organizations can help harness the power of all the investments that have been made in technology and business process redesign, and improve results for patients and other healthcare stakeholders. However, most healthcare organizations have scarce resources to execute their business strategies, and IG program efforts must compete with other priorities. The business case must be made that once embedded, a robust IG program can yield significant benefits in improving patient care and outcomes, protecting privacy, assuring compliance, and preparing for and executing litigation requests, while reducing the costs of these key business activities.

Conclusion

Where should healthcare organizations start? How do they embark on an IG program? First, an assessment of the current state of the organization's information handling processes should be conducted, including an information inventory of all information assets and the creation of a data map. A data map shows where information is stored, and may include diagrams of information inflows and outflows. It is particularly helpful in identifying where sensitive data resides, including PHI, PII, and credit card information (PCI). Once identified and located, measures such as applying encryption can be implemented to better secure and control information.

When making the case for launching an IG program, practitioners must highlight the positive and demonstrate that improved patient outcomes, reduced legal risk, and lower cost structures are possible. They must also emphasize the business risks of indecision by showing the impact of data breaches and information loss which occur almost daily. A survey of 5,000 US consumers by security firm Carbon Black showed that over two-thirds of those surveyed would consider leaving their healthcare provider if it were the target of a ransomware attack.[50] So there can be real financial consequences if management in healthcare organizations does not take proactive steps to implement IG programs.

Healthcare organizations cannot afford to wait any longer; continued procrastination will only compound the problem and expose the organization to undue business and legal risk. And it is management that will ultimately be held accountable.

NOTES

1. "What is Information Governance?" *Information Architecture Inc.* (blog), accessed August 29, 2017, www.informationarchitected.com/blog/what-is-information-governance/.

2. Iron Mountain, "The IG Initiative Definition of Information Governance," accessed August 28, 2017, www.ironmountain.com/Knowledge-Center/Reference-Library/View-by-Document-Type/General-Articles/T/The-IG-Initiative-Definition-of-Information-Governance.aspx.

3. ARMA International, Glossary of Records Management and Information Governance Terms, 5th ed. (ARMA TR 22-2016) (Overland Park, KS: ARMA International, 2016), 43.

4. International Organization for Standardization (ISO), *ISO* 15489-1, 2nd edition 4-15-2016 Information and documentation—Records management—Part 1: Concepts and Principles (Geneva: ISO, 2016), 2.

5. Richard Pearce-Moses, s.v. "information," Glossary of Archival and Records Terminology, American Society of Archivists, accessed August 29, 2017, www2.archivists.org/glossary/terms/i/information.

6. Oxford Dictionaries Online, s.v. "information," accessed August 29, 2017, https://en.oxforddictionaries.com/definition/information.

7. Keith D. Foote, "Data Governance and Information Governance: Contemporary Solutions, "DATAVERSITY, September 13, 2016, www.dataversity.net/data-governance-information-governance-contemporary-solutions/.

8. *ISO* 15489-1, 2nd edition, 3.

9. Glossary of Archival and Records Terminology, s.v. "document," accessed August 29, 2017, www2.archivists.org/glossary/terms/d/document.

10. Chad Brooks, "Document Management Systems: A Buyers Guide," *Business News Daily,* January 19, 2017, www.businessnewsdaily.com/8026-choosing-a-document-management-system.html.

11. Christine Taylor, "Structured vs. Unstructured Data," *Datamation,* August 3, 2017, www.datamation.com/big-data/structured-vs-unstructured-data.html.

12. Merriam-Webster Online, s.v. "information," accessed August 29, 2017, http://unabridged.merriam-webster.com/unabridged/information.

13. SearchStorage, s.v. "information life cycle management," last modified September 2005, http://search storage.techtarget.com/definition/information-life-cycle-management.

14. Modeling Cross-Domain Task Force, "Appendix 16: Overview of the Records Continuum Concept," in *International Research on Permanent Authentic Records in Electronic Systems* (InterPARES) 2: *Experiential, Interactive and Dynamic Records*, Luciana Duranti and Randy Preston, eds. (Padova, Italy: Associazione Nazionale Archivistica Italiana, 2008), www.interpares.org/display_file.cfm?doc=ip2_book_appendix_16.pdf.

15. Karen A. Hobert, Gavin Tay, and Joe Mariano, "Magic Quadrant for Enterprise Content Management," October 26, 2016, Gartner, https://www.gartner.com/doc/reprints?id=1 -3KZPGDB&ct=161031&st=sb.

16. Venus Tamturk, "Hyland Completes Acquisition of Lexmark's Perceptive Business," *CMS Connected,* July 12, 2017, www.cms-connected.com/news-Archive/July-2017/Hyland -Completes-Acquisition-of-Lexmark-s-Enterprise-Content-Management-Unit-Perceptive.

17. *Glossary,* s.v. "What is Enterprise Content Management (ECM)?" Association for Information and Image Management (AIIM), accessed September 1, 2017, www.aiim.org/What-is-ECM -Enterprise-Content-Management#.

18. "What is Enterprise Content Management (ECM) Software?" *Gartner Peer Insights,* accessed September 1, 2017, https://www.gartner.com/reviews/market/enterprise-content -management.

19. Hobert, Tay, and Mariano, "Magic Quadrant for Enterprise Content Management."

20. John Mancini, The Next Wave: Moving from ECM to Intelligent Information Management Association for Information and Image Management (AIIM), 2017, accessed August 27, 2017, www.aiim.org.

21. Michael Woodbridge, "The Death of ECM and Birth of Content Services," *Gartner Blog Network* January 5, 2017, http://blogs.gartner.com/michael-woodbridge/the-death-of-ecm-and-birth-of -content-services/.

22. Ibid.

23. Ibid.

24. Mancini, "The Next Wave."

25. Ibid.

26. National Archives and Records Administration (NARA), "Fast Track Products," accessed September 1, 2017, www.archives.gov/records-mgmt/policy/prod6a.html.

27. Patricia Manning, "Competency Statement E (e-Portfolio Prepared in Partial Fulfillment of MARA Degree)," unpublished essay, 2011.

28. For additional information, consult the updated Guide to Commonly Used National and International Records Management Standards and Best Practices (2017) developed by Virginia A. Jones, CRM, FAI. The guide is available at no cost from the ARMA International Education Foundation website at http://armaedfoundation.org/research-reports/.

29. Joint Interoperability Test Command (JITC), "RMA Product Register," accessed September 1, 2017, http://jitc.fhu.disa.mil/projects/rma/reg.aspx.

30. *"Model Requirements for the Management of Electronic Records,"* (MoReq), "MoReq2010," accessed September 1, 2017, www.MoReq.info/. This site provides documents for download as well as information on becoming a MoReq educator, translator, or test center.

31. If you are a member of a professional association and feel you can contribute to the development of a standard, technical report, or guideline, consider becoming involved with your professional organization's standards development initiatives.

32. InsideBigData, "The Exponential Growth of Big Data," February 16, 2017, https://insidebigdata.com/2017/02/16/the-exponential-growth-of-data/.

33. Merriam-Webster Online, s.v. "regulation," accessed September 1, 2017, http://unabridged.merriam-webster.com/unabridged/regulation.

34. Cornell University Law School, Federal Records Act of 1950, 44 USC § 2901 et seq., *Legal Information Institute,* accessed September 1, 2017, www.law.cornell.edu/uscode/html/uscode44/usc_sup_01_44_10_29.html.

35. SearchCIO, Sarbanes-Oxley Act (SOX), accessed September 1, 2017, http://searchcio.tech target.com/definition/Sarbanes-Oxley-Act.

36. Financial Industry Regulatory Authority (FINRA), "Regulatory Notice 17-18—Social Media and Digital Communications: Guidance on Social Networking Websites and Business Communications," April 2017, https://www.finra.org/sites/default/files/notice_doc_file_ref/Regulatory-Notice-17-18.pdf.

37. US Government Printing Office, Health Insurance Portability and Accountability Act of 1996, H.R. 104-191, 104th Cong. (1996), accessed September 1, 2017, www.gpo.gov/fdsys/pkg/PLAW-104pub1191/content-detail.html.

38. Cornell University Law School, "Electronic Signatures in Global and National Commerce," 15 USC § 96, *Legal Information Institute,* accessed September 1, 2017, www.law.cornell.edu/uscode/15/usc_sup_01_15_10_96.html.

39. Arielle Castro, "E-Signature Market Update: What to Expect in 2017," *RPost* (blog), December 19, 2016, www.rpost.com/blog/e-signature-market-update-expect-2017/.

40. The *Federal Rules of Civil Procedure* can be viewed at www.law.cornell.edu/rules/frcp.

41. Olivia Gerroll, "Rule 1, 16, 26, 34, 37: FRCP Amendments Pertaining to eDiscovery," *D4,* March 9, 2016, http://d4discovery.com/discover-more/2016/3/the-2015-amendments-to-the-frcp-that-pertain-to-ediscovery#sthash.ppDeMjR1.dpbs.

42. JDSUPRA, "Court Approves Defendant's Proposed Sampling Production Plan: eDiscovery Case Law, May 5, 2017, www.jdsupra.com/legalNews/court-approves-defendant-s-proposed-42450/.

43. Sedona Conference, "The Sedona Conference Commentary on Proportionality in Electronic Discovery," *The Sedona Conference Journal* 18 (May 2017), 141–76.

44. SearchStorage.co.UK, U.K. Data Protection Act 1998 (DPA 1998), last modified January 2008, http://searchstorage.techtarget.co.uk/definition/Data-Protection-Act-1998.

45. European Union, Directive 95/46/EC of the European Parliament and of the Council on the Protection of Individuals with Regard to the Processing of Personal Data and on the Free Movement of Such Data, October 24, 1995.

46. AHIMA. "Information Governance Glossary." accessed April 26, 2018, www.ahima.org/topics/infogovernance/ig-glossary.

47. Dan Munro, "U.S. Healthcare Ranked Dead Last Compared to 10 Other Countries," *Forbes/Pharma & Healthcare,* June 16, 2014, https://www.forbes.com/sites/danmunro/2014/06/16/u-s-healthcare-ranked-dead-last-compared-to-10-other-countries/#89ab65a576fd.

48. Jen Christensen and Elizabeth Cohen, "Medical Errors May Be Third Leading Cause of Death in the U.S," *CNN,* May 4, 2016.

49. Jessica Davis, "7 Largest Data Breaches of 2015," *Healthcare IT News,* December 11, 2017; Cameron F. Kerry, "Lessons from the New Threat Environment from SONY, Anthem and ISIS," Brookings, March 26, 2015, https://www.brookings.edu/blog/techtank/2015/03/26/lessons-from-the-new-threat-environment-from-sony-anthem-and-isis; "Major 2016 Healthcare Data Breaches: Mid-Year Summary," *HIPPA Journal,* July 11, 2016, https://www.hipaajournal.com/major-2016-healthcare-data-breaches-mid-year-summary-3499.

50. Viscuso, Michael, "Ransom-Aware: Carbon Black Survey Finds 7 of 10 Consumers Would Consider Leaving a Business Hit by Ransomware," Carbon Black, May 25, 2017, https://www.carbonblack.com/2017/05/25/ransom-aware-survey-finds-7-of-10-consumers-would-consider-leaving-a-business-hit-by-ransomware/.

CHAPTER 3

Records and Information Creation and Capture, Classification, and File Plan Development

INTRODUCTION

In 2025, the world will create and replicate 163 zettabytes (ZB) of data, a tenfold increase over 2016. IDC (International Data Corporation) categorizes this data into four types:

- **Entertainment:** Image and video content created or consumed for entertainment purposes.
- **Non-entertainment image/video:** Image and video content for non-entertainment purposes, such as video surveillance footage or advertising.
- **Productivity data:** Traditional productivity-driven data such as files on PCs and servers, log files, and metadata.
- **Embedded:** Data created by embedded devices, machine-to-machine, and IoT.[1]

Much of digital data (embedded data) is created automatically and is ephemeral (transitory) in nature. In the world of information management, *transient data* are created within an application session. It passes quickly into and out of existence producing results beyond itself. At the end of the session, it is discarded or reset back to its default and not stored in a database.[2] Transitory digital data should not be confused with transitory records. *Transitory records* are those only needed for a short time. They can be used or acted upon and then destroyed. They do not contain information that will be needed in the future. In this chapter, we'll deal specifically with records and information that result from business activities (productivity data) conducted using some of the many systems, components, networks, applications, and services employed by users at home and at work.

When discussing records and information creation and capture, it is necessary to consider storage issues, which influence our attitude toward creation. The use of public, private, and hybrid cloud storage environments continues to grow. Organizations that have invested heavily in their own data centers will continue to support them for some time, especially for storage of sensitive data, while making a gradual move to the cloud. Hard disk drives, NAND flash storage (as well as emerging storage technologies similar to flash) are used in data centers, as are tape and optical storage for data less frequently accessed.

The core technology for data storage, especially magnetic disks, has progressed rapidly. According to IBM scientists, who in 2017 set a new world record in tape storage, "tape storage is still considered the most secure, energy efficient and cost-effective solution for storing enormous amounts of back-up and archival data, as well as for new applications such as Big Data and cloud computing." The new product has a potential to record 330 terabytes (TB) of uncompressed data (the equivalent of 330 million books) on a single tape cartridge that fits in the palm of your hand.[3]

Although great strides have been made in the area of data storage technology, additional research and development are needed to address, among other issues, the lack of standards for software (e.g., proprietary word processing formats); systems requirements needed to support data privacy, access limitations, and retention requirements; and the development of sustainable economic models to support data access and preservation over the long term.

RECORDS AND INFORMATION CREATION AND CAPTURE

Records are a *subset of information* created and captured as evidence of business decisions, actions, or transactions. All records, including business email and other electronic records, created or received, should be managed. Regardless of the methods used to create and capture records (manual or automated process), users sometimes have difficulty identifying a *record*. The fact that there is no universal definition of a record contributes to the confusion. Many believe it is time to move beyond the need to define a record and manage all information based on its value to the organization.

Creating Records

Information is a valuable business asset that can help an organization achieve its goals by supporting business activity; examples include data sets and technical manuals. Information, though, is not evidence of an activity and is not a record unless it possesses these additional characteristics:

- **Authenticity:** An authentic record can be proven to be what it purports to be, created or sent by the person purported to have created or sent it, and created or sent at the time purported.
- **Reliability:** A reliable record can be trusted as a full and accurate representation of the transactions, activities, or facts to which it attests.
- **Integrity:** A complete and unaltered record is said to possess integrity.
- **Usability:** A usable record can be located, retrieved, presented, and interpreted.

Records provide evidence of work activity and help the organization conduct its business in an efficient and accountable manner.

At one time, organizations had limited tools with which to create records, and only a few people within the organization had the authority to create records. In the mid-1950s, for example, an executive would dictate a letter to a private secretary who would type information onto paper for his signature as shown in figure 3.1.

Once signed, the original correspondence would be mailed to the intended recipient and a copy would be filed in a file drawer. Office copiers were not necessary because the

FIGURE 3.1 A secretary takes dictation on a typewriter, 1954.

SOURCE: Art Resource, NY. Photo: bpk, Bildagentur

secretary used carbon paper to make one or more duplicates on a thin, lightweight, strong paper called *onionskin* at the same time that the original was typed. Access to the organization's official copy was limited. Therefore, privacy and security measures were less complicated than they are today.

Advances in information technology changed the methods used to create and capture records by making the job of the secretary easier through the introduction of electronic typewriters and word processors and, eventually, by virtually eliminating the position of secretary in most organizations.

Today, thanks to the introduction of computer and communications technology, networking, the World Wide Web, social media, cloud computing, the Internet of Things, and more, records creation and capture are the work of all staff—or of no staff at all (e.g., sensors and blockchain technologies). Therefore, recordkeeping must be considered integral to the activities that promote the core mission of the business unit or organization and not as an add-on. The extent of the tasks that must be performed by staff is, of course, impacted by the degree of automation that can be applied.

Recognizing the value in information that does not fit the definition of a record, the National Archives of Australia explains that good information and records management allow employees, contractors, and consultants to properly manage both information and records to:

- find documents or information when needed,
- reuse work that the individual or someone else has done in the past,
- find the most recent version of a document,
- show evidence of why a particular decision was made and by whom, and
- protect themselves, their clients, the public and the Australian Government.[4]

Knowing what records to create involves:

- using work process analysis to identify the records needed to document business or work processes;
- understanding the legal and regulatory requirements that impact the organization, including internal policies, procedures, and directives; and
- assessing the risks of failing to create records.

Records creation and capture can be integrated into business rules for workflow and transaction systems. Records can also be created as a deliberate action after the event, such as documenting the minutes of a meeting from recordings made during the meeting.

Capturing Records

In records management terms, *capturing a record* means ensuring that the record—for example, a receipt, contract, or directive—becomes fixed so that it cannot be altered or deleted. This is different from the use of the term *capture* to denote the process of collecting information and delivering it into business applications and databases for further action. Dynamic records—such as those created as the result of a comment on a blog, a post to a social networking site, or an entry on a wiki site—pose unique challenges because the information may be both captured for further action and deemed a record that must be preserved in an unalterable state.

Records are captured by a records system if they meet certain business, legal, or other requirements identified through appraisal. Capture involves the:

- assignment of a unique identifier (either machine-generated and readable, or human readable);
- capture or generation of metadata about the record at the point of capture; and
- creation of relationships between the record and other records, agents, or business.[5]

These goals can be accomplished through the use of explicit metadata persistently linked with the record (i.e., embedded in, attached to, or associated with the specific record).

Have you thought about the correlation between the legalization of marijuana and the growth in volume of physical records? If you worked in the County of Denver, this would have been on your mind even before the sale of marijuana was approved. The County faced the challenge of capturing and managing a backlog of paper documents and developing a process to implement scanning into a document management system going forward. The process used to manage the deluge is described in the TAB Success Story.

TAB Success Story: How the City and County of Denver handled an unprecedented surge in retail marijuana license applications.

In October 2013, the City and County of Denver's Department of Excise and Licenses began accepting licenses for retail marijuana sales. Applications grew to ten times the normal volume in just a few months. Turnaround time and, therefore, customer service suffered. Two problems needed to be resolved: (1) how to handle the backlog and (2) redesign of the business process to accommodate the "new normal." The process involved seventeen different documents for each application, including insurance and background checks. The backlog alone consisted of over 2,000,000 documents—all paper. Tab's FutureRMS app (see tab.com) was employed to provide the expertise needed to manage the situation. Records management best practices for physical collections were implemented to handle the backlog, resulting in placing documents in proper file folders or pocket folders in their correct locations on shelves and creating an inventory listing of all folders and pockets. The process going forward involves scanning physical records, mapping workflows in a document management system, and implementing a day-forward scanning process.

Records Capture Methods

Records capture can occur manually after creation if using a paper-based filing system (e.g., by printing and filing an email message). Records can be captured automatically at the time of creation, if an electronic system is used. For example, records can be captured upon receipt of physical documents (as in the case of marijuana license applications) by scanning into an electronic system. Capture can be accomplished by automatic transfer of email to an archive server (repository) based on keywords or metadata such as sender, recipient, date, and terms found in the subject line or text of the message. Records on third-party systems used for outreach, such as blogs, may be captured upon creation if the content is static in nature or after creation if the content is dynamic. Table 3.1 lists some of the ways that an organization can capture content.

Social media tools present unique challenges to the organization. Pressured by consumers and enterprises alike, sites such as Facebook provide tools to allow the user to download information. Competition also spurs social networking providers to innovate. In an attempt to distinguish itself from other social networking sites, Google+ offers a number of

TABLE 3.1 Records can be captured either manually or automatically by the employee, the organization, or a third-party.

PAPER-BASED FILING SYSTEM	ELECTRONIC SYSTEM	THIRD-PARTY SYSTEM
Printing an electronic document (e.g., an email) to place in a file folder housed in a file cabinet	Registering an electronic document in an electronic records management system (manual)	Contracting with a cloud-based service provider (e.g., Smarsh) to harvest (or accept transfer of) and store electronic content for the organization
Making a photocopy of an original document sent by your organization and placing it in a file folder	Entering data into an electronic system, which then saves the data automatically	Using a web crawler (e.g., Internet Archives' Heritrix) to collect digital objects over the Internet
Receiving a physical copy of a signed contract and placing it in a fireproof vault	Scanning and digitizing an old photo to store in an electronic records management system	Use tools provided by third-party sites to download your data (e.g., download all data stored within Google products with the use of *Google Takeout*)

ways to export data, including a feature called Google Takeout. Google Takeout, also available as a stand-alone service, allows users to export contacts, photos, profiles, and streams of posts with a single click. In addition, data can be downloaded from a number of other Google products, including Blogger, Calendar, Google Drive, Gmail, and YouTube.[6] Examples of methods currently employed to capture and manage social media records will be presented in chapter 7.

One estimate claims that 77 percent of the American population owns a smartphone and more than 85 percent of physicians and practices use mobile devices daily. The use of these devices and medical software applications is known as mHealth, or mobile health-care.[7] Software applications for mobile devices are available, and data created by physicians, healthcare professionals, and patients using those devices must be captured as well.

By the time you read this text, the technology landscape will have changed. Scan the horizon not only for new technologies but also for vendors who provide software solutions that make it easier to capture records created through those technologies.

Because information creation and capture is the work of all staff to some extent, the organization must provide its employees with these tools:

- policies, procedures, and guidelines
- effective information technology systems
- records management compliance program
- staff training

Mobile Records Management

Not only are mobile devices used to create records—they can also be used to track, organize, and manage information. Some of the ways in which Tab's Fusion RMS mobile app is used for records management are:

- accessing documents using a meta-tag search feature
- documenting file transfers to update the chain-of-custody of physical files
- reading barcodes using the built-in camera on the smartphone or tablet (see http://fusionrms.tab.com/what-is-mobile-records-management/).

CONTROLLED LANGUAGE AND RECORDS CLASSIFICATION

Once records are created and captured, they must be managed in a way that allows the right record to be located at the right time and in a usable form. Non-records can also have evidentiary or informational value for the organization, so decisions must be made that relate to the management of all information of value. Traditionally, controlled language was developed to identify terms used for titling or indexing records. Those terms were incorporated into a thesaurus used to classify records (grouped together under a specific label) or to select indexing terms for the record. These terms were used for broad subject areas and were not closely related to business functions. More recently, classification has gone beyond developing an alphabetical listing of terms for indexing and grouping to developing a functional classification scheme based on an organization's business functions, activities, and transactions.

Controlled Language

Controlled language, also called *controlled vocabulary,* is a way to organize information in "an agreed-upon use of language in a predetermined or predictable way for description of organizational information resources, regardless of the format of the resource (media neutral)."[8]

Several controlled language (vocabulary) tools are available, including an index, a glossary, a folksonomy, a taxonomy, a thesaurus, and an ontology. When placed on a semantic richness continuum, they appear as shown in figure 3.2.

- An index is an ordered list of controlled language terms that points to the location of information related to each term.[9]
- A glossary, also known as a vocabulary, is an alphabetical list of terms in a domain of knowledge with the definitions for those terms.[10]
- A folksonomy, a contraction of the words folk (person) and taxonomy, is an [unstructured] system of classification that makes use of terms that occur naturally in the language of users of the system.[11]
- A taxonomy is a subject-based classification scheme used to arrange terms in a controlled vocabulary into a hierarchical structure that shows parent-

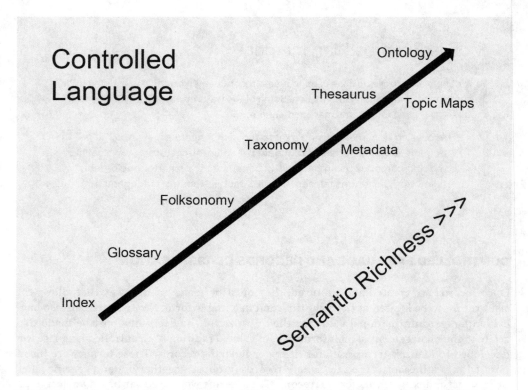

FIGURE 3.2 Semantic richness of controlled language facilitates search and retrieval.

child relationships. In a simple taxonomy, each item being classified fits into just one place in the taxonomy, with a single parent and any number of children.[12]

- A thesaurus is a controlled vocabulary of terms arranged in a structured order and with relationships between terms indicated with standardized designations that are used to aid document indexing and searching.[13] The following are examples of properties describing subjects:

    - *BT (broader term)* refers to a term above a given term in a hierarchy that is wider in scope or less specific in meaning (e.g., BT = reading materials).
    - *NT (narrower term)* refers to a term below a given term in a hierarchy that is narrower in scope or more specific in meaning (e.g., NT = volume).
    - *USE (preferred term)* refers to another, synonymous term that should be used instead of the given term (e.g., USE = book).
    - *RT (related term)* refers to a term related to the given term that is neither a synonym nor a broader term (e.g., RT = leisure reading).

- An ontology is a working model of entities and interactions in some domain of knowledge or practice, such as transportation.

In 1993, Stanford University artificial intelligence specialist Tom Gruber described ontology as "the specification of conceptualizations used to help programs and humans share knowledge."[14] This is accomplished using a set of concepts—classes (or sets), attributes (or properties), and relationships (or relations among class members)—that are specified in some way to create an agreed-upon vocabulary for exchanging information.

Two terms in figure 3.2 represent related but dissimilar concepts:

- Metadata is information about an asset beyond the file name. It is an attribute or element that helps define an "object" (e.g., document, database, image, or presentation). It can be used as a finding aid, but it is not a system of classification. Tools like thesauri provide statements about "subjects" used in classification. Subject-based classification uses subjects in metadata.
- Topic maps combine classification and metadata. They are organized around topics (subjects). But, because a subject can be anything, we can use objects described by metadata as a special kind of subject. This allows us to create a subject for those objects, such as document. We can express the metadata describing the new subject (document-object) using names (e.g., authors), occurrences (e.g., events/activities), and associations (e.g., employee).

Let us now turn our attention now to the ways in which classification systems are used in the business environment.

Classification and Filing Systems

Classification is defined as the organization of materials into categories according to a scheme that identifies, distinguishes, and relates the categories.[15] Classification systems can be used to impose some kind of order on the chaos that results from the growth of information by grouping like objects together. Remember the clay tokens used in Mesopotamia in 4000 BCE that were discussed in chapter 1? Some of the engraved symbols represented not only the quantity, but also the type, of animal. The symbols representing different types of animals comprised a form of classification scheme.

There are many different classification schemes, but we'll cover just a few in this chapter. In the first half of the twentieth century, manual filing systems tamed the chaos that arose from the growth of records attributed to the typewriter. Paper files were most often organized according to one of these filing methods: alphabetic, numeric, geographic, subject, and chronological. Many organizations must still deal with their legacy paper documents. Although that is changing, change takes time. For example, in 2012, the Executive Office of the President released the *Managing Government Records Directive,* which required federal agencies to manage both permanent and temporary email records in an accessible electronic format by 2016 and to manage all permanent electronic records in an electronic format by 2019.[16] By 2017, progress toward these goals had been made, but there was still a need for improvement according to the *Federal Agency Records Management Annual Report for 2016.*[17]

In the 1960s, the emergence of mainframe computers brought about the desire to computerize filing systems. At the same time, text indexing systems and sophisticated search algorithms came into use to classify and locate data. Don't allow the focus on digital information to lead you to dismiss simple classification schemes completely. The alphabetic scheme used to organize and classify paper records can be used to control digital records as well.

Alphabetic, Subject, and Numeric Filing

Although digital records may be created by employees using devices such as computers, smartphones, and iPads, at least some of those businesses have paper files. A visit to the dentist's office underscored this fact for me. A patient scheduling system allowed for computerized scheduling of appointments, but copies of dental charts, insurance forms, and even X-rays were placed into paper file folders on open shelving.

Alphabetic Filing System

A system in which files and documents are arranged in alphabetic order from A to Z is known as *an alphabetic filing system*.[18] It's an easy and effective organizational system that has one primary goal—fast retrieval of important documents. Records stored as hard copies are often filed alphabetically (see figure 3.3). Computer files can also be organized alphabetically into folders labeled with the letters of the alphabet.

Setting up an alphabetic filing system using system folders is one option for organizing client files. We often see this system in small law offices, where a simple folder structure based on client names stored alphabetically is created on *a shared drive*. The client folders may be subdivided into folders based on the subject of the contents, such as correspondence, deposition, and evidence. Access to the shared folders is provided on an as-needed basis for attorneys, paralegals, and other support staff. Without the benefit of document management, enterprise content management, and/or records management software, this may be the best option.

Subject Filing System

A *subject filing system* is one in which each document relates to a specific subject matter and is arranged in alphabetical order by subject.[19] In a document-based system, subject filing requires someone to analyze each document to determine the subject. Cross-referencing is required if more than one subject is contained within the same document.

Many small, local governments use a subject filing system that is arranged alphabetically. The categories are arranged according to the types of activities taking place, and each category usually contains several subcategories. The state of North Dakota's Information Technology Department (IDT) provides guidance on the effective management of electronic records. This guidance includes the recommendation that each state agency develop a standard naming convention for electronic documents based on its program needs, but that they should consider using the State's Subject Classification

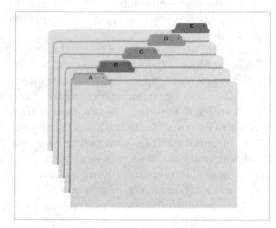

FIGURE 3.3 Alphabetic filing guides reduce filing and location time by subdividing a file drawer.

Courtesy of the Smead Manufacturing Company, www.smead.com/.

TABLE 3.2 Examples of categories included in North Dakota Subject Classification System.

#	CODE	SUBJECT	DEFINITION
01	(ACT)	ACCOUNTING	All functions involved in a financial transaction.
14	(AOC)	ASSOCIATIONS	Information concerning organizations outside of the department (corporate data, membership rosters, institutes, trade groups).
30	(C/L/A)	CONTRACTS/ LEASES/ AGREEMENTS	Information or documents regarding office agreements, leases, and contracts.
60	(PER)	PERSONNEL	Any information relating to personnel of the agency.
75	(SA)	SAFETY/SECURITY	Records relating to operating safety requirements, precautions, protection from damages, risk, injury, and reports pertaining to safety.

SOURCE: North Dakota State Government, ITD, "Electronic Records Management Guidelines," revised July 10, 2017, https://www.nd.gov/itd/standards/electronic-records-management-guidelines.

System when creating directories and subdirectories. Five of the thirty-one subjects are shown in table 3.2.

Numeric Filing System

A *numeric filing system* is any classification system designed to arrange records based on numbers that are assigned or taken directly from a record (e.g., a purchase order). Decimal numeric filing arrangements are the most commonly used numeric filing method, and the best-known system of this type is the Dewey Decimal Classification System (DDC) developed for libraries in the late 1800s; the current version, DDC 23, was released in 2011. DDC specifies ten main classes divided into ten subclasses, which are further divided into ten subdivisions. A code known as a *numeric call number* is assigned to each book or other resource based on where the content falls within the taxonomy. WebDewey, an online version of DDC, provides access to the DDC 23 database including automatic updates to the system.

Other Options for Libraries

At the turn of the twentieth century, the Library of Congress developed its own classification system to categorize books and other items. It has twenty-one subject categories.

In keeping with the move away from print materials, the LC no longer provides print publications. However, a web-based subscription service, Classification Web, features the entire Library of Congress Classification System and complete Library of Congress Subject Headings (LCSH) and Name Headings for a fee. The Classification Web is updated daily, and a free trial is available through the LC website.[20]

Example of a Numeric Filing System

The Dewey Decimal System has ten main classes:

000   Computer Science, information and general works

100   Philosophies and psychology

200   Religion

300   Social sciences

400   Language

500   Science

600   Technology

700   Arts and recreation

800   Literature

900   History and geography

SOURCE: OCLC, "Dewey Decimal Classification Summaries," accessed May 12, 2018, https://www.oclc.org/en/dewey/features/summaries.html#hi.

Determining what classification system is best for users is not an easy task. The Randolph C. Watson Library at Kilgore College provides a table to help those familiar with the DDC understand where to find the material they are seeking under the LCSH; for example, Dewey Subject Area *160 Logic* translates to *BC Logic* for the LC Subject area. However, *070 Journalism, Publishing, News media* translates to *AN Newspapers* in LC Subject area.[21]

Some librarians unhappy with the weaknesses of both the Dewey Decimal System and the Library of Congress Classification System began as early as 2007 to use a simplified subject-based taxonomy similar to the classification system found in bookstores.[22] Works classified according to the BISAC (Book Industry Standards and Communications) Subject Heading list enhance the browsing experience of patrons unfamiliar with both the Dewey Decimal System and the Library of Congress Classification System.[23] An example of a BISAC subject heading with additional subheadings (more specific headings) is:[24]

LC0002000 LITERARY COLLECTIONS / American / General.

Dewey Services, provided through OCLC, discontinued mapping between DDC and LCSH in 2006 in order to divert resources to a project to add DDC numbers to the authority records for BISAC subject headings.

Chronological and Geographic Filing Systems

A *chronological filing system* is arranged by date and can be used to organize business records such as invoices, purchase orders, and bills of lading. If using a file folder, the newest records go in the front. If using a computer, a field to hold the date of the transaction is included in order to allow the software to find the date in question and retrieve the appropriate document. If more than one document has the same date, a search is conducted on a secondary field as well. This system is most useful for small files and records with a short life span so that older files can be purged to make room for more recent records.

Library of Congress Classification Outline

The Library of Congress Classification Scheme includes twenty-one categories:

A   General Works

B   Philosophy, Psychology, Religion

C   Auxiliary Sciences of History

D   World History and History of Europe, Asia, Africa, Australia, New Zealand, etc.

E   History of the Americas

F   History of the Americas

G   Geography, Anthropology, Recreation

H   Social Sciences

J   Political Science

K   Law

L   Education

M   Music and Books on Music

N   Fine Arts

P   Language and Literature

Q   Science

R   Medicine

S   Agriculture

T   Technology

U   Military Science

V   Naval Science

Z   Bibliography, Library Science, Information Resources (General)

SOURCE: Library of Congress, "Library of Congress Classification Outline," accessed May 12, 2018, www.loc.gov/catdir/cpso/lcco/.

A *geographic filing system* classifies records according to geographic location. The Standard Geographical Classification (SGC) is Statistics Canada's official classification system for geographic areas in Canada. SGC 2016 provides standard names and codes for the geographical regions of Canada (Level 1), followed by provinces and territories (Level 2), census divisions (Level 3), and census subdivisions (Level 4).[25]

BUSINESS CLASSIFICATION SCHEMES

ISO 15489-1:2016 defines *classification* as the "systematic identification and/or arrangement of business activities and/or records into categories according to logically structured conventions, methods, and procedural rules."[26] *Business classification* is the process that helps an organization describe, organize, and control information. Business classification systems are built upon an analysis of the organization's business activities. The business classification scheme is used to link records to their business context and is necessary to capture full and accurate records.

Functional Classification Scheme

Since the release of ISO 15489 in 2001, classification based on organizational functions and activities has been the preferred method to control information and records. Classification by function is based on the context of a record's creation and use rather than content alone. *Classification by function* means classification according to why the record exists and not what it is about (subject). Functions consist of activities, which consist of transactions.

The main functional high-level categories used in the example in figure 3.4 along with the unique three-letter identifier for each are:

- Firm Administration (FRM)
- Sales and Marketing (MKT)
- Finance Department (FIN)
- Information Management (INF)

- Reference (REF)
- Human Resources (HUM)
- Legal (LEG)
- Operations (OPS)

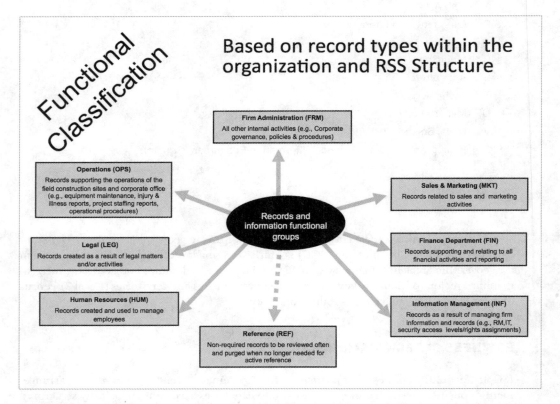

FIGURE 3.4 Major headings of functional classification scheme derived from records and information functional groups.

SOURCE: Unpublished report. Courtesy of MARA graduate C. J. Rodriguez.

A functions-based classification system offers several benefits because it:

- provides an understanding of the relationship between the business and its records;
- identifies records that should be created for their evidential value;
- identifies high-priority records that should be captured because of their business value;
- facilitates retention decisions; and
- allows retention requirements to be determined at the point of creation.[27]

Records Classification Schemes

Records classification is the process followed to categorize or group records into retrieval units. A records classification scheme is also referred to as a *file plan*. The records classification scheme is a tool used to classify records and other business information based on the business activities that generate records. It is derived directly from the organization's business classification scheme.

The records classification scheme is often represented as a directory or folder structure, especially in electronic records management systems (as shown in figure 3.5) and it can provide two, three, or sometimes four levels. The hierarchical structure orders or ranks *function > activity > topic > subtopic*. When implemented within a business information system, it controls the vocabulary used, ensures consistency of information description, and facilitates the capture, titling, retrieval, maintenance, and disposal of records and other information.

As with any hierarchical scheme, navigational paths (such as links) exist between related terms, but those paths are limited to the relationships within the structure and the terms used for classification. A second classification tool, the *functional thesaurus*, can be built from the same business classification scheme, but the terms would be listed in alphabetical order.

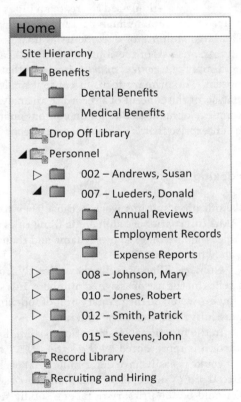

FIGURE 3.5 Hierarchical representation of a file plan for a human resources function.

SOURCE: Don Lueders, "Introducing the SharePoint 2010 Records Center," SharePointRecordsManagement.com (blog), May 2, 2010, http://sharepoint.recordsmanagement.com/2010/05/02/introducing-the-sharepoint-2010-records-cdener/. Courtesy of SharePointRecordsManagement.com.

Auto-Classification

Auto-classification (automatic classification) is the "process of using electronic systems to encode rules and apply them to records in order to categorize and sort them.[28] Auto-classification software mines the content of structured and unstructured data files, analyzes the content based on defined rules and workflows, and categorizes the files based on metadata, words, or phrases. The categories can be associated with retention schedules and security classifications. Documents can be archived, disposed of, and even placed on legal hold based on the organization's records management policy. Auto-classification is becoming an important part of an organization's information governance strategy resulting in improvements in user productivity and satisfaction. Grouping files based on categories or characteristic can aid in compliance and reduce litigation risks. Employing auto-classification tools to search for the presence of PII or other sensitive content can help protect the organization against data breaches and lower eDiscovery costs.

INDEXING, CONTENT ANALYSIS, AND FILE PLAN DEVELOPMENT

The primary method used to create an index for records and information management has evolved from humans analyzing and then indexing individual documents to computers that scan large volumes of documents against controlled terms and indexing them automatically. An analysis of the content of records can provide the controlled terms used in indexing. Simply put, *content analysis* is a term that can be applied to all examinations of message content. The primary focus of content analysis, however, has expanded from conceptual analysis of the content of a record to an analysis of the relationships between concepts. File plan development also relies on content analysis to describe and categorize the content in the enterprise that is or may become a record.

Indexing

Classification systems work because they follow predefined rules to ensure consistency. ARMA International's alphabetic filing rules establish an index order of units for personal names that are indexed by surname and then first name followed by initial or middle name as shown in table 3.3.

Numeric filing uses numbers directly from a record such as a purchase order number or relies on the use of assigned numbers. In a straight-numeric filing system, purchase order numbers would be the primary unit of indexing, and the purchase orders would be arranged consecutively in ascending order.

In the functional classification system illustrated in figure 3.4, the sales and marketing function is represented by the letters MKT and the legal function as LEG. The organization could as easily have determined that each function should be represented numerically instead, for example, Sales and Marketing as 10 and Legal as 20. If so, the numbers 10 and 20 would be the primary numbers; subdivisions would then be identified by appending a second number, and so on. This is known as a duplex-numeric system because two or more sets of codes are used.

The chronological filing system is a type of numeric arrangement, but dates are used as indexing units. The most common order is year, month, day as in 2020-05-03 to denote May 3, 2020, as specified in *ISO 8601—Data elements and interchange formats—Information interchange—Representation of dates and times*. Under this system, the document with the most current date is placed at the front of a physical file folder.[29]

TABLE 3.3 Example of indexing order within an alphabetic filing system.

PERSONAL (FILE) NAME	FIRST UNIT	SECOND UNIT	THIRD UNIT
Jane A. Doe	Doe	Jane	A.
Jane Alexandra Doe	Doe	Jane	Alexandra

An Introduction to Content Analysis

Content analysis (also called content analytics) is defined as a research tool used to determine the presence of certain words or concepts within texts and sets of texts.[30] It is also defined as a research technique for making replicable and valid inferences from texts (or other meaningful matter) to the contexts of their use.[31]

Recently Big Data technologies have been recognized as tools that can add insight into records and information an organization possesses. One example is IBM's Watson Content Analytics, which can collect and analyze both structured and unstructured content found in databases, email, documents, websites, and more. The text analytics result in a searchable index that can be queried to find and retrieve relevant documents from a ranked list of results.[32]

As early as the 1930s, content analysis was used in military intelligence to analyze communist propaganda and military speeches for themes by searching for the number of occurrences of particular words and phrases.[33] Today content analysis is used in several fields, including marketing and media studies, sociology and political science, and literature and rhetoric. It can include visual documents as well as text, and the focus is on phrases and categories rather than simple words. Two categories of content analysis are *conceptual analysis* and *relational analysis*.

The examination of text for the existence of certain words is an example of conceptual analysis. *Text content analysis tools,* for example, can provide statistics about the text (written content)—such as word count, number of sentences, and reading ease—to help you improve your writing. This type of tool is built into most word processing programs but also exists as stand-alone software or services.

Some content analysis tools not only report the existence of certain words and phrases but also perform tasks such as extracting metadata and hyperlinks, classifying documents, and detecting language and encoding. This type of tool is particularly suited to information retrieval and extraction projects and is an important part of text-mining tools.

Relational content analysis has been termed *semantic analysis.*[34] It goes beyond determining the presence of concepts by looking for meaningful (semantic) relationships between those concepts. In chapter 1, you were introduced to the Semantic Web that facilitates data sharing and reuse across application, enterprise, and community boundaries. The Semantic Web employs semantic ontologies (controlled vocabularies) to accomplish this task.

When we enter data into a database, the application controls the data. In order to retrieve the data, we look for the file in question and then open it in the appropriate application. By contrast, the Semantic Web allows a person—or a machine—to start out in one database and then move through other databases about the same topic seamlessly and effortlessly (see figure 3.6).

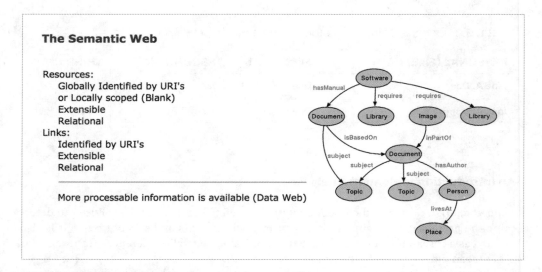

FIGURE 3.6 The Semantic Web.

SOURCE: Eric Miller, "Weaving Meaning: An Overview of the Semantic Web." World Wide Web Consortium, November 20, 2004, https://www.w3.0rg/2004/Talks/1120-semweb-em/slide17–0.html. Copyright © 2004 World Wide Web Consortium (Massachusetts Institute of Technology, European Research Consortium for Informatics and Mathematics, Keio University). All Rights Reserved. www.w3.0rg/Consortium/Legal/2002/copyright-documents-20021231.

Paypal's Praveen Alavilli described the semantic world on the web as "one giant labeled, directed multigraph of people, things, and relationships."[35] The term *labeled* refers to the use of vocabularies and data formats that enable semantics on the web.

The terms *Semantic Web* and *linked data* have received much less attention in the last few years due to the lack of easy-to-use tools to deal with large volumes of diverse data and the quality and quantity of mappings between related data. This doesn't mean that the Semantic Web is no longer important—just not as an end in itself. Indications are the Semantic Web and semantic technologies and techniques are being absorbed into the larger artificial intelligence field.[36]

Content Analysis and File Plan Development

The terms *content analysis* and *file plan* are most often used to refer to elements of an electronic content or records management system. The file plan lists the records in the organization and describes how they are organized and maintained. There is more to file plan development than one might think when looking at an image that represents a records classification hierarchy (file plan) as shown previously in figure 3.5. The file plan also describes, for each type of record in the enterprise, where the records should be retained, the policies that apply to them, how they need to be retained, how they should be disposed of, and who is responsible for managing them. Procedures for amendments and additions must be documented, and responsibility for the control of the file plan (e.g., evaluating and updating) must be assigned. It is wise to identify all regulatory, operational, and societal recordkeeping requirements before completing the records classification scheme.

RECORDS MANAGEMENT METADATA

Metadata for records, as described in the updated basic records management standard ISO 15489-1:2016, is "structured or semi-structured information, which enables the creation, management, and use of records through time and within and across domains."[37] Records management has always managed metadata. When dealing with paper records, metadata such as author, subject, and title of records were implicit in the record and were used to index records for filing. In the digital world, metadata needs to be explicitly documented in order to describe the content, business context, structure (e.g., form and format), relationships with other records and other metadata; identifiers and other information needed to retrieve and present the record; and the business actions and events that involved the record throughout its existence.

Metadata are used to define a record at the point of capture so that it is fixed into the business context and management control is established over it. It will continue to be applied throughout the record's lifecycle, essentially documenting the record's provenance (i.e., origins, custody, and ownership). It ensures the authenticity, reliability, usability, and integrity of the record and can be used as evidence of transactions and activities (see sidebar, Production of ESI and Metadata for e-Discovery).

The metadata itself is considered a record and must be managed as such. It must be protected from loss, unauthorized deletion, and unauthorized access, and it must be retained or destroyed according to the requirements identified during appraisal.[38] Court opinions continue to evolve regarding the evidential value of metadata and should be monitored. The attention paid to this topic indicates that the organization will be at risk if it does not capture and manage metadata along with the record.

Records Management Metadata Standards

The importance of creating, capturing, and managing metadata at every stage of a record's lifecycle is evident. But, which metadata? Records management standards and technical reports were introduced in a sidebar in chapter 2. Let's see how RIM standards apply to managing metadata for records.

There are three specific international standards related to managing metadata for records within the framework of ISO 15489:

- ISO 23081—Part 1: Principles
- ISO 23081—Part 2: Conceptual and Implementation Issues
- ISO 23081—Part 3: Self-Assessment Method

ISO 23081:1-2017—Part 1: Principles

First released in 2006, this international standard was updated in 2017. It sets the framework for creating, managing, and using records management metadata and explains the principles that govern them. It addresses the relevance of records management metadata in business processes and the different roles and types of metadata that support business and records management processes. As is the nature of standards, this document tells the reader what to do but not how to do it. This standard makes clear that different perspectives on records management metadata are possible and may coexist. They include:

Production of Electrically Stored Information and Metadata for e-Discovery

The best answer to the question of whether a plaintiff can be compelled to produce metadata is "that depends." However, the following court cases indicate that it is best to be prepared. Some courts are taking a favorable view on requests for electronically stored information (ESI) with accompanying metadata.

In *Morgan Hill Concerned Parents Association v. California Department of Education,* Magistrate Judge Allison Claire of the US District Court Eastern District of California signed an order on February 1, 2017, ordering that the "Plaintiffs' motion to compel is GRANTED, as follows: Within thirty days, CDE shall produce all ESI in native format with all metadata attached. Any ESI that has already been produced in another format shall be reproduced in native format with all metadata attached ."*

"In *Singh et al. v. Hancock Natural Resources Group, Inc. et. al., No. 15-1435 (E.D. Cal., Dec. 29, 2016),* California Magistrate Judge Jennifer L. Thurston granted the defendants' motion to compel (in part), ordering the plaintiffs to 'produce all emails and other documents sought by the defendants in the format demanded with the accompanying metadata from the native computer.'†

The Magistrate Judge in the US District Court, District of Connecticut, in *Prezio Health Inc. v. Schenk et. al.,* granted "in part the Plaintiff's Motion to Compel to the extent that an in camera review is ordered, which depending on the content of the documents, may be followed by production of the metadata." Defendants were required to submit the requested documents to this Magistrate Judge's Chambers on or before September 4, 2015.‡

In *7-Eleven, Inc. v. Sodhi,* Magistrate Judge Joel Schneider ordered that by March 1, 2015, "7-Eleven *shall produce the requested metadata* for the documents identified in Plaintiff's moving papers." He also "ordered that the Order is entered *without prejudice to Plaintiff's right to request additional metadata.*"**

* Justia Dockets & Filings, "Morgan Hill Concerned Parents Association v. California Department of Education, February 1, 2017, https://docs.justia.com/cases/federal/district-courts/california/caedce/2:2011cv03471/233488/287.

† Doug Austin, "Court Orders Plaintiff to Produce Emails with Original Metadata: eDiscovery Case Law," February 3, 2017, https://www.ediscovery.co/ediscoverydaily/electronic-discovery/court-orders-plaintiff-produce-emails-original-metadata-ediscovery-case-law/.

‡ Justia Dockets & Filings, "Prezio Health Inc. v. Schenk et al.," August 25, 2015, https://docs.justia.com/cases/federal/district-courts/connecticut/ctdce/3:2013cv01463/102297/77.

** Justia Dockets & Filings, "7-ELEVEN, INC. v. SODHI, No. 3:2013cv03715 - Document 291 (D.N.J. 2015)," modified March 18, 2015, https://law.justia.com/cases/federal/district-courts/new-jersey/njdce/3:2013cv03715/290844/291.

- metadata that document the business perspective, where records management supports business processes;
- metadata that document the records management perspective, where metadata capture the characteristics of records and their context, and support management over time; and
- metadata that document the use perspective within or outside the records creating business context, where metadata enable the retrieval, understandability, and interpretation of records.[39]

ISO 23081-2:2009—Part 2 Conceptual and Implementation Issues

This technical specification supports Part 1 of the standard. It does not prescribe a specific set of metadata elements, but it does identify generic types of metadata that fulfill the requirements for managing records. No metadata schema is presented; organizations are expected to select specific metadata to meet their own business requirements.

The phrase *metadata for managing records* as "structured or semi-structured information that enables the creation, registration, classification, access, preservation and disposition of records through time and within and across domains" is defined in this document.[40] Metadata for managing records describes the attributes of records to enable their management and use or reuse. But the metadata also document the relationships between records and the agents that make and use them and the events or circumstances in which the records are made and used (relationships such as those illustrated in figure 3.7).

A metadata model for managing records groups metadata elements into six categories, as shown in figure 3.7. Metadata elements are recommended for each of these six categories. For example, the following elements are recommended description metadata:

- Title
- Classification
- Abstract
- Place
- Jurisdiction
- External Identifiers

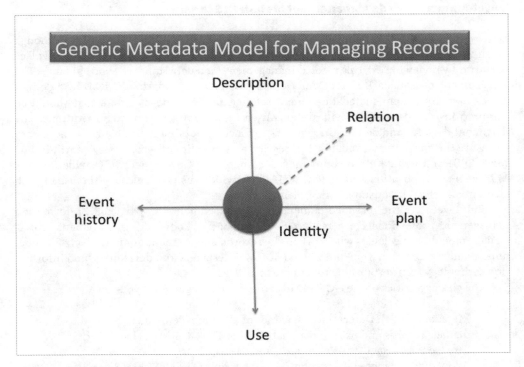

FIGURE 3.7 Metadata Model as described in ISO 23081-2:2009.

A logical plan showing the relationships between all metadata elements identified, called a *metadata schema*, must be created. The metadata schema incorporates a set of rules to enable the management of metadata; for example, rules related to semantics (e.g., agreement about the meaning of elements, such as author or title) and syntax (rules to convey semantics and structure of the expression of the values).

ISO 23081-3:2011—Part 3: Self-Assessment Method

Part 3 provides guidance on conducting a self-assessment on records metadata created in relation to the creation, capture, and control of records. It was designed to identify an organization's current state of records metadata readiness and the risks associated with the current state and to give direction on how to improve the organization's readiness. The self-assessment method considers two levels: the metadata framework level and the systems level.

The set of metadata framework criteria rates how well an organization has established a framework to meet key recordkeeping metadata criteria. It addresses nine main criteria independent of specific systems, such as metadata strategy, policies and rules, and metadata structures, including schemas and encoding schemes. The set of twenty criteria for systems and system-related projects includes criteria such as the implementation of metadata elements into systems and the management of the metadata process.

Developing a Records Management Metadata Schema

Developing a metadata schema for records management can be time-consuming. Although organizations are expected to define their own metadata elements and schema, a good place to start is by reviewing existing records management metadata standards and guidance. The Government of Canada Records Management Metadata Standard (GC RMMS)[41] defines a records management metadata element set that outlines the metadata that should be captured in records management systems used by federal government institutions. The document declares and defines the semantics of a core set of metadata elements necessary to ensure the authenticity, reliability, integrity, and usability of records as set forth in ISO 15489:2001 and ISO 23081. A companion document, the Government of Canada Records Management Application Profile (GC RMAP), provides business rules for the use of each element and the relationships among elements.[42]

Employees are the intended audience for the documents, in particular, information management professionals (especially records managers), knowledge management professionals, metadata specialists who work in the records management domain, electronic document and records management system (EDRMS) designers and developers, and information technology staff responsible for supporting EDRMS.

The characteristics of the GC RMMS can be used as a guide for your own work:

- Metadata model: Determine the names of all of the elements to be used to manage records and list them alphabetically. The GC RMMS has identified fifty elements, such as title, creator, and description.
- Adopt existing metadata elements when possible. The GC RMMS has adopted seven Dublin Core descriptive metadata elements: creator, description, identifier, language, subject, title, and type.
- Determine the convention to be used to format the names of the declared elements. The GC RMMS uses the following convention: lowerCamelCase.

The character strings' remaining element names must remain unchanged; this is essential when translating a human readable GC RMMS document into a machine-readable format (e.g., XML) and for ensuring interoperability.

- Describe the attributes of each metadata element. For the seven Dublin Core descriptive metadata elements, the attributes are name, URI, and definition. For example, the metadata element Subject would be described in this way:

ATTRIBUTE	VALUE
Name	Subject
URI	http://purl.org/dc/elements/1.1/subject
Definition	The topic of the content of the resource

- Describe the attributes of each metadata element created for the organization. For example, the metadata element Disposition Action would be described in this way:

ATTRIBUTE	VALUE
Name	dispositionAction
Definition	The action that will be taken on the records or file on expiry of its retention period
Value Domain	Enumerated strings of text representing disposition actions
Datatype Name	String

Metadata are essential to ensuring that records and information will survive and continue to be accessible into the future. Records professionals should be prepared to work with information managers and vendors to define metadata requirements, develop metadata policies and strategies, and monitor metadata creation.

SUMMARY

This chapter began with the statement, "In 2025, the world will create and replicate 163 ZB of data, a tenfold increase over 2016." Estimates such as this are becoming meaningless to most of us. But what we do understand is that the volume, velocity, and variety of data, information, and records will continue to grow, and we must take a proactive approach to govern it. This digital data can be divided into three categories:

- Transient data created within an application session and discarded or reset to its default by the end of the session.

- Transitory records needed for a short time that are used or acted upon and then destroyed.
- Records that result from business activities that must be retained as essential records to ensure business continuity or for administrative, regulatory, fiscal, and historical purposes.

Records creation can occur in numerous ways using a variety of devices, including laptops, iPads, smartphones, and smart appliances (e.g., refrigerators and automobiles).

Records capture ensures that the record is fixed (unalterable) as evidence of an activity or event. Metadata are captured with the record and continue to accrue throughout its lifecycle. The method of capture depends on the method of creation (e.g., email received, posts on social networks, or data entered into database as the result of a business transaction) and initial location of the information (e.g., enterprise system or third party).

Once records are identified and captured, they must be managed. Controlled language and classification systems are used to impose order. Classification schemes range from simple alphabetic and subject filing systems to business classification schemes and records classification schemes (file plans). Before completing the records classification scheme, all recordkeeping requirements, such as applicable regulations, must be identified. Auto-classification tools are becoming more prevalent and powerful.

Beyond content analysis, file plan development includes records description, policies, retention and disposition requirements, and responsibility for controlling the file plan.

The key to managing electronic records is the use of metadata. Records management has always managed metadata. When dealing with paper records, metadata were implicit in the record, but in the digital world, metadata must be explicitly documented in order to describe the content, context, and structure of records and their management through time and within and across domains.

Before moving on to chapter 4, read the paradigm contributed by Peg Eusch, CRM. Peg retired from her position as University Records Officer, University of Wisconsin—Madison, on June 8, 2017. Within the University's decentralized records management structure, she served as the university-wide consultant providing advice and education. She reminds us there is more than one way to view the concept of a file plan. As one of her last professional activities, Peg agreed to share her unique approach to using the elements of file plan development to train employees within the University's decentralized records management structure.

PARADIGM

University Records Management File Plans

Peg Eusch, CRM
University Records Officer, University of Wisconsin–Madison

Introduction

The University of Wisconsin–Madison was founded in 1848. It comprises thirteen schools and colleges, 21,796 faculty and staff, and 43,338 students. The UW–Madison Archives was founded in 1951. As a result of the changing needs and management of campus records, the Records Management Program was founded in 1985. The Records Management Program is housed in the University Archives and reports through the General Library System.

The UW-Madison University Records Management program is managed in accordance with the UW Board of Regents Records Management Policy 3-2 and the Wisconsin Public Records Board requirements for records management programs. The program follows *ISO 15489 for Records Management* and ARMA International's eight Generally Accepted Recordkeeping Principles aka "The Principles" of Transparency, Availability, Compliance, Accountability, Protection, Integrity, Retention and Disposition. The University Records Management Advisory Group (URMAG) endorsed these principles in 2010.

Currently the Records Management Program is staffed by one full-time employee, the University Records Officer. There were two Records Management Student Assistants for 2016–2017.

Records management is an essential part of all university employees' daily activities. University employees, at all levels, use, distribute, and retain university records from record creation through disposition. University records are important assets in the operation of the University and should be organized, accessed, and managed in accordance with records management best practices, such as the Generally Accepted Recordkeeping Principles, in all formats and media. An organized workplace is more conducive to creating new ideas and improved efficiencies.

The University Records Manager/Officer plans, organizes, and directs activities of the university's Record Management Program by communicating record policies and industry best practices for university records. There are many facets to the Records Management Program that bring information value and reduce risk to the UW–Madison campus. The University Records Officer serves on a variety of university committees across campus that are concerned with records and information management issues and relies on the University Records Management Advisory Group (URMAG) to support and give direction to Records Management initiatives.

Problem Statement

Communication and training are an ongoing challenge in this decentralized environment on campus for the University Records Officer. Consultation is a large part of the University Records Officer responsibilities. During these visits, the Records Officer learned that when an employee departs, the next employee coming into the position is unaware of what the records management processes were and what types of records are created. This inconsistent management of records has the potential to lead to increased records control risks and legal risks in the management of university records. The Records Officer has recommended to the campus that there should be some kind of documentation to demonstrate what the department or unit is doing with regard to the information it captures and maintains through the records lifecycle. One way to do this is through the use of a Records Management File Plan for transparency in the records processes.

Approach Taken

A change in thought and approach came about because of a presentation on file plans given in the fall of 2015 by one of our ARMA Milwaukee Chapter members, Herb Foster, CRM. His presentation provided the basis and ideas for reevaluation and revamping the information being conveyed in presentations from the traditional *"What Is Records Management?"* to those on how employees could put records management into practice to better manage the information that they create and store. Covering records management through the elements in the file plan touches all areas and questions employees have and underscores that records management is more than just retention. Some examples are: what is a public record and non-record, records and email, records and digital imaging, and retention and disposition. The file plan is used in a slightly different capacity than the traditional concept of a file plan in a spreadsheet. The idea is to provide an outline and understanding of records management concepts and also provide a way to apply these concepts to practice on the university campus. The file plan also complies and integrates with ARMA International's Generally Accepted Recordkeeping Principles.

The University Records Management File Plan

The Records Management File Plan creates the road map for the management of records. It is the Who, What, When, Where, Why, and How of managing records within the department or unit. The university department or unit creates its own Records Management File Plan to demonstrate how information is created and managed, where it is stored, and what processes it is using. There are ten elements covered in the Record Management File Plan, as shown in figure 3.8.

1. *Document:* What type of information does the department or unit create?
2. *Record Organization:* What filing structure and naming conventions are used to manage the information?

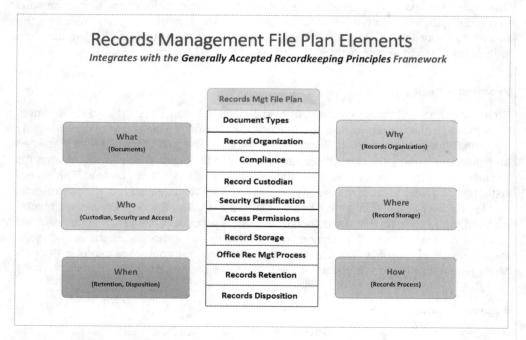

FIGURE 3.8 Records Management File Plan elements.
Courtesy of Paradigm author, Peg Eusch, CRM.

3. *Compliance Requirements:* Are there any legal or regulatory requirements that need to be identified in complying with retention and the management of records?
4. *Record Custodian:* Is there a role that has been designated as responsible for the department or units records?
5. *Security Classification:* Has there been appropriate security applied to the information managed based on the categories Restricted, Sensitive, Internal or Published/Public?
6. *Access Permissions:* Have the appropriate access permissions been evaluated and been given?
7. *Record Storage:* Where are all the repositories where records are being used and stored—in both electronic and paper formats?
8. *Records Management Process:* Is there transparent documentation of the records processes and creation of the File Plan for each department or unit?
9. *Records Retention:* Is knowledge of where to find the university retention schedules and department unique schedules and how long to maintain records being shared?
10. *Records Disposition:* Does the department understand what events trigger the retention schedule and the appropriate disposition?

This is covered through University training, which consists of the presentation given to department and units as well as the job aid and file plan template for departments or units to use to guide them through all ten elements.

The file plan is used for:

- training new employees in how records are managed within the department/unit
- identifying records consistently
- retrieving records in a timely fashion
- disposing of records no longer needed
- meeting legal and organizational requirements
- providing transparency in how records are managed

Information on the Records Management File Plan can be found on the UW–Madison Records Management website. (https://www.library.wisc.edu/archives/records-manage ment/training/organizing-university-records-for-departments-and-units/.)

Conclusion

Incorporating records management into the File Plan presentation and guidance was important to show how records management is used and to make the concepts easier for employees to understand. The information has been well received and provides options for improved recordkeeping and for opening the discussion of records management challenges.

Next Steps

The UW–Madison Records Management Program will continue to educate employees regarding their responsibility for management of records and best practices. The Records

File Plan is just one of many record concepts and issues that are being addressed with university employees. More information can be found on the UW-Madison Records Management website. https://www.library.wisc.edu/archives/records-management/.

NOTES

1. David Reinsel, John Gantz, and John Rydning, "Data Age 2025: The Evolution of Data to Life-Critical," *IDC White Paper,* April 2017, p. 12, https://www.seagate.com/files/www-content/our-story/trends/files/Seagate-WP-DataAge2025-March-2017.pdf.

2. *PC Magazine Encyclopedia,* s.v. "transient data," PCMag.com Encyclopedia, accessed September 2, 2017, www.pcmag.com/encyclopedia_term/0,2542,t=transient+data&i=53093,00.asp.

3. IBM,"IBM Sets New Record for Magnetic Tape Storage; Makes Tape Competitive for Cloud Storage," August 2, 2017, www-03.ibm.com/press/us/en/pressrelease/52904.wss.

4. "Everyone Working for Government," National Archives of Australia, accessed September 2, 2017, www.naa.gov.au/information-management/getting-started/for-everyone-who-works-for-government/index.aspx.

5. International Organization for Standardization (ISO), *ISO 15489-1 2016. Information and documentation—Records management—Part 1: Concepts and principles,* 16.

6. Google Takeout, accessed September 2, 2017, https://takeout.google.com/settings/takeout.

7. Sarah Krizanic, "Mobile Devices and Applications are Transforming Clinical Practice," *California Healthcare News,* August 7, 2017, www.cahcNews.com/articles/08-2017/ca-skrizanic-0817.php.

8. ARMA International, *Controlled Language in Records and Information Management* (Lenexa, KS: ARMA International, 2008), 5.

9. Ibid., 7.

10. *Wikipedia,* s.v. "glossary," last modified September 7, 2017, http://en.wikipedia.org/wiki/Glossary.

11. *Dictionary.com,* s.v. "folksonomy," accessed September 7, 2017, http://dictionary.reference.com/browse/folksonomy.

12. *Merriam-Webster Online,* s.v. "taxonomy," accessed September 7, 2017, https://www.merriam-webster.com/dictionary/taxonomy.

13. ARMA International, ARMA TR 22:2016, *Glossary of Records Management and Information Governance Terms* (Overland Park, KS: ARMA International, 2016), 52.

14. Thomas R. Gruber, "Toward Principles for the Design of Ontologies Used for Knowledge Sharing" (Technical Report KSL 93-04, Knowledge Systems Laboratory, Stanford University), paper presented at the International Workshop on Formal Oncology, Padova, Italy, March 1993, www-ksl.stanford.edu/KSL_Abstracts/KSL-93-04.html. Gruber has since updated this definition: "In the context of computer and information sciences, an ontology defines a set of representational primitives with which to model a domain of knowledge or discourse. The representational primitives are typically classes (or sets), attributes (or properties), and relationships (or relations among class members)" (http://tomgruber.org/writing/ontology-definition-2007.htm). However, the original definition is better suited for our purposes.

15. Richard Pearce-Moses, s.v. "classification," *Glossary of Archival and Records Terminology,* American Society of Archivists, accessed September 7, 2017, https://www2.archivists.org/glossary/terms/c/classification.

16. Executive Office of the President, *Memorandum for the Heads of Executive Departments and Agencies and Independent Agencies,* August 24, 2012, https://www.archives.gov/files/records-mgmt/m-12-18.pdf.

17. Laurence Brewer, *Memorandum to Federal Senior Agency Officials for Records Management and Agency Records Officers: Federal Agency Records Management Report,* September 28 2017, https://www.archives.gov/records-mgmt/memos/ac39-2017.

18. ARMA TR 22:2016, *Glossary of Records Management and Information*, 2.

19. Ibid., 51.

20. Library of Congress, *Classification Web,* accessed September 8, 2017, www.loc.gov/cds/classweb/.

21. "Library of Congress vs. Dewey Decimal," Randolph C. Watson Library, Kilgore College, accessed September 8, 2017, http://library.kilgore.edu/library/lc_dewey.htm.

22. Barbara Fister, "The Dewey Dilemma," *Library Journal,* May 20, 2010, http://lj.libraryjournal.com/2010/05/public-services/the-dewey-dilemma/.

23. Book Industry Study Group (BISG), *Complete Subject Headings List, 2016 Edition,* accessed September 8, 2017, http://bisg.org/page/BISACEdition.

24. BISG, *Complete Subject Headings List,* s.v. "literary collections," http://bisg.org/page/LiteraryCollections.

25. Statistics Canada, "Geographic Classifications (SGC) 2016—Volume I, The Classification," last modified May 16, 2016, www.statcan.gc.ca/eng/subjects/standard/sgc/2016/index.

26. ISO 15489-1:2016, 2.

27. Jay Kennedy and Cherryl Schauder, *Records Management: A Guide to Corporate Recordkeeping,* 2nd ed. (Melbourne: Longmans, 1998), 115.

28. ARMA International, *ARMA TR 22:2016, Glossary of Records Management and Information Governance Terms* s.v. "automatic classification." (Overland Park, KS: ARMA International, 2016), 5.

29. Additional examples of indexing methods can be found in ARMA International, *Establishing Alphabetic, Numeric, and Subject Filing Systems* (Lenexa, KS: ARMA International, 2005). Users referring to this guide are presented with specific rules that must be followed to ensure that records can be retrieved quickly and easily when necessary.

30. The term *texts* is used broadly to include books, essays, interviews, discussions, newspaper articles, speeches, conversations, advertising, theater, informal conversations, or any occurrence of communicative language.

31. See Google Books for excerpts from books discussing content analysis: http://books.google.com/ooks?hl=en&lr=&id=q65703M3C8cC&oi=fnd&pg=PA3&dq=%22content+analysis%22+%2B+records&ots=bK8kBYGdwW&sig=WttW3p0Gquh1APRUXRdQa50FJfQ#v=onepage&q=%22 content%20analysis%22%20%2B%20records&f=false.

32. IBM, IBM Watson Content Analytics 3.5.0: Product Overview, accessed September 8, 2017, https://www.ibm.com/support/knowledgecenter/en/SS5RWK_3.5.0/com.ibm.discovery.es.nav.doc/iiypofnv_prodover_cont.htm.

33. C. W. Roberts, "Content Analysis," in *International Encyclopedia of the Social and Behavioral Sciences,* accessed September 8, 2017, http://dx.doi.org/10.1016/B0-08-043076-7/00707-5.

34. Michael E. Palmquist, Kathleen M. Carley, and Thomas A. Dale, "Applications of Computer-Aided Text Analysis: Analyzing Literary and Nonliterary Texts," in *Text Analysis for the Social Sciences: Methods for Drawing Statistical Inferences from Texts and Transcripts*, ed. Carl W. Roberts (Mahwah, NJ: Lawrence Erlbaum Associates, 1997).

35. Sean Golliher, "SemTech 2011 Coverage: PayPal Discusses Social Commerce and the Semantic Web, *DATAVERSITY,*" June 13, 2011, www.dataversity.net/semtech-2011-coverage-paypal-discusses-social-commerce-and-the-semantic-web/.

36. Jennifer Zaino, "2017 Trends for Semantic Web and Semantic Technologies," *DATAVERSITY,* November 29, 2016, www.dataversity.net/2017-predictions-semantic-web-semantic-technologies/.

37. ISO 15489-1:2016, 2.

38. Ibid., 6.

39. International Organization for Standardization (ISO) *ISO 23081-1:2017 Information and Documentation—Records management processes—Metadata for records—Part 1: Principles* (Geneva: ISO, 2017), 4.

40. International Organization for Standardization (ISO), *ISO 23081-2:2009 Information and Documentation—Managing Metadata for Records—Part 2: Conceptual and Implementation Issues* (Geneva: ISO, 2009), 2.

41. Library and Archives Canada. (2006, February 7). *Government of Canada Records Management Standard,* February 7, 2007.

42. Ibid.

CHAPTER 4

Records Retention Strategies

Inventory, Appraisal, Retention, and Disposition

INTRODUCTION

The debate over keeping information forever versus following a records retention and disposition policy is ongoing. Some experts believe that all information has potential value and should (and could) be preserved permanently. They point to the decreasing cost of storage and the increasing capacity of storage media, especially the advantages presented by cloud storage. Other experts adhere to the lifecycle model of records management and advocate for destruction of records that no longer have value. They point to the cost of locating and redacting information requested in the course of litigation (even when using auto identification and redaction tools) and the danger of exposing personally identifiable information if proper controls are not in place. Robert J. Johnson, author of *Information Disposition: A Practical Guide to the Secure, Compliant Disposal of Records, Media and IT Assets,* makes what is to my mind a profound statement when he says, "All information and all media will eventually be discarded."[1] Disposition of information no longer of use to the organization is one way to "protect" that information from improper disclosure at this vulnerable point in its life cycle.

> **Even if you can keep information forever, should you?**

Organizations are faced with compelling reasons to retain records for use in conducting business and to comply with existing laws and regulations. They must conduct a cost-and-risk assessment to decide if they will retain all information permanently or dispose of it. The purpose of this chapter is not to resolve the debate over the *keep everything forever storage retention strategy* versus the traditional *records retention and disposition strategy*. Instead this chapter will provide records retention strategies useful to those organizations that include disposition as part of their overall information governance approach.

RECORDS INVENTORY

New businesses are often so consumed with their core mission that records management is an afterthought. By the time those in charge finally understand the necessity of developing a strategic approach to records and information management, records exist in a variety of formats stored in a multitude of equipment types and locations, often putting the organization at risk. That makes the task of ensuring that records and information are managed

Statewide Agencies Records Retention Schedule
Agency Schedules/Office of the Secretary of the Commonwealth/Corporations
Division/Certificates of Organization for LLC

Schedule Number and Title	Total Retention	Schedule Description
G12-05 (c) **Certificates of Organization for Limited Liability Companies Filed Pursuant to MGL c. 156C: Microfilm duplicate** _Retain until administrative use ceases._		
G12-05 (b) **Certificates of Organization for Limited Liability Companies Filed Pursuant to MGL c. 156C: Microfilm master** _Permanent._		
G12-05 (a) **Certificates of Organization for Limited Liability Companies Filed Pursuant to MGL c. 156C: Paper copy** _Retain 85 years after microfilming and public hearing._		

FIGURE 4.1 Retention requirements for one type of record (Certificates of Organization for Limited Liability Companies) stored on paper and microfilm.

SOURCE: "Massachusetts Statewide Records Retention Schedule, Quick Guide," Schedule Number: 01–17, 282. www.sec.state.ma.us/arc/arcpdf/MA_Statewide_Records_Schedule.pdf.

properly much more difficult. A records inventory is the first logical step in establishing a records retention and disposition program where none exists.

Businesses with established records and information management programs must continue to audit compliance and make adjustments to their policies and practices based on internal factors (e.g., reorganization, acquisitions, and mergers) and external events (e.g., changes in laws and regulations). A periodic records inventory is necessary to ensure that the organization understands what types of records exist, in what format, and where they are stored.

ARMA International defines _records inventory_ as "a detailed listing that includes the types, locations, dates, volumes, equipment, classification systems, and usage data of an organization's records."[2] This definition can be applied to both physical and electronic records inventories.

Although we are swiftly and surely moving toward a digital world, a records and information management professional must acknowledge and be equipped to manage paper records until they are either digitized and the paper version can be disposed of, or until their retention requirements have been met.

Even in offices where paper records need not be retained if the records are available in alternate formats (e.g., microfilm), many offices will maintain a hybrid system for years, as shown in figure 4.1.

Some inactive records have long-term retention requirements and back-scanning can be cost prohibitive. In addition, if paper records of historical value exist, they must be identified and managed in a way that ensures their physical survival.

Inventory of Physical Records

Records can be stored on different types of physical media, such as paper, CDs, videocassettes, microfilm, magnetic tape, and xray film. Architectural models made out of balsa wood may even be considered records that must be managed. The records inventory can be

Physical Record Example

A commission resurveying the North Carolina–South Carolina boundary in 1928 found a longleaf pine that had been blazed to mark the boundary in 1735. They felled the tree, replaced it with a stone marker, and gave one-half of the blazed section of the tree to each state. The South Carolina State Archives holds many maps and plats serving as legal records of boundaries of various kinds, but this tree section is unique and one of the most unusual records in the holdings of the State Archive.

SOURCE: Image courtesy of the South Carolina Department of Archives and History.

used to develop a retention schedule, provide input to the vital records protection program, and identify potential improvements to the records and information management program for both active and inactive records.

A necessary component of any successful project is support from top management— preferably in the form of a directive from the organization's president or chief operating officer to all employees who will be involved in the records inventory project. Additional champions within the organization should be identified, including managers from finance, legal, information management, and human resources. The project can be accomplished by internal records and information management staff, departmental staff, or an outside consulting firm. Each approach has advantages and disadvantages. The budget allocated for the project and the time frame within which it must be accomplished will be determining factors.

The internal records and information management staff will have a good understanding of the records held by the organization and the individuals they need to work with to conduct the inventory. But they may not have the time needed to conduct a physical inventory. The work-unit staff would know what records are created and where they are located, but they may be reluctant to point out any weaknesses in their system. An outside consultant would be objective and have the experience necessary to conduct the records inventory, but there may be internal resistance and the cost for an outside consultant would be higher than if internal staff were used.

Pre-inventory Steps

Once support from top management has been obtained, champions have been identified, and the project manager has been appointed, the following pre-inventory steps should be taken:

- Clarify the records inventory objectives and strategies.
- Design the inventory form and accompanying directions. Blank forms are available from ARMA International, and many examples, such as the

Main State Archives Records Series Inventory illustrated in figure 4.2, are available online.

- Staff and train the project team. Provide them with an organizational chart describing the main functions of each office along with the necessary supplies to inventory physical holdings, including blank inventory forms;

Maine State Archives	Archives Use Only (applies to new schedules)		
RECORD SERIES INVENTORY	Agency No.	Schedule No.	Series No.

Department	Bureau/Division		Date
Person to Contact	Telephone No.	Location of Records	

Contact person's mailing address

Series title

Description of Records: Why does the agency keep these records—what program or programs do they support? How are the records used, and by whom? What might be found in a typical file? *(Please include samples with inventory form; you may black out identifiable personal information if this raises confidentiality concerns. Also, please spell out all acronyms.)*

Frequency of Use: At what point does each file become "closed" as far as your business needs are concerned and how often do these files need to be accessed?

Arrangement: ☐ Alphabetically ☐ Chronologically ☐ Geographically ☐ Case number ☐ Other _____

These records are retained by: ☐ Calendar Year (1/1 – 12/31) ☐ State Fiscal Year (7/1 – 6/30) ☐ Federal Fiscal Year (10/1 – 9/30)

Media Type: ☐ Paper ☐ Microfilm ☐ Microfiche ☐ Audio Tape ☐ Digital File ☐ CD ☐ Photograph ☐ DVD/Video ☐ Other _____

Date of Oldest File	Volume in Cubic Feet if Applicable	Annual Rate of Accumulation if Applicable	Filing and Storage Equipment *(How are records stored)*

Can the same information be found in other records? *(If yes, please explain. We are asking this because it's important to know where the State would go to reconstruct the records, in case of disaster.)*

Are records confidential? ☐ no ☐ yes   If yes, which statutes or regulations apply?

How long do you need to store these records (total for paper files should not exceed 20 years):

In Your Agency	In the Records Center	Archives or Destroy *(your recommendation)*

What Statutes, law, regulations or research information did you use to determine your retention periods?

Signature of Agency Records Officer (Other Agency Head – Please specify)	Date

MSA/RM 59/Rev. 072012

FIGURE 4.2 Records Series Inventory form.

SOURCE: Maine State Archives, MSA/Records Management, 5/29/2015, www.maine.gov/sos/arc/records/state/inventoryinfo.pdf.

adhesive labels to identify records and containers and to show they have been inventoried; and equipment including flashlight, gloves, and dust masks for use in storage areas.

- Communicate to staff and management about the project. Allay the fears of those representing each work unit to be inventoried and explain that this is an inventory and not an audit.
- Conduct a preliminary survey to identify the location of records, estimate their total volume, flag hazards, and note any problems with space and storage.
- Establish a work schedule that includes dates, locations, and contacts for each unit to be inventoried that provides flexibility. Other activities (e.g., budget deadlines) may take priority within units and need to be accommodated.

Conducting the Inventory Steps

The following are the recommended steps to take when conducting a physical inventory:[3]

- Draw a map of the physical layout of each area, numbering each piece of storage equipment and noting the location of each records series. Record all records such as correspondence, photographs, reports, and maps that are evidence of the organization's activities. Disregard all non-records such as magazines, catalogues, blank forms, books, and pamphlets.
- Inventory the records as a series, that is, a group of identical or related records that can be evaluated as a unit because they are normally filed, used, and disposed of as a unit. Record the information on an inventory form. Complete a separate form for each location where records in the same series are filed or stored. The information from all forms related to one series will be consolidated onto a master inventory and used to develop a records retention and disposition schedule.
- Store the inventory data in a database developed in-house (e.g., using Microsoft Access), in records management software purchased specifically for the task, or in a content management system with records management functionality. A system to manage physical assets as well as electronic records provides additional advantages. For example, one solution allows users to manage both the physical document and an electronic copy if both must be retained. A double-click on the electronic copy will bring up the location of the physical record. Once the retention requirements have been met, the system alerts the appropriate party to destroy both copies.

Completing the Records Inventory Form

An inventory form similar to the one illustrated in figure 4.2 must be completed for each records series. The method described here takes an *archival approach* by starting at the end of the workflow, and accepting the fact that existing records must be managed. Complete the inventory form by performing the following steps:

- Visit or contact all functional areas within the organization.
- Locate, identify, and inventory their records.

- Complete one form for each records series title. All records in a series must have the same retention period. If a record exists that does not fit within established series, create a new record series. Note whether the records are original or a duplicate as well as the medium on which they are stored.
- If the information is not available from the representative of the functional area, check the applicable data privacy classification laws and business practices for data in the record series.
- The retention requirements are based on legal, fiscal, and administrative requirements. If the retention periods are not known, or need to be verified, identify state and federal laws that prescribe a retention period for the records and check the state and federal audit requirements as well. Note that for this particular form, retention requirements will be stated in terms of length of time the records have been in the office, storage area, and records center. The retention period can be expressed in terms of time, for example, retain three years, or in terms of an event or action, for example, retain six months after audit.

Inventory of Electronic Records and Electronic Systems

Records and information managers must know the electronic records created and the systems involved in order to develop a plan to manage those e-records.

Location of Electronic Records

An electronic records inventory will form the basis for management decisions and assist organizations in fulfilling their current and future obligations when faced with e-discovery and/or Freedom of Information (FOI) requests. The electronic records inventory is more challenging than a physical records inventory and requires assistance from information technology (IT) as well as input from users of the information and communication systems. The information gathered will feed into the development of the file plan discussed in chapter 3 and will be a key element when developing requirements for the organization's electronic records management system discussed in chapter 6.

The electronic records inventory will include both structured records (e.g., database-driven such as payroll records) and unstructured records (e.g., photos, email, and presentations). In addition to electronic records housed within an electronic records management system, active records are maintained in the organization's business systems and stored in third-party systems and on mobile devices. The result is that organizations are faced with electronic records in a variety of formats stored in multiple locations that can be categorized as follows:

- **Centralized information systems:** Centralized information communications technology systems are installed and operated by the information technology department; they include email servers, content/document/records repositories, enterprise-wide application servers (e.g., enterprise-wide geospatial information systems), and legacy systems (obsolete information technology). Organizations operating from multiple physical sites benefit from centralized systems that provide instant access to updated, consistent information.

- **Decentralized information systems:** Decentralized computing occurs when work units have a high degree of local autonomy in developing their information technology resources and specific needs not relevant to other work units in the organization (e.g., a 911 computer dispatch system used by the local fire department).
- **Personal work stations and storage devices:** Decentralized computer systems pose fewer problems than other decentralized locations within which records may reside, such as PC hard drives, laptops, digital cameras, smartphones, and tablets.
- **Third-party systems:** The internet, Web 2.0, social media, cloud computing, and the Internet of Things have changed the way organizations conduct business. Organizations interact with their current and potential customers on social networking sites hosted by third-party providers, often creating records that must be managed. They take advantage of the benefits offered by cloud service providers, which can result in records that are stored on computers located outside of the country in which the organization does business. And increasingly they gather data from sensors embedded in high-tech devices employed in "smart cities," "smart homes," "smart warehouses" and "smart offices."

The electronic records inventory should concentrate on logical collections of records grouped by business function or subject rather than by physical location. Many of the steps involved in preparing for and conducting an electronic records inventory mirror those involved in a physical records inventory. However, rather than a map of the physical layout of an office area or records storage center, a data map can be used as a diagram of agency-owned information and communication tools and technologies.

IT should maintain a data map for centralized systems and decentralized systems for which they have responsibility. The data map should also include information hosted at social media sites and by third-party providers. Individuals familiar with information and communication technology within each work unit will need to be interviewed to identify any information systems or storage locations not already included on the data map.

Electronically Stored Information Data Mapping

Data mapping is not a new concept, but it is used in two different ways. In the first instance, data mapping specifies how one information set relates, or maps, to another. The relationships between the data are key for migration and integration projects. However, data mapping in the second instance is a comprehensive inventory of a corporation's IT systems that store information. This "defensible inventory" is important for litigation and other proceedings.

The data map shown in figure 4.3 identifies the locations of electronically stored information (ESI) for which the Florida Attorney General's Office is responsible: individual agency workstations, shared drives, database repositories, servers, archives, home computers, telephones and pagers, storage media, and cloud storage.

Inventorying provides intellectual control over electronic systems (network applications, backups, and legacy media). This inventory often contains information as to the number and size of files residing in email accounts or shared folders, but it rarely explains the types of information produced by the systems. Electronically stored information data

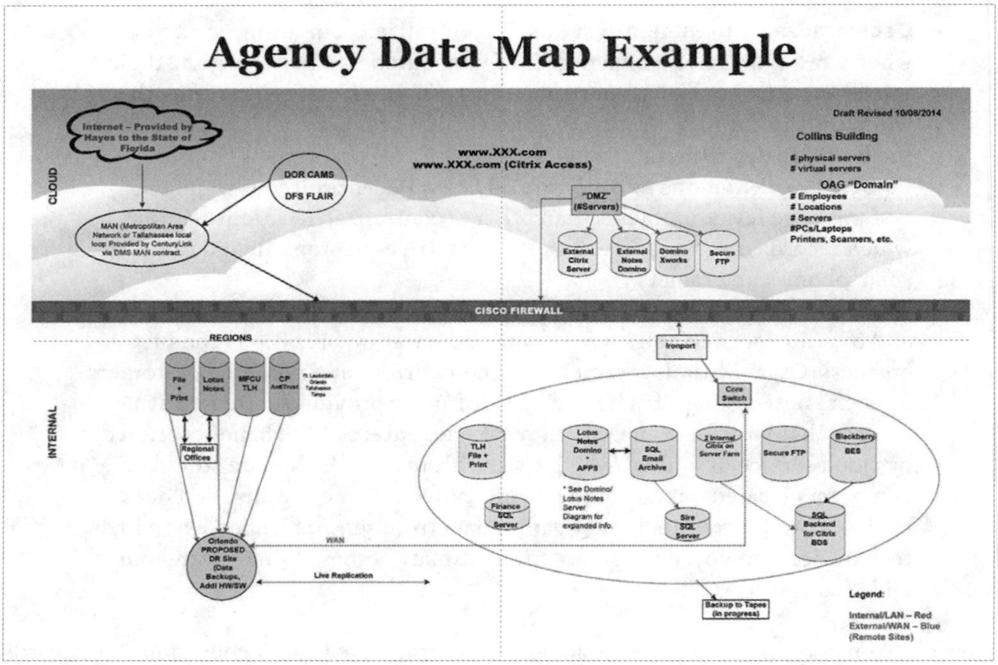

FIGURE 4.3 Florida Attorney General data map example.

SOURCE: Florida State College of Law Research Center, http://guides.law.fsu.edu/ediscovery/datamaps
License: CC BY-ND 4.0.

maps must be accompanied by additional information that can be used to develop effective records management, records retention, and litigation hold policies and procedures.

ESI data maps show the logical relationship between the systems and repositories and backup systems. They allow the organization to better understand the current state of storage, identify sensitive data in unknown areas of the network and remediate, and gain visibility into risky data usage patterns in order to secure data and prevent loss.

The process of creating the data map involves compiling a complete list of all systems used, including communication and collaboration tools. A list of business processes should also be compiled and then compared with the system list to ensure that all electronically stored information is accounted for. A list of roles, groups, and users involved in the business processes should also be developed. Off-site or third-party storage systems used for communications, cost-efficiency, or disaster recovery should be identified.[4] Mobile devices used when working remotely and equipment used in home offices may also contain business records and should be included.

Social media enterprise solutions may be implemented internally and belong on the data map. If the organization uses social media tools provided by commercial entities or takes advantage of cloud services, the data map must be modified to specify the information hosted by these third-party providers as well. The data map(s) supplemented by charts, lists, and tables, with supplementary illustrations and analyses that describe the information and the infrastructure and systems that host the information, provides a "total information systems overview" one can equate to a *data atlas*.[5]

Completing the Electronic Records Inventory

The scope of the electronic records inventory project must be considered during the planning phase. Enterprise-wide inventories may be accomplished as part of one project in small- or medium-sized organizations, but limiting the scope of the project is a better way to approach an electronic inventory project in a large organization. Project managers understand the wisdom of tackling the low-hanging fruit (projects and people most likely to ensure success), so that success can be demonstrated and built upon.

Although the data map is invaluable, users of the information systems must also be surveyed. The electronic records inventory can be approached in one of three ways:

1. Require that representatives of each work unit complete an electronic records inventory for their area. The questionnaire should be submitted to the project manager, who would contact the persons completing the inventory form if there were questions.
2. Assign the task of completing the records inventory form to the records manager or other member of the records inventory team. The form should be completed during interviews with work unit liaisons and those using the information systems within each area.
3. Implement a hybrid approach. Ask the work unit representatives to complete and submit the form. Use the form as a basis for the interviews to follow. Additions and corrections should be made based on the information gathered during the interview.

Examples of electronic records inventory forms, similar to the physical records inventory forms, can be found online. If used, liaisons are advised to use the form to add, change, or delete a records series on the related records retention schedule.

Two most important questions that need to be answered are: (1) what systems are in use? and (2) what records series are in each system? However, some organizations may seek more detailed information. The Electronic Records Inventory Worksheet employed by the Indian Health Service, the federal health program for American Indians and Alaska Natives, is shown in figure 4.4.

This form requires additional information, such as system owner, information owner, data backup/frequency, backup location, retention of records, and authority for retention. This information can be used to create or update a records retention schedule and can be factored into migration and preservation decisions for records with long-term retention requirements.

Once the electronic records inventory project has been completed, the records manager or other person conducting the electronic records inventory must ensure the information provided is interpreted accurately. If a questionnaire was completed and submitted by a work unit, the responses should be reviewed with the unit records liaison or other person who completed the form. If the survey/interview method was used, the person conducting the interview should prepare a summary of the results of the inventory and submit it to the interviewee for editing, if necessary, and approval.

An analysis of the results of physical and/or electronic inventories can be used to identify:

- obsolete and/or duplicate records and documents that can be consolidated or disposed of

- location of information to respond more quickly to discovery requests
- records most critical to business continuity in the event of a disaster
- current and future storage needs

When describing the process of completing an inventory, interviews with records creators were included. Those interviews could be used not only to ask about the current records but also about the business process. However, an analysis of the business process can be conducted independently of the records inventory.

IHS-971 (02/2016)

ELECTRONIC RECORDS INVENTORY WORKSHEET

General Information

Agency: **Indian Health Service**		Date:	
1. Location Name:	2. Office/Division/Section:	3. Building/Room Number:	
4. Name of Person Taking Inventory:	5. Phone Number:	6. Contact E-mail address:	

Electronic Records Information

7. Name of Electronic System:

8. Application Name:

9. Information Owner:

10. System Owner:

11. System is: ☐ Commercial off the shelf   ☐ Custom, In-house

12. Electronic Records Description:

13. Inputs/Source Documents: (hard copy forms and hard copy documents that are scanned (e.g. correspondence, reports, still pictures, maps, etc.))

14. Outputs: (what types of reports are generated from application)

15. Is there a register, index, etc. to the records?   ☐ Yes   ☐ No

16. Are data files backed-up? ☐ Yes   ☐ No   Frequency:

17. Where are the data backups stored?

18. How long are records kept?   ___ Years(s)   ___ Month(s)

19. Retention is based on: ☐ Statute or Law   ☐ Regulation   ☐ Industry Standard

20. If question #18 is not applicable, then recommend a retention period:

FIGURE 4.4 Electronic records inventory worksheet.

SOURCE: Indian Health Service, https://www.ihs.gov/ihm/includes/themes/responsive2017/display_objects/documents/pc/dsp_ihm_pc_p5c15_ap_b.pdf.

RECORDS APPRAISAL

The 2016 update of the ISO 15489 records management standard introduces the concept of records *appraisal* as: "the process of evaluating business activities to determine which records need to be created and captured and how long the records need to be kept."[6] The difference between the results of the inventory and the appraisal is that one determines what is being/has been retained while the other determines what should be captured and retained.

In order to determine what evidence of business should be retained, the person performing the appraisal must understand: (1) the nature of the business in the context of its legal, resourcing, and technological environment, and (2) the risks to which it is exposed and how those risks can be managed through the creation, capture, and management of records (ISO 15489:2016).[7]

Business Records Requirements

ISO 15489-1:2016 further states that records requirements are derived from business needs, legal and regulatory requirements, and community or societal expectations. Obviously, identifying the business records requirements necessitates working with all stakeholders, including representatives from business units, legal, information technology, and risk management.

Business Needs

Asking representatives from business units to describe their process will reveal points at which documentation (a record) is created to serve a business need. For example, the purchasing process involves the creation of both a purchase requisition form (seeking approval to order) and a purchase order (placing the order with the vendor). Both must be created and provide evidence of a business activity, but as you might already suspect, one retains its value longer than the other. In this case, the retention periods are different: commonly three years for the requisition form and seven years for the purchase order. In electronic systems, metadata and linkages between these two and other records must be maintained.

Legal and Regulatory Requirements

The legal and regulatory environment is becoming more complex due to an increasing number of laws and regulations and new business models that facilitate commerce across jurisdictional boundaries. For example, the European Union's GDPR (General Data Protection Regulation) that became effective May 25, 2018, impacts businesses outside of the European Union, because the legislation applies to anyone with an establishment or equipment inside the EU; anyone who offers goods and services (even if they are free) to EU residents; and anyone who monitors the behavior of EU residents.[8]

Risk Management

Risk management involves identifying, assessing, and controlling threats to an organization. Today, many risks arise from the improper handling of an organization's records and information. Some also arise from the response taken immediately after an incident. For example, in 2017, Equifax (a company that keeps financial details about all Americans to gauge how much of a risk they are when applying to borrow money) disclosed that vital data about 143 million Americans was exposed. Immediately after the announcement, which took place one month after the actual incident, the company compounded the negative publicity by offering affected customers free credit-file monitoring and identity-theft protection but included fine print stating that acceptance of the offer would require customers to use a private third-party arbitration service to resolve any disputes (i.e., they could not file a lawsuit). Reaction to the event and the organization's response resulted in calls for formal investigations, damage to the firm's reputation, and a drop of 25 percent in the value of its stock.[9]

Primary and Secondary Value of Records

Records are created and maintained to provide evidence of and value to the organization (primary value) but that value may extend beyond the purpose for which they were created (secondary value). Records can meet one or more of the following four requirements:

- administrative (operational)
- fiscal
- legal (and regulatory)
- historical (research/archival)

When possible, archival records should be identified during the appraisal process to ensure proper maintenance until such time as the record is transferred to an archive.

Administrative (Operational)

Records that meet administrative needs aid in the conduct of day-to-day business, define policy and procedures, or ensure administrative consistency and continuity. Administrative (operational) records include directives/policies/procedures; organizational charts; general correspondence; minutes of official meetings; and personnel records.

Fiscal

Records that satisfy fiscal requirements may be necessary to conduct current or future business or provide evidence of financial transactions and the movement and expenditure of funds. These records include financial audit reports, accounting journals and ledgers, tax receipts; annual budget documents, and payroll records.

Legal (and Regulatory)

Records that satisfy legal requirements are those that document and protect the rights and interests of an individual or organization, provide for prosecution or defense of litigation, demonstrate compliance with laws and regulations, and/or meet other legal needs. These records include contracts, titles, claims, deeds, and birth certificates.

Historical (Documentation or Research/Archival)

Records that satisfy historical requirements are useful or significant for documenting and understanding the past. These records may have had primary value for the organization at one time but are no longer needed for administrative, legal, or fiscal purposes. They do, however, contain authentic evidence of an organization's policies, decisions, operations, or other activities that should be retained. They often document the development of a government and its policies, provide evidence of the lives and activities of people, describe social and economic conditions, and record the development of community and business. Records of historical interest may include correspondence (authored by or received by a significant person, such as the founder of the organization or the president of the country); US military records; birth, marriage, and death records; meteorological (weather and climate) data; and legal opinions.

Primary and Secondary Value of Records

The *primary value* of records—those that satisfy administrative (operational), fiscal, and legal requirements—is derived from the original use for which they were created. Traditionally administrative and fiscal records are considered transient by archivists, and records must possess other values to be considered archival.

Records have *secondary value* when they are useful or significant for purposes other than that for which they were originally created. Secondary value includes records that satisfy information or evidential needs as well as research interests. US Census records, for example, provide evidence of the size and composition of the US population only until the next census is published. But the content of census records provides information of value to researchers long after its evidential value has expired.

Records that meet legal requirements can have primary or secondary value, depending upon the purpose and function of a record. A contract, for example, is a legally enforceable agreement between two or more persons that documents specific actions on the part of each party (primary purpose). However, the contract may continue to meet legal requirements after final settlement if the contract period is less than the relevant statute of limitations (secondary legal value).

Essential (vital) records may be identified as part of a paper or electronic records inventory or may be the subject of a separate essential (vital) records inventory. Essential records and their relationship to disaster preparedness and recovery and to business continuity are covered in chapter 8.

Records Series

The common unit for organizing and controlling files in the United States is a *records series*. Records are grouped together, either through physical or intellectual control, because they relate to a particular subject or function, result from the same activity, document a specific type of transaction; take a particular physical form; or have some other relationship arising out of their creation, receipt, maintenance, or use.[10]

Consider the different types of documents you used to prepare last year's federal tax return. Whether you mailed your hard-copy return or filed electronically, the supporting documentation must be retained to provide evidence for the figures you used on your tax return in case of an audit. If you file electronically, you are urged to print (either as hard copy or to a PDF file) your tax return and keep a copy for your records along with the supporting documentation.

A copy of the forms you submitted and the supporting documentation comprise a records series that could be named "2020 Tax Returns." You might decide to separate the various documents used to prepare your tax returns into two folders, one for "State Tax Returns" and another for "Federal Tax Returns." The resulting hierarchy is shown in figure 4.5.

Once you determine how to organize these records, the next question is "how long should you keep them?" If you file a claim for a refund, for example, the Internal Revenue Service (IRS) has three years from April 15 of the year due, or from the date you actually filed if later, to audit your tax returns. Unless you believe the IRS will initiate proceedings against you for tax fraud, you can probably dispose of your records after the three-year period expires.

Notice the conditional term *probably*. Retention periods can be affected by other factors, such as claiming loss for worthless securities or failing to report all of your income. The tax code and retention requirements are even more complex for businesses, including self-employed individuals and small businesses, partnerships, and international corporations. A records manager must follow a similar but more complex thought process to determine what constitutes a records series. Each record series must be controlled by a records schedule that provides mandatory instructions for the retention and disposal of records. In order to determine the retention period for each records series, research needs to be conducted into prevailing legal and regulatory requirements. This process can be used to determine the retention requirement for all types of records, including those that present the public face of the organization online, website records.

WEB RECORDS:
IDENTIFYING, CAPTURING, AND SCHEDULING

Of course, there is no records series named "Web Records." The term is used to help us focus on the considerations that must be made when planning to manage web-based records—a concern for almost every public and private organization.

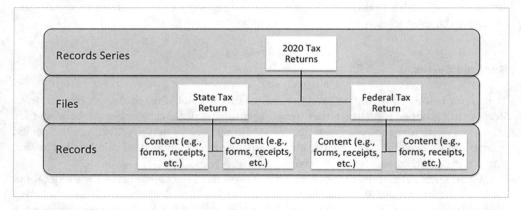

FIGURE 4.5 Anatomy of a records series.

Recordkeeping Roles and Responsibilities

Individuals with responsibilities related to website records management may include content providers, website managers, records professionals, archivists and/or librarians, legal services, and end users. Their duties must be clarified.

Recordkeeping Requirements for Web-Based Records

Web-based records are subject to the same requirements as paper-based or other electronic records. They must be retained and disposed of in accordance with retention and disposal schedules based on their administrative (operational), legislative, financial, and historical value. In some cases, content displayed on a website is information held elsewhere in hard copy or electronic format. The online digital representation disseminates information to a broader audience. The original records may already be managed by a recordkeeping system. However, if records contained on a website are not being kept in another form, it is essential to ensure that they are managed by the organization's recordkeeping system. Approaches to managing web-based records will differ based on the type of content contained: static or dynamic.

Static Web Content

A *static webpage* displays the content to each viewer in the same way. Static content can be developed quickly through the use of website development tools that publish HTML files for upload to the web or using a website content management system. Pages that represent static content considered records can be captured by a records management system before posting. A set of recordkeeping rules to provide guidance for custodians of the content (whether content contributors, website managers, or others) might include:

Addition of content:

- No action is required when the content published on the website already exists in a record controlled by the organization's recordkeeping system.
- If new versions of documents are added to websites or changes are made to existing content (excluding minor changes such as the correction of spelling errors), a copy of the updated document should be retained.
- Content must be published with metadata to provide context (e.g., date of approval, authorization, disclaimer, copyright notice).

Removal of content:

- If a complete and current copy of a file published via the Web is managed by a recordkeeping system or is held by the initiating party, it may be deleted from the website at any time.
- If a copy of the web-based record is not managed by the recordkeeping system or elsewhere, it may be deleted from the website only when all records retention requirements have been met.

- If the records are required for audit or legal purposes, or relevant to an e-discovery or Freedom of Information (FOI) request, they must not be modified or destroyed even if their retention requirement has been met. A legal hold must be put into effect following procedures in place for all records (e.g., the legal department notifies the records manager, who then advises the IT security manager).

Preservation for archival purposes:

- If most of the content is held in a content management system or controlled by a recordkeeping system, periodic snapshots may be appropriate to create an accurate archive of a significant portion of the website at a particular point in time. A risk assessment should be conducted to determine which portions of the website(s) should be included and the frequency of the snapshots (e.g., annually or when major changes have been made to the design and/or content).
- Records created by capturing snapshots must be managed according to accepted recordkeeping principles (e.g., not overwritten until retention periods have been met and migrated through upgrades of hardware and software to ensure their continuing usability and authenticity).
- Snapshots are not recommended for websites that incorporate highly dynamic functionality, including databases and e-commerce transactions.

In general, snapshots are suitable for the static websites but not appropriate for dynamic websites.

Dynamic Web Content

To help us understand the differences between early static websites and today's interactive sites, we can use the Internet Archives' Wayback Machine to locate an image of an earlier site (see figure 4.6). The 1996 WhiteHouse.gov site contains only text and links to other textual documents and does not allow for public comments. You can imagine the ease with which records could be managed, because content could reside in the same location as other electronic documents not posted to the Web. For historical purposes, a periodic screenshot is sufficient, because the page would be changed very little over time.

A *dynamic webpage* is one that delivers custom content and is generated in response to a user request, drawing content from a database and displaying the content in a prede-termined format.[11] Dynamic sites often contain links to other sites, including social media sites that should be captured and preserved if a complete picture of the ways in which the organization communicates is desired. The current White House website contains dynamic elements and encourages interactivity with the public. Users can register to receive updates, view featured videos, and tune in to live events as they occur. The site encourages the public to become involved in government by creating and signing petitions. Links to the following social media tools are located at the bottom of the home page: Facebook, Twitter, and Insta-gram. In addition, web pages for the president, first lady, vice president, and second lady can be reached through links on the main site—each with a link to their Twitter account. The Twitter accounts are also covered by the Presidential Records Act and must be preserved.

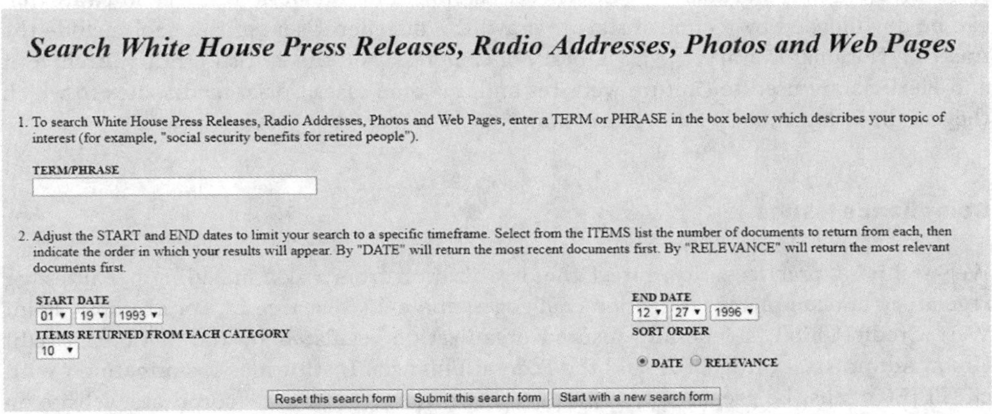

Search *White House Press Releases, Radio Addresses, Photos and Web Pages*

1. To search White House Press Releases, Radio Addresses, Photos and Web Pages, enter a TERM or PHRASE in the box below which describes your topic of interest (for example, "social security benefits for retired people").

TERM/PHRASE

[   ]

2. Adjust the START and END dates to limit your search to a specific timeframe. Select from the ITEMS list the number of documents to return from each, then indicate the order in which your results will appear. By "DATE" will return the most recent documents first. By "RELEVANCE" will return the most relevant documents first.

START DATE
[01 ▾] [19 ▾] [1993 ▾]

ITEMS RETURNED FROM EACH CATEGORY
[10 ▾]

END DATE
[12 ▾] [27 ▾] [1996 ▾]

SORT ORDER
◉ DATE ○ RELEVANCE

[Reset this search form] [Submit this search form] [Start with a new search form]

FIGURE 4.6 Whitehouse.gov site in 1996 (Web 1.0).

SOURCE: Internet Archive Wayback Machine, accessed October 19, 2017, https://web.archive.org/web/19961227062541/http://whitehouse.gov/.

Although the files that made up presidential administration websites are preserved in the *Executive Office of the President Electronic Records Archive,* their interfaces are not. Therefore, NARA provides links to the WhiteHouse.gov websites for President William Jefferson Clinton (1993–2001), President George W. Bush (as archived 2009), and President Barack Obama (2009–2017) as part of the Presidential Libraries sub-site.[12]

Data retention decisions must be made about the content contributed by the public so that information that could constitute an invasion of privacy is not released. However, access to this information may be the subject of a Freedom of Information request five years after the end of the current administration. NARA or the White House may dispose of information lacking historical value. Currently, the White House has the following retention requirements:

- Server log entries are retained for one year.
- Cookie data linked to individual users are retained for thirteen months.
- Other cookie data and automatically generated email data may be retained by the White house until the end of the current administration.[13]

Web Archiving

As mentioned earlier, creating snapshots of websites may be acceptable for historical purposes when preserving static websites, but that method is not suitable for dynamic websites.

In addition to hosting the Wayback Machine, a public archive containing over 306 billion webpages from 1996 through October 20, 2017, the Internet Archive provides a web archiving subscription service, Archive-It, which allows institutions to build and preserve collections of born-digital content.[14] Archive-It partners can harvest, catalog, manage, and browse the archived collections. The collections are hosted at the Internet Archive data center and are accessible to the public via full-text search. Another tool developed by the Internet Archive is Heritrix.[15] This is an open-source, scalable Web crawler capable of fetching, archiving, and analyzing internet-accessible content. Heritrix is free software that can be downloaded by technical staff to crawl the internet. Users of this tool include the Austrian National Library, the US Library of Congress, and the British Library. Archive-It and Heritrix are used to capture websites and, in some cases, social media sites to which they are linked, primarily for preservation.

Compliance Issues

Web-archiving practices can protect the organization from risks, including penalties for regulatory noncompliance, litigation challenges, and e-discovery costs. For example, Point West Credit Union, a federally insured organization regulated by the National Credit Union Administration (NCUA) and the Federal Financial Institutions Examination Council (FFIEC), must be prepared to reproduce any given page from its corporate website on any given day over a three-year period. They transitioned from keeping track of changes on their website in a spreadsheet to using Smarsh's Web Archiving Tool to capture and manage all content.[16] In addition to web content, this solution can be used to archive email, instant messages, text messages, and social media as well. Tools are provided to allow customers to export all content without data-related fees; however, assistance (and storage media) can be provided for nominal hourly fees.

LEGAL AND REGULATORY COMPLIANCE

As illustrated by the Point West Credit Union example, organizations must comply with the recordkeeping requirements established by the entities that exercise control over them.

Federal and State Laws

In the United States, some regulations apply to organizations in general, such as accounting and tax laws; others apply to organizations within specific industries, such as healthcare. Some are imposed by the federal government, whereas others are imposed by the state or local governments. Retention requirements often vary across jurisdictions. Florida, for example, requires public hospitals, healthcare facilities, and medical providers to maintain master patient indexes (including patient name, number, birth date, date of admission, and date of discharge where applicable) for ten years.[17] Texas requires master patient indexes to be retained permanently.[18]

Statutes of Limitations

Statutes of limitations are federal or state laws that restrict the time in which legal proceedings can be brought against a defendant in either a civil or criminal matter. In Alabama, a product liability action must be brought "within two years from the time when the injury is or should have been discovered."[19] In Louisiana, action must be taken "within one year from the time when the injury occurred."[20] In Massachusetts, however, action must be brought "within three years of the date on which the injury occurred."[21]

Audit Period

There are different types of audits. "Generally, the IRS can include returns filed within the last three years in an audit. Additional years can be added if a substantial error is identified. Generally, if a substantial error is identified, the IRS will not go back more than the last six years."[22] The Securities and Exchange Commission requires accounting firms to retain certain records relevant to their audits and reviews of issuers' financial statements for seven years.[23] Records to be retained include the accounting firm's work papers and certain other documents that contain conclusions, opinions, analyses, or financial data related to the audit or review.[24] According to the Massachusetts Society of Certified Public Accountants, a corporation's internal audit records should be retained six years, but a public audit report must be retained permanently.[25]

Administrative Needs

The retention requirements for records with administrative or operational value would not be discovered during legal research but would be revealed based on input from records creators and users. The information gathered through records appraisal and legal research is used to develop the records retention and disposition schedule. Contrary to advice to consider the risks associated with the retention and disposition of records in ISO 15489-1:2016, I would not factor risk in just yet. It is important first to identify how long the records *should be* retained based on legal and regulatory requirements. Adjustments, if desired, can be made later.

DEVELOPING A RECORDS RETENTION AND DISPOSITION SCHEDULE

The primary purpose of a records retention and disposition schedule is to ensure that records are retained only as long as necessary and then disposed of when they no longer have value.

The benefits of developing a records retention and disposition schedule to facilitate disposal of physical records are well-documented. They include a reduction in time to locate and retrieve desired information as well as a reduction in costs associated with the equipment, space, staff, and/or services needed to manage those records.

When the discussion turns to electronic records, however, the benefits are less clear. First, electronic records are not as visible as physical records. They take up less space on storage devices that are constantly increasing in capacity and decreasing in price. However, the cost of identifying and disposing of electronic records residing both under the direct control of the enterprise and under the control of third-party providers can exceed storage costs.

There are advantages to disposing of electronic records, which include mitigating the risk of retaining records that could be used against the organization (the proverbial *smoking gun*); reducing the cost of locating the requested records in response to e-discovery and/or Freedom of Information requests; and reducing the cost of inspecting records to redact PII, such as social security numbers, credit card numbers, address information, and driver's license numbers.

Retention Schedule Considerations

The following list of questions should be answered before the actual work begins on the development of the records retention and disposition schedule:

- Is there an existing records retention and destruction schedule or are you creating it from scratch?
- What is the scope of the retention schedule—enterprise-wide or focused on one function or work group?
- Will you use a functional retention schedule or one related to the organization's structure?
- Were a records inventory and business process analysis completed recently? If so, you may have already gathered much of the information you need. If not, both should be completed before proceeding further.
- Will a general records schedule be prepared for records that exist in departments, agencies, and work groups across the enterprise?
- Have legal/regulatory considerations been researched? If so, you can use that information for the schedule. If not, determine who will conduct the research and monitor any changes in legislation. This research feeds into the records schedule and must be completed first.
- Will electronic records be included in this retention/disposition schedule or will separate records retention and disposition schedules be prepared for physical and electronic records?
- What resources are available to develop and maintain the retention schedule(s), such as records retention scheduling software and a records legal research database?

Records Retention and Disposition Schedule

The records retention and disposition schedule is created after the records inventory, business process analysis, and legal/regulatory research have been completed. The format used to record information will differ, but common elements will be included in every schedule. This information may be gathered manually, but it should be managed through the use of a database or records retention software program.

The most common elements include the records series, record title and description, records office, retention requirement (often specifying location for active and inactive files), and disposition method. If a functional classification is used, the function (e.g., fiscal), and the record category (e.g., fiscal: budget and budget control) will be included. Additional information may include storage medium, volume of records, effective date, and revision number and date.

The University of California allows the public to search its web-based *Records Disposition Schedules Manual*. Figure 4.7 is the result of a general search on the entire retention schedule.[26]

Notice the distinction between administrative records in the second and third rows—one class requires permanent retention although the other can be deleted or destroyed five years after the end of the physical year in which they were created.

Software and services can be acquired from vendors such as RecordLion[27] that automates tasks based on rules-based recordkeeping. For example, records are categorized and automatically declared based on classification rules; retention periods are based on triggers (e.g., calendar events, business system events, or rules based on any combination of available metadata); and disposition is automated, including approvals, review periods, destruction certificates, and an audit trail.

Zasio's *Versatile Enterprise* software manages the complete lifecycle of physical (e.g., documents and boxes) and electronic records (e.g., word processing and email). Figure 4.8 displays a user-friendly records series dialog box for Accounts Payable records, with retention requirements based on the date of creation.

Even for an electronic system, a retention schedule takes a great deal of time to create and maintain because it is based on classification rules someone must create. That's one of the reasons some records managers prefer the concept of *big buckets.*

Big Buckets and Records Retention Schedules

Big buckets is a method used to simplify records retention schedules by consolidating record types related to the same business function or process with similar retention requirements into bigger retention buckets (records series). The fewer buckets, the fewer retention choices, and the greater likelihood of compliance with the organization's retention schedule.

There are also challenges to the big buckets approach. One is the need to manage exceptions, such as event-driven retention requirements. For example, two records titles may have a retention requirement of ten to twenty-five years, but the triggers can be different. The trigger for one can be the phrase *after the last update,* although the trigger for the other can be *after the last date of activity.* If the *last update* does not take place on the *last date of activity,* these are two different triggers.

Search Results:

The items from the existing schedule that have not been superseded are in this database.
New items have a * after the number.

261 records found for "*"

Records Code	Function	Function Description	Category	Category Description	Sub-Category Title	Keywords	Retention Period	Retention Rule	Comments
0001*	01. General Routine Office Transitory Records	Transitory records document routine general office activities. In this context the word "routine" more...	1. General Routine Office Transitory Records	Transitory records document routine general office activities. In this context the word "routine" more...		routine internal reports, routine internal reviews, routine internal plans, letters, more...	Official Record: Retain records for no longer than one year after their administrative use more...	Delete or destroy after the retention period has lapsed	View
0002A*	02. Program Administration Records	Program administration records document the activities involved in managing and/or running the more...	A. Program administration records of enduring historical value	A. Program administration records of enduring historical value are those significant records that more...		academic plans, long range development plans, Physical Design Frameworks, policy, policies, more...	Official Record: Permanent, subject to University Archives review. Coordinate the transfer of more...	Permanent records	View
0002B*	02. Program Administration Records	Program administration records document the activities involved in managing and/or running the more...	B. Operational program administration records	Operational program administration records do not have enduring historical value, but serve to more...		letters, acknowledgem... memos, notes, transmittals, e-mail messages, demonstrate m...	Official Record: Retain records 5 years after the end of the fiscal year in which the records are more...	Delete or destroy after the retention period has lapsed	View

FIGURE 4.7 Portion of the University of California records retention schedule.

SOURCE: http://recordsretention.ucop.edu/index.php/du/retentionSchedules/recordCategory.

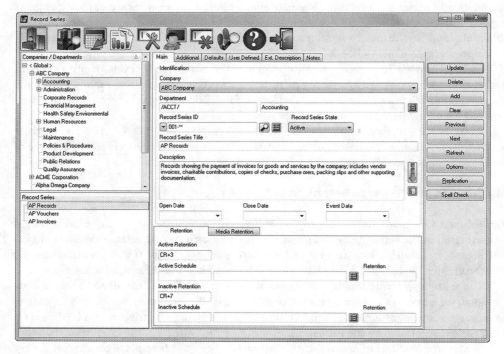

FIGURE 4.8 Versatile enterprise records series dialog box.

Courtesy of Zasio Enterprises, Inc.

Developing a big bucket retention schedule requires the same initial steps we've already discussed, including organizing the information by business function and records series, performing a business process analysis, conducting legal research, and identifying the retention periods for all records—those that are governed by legal and regulatory requirements and those that are not.

Once those tasks are accomplished, attention can be turned to creating the big buckets. In her 2008 article, "How to Win the Compliance Battle Using Big Buckets," Dr. Susan Cisco makes recommendations for developing new retention schedules and updating existing schedules, including:[28]

- Map the records to the correct legal groups. These will form the first round of buckets (records series).
- Consolidate those buckets into fewer buckets by assigning the longest retention period in a group of consolidated buckets to form new bigger buckets.
- Develop crosswalks to legacy content classified by a traditional records schedule and update retention requirements for physical and electronic records to reflect the new, bigger retention buckets.
- Conduct a pilot implementation, analyze feedback, and make modifications before introducing the big bucket retention and disposition schedule enterprise-wide.

NARA provided guidance for federal agencies wanting to create a flexible Big Bucket or large aggregation schedule for their records in "NARA Bulletin 2010-03, Subject: Flexible Scheduling."[29] Supporting materials include an example of the type of crosswalk Cisco recommended in her article.

Several requests for records disposition authorities to move to a Big Bucket approach have been approved for US federal agencies since then. One was a request by the *Centers for Medicare and Medicaid Services,* to use nine buckets for all of its records. The Request for Records Disposition Authority for Bucket 3—Financial Records (programmatic) was first certified in 2015 and revised and approved by the Archivist of the United States in 2017. The crosswalk submitted reveals Big Bucket 3 replaces twenty-six previous items.

NARA committed to a five-year (2013–2017) project to update and revise its General Records Schedules, resulting in fewer buckets and either an increase or decrease in the retention period for records. Figure 4.9 shows one section of a crosswalk between the new records series and the old records for General Records Schedule 4.2: Information Access and Protection Records.

Aggregating records series into big buckets involves making risk-management decisions related to keeping records too long or not long enough. Notice in figure 4.8 that the original retention period for item 020 ranged from two years to six years. However, under the big bucket schedule, the retention period for each of these records series is six years. Larger buckets will make it easier for auto-categorization tools to make more accurate and consistent classification decisions.

Once the records retention and disposition schedule has been completed, operating procedures must be updated to reflect changes to existing operations. The operating procedures and records schedules should be included in a repository to be shared with all stakeholders (e.g., legal counsel, chief operating officer, chief financial officer, etc.) for their comments, approval, and signature. Once modifications are made, the parties satisfied, and the

Transmittal No. 27
January 2017

General Records Schedule 4.2

New GRS 4.2				Old GRS			
GRS No.	Item No.	Retention	ERA Number/ Disposition Authority	GRS No.	Item No.	Retention	Disposition Authority
				14	15	2 years	N1-GRS-98-2, item 12
4.2	001	3 years	DAA-GRS-2016-0013-0003	14	26	2 years	N1-GRS-98-2, item 13
				18	1	2 years	GRS 18, 1960, item 2
				14	1	3 months	N1-GRS-98-2, item 10
4.2	010	90 days	DAA-GRS-2013-0007-0001	14	2	3 months	GRS 14 (1952), items 2 and 3
				23	7, first bullet	When no longer needed	N1-GRS-04-5, item 1
				14	11a1	2 years	NC1-64-77-1, item 16a1
				14	11a2a	2 years	NC1-64-77-1, item 16a2a
				14	11a2b	6 years or 3 years or with related records	NC1-64-77-1, item 16a2b
				14	11a3a	6 years	NC1-64-77-1, item 16a3a
				14	11a3b	6 years or 3 years or with related records	NC1-64-77-1, item 16a3b
				14	12a	6 years or 3 years	N1-GRS-87-4, item 17a
				14	21a1	2 years	NC1-64-77-1, item 25a1
				14	21a2a	2 years	NC1-64-77-1, item 25a2a
				14	21a2b	4 years or 3 years or with related records	NC1-64-77-1, item 25a2b
4.2	020	6 years	DAA-GRS-2016-0002-0001	14	21a3a	5 years	NC1-64-77-1, item 25a3a
				14	21a3b	4 years or 3 years or with related records	NC1-64-77-1, item 25a3b
				14	31a1	2 years	N1-GRS-87-7, item 31a1
				14	31a2a	2 years	N1-GRS-87-7, item 31a2a
				14	31a2b	4 years or with related records	N1-GRS-87-7, item 31a2b
				14	31a3a	5 years	N1-GRS-87-7, item 31a3a
				14	31a3b	4 years or with related records	N1-GRS-87-7, item 31a3b
				14	31c	When requested docs are declassified or destroyed	N1-GRS-87-7, item 31c
				14	32a	4 years	N1-GRS-87-7, item 32a
				4.2	020	6 years	DAA-GRS-2013-0007-0002

FIGURE 4.9 Portion of General Records Schedule Crosswalk, The General Records Schedules, Transmittal 27, NARA, January 2017.

SOURCE: NARA, https://www.archives.gov/files/records-mgmt/grs/grs-trs27.pdf.

procedures and schedules approved, the information can be published and training can be provided.

The records manager's job doesn't end with implementation and training. A program compliance review must be designed to audit the destruction or transfer of records scheduled for disposition. Notices of noncompliance must be sent when necessary. The records manager should also scan the internal environment for changes that may require an adjustment to the records retention and disposition schedule and monitor the external environment to see how legal and regulatory changes might impact the records retention and disposition schedule.

SUMMARY

The primary purpose of a records retention and disposition schedule is to ensure that records are retained only as long as necessary and then disposed of when they no longer have value. The information gathered through the records inventory, records appraisal process, and legal research is used to complete the records retention and disposition schedule.

The records inventory provides a detailed listing of all records held by the organization, both physical and electronic. Tools such as floor plans of records storage areas and data maps of computer systems are helpful in conducting the records inventory.

To determine records retention requirements, records are appraised based on their current operational, regulatory, legal, fiscal, and historical value, and legal research is conducted to identify governing laws and regulations.

Related records are grouped into records series and evaluated as a unit for retention purposes. Retention requirements are assigned. This information is recorded on the records retention and disposition schedule, along with additional information such as the office of record, location of record, and method of disposition.

Attention must be paid to all records, including those residing on corporate websites. The content on static web pages may be copies of content held elsewhere; however, content on dynamic sites may be considered records that must also be governed by a records schedule.

Aggregating records series into big buckets is an alternative approach to the traditional records series that makes it easier for employees and auto-categorization tools to make more accurate and consistent classification decisions.

The records retention and disposition schedule, along with accompanying operational procedures, must be made available to all employees who are assigned records management responsibilities. This information can be disseminated through the publication of records retention and disposition guidelines and through employee training programs. Tools needed to support retention and disposition should be integrated into communication and information systems during the planning phase to remove the burden for retention and disposition decisions from the user when possible. The destruction or transfer of records that have met their retention requirements should be audited to ensure that the organization is in compliance. Both the internal and external environment should be monitored for changes that might impact the records retention and disposition schedule.

This chapter culminated with a discussion of big buckets proposed by Susan Cisco in 2008. Much has changed in the intervening years, but much remains the same. Organizations continue to face issues related to retention and disposition of information assets. In her contribution to this chapter, Susan Cisco takes advantage of the need to revise a retention schedule to launch an information governance program.

PARADIGM

Leveraging a New Retention Schedule to Launch an Information Governance Program

Susan Cisco, PhD, CRM, FAI
Information Governance Subject Matter Expert and Educator

Introduction to Project

Two financial firms merged to form one consolidated operation. Each had its own records and information management systems, processes, and retention schedule. As the new firm (the "Firm") consolidated systems and processes, no systematic deletion or destruction of information took place because there was no master retention schedule to ensure consistent and defensible disposition.

In the highly regulated broker-dealer industry, clients and regulators expect that firms retain and dispose of information appropriately and compliantly. Information governance mistakes can be costly for broker-dealers so the stakes are high. In 2016, the Financial Industry Regulatory Authority (FINRA) handed down $14.4 million in fines to a dozen firms for breaches related to improper retention of electronic records and potential harm to investors. Because the Firm aspires to be the best, information governance is a high priority.

Problem Statement

The Firm is transparent about the critical, ongoing need for a comprehensive oversight and governance process to protect its proprietary information and clients' PII. This and several other factors contributed to its decision to launch an IG Program. They included:

- *Enhanced Defensible Information Disposition Process.* The Firm wanted to update its master retention schedule to enhance the process for the consistent, systematic, and defensible disposition of redundant and obsolete information. Some information was being retained indefinitely and often in duplicate.
- *Risk from Over Preservation of Information.* Retaining redundant and obsolete information introduced risk to the Firm and its clients, including exposure to security breaches of private information and industry sweeps of firms by regulatory agencies. The SEC, for example, can and does conduct risk-based examinations of broker-dealers to assess their compliance with SEC Rule 15c3-3.
- *Real Estate Consolidation.* The Firm had to consolidate operations. With an updated retention schedule, they anticipated the disposition of mostly physical eligible and redundant information prior to the move, saving them time and money.
- *Biggest Pain Point of Employees Is Finding Information.* The Firm used an online polling system and learned that finding information is a significant problem for many employees. If they cannot locate and access needed

information in a timely fashion, clients may lose confidence and trust in the Firm, and regulatory agencies may monitor them more frequently—risks the Firm wanted to mitigate.

Approach Taken

In the first year after the merger, the Firm launched its IG Program by establishing a framework of roles, policies, standards, and metrics to ensure the effective and efficient use of information:

- *The Information Governance Security Committee*—Established the Information Governance Security Committee to oversee information security, privacy, and governance in a proactive manner; ensure the establishment of strategies, controls, methodologies, and frameworks to protect information resources/assets; and ensure the Firm is abiding by the IG policies and retention schedule. The committee meets monthly.
- *IG Policies*—Updated the Records Management Policy, Data Classification Policy, and Data Backup/Recovery Policy.
- *Up-to-Date and Approved Retention Schedule*—Consolidated three existing retention schedules into a single "master" retention schedule containing 119 record series or buckets in a twelve-week project that included:

  - Development of a new retention schedule classification scheme and mapped information from the three existing retention schedules to the new scheme.
  - A third-party legal services provider identified the legal and regulatory requirements for retention, privacy, and storage format for US federal as well as for the 21 states in which the Firm operates. The requirements were then mapped to the associated record series in the retention schedule classification scheme—producing the first draft of the Firm's new, consolidated retention schedule.
  - Gathering feedback and validation on the draft retention schedule during which the Firm met with Subject Matter Experts (SME) at all levels across the Firm. Fifty SMEs met in groups of two to six participants in two separate review sessions. They were asked to:

    - Identify any gaps in coverage of business functions and processes.
    - Review legal retention recommendations for reasonableness.
    - If the retention requirement of the business is longer than the legal retention requirement, provide justification for extending the retention period.
    - For records series without legal retention requirements, provide the business requirement for retention (38 percent of the record series had no federal or state requirements for retention, and SMEs made retention recommendations).

- A presentation of the final draft retention schedule to the Information Governance Security Committee and General Counsel, which included three requests to extend retention periods. The retention schedule and requests to extend retention were approved.

- Presentation to the Firm's Board of Directors for final approval.
- *Employee Training and Awareness Program*—Committed to establishing a network of IG Coordinators across the Firm, training all employees on IG policies and procedures, and monitoring for compliance with IG policies and the retention schedule.

Results

Once the IG policies and retention schedule were approved, the Firm targeted quick wins while at the same time planning for the rollout of the IG Program across the Firm.

Quick Wins

- Identified approximately 25,000–35,000 backup tapes that had satisfied their retention requirement and could be destroyed. The Firm paid for the one-time secure destruction by a third party and estimated off-site storage cost savings of $4,000 per month going forward. In addition, the defensible disposition of the obsolete data immediately reduced unnecessary liability to the Firm during litigation or regulatory inquiry.
- Sought out caches of paper originals maintained after scanning because the Firm considered scanned images to be the "official" record. On a trip to a branch office, the Firm's General Counsel identified a large volume of paper files eligible for destruction pursuant to the Retention Schedule, which were scheduled for immediate secure destruction.
- In the consolidation of operations, the Firm securely disposed of fifteen filing cabinets of duplicates and obsolete information and reclaimed more than 100 square feet of expensive office real estate. More cleanup is expected before the consolidation is complete.

Rollout of the IG Program across the Firm

- Used Firm's in-house media (newsletters, blogs, etc.) to make employees aware of the IG Program and its activities.
- Initiated plans to:
  - Communicate directly with managers and supervisors on details of the IG Program rollout.
  - Identify IG Coordinators, at least one per department plus one backup.
  - Implement the annual information survey required in the Firm's policy.
  - Provide an IG portal for IG Coordinators and casual users to access details on the firm's IG Program including how long to retain a specific record and where to get help with retention and disposition.
  - Require annual certification of employees for compliance with the IG Program.
  - Require web-based training for all employees.
  - Include the IG Program overview in new employee orientation.

Lessons Learned

- *Resistance.* When resistance is met, dig into the problem to understand all points of view and collaborate to identify a solution. Sometimes it may be necessary to engage senior leaders or third parties to adjudicate decisions such as requests to extend retention periods beyond the legal requirement. Of course, when litigation or investigations are anticipated or under way, destruction of information responsive to a matter is suspended until the matter is settled.
- *All Information Needs a Retention Period.* Determine retention requirements for information that is not covered by the retention schedule such as drafts, duplicates, and convenience copies. For this Firm, the policy states that information having short-term or transitory value is to be retained only as long as needed for short-term operational purposes and then disposed of.

Conclusion

As the custodian of clients' personal and private information and due to the strict guidelines imposed by regulators, the Firm acknowledges the critical, ongoing need to provide a comprehensive oversight and governance process to protect its information assets. In the first year of its IG Program, the Firm sought to take small, prioritized steps in building the program rather than "boiling the ocean" in an attempt to address all of the Firm's IG issues at one time. The Firm thinks training and awareness are paramount in the transition to more IG controls and will require annual training for all employees. The Firm knows there are technical solutions available to support the Firm's IG program; however, a better understanding of what employees and clients need is the first priority. Finally, the Firm is committed to collecting metrics and monitoring for compliance with IG policies and the retention schedule.

NOTES

1. Robert J. Johnson, *Information Disposition: A Practical Guide to the Secure, Compliant Disposal of Records, Media and IT Assets* (Phoenix, AZ: NAID, 2017).
2. ARMA International, ARMA TR 22:2016, Glossary of Records Management and Information Governance Terms (Overland Park, KS: ARMA International, 2016), 2.
3. Suzanne Etherington and Ann Marie Przybyla, *Inventory and Planning: The First Steps in Records Management* (Archives Technical Information Series #76), New York State Archives, 2003, accessed September 13, 2017. www.archives.nysed.gov/common/archives/files/mr_pub76.pdf.
4. Ganesh Vednere, "The Quest for eDiscovery: Creating a Data Map," *Infonomics* 23, no. 6, 28–33.
5. Wayne Wong, "Managing Your Way to Data Compliance with a Data Atlas," *Information Management* (January/February 2012), 21–25.
6. International Organization for Standardization (ISO), *ISO 15489-1:2016 Information and documentation—Records management—Part 1: Concepts and principles,* 10.
7. Ibid.
8. Mike Carthy, "10 Things You Need to Know about the GDPR," *Information and Records Management Bulletin* (March 2017), 196.
9. Ken Sweet, "Getting Up to Speed on the Equifax Data Breach Scandal," ABC News, September 11, 2017, http://abcNews.go.com/Technology/wireStory/speed-equifax-data-breach-scandal-49771561.

10. US Department of the Interior, "What is a Records Series." *Records Management Questions,* accessed September 14, 2017, https://www.doi.gov/ocio/policy-mgmt-support/information-and -records-management/records-management-questions.

11. ARMA International, *Website Records Management* (Overland Park, KS: ARMA International, 2009).

12. Presidential Libraries, "Archived Presidential White House Websites," last reviewed January 18, 2017, https://www.archives.gov/presidential-libraries/archived-websites.

13. White House.gov, "Privacy Policy," accessed October 20, 2017, https://www.whitehouse.gov/ privacy#section-340861.

14. Internet Archive Wayback Machine, accessed October 20, 2017, https://archive.org/web/.

15. Heritrix, accessed October 20, 2017, https://webarchive.jira.com/wiki/spaces/Heritrix/overview.

16. Smarsh, "Point West Credit Union Uses Smarsh Web Archiving for Compliance Peace of Mind," accessed October 20, 2017, www.smarsh.com/case-studies/point-west-credit-union.

17. Florida Department of State, "General Records Schedule GS4 for Pubic Hospitals, Health Care Facilities, and Medical Providers," State Library and Archives of Florida, December 1997 (technical updates May 2007), 6, https://www.unf.edu/uploadedFiles/anf/controllers/records_management/ GS04_Retention_Schedule_for_Health_Care_Facilities.pdf.

18. Texas Department of State Health Services, "State of Texas Records Retention Schedule," May 1, 2016, p. 3, www.dshs.state.tx.us/Records/MentalHealthHospitals.pdf.

19. FindLaw, "Time Limits for Filing Product Liability Cases: State-by-State," accessed September 14, 2017, http://injury.findlaw.com/defective-dangerous-products/defective-dangerous-products-law/ state-time-limits-for-filing-product-liability-cases.html.

20. Ibid.

21. Ibid.

22. Internal Revenue Service (IRS), "How Far Back Can the IRS Go to Audit My Return?" IRS Audit FAQs, last modified September 11, 2017, https://www.irs.gov/businesses/small-businesses-self -employed/irs-audits#far-backs.

23. Securities and Exchange Commission, "SEC Adopts Rules on Retention of Records Relevant to Audits And Reviews" (2013), accessed September 14, 2017, https://www.sec.gov/news/ press/2003-11.htm.

24. Ibid.

25. Massachusetts Society of Certified Public Accountants, Inc., *The Record Retention Guide,* 2004, 3, www.cpa.net/resources/retengde.pdf.

26. University of California, "Records Disposition Schedules Manual," accessed September 14, 2017, www.ucop.edu/recordsretention/.

27. RecordLion. "Records Management Software," accessed September 14, 2017, www.recordlion.com/ solutions/objective/records-management/.

28. Susan Cisco, "How to Win the Compliance Battle Using 'Big Buckets,'" *Information Management* (July–August 2008), http://content.arma.org/IMM/JulyAug2008/How_to_win_the_compliance _battle.aspx.

29. National Archives and Records Administration (NARA), "NARA Bulletin 2010–03: Flexible Scheduling," Records Managers, May 3, 2010, https://www.archives.gov/records-mgmt/ bulletins/2010/2010–03.html.

CHAPTER 5

Records and Information Access, Storage, and Retrieval

INTRODUCTION

The active phase of the records lifecycle is one in which records managers traditionally had little involvement. Paper records were stored in offices close to those who had reason to refer to them during the conduct of business. Office workers were responsible for designing and implementing filing systems, and records managers received custody of the records when they became inactive.

The introduction of digital information and electronic information systems took some of the responsibility out of the hands of office workers but placed it into the hands of the information technology department. Records managers still had little involvement with the active use of the information in the systems and devoted time to such activities as writing policies and procedures, developing retention and disposition schedules, caring for inactive records, and overseeing the disposition of records either through destruction or transfer to an archives.

Recently, however, the explosion of digital information and the proliferation of electronic information and communication systems have transformed the way records management is perceived and practiced. Records have value both for their content and as evidence of communications, decisions, and actions. Records and information professionals are expected to understand the business processes, identify records-related risks, and partner with other stakeholders to ensure that the implementation and use of new systems and emerging technologies will comply with governing laws and regulations. The Australian government terms this new era of records management *digital records and information management.*[1]

Today almost all records are created digitally, but some paper-based practices still exist. The records manager can help the organization make a transition from the practice of retaining paper records to a digital records and information program by identifying existing work processes and determining where paper-based practices can be replaced by digital practices. This requires an understanding of information systems used to conduct daily operations.

In the previous chapter, you were introduced to an archival approach to identifying records by starting at the end of the workflow, identifying records in existence, and ensuring they are managed according to a records retention and disposition schedule. But there is a second approach, known as the *systems analysis approach.* This approach requires the records manager to start at the point of creation (or planning, when possible), following each step of the workflow to identify the type of records created and indicating the records series to which the resulting records belong. Because records and information managers are increasingly part of an information governance team, an understanding of the business process is essential not only to identify and manage records but also to improve the process. During this active phase of the information lifecycle, records and information managers can contribute their expertise to decisions being made about workflow processes, access controls, storage systems, metadata, and the search and retrieval processes.

Operational efficiency can be enhanced when automated processes are introduced or improved. In most cases, business practices will be changed to fit the new and improved process. The activity of reviewing existing business practices in order to make these changes is called *business process analysis*. Two approaches that can be used to better understand current business practices are *business process mapping* and the development of *workflow diagrams*.

BUSINESS PROCESS MAPPING AND WORKFLOW PROCESS

Business process mapping and workflow diagrams can help an organization identify records, streamline its operations, reduce redundant work tasks—and therefore duplicate records—and improve efficiency.

Business Process Mapping

A business process identifies how work is done within an organization, not what is done. "Business process mapping is a way to visualize what a business does by considering roles, responsibilities and standards."[2]

Organizations create value for their stakeholders by developing more efficient and effective operations; this is called *business process improvement*. The process can be illustrated as a series of activities that contribute to a specific output. Those same activities contribute to the creation of records that must be captured and managed. Purchasing, for example, is a straightforward function found within any organization. However, the missions of purchasing departments may vary. The purchasing department of the University of Alabama has developed the following mission and vision statements to guide its practices:

> The Purchasing Department's **mission** is to continually identify and incorporate innovative purchasing practices that will support the teaching, research, and service efforts of The University of Alabama.
>
> Our **vision** is to create customer satisfaction by providing value and efficiency to each purchase request while adhering to University policy, state law, and sound business practices.[3]

Before the purchasing department can take control of the purchasing process, a requisition must be submitted by the requesting department and approved by those with authority to do so. Although a number of individuals may be involved in the requisition and purchase process, the primary user is concerned with one thing—ordering and receiving the necessary goods and services.

Once the goods or services have been received, two different documents may also be received: the bill of lading and a vendor invoice. The bill of lading is the official document prepared by the carrier duly accepting goods for shipment containing information, which includes the item, quantity, value, date, and more.[4] This bill of lading is a contract to carry goods to the intended destination. It is the basis by which the seller can claim consideration (bill for the products) and the buyer can take delivery of the goods. The vendor invoice is a bill generated by the vendor and submitted to the purchaser once delivery is made.

Workflow Diagrams for a Paper-Based Business Process

Workflow is a term used to describe the tasks, procedural steps, organizations, or people involved, required input and output information, and tools needed for each step in a business process.[5] A workflow diagram is used to visually represent the components of the business process. The workflow will vary from one organization to another depending upon the size of the organization and the organizational structure. An example of a manual requisition/purchase ordering process for an organization that has a purchasing department is shown in figure 5.1.

In this manual system, we follow the process from the creation of a *purchase requisition* through the approval process and receipt of a purchase order by the vendor.

Although not illustrated in figure 5.1, the bill of lading is returned to the purchasing department to provide evidence of delivery. A vendor invoice may accompany the delivery or be sent to the purchasing department separately. If it accompanies the bill of lading, it is also sent to purchasing marked with the corresponding purchase order number for verification purposes. Upon verification, the purchasing department sends the vendor invoice to the accounts payable department for payment (if it has not been prepaid). The original paper invoice is retained by accounts payable, often for the remainder of the current

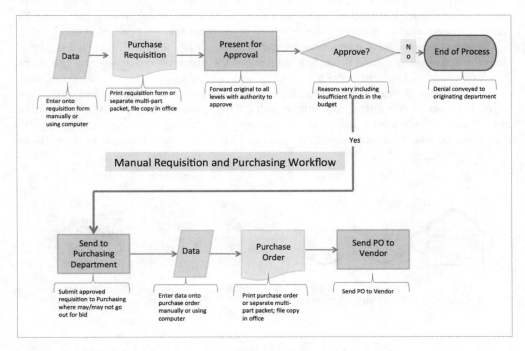

FIGURE 5.1 Workflow for manual requisition and purchasing process.

fiscal year plus six years. A copy of the purchase order is filed and retained by the initiating department and the purchasing department according to the records retention schedule, commonly three years within the purchasing department but only one year within the department that requested the order. The retention periods and departments involved may differ from one firm to another.

Within this manual process, the same data may be entered more than once and duplicate copies of documents are likely to exist within and across departments. An analysis of the workflow can result in savings of time and space if the manual process is modified—but the ideal solution is to automate this process.

Workflow Diagrams for a Digital Process

Today, most records—including purchase orders—are born digital. They are created using a variety of software and technologies, many with a web-based interface. And because of the ease of access to digital records, use takes on a whole new meaning. Let's return to the purchase order as an example of an automated requisition and purchasing system, the records created, and the operational and informational value that can be derived.

The requisition creation and approval process can be made more effective through the use of an automated requisition system that focuses on efficient workflow. User security measures ensure that the end user preparing the purchase requisition can access only her or his own accounts. The end user may be required to enter quotes for the requested items. Those quotes may be electronically attached or scanned into the requisition maintenance screen for future reference.

The workflow process informs those with the authority to approve purchase requisitions that there are requisitions awaiting approval. In some organizations, there may be more than one level of approval. The purchase requisition may be rejected at any level of the approval process for various reasons, for example, if the amount requested is higher than the approved spending limit. The outcome of the purchase requisition process is the purchase order as shown in figure 5.2.

The features of an automated requisition/purchasing process are many and can extend beyond the act of submitting a purchase order. The basics of the automated requisition process can include adding and maintaining suppliers, adding new requisitions, requisition approval workflow, requisition revisions and cancellations, converting requisitions to

FIGURE 5.2 Automated requisition/purchase order workflow.

purchase orders, receiving processes, invoice matching, and closing purchase orders and requisitions.

In spite of the benefit of automating the requisition and purchase process, users accustomed to shopping online understand there is a better way to gather information and complete requisition requests—such as access to online catalogs and a shopping cart. And accounts payable personnel recognize the value of integrating the purchasing process with accounts payable systems. Vendors taking advantage of these new opportunities to satisfy the needs of the customers offer e-procurement (procure-to-pay) options.

e-Procurement and Procure-to-Pay Suites

"e-Procurement (electronic procurement) is the business-to-business (B2B) requisitioning, ordering, and purchasing of goods and services over the internet."[6] From the employee's perspective, this is an attractive option that allows him or her to select the needed items (i.e., those that match the procurement office's requirements for cost, quality, and supplier) from online catalogs; complete a requisition for the items; and track delivery status.

Figure 5.3 illustrates the Purchase-to-Pay process (also known as Procure-to-Pay and P2P) offered by Basware (one of only three leaders in Gartner's 2016 Magic Quadrant for P2P Suites). As seen in figure 5.3, creation involves visiting the marketplace and placing needed items in a shopping cart. In addition, the process involves reconciling invoices with purchase orders as well as payment plans and taking advantage of discounts when warranted. When the invoices are reconciled, an "ok-to-pay" trigger is sent to the accounting

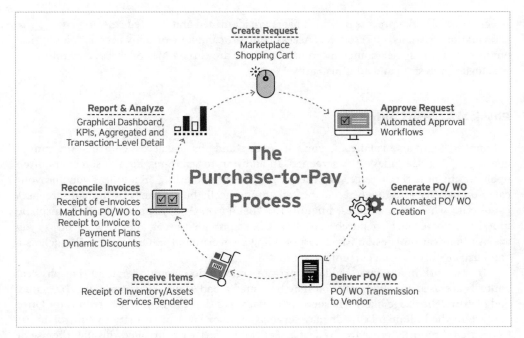

FIGURE 5.3 Purchase-to-Pay Process offered by Basware.

SOURCE: www.basware.com5.

system. A dashboard allows the organization to analyze transactions and generate reports that can be used to consolidate suppliers, negotiate better pricing, improve time between delivery and payment for invoices to take advantage of discounts, and more.

Among the benefits of moving to a P2P process are:

- reduction in operational expenses
- increased user adoption on the requisition end
- supplier consolidation based on analysis of reports
- on-time payments through automatic reconciliation of invoices and receipts
- reduction of spending on Accounts Payable (AP) through automation
- improved discount capture ratio through AP automation solution

In 2017, Basware released a whitepaper citing three disruptive trends that will shape the finance and procurement process going forward: 1) artificial intelligence (AI) and robotic process automation (RPA), 2) predictive analytics, and 3) Blockchain technology. The best advice they give is to hire people that have the breadth of skills to work alongside technology and provide on-going training to current staff to prepare them for these new possibilities.[7]

Regardless of the system, one thing is certain: controls are necessary to ensure that only authorized individuals have access to the system. That access will be conditional based upon roles and responsibilities.

ACCESS CONTROLS

Access control is the process by which users are identified and granted certain privileges to information, systems, or resources. Access controls can allow or deny access to a physical environment or an electronic environment. There are three types of access control methods: logical, physical, and administrative.[8]

Physical Access Controls

Attempt to board an airplane and you will understand physical access controls. You cannot check your luggage unless it is screened. In addition to scanning, human screeners often open and inspect the luggage. You cannot get into the boarding area unless you and your carry-on baggage are screened, most often automatically but at times by human screeners conducting what, in some cases, amounts to a "pat down." And, you can't board the airplane unless you prove you have purchased a ticket, been provided a seat, and are who you say you are. Authentication is established by providing a government-issued picture ID such as a valid driver's license or a current passport.

If you work in any large public or private organization, you understand that physical controls are used there as well. You may be issued a badge with your employee ID, name, and picture. The badge likely will serve as a smart card that can be read electronically. Once you are in the building, keypads may serve as another layer of security to control access to restricted rooms. Access to physical assets can be further controlled through the use of containers such as file cabinets, safes, or vaults that are protected and require codes, keys, or combinations to open.

In 2017, the Apple iPhone X was announced. Its most exciting feature was Face ID—facial recognition used to unlock the screen. The intended benefits are increased user convenience and security. Apple claims Face ID is more reliable than Touch ID (fingerprint recognition). The chance of someone else unlocking your phone with Touch ID is one in 50,000, but with Face ID it is one in a million.

Face ID is accomplished by the use of a camera and 3-D scanner to both record an image and measure the contours of facial features using 30,000 invisible points to create a 3-D map that can be read by an infrared camera. An infrared light is beamed at the user's face to help recognize it even in the dark, and the camera can adapt to the user's physical changes.

Concerns over successful attempts to beat facial recognition in the past using pictures and models of the subject's face were dismissed because of the unique 3-D process Face ID employs. Concerns linger, however, because if someone does find a way to fool the system, they can do so forever. Passwords can be changed easily; the contours of your face cannot. In addition, it is easier to coerce you to unlock your phone by positioning the camera in front of your face than forcing you to reveal a password.

SOURCE: Bloomberg Business Week, "Why iPhone X Face Recognition is Cool and Creepy," accessed September 23, 2017, https://www.bloomberg.com/news/articles/2017-09-15/why-iphone-x-face-recognition-is-cool-and-creepy-quicktake-q-a

Some corporate biometric access control systems based on a card, pin number, or fingerprint can handle thousands of users and be configured via a secure connection from any standard web browser. Access policies, user management, and reporting can be controlled from an administrator's desk. Of all the biometric devices and scanners available today, iris cameras are considered the most accurate. They perform recognition detection based on an analysis of patterns visible within the iris of an eye.

Physical access controls can be breached, some more easily than others. IDs can be forged and buildings can be entered by waiting for someone else to open the door and walking in behind them as if you belong. Security requires layering the access controls in the hopes that a breach at one layer (e.g., workplace perimeter) will be discovered when the person moves on to the next layer (e.g., building), and the next (e.g., secure room).

Logical/Technical Access Controls

Protecting electronic information involves both physical and logical access controls. Logical access controls often entail the use of multiple security controls and authentication techniques. Logical access controls are found in databases, applications, servers, and even in transit. Access to critical data should be determined by a person's role, and the need for access should be reviewed regularly.

The information technology (IT) manager must work with the business unit managers (data owners) to determine what access an employee should have to business information systems; for example, who needs access to the requisition and purchase order process in our previous example. Access could be extended to stakeholders outside of the organization, including vendors and clients. The records manager could work with IT to determine where records are created, how they are captured, and who needs access.

When used by a firm that allows access from outside the country, IT access policies should be set by geographic region and then by user roles and responsibilities. This approach will help the firm comply with differing international standards for privacy. Just as with ID badges for physical control, identification credentials (e.g., a digital signature) must be issued to authenticate the user. Three factors can be required for authentication:

- something you know (e.g., a password)
- something you have (e.g., a certificate with associated private key or smart card)
- something you are (e.g., a biometric such as fingerprint, iris, or facial recognition)[9]

Authentication assurance increases with the addition of a second and third authentication technique. In addition to establishing proof of identity, authorization to access the asset must be confirmed.

Today's technology allows employees to engage in *telework* (also called remote or virtual work), and organizations in the public and private sectors are taking advantage of its benefits. This means, however, a growing number of individuals need access to sensitive information from outside the corporate firewall. Access can be provided through a virtual private network (VPN), which requires encryption and authentication of the remote client prior to access.

Access controls must also take into account mobile users of the system. In addition to the physical and logical access controls already discussed, networks can be made more secure to prevent unapproved access that could result in loss for the organization. These access controls would be applied by those responsible for information security. Two examples are:

- a remote access server (RAS) or network access server (NAS) that functions as the access control point to allow or deny access to the local network; and
- firewalls that control traffic flow between a trusted network and an untrusted network.

Access Controls and Cloud Computing

Access control is a key concern when a firm moves critical applications and sensitive information to public and shared cloud environments. Cloud providers—such as Amazon, IBM, Google, Salesforce.com, and Microsoft—must provide access controls at least as robust as those employed by the client firm. Humans are still a factor, and employees of the firm providing cloud services must be screened and trained to the same standards as the client firm's own employees. Physical location of the cloud provider's data center must be evaluated for its physical security features, including authorized access and network requirements.

A service level agreement (SLA)—also known as a terms of service (TOS) agreement—is your contract with the cloud provider. Read it carefully, understand the contents, and negotiate the terms where possible to reduce risks to your organization.

When evaluating the feasibility of contracting with a cloud service provider, keep in mind that access is dependent upon the internet. How will the organization operate if

Factors to Consider When Selecting a Cloud Vendor

- certifications and standards
- technologies and service road map
- data security, data governance, and business policies
- service dependencies and partnerships
- contracts, commercials and SLAs
- reliability and performance
- migration support, vendor lock, and exit planning
- business health and company profile

Cloud Industry Forum, "8 criteria to ensure you select the right cloud service provider," accessed January 28, 2018, https://www.cloudindustryforum.org/content/8-criteria-ensure-you-select-right-cloud-service-provider

internet access is interrupted at either the vendor's or the organization's location? This is an issue that must be addressed in relation to the organization's disaster preparedness and business continuity plan for major interruptions. But minor interruptions due to network saturation, bandwidth capacities, and incompatibility with the organization's architecture will also adversely impact business operations.

Administrative Access Controls and Social Media

A third method to control access results from administrative action that includes developing policies and procedures, providing education and training, and monitoring and evaluating use. These controls must remain current to reflect the use of emerging technologies and evolving laws and regulations. In order to protect the organization from risk related to social media use, access control processes should complement the social media and records management policies. Social media used to reach out to the public involves technologies controlled by third-party providers; content may be stored in multiple locations; content may be created by multiple collaborators; and interactive content management may be a requirement. Many of the factors to be considered when selecting a cloud provider apply when evaluating the use of social media.

Although most employees will engage in social media activities in their private lives, social media activities on behalf of the firm can be limited to authorized employees. Those employees should understand their roles and responsibilities. They should be provided user IDs and passwords to access the account(s) and to speak on behalf of the organization. The best protection for both the individual engaging in social media interactions and the organization requires the development of clear but comprehensive social media and records management policies followed by employee education and training.

ACTIVE STORAGE SYSTEMS

Records in the active phase of the records lifecycle are stored in a way that allows daily access and use. Physical records can remain in file cabinets in the office environment, close to those who refer to them in the course of business. In education, for example, student folders with documentation of courses required for programs, courses already taken, and courses planned might be located in the advisor's office, easily accessible for use during meetings with students. When use drops off, such as when a student graduates or transfers to another school, permanent records are often microfilmed and stored in physical control containers, such as vaults.

In an electronic environment, information used in the course of business is also stored in a manner that allows immediate access. For example, student information today most likely resides in a student information system (SIS), also known as a student records system (SRS). The SIS is a software application used to organize student information and conduct operations. The systems vary in size, scope, and capability, and the functions of the system can support admitting, advising, and registering students; recording grades; and storing student records. In addition to allowing the advisor access to information about a student, the same information can be made available to multiple users—including the student—simultaneously. Access rules can be set up to allow access only to the information users need to perform their work.

Retention requirements must be considered when deciding upon the storage medium used. For example, the University of Pennsylvania's current Records Retention Schedule that sets the requirements for student records is shown in table 5.1.[10]

The schedule shown in table 5.1 mandates that transcript requests should be disposed of after one year. They can be digitized and stored electronically or stored as paper in a file folder in a cabinet in the office until the end of that year. Grades should be retained permanently. If they are retained electronically, they could remain in the SIS for fast retrieval, but their use would diminish over time. Transfer to a more permanent medium such as

TABLE 5.1 University of Pennsylvania records retention schedule: Academic/student records.

RECORD TYPE	RETENTION PERIOD
Admission records	10 years
Grade records	Permanent
Other academic records	5 years
Career planning and placement	4 years
Class schedules	Transfer to UARC after 2 years; permanent
College Catalog	Transfer to UARC after 2 years; permanent
Degree audit records	5 years after date of last attendance
Disciplinary action records	5 years after graduation or date of last incidence
Student academic files (departmental)	5 years
Transcript requests	1 year

SOURCE: University of Pennsylvania, University Archives and Records Center, "University of Pennsylvania Records Retention Schedule: Academic/Student Records," University Records Center. Last modified June 17, 2011, www.archives.upenn.edu/urc/recrdret/studtacad.html.

microfilm for long-term storage may be a more viable option than managing the information in a database permanently.

According to the university guidelines, the office of origin has the option of maintaining most records in their office or of transferring them to the university records center. In some cases, however, permanent records, including class schedules and the college catalog, *must* be transferred to the university archives and records center. Inactive records management and long-term preservation will be discussed further in chapters 11 and 12.

Student information systems can be integrated with other tools, such as learning management systems (LMS) used for online instruction. If so, grades computed in an LMS could be transferred electronically into the SIS at the end of the term. Grades stored in a grade book database in the LMS and transferred to the SIS utilize structured data, that is, in columns and rows of data.

In addition to the information stored in databases, other systems—both paper and electronic—hold different types of data. Student requests for transcripts, for example, may arrive in the mail in the form of a letter. Regardless of whether the letter is filed in a physical file or scanned into a content management system, the data contained is unstructured and difficult to search. Schools also provide information for prospective and current students on their website in addition to or in place of the traditional print catalog. Data contained in webpages may be stored in a web content management system with associated metadata to enable search and retrieval based on content. That data is considered *semi-structured*.

Structured, Unstructured, and Semi-Structured Data

The terms *structured data, unstructured data,* and *semi-structured data* have long been used by professionals in the information technology sector. Because a team approach is needed to manage information and records today, records and information managers should understand the vocabulary that may be used by other members of the information governance team. More important, though, is understanding the systems that manage these types of data. Simply put, structured data is synonymous with database data managed by database management systems and unstructured data with electronic objects managed by electronic document, electronic content, and electronic records management systems.

Nutrition Facts	
Serving Size 1/2 cup (115g)	
Servings Per Container About 4	
Amount Per Serving	
Calories 250	Calories from Fat 130
	% Daily Value*
Total Fat 14g	22%
Saturated Fat 9g	45%
Cholesterol 55mg	18%
Sodium 75mg	3%
Total Carbohydrate 26g	9%
Dietary Fiber 0g	0%
Sugars 26g	
Protein 4g	
Vitamin A 10%	Vitamin C 0%
Calcium 10%	Iron 0%
* Percent Daily Values are based on a 2,000 calorie diet.	

Structured Data

Most of us consult structured data every time we visit the grocery store. The data listed on product labels as "Nutrition Facts" is structured data (see figure 5.4).

However, the term *structured data* refers more commonly to a database where specific information is stored based on a methodology of columns and rows. Databases can be classified

FIGURE 5.4 Nutrition labels contain structured data. The Entity is "Nutrition Facts" for this particular product. The Attributes are Calories, Total Fat, Cholesterol, and so on.

Structured Data		
ID	Name	Grade
1	Student Name No. 1	B
2	Student Name No. 2	A
3	Student Name No. 3	B+
4	Student Name No. 4	B
5	Student Name No. 5	A-
6	Student Name No. 6	B
7	Student Name No. 7	A
8	Student Name No. 8	C
9	Student Name No. 9	B
10	Student Name No. 10	A

FIGURE 5.5 Structured data can be replaced by the term *database data,* because this describes the format and presentation requirements of this information.

based on the content type, for example, bibliographic, document-text, statistical, or multimedia objects. They can also be classified according to their application, such as accounting, movies, manufacturing, or insurance. Metadata associated with each of the records within the electronic file are used to display those records within columns and rows as shown in figure 5.5. Structured data are easily searched, mined, and manipulated.

Data Presentation

Reports, tables, and charts provide snapshots of data in the database at specific points in time. These formats make it easier for the busy individual to derive meaning from the data stored in a database. For example, the fact that a grade of B was earned by 40 percent of the students although a grade of C was earned by only 10 percent is easily and quickly understood by those viewing figure 5.6.

Reports, tables, and charts produced from data in the database can be managed with software intended to manage unstructured objects, for example, electronic document management, electronic content management, and electronic records management system software.

Relational Database Management Systems (RDBMS)

The student grades example in figure 5.5 displayed information from one database table that contained the student ID, student name, and student grade. But, popular database management systems are relational systems (RDBMS) that store data in collections of tables (also called entities). Each table consists of columns (properties of the table referred to as fields, such as student name and grade) and rows (also called records, such as an individual student's record) as shown in figure 5.7.[11] Relations are defined between tables for cross-referencing using a primary key, for example, the ID assigned to each student. Data can be pulled from more than one table in a relational database to create a record (student scores on assignments and tests, for example).

Information technology personnel are usually responsible for managing the relational database, but they may not understand the records retention implications of creating records using data from tables in a relational database. Because the official record is comprised of the tables' fields, rows, and elements, plus the relationships between the tables, the record will be incomplete if one table containing information used to build the record is missing. RIM professionals must ensure that the records retention schedule is modified so that when it is applied to structured content, none of the tables are removed prematurely. This involves working with IT, and under certain circumstances the vendor, to explain what the different records series mean and how to apply the records retention schedule so that data are not disposed of without consideration of the relationships between that data and other data in the database.

Unstructured Data

IDG estimates unstructured data is growing at the rate of 62 percent per year, and that by 2022, 93 percent of all data in the digital universe will be unstructured, primarily from the emergence of social media networks; customer information from telcos and utilities such as call history, messaging logs, and usage trends; and information services such as traffic data, weather information, and stock indices.[12]

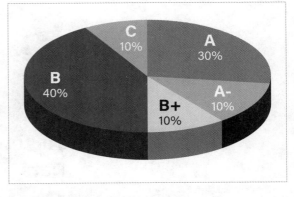

FIGURE 5.6 End-of-term letter-grade distribution for students in one class.

Unstructured data has no well-defined model or schema for accessing information and typically includes digital images and objects, text, and other data types not part of a database (see figure 5.8). Email messages, instant messages, Word documents, images, PowerPoint presentations, blogs, Twitter posts, and MP3 files are all examples of unstructured data.

An easy way to determine if an item is unstructured is by asking if it is easily searchable (i.e., without adding metadata or using a crawler like an index server). If the answer is no, it is unstructured data. One of the biggest challenges facing organizations today is discovering a way to extract value from the vast amount of unstructured data produced. Organizations can capitalize on this vast amount of data by applying business intelligence applications and technologies for gathering, storing, analyzing, and providing access to unstructured data in order to help the enterprise make better business decisions.[13]

Wall Street traders, for example, found they can use computer programs to monitor and decode words, opinions, and even keyboard-generated smiley faces posted on Twitter. Johan Bollen, a professor at Indiana University and coauthor of the study linking Twitter

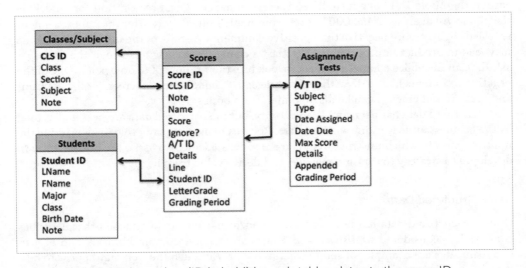

FIGURE 5.7 The Primary key (ID in bold) in each table relates to the same ID in another table.

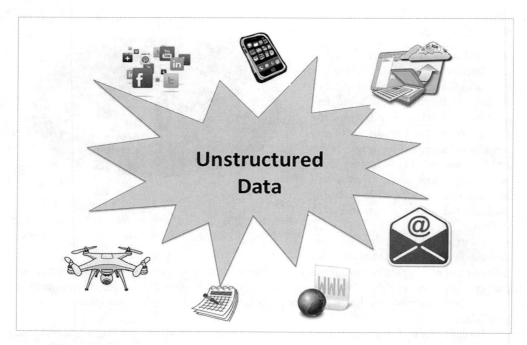

FIGURE 5.8 Unstructured data examples.

mood measurement to stock market performance, claims an 87 percent accuracy rate in using Twitter mood measurements to predict Dow stock prices three to four days later.[14] The "Bollen Study" remains the most cited paper investigating the link between sentiment data and predictive models for trading.

This type of knowledge about human emotions can be used as a basis for placing trades that profit from the information. Organizations can use sentiment analysis to gauge the reception a newly announced (but not yet available) product is receiving. As mentioned earlier, the Apple X iPhone introduced FaceID, enhanced facial recognition for unlocking the phone. An analysis of 150,000 Twitter comments immediately after the announcement revealed slightly more negative than positive comments. A study of the negative comments may lead to product improvement or at least a change in messaging. One of the messages asked, "Can the police compel a suspect to look into their iPhone X to unlock it?" One of the negative comments had to do with product design, "The iPhone X's screen is all glass front and back. So if it cracks I can be disappointed from both sides."[15]

Structured data has been an IT-led activity, but unstructured data are best understood by the business units working with the data. Records managers play a role in identifying the multiple ways in which unstructured data are generated and can assist the organization in developing a strategy to capture, manage, and derive value from it.

Semi-Structured Data

Once unstructured data has been organized and/or has metadata attached that describes content, it is considered *semi-structured*. SharePoint lists, document libraries, and project and team sites are examples of semi-structured data. Although the web may appear to be a vast database, most of the information on the web consists of unstructured data. Hypertext

```
<h1> Bibliography</h1>
<p><cite>Title of Book </cite>
Author 1, Author 2, Author 3<br>
Publisher, Date of Publication</p>
```

HTML
1. *provides structure*; for example,
   text between <p> and </p> is
   one paragraph,
2. *define content*; for example,
   <cite> and </cite> is used to
   define a phrase between the
   tags as a reference source.
3. *specifies appearance*; for
   example, text between <cite>
   and </cite> will typically be
   displayed as italics.

```
<Bibliography>
    <book> <title> Title of Book 1</title>
           <author>author 1</author>
           <author>author 2</author>
           <author>author3</author>
           <publisher> Publisher </publisher>
           <year> year </year>
    </book>
</bibliography>
```

XML *describes content*; for example, the text
between the tags <author> </author> is
described as the author of a work.

FIGURE 5.9 Comparison of HTML and XML markup.

Markup Language (HTML) is the publishing language of the Web, and it is used to provide structure that tells the web browser how to present the page. But webpages marked up with HTML tags cannot be queried based on those tags. When the Extensible Markup Language (XML) is used to describe the content of the HTML document, those documents can be queried based on that content. XML is not a replacement for HTML; it doesn't do anything except wrap information in tags that can be used by software to send, receive, or display it.

In figure 5.9, the HTML tags <h1> </h1> surrounding the word *bibliography* tell the web browser that the word should be displayed as a header (large, bold). The <p> </p> tags tell the browser the content between the opening and closing tags should be treated as a paragraph, which means adding a blank line before and after. The <cite> </cite> tags instruct the browser to tag the words between the opening and closing tag as a title of a work and to display the title in italics. The <br> creates a line break on the webpage. These tags provide display instructions to the browser, but they don't facilitate search and retrieval of a work based on the title, any of the authors, the publisher, or the date of publication.

XML is a markup language for documents that contain structured information. However, because XML files don't conform to the formal structure of tables and data models associated with databases, information contained within an XML document is considered semi-structured. In addition to web documents, semi-structured data can be found in e-commerce transactions, mathematical equations, vector graphics, object metadata, and server application programming interfaces (APIs).

Big Data

Now let us turn our attention to the pie chart in figure 5.10 illustrating distribution of the 58 million strong Hispanic population in the United States at the start of 2016 based on data

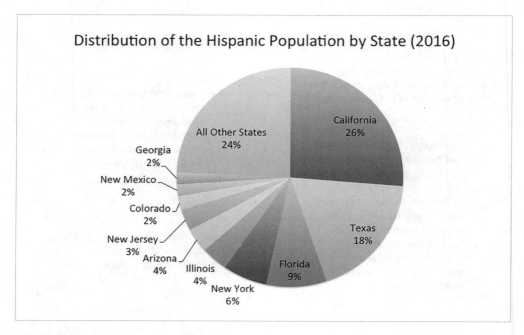

FIGURE 5.10 Distribution chart illustrating Hispanic population by state adapted from two data sources.

SOURCE: Pew Research Center and "How the U.S. Hispanic Population is Changing." www.pewresearch.org/fact-tank/2017/09/18/how-the-u-s-hispanic-population-is-changing/.

from 2015 American Community Surveys. This type of data is considered Big Data, which is difficult to work with using traditional data management options.

Big Data can be defined as "data so large that it is difficult to process with traditional database and software techniques."[16] The term can be used to describe both structured and unstructured data "consisting of billions to trillions of records of millions of people—all from different sources (e.g., web, sales, customer contact center, social media, mobile data, and so on)."[17] Big Data could be used to describe the tools and techniques used to manage Big Data sets. Challenges and opportunities are presented by three properties of Big Data: volume, variety, and velocity.

Organizations can incorporate Big Data techniques into their existing architecture. For example, radio frequency identification (RFID) tags can be used to track every product manufactured by an organization and stocked in product warehouses and consumer stores around the globe, providing updates that can be used to understand what is being purchased and where. Market intelligence can be mined from billions of tweets that are posted to Twitter each month. Complex machinery producing terabytes of data per hour can be monitored and examined by engineers in near real time or can be mined later for engineering improvements.

Cloud technologies are increasingly used to store and process large amounts of data. Enterprise Integration Platform as a Service (iPaaS), first used for "cloud service integration (CSI) and application to application (A2A) integration is increasingly used for business to business (B2B) integration, mobile application integration (MAI), API (application programming interface) publishing, and Internet of Things (IoT) integration."[18]

Data Mart, Data Warehouse, and Data Lake Systems

One way to gain valuable insights from the huge amounts of fast-flowing data facing large enterprises today is to transfer a copy into a data warehouse where it can be queried and analyzed without negatively impacting the transaction system. In a 2016 report issued by Amazon Web Services, a *data warehouse* is described as "a central repository of information coming from one or more data sources. Data typically flow into a data warehouse from transactional systems and other relational databases, and typically includes structured, semi-structured, and unstructured data."[19]

As defined by Bill Inmon, the "father of data warehousing," a data warehouse is a "subject-oriented, integrated, time-variant and non-volatile collection of data in support of management's decision-making process." Ralph Kimball, the "father of business intelligence," preferred a more simple definition with the focus on function: "A copy of transaction data specifically structured for query and analysis."[20] Both Inmon and Kimball recognized the need to bring copies of valuable data together so that it can be queried and analyzed to support strategic decision-making. The difference in their philosophy rests mainly on which comes first, the data warehouse or subsets called data marts.

A *data mart* is a specific, subject-oriented repository of data gathered from operational data and other sources and designed to serve the needs of a particular community (e.g., a specific department or team) of knowledge workers. The key objective is to provide the

TABLE 5.2 Data warehousing and data marts—two perspectives.

	BILL INMON	RALPH KIMBALL
Father of . . .	Data warehousing Credited with coining the term "data warehouse"	Business intelligence Credited with defining the concepts behind "data marts"
Definition of data warehouse	A subject-oriented, integrated, time-variant, and nonvolatile collection of data in support of management's decision-making process.	A copy of transaction data specifically structured for query and analysis.
Focus	Design	Functionality
Paradigm	An enterprise has one data warehouse, and data marts source their information from the data warehouse.	Data warehouse is the conglomerate of all data marts within the enterprise. Information is always stored in the dimensional model.
View of data marts	Data warehouses can become enormous, with hundreds of gigabytes of transactions. As a result, subsets, known as "data marts," are often created for just one department or product line.	Start with building several data marts that serve the analytical needs of departments, followed by "virtually" integrating these data marts for consistency through an information bus.

NOTE: Data warehouses in most enterprises resemble Kimball's idea because they start out as a departmental effort, originating as a data mart. Once additional data marts are added, a data warehouse is created.

business user with the most relevant data as quickly as possible. The *data warehouse* is a central aggregation of data (which can be distributed physically) that starts from an analysis of what data already exists and how it can be collected and later used.[21] A comparison of the two perspectives is provided in table 5.2.

Both the data warehouse and data mart organize data to fit the context of the database scheme into which it is transferred. Another option is to retain the data in its structured, semi-structured, unstructured raw format in a *data lake*. Data lakes add structure to the data only once it has been transferred back out to the application layer, as illustrated in figure 5.11.

Integration Platform as a Service (iPaaS) solutions typically include capabilities such as data mapping and transformation as well as integration flow development and life cycle management tools. One provider considered "the" leader in the 2018 Garner Magic Quadrant is Informatica. This firm provides various options of cloud integration capabilities that include data lake management.[22]

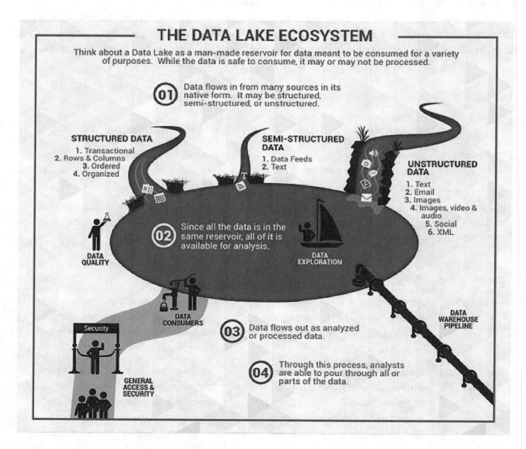

FIGURE 5.11 Data remains in lake in native form until processed.

SOURCE: Dunn Solutions Group, www.dunnsolutions.com.—a digital transformation consultancy focusing on analytics and e-commerce automation

Records managers immediately recognize that the contents of data warehouses, data marts, and data lakes are duplicates of data already in existence. The question is, "Are the data stored in data warehouse records?" Some believe "they are and the records manager should have overall responsibility for the data."[23]

SEARCH AND RETRIEVAL PROCESS

The search and retrieval process is dependent upon the storage system(s) in use. Storing data is one side of the coin; the other side is being able to retrieve it. Let us look at each data type—structured, unstructured, semi-structured—and some associated search and retrieval methods.

Structured Data: Search and Retrieval Methods

From a user standpoint, it is not necessary to understand how to program a database, but it is important to understand how to use a database management system and its search and retrieval mechanisms to obtain the desired information.

Structured data are stored in a database that can be presented in tables comprised of columns and rows. Programming languages have been developed to manage structured data. Structured Query Language (SQL), which is an American National Standards Institute (ANSI) and International Organization for Standardization (ISO) standard, is the original data definition and query language for updating, deleting, and requesting information from databases. The program runs on a server interpreting actions taken by users who manipulate the data using tables, columns, rows, and fields. The client programs send SQL statements to the server for processing. The replies are returned to the client program.

A database management system is necessary to access and process data contained in the SQL database. MySQL is a popular open-source database management system used in web applications. SQL is also used in commercial applications.

Structured Search and Retrieval Example: Lexis/Nexis

LexisNexis is a subsidiary of the RELX Group (formerly Reed Elsevier). The group started in 1970 as a database named LEXIS that was a continuation of the Ohio State Bar's efforts to offer full-text searching of all Ohio court cases. By the time it went public in 1973, it had added New York cases to the database. In 1980, the database contained all of the US federal and state cases, and the NEXIS service was added to give journalists a searchable database of news articles.

If you visit LexisNexis Support, you will encounter an abundance of resources available to help the researcher.[24] Basic search tips make recommendations on the use of capital letters, connectors, noise words (*stop words* such as *a* and *the* that are disregarded in a search), developing a search request, and an introduction to traditional Boolean searching. To find documents concerning employee drug tests, for example, you might use this search request: *Drug w/5 test or screen! w/10 employ!* This search request is not natural language. The user must learn how to search on this system in order to locate the desired information. And this is only one type of system. Search tips for other databases reveal different strategies that must be employed by the user.

Basic Search Terms

keyword search: A type of search that looks for matching documents that contain one or more words specified by the user. This is a good option to find a document when you do not know the authorized subject heading or the complete name of the author of the document.

Boolean search: A type of search allowing users to combine keywords with operators such as AND, NOT, and OR to make keyword-based text searches more precise. Boolean operators can be used with most databases and web-search engines.

faceted search: Also called *guided navigation,* faceted search is a type of navigation model that leverages metadata fields and values to provide users with visible options for clarifying and refining queries. Faceted searches allow the users to filter data through multiple paths and different ordering. Database-driven e-commerce catalogs include the facets price range, color, brands, and more.

field search: A search for a term or a number within a data field of a document or database. An online telephone directory allows users to search within fields.

full-text search: A search that compares every word in a document, as opposed to searching an abstract or a set of keywords associated with the document. Most web search engines perform this type of search.

inverted index search: A search using an index of unique words appearing in any document, and for each word a list of documents in which the words appear.[*]

structured search: A search method that uses the structure of data that has an inherent structure—such as dates, times, and numbers, even text such as names of colors.[†] The three types of structured searches are: Boolean (Structured Query Language, or SQL) search, keyword (vector) search, and reverse indexes.

vector search model: The vector model considers a search query as a vector in keyword space and then scores the items located based on the distance from the query calculated by counting the number of times keywords appeared in each document, the size of the document, and the density of the keywords in the document.

[*] Inverted Index, Elastic, accessed November 18, 2017, https://www.elastic.co/guide/en/elasticsearch/guide/current/inverted-index.html.
[†] Structured Search, Elastic, accessed November 18, 2017, https://www.elastic.co/guide/en/elasticsearch/guide/current/structured-search.html.

Search and Retrieval Options: Library of Congress

Note the search options available for the Library of Congress (LC) Online Catalog shown in figure 5.12. One search method allows the user to insert a subject keyword. This allows a search for any word or phrase found in one of the subject heading controlled vocabularies used at the LC. If the user doesn't know what words are in the controlled vocabulary, he or

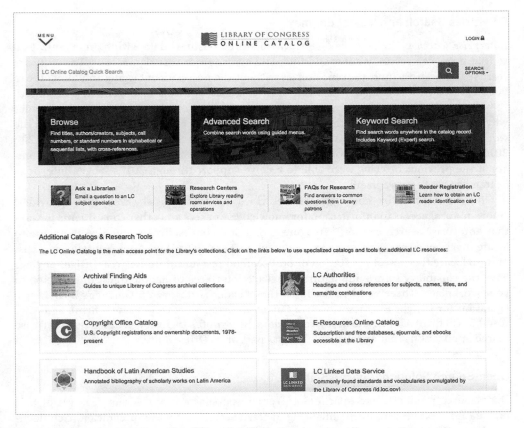

FIGURE 5.12 The Library of Congress Online Catalog.

SOURCE: Library of Congress, https://catalog.loc.gov/.

she can view the latest edition of the *Library of Congress Subject Headings* (*LCSH*), which is now part of the Library of Congress Classification Web subscription service.[25]

Structured data can present the desired results if the user knows how to conduct a search. Business units should provide training to employees who are the end users of the systems. Records managers should understand the types of records generated by these systems, where they reside, and how they can be managed. The IT department in most cases will *own* the systems and have ultimate responsibility for the information managed, but effective information governance requires that all stakeholders are involved. If the systems are used to share information with the public, instructions to facilitate search and retrieval must be provided.

Unstructured Data: Search and Retrieval Methods

Data volume is set to grow 800 percent over the next five years, and 80 percent of it will be unstructured data.[26] This fact raises the question of how can we determine its value and put it to use. Enterprise search solutions, now dubbed "Insight Engines" by Gartner, can help the organization do just that.[27]

Enterprise Search and Insight Engines

Enterprise search is the organized retrieval of stored business data within an organization so that users can securely enter and find data across enterprise databases.[28] The software searches data across multiple repositories without the necessity of tagging and filing. It can be integrated with data analytics, business intelligence, and data management solutions.

Workers accustomed to performing Google searches in their private lives may wonder why a simple Google-like search couldn't be used to locate and retrieve information in the workplace. Actually, Google had such a product, the Google Search Appliance, from 2012 to 2016, but discontinued the appliance in favor of a cloud-based solution. Because customers of the previous offering were able to receive support through 2017, Google Enterprise Search has yet to prove itself.

Insight engines, by contrast, are described as "enterprise search that [provides] "more-natural access to information for knowledge workers and other constituents in ways that enterprise search cannot.[29] Imagine giving oral commands to your search engine to locate that needed email message or document, just as you use Siri, Apple's intelligent assistant, to locate the closest gas station or best seafood restaurant in the area. Insight engines have the capability to provide natural language interfaces to handle questions specific to your workplace. Three vendors occupied the "Leader" category on Gartner's 2017 Magic Quadrant for Insight Engines: Coveo (a Canadian firm), Sinequa (a French firm), and Microsoft (a US firm). Unlike the first two vendors, Microsoft's inclusion is based on enterprise search applications that are available only as part of its Office Suite.

Open-Source Solution: Apache Solr

Open-source products, like Apache Solr, remain popular options. Major features of Solr include full-text search, hit highlighting, faceted search, database integration, rich document (e.g., Word, PDF) handling, and geospatial search.[30] Products like Lucidworks' Fusion 3 integrate with Solr to allow users to set up capabilities using both an "Index Workbench" and a "Query Workbench."[31] Solutions such as Apache Solr require more IT expertise than an out-of-the box or cloud-based solution. However, in the long run, an open-source solution may be less expensive. These are factors that must be considered when determining the best search and retrieval solution for the enterprise. The role of the records manager is to keep abreast of search and retrieval options and to provide input from a records management and user perspective.

Semi-Structured Data: Search and Retrieval Methods

Semi-structured data are often grouped with unstructured data when discussing search and retrieval methods. Two examples of search and retrieval methods are especially useful when working with semi-structured data.

Extensible Markup Language (XML)

As stated previously, Extensible Markup Language (XML) is a markup language developed to describe the content of web documents. It uses standard descriptions for labeling digital information and automates the identification of material and exchange of data between computers. Data are stored within XML tag sets so that it can be searched, transmitted, or updated by any application that recognizes XML tags. XML can be used to label the information content of diverse data sources, including structured and semi-structured documents, relational databases, and object repositories.

An advantage of a search for XML documents is increased precision in search results. Consider a search for a document written by an author named *Black* using a full-text search. The query might return documents with black as a color or black as a mood. Even the addition of the word *author* to create a Boolean search term of *Black AND author* may not reveal the required results if the word *author* is not included in the document and instead the contribution by the author is written as *contributed by.* However, if the author's name were marked up using XML as *<author>Black</author>,* the search would be more precise.

XML tags provide structure, but the tags themselves are not standardized. Unlike HTML's predefined tags, any individual, organization, or industry can define their own XML tags. This is an advantage in that the organization or industry can use XML tags relevant to its situation. But the disadvantage is the resulting inconsistency across organizations and industries. This can be illustrated by the *<author> </author>* tag set used previously. What if the document was marked up using the tags *<contributor> </contributor>* instead of *author?* A search for author would not produce the desired results.

Two methods can be employed to express the XML system used:

- Document type definition (DTD) lists what tags can be used with the XML document along with their content and relationships to one another.
- XML schema—the newer, more powerful approach—provides the rules an XML document has to follow.

XML schemas (documents defining the *legal* building blocks of an XML document) do much more than describe the elements that can appear in a document, such as *author* or *contributor.* They also define, among other things, attributes that can appear in a document and the default and fixed values for elements and attributes. Schemas set expectations. For example, the format of a date can be confusing. In some countries *6-11-2021* is interpreted as June 11, 2021, but in others as November 6, 2021. The schema can ensure mutual understanding of the date by setting the date element with a data type like this:

<date type="date">2021-06-11</date>

The XML data type *date* requires the format of *YYYY-MM-DD* and ensures an understanding of the content because the XML date is always formatted as *YYYY-MM-DD.*

Vendors contribute to the problem when they use nonstandard XML tags in their products. But they can also be part of the solution. OASIS (Organization for the Advancement of Structured Information Standards) is a not-for-profit consortium that drives the development, convergence, and adoption of open standards. A technical committee of OASIS comprised of several large technology vendors—including Microsoft, IBM, RedHat, and SAP—developed the Open Data Protocol (OData) specification to simplify data sharing across disparate applications in the enterprise, Cloud, and mobile devices. The specification defines an XML representation of the entity data model exposed by an OData service. Their work resulted in the development of two ISO standards: *ISO/IEC 20802-1:2016 Information technology—Open data protocol (OData) v4.0—Part 1: Core* and *ISO/IEC 20802-2:2016 Information technology—Open data protocol (OData) v4.0—Part 2: OData JSON Format.*

This brief discussion is not meant to tell you all you need to know about XML or the open-standards initiative. Rather, it is included to provide a glimpse into the technology in use or in development that will impact information systems that create, store, and manage information assets.

Semantic Search

Semantics refers to the meaning of words. A *semantic search,* therefore, will search and discover the meaning of words and not just their occurrence. The concept of a *semantic network model* was coined in the early 1960s, but it was not until the advent of the World Wide Web that the concept of the Semantic Web (Web 3.0) was introduced as an extension to enable people to share content beyond the boundaries of applications and websites. Unlike the relationships built using hyperlinks within webpages, on the Semantic Web the relationships are named and understood; for example, a relationship binding a person and his or her email address.

Semantic search engines return results based on their ability to understand the definition of the word or term being searched for and to understand the context in which the words are used. According to the World Wide Web Consortium (W3C), the vision for the Semantic Web is to extend the principles of the Web from documents to data.[32] The inability to easily share information residing in disparate repositories (silos) is a major deterrent to the efficient use of an organization's information assets. The integration of independent silos of data is one application that would benefit from semantic search.

Figure 5.13 illustrates the two-way relationship that exists between a purchase made and various facets of that purchase. This relationship can provide the basis for a *semantic faceted* search in which users explore a collection of items (purchases) by browsing their conceptual dimensions (facets) and their values (facet values).[33]

Note the relationships expressed in figure 5.13. They can be expressed as *the purchase of a "good book" was made for $30 by Scott from books.com as a birthday present.* The name of the recipient could be another facet providing additional information. A search on almost any one of these facets can provide valuable business intelligence. For example, who made this purchase? Scott. What do we know about Scott and how do we act on that knowledge? Two facts are apparent:

- He liked that *good book*. Maybe he will like similar books? Who else bought the *good book*? What other books did they purchase recently? Maybe Scott should be informed in case he'd like to buy those, too.
- He bought it as a birthday present for Zoe Franks. Perhaps he'd like to register the recipient of the gift in a birthday registry. Reminders of Zoe's birthday may result in repeat sales.

You were introduced to ontologies in chapter 3. The data in parentheses in the chart, for example, (allValuesFrom), are properties in the *Web Ontology Language* (OWL) vocabulary. OWL is a semantic markup language for publishing and sharing ontologies on the World Wide Web.[34] OWL was developed as a vocabulary extension of the *Resource Description Framework* (RDF). *RDF* is the standard model for data interchange on the web that allows structured and semi-structured data to be mixed, exposed, and shared across different applications.

METADATA AND METADATA STANDARDS

Archivists and records managers have long used metadata to create finding aids, file lists, inventories, and file plans. Records managers also capture metadata to manage records in records management systems. You became familiar with records management metadata in chapter 3. This chapter will introduce you to metadata used for different types of digital objects, including images, publications, and rights management.

Metadata is structured information that describes, explains, locates, or otherwise makes it easier to retrieve, use, or manage an information resource.[35] A metadata framework involves five components:

- **Schema:** a systematic, orderly combination of elements and terms
- **Vocabulary:** the value that would be entered into the schema
- **Conceptual model:** a model describing how all the information and concepts in a resource relate to one another
- **Content standard:** a standard that describes how vocabularies should be entered within the metadata schema categories
- **Encoding:** a method used to present the metadata (e.g., XML)

In 1995, work began on a set of metadata elements that would provide a basic group of text elements to describe and catalog digital resources. At the time, fifteen text fields were

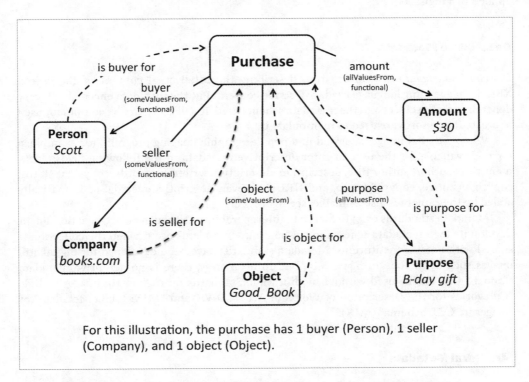

For this illustration, the purchase has 1 buyer (Person), 1 seller (Company), and 1 object (Object).

FIGURE 5.13 Semantic search explores relationships between an instance (purchase) and its facets.

developed and called the *Dublin Core* after Dublin, Ohio, where the work originated. The Dublin Core metadata element set is now an international standard, *ISO 15836:2009 Information and Documentation—The Dublin Core Metadata Element Set.*[36] A Dublin Core metadata record can describe physical resources, digital materials, or composite media, such as webpages. The original fifteen elements are shown here:

- Title
- Creator
- Subject
- Description
- Publisher

- Contributor
- Date
- Type
- Format
- Identifier

- Source
- Language
- Relation
- Coverage
- Rights

The Dublin Core allows for extensibility; the elements can be added to and built upon to meet the needs of the organization. Metadata can be stored with the digital object or separately in a database. When metadata are associated with a digital object, the elements are encased in a tag and the source is identified by a *dc* for Dublin Core as in this example:

<dc:creator>Samantha Franks</dc:creator>

In this example, Samantha Franks is added as descriptive metadata to credit her as creator of the work. In addition to descriptive metadata, structural and administrative data can be applied to a digital object.

Descriptive Metadata

Descriptive metadata are information describing the intellectual content of the object. XML is an encoding language used to describe content. But the metadata encoded will vary depending on the object and the metadata schema used. It will even vary by equipment used to create it and software used to manipulate it.

When a digital image is viewed in a popular graphic imaging program, for example, a form is available for the user to enter descriptive metadata in the following fields: document title, author, author title, description, description writer, keywords, copyright status, copyright notice, copyright info, and URL. However, descriptive metadata automatically added by the camera is also available (see figure 5.14).

Metadata standards exist to facilitate interoperability. Although an organization might develop its own metadata schema for in-house use, problems occur when the collection is shared with outside institutions. Metadata standards have been developed for digital still images such as the one in figure 5.14, but unfortunately, there is no definitive metadata standard that can be used without modification. Standards for digital still images include "Categories for the Description of Works of Art" (CDWA) and "MIX: NISO Metadata for Images in XML Schema" (MIX).[37]

Structural Metadata

Structural metadata describes the physical and/or logical structure of complex digital objects, for example, how scanned pages should be assembled into a book. It can be used to describe the relationships between an object's component parts and is often used to facilitate navigation and presentation of complex items. The content organized by a structural metadata map may be a mix of digital content files, including structured or unstructured text, images, audio, video, and/or applications (e.g., PDF).

Scanned Books and Publications

When considering a structural metadata scheme, it is necessary to consider the type of digital items being modeled and how they will be used. Scanned pages of a book would best be marked up in the Metadata Encoding and Transmission Standard (METS). One benefit of using METS for digital libraries is the number of page-turning applications that understand METS.

METS is a standard for encoding descriptive, administrative, and structural schema for digital objects. It was developed in 2001 for the Digital Library Federation (DLF), was approved as a NISO standard in 2004, and is maintained by the Library of Congress.[38]

The METS XML document format consists of seven major sections: header, descriptive metadata, administrative metadata, file section, structural map, structural links, and behavior.[39] However, the heart of the document format is the overall structure contained in a structure map between the following tags:

<mets:structMap TYPE="physical"> </mets:structMap>

Those responsible for libraries and archives in the public and private sectors should become familiar with METS XML to understand the type of metadata available for digital library objects they access or acquire and in order to make informed decisions on methods that can be used to scan and make available complex digital objects.

Electronic Books (e-Books)

What about e-books? Publishers suffering from a downward spiral in sales of print materials now embrace the electronic publishing environment. In October 2011, the International

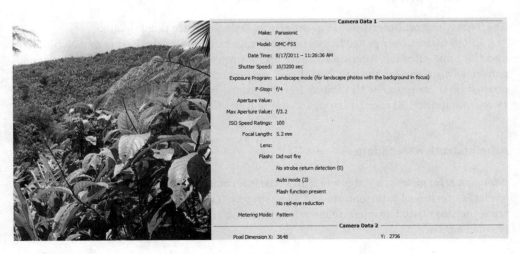

FIGURE 5.14 Metadata added to image file by camera.

Digital Publishing Forum (IDPF), the trade and standards association for the digital publishing industry, approved the EPUB 3 specification as a distribution and interchange format standard for digital publications and documents including textbooks; digital magazines; and educational, professional, and scientific publications. The most recent version, EPUB 3.1, is a family of specifications that define a means of representing, packaging, and encoding structured and semantically enhanced web content for distribution in a single file container.[40]

The file extension, .epub (EPUB), is an XML format for reflowable digital books and publications. It is composed of three open standards: the Open Publication Structure (OPS), Open Packaging Format (OPF), and Open Container Format (OCF). EPUB allows publishers to produce and distribute a single digital publication file and provides consumers with interoperability between software/hardware for unencrypted reflowable digital books and publications.

The Open Publishing Structure (OPS) combines subsets and applications of other specifications to facilitate the construction, organization, presentation, and interchange of electronic documents. Among the other specifications are XML, Digital Talking Book (DTB), Scalable Vector Graphics (SVG), and Cascading Style Sheets (CSS).

Not many records and information managers will find themselves responsible for creating EPUBs, but if necessary, enterprise content publishing solutions are emerging to allow technical communication authors and software development teams to convert and publish high volumes of content from Microsoft Word and Adobe InDesign CS to common formats including PDF and e-books. In addition, records and information managers may need to provide input into editing the metadata that accompanies e-books they acquire, especially if working in a corporate archives or library.

EPUB metadata editors are appearing on the scene, and certain batch operations are allowed. The following metadata fields are available:

- Title
- Creator
- Series
- Series Index
- Publisher
- Date (original publication)
- Type
- Format Identifier
- Source
- Language

The Title, Creator, Description, Publisher, and Date fields are prepopulated.

EPUB files can be opened in most e-book readers, including the Barnes and Noble Nook and the Kobo eReader. Amazon's Kindle uses a proprietary format, AZW, but files can be converted to a similar format, MOBI, for reading on the Kindle. EPUB files can also be opened on a computer with various free programs, including Calibre, Adobe Digital Editions, Mobipocket Reader Desktop, and Apple Pages for the Mac.

Administrative Metadata

Administrative metadata states when and how information resources were created, file type and other technical information, and access rights. Two types of administrative data that are sometimes listed as separate metadata types are *rights management metadata* and *preservation data*.

Rights Management

Increasingly those publishing on the Web are turning to Creative Commons, a nonprofit organization that allows anyone who publishes on the Web to license their work using a three-layer design: legal code, human readable language, and machine readable version using *CC Rights Expression Language* (CC Rel). This language uses a combination of HTML and RDFa to embed license information into a webpage as shown in figure 5.15.

Archivists and records and information managers should understand Creative Commons licensing (see http://creativecommons.org/).

Preservation: METS and PREMIS

Earlier you were introduced to METS and learned that it is a standard for encoding descriptive, administrative, and structural schema for digital objects—types of metadata relevant to preservation. Although the schema was developed originally for digital libraries, its use has been extended to digital repositories and preservation. Archival objects must retain the characteristics of fixity, viability, renderability, understandability, and/or authenticity. The Preservation Metadata: Implementation Strategies (PREMIS) working group released version 3 of the *PREMIS Data Dictionary for Preservation Metadata* in June 2015 to address these challenges.[41] A data model was developed to organize the semantic units in the dictionary into four activities important to digital preservation: Rights, Events, Agents, and Objects.

"PREMIS Preservation Metadata XML Schema version 3.0" was released January 18, 2016. Both METS and PREMIS are XML schema. PREMIS can reside within a METS document. METS can provide the structure and transferability, and PREMIS can provide the information about a digital object necessary for digital preservation actions. The Library of Congress has prepared guidance on how the PREMIS and METS tags should be integrated.[42]

FIGURE 5.15 Example of Creative Commons Rights Expression Language used to embed license information on a webpage.

SUMMARY

The growth of digital information has transformed the way records management is perceived and practiced. Today's records and information professionals, who once primarily managed inactive records and made arrangements for destruction or transfer to an archives, now use their expertise to improve active records and information management.

Today's records and information management professional must master more than one knowledge domain. He or she must understand the mission and goals of the organization and the work of business units. At the same time, he or she must understand information technology well enough to provide value to discussions related to information systems and must understand archives well enough to ensure that records are captured, managed, and preserved as long as they have value.

This expanding role requires that the new records professionals understand business and information systems and be able to evaluate their effectiveness through the use of business process mapping and workflow diagrams. They must also understand structured, unstructured, and semi-structured data and be able to develop or recommend search and retrieval tools and strategies appropriate for each type of data.

Metadata plays an important part in information search and retrieval. The new records and information professional must understand metadata and become familiar with metadata schema and standards of use in her or his industry.

Records and information professionals can also participate in the development of physical, logical, and administrative access controls. They can address the importance of adhering to established procedures and play a prominent role in negotiating service level agreements with third-party providers, including social networks and vendors of cloud computing services.

Becoming involved in business process improvement is one way to add value to the organization; a similar approach can be applied to the process used to manage records and information. In her contribution to chapter 5, Charlene Cunniffe, Associate Director of HRM, explains how a Continuous Improvement process using Lean practices can be implemented to improve Records and Information Management programs.

PARADIGM

Introduction of Continuous Improvement in Records Management Programs and Processes Using Lean Practices

Charlene Cunniffe
Associate Director, Information and Records Management

Introduction

Lean thinking begins with an understanding of two critical concepts: value and waste. Most of the tools and techniques used in Lean Continuous Improvement exercises focus on (a) identifying value creation for the customer, the value-added steps a customer is willing to pay for, or (b) reducing waste, generally by reducing the number of steps in a process or the time it takes to complete an end-to-end process. Lean continuous improvement also identifies and eliminates any rework and defects. Removing non-value-added activities (what the customer does not care about or is unwilling to pay for) is part of Lean analysis. A case study approach is used to illustrate the application of Lean practices to a real-world situation.

Problem Statement

One of the constant challenges for large multinational organizations is the continual merger, acquisition, and divestiture activity experienced as the organization assesses its product portfolio and market position, and refocuses its efforts to maximize shareholder value.

In the records management world of this type of organization, there are many challenges arising from the constant churn and restructuring. Records managers may participate in the closure of sites no longer needed due to low product sales or the decision to no longer produce a product. There may be efforts made to squeeze more people in a new working space in high price-per-square-foot locations. This might mean that the records management staff concentrates on reducing paper in those locations. Another possibility may be that the company merges with a similarly sized company, which could result in the need to make a decision about which processes are adopted—those of Company A or Company B? Which company's retention schedule will be used?

Approach Taken

Each organizational change scenario results in the need to streamline processes and harmonize the way that employees approach information management. At one large pharmaceutical company, several mergers, acquisitions, and continual growth resulted in disparate systems and processes throughout the shared services organizations including those in IT, Records Management, Finance, Procurement, Human Resources, and more. A decision was made to adopt a Lean approach to analyzing and dealing with the systemic issues in order to identify the best system or process for the company as it currently existed. Efforts were made transversally across all the shared services organizations to work on improving cross-functional solutions, and to take a new look at what end-to-end processes could be developed to respond quickly to evolving organizational needs.

To improve processes in the Information and Records Management department, several kaizens (multiday continuous improvement workshops) were held on several RM-related subjects, focusing team efforts on an analysis of current state and a determination of how the group could move forward to improve processes that impacted not only RM but related groups—IT, legal, and compliance, for example.

To introduce the concepts and tools of Continuous Improvement and Lean to the records management team, one specific issue was addressed. An ongoing challenge for the US Information and Records Management (IRM) of the organization was to harmonize the approach to off-site storage and to reduce the complexity of the process for company end users. At some locations, the end users were encouraged to independently index and pack records for off-site storage, complete data entry into the vendor system, and take responsibility for quality checking the box content and indexes. No entry was made into the central non-vendor management system. At the company headquarters, all boxes going off-site were directly collected and managed by RM staff, who verified the contents of the box against the index and entered the data into a records management system maintained by the company itself, not the off-site storage vendor.

The IRM team consisted of five professionals in two major hubs, located in Massachusetts and New Jersey. IRM had hired several contractors to work at each site on off-site box storage as demand increased and the team started to have some concerns about quality in the decentralized process location. As valued partners, the on-site supervisor from each contractor group was invited to participate in analyzing the existing process and helping to determine the future state of the off-site storage process. It was important to the team to improve and maintain a quality records lifecycle process for physical records.

The IRM team was guided by two trained Lean leaders who were not members of the IRM organization, who had not had any real interaction with the group, and who did not have much knowledge of the work that IRM did. They followed the company-established protocol for conducting a kaizen. There were two phone meetings before the actual event with a subset of the team to discuss the kaizen—what the purpose was, who might be the right participants, and what Lean tools would be employed to deliver the right results for this project, which was very different from a more traditional kaizen that might focus on logistics or manufacturing steps.

The initial kaizen was held with five team members. The Senior Director of IRM was the project sponsor, and his manager was the Executive Sponsor of the effort, ensuring executive support and necessary resources such as budget for travel. The team met for four days. One of the intangible benefits to this meeting was introducing members of the team to each other in person, which led to smoother team interactions and better communication between sites for future efforts.

The team was led through exercises including the establishment of a kaizen charter—including a problem statement, a list of participants and their roles, goals, metrics of success, and scope. For this introductory kaizen, the following were developed for use of the Continuous Improvement (CI) team:

Identifying an Opportunity

The average turnaround time needed to complete an IRM service request from start to finish is approximately five business days. The current process for requesting services includes three separate points of request vehicles (in-person, electronic, phone). There are also four different spreadsheets used to track requests resulting in duplicative efforts, confusion, and addition of non-value added time.

Goal Statement

- develop a harmonized process to create, track, and report on IRM service requests
- reduce the number of failed delivery attempts for box retrievals by 35 percent
- reduce the average turnaround time for search requests by 20 percent
- as one IRM, continue to meet or exceed the 95 percent KPI level

The team also created mechanisms for more fluid box request processing through a central mailbox shared by members of all sites. Steps were reduced in the process, time to results was reduced, and metrics reporting was set up.

Results

Members of IRM felt that their efforts had many measurable results in the ninety days allotted to improve the process, and which continue today. Longer-term projects and issues were identified as a side effort of the kaizen, leading to future kaizens and CI efforts for the team. Other IRM team members participated in many more kaizens to improve not only IRM processes but also work between IRM and other organizations, including IT, Legal, Procurement, Facilities Planning, and Human Resources.

Two years after the initial kaizen, the same team met again, this time under the direction of one of its own members who had become a Lean leader, to revisit their harmonized process after changes in the organization and the team. The former "future state" had become the "current state," but times had changed and there was a need to adjust several parts of the process to accommodate a new acquisition that brought additional sites and personnel to fit into the process.

Training in and practice of Continuous Improvement efforts using Lean methodology has made the IRM team more efficient and effective. The team is quick to point out areas that could benefit from immediate "quick wins" and are also regularly eager to put their heads together for informal or formal CI efforts focusing on other processes on which the group relies.

Conclusion

The application of Lean practices in a real-world records management environment created great opportunities for team building and continuous process improvement in several processes of the operational records program. Using such Lean tools as a kaizen Charter, Voice of the Customer exercises, a Value Stream Map, an implementation plan, and defined metrics of success, the records management team created the universe of shared expectations, roles, responsibilities, and quick-win goals. A kaizen readout to all the team and its sponsors demonstrates the Lean methods used and defines the expected successes. A benefit effort matrix helps define the expected quick wins to be accomplished in thirty to ninety days as well as identifying what the team could work on for future kaizens or long-term projects.

NOTES

1. National Archives of Australia, "Digital Records," accessed September 27, 2017, www.naa.gov.au/information-management/digital-transition-and-digital-continuity/digital-transition-policy/digital-transition/index.aspx.
2. SmartDraw, "Business Process Mapping," accessed September 27, 2017, https://www.smartdraw.com/business-process-mapping/.
3. The University of Alabama, "Mission/Vision Statement," Procurement Services, accessed September 23, 2017, www.missiontexas.us/city-departments/purchasing-department.
4. Legal-Explanations.com, s.v. "bill of lading," accessed September 27, 2017, www.legal-explanations.com/definitions/bill-of-lading.htm.
5. Faufu Oluwatoyin Raheem, "Human Workflow Task for ONE-Admin of Mediator for the Interaction of Internet Protocol Network and Transport Network Management System," *The IUP Journal of Knowledge Management*, 14, no. 3, 23–43.
6. TechTarget, "e-Procurement (Supplier Exchange)," accessed September 27, 2017, http://searchcio.techtarget.com/definition/e-procurement.

7. Basware, "3 Disruptive Trends Shaping the Future of Finance and Procurement," accessed May 13, 2018, https://www.basware.com.

8. Matthew Greenwell, *Defense-in-Policy Begets Defense-in-Depth,* SANS Institute, March 26, 2015, https://www.sans.org/reading-room/whitepapers/leadership/defense-in-policy-begets-defense-in-depth-35882.

9. Kyle O. Bailey, James S. Okolica, and Gilbert L. Peterson, "User Identification and Authentication Using Multi-Modal Behavioral Biometrics," *Computers and Security* 43 (2014), 77–89.

10. University of Pennsylvania, University Archives and Records Center, "University of Pennsylvania Records Retention Schedule: Academic/Student Records," University Records Center, last modified June 17, 2011, www.archives.upenn.edu/urc/recrdret/studtacad.html.

11. The term *record* when referring to rows in a database is different from the term *record* defined in ISO 15489-1:2016.

12. Headwaters Group, "Your Unstructured Data is Sex—You just Don't Know It," May 23, 2017, http://content.theheadwatersgroup.com/blog/your-unstructured-data-is-sexy-see-how; Eileen Yu, "Oracle Looks to Clear Air on Big Data," *ZDNet,* October 4, 2012, www.zdnet .com/oracle-looks-to-clear-air-on-big-data-7000005211.

13. SearchDataManagement, s.v. "business intelligence (BI)," accessed September 27, 2017, http://searchdatamanagement.techtarget.com/definition/business-intelligence.

14. Adam Shell, "Wall Street Traders Mine Tweets to Gain a Trading Edge," *USA Today,* May 4, 2011, www.usatoday.com/money/perfi/stocks/2011-05-03-wall-street-traders-mine-tweets_n.htm.

15. Patrick Whatman, "Apple Event: What We Learned from 500,000+ Social Mentions," September 13, 2017, www.business2community.com/mobile-apps/apple-event-learned-500000-social -mentions-01917637#0iBSSd885887Wih0.97.

16. *Webopedia,* s.v. "big data," accessed September 27, 2017, www.webopedia.com/TERM/B/ big_data.html.

17. Ibid.

18. Gartner. "Magic Quadrant for Enterprise Integration Platform as a Service," March 2017, https://www.gartner.com/doc/reprints?id=1-3X0Y452&ct=170403&st=sb.

19. AWS, "What is a Data Warehouse?" accessed September 27, 2017, https://aws.amazon.com/ data-warehouse/.

20. Bill Inmon, "A Tale of Two Architectures," *Scribd,* accessed April 30, 2018, https://www.scribd.com/ document/52332955/A-TALE-OF-TWO-ARCHITECTURES.

21. Ibid.

22. Informatica, 2018, https://www.informatica.com.

23. Edward Atkinson, "Data Warehousing—A Boat Records Managers Should Not Miss," *Records Management Journal* 11, no. 1, 35–43.

24. LexisNexis, "Search Basics," Lexis Advance Support and Training, accessed May 13, 2018, https://www.lexisnexis.com/en-us/support/lexis-advance/search-basics.page.

25. Library of Congress Classification Web, accessed September 24, 2017, www.loc.gov/cds/classweb/.

26. Headwaters Group, "Your Unstructured Data is Sexy.

27. Gartner, (2017, March 30), "Magic Quadrant for Insight Engines," accessed September 24, 2017, https://www.gartner.com/doc/reprints?id=1-3WQ4EMP&ct=170330&st=sb.

28. G2 Crowd, "Best Enterprise Search Software, accessed September 24, 2017, https://www.g2crowd.com/categories/enterprise-search.

29. Kamran Khan, "Here's Why Insight Engines Are the Next Big Thing," *CMSWire,* August 8, 2017, www.cmswire.com/digital-workplace/heres-why-insight-engines-are-the-next-big-thing/.

30. Apache Solr, Apache Software Foundation, accessed September 24, 2017, http://lucene.apache.org/ solr/.

31. Enterprise Search, "Lucidworks 3 Released!" January 25, 2017 www.enterprisesearchblog.com/open-source/.

32. World Wide Web Consortium (W3C), "Semantic Web," accessed September 24, 2017, https://www.w3.0rg/standards/semanticweb/.

33. Weize Kong, "Extending Faceted Search to Open-Domain Web," *ACM SIGIR Forum* 60, no. 1 (June 2016), 90–91.

34. World Wide Web Consortium (W3C), "Web Ontology Language (OWL)," W3C Semantic Web, September 24, 2017, https://www.w3.org/2001/sw/wiki/OWL.

35. National Information Standards Organization (NISO), *Understanding Metadata* (Baltimore, MD: NISO, 2017), 1, www.niso.org/apps/group_public/download.php/17446/Understanding%20Metadata.pdf.

36. International Organization for Standardization (ISO), *ISO 15836:2009 Information and Documentation—The Dublin Core Metadata Element Set* (Geneva: ISO, 2009).

37. The Getty Research Institute, "Categories for the Description of Works of Art," J. Paul Getty Trust, last modified October 6, 2015, www.getty.edu/research/publications/electronic_publications/cdwa/index.html; Library of Congress, "MIX: NISO Metadata for Images in XML Schema," last modified November 23, 2015, www.loc.gov/standards/mix.

38. Library of Congress, "Metadata Encoding and Transmission Standard (METS)," last modified August 18, 2017, www.loc.gov/standards/mets/.

39. Library of Congress, "METS: An Overview and Tutorial," last modified March 30, 2017, https://www.loc.gov/standards/mets/METSOverview.v2.html.

40. Idpf. (2017, January 5). EPUB 3.1, latest version January 5, 2017, accessed September 24, 2017, www.idpf.org/epub/31/spec/epub-spec.html#sec-epub-specs.

41. PREMIS Editorial Committee, PREMIS Data Dictionary for Preservation Metadata, Version 3, Library of Congress, June 18, 2016, www.loc.gov/standards/premis/index.html.

42. Ibid.

CHAPTER 6

Electronic Records and Electronic Records Management Systems

INTRODUCTION

In the previous chapter, we explored the active phase of the records and information lifecycle, focusing on systems and methods used to access, store, and retrieve data for operational needs and to be used in decision-making. You learned that records managers, although identifying records created by or residing in information systems, can contribute to the organization by analyzing workflows and streamlining business processes. You were introduced to search and retrieval methods for structured, unstructured, and semi-structured data, as well as metadata standards that facilitate search and retrieval.

You also learned that information has value, whether considered a *record* or not. But not all information should be retained indefinitely for various reasons, including the cost of responding (locating, retrieving, reviewing, redacting, presenting) to e-discovery and Freedom of Information requests in today's litigious and open society. In this chapter, we'll turn our attention to the subset of information termed electronic records and the use of technology to manage them.

ELECTRONIC RECORDS

Information stored on paper or microfilm can be read by the human eye. An electronic record is invisible and indiscernible to a user until the system produces an image or sound.[1] US National Archives and Records Administration (NARA) regulations (36 CFR 1234.2) defines an electronic record as "any information that is recorded in a form that only a computer can process and that satisfies the definition of a record."[2] ISO *16175-1:2010* defines an electronic record as a "record on electronic storage media, produced, communicated, maintained and/or accessed by means of electronic equipment."[3] Examples of electronic records include email messages, word processing documents, electronic spreadsheets, digital images, databases, video and audio files, voicemail, webpages, text messages and data stored in geographic information systems (GIS).

Electronic records reside in a variety of devices and locations depending on how they are created and by whom, as well as where they are within the records management lifecycle. For example, employees can create records away from the office and store them on USB flash drives, tablets, and smartphones. Employees working within the enterprise may store records on personal computer (PC) hard drives, network drives, and compact discs (CDs).

Information technology (IT) departments can move records to magnetic tapes for storage. Electronic records may reside in third-party systems controlled by vendors, for example, blog posts, tweets, and profiles posted to social networking sites or customer data stored in applications hosted by a software-as-a-service (SaaS) vendor providing file sharing/collaboration tools such as Box, Dropbox, or iCloud.

One example of the increasingly widespread acceptance of a digital record is the stock certificate, which once was one of the most important pieces of paper in the life of an investor. Today, the paper stock certificate is becoming a historic relic. Most Wall Street firms will produce paper stock certificates upon request, but they may charge a fee to handle the transaction. The Walt Disney Company, for example, will send a nonnegotiable "Disney Collectible Shareholder Certificate" adorned with Disney characters to investors for $50 plus tax upon receipt of a Registered Shareholder Verification Form. These are often purchased as gifts to commemorate the purchase of the actual gift—Disney shares. The certificate has no value because stock ownership is tracked electronically in order to eliminate the loss of certificates and simplify the transfer or sale of shares.[4]

In the past, records managers were responsible for retention and disposition of records that were no longer actively used by employees of the organization. But one major difference between then and now is the focus on the user, who may derive value from access to records that in the past were inaccessible (e.g., information in paper documents or on magnetic tapes stored in a records center). Another major difference is the diversity of systems employed today that create digital records. In some cases, it makes sense to control the records in the system of origin rather than move them to a records repository.

Electronic records must be identified regardless of their origin and location so that they can be controlled by the organization's records retention program. The timely disposition of records will reduce storage costs and mitigate risk related to legal and regulatory record-keeping requirements that otherwise would be incurred by retaining records that no longer have value.

ENTERPRISE INFORMATION SYSTEMS (EIS)

Electronic records can be produced by systems that serve the specific needs of one department or function (e.g., customer relationship management). However, in 2005, the term *enterprise information system* came into use to represent the integration of information systems that include web-enabled features. Key business processes integrated into a single software system enable information to flow seamlessly throughout the organization. Supply chain management is an area that benefited greatly from the integration of multiple systems into one in which every business unit along the supply chain has access to the same information (see figure 6.1).

Wal-Mart's supply chain management practices present a classic example of how an investment in information technologies to facilitate information sharing can result in increased efficiency in operations and better customer service. In large part due to information technologies, Wal-Mart was the first nonindustrial service business in the United States to rise to the top of the corporate rankings.[5]

Logistics, as described by David Andries, Vice President of UPS Customer Solutions, is about "implementing efficiencies across a business's entire supply chain that help them achieve their strategic goals"[6] United Parcel Service (UPS) attributes its success to its logistics activities—which include air and ground delivery, as well as warehousing and supply chain management—and its superior customer service, which allows customers to track their shipments online.

Although its ability to present customers with options based on advanced analytics is legend, Amazon.com is another company that excels when it comes to supply chain management; for example:

- In 2013, Amazon announced Prime Air, a delivery service that would use drones to deliver packages. At the time, the United States considered drones that fly outside a human's line of sight illegal, but the British government began testing of drones for delivery.
- In 2015, Amazon received a license from both the United States and China to act as a freight forwarder for ocean container shipping, essentially allowing it to buy space on container ships at wholesale rates and sell at retail.
- In 2015, Amazon filed a patent to build beehive-like towers in urban areas to serve as multilevel fulfillment centers for delivery drones to take off and land. These "beehives" would support truck deliveries and include self-service areas for customers to pick up items.
- In 2016, Amazon introduced its Air Cargo service based on a deal to lease Boeing 767 aircraft to shuttle merchandise around the United States. The intent is not to compete with other carriers but to increase capacity that will allow customers to purchase later in the day and still receive next-day and two-day deliveries.[7]

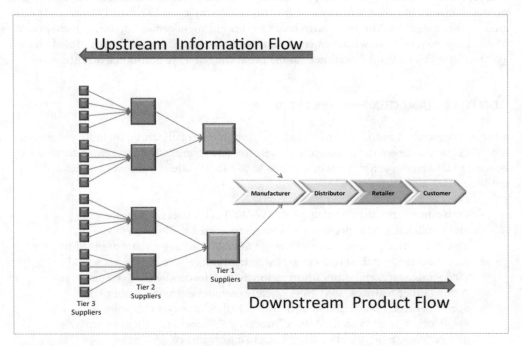

FIGURE 6.1 Supply chain management improves operations with information flowing both upstream to suppliers and downstream to customers.

- In 2016, Amazon was awarded a patent for blimps stocked with drones to serve as airborne warehouses circling over cities at 45,000 feet to launch drones to fulfill orders.[8]
- In 2017, Amazon made its application for the "beehive" patent public.[9]

These steps by Amazon are expected to reduce shipping expenses and reliance on third-party logistic providers like UPS.

Of interest to note is that in 2017, the Trump administration began instituting a program to expand drone testing in the United States that would allow beyond-visual-line-of-sight flights, nighttime operations, and flights over people. The same year, the Federal Aviation Administration (FAA) granted CNN the first waiver to fly drones in crowded areas.[10] This initiative will pave the way for Amazon's use of drones in populated areas.

The examples are provided to underscore the primary reason for electronic information systems. *They are not implemented to create records.* They are implemented to help the business improve operations, with an eye to increasing customer satisfaction. Records are created, though, and the organization has an obligation to manage them. Stop to consider the Amazon example and all the ways in which records are created, starting with the idea protected by a patent and ending with delivery of the desired item by drone. Obviously traditional methods of managing records and information are incapable of meeting the challenge.

One school of thought is that if records are stored in an enterprise-wide information system, they will be easier to manage because the records will be controlled by one system. The introduction of enterprise-wide information systems has simplified the task of locating and capturing records. EIS, though, are not the solution to records management challenges unless electronic records management functions are employed to control the records created by those systems. You were introduced to content management systems in chapter 2. Their use is so pervasive within organizations today—often integrated with records management systems and collaboration systems—that they deserve additional attention.

CONTENT MANAGEMENT SYSTEMS

Content is described as the electronic information in an organization, including electronic records, email, and even the organization's website. The term *content management system* can be used to describe specific types of systems in use for different purposes or within different industries, for example:

- **Web content management systems (WCMS)** allow users "to create, edit, and publish digital content such as text, embedded audio and video files, and interactive graphics for websites."[11] Most WCMS use a database to store and control a dynamic collection of web material (e.g., text, photos, sound, video, metadata, and other information assets) needed by the system. Among other features, a WCMS typically includes automated templates, access control, easily editable content, workflow management, content syndication (such as content distribution by RSS feeds to other systems), and versioning (which allows roll-back to a previous copy).
- **Industry-specific web content management systems** are available, such as the one provided by Influence Health. Its Content Management

System (CMS) allows for the creation of hospital websites, landing pages, micro sites, and mobile sites through an authoring and editing platform that requires no coding. Images, videos, and other digital assets can be uploaded. Content can be delivered not only through the website but also to smartphones tablets, and more. The system can be integrated with customer relationship management (CRM), marketing automation, enterprise, and analytics platforms through the use of pre-built connectors.[12]

- **Social content management systems** can combine social networking applications (e.g., blogs, wikis, image sharing) into one suite to make it easy to manage and share social content without building silos of information. Enterprise social content management systems can authenticate users with a single sign-on, approve content with integrated workflow, and meet key compliance requirements. They allow the organization to capture, manage, and leverage social content generated from a wide variety of locations and devices. In some cases, social media can also be integrated with an organization's existing enterprise content management system to enable the enterprise to store and manage its unstructured social content in the same repository.

- **Mobile content management (MCM) systems** can be employed when employees use their own devices for both personal and work-related activities. According to The Sedona Conference Commentary on BYOD (2018), employee-owned devices that contain unique, relevant ESI should be considered sources for discovery.[13] One of the challenges of the bring your own device (BYOD) movement is the fact that it is difficult to separate work-related and personal communications. Software is available to provide separate containers for data on the same device—one for personal applications controlled by the user and the other for corporate applications controlled by a corporate administrator. The corporate administrator can, for example, allow or prohibit saving data on the device, encrypt stored data, configure application start authentication, and control internet access, SMS and calls. One benefit for departing employees is that containerized data can be wiped from the device without impacting personal data.[14]

The web content management market is expected to grow by 2.5 times by 2022 because of B2B companies adopting CMS for mobile and social content management as well as artificial intelligence capabilities and natural language processing.[15]

ENTERPRISE CONTENT MANAGEMENT SYSTEMS (ECMS)

Enterprise content management systems (ECMS) are used to control unstructured content so that the information can be used in daily operations. But they are also designed to protect digital documents (primarily text and graphics) that serve as accurate and complete evidence of transactions. Those records are regulated and contained, easy to search, and include core elements such as facts, dates, and commitments.

According to AIIM, ECMS can perform five major functions:

- **Capture:** Create, obtain, and, organize information.
- **Manage:** Process, modify, and employ information.
- **Store:** Temporarily back up frequently changing information in the short term.
- **Preserve:** Back up infrequently changing information in the medium and long term.
- **Deliver:** Provide clients and end users with requested information.[16]

An organization may employ one or more ECMS to control the flow of information and manage its records. Electronic records management functionality may be integrated into a new ECMS or built upon the ECMS already in place. ECMS were initially used to manage records that provide evidence of business transactions. Today's ECMS must also be able to manage information resulting from social media and collaborative technologies. ECMS can be integrated with business processes, business rules technologies, and analytics to offer more than just the information stored. Content analytics, for example, can glean business intelligence out of unstructured content to discover patterns that provide additional insight into the business, such as patterns that reveal the factors that lead to customer churn (lost customers).

Some enterprise content management systems, such as M-Files, include artificial intelligence (AI)-based capabilities. M-Files acquired Apprento, a Canadian developer of AI and natural language technology, to enhance its content management offerings. M-Files uses the Apprento Business Context Engine to automate metadata management. Natural language processing is employed to understand semantics and concepts in content. For example, M-Files is able to identify the "customer" in a "contract." This ability to understand the content in business documents automates workflow and document filing.[17]

ELECTRONIC RECORDS MANAGEMENT

The term *electronic records management* (ERM) as defined by ARMA International presents two different scenarios—one in which an electronic system manages all records (including paper and microfilm) and another in which an electronic system applies records management principles to electronic records.[18] In 2000, NARA provided clarification by stating that the word *electronic* in ERM refers to automation, not to the nature of the record (see figure 6.2).[19]

On November 28, 2011, President Barack Obama took steps to improve records management within the US federal government by signing the Presidential Memorandum— Managing Government Records.[20] As a result, on August 24, 2012, federal agencies were directed by the Office of Management and Budget (OMB) and National Archives and Records Administration (NARA) through *M-12-18: Managing Government Records* to pursue the following goals:

1. By 2016, manage both permanent and temporary email records in an accessible electronic format.
2. By 2019, manage all permanent electronic records in electronic format. Of note is the strong recommendation that agencies consider the benefits of digitizing permanent records created in hard-copy format or other analog formats (e.g., microfiche, microfilm, analog video, analog audio).[21]

A preliminary analysis of the reports submitted from Executive Branch departments and agencies by the March 17, 2017, deadline indicated most federal agencies were managing their email electronically and have met the target set for them. However, this data also shows that improvements are still needed to meet the success criteria set out by David S. Ferriero, the Archivist of the United States, in April 2016, which are categorized into four groups: *policies, systems, access,* and *disposition.*[22] In addition, it was noted that some agencies may have specific email management requirements related to issues such as the US Freedom of Information Act and Privacy Act; classified information; and cyber security. Because our chapter is about Systems, let's review NARA's expectations and success criteria for government electronic systems.

The basic expectation is:

> Agencies must have systems in place that can produce, manage, and preserve email records in an acceptable electronic format until disposition can be executed. Additionally, systems must support the implementation of agency policies and provide access to email records throughout their lifecycle.[23]

Success for such systems would look like:

> Your agency's systems and business processes support the management of email records in accordance with all applicable requirements including the manual or automatic

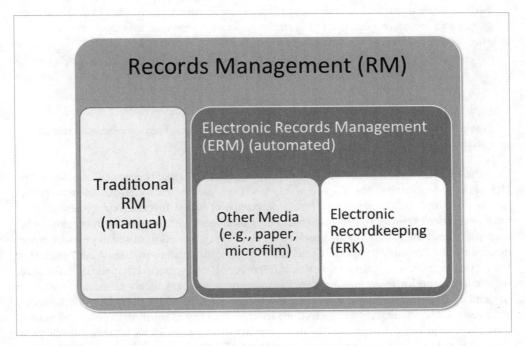

FIGURE 6.2 Context for Electronic records management (ERM).

SOURCE: Adapted from Information at National Archives and Records Administration (NARA). "Context for Electronic Records Management (ERM)," Records Managers, last updated March 27, 2000, https://www.archives.gov/records-mgmt/initiatives/context-for-erm.html.

Capstone-based Approach to Email Management

This approach simplifies the records schedule for email and reduces the records management burden on users by:

1. Basing email records retention on the mailbox owner's role in agency rather than on the content of each email record, and
2. Automating email capture and management according to the simplified, role-based Capstone retention periods.

NARA's General Records Schedule (GRS) for email managed under the Capstone approach specifies three retention periods: *permanent* for Capstone officials (e.g., heads of agencies, assistants to heads of agencies, directors of significant program offices and principle management positions such as Chief Operating Officer or Chief Knowledge Officer); *Temporary. Delete when 7 years* old unless required for business use for email of non-Capstone officials, their staff and contractors; and *Temporary. Delete when 3-years-old* unless required for business use. This applies to non-supervisory positions carrying out routine and/or administrative duties.

The permanent requirement applies to all existing accounts of the Capstone official including legacy email accounts and accounts managed by staff, regardless of the address names on the accounts (e.g., nicknames, office, title, names). It also applies to personal email accounts used for agency business. When personal accounts are used, "a complete copy of these records must be forwarded to an official electronic messaging account of the officer or employee not later than 20 days after the original creation or transmission of the record."

SOURCE: General Records Schedule 6.1, accessed October 19, 2017, https://www.archives.gov/files/records-mgmt/grs/grs06.1.pdf

execution of their disposition whether using a Capstone-based or content-based record schedule.[24]

The Internal Revenue Service (IRS) is one agency that failed to meet the deadline. The IRS plans to implement the Capstone approach recommended by NARA to manage the content within 190,000 mailboxes for three groups of users: forty senior agency officials with permanent retention, two hundred senior managers with temporary retention of fifteen years, and the remaining end users with temporary retention of seven years. A report created by the Treasury Inspector General for Tax Administration in August 2017 indicated the IRS met nineteen of thirty-two criteria (59 percent) and specified that additional efforts were needed to ensure an email records management solution meets all requirements by the end of 2017 (more than a year after the target date).[25] Failure to meet the criteria on time resulted in the inability to reap the expected benefits of minimizing cost, increasing efficiency, improving documentation of agency actions and decisions, and transferring historical records with permanent retention to the NARA.[26]

All criteria for the *Disposition* category were reported as having been met. And only two of the criteria for the *Policies* section were not met: periodic compliance audits and training. Neither could be approached until the system was in place. A sample of the requirements still under development for both *systems* and *access* indicate functional requirements that must be addressed:

- **Systems:** Maintain the content, context, and structure of the records; associate email records with the creator, their role, and their agency; migrate email from one system to another, or to an email archiving application to ensure consistent access; and retain the components of email messages including labels that identify each part of the header, the message content, and any attachments.
- **Access:** Use, retrieve, and interpret email records throughout the entire NARA-approved retention period; access email from current and departed employees; perform a federated search across multiple email accounts or multiple systems to find the email necessary for agency business; and use digital signatures or encrypted technology for email where email can be used and retrieved across the record lifecycle.

These goals can be accomplished only by implementing the right type of electronic system: one that supports records management and litigation requirements, including the capability to identify, retrieve, and retain the records for use if needed.

ELECTRONIC RECORDS MANAGEMENT SYSTEMS (ERMS)

ERMS consists of "software, hardware, policies, and processes to automate the preparation, organization, tracking, distribution, and disposition of records regardless of media."[27] The system must include retention scheduling and disposition.[28]

An ERMS is sometimes referred to as a records management application (RMA). The ERMS/RMA selected to manage records will depend upon organizational needs and the functionality provided by various products. The primary management functions of an ERMS/RMA are categorizing and locating records and identifying records due for disposition. EMRS/RMA software also stores, retrieves, and disposes of the electronic records in its repository.

Functional requirements must be identified before deciding to acquire an electronic records management solution. Typical functions of an ERMS/RMA include:

- Marking an electronic document as a read-only electronic record.
- Protecting the record against modification or tampering.
- Filing a record against an organizational file plan or taxonomy for categorization.
- Marking records as essential (vital) records.
- Assigning disposal (archival or destruction rules) to records.
- Freezing and unfreezing disposal rules.
- Applying access and security controls (security rules may differ from the source electronic document in an EDMS or ECMS).
- Executing disposal processing (usually an administrative function).
- Maintaining organizational/historical metadata that preserves the business context of the record in the case of organizational change.
- Providing a history/audit trail.

ELECTRONIC RECORDS MANAGEMENT SYSTEMS GUIDANCE

Guidance is available for both the vendors who develop records management applications and the users of such systems. Two publications many records managers are familiar with are:

- The US Department of Defense's *DoD 5015.02-STD: Electronic Records Management Software Applications Design Criteria Standard.*[29]
- The European Commision's *Modular Requirements for Records Systems* (MoReq2010)[30]

Neither *DoD 5015.02* nor *MoReq2010* has been endorsed by a standards development body to become a de jure standard, but both documents may be considered de facto standards due to their universal appeal, availability, and adoption.

DoD 5015.02-STD: Electronic Records Management Software Applications Design Criteria Standard

DoD 5015.02-STD, published by the US Department of Defense (DoD), provides guidance for electronic records management information systems development. This standard presents mandatory baseline functional requirements—as well as requirements for classified marking, access control, and other processes—and identifies non-mandatory but desirable features. Version 3 of the standard, issued in 2007, incorporates baseline requirements for RMA-to-RMA interoperability and archival transfer to the NARA.[31]

As technology changes, so must guidance. In August 2017, Department of Defense Instruction Number 5015.02 updated a previous Department of Defense Directive—both of which are related to the Department of Defense Records Management Program.[32] Several changes were made, including the use of the term *essential records* in place of *vital records* and the addition of the term *IT services* to *EIS systems*. Several major changes reflect the goals of M-12-18: *Managing Government Records Directive* and the numerous instances of the misuse of email by officials, employees, and subcontractors at all levels of government. As you read the following additions to the instructions, think about actual events that may have precipitated their inclusion:

- **Applicability:** This instruction applies to information created, received, collected, processed, maintained, disseminated, disclosed, or disposed of by or for the DoD, in any medium or form, including information managed by DoD or a third party on behalf of DoD.
- **Policy:** It is DoD policy that
    - Records created, sent, or received using electronic messaging accounts must be managed electronically, including the capability to identify, retrieve, and retain records for as long as they are needed.
    - Records and non-record materials are government-owned and cannot be copied or removed from government custody or destroyed, except as authorized.
    - Nonofficial electronic messaging accounts, with very few exceptions, must not be used to conduct official DoD communications. If a DoD

employee uses a nonofficial electronic messaging account, the employee must copy the message to his or her official electronic messaging account when the record is first transmitted, or must forward a complete copy of the record to their official electronic messaging account within 20 days of the record's original creation or transmission.[33]

RMA products are tested for compliance with *DoD 5015.02-STD*, and certification by the Defense Information Systems Agency's (DISA) Joint Interoperability Text Command (JITC) indicates the product has met the baseline requirements for electronic recordkeeping for Department of Defense organizations. The JITC RMA Product Register publishes the test results online (as shown in figure 6.3).

Note the plus signs in the Vendor column in figure 6.3. Select one to learn more about that product. For example, a detailed report for the third listing, IBM Enterprise Records v5.1.x, indicates the following among the other useful features demonstrated: document imaging capability, bar-coding capability, workflow and document management features, print file label capability, and web capability.

Note also in figure 6.3 the column labeled "FOIA & PA." Products certified compliant with both the Freedom of Information Act (FOIA) and the Privacy Act (PA) will have a checkmark in that column.

Using DoD 5015.02-STD Outside the Federal Government Sector, the ARMA technical report introduced in chapter 2, identifies gaps in the standard's requirements where records management functions—such as bar coding, folder and box labels, physical records tracking systems, integration with offsite storage facilities, and development of (mandatory) destruction certificates—are not addressed.[34]

Modular Requirements for Records Systems (MoReq2010)

The *MoReq2010* specification was designed for users of electronic records, experts in records management, and suppliers of ERMS software outside of the United States. Launched in

RMA PRODUCT REGISTER

Updated: 9/19/2017 7:27 AM

Vendor	Product	Valid Thru	Baseline	Classified	FOIA & PA	RMA OS	RMA DB	RMA Email
+ Open Text Corporation	Vignette Record Manager v8.1	Perpetual	X	X		MS Windows Server	Oracle	MS Outlook
+ Gimmal LLC	Gimmal Compliance Suite for Microsoft® SharePoint® 2010	Perpetual	X	X		MS Windows Server	MS SQL Server	MS Outlook
+ IBM Corporation	IBM Enterprise Records v5.1.x	Perpetual	X	X		IBM AIX, MS Windows	IBM DB2, MS SQL	IBM Lotus Notes, MS Outlook
+ Feith Systems and Software, In...	Feith RMA iQ (formerly known as Feith Document Database 8)	Perpetual	X	X	X	MS Windows	MS SQL Server, Oracle	MS Outlook

FIGURE 6.3 DoD 5015.02-STD compliance test results are shown on the RMA Project Register webpage.

SOURCE: Joint Interoperability Test Command (JITC). "RMA Product Register," Records Management Application (RMA), accessed October 7, 2017, http://jitc.fhu.disa.mil/projects/rma/reg.aspx.

May 2011, this version contains functional and nonfunctional requirements for records systems as defined by ISO *15489-1:2001 (MoReq2010 has not yet been updated to reflect ISO 15489-1:2016). MoReq2010* does not specify any records system, but it outlines the essential elements a records system should possess.[35] It defines the core functionality required of records systems for public and private sectors. Because it is a modular specification, it can be extended to allow for specialized application in different jurisdictions, markets, and industry sectors, including healthcare, finance, defense, and legal.

In previous specifications of *MoReq*, an ERM system was visualized as a stand-alone content repository situated alongside other content repositories. *MoReq2010* however, views ERM as a capability that could be integrated within each separate application used or could sit behind those applications and manage records within them. For organizations that have invested heavily in different types of electronic systems, the view of one user interface and one repository/server is unrealistic. The introduction and rapid adoption of products such as SharePoint for collaboration have introduced the potential for collaborative silos and further complicates the issue.

MoReq2010 is described as the first of a new generation of systems and processes that will enable a single view of records and archives. Interoperability is achieved by abstracting metadata from the underlying document repository, database, middleware, and operating system. This specification provides a layer of RM-inspired middleware between the underlying infrastructure and every application and service, which should provide a RM policy from cradle to grave.

MoReq2010 "enables commercial and government organizations to secure and develop critical information independent of email, document and content management, cloud and mobile systems, so that when systems are changed, updated, migrated or integrated, the security, value and probity of the records is maintained."[36] Figure 6.4 illustrates the components of a MoReq-compliant records system.

The *MoReq2010* accreditation, certification, and testing program was announced in December 2011, and the first accredited test center, Strategy Partners, was named. The DLM

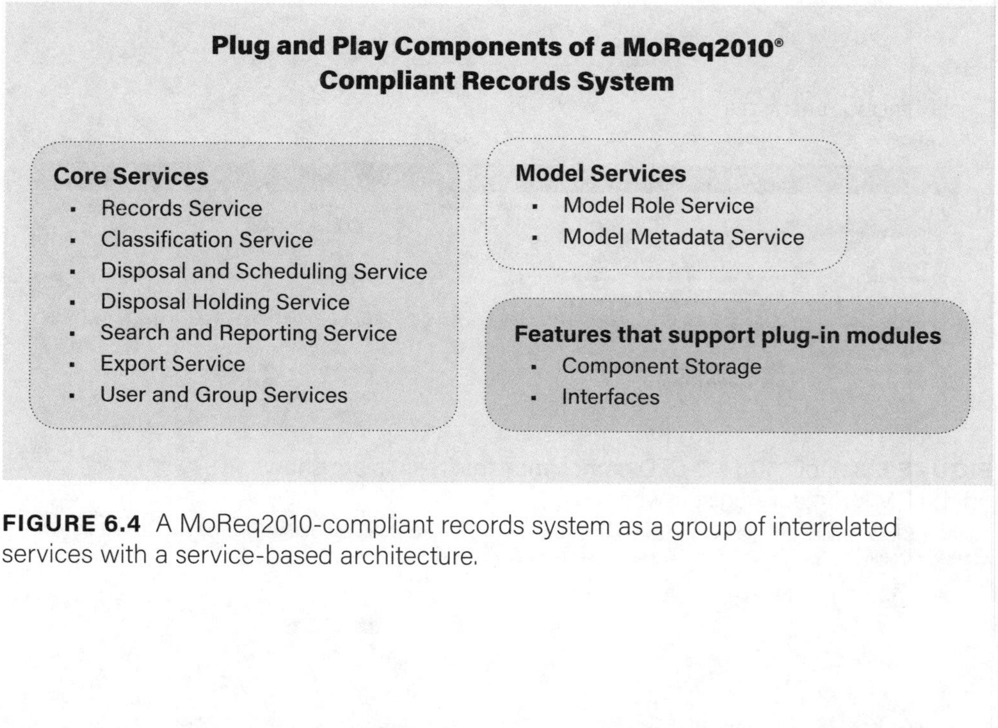

**Plug and Play Components of a MoReq2010®
Compliant Records System**

Core Services
- Records Service
- Classification Service
- Disposal and Scheduling Service
- Disposal Holding Service
- Search and Reporting Service
- Export Service
- User and Group Services

Model Services
- Model Role Service
- Model Metadata Service

Features that support plug-in modules
- Component Storage
- Interfaces

FIGURE 6.4 A MoReq2010-compliant records system as a group of interrelated services with a service-based architecture.

Forum serves as the certifying body.[37] Whereas earlier versions of MoReq were very popular, as of this writing, MoReq2010 has not garnered wide support and the project appears to have stalled. This could reflect the trend toward integration of systems by vendors of products and services that do so without referencing MoReq or seeking certification.

Electronic Records Management System Functionality

The scope of the electronic records management system will be determined by other systems already in place, the functional requirements identified by the organization, and the resources available. Organizations have several options and can install:

- separate systems for electronic and paper records;
- a single system for all records, both physical and electronic;
- separate systems for some records types, such as email and IM; and
- a separate system (or systems) for functional areas or subgroups.

The most pressing challenge is to acquire a records management system that works with existing and planned business systems. This section provides examples of several different frameworks for integration to help you visualize where records under the control of a records management system might reside and how those systems could interact with one another.

Integration of EDM and ERM Systems

The technical report *ANSI/AIIM/ARMA TR48-2006 Revised Framework for Integration of Electronic Document Management Systems and Electronic Records Management Systems* proposed three approaches to implementing an integration of an electronic document management system (EDMS) with an electronic records management system (ERMS).[38]

The first model illustrated the integration of a stand-alone EDMS with a stand-alone ERMS. This situation exists, for example, when an EDMS is in place and the organization decides to implement a separate ERMS system (see figure 6.5). The existing EDMS interface and repository/server are used to manage documents produced in other systems. Documents considered records but residing in the EDMS could be classified as records by linking them to an ERMS folder. Both physical and electronic documents created in other systems (for example, email messages) could be declared and classified directly into the ERMS. An email attachment could be classified into the ERMS if considered a record or into the EDMS if considered a work in progress.

The second and third models show how one user interface could manage documents and records in either a single repository/server (Model 2) or in separate repositories/servers for the EDMS and the ERMS (Model 3). From these early attempts to integrate the functionality of EDM and ERM systems came the term *electronic document and records management system* (EDRMS).

A full-featured EDMS with built-in ERMS is portrayed in Model 2. This product is the result of acquisitions of ERMS by vendors of EDMS to add records management functionality to their products. Management is simplified by providing the user with a single interface and single repository/server (see figure 6.6). Documents stored directly within the EDRMS along with their associated metadata utilize a consistent metadata schema. However, some

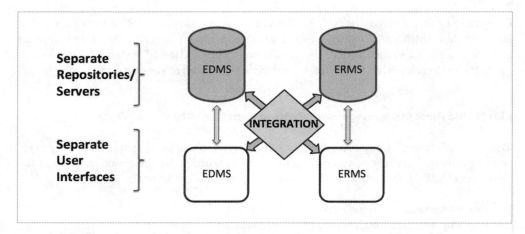

FIGURE 6.5 Model 1—Integration of stand-alone EDMS with stand-alone ERMS.

electronic information, such as email, will have to be imported from other systems, and their associated metadata will differ. Documents produced by other systems are saved to the EDRMS first and then declared, classified, and managed as records. An EDRMS can also identify and track physical documents such as incoming mail and patient records using bar code labels or RFID (radio frequency identification) smart labels.

The third approach integrates electronic records management functionality into the EDMS repository (see figure 6.7). The user interface interacts with the EDMS repository/server, which then interacts with the ERMS. The records remain in one location, and the metadata residing within the ERMS is used to point to and manage them. The ERMS manages the enterprise file plan, retention schedule, and disposition processing.

Enterprise Content Management Systems and Records Management Functions

The previous models were designed at the same time the concept of enterprise content management systems was gaining momentum. Although one might say ECM goes back almost thirty years to the introduction of computer networks and document scanners, it wasn't until the early 2000s that managing web content and websites as corporate assets came under the control of ECM. In 2004, Gartner introduced the Magic Quadrant for ECM, which it described as "the convergence of document management, Web content management, and other content technologies into a comprehensive suite."[39] At the time, six components were reviewed, and one of them was "records management for legal or regulatory purposes, long-term archiving, and automation of retention and compliance policies."[40]

In November 2016, Gartner released a critical capability report for ECM products[41] and scored fifteen ECM products on five factors: personal and team productivity; records management and compliance; process applications; content ecosystem; and digital Transformation/modernization. The fifteen vendor products listed in rank order from highest to lowest were OpenText, IBM, Dell ECM, Hyland, Laserfiche, Oracle, Lexmark, M-Files, Alfresco, Objective, Newgen Software, SER Group, Xerox, Microsoft, and Everstream.

In 2017, Gartner declared ECM dead for one specific reason—it was not meeting expectations. ECM promised to deliver the following benefits:

- regulatory compliance and risk management
- retention and dissemination of business knowledge
- cost and process efficiencies
- innovation and ways of working.

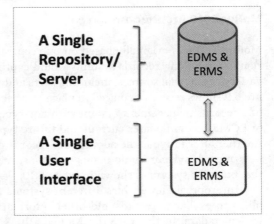

FIGURE 6.6 Model 2—EDRMS (integrated EDMS with ERMS).

The ECM platform appeared to successfully enable only one of the four benefits: regulatory compliance. In reality, most organizations have more than one repository, and the integration required to share business knowledge is challenging.[42]

The cloud, social networks, and mobile and analytics technologies require a different approach. Therefore, Gartner proposed the concept of the *Content Services Platform* (CSP) as the next stage of ECM. The core of CSP is an integrated set of content-related services and microservices, repositories, and tools that can be extended and adapted. The first Gartner Magic Quadrant for Content Service Platforms (2017) included some familiar vendor products, such as OpenText, Microsoft, IBM, Alfresco, and Laserfiche. But it also included vendors that would not have been considered in the ECM market, such as those that serve a single vertical market or those that offer strictly platforms and not package solutions, including Box, iManage, Comarch, Micro Focus (HPE Software), and Nuxeo.[43]

MoReq2010 moved beyond the concept of integrating either an EDMS or an ECMS with an ERMS to the integration of records management functions within all business systems.

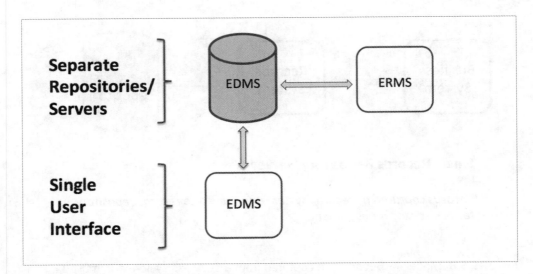

FIGURE 6.7 Model 3—Integration of ERMS into an EDM repository/server.

MoReq2010 Architecture

MoReq2010 was originally based on one centralized repository model where an organization's stand-alone records systems would capture records into its own repository from a variety of external sources, including users and other business systems (see figure 6.8). Figure 6.9 shows records managed in place by a records management system. This integration of a records management system with any type of business system rather than an EDMS or ECMS accommodates current and future types of business systems that create records. Another alternative is the adoption of records controls by the business system. This business/records system would manage only a specific set of records captured or generated by that business system as shown in figure 6.10.

Interoperability enables different systems with different features from different suppliers to exchange records and other information. This is accomplished using standardized metadata, in this case the MoReq2010 XML schema. For testing and certification, MoReq2010 requires that records systems be measured against the MoReq2010 model metadata service in one of two ways:

- The records system implements the MoReq2010 model metadata service in full.
- The records system implements its own native metadata model and (1) demonstrates that its native metadata model is equivalent to the MoReq2010 model metadata service, and (2) that it can convert its native metadata into the same XML format used by the MoReq2010 model metadata service.

The examples presented in figures 6.8, 6.9, and 6.10 represent three records control options, any combination of which may be employed within an organization to manage electronic records:

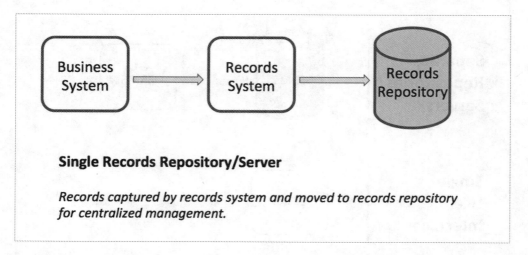

Single Records Repository/Server

Records captured by records system and moved to records repository for centralized management.

FIGURE 6.8 Model 4—Records are captured from a business system and moved into a records repository for control by the records system.

- intellectual and physical control of records within a records repository,
- intellectual control of records housed in a document management system or enterprise content management system, or
- intellectual control of the records housed within business systems (e.g., an email system, an accounting system, or a GIS).

In some cases, the electronic records systems will also exert intellectual control over physical records housed on- or off-site.

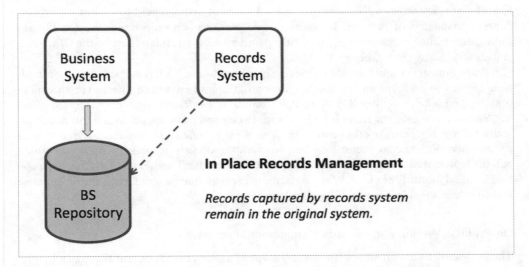

FIGUE 6.9 Model 5—Records managed by a records management system regardless of their location.

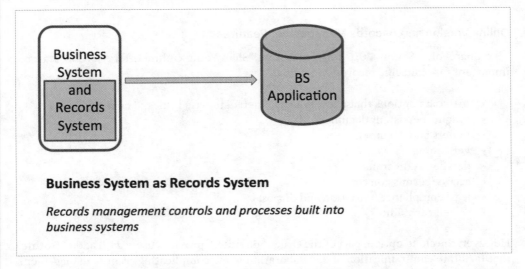

FIGURE 6.10 Model 6—Records management functionality built into a business system.

Records management functionality has been considered an essential component of document management, electronic content management, and now content service platforms. The ideal situation is to have records management capabilities integrated into the solution; however, even when that is the case, it may not be enough to meet the needs of the organization. To see how complicated this issue has become, we'll use SharePoint On-Premise and Office 365/SharePoint Online as an illustration.

SHAREPOINT AND RECORDS MANAGEMENT

SharePoint is known as a collaboration tool, a document management tool, or an enterprise content management product. It comes in two versions—an on-premise version (SharePoint Server 2016 at the time of this writing) and an online version (part of the Office 365 suite, called SharePoint Online).

An organization must decide if one or a combination of both is suitable based on multiple factors. SharePoint on-premise requires an IT team to maintain the server and apply updates and patches. Office 365/SharePoint online is a software-as-a-service (SaaS) offering. With a cloud offering there is no hardware to buy and software updates occur automatically. Of course, there are other considerations—cost for one and compliance requirements for another. With the on-premise option, an investment must be made in hardware, which will be depreciated over time. The cloud option, on the other hand, is an operating expense, that is billed monthly per user. When it comes to records management, both the on-premise and the cloud version have functionality built in.

On-Premise Version and Records Management Features

The on-premise version allows the management of unstructured content through a hierarchy of site collections: sites/sub-sites, document libraries, (folders/document sets), and documents. Document libraries can be used to store and manage records—essentially becoming logical containers or aggregations of records like files in a traditional EDRM system.

Online Version and Records Management Features

Like SharePoint Server 2016 for on-premise, SharePoint Online offers several features important for managing records, including:[44]

- metadata options that allow multiple metadata-based rules to be set
- unique, persistent document ids
- folders and document sets
- versioning
- detailed audit trails
- access/permission controls
- legal compliance/retention and disposal
- search capabilities

However, the cloud option, part of the Office 365 suite,[45] provides users with added features that facilitate communication and collaboration while complicating records management, including but not limited to:

- Office 365 Groups, each with its own SharePoint site
- Teams, a chat-based workspace
- OneDrive for Business, a personal version of SharePoint
- Yammer, a microblogging and collaboration tool (asynchronous communication)
- Skype for Business
- Outlook for email
- Delve, a data visualization and discovery tool
- Planner, a planning application to organize teamwork
- Sway, an app to create and share interactive reports, presentations, and personal stories

Consider the ramifications—SharePoint is only one part of Office 365 and users can elect to work with any of the options enabled. They can store files in OneDrive, communicate with those outside the organization through Yammer, upload files to a document library in a team site, and more. Some of these settings can be disabled for added control. Even so, users who are more creative and productive working in a lightly controlled environment would object. To further complicate matters, a hybrid approach—using both SharePoint on-premise and online—is possible. Planning before implementation and rollout is essential. This is where records management expertise is invaluable!

Implementing Records Managers in both SharePoint On-Premise and SharePoint Online

There are three approaches:

1. Within SharePoint, you can create a *Records Center* to serve as a repository for copies of documents when they become records.
2. You can manage records in place without copying or moving documents to a special repository by declaring the document a record and then applying security, retention, and disposition properties to it.
3. You can use a hybrid approach by managing active documents in place for a set period and then moving them to a records center when no longer actively in use.

Records retention policies are set in the Security and Compliance Center. Two retention policy subsections (options) are (1) retention-based policies meant to be used for global policies, such as retention of email not governed by other retention policies, and (2) label-based policies mapped to individual classes in a retention schedule or disposition authority (as is done in the Australian recordkeeping context).

Enhancing SharePoint Records Management Functionality

Remember the RMA Product Register in figure 6.3? As strong as its records management features appear, Microsoft SharePoint is not on the list.

A report produced by a committee of the InterPARES Trust research project found, "Office365/SharePoint online has limited retention and disposition features that may be sufficient for smaller organizations or for initial installations to better understand its capabilities. However, those who demand more robust records management functionality would be wise to look at the integration of third-party solutions."[46]

One such product, the Gimmal Compliance Suite, which is on the RMA Product register, can use SharePoint architecture and taxonomies to extend the following record management functions for both SharePoint on premise and SharePoint online:

- File plan and retention schedule management
- Classification and identification
- Record declaration
- Retention

- Disposition
- Auditing
- Email
- Physical records
- Legal holds

A comparison of features included in Office 365 out of the box with those when Gimmal's software is added is shown in figure 6.11. Although these features may change by the time you read this, it gives you an idea of how gaps between what you need to manage your records and what is provided in the solution you choose can be filled in by a second product.

FEATURES	Office 365	Office 365 + Gimmal
Automatic declaration of records at creation.	✓	✓
Manual record declaration in addition to automated processes.	✓	✓
Create rules to declare records based on conditions of an item (e.g., metadata).	✗	✓
Lifecycle-based control throughout the life of the record.	✗	✓
Support Records Centers—but declaration of records can occur in any suitable location.	✗	✓
Declare records in OneDrive for Business, Office 365, or legacy My Sites from one solution.	Limited	✓
Declare and manage physical and digital records regardless of location.	✗	✓
Manage essential records in SP while ensuring security at all times.	✗	✓

FIGURE 6.11 Records declaration feature from the SharePoint-Gimmal Matrix.

SOURCE: Created by author based on information provided on Gimmal's website, https://www.gimmal.com/.

This type of extender is now also available from Gimmal for other electronic systems—legacy ECM solutions, file shares, OneDrive for Business, and Box—due to Gimmal's acquisition in early 2017 of RecordLion, an information governance and records management software company. And there is competition in this marketplace as well from vendors such as Collabware and Colligo. Another option, Records 365, was built especially for Office 365.

Responding to client needs, in September 2017 Microsoft announced new data governance features would be added in Office 365. Among them are three powerful tools to govern data, information, and records:

- **Records management dashboard:** The dashboard will provide an overview of all disposition activity.
- **Access governance dashboard:** This dashboard, which supports data leakage controls, will show any items that (a) appear to contain sensitive content and (b) can be accessed by "too many" people.
- **Autosuggested records retention policies:** The system can identify groups of records that do not seem to be subject to a suitable retention policy and make a recommendation to create one.[47]

DATA AND SYSTEM MIGRATION

Storing digital objects in a repository, identifying records, and managing them using an electronic records management system are important, but that is not the end of the records management process. The records must be managed "over time" as dictated by records retention requirements. Because some records have retention requirements that extend beyond the expected life of the systems in which they reside, the records manager must also understand the issues involved in migrating content from one system to another.

Data Migration Issues

Data migration issues must be addressed before moving on to system migration issues. Among the data migration considerations are:

- **Data identification:** Identify all source data that must be migrated to the target system and where it is located. Identify gaps between the data required in the target system and the data existing in the source system. Consolidate data from more than one source system if necessary to fill in the gaps.
- **Unique identifiers:** When records from two or more databases are consolidated into one database during migration, there is a possibility that the same identifier is used more than once. For example, one database may use the prefix "P" for the planning whereas a second database uses the prefix "P" for purchasing. If conflicts are identified, a business rule can be written to change one of the identifiers (e.g., PR for purchasing or PL for planning) to avoid duplication and facilitate search and retrieval.
- **Data quality assessment:** Examine the value of the data. Remove duplicate data and identify data that no longer has value before implementing a system migration.

- **Metadata identification:** Decide which metadata should be migrated and which metadata are no longer relevant. Document the rationale behind these decisions.
- **Explicit metadata fields:** Search and retrieval depends upon the existence of explicit metadata. If the current system does not store all necessary metadata as required (e.g., separate fields for first name and last name), establish those new fields. If the current system applies metadata through inheritance from a parent record (e.g., disposal after audit), enter the metadata as an explicit value or preserve the functionality that will allow the value to be inherited from a parent record.

System Migration Issues

Systems may be upgraded or replaced to accomplish business goals, including enhanced security, increased productivity, and decreased costs. In addition, mergers and acquisitions can force an organization to transfer its data to a system used by a company with which it has merged. Among the issues to be considered when migrating content to new systems are:

- **Metadata mapping:** Content migration is challenging due to the potential loss of quality of existing metadata. It is important to map metadata between the existing business system and the new one. The metadata that must be mapped is metadata about the types of objects the application can hold (entities); a description of the document/object; the actions that users can perform on the entities (functions); and the roles users can be assigned (collections of functions users can perform such as access, view, download content).
- **Records management metadata:** Records management metadata—including records management controls (disposal authorities, security classifications, and record classification tools); metadata to automate activities; and metadata used to aggregate related documents into files, volumes, or series—must also be migrated.
- **Consider the alternative:** Migration can be time-consuming and costly. An alternative to migration is to use the new system going forward and maintain the legacy system to manage existing content. Disadvantages to this approach include the cost of maintaining both systems (e.g., licensing fees and technical support); loss of productivity because users will be required to use both systems to access information; and eventual loss of employees who know how to use the older system.
- **Keep abreast of new systems and standards:** With the increased popularity of cloud solutions, organizations should be aware of the issues and strategies related to data migration to the cloud. Those wishing to take advantage of cloud migration without jeopardizing mission-critical information should consider a private cloud or a hybrid approach to maintain some data behind the organization's firewall. A review of the current information governance strategy is also necessary to address security and control issues introduced by moving to the cloud.

System Migration Process

Records managers who understand integration challenges are prepared to work with information technology personnel to plan and manage system migration. They can, for example, assist during the pre-migration and post-migration testing phases to ensure the output is accurate and complete, monitor data quality in the new system, and help prepare for the next migration.

Additional guidance on managing the migration of digital records is available from several sources, including the State Records Authority of New South Wales. Guideline 22, Section 4 of the *Government Recordkeeping Manual*, "Effectively Manage the Migration of Your Digital Records," which provides a wealth of information to help manage the migration of digital records.[48] The topics covered include key record requirements critical to maintaining record authenticity, integrity, reliability, and usability during migrations; data and system issues to consider when developing a migration plan; the use of contractors to perform migrations; pre- and post-migration testing; and creating records of the migration.

RECORDS MANAGEMENT IN THE CLOUD

What should be done about records residing on third-party servers? One option is to capture those records (e.g., tweets and posts) and bring them into an in-house system. Another option is to manage those records in the cloud. To decide which option is most appropriate for any organization, it is important to understand cloud computing.

Cloud computing involves web-based hosted services divided into the following three basic categories:

- **Software as a service (SaaS):** Software as a service means delivering software over the internet, eliminating the need to install the software on the organization's own computers. Examples include Office 365 and Google Apps.
- **Platform as a service (PaaS):** The best-known example comes from Salesforce.com, which has been providing customer relationship management (CRM) applications since 1999. Salesforce.com offers a set of tools and application services called *Force.com* that internet service vendors and corporate IT departments can use to build new and better applications for tasks such as human resource management (HRM), supply chain management (SCM), and enterprise resource planning (ERP).
- **Infrastructure as a service (IaaS):** Infrastructure as a service is the delivery of computer infrastructure—generally virtualized platform environments— as a service. This service typically is considered a utility, like electricity and water, which is billed based on the amount of resources consumed. Amazon .com Web Services and Rackspace Openstack Cloud are two examples of this type of cloud service.

Cloud computing offers the following benefits:

- highly efficient storage of records that are rarely accessed but must be maintained, such as old email messages and documents.

- economies of scale, giving the organization access to records platforms, functionality, and preconfigured compliance-driven solutions that were previously unaffordable.

Some cloud providers will likely fail or be forced to change their business models, resulting in a reduction of the functionality delivered for a specific price. In addition, as the sector matures, mergers and acquisitions will reduce the number of products we're familiar with while introducing new options.

Due diligence is advised, but it is not always easy to predict future events. In the case of cloud computing, it is essential to understand customer rights to terminate the agreement, migrate to another service, or fall back to a pre-cloud contract if one existed.

PLANNING AND MANAGING AN ELECTRONIC RECORDS MANAGEMENT PROGRAM

The information in this chapter is provided to help you better understand electronic records and the systems that create and manage them. Selecting and implementing the ERM system is one phase in planning and managing an electronic records management program outlined as follows:

1. Conduct an electronic records survey.
2. Plan the electronic records management project.
3. Select and implement the ERM system.
4. Advocate effective electronic records management.
5. Manage organizational change.

The ERM program is one aspect of the organization's overall records management program.

SUMMARY

Electronic information systems are employed to improve the efficiency and effectiveness of an organization, not to create records. However, information is created by these systems, and a portion of that information is comprised of records that must be managed to meet compliance requirements and to provide evidence of business transactions.

Web and social media technologies have changed the way we communicate, collaborate, and interact with others within and outside of the enterprise. They also generate information, some of which are records. Records and information managers play a vital role in identifying records and providing guidance to those responsible for capturing and managing them.

Various content management systems can be used to control unstructured content, including web content management systems, enterprise content management systems, and social content management systems. Electronic records management systems can be integrated with other business systems to manage the records residing in the systems of origin. Typical electronic records management system functions include protecting the record against modification or tampering, marking records as essential, and freezing and unfreezing disposal rules.

Two de facto standards that provide guidance to vendors creating records management applications are the US Department of Defense's *DoD 5015.02-STD: Electronic Records Management Software Applications Design Criteria Standard* and the European *MoReq2010: Modular Requirements for Records Systems.*

Organizations have several options for implementing records management systems, including installing separate systems for electronic and paper records or installing a single system for both electronic and physical records. Several approaches to integrating electronic records management systems with other electronic systems exist. And connectors and extenders can be installed to enhance records management features built into business systems.

The useful life of records and information often extends beyond the lives of the systems in which they are created and stored. Migration is an activity that transfers records and information from one system to another so they can be read and used as long as necessary. Records managers can contribute to data and system migration operations in various ways, including identifying records and the metadata required to describe and manage those records.

The growing trend to take advantage of cloud computing services presents additional records management opportunities and challenges.

In the next chapter, we'll explore emerging technologies and their impact on records management. But before we do that, Morgan King, Director and Head of Records and Information Management, and Stephen Aaronson, Director and Head of IT Legal, explain how they teamed up to implement a full-service ERMS at a leading global biotechnology company in their paradigm.

PARADIGM

The Art and Science of ERMS Deployment

Morgan King
Director and Head of Records and Information Management, Shire Pharmaceuticals

Stephen Aaronson
Director and Head of IT Legal, Shire Pharmaceuticals

The days of manual and paper-based processes are gone. Technology is the core infrastructure that runs all businesses. Because employees can instantaneously duplicate data for their convenience, Electronically Stored Information (ESI) is growing at an unprecedented rate. Enterprises are employing a myriad of vehicles for storing and providing access to information. These include traditional client servers, cloud-based solutions, mobile devices, and other computing systems. Demand and pressures for state of the art information technology-based solutions and delivery vehicles are increasing exponentially. Although these solutions are generally regarded as readily available commodities and vendors are marketing them to leaders of core business functions as "must haves" to remain innovative, companies are challenged to keep their IT costs relatively flat.[49] Technology is not free.

This creates a fiscal paradox for companies: it is necessary to keep investments in information technology solutions flat while growing the technology footprint. With these conflicting pressures in play, organizations are challenged to prioritize investments in information technology. They must balance running the business (or keeping it afloat) and optimizing the business through investments in technology and process innovation. *At the center of this paradox is information.*

Further compounding this central tension between cost reduction and growth is the fundamental pressure on many organizations to mitigate risks and satisfy regulators. Depending on the industry, there are different rules and regulations for storing and retaining information that is considered a company record. Failure to protect this information can lead to damages associated with liabilities, license to operate, loss of intellectual properties, sanctions, or damage to corporate image. Many companies that are faced with the demand to manage regulatory and legally complex risks first begin by establishing a records and information management (RIM) presence in the organization. This may be one individual for smaller companies or an entire team of personnel in larger organizations. In an exclusively paper world, the mere presence of a RIM expert, the institution of policies, and the education of staff on principles and best practices would entail risk. However, we do not live in such a world.

Companies must now address dynamic ecosystems of information in a variety of formats and silos. Records and information management must be partnered with other functions concerned with information, most pointedly, the information technology function. See table 6.1 for details.

Beyond partnership, technology and automated process are required to achieve the level of systematic control that legal and regulatory authorities now expect organizations to meet.

Electronic records management systems (ERMS) assist with applying systematic processes and controls to mitigate the risks that could lead to damages. An ERMS requires significant investment that must be justified, vetted, and prioritized against the other demands for investments in information technology.

In the past, justification for an ERMS focused mainly on intangible needs—to have good practices, the ability to locate information, or the damages that may result if there was failure to comply with regulations. This was an extension of the risk mitigation rationale that led companies to institute a records and information management program in the first place. However, as companies face the "pull" of the information paradox—*the demand to reduce cost*—the high price tag and resource requirements attached to robust ERMS implementations become a major deterrent. When faced with these figures and options, companies may be more willing to accept risk and hope that policies and training are enough.

The damages that RIM professionals may often dangle in front of management to try to make the case for investments in technology are "what if" scenarios that are difficult to quantify. They can be viewed as scare tactics or fear-mongering. Companies may be willing to accept the risk of not having an ERMS. Their rationale may be that these damages will never occur and that their investment in RIM personnel and organizational education is appropriate. In our experience as leaders in IT and RIM, rather than focusing on the intangibles, successful business cases shift the focus towards the tangibles and how an ERMS can be viewed as the "push" of the information paradox—*paving the way for innovation and growth.*

The tangible benefits of a full service ERMS are associated with reducing storage costs by eliminating ROT (redundant outdated and trivial content) and records and information that do not need to be retained, freeing up operating and infrastructure expenses

TABLE 6.1 How will you partner?

Who?	Description	Responsibilities with respect to ERMS
Records and Information Management	The individual or team accountable for implementing records and information management policies, standards, procedures, and guidelines and training the organization on good records management practices	• Set the business policies for operating the ERMS. • Responsible and accountable for training. the organization to ensure appropriate use. • Socialize tool and promote user adoption. • Gather metrics to assess and manage ERMS performance. • Identify new business use cases/ opportunities to enhance tool performance over time. • Defend tool in audits and investigations.
RIM IT Business Partner	The individual or team responsible for partnering with RIM to support technology solutions for records and information management	• Envision (in partnership with RIM) the technology required to support records and information management requirements. • Architect solutions. • Procure the ERMS. • Deploy the ERMS—includes validation and documentation to support the system in a highly regulated environment such as healthcare. • Run the ERMS—ensure the system does what it is supposed to do, respond to user experience feedback, and make incremental process improvements over time. • Enable system upgrades, migrations, and enhancements as appropriate.
RIM Liaisons	Records and information management subject matter experts within business functions.	• May serve as testers/or pilot participants as an ERMS is rolled out. • Serve as "change champions" as the tool is socialized to the organization. • Utilize the ERMS to appraise and archive content. • Provide feedback to RIM and IT to ensure tool meets their needs.
Information Owners or Custodians	The owners or custodians of records and information	• Utilize the ERMS to appraise and archive content. • Provide feedback to RIM and IT to ensure tool meets their needs.
Senior Management	Senior leaders in the organization—often have a direct leadership line to RIM and RIM IT (in our case these are leaders in Legal and IT).	• Serve as executive sponsors for business cases. • Provide buy-in and funding for ERMS projects. • Monitor progress as tools are deployed by receiving sponsor updates from RIM and IT.

TABLE 6.2 Metrics and assigned responsibility.

What?	Who Captures?
License/Maintenance cost	IT system owner of tool or infrastructure
Storage cost	IT system owner of tool or infrastructure
GB of data ingested	RIM team/RIM IT business partner
Data disposed per policy	RIM team/RIM IT business partner
Systems archived/decommissioned	RIM team/RIM IT business partner

by eliminating legacy or redundant systems, enabling human resource productivity gains to focus on other business critical activities through efficient information searches and retrieval, and accelerating associated tasks. These gains are realized while remaining compliant with legal and regulatory requirements. How a team arrives at the tangible benefits is both an art and a science; a framework for value capture must be artfully designed by individuals who also understand all the variables in the landscape that can be applied mathematically to demonstrate the profitability of the initiative. Table 6.2 provides details.

As for the framework, those endeavoring to build an ERMS must understand the landscape in which it will operate. This includes an understanding of where records are located, record types, information custodians and owners, time spent managing the records, the space they consume, application and infrastructure licensing, and infrastructure run rates. This foundational information must be gathered in tandem by RIM and IT professionals to engineer a comprehensive suite of tools to address business needs and drive growth.

As for the mathematical algorithms, productivity calculations can be done with the help of an organization's HR department. If you think of an ERMS as stock, it can yield high dividends that can be immediately reinvested in running the business or cashed in. The license, maintenance, and storage costs of retiring systems and reducing the organization's storage footprint are straightforward once the mechanism for capturing the metrics is established and consistently deployed. Once the metrics are captured, they can be used by your team to demonstrate the value of your investments. In many industries, the ability to do so is a required competency in order to continue to operate and further develop the program.

In our experience, taking the time to develop a robust strategy for your ERMS prior to deployment is critical to success. Building a meaningful file plan, investing in the right technology, and deploying it in such a way that it becomes an accelerator rather than a hindrance to the business will inevitably lead to meaningful savings. It will also lead to an appreciative organization that is no longer held captive by the costs and operational burdens of historical data.

NOTES

1. *Glossary of Archival Language for Archives in Tennessee,* s.v. "electronic record," accessed October 7, 2017, www.expertglossary.com/definition/electronic-record.
2. National Archives and Records Administration (NARA), s.v. "electronic record," "Context for Electronic Records Management [ERM], accessed October 7, 2017, https://www.archives.gov/records-mgmt/initiatives/context-for-erm.html.

3. International Organization for Standardization (ISO), *ISO 16175-1:2010—Information and Documentation—Principles and Functional Requirements for Records in Electronic Office Environments—Part 1: Overview and Statement of Principles* (Geneva: ISO, 2010).

4. Broadridge Financial Solutions, "Welcome Disney Shareholders," accessed October 7, 2017, http://shareholder.broadridge.com/disneyinvestor/#navTabs4.

5. Laurent Belsie, "Wal-Mart: World's Largest Company," *The Christian Science Monitor,* February 19, 2002, www.csmonitor.com/2002/0219/p01s04-usec.html.

6. UPS, "Defining Logistics, How it Relates to Your Supply Chain—And Why It's Crucial for Your Company," accessed October 7, 2017, https://www.ups.com/us/en/services/resource-center/Logistics-Definition.page.

7. Michael Bentley, "Fighting Amazon's Supply Chain Takeover," *Logistics Management,* January 3, 2017, www.logisticsmgmt.com/article/fighting_amazons_supply_chain_takeover.

8. Arjun Kharpal, "Amazon Wins Patent for a Flying Warehouse That Will Deploy Drones to Deliver Parcels in Minutes," CNBC, December 30, 2016, https://www.cnbc.com/2016/12/29/amazon-flying-warehouse-deploy-delivery-drones-patent.html.

9. Kayla Yurieff, "Amazon Patent Reveals Drone Delivery 'Behives,'" *Money,* June 23, 2017, http://money.cnn.com/2017/06/23/technology/amazon-drone-beehives/index.html.

10. Marco Margaritoff, "Trump Administration Expands Drone Use to Beyond Visual Line of Sight," *The Drive,* October 25, 2017, www.thedrive.com/aerial/15458/trump-administration-expands-drone-use-to-beyond-visual-line-of-sight; Margaritoff, "FAA Grants Waiver Allowing CNN to Fly Drones Over Crowds," *The Drive,* October 18, 2017.

11. G2 Crowd, "Best Web Content Management Systems," accessed October 7, 2017, https://www.g2crowd.com/categories/web-content-management.

12. Influence Health, "Content Management System (CMS) by Influence Health," accessed October 7, 2017, https://www.influencehealth.com/consumer-experience-platform/content-management-system.

13. Kaspersky Lab, "Multilayered Security, Management and Control for All Mobile Endpoints," accessed April 28, 2018, https://media.kaspersky.com/en/business-security/kaspersky-mobile-security-datasheet.pdf.

14. The Sedona Conference, "Commentary on BYOD: Principles and Guidance for Developing Policies and Meeting Discovery Obligations," 2018, https://thesedonaconference.org/publication/Commentary%20on%20BYOD.

15. Sudipto Ghosh, "Content Management Systems with Web Analytics & Social Media Integrations Key to Industry," *Market Technology Insights,* March 31, 2017, http://martechseries.com/content-marketing/content-management/content-management-systems-with-web-analytics-social-media-integrations-key-to-industry/.

16. AIIM, "What Is Enterprise Content Management (ECM)?" accessed October 7, 2017, www.aiim.org/What-is-ECM-Enterprise-Content-Management.

17. Rick Whiting, "M-Files Adding AI Capabilities to Its Content Management System with Acquisition," CRN, August 29, 2017, www.crn.com/news/applications-os/300091296/m-files-adding-ai-capabilities-to-its-content-management-system-with-acquisition.htm.

18. ARMA International, s.v. "electronic records management (ERM)," *Glossary of Records and Information Management and Information Governance Terms,* 5th ed., p. 18, ARMA International TR 22-2016. (Overland Park, KS: ARMA International, 2016).

19. National Archives and Records Administration (NARA), "Context for Electronic Records Management (ERM)," Records Managers, last reviewed May 10, 2017, www.archives.gov/records-mgmt/initiatives/context-for-erm.html.

20. Barack Obama, "Presidential Memorandum—Managing Government Records," WhiteHouse.gov, November 28, 2011, www.whitehouse.gov/the-press-office/2011/11/28/presidential -memorandum-managing-government-records.

21. Executive Office of the President, "M-12-18: Memorandum for the Heads of Executive Departments and Agencies and Independent Agencies," August 24, 2012, https://www.archives.gov/files/records-mgmt/m-12-18.pdf.

22. David S. Ferriero, "Criteria for Managing Email Records in Compliance with the Managing Government Records Directive (M-12-18)," April 6, 2016, p. 2, https://www.archives.gov/files/records-mgmt/email-management/2016-email-mgmt-success-criteria.pdf.

23. Ibid., p. 3.

24. Ibid.

25. Treasury Inspector General for Tax Administration, "Additional Efforts Are Needed to Ensure the Enterprise E-Mail Records Management Solution Meets All Requirements Before Deployment, Ref. No. 2017-20-039," August 7, 2017, https://www.treasury.gov/tigta/auditreports/2017reports/201720039fr.pdf.

26. Ibid., p. 10.

27. ARMA International, s.v. "electronic records management system (ERMS)," *Glossary of Records and Information Management and Information Governance Terms,*18.

28. Ibid.

29. Department of Defense, *DoD 5015.02-STD: Electronic Records Management Software Applications Design Criteria Standard* (Washington, DC: United States Department of Defense, April 25, 2007), www.dtic.mil/whs/directives/corres/pdf/501502std.pdf.

30. DLM Forum Foundation, *MoReq2010: Modular Requirements for Records Systems,* accessed October 7, 2017, http://MoReq.info/.

31. *DoD 5015.02-STD: Electronic Records Management Software Applications Design Criteria Standard.*

32. Department of Defense Instruction, Number 5015.02, Incorporating Change 1, (August 17, 2017), www.esd.whs.mil/Portals/54/Documents/DD/issuances/dodi/501502p.pdf?ver=2017-08-17 -142503-963.

33. Ibid.

34. ARMA International, *Using DoD 5015.02-STD outside the Federal Government Sector,* ARMA TR 04–2009 (Lenexa, KS: ARMA International, 2009).

35. DLM, "About MoReq2010."

36. Gareth Morgan, "Leading Vendors Collaborate for Records Management Scheme," Computing.co.uk, July 14, 2011, www.computing.co.uk/ctg/news/2094155/leading-vendors-collaborate -records -management-scheme.

37. DLM is an acronym for Document Lifecycle Management. The DLM Forum is a European community of parties interested in archive, records, document, and information lifecycle management.

38. AIIM International, *ANSI/AIIM/ARMA TR48-2006 Revised Framework for Integration of Electronic Document Management Systems and Electronic Records Management Systems* (Silver Spring, MD: AIIM International, 2006).

39. James Lundy, Kenneth Chin, and Karen M. Shegda, "Start Planning for Enterprise Content Management," Gartner, November 16, 2004, https://www.gartner.com/doc/461344/start-planning -enterprise-content-management.

40. Brice Dunwoodie. "Vignette a Leader in ECM Magic Quadrant," *CMSWire,* October 25, 2004, www.cmswire.com/cms/enterprise-cms/vignette-a-leader-in-ecm-magic-quadrant-000459.php.

41. Karen M. Shegda and Gavin Tay, "Critical Capabilities for Enterprise Content Management," *Gartner Report,* November 29, 2016, www.project-consult.de/files/Gartner_ECM_Critical _Capabilities_2017_Jan2017.pdf.

42. Michael Woodbridge, "The Death of ECM and Birth of Content Services," Gartner, January 5, 2017, http://blogs.gartner.com/michael-woodbridge/the-death-of-ecm-and-birth-of-content-services/.

43. Karen A. Hobert, Michael Woodbridge, and Joe Mariano, Gavin Tay, "Magic Quadrant for Content Services Platforms," Gartner, October 5, 2017, https://www.m-files.com/en/Gartner-Magic -Quadrant-CSP-2017.

44. Andrew Warland, "How Office 365 Challenges Traditional Records Management Practices," blog post, September 27, 2016, https://andrewwarland.wordpress.com/2016/09/27/how-office -365-challenges-traditional-records-management-practices/.

45. Microsoft Office, Get the Most from Microsoft Office, accessed October 12, 2017, https://products.office.com/en-us/business/get-office-365-for-your-business-with-latest-2016 -apps?&WT.srch=1&wt.mc_id=AID623587_SEM_udcTpKDH.

46. Patricia Franks, et al., "Retention and Disposition in a Cloud Environment, Final Report," May 17, 2016, InterPARES Trust, 15. https://interparestrust.org/assets/public/dissemination/ NA06_20160902_RetentionDispositionInCloud_FinalReport_Final.pdf.

47. Andrew Warland, "Office 365—New Data Governance and Records Retention Management Features," blog post, October 7, 2017, https://andrewwarland.wordpress.com/2017/10/07/ office-365-new-data-governance-and-records-retention-management-features/.

48. State Records Authority of New South Wales, "Effectively Manage the Migration of Your Digital Records (Guideline 22)," revised February 2015, https://www.records.nsw.gov.au/recordkeeping/ advice/effectively-manage-digital-records-migration.

49. Charles McLellan, ""IT Budgets 2016: Surveys, Software and Services, ZDNet," October 1, 2015, www.zdnet.com/article/it-budgets-2016-surveys-software-and-services/.

CHAPTER 7

Developing and Emerging Technologies and Records Management

INTRODUCTION

Each year, analysts, futurists, and others attempt to identify the technologies most likely to alter industries, fields of research, and even the way we live. Many of those emerging technologies will impact the way records and information are created, stored, used, disposed of, and preserved. Some of the predictions made, if they materialize, will change the way we answer such questions as:

- What is a record?
- How can we capture it?
- How can we preserve it?

Recordkeepers must consult a variety of sources to stay abreast of emerging technologies and trends. Emerging technologies are "new technologies that are currently developing or will be developed over the next five to ten years, and which will substantially alter the business and social environment. These include information technology, wireless data communication, man-machine communication, on-demand printing, biotechnologies, and advanced robotics."[1] It is important to keep in mind that emerging technologies are not only technologies that have not yet been introduced to the consumer market but also those that have been introduced and are in the process of refinement while in use—those are referred to as developing technologies in this work.

DEVELOPING TECHNOLOGIES: SOCIAL MEDIA

In the first edition of this book, social media was considered an emerging technology. Today, most of us can identify at least one tool we use in our everyday lives from those included in figure 7.1. Because of the speed at which social media is evolving, social media is considered a *developing technology* still worthy of consideration in this chapter.

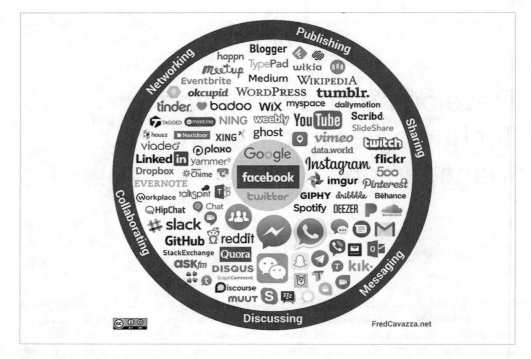

FIGURE 7.1 Social Media Landscape 2017.

SOURCE: FredCavazza.net, CC 4.0, https://creativecommons.org/licenses/by/4.0/.

SOCIAL MEDIA AND RECORDS MANAGEMENT

The term *social media record* is being used in this instance to represent all records posted to, created through, or residing in social media technologies. Many of these records could potentially be classified under existing series titles, such as electronic communications or press releases. If the content represents a new record series, the records retention schedule must be updated.

Social media records can reside in social media technology hosted by third-party providers or hosted by the organization itself. Social media technology hosted by the organization provides a greater degree of control over the content and is ideal for projects that don't require participation by the general public or that require high levels of security. When the intent of the social media initiative is outreach to the public, the use of popular social networks hosted by third parties is the best approach.

In the early days of social media use, those responsible for records management often learned about social media initiatives after they had been implemented. This was the case within the executive branch of the US federal government in January 2009 when President Obama directed all federal agencies to create an environment of openness and transparency. Soon after, social media teams were formed and social media outreach initiatives were launched. These employees were the innovators and early adopters who paved the way for the rest of the government agencies.

In October 2010, the US National Archives and Records Administration (NARA) published "NARA Bulletin 2011-02: Guidance on Managing Records in Web 2.0/Social Media

Platforms."[2] That same month a study was released by the IBM Center for the Business of Government titled "How Federal Agencies Can Effectively Manage Records Created Using New Social Media Tools."[3] In March 2011, the American Council for Technology and Industry Advisory Council, a nonprofit public-private partnership dedicated to improving government through the application of information technology, identified the following challenges presented by emerging technologies:

- identification of a record
- capture of the record
- retention of the record
- scheduling/distribution/disposition of the record
- staffing and education (for employees, including executives)[4]

These challenges are like the challenges recordkeepers faced before social media, and the recommended actions remain the same:

- updating RIM policy "before" using social networks
- updating the RIM training course
- defining and applying strict access controls
- defining a record and determining its status
- developing and applying a comprehensive records retention schedule

Although the responsibilities remain the same, the policies and practices must be adjusted.

The 2016 *Records Management Self-Assessment Report* completed by 257 federal agencies revealed that after email management, information generated through electronic communication was their biggest challenge. Only 56 percent (143 of 256) of agencies reported having documented and approved policies and procedures in place to manage electronic messages (including text, chat/instant, and voice), as well as messages created in social media tools or applications, and only 30 percent of agencies had approved records schedules to cover the same types of electronic messages.[5]

Identifying Social Media Records

According to Arian Ravanbakhsh, Supervisory Records Management Policy Analyst in the Office of the Chief Records Officer at NARA, "Social media content and electronic messages related to the conduct of agency business are presumed to be Federal Records."[6] "NARA Bulletin 2011-02" contains a non-exhaustive list of questions that employees can use to help determine record status.[7] The list provided here uses the term *organization* for the term *agency* in the original list.

- Is the information unique and not available anywhere else?
- Does it contain evidence of the organization's policies,
  business mission, etc.?
- Is this tool being used in relation to the organization's work?
- Is the use of the tool authorized by the organization?
- Is there a business need for the information?

Additional guidance is provided in the following documents:

- NARA Bulletin 2014-02: Guidance on Managing Social Media Records
- NARA Bulletin 2015-02: Guidance on Managing Electronic Messages

NARA Bulletin 2014-02 reminds agencies that content created on social media platforms, including Twitter, is likely to be a federal record. Content posted to third-party sites must be captured and managed according to the agency's policy. Some may be temporary records that have transitory, short-term, or long-term retention requirements, but others may be permanent records requiring eventual transfer to NARA for preservation.[8]

NARA Bulletin 2015-02 applies to text messaging, chat/instant messaging, direct messaging functionality in social media tools or applications, voice messaging, and similar forms of electronic messaging systems. These messages must also be scheduled for disposition based on the author and content. As with email, electronic records created or received in a personal account but which meet the definition of a federal record must be forwarded to an official messaging account within twenty days.[9]

Even when social media content does not rise to the level of a record according to the definition in use, the organization may still be responsible for managing the non-record content. For example, an organization may consider a social networking profile a record but consider comments non-records. That decision will have an impact on what must be retained according to the records retention schedule. It does not, however, absolve the organization from monitoring and evaluating the comments. Security and privacy risks emerge, for example, through posts that reveal trade secrets or those that violate company policy.

Understanding the Origin of Social Media Records

The New York State Archives offers three models for managing the development of content for social media sites based on an organization's desire for control and appetite for risk: (1) the Centralized Approach with strict controls and low risk, (2) the Decentralized Approach with control distributed to units of the organization and moderate risk, and (3) the Laissez-Faire Approach with no internal controls resulting in high risk.[10] The last approach is the most troublesome for the organization and should be remedied as quickly as possible. Although a centralized approach is the least risky (other than not engaging in social media at all, which is *not* an option), in larger organizations, the decentralized approach may make the most sense. For example, more than 200 employees of NARA contributed to 130 social media accounts on 14 different platforms, generating over 250 million views in 2015.[11]

In a recent study of the use of social media by twenty local governments—ten in the United States and ten in Canada—the communications or public relations department most often managed social media. As one public relations manager explained, "social media has the same value implication as a press release, and we need to select the staff as we would any other media spokesperson so that they are approved and then equipped for success."[12]

Although it is possible to submit content to social media sites manually, there are tools that can automate the process regardless of the number of accounts managed. HootSuite provides a dashboard that allows the user to add accounts, schedule posts across major platforms, and add account managers.[13] HootSuite's real-time analytics makes it easy to spot trends and drill down for insights into how the social content is performing.

Capturing Social Media Records

The methods used for the development of content for social media sites have a direct bearing on the methods that could be used to capture social media records. Capture methods also depend on the social media technology and the tools available to the organization. NARA Bulletin 2014-02 suggests the following options—some also suitable for capturing website records:

- using web crawling or other software to create local versions of sites;
- using web capture tools to capture social media;
- using platform specific application programming interfaces (APIs) to pull content;
- using RSS Feeds, aggregators, or manual methods to capture content; and
- using tools built into some social media platforms to export content.[14]

To this list we should add using social media archiving and compliance services.

We will now analyze the content contained within three popular social media technologies—blogs, microblogs, and social networking sites—to consider alternate methods to capture content from two different perspectives, the federal government and the finance industry.

The methods used to determine how best to manage content today can also be applied to technologies, tools, and services not yet in existence.

Blogs, Microblogs, and Social Networking Sites

Blogs

Blogs contain only four significant sections: the header, the content area, the footer, and the sidebar. Organizations that allow comments can delete those that are deemed unacceptable (backed by a policy explaining what is unacceptable). An archive may be maintained for public access. Blog content is fairly simple to capture, because content is created and then uploaded and comments are not necessarily considered records. Here are several options:

- If the blog does not contain comments, the blog posts can be captured and saved to a content management system before they are uploaded to the site.
- If the blog contains comments, an RSS feed can be used to capture comments and forward them to the organization. Some organizations use a sampling technique to capture some but not all the comments made by visitors to the blog.
- If the entire blog, not individual posts, rises to the level of a record, the entire blog site can be captured in the same way a website is captured. For example, content can be harvested using Archive-It and hosted at the Internet Archive data center for public access.
- If the blog is to be retained by the organization—as is the case with the National Library of France—robots, or bots, can be used to carry out bulk harvesting to capture a blog at specific points in time.

Today blogs are often used as websites, with 91 percent of all blogs and 62 percent of the blogs of the top fastest growing companies running on WordPress.[15] WordPress allows administrators to export the content of their blogs to an XML file or export directly to a new WordPress site. Options are available to export All, Posts, Pages, or Feedback. For those who want to transfer to another blog site but don't want to transfer themselves, a Guided Transfer Option is available for a fee.

Microblogs

Twitter has become synonymous with the term *microblog*. Tweets can be posted in a number of ways, including by email, text messaging, instant messaging, through the Twitter website, or by using a social media management tool with a dashboard. One of the easiest ways for an individual to archive tweets is by grabbing the RSS feed for the tweet stream of choice and then adding it to a preferred RSS reader, such as Feedly or NewsBlur. Instagram and Tumblr are also considered microblogs.

Enterprise microblogs are business tools that enable users to communicate, collaborate, and share files with those who are provided access to the network. Two prominent enterprise social networking tools that began as microblogs are Salesforce Chatter and Microsoft's Yammer. These enterprise social networks can be used as desktop or mobile applications or through integration with business applications.

Salesforce Chatter is marketed as the #1 Enterprise social network. It can be extended to allow customer social networks. Users can follow people or records (accounts, cases, opportunities, etc.). Application data (e.g., Microsoft Office documents, PDFs, and image files) can be previewed in the user's Chatter feed. Chatter posts, including those posted from Chatter Mobile, are stored forever unless deleted by an administrator or user. Apps are available to extend the functionality. One app, Chatter Compliance, allows system administrators to archive and search Chatter posts, comments, and private messages. Another app, Archiver For Chatter, accomplishes compliance with FINRA, SEC, and HIPAA by sending a copy of the post and related content to the journaling mailbox specified for long-term retention.

Chatter can be integrated with other applications. For example, customers who use Salesforce Customer Relationship Management can integrate an app called Shipmate for UPS by Zenkraft to prepare shipments and print labels using data in Salesforce CRM. Shipmate is "made social" by integrating with Chatter to track shipments to customers without having the tracking number or logging into a separate system.

Yammer Basic is available for free if you register with a valid company email account. One fee-based version allows access to both the enterprise social network and SharePoint Online. The enterprise version provides administrative features that include customization of the network, user management, security tools, and keyword monitoring. Administrators can export data for legal and regulatory compliance and lock down content as final to prevent editing and new versions. Files and notes can be marked as official and read-only. Those files and notes most actively shared, commented on, viewed, or marked as official appear higher in search results and content directories.

Social Networking Sites

You were introduced to Facebook and LinkedIn earlier. Facebook provides the option to *Download a copy of your Facebook data at the bottom of General Account Settings*. The user can instruct Facebook to create an archive of photos, posts, messages, and other information.[16] An expanded archive can also be downloaded that includes historic information such as the mobile phone numbers added to the account, a list of log-ins stored for the account (which is not complete), and the IP addresses from which the user logged out. It even includes facial recognition data—a unique number based on a comparison of the photos in which you're tagged. Facebook uses this data to help others tag you in photos.

The process of downloading data from Facebook is time-consuming. Persons must use their ID and password to log in and request the download. When the data are archived, an email is sent to the address on the account for confirmation. This process only provides data up to a specific time, so if this method is used, a regular schedule should be developed and adhered to.

LinkedIn's user agreement contains the following statements: "Both you and LinkedIn may terminate the Agreement and your account for any reason or no reason at any time, with or without notice."[17] LinkedIn allows users to download an archive of their data in two stages. Within minutes of making a request, an email is sent with a link to a page where messages, connections, and contacts can be downloaded. Within twenty-four hours, a second email is sent containing a link to a page from which the full archive, including activity and account history, can be downloaded.

As illustrated by these two examples, if an organization chose to download its own data from Facebook and LinkedIn, a great deal of time would be required.

Two approaches to manage social media records are discussed next, one practiced by the Executive Office of the President of the United States and another recommended for members of the finance industry. They illustrate approaches that are dependent upon a number of factors, including governing regulations.

Executive Office of the President

President Barack Obama was known as the "first social media president." Between 2009 and 2017, the Office of the President rolled out a revamped WhiteHouse.gov site featuring a blog, RSS, and an email list. From 2009, the Office of the President communicated with the public through social media accounts including Facebook, Flickr, Vimeo, iTunes, MySpace, Instagram, Snapchat, and Twitter.[18] As with other presidential records, the content of these sites belong to the public. The *digital transformation process* upon the end of the Obama presidency and the start of the Trump presidency had to address three issues: transfer of the accounts to the incoming president, transfer of social media content to NARA, and making the content accessible to the public. Before President Donald J. Trump took office, the following are just some of the actions taken:

- @POTUS, with its 11 million followers but no tweets on the time line, was made available for use by President Trump on January 20, 2017.
- @POTUS44 was created to retain the tweets on Twitter as an accessible archive of President Obama's use of Twitter (see figure 7.2).
- President Obama's tweets were also transferred to NARA to be preserved and made accessible alongside other presidential records.
- An Obama White House Instagram account was created as an accessible archive at https://www.instagram.com/ObamaWhiteHouse/.
- An accessible archive of the Obama White House Facebook page was created at https://www.facebook.com/ObamaWhiteHouse.

- The Facebook and Instagram accounts were renamed to "44" user names and preserved by NARA.

A similar process was planned for other social media accounts including YouTube and Tumblr.[19]

ArchiveSocial developed The Obama White House Social Media Archive, shown in figure 7.3, to allow the pubic to query the content of all White House social media platforms at once.

Visit the fully searchable Social Media Archive to examine 250,000 social media records from more than 100 official White House social media profiles. Among them are the White House Facebook page, the First Lady's Instagram feed, and the @POTUS Twitter time line.

The Finance Industry

The finance industry utilizes blogs, microblogs, and social networking sites to reach out to current and prospective clients. Here, too, we can look to laws and regulations to provide guidance.

The Finance Industry Regulatory Authority (FINRA) was established to protect American investors by making sure the securities industry operates fairly and honestly. FINRA oversees nearly 3,800 broker dealer firms with approximately 634,000 brokers. FINRA has been providing guidance to its members about social media communications since it issued Regulatory Notice 10-06 in 2010 followed by Regulatory Notice 11-39 in 2011. Both notices made it clear that "every firm that intends to communicate, or permit its associated persons to communicate, through social media sites must first ensure that it can retain records of those communications as required by Rules 17a-3 and 17a-4 under the Securities and Exchange Act of 1934 and NASD Rule 3110."[20] Firms were instructed to retain all social media activities for not less than three years, the first two in an easily accessible place.[21]

FIGURE 7.2 Accessible archive on Twitter for President Barack Obama.

SOURCE: https://twitter.com/potus44?lang=en.

The treatment of blogs and social networking sites such as Facebook, Twitter, and LinkedIn under FINRA Rule 2210 depends on whether the content is static or dynamic.[22] Static blog posts, for example, constitute advertisements and require approval prior to posting. If the blog allowed users to engage in real-time interactive communications, the blog is considered an interactive electronic forum, and the contents do not need preapproval. Static content on social networking sites needed preapproval, but dynamic content on those same sites does not. According to FINRA, third-party posts are not records unless endorsed by a representative of the firm. Actions have consequences. Do not *favorite* or *like* third-party posts and be careful of retweets.

FINRA Regulatory Notice 12-29,[23] with an effective date of February 4, 2013, reduced the number of communication categories from six to three: institutional communication (distributed only to institutional investors), retail communication (distributed or made available to more than twenty-five retail investors within any thirty calendar-day period), and correspondence (distributed or made available to twenty-five or fewer retail investors within any thirty-day calendar period). Social media communications fall under the retail communication category and they:

- are exempt from pre-use approval requirements (no approval needed before posting);
- must be managed "after" posting;
- must comply with NASD Rule 2210(b)(4)(A) concerning recordkeeping requirements; and
- must be retained for a period of three years (two years on the premises).

In 2014, FINRA conducted a review of its communication rules. Several issues were raised by survey participants including the need for additional guidance on how to distinguish

FIGURE 7.3 Social Media Archive captured and managed by ArchiveSocial.

SOURCE: https://archivesocial.com/whitehouse/.

between static and interactive content and clarification of rules applied to web, social media, and mobile content.[24] As a result of the review, Regulatory Notice 17-18, "Social Media and Digital Communications," was released in April 2017. Illustrating the evolving nature of communication technology, the following guidance was provided related to text messaging:

> Every firm that intends to communicate, or permit its associated persons to communicate, with regard to its business through a *text messaging app or chat service* must first ensure that it can retain records of those communications as required by SEC Rules 17a-3 and 17a-4 and FINRA Rule 4511. SEC and FINRA rules require that, for record retention purposes, the content of the communication determines what must be retained.[25]

When it comes to FINRA rules and guidance, there is no fresh start—each builds upon or modifies previous instructions. Keeping up with the changes to ensure the firm understands what it must do to be in compliance is a time-consuming task. Ensuring compliance is an added challenge. You've already been introduced to several services that provide archiving solutions for financial advisors—including Smarsh and ArchiveSocial. Another, GlobalRelay, was designed specifically to meet the recordkeeping and compliance requirements of the financial industry put in place by the Security and Exchange Commission (SEC), the Financial Industry Regulatory Authority (FINRA), and the *Federal Rules of Civil Procedure* (FRCP). It captures and archives an authentic and complete record of more than forty-five data types including social media, instant messages, and mobile messages.[26]

Records Scheduling Challenges and Solutions

Some social media records can be considered duplicate records. This can easily be understood in the case of a video created in-house and uploaded to YouTube. The original is often stored within the enterprise in its native format and the version posted to the social media site is considered a copy. In a traditional paper-based world, a copy is assigned a shorter retention period than the original. The copy is destroyed based upon the retention schedule. In reality, once a digital object is shared through the use of a social media, it is unrealistic to believe that all copies can be disposed of according to a retention schedule. Although an enterprise may have a terms of service agreement that allows it to close an account and remove the content, due to the viral nature of social networking, it is extremely likely that copies will exist that cannot be located and destroyed.

Once records are captured into an enterprise content management, records management system, or other digital repository, records retention requirements can be applied. The granular nature of retention schedules designed for paper-based records poses a problem to those attempting to manage records created by social media technologies and provides additional support for the big buckets approach to records retention introduced in chapter 4.

Automated solutions are the best option to records identification, capture, and scheduling for organizations large and small, public and private. Unfortunately, some organizations continue to place the ultimate responsibility for records management decisions on the creators of the records, and mistakes are made. To protect the organization and its employees, social media policies are needed.

Social Media Policy Development

Policies are high-level plans that embrace the general goals and acceptable procedures of an organization. They are established to document a definite course or method of action. Most firms have more than one policy—such as those for records management and electronic communication.

The social media policy may start out simple if the organization is in the early stages of embracing social media technology. It will grow as the company becomes more deeply or broadly engaged. The policies will contain general guidelines governing employee behavior as well as more specific information related to social media technologies used by the organization. All stakeholders, including information technology, business units, human resources, records management, marketing, and compliance, must be involved in developing the policy. Some organizations have social media teams. Members of this team can form the core of the social media policy development committee. A number of organizations have posted their social media policies online. For example, IBM published the "IBM Social Computing Guidelines" for blogs, wikis, social networks, virtual worlds, and social media online on its website.[27] The Social Media Governance website hosts a database with links to almost 200 social media policies.[28] Review some of these before beginning to write your own social media policy.

General Social Media Policy Contents

The social media policy should address security, privacy, and communications issues, as well as records management. At a minimum, include the following general information:

- Specify who is authorized to represent the organization in social media (e.g., representatives from marketing or communications).
- Encourage employees to include a standard disclaimer when publishing content that makes clear that the views shared are representative of the employee and not necessarily of the organization.
- Specify who is authorized to create social media accounts for your organization and/or provide an online form to allow an employee to apply for one or more social media accounts.
- Clarify the content of messages to be shared through social media on behalf of the organization; for example, sharing of personal messages on organization social media sites may be prohibited.
- Specify the criteria to be followed before implementing a new social media initiative to obtain approval that will guarantee the resources needed to ensure success.
- Include a reference to your organization's records management policy within the social media policy.

Social Media Strategy

The use of social media and other electronic communication tools is now an integral part of every organization's daily operations. To take advantage of the benefits and minimize the risks, a strategy should be developed, implemented, reviewed, and revised. Employees at NARA were pioneers in adopting the use of social media for themselves and provided guidance to other federal agencies. NARA's Social Media Strategy for Fiscal Years 2017–2020 identifies four main goals: Tell Great Stories; Deepen Engagement; Grow Our Audience; and Cultivate a Community of Practice.[29] All strategies and actions are designed to help NARA reach those goals. Equally important is the inclusion of metrics in the form of "data in action" to help the agency provide content of value and interest to the public. It is important to collect not only statistics that reveal how many people were reached and who they are, but also what actions they took as a result of visiting the site, such as commenting, sharing, liking, replying. Beyond the number of comments, the NARA metrics look at the kinds of comments—what is the sentiment of the reaction exhibited by visitors to the site?

Integration with the Electronic Content/Records Management System

Leaders of large companies acknowledge the fact that there will never be one repository for all content. That means, for content to be managed by a records management system, a connection must be made from different source systems. Let's look at one example.

Enterprise Social Media and Electronic Records Management

We'll use Salesforce Chatter, discussed previously, to demonstrate one potential solution to apply records management control to data created in the clouds.

Salesforce is the leader in CRM cloud services. Chatter is built on the Force.com platform that also enables the CRM software. Chatter feeds are stored permanently unless deleted by an administrator or user. The Salesforce customer who has records from both business transactions and social interactions that must be managed can store those records in an electronic content management system like Open Text's Extended ECM for Salesforce, which possesses the following capabilities: Document Management, Records Management, Capture, Archiving, Workflow, and Collaboration.[30]

This example specifies specific products, but the process used to determine the solution is the important lesson. As a records manager, you will need to understand transaction and social systems and then conduct some research in order to determine the best content/records management solution.

Public Social Media and Electronic Records Management

The best approach to capturing content is to employ an automatic archiving solution. Recently, a number of social media archiving solutions for business compliance and records management have come on the market. Two examples already mentioned are ArchiveSocial and Smarsh.

The ArchiveSocial system is entirely web-based and archives data from social networking platforms including Facebook, LinkedIn, Twitter, Instagram, YouTube, Vimeo, Flickr, Pinterest, and Google+. ArchiveSocial features a sophisticated search interface for filtering social media content and generating PDF exports of the entire social media conversation surrounding the key words searched (see figure 7.4). Records can be viewed in their original context with the Social Media Replay feature, and changes over time (e.g., edits, deletions, hidden content) can be viewed using Version History. ArchiveSocial maintains the native format of each record with metadata. A time-stamped digital signature applied to each individual record establishes proof of authenticity when providing electronic records as evidence in response to an e-discovery request. Government agencies, faced with a growing number of Freedom of Information requests, can simplify search and retrieval of requested public records using this solution.

Smarsh is an SaaS firm that provides hosted archiving and compliance solutions for archiving electronic communications, including email, instant messaging, and social media platforms (e.g., Facebook, LinkedIn, and Twitter). Captured content is preserved in redundant, geographically dispersed data centers and burned to WORM optical storage. The content is accessible via a web-based management console, and it is possible to track the entire thread of social media posts from multiple individuals, providing context to the conversation. Records are retained according to the organization's retention policies, including legal holds. Administrators can retrieve as many messages as necessary in original form on demand. They can download content to a PC or portable media device, or export it for e-discovery in the electronic discovery reference model (EDRM) XML interchange format schema and transfer it to document review and processing systems. Part of this service is delivery of monthly copies of data on encrypted DVDs. Integration with enterprise social collaboration tools is possible.

These examples are provided to help you understand the logic behind developing records management solutions for records created through the use of social media. By the time

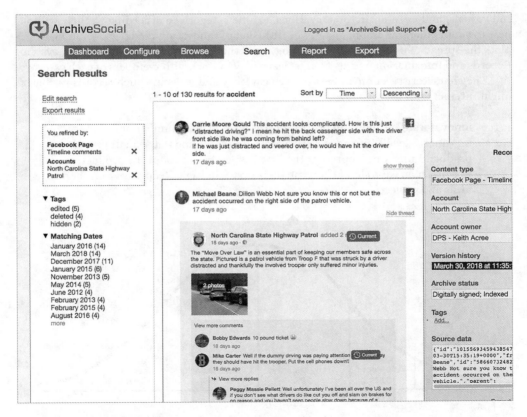

FIGURE 7.4 ArchiveSocial interface showing Facebook page posts and underlying metadata.

SOURCE: Courtesy of ArchiveSocial, http://archivesocial.com/.

you read this, the landscape will have changed dramatically. But what will still be important is that you are prepared to investigate and understand solutions that will help you manage your organization's records and information. A similar thought process can be applied to new emerging technologies demanding attention from records and information managers. How do we know what they are? The next section provides some suggestions.

DIFFUSION OF INNOVATION AND TREND SPOTTING

As we experienced with the evolution of social media, emerging technology will always require updates and adjustments to records management practices. Records and information managers must not only deal with *what is* but must also be prepared for *what will be*. This is not an easy task but one that can be accomplished by identifying emerging technologies, monitoring their adoption rate, and evaluating their potential impact on the RIM program.

Diffusion of Innovation

Individuals, and even entire organizations, can be categorized according to their willingness to adopt emerging technologies. The diffusion of innovation model shown in figure 7.5 plots the spread of a new idea or technology over time among members of a social system. Records and information managers must learn how to work with members of each category.

The characteristics of members of each category and ways in which records managers might interact with them follow:

- **Innovators:** The adoption process begins with a small number of visionary, imaginative, well-informed risk-takers who are willing to try an unproven product. Innovators represent the first 2.5 percent to adopt the product. Records managers should become their first followers. Keep an eye on their ideas and projects.

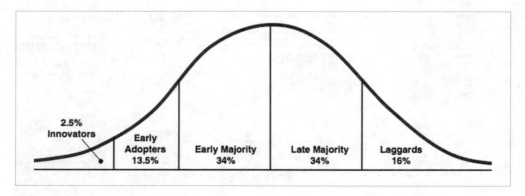

FIGURE 7.5 Diffusion of innovation based on categories of adopters.

SOURCE: Wikipedia, s.v. "Innovation Adoption Lifecycle," by Everett Rogers, last modified December 30, 2011, https://upload.wikimedia.org/wikipedia/en/archive/4/45/20110714211709%21DiffusionOfInnovation.png.

- **Early adopters:** Once benefits begin to become apparent based on the positive response of innovators, early adopters begin to purchase the product or subscribe to the service. Early adopters tend to be educated opinion leaders and represent about 13.5 percent of consumers. Records managers should foster relationships with this group and offer to assist them to identify and resolve records management challenges. They enjoy talking about their initiatives and welcome the opportunity to be part of a pilot records management project.
- **Early majority:** Members of this group are careful and tend to avoid risk. The early majority adopts the product once it has been proven by the early adopters. They rely on recommendations from others who have experience with the product or initiative. They look for simple, proven, better ways of doing what they already do. The early majority represents 34 percent of consumers. Records managers should be prepared to provide rationale and guidance to this group in managing records created using emerging technologies.
- **Late majority:** Members of this group are conservative pragmatists who avoid risk. They are somewhat skeptical and will acquire a product or subscribe to a service only after it has become commonplace. The late majority represents about 34 percent of consumers. In the product world, their only fear is of not fitting in; this carries over to the workplace. Records managers should be prepared to provide concrete examples of how the members of the previously described categories address records management considerations surrounding emerging technology and the benefits they derive from doing so.
- **Laggards:** Laggards hold on to the status quo as long as possible. They avoid change and may not adopt a new product or service until traditional alternatives no longer are available. Laggards represent about 16 percent of consumers. Records managers should be prepared to address their criticisms and provide as much information as possible about the new products or procedures. Like the late majority, they should see examples of how others have successfully adopted the innovation. They may need to be granted a great deal of control over when, where, how, and whether they will modify their behavior to manage records resulting from new technology.

Trend Spotting

Those responsible for records management within an organization should scan the environment to spot emerging technologies and trends that may impact RIM in the future.

Learn to Trend-Spot

Trend spotters identify changes taking place in both the short term and long term and share stories about the value of the change in order to influence others to adopt that change. Trend spotting is an industry, and expert trend spotters (e.g., forecasters and futurists) can be employed to help an organization understand both tangible (e.g., smartphones) and intangible (e.g., expectations) trends.

You can spot trends yourself by using these approaches:

- Listen to others around you. Identify the innovators and early adopters in your organization. Get involved in innovative projects to experience change yourself.
- Listen and learn from those outside of your organization. Attend conferences and trade shows, speak to colleagues, and understand what is important to them before you see it in print.
- Watch/read/browse journals, newspapers, and the internet. Learn what is happening with emerging technologies, in records management and related fields, and in the industry in which your organization operates.
- Look more broadly at other industries that may impact your own.
- Use software and/or services for spotting trends. Search the internet for trend-spotting software and services.

Trend-Spotting Service: Google Trends

Google Trends is a free online service that allows a search of one or multiple terms to determine the world's interest in topics of your choice (www.google.com/trends/). You can search in *real time* (a feature added in 2016) to get the results of a random sample of searchers over the last seven days or in *non-real time*. The non-real time search provides another random sample of the full Google dataset that can go back anywhere from 2004 to approximately thirty-six hours ago.

You can compare results for five different topics at one time. The results are plotted on a line graph showing interest over time and they are plotted on a map chart to indicate interest by region. Queries related to the search terms are also presented.

A search on three key terms—social media, cloud computing, and artificial intelligence—between 2004 and 2017 clearly shows an increasing interest in social media; however, interest in cloud computing peaked in 2011 and has trended downward since then (see figure 7.6). The data on cloud computing reinforces a 2011 prediction by International Data Corporation (IDC), that *cloud computing* as a buzzword will decrease as the use of cloud services becomes part of the mainstream.[31] What some may find surprising is that the current increased interest in artificial intelligence has not yet brought that search term in line with the interest expressed in January of 2004.

Journals and Research Firms

A number of analysts and research firms provide information on technologies and trends that you will find useful. A description of three of those resources—*MIT Technology Review,* International IDC, and Gartner—as well as examples of recent predictions, follow. Note the references to different groups along the diffusion of innovation curve shown in figure 7.1 in their predictions.

The MIT Technology Review, published by the Massachusetts Institute of Technology (MIT), identifies emerging technologies and analyzes their impact for technology leaders, business leaders, and researchers who create and fund the innovations that drive the global economy. *MIT Technology Review* is "a global community of business and thought leaders, innovators and early adopters, entrepreneurs and investors, as well as all of MIT's alumni."[32]

Don't limit yourself to monitoring trends within your own industry. Advances in another industry may have a significant impact on your work in the future.

On the May 2017 list of ten breakthrough technologies are those that can help fight cancer, reverse paralysis, and create cheap and continuous power. One device that appeals to individuals wishing to capture a 360-degree record of their experiences is the "360-degree selfie." Although it has been possible to record 360-degree photos and videos for some time, the process was time-consuming and expensive. Today, several cameras, such as the ALLie Camera that retails for less than $500, support fast stitching (to produce the 360 degree effect) and live-streaming to share what is recorded. Journalists from various news outlets use similar cameras (e.g., the Samsung Gear 360) to produce spherical photos and videos that document events such as hurricanes and visits to refugee camps.[33]

Let's consider this particular innovation—360-degree selfie cameras—in terms of relationship to law enforcement and RIM. In the United States, police officers are required to file reports of incidents, crimes, arrests, and accidents investigated. The reports describe what was done, what was not done, and why. They may include a description of sounds, bloodstains, statements, demeanor of witnesses, and more. The majority of these are considered public records, which can be read by insurance companies, attorneys, journalists, and other interested parties. In many cases, dash cams on police vehicles provide an unbiased view of the event that occurs in front of the dash cam. A growing number of localities across the nation are beginning to allocate funding for body cams that, again, allow us to view what is directly in front of the officer. But that is not the complete picture. Often, what is occurring directly around the immediate environment is also important and should

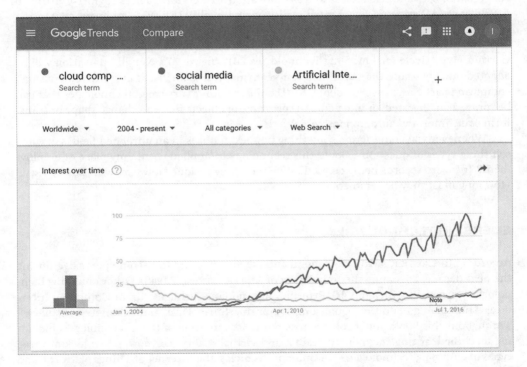

FIGURE 7.6 Results of a Google Trends search on three topics: Cloud computing, social media, and artificial intelligence.

be part of the record; 360-degree recordings would expand the picture to provide this additional information. What may be surprising to some is that police officers often write up their reports without being able to view the video first. That, too, is slowly changing. In March 2017, a House committee voted 17-0 to allow police officers in Tallahassee, Florida, to view the footage from their body cameras before submitting reports or responding to complaints.[34]

IDC is a provider of market intelligence, advisory services, and events for the information technology and telecommunications markets. More than a decade ago, IDC began documenting the emergence and evolution of the third platform, which is built on cloud, mobile, Big Data/analytics, and social technologies. Adoption of these technologies has prompted a digital transformation that, according to Frank Gens, Senior Vice President and Chief Analyst at IDC, has resulted in a shift in digital transformation efforts from "project" or "initiative" status to strategic business imperative.[35]

Emerging technologies may be considered *disruptive technologies,* a term coined by Clayton M. Christensen in 1995 to describe a new, emerging technology that replaces an established one. By 2003, Christensen had replaced the term *disruptive technology* with the term *disruptive innovation* to broaden the concept to include the strategy or business model that the technology enables that creates the disruptive impact.[36] Traditional examples of disruptive innovations (also termed disruptive technologies by some) are the automobile and the computer. More recent examples are the Internet of Things and blockchain technology. *Innovative accelerators* are used to advance (kick start) disruptive innovation initiatives. According to IDC, nearly 75 percent of IT spending by 2019 will be for third platform core technologies and services, as well as innovation accelerators such as cognitive/artificial intelligence (AI) systems, augmented reality/virtual reality (AR/VR), and next-generation security.[37]

Gartner, an information technology research and advisory company, published the Gartner Hype Cycle for Emerging Technologies 2017 (figure 7.7). Not all innovation will be adopted quickly—note the more than ten-year time frame for *smart dust* (extremely small computing particles, sensors, robots, RFID chips, or other very small technologies that can be sprayed on, ingested, or injected), 4-D printing (of objects that can change shape or transform over time), and autonomous vehicles.

Whenever you come across something new, even if it is in an unrelated field, ask yourself these types of questions: Could this technology be applied within my place of employment? If so, are records being created? Where do they reside? How can/will they be used? How long must they be retained?

EMERGING TECHNOLOGIES

According to Gartner, Artificial General Intelligence is going to become pervasive during the next decade, becoming the foundation of AI as a Service (AIaaS). Other emerging technologies to monitor include: 4D Printing, Autonomous Vehicles, Brain-Computer Interfaces, Human Augmentation, Quantum Computing, Smart Dust, and Volumetric Displays.[38] Throughout this book, you'll come across references to some of these technologies including machine learning, augmented reality, and virtual reality. For now, let us look at three types of emerging technologies—autonomous vehicles, the Internet of Things platform, and blockchain technology —to see if and how they might impact records and information management.

Autonomous Vehicles

Billionaire tech investor Jim Breyer predicts artificial intelligence (AI) will be five to ten times bigger than the social media market, especially when AI's self-learning capabilities are applied to the healthcare and finance fields.[39] However, one exciting application of AI that might be relevant to the majority of us is autonomous vehicles (i.e., smart cars).

Smart cars learn to drive as humans do—by looking at the road ahead and making decisions. Also like humans, they learn from their mistakes. Google is developing an algorithm to allow cars to learn to drive—expect that release in 2020. Tesla's smart cars have been on the road for a few years now, but the autopilot system is not yet fully functional.

What does this have to do with records management or information governance? Quite a bit! Because intelligent systems in smart cars can respond to voice comments, it is conceivable for them to record all conversations taking place in the vehicle. In the case of an accident between two vehicles, both vehicles could immediately send accident information to law enforcement and emergency responders. Included among the data gathered may be facial images of those inside or outside of the vehicle; facial recognition can be employed to identify those involved.

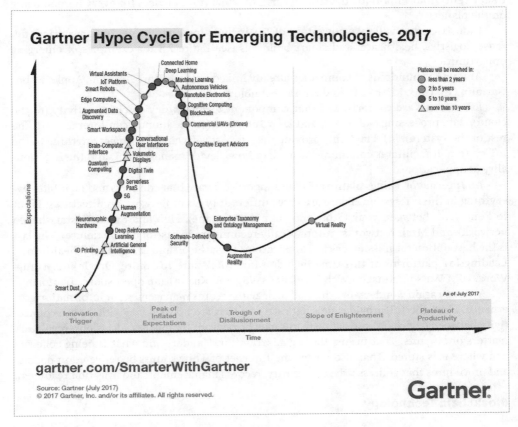

FIGURE 7.7 Gartner's Hype Cycle for Emerging Technologies 2017.

SOURCE: Gartner (August 2017).

Beside information about the accident itself, other data will be gathered, such as the identity of the driver and all passengers, start and end points, travel route, time and date of trip, speed (continuously monitored), and payment (a growing trend for rental automobiles). The data will most likely be stored in the cloud, and the data controllers will most likely be automakers and rental car companies who may find it lucrative to sell this information to others, including government, insurance companies, and other businesses. For example, city transportation departments would benefit from understanding when most accidents occur to prioritize road safety projects. And insurance companies may interpret the data sent by smart cars and determine you are a poor driver of your regular car, which could result in an immediate increase of your premium.

Internet of Things Platform

The Internet of Things (IoT), born sometime between 2008 and 2009, is basically a network connecting any device with an on/off switch to the internet and to one another. The IoT can include devices as near to you as your home washer and dryer or devices as remote as the drill on an oil rig or the jet engine of an airplane. These devices can collect and exchange data using embedded sensors. Business Insider Intelligence estimates there will be more than twenty-four billion IoT devices on earth by 2020 (four devices for every human being on the planet).[40]

Industries that will take advantage of IoT include manufacturing, transportation, defense, logistics, healthcare, and smart buildings (see figure 7.8 for examples of emerging opportunities).

Among the hundreds of companies already linked to the IoT are Amazon, Apple, Fitbit, Garmin, GE, IBM, Microsoft, and Zebra Technologies.[41]

IoT systems are comprised of four components: sensors/devices, connectivity (to the cloud), data processing (software), and User Interface (so the human can interact with the rest of the system). IoT Platforms provide the support software to connect anything to the IoT system. It facilitates communication, data flow, device management, and the functionality of applications.

An Internet of Things platform is the support software that connects and facilitates everything in the IoT system. There are three different types of network architectures: Point to Point (e.g., between your Fitbit and your smartphone), Hub and Spoke (a star-shaped network), and Mesh Networks (automatically reconfigure in case of device failure). The last is the best option for mission critical applications (e.g., the oil and gas industry, healthcare). Leading IoT platforms at this time include Microsoft Azure IoT Suite, Oracle IoT, ThingWorx, IBM Watson, Amazon Web Services (AWS), and Kaa IoT (an open-source platform).

You may again wonder what this had to do with records management or information governance. First, the IoT provides new data streams that are not possible without the connectivity between devices. Those data streams may be relevant for business decisions, regulatory matters or lawsuits. That means the organization must understand what is being collected and where it is stored. That also means the Internet of Things must be reflected in policies and procedures that address privacy, security, records management, and litigation readiness.

Blockchain Technology

Blockchain is a digitized, decentralized, immutable ledger for recording the history of cryptocurrency transactions. It was developed as the accounting method for the virtual currency

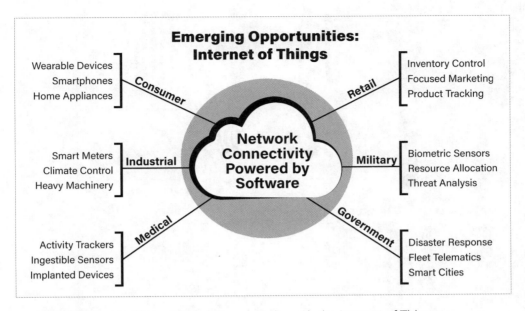

FIGURE 7.8 Exchanging and analyzing data through the Internet of Things.

Bitcoin. Bitcoin (Bitcoin.org) uses peer-to-peer technology, eliminating the need for a central authority or bank; all transactions are carried out by the network. Notice that in figure 7.7, Blockchain technology is moving down from the peak of inflated expectations toward the trough of disillusionment. That is likely to be a temporary readjustment of expectations as we are now beginning to see other vendors provide business applications of blockchain technology without the need for cryptocurrency exchange. Leaders in the Blockchain as a Service (BaaS) field are Microsoft, IBM, and Deloitte. (See figure 7.9.)

Another firm, Factom, provides technology that can be adapted to almost any organization. Although it does issue its own cryptocurrency, called *Factoids*, it separates the blockchain from the currency, enabling use for events outside of monetary transfers. Factom has been working with the US Department of Defense and the Bill and Melinda Gates Foundation to develop new ways to secure records. Their goal is to use their blockchain-based software system to record, manage, and share records while ensuring sensitive information is appropriately shared and privacy is respected.

> The blockchain is an incorruptible digital ledger of economic transactions that can be programmed to record not just financial transactions but virtually everything of value.
>
> —Don and Alex Tapscott, authors, *Blockchain Revolution* (2016), https://www.linkedin.com/pulse/whats-next-generation-internet-surprise-its-all-don-tapscott/

You may remember the banking crisis of 2007 that resulted in millions of mortgage foreclosures over the next few years. Since then over 6.2 million families have lost their homes.[42] The first decision in the "produce-the-note" defense occurred in 2007 when a federal judge in Cleveland threw out fourteen foreclosures by Deutsche Bank National Trust Co. Although at least one of the families eventually lost their home, the decision was

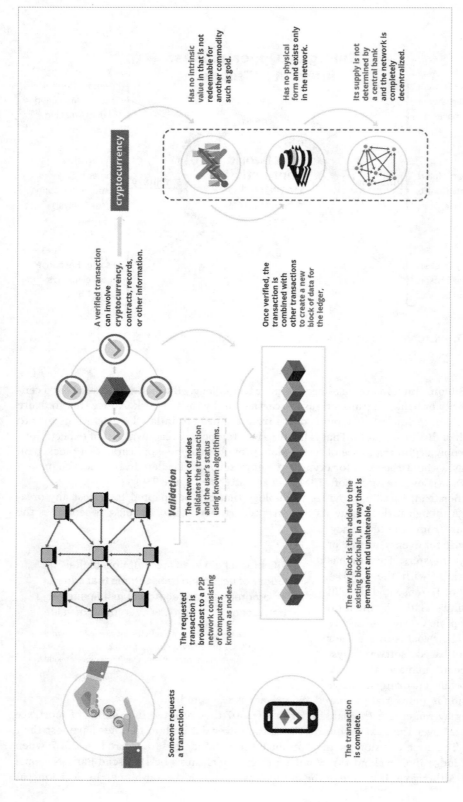

FIGURE 7.9 Transaction processing using blockchain technology.

SOURCE: BlockGeeks, https://blockgeeks.com/guides/what-is-blockchain-technology/

considered a success in keeping the families in their homes a while longer, and it alerted the mortgage industry to the consequences of poor recordkeeping.[43] However, as recently as 2016, staffing firms were recruiting default breach specialists to locate missing documents needed to complete the *chain of title* prior to foreclosure referral. How much easier and less expensive it would be to do it right the first time!

Released in 2016, Factom Harmony is a blockchain solution for the mortgage industry. The average mortgage loan produced 500 documents in 2014. The industry itself produces five trillion pages of new documents each year, with a need to keep forty trillion pages of mortgage history. As illustrated by the "produce the note" defense to prevent or delay foreclosure, the biggest challenge occurs when the mortgage company is asked to re-create a decision (not a document) years later. Using blockchain technology, this required data can be provided.

SUMMARY

Social media is included in this chapter not because it is a new, emerging technology, but because it is a developing technology that continues to challenge records and information managers. The good news is that solutions to capture and manage social media content, including enlisting the services of a social media archiving provider, are also evolving.

Although records and information managers deal with day-to-day responsibilities, they must also scan the horizon for emerging technologies that may impact their RIM programs in the future. One way to keep abreast of emerging technologies is to identify trends. This can be accomplished by listening to others within and outside your organization; watching, reading, and browsing journals, newspapers, and the internet; looking more broadly outside of your own industry; and using software and/or services to spot trends.

The diffusion of innovation model introduced in this chapter plots the adoption of new technology over time. In addition to understanding how society at large adopts new technology, it is necessary to understand how members of the organization attempt to implement it in the workplace. The Gartner Hype Cycle model provides an overview of emerging technology through its various stages from innovation through productivity. Three of those innovations, autonomous vehicles, the Internet of Things platform, and blockchain technology were examined to better understand how they might impact records and information management and information governance. You can use a similar approach to explore the potential impact of other emerging technologies.

One of the emerging technologies introduced in this chapter is blockchain technology. On the Gartner Hype Cycle (figure 7.3) it is represented as moving down the Peak of Inflated Expectations into the Trough of Disillusionment. However, by mid-2017 it became a hot topic in various industries including healthcare, banking, and the travel industry. All indications are that blockchain technology may move into the Slope of Enlightenment more quickly than many other emerging technologies.

Dr. Victoria Lemieux, an associate professor at the University of British Columbia (UBC), leads the University's research effort Blockchain@UBC. In her contribution to this chapter, Dr. Lemieux provides an introduction to this emerging technology as applied to recordkeeping and presents questions that should be asked and answered before an organization can determine if blockchain technology is appropriate for them.

PARADIGM

Blockchain Technology and Recordkeeping

Victoria L. Lemieux
Associate Professor, Archival Science
The University of British Columbia, Vancouver, Canada (vlemieux@mail.ubc.ca)

B lockchain is a novel technology that is often described as a distributed ledger. In block-chain systems, transaction records are grouped into blocks that are cryptographically secured in an append-only, time-ordered chain to provide, at least in theory,[44] an immutable ledger. In addition, the ledger is copied to distributed computer nodes communicating with one another via a peer-to-peer, mesh network.[45] The unique combination of cryptographically chaining transactions together and distributing copies of the ledger to many nodes permits detection of any alteration of the transaction records, allows parties to transact business without necessarily trusting one another, and creates a transparent and immutable[46] record. Increasingly, the business rules that determine when and how a transaction will take place are encoded into computer code in "smart contracts" and executed automatically on the blockchain. This allows different types of transactions to take place autonomously on a blockchain, without any human intervention.[47]

Just like other technologies before it, blockchain technology is beginning to transform the way that organizations communicate and keep records. All around the world governments and businesses are piloting the use of blockchain technology in a wide variety of sectors, including in the medical, real estate, financial, and education domains. An ongoing study of different types of blockchain projects for recordkeeping suggests that there are currently three basic types of blockchain solutions in operation today (see figure 7.10).[48] In the "mirror" type, the blockchain serves as a repository of "digital fingerprints," or hashes, of the records in an originating system. In the "digital record" type, records are no longer just mirrored or fingerprinted on chain but are actively created on chain in, for example, the form of smart contracts. Finally, in the "tokenized" type, not only are records captured on chain, but assets, such as land, agricultural products, and creative works, are represented and captured on chain by linking them to an underlying cryptocurrency or digital token.

Given the way in which blockchain technology is beginning to transform organizational communication and recordkeeping, information governance professionals may be called upon to help their organizations decide whether they need a blockchain solution and, if so, how to go about implementing one.

In thinking about the application of blockchain technology, the first decision an organization must make is whether a blockchain solution is necessary. Many organizations are simply jumping on the blockchain bandwagon, possibly for fear of being left behind.[49] Before considering whether to launch a blockchain project, however, organizations should consider whether blockchain technology is the right direction to take. Typical questions for consideration include:[50]

1. *Is your organization happy with its current recordkeeping system (e.g., a relational database)?* All organizations keep records of transactions in some kind of system, but often that system of recordkeeping may not work well for the organization. If not, there may be an opening to improve an organization's recordkeeping

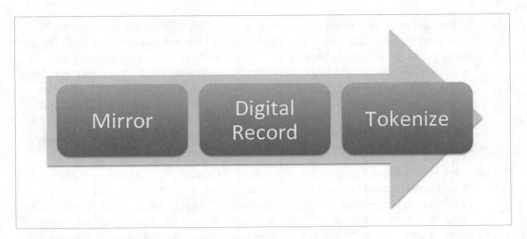

FIGURE 7.10 A Typology of Blockchain Recordkeeping Solutions.

SOURCE: Victoria L. Lemieux , "A Typology of Blockchain Recordkeeping Solutions and Some Reflections on Their Archival Implications," *2nd IEEE Big Data Workshop on Computational Archival Science.* Figure is Victoria L. Lemieux's own rendering.

by applying blockchain technology. In some cases, an organization may be reasonably happy with its current technology but still motivated to explore the application of blockchain technology to avoid being "disrupted" or to take advantage of a strategic business opportunity offered by blockchain that is not available with its current technology solution.

2. *Do you need to ensure that multiple parties, who do not inherently trust one another, can each see and attest to a synchronized authoritative source of the "truth"?* If the application area for blockchain technology that your organization is considering does not involve multiple parties to a business transaction who need to update a shared recordkeeping system (e.g., database) to which they must refer back for trustworthy evidence of completed business transactions, then blockchain technology may not be needed. Some also argue that blockchain systems are most applicable to situations in which the transacting parties do not necessarily need to identify themselves or trust one another.[51]

3. *Do you need a guarantee that any party creating transactions between untrusted organizations or multiple jurisdictional boundaries is following the same known set of rules?* When multiple stakeholders interact with one another in a business transaction according to a shared and known set of business rules there may be an advantage to using blockchain technology, especially when those stakeholders do not necessarily trust each other and also collectively need to add records to a recordkeeping system in the process of completing a transaction. An example would be an online marketplace where the buyer and seller do not necessarily know or trust one another and want to exchange goods for currency.

4. *Do you have reasons why you would want to eliminate or reduce the role of an intermediary, such as high transaction costs (e.g., a clearing house or a bank with high fees)?* Middlemen, who act as disinterested intermediaries to facilitate business transactions among stakeholders, typically add expense and complexity

to the execution of organizational transactions. Think about the fees that banks charge to transfer funds from one person to another, for example. Additionally, in some contexts, the trusted intermediaries prove to be not so trustworthy after all (e.g., officials who accept bribes to make fraudulent accounting entries). In such cases, the potential to eliminate intermediaries through applying blockchain's peer-to-peer transaction capabilities can be an attractive way to cut costs and reduce the risk of fraud or tampering. If your organization is the middleman, you may want to begin experimenting with blockchain technology to avoid being suddenly disrupted by it.

5. *Do you care about highly secured methods of transacting?* Blockchain's use of cryptographic techniques and distribution of copies of the ledger make it a relatively secure form of transacting business. This is not to say that it is without security or other information risks, however.[52] In addition, blockchain solutions come in many varieties and use different consensus mechanisms (or means of chaining together blocks of business transactions),[53] each of which may trade off security to maximize other capabilities, such as speed and transaction throughput. In recommending the application of blockchain technology, information governance professionals need to understand the implications of these design trade-offs for the application of blockchain technology within their organizations.

6. *Do you need stakeholders to have the ability to access shared evidence of business transactions?* Blockchain technology creates a transparent record of transactions in the form of a hash indicating those transactions that have been securely added to the chain. Each node in the blockchain's distributed network keeps a full or partial copy of the ledger so that it is always possible to check whether a transaction is legitimate or not. Through the use of blockchain search interfaces, such as the Block Explorer for the Bitcoin blockchain, it is possible to search for and confirm the existence and legitimacy of transactions.[54]

7. *Do you need something that helps ensure that assets are not used or "spent" twice?* Blockchain technology solves what is called the "double spending" problem. For example, if you have a house that you are selling to a buyer, that buyer wants assurance that you cannot turn around and sell the same house to someone else before they have a chance to occupy it. Blockchain's unique design makes sure that you can only use or spend an asset once, not twice.

8. *Do you need a guarantee that transactions have not been tampered with or altered?* In the digital era, when records are often subject to intentional or accidental alteration, it is important to be able to detect if the integrity of records has been affected. Through the use of digital signatures, which produce a unique hash fingerprint of records, it is relatively easy to detect if records entered into a blockchain have been altered by comparing the hash of those records in the blockchain with a subsequent hash of the same records. If the two hashes do not match, the integrity of the records may be in question.

9. *Do you need to maintain data synchronization, consistency, and integrity across multiple data stores that may transcend untrusted organizations or other such jurisdictional boundaries?* Because blockchain technology operates as a distributed system in which there are multiple copies of the ledger kept by the

nodes, or participants, in the network, records of transactions are synchronized and consistent across the network, and their integrity can always be checked. If a copy of the ledger held by one node does not match copies held by other nodes, then it may be untrustworthy and need to be eliminated from the distributed ledger.

10. *Does your organization operate in a fluid regulatory environment rather than an established, tightly regulated space?* The more highly regulated and tightly controlled the institutional context in which a potential blockchain solution may be implemented, the more difficult it may be to make the transition to a blockchain solution. Generally speaking, early adopters of blockchain solutions are emerging where regulation and institutions are weak, which presents an opportunity for blockchains to be applied to solve a problem as opposed to disrupting an existing stable environment.

If the answer to all or most of these questions is "yes," then blockchain technology is the way to go. If not, then more traditional technologies may be best.[55] For most organizations, the answers to these questions will not be a binary yes or no, but a matter of degree. Organizations operating in areas with weak state institutions (e.g., lesser-resourced nations) or that must interact with costly intermediaries (e.g., finance), and that have a high risks and costs associated with establishing the provenance of commodities such as diamonds and food, may be experiencing enough "pain points" to take on the risk of being early blockchain system adopters. For other organizations, it may make more sense to wait until blockchain technology becomes cheaper, more developed and more accessible.

Having determined that, in theory, blockchain technology is suited to your organization's use case, the path to practically validating its suitability and the process of digital transformation can be a long and complex one. For one thing, blockchain technology is still evolving and changes to its design and configuration are occurring at a fast pace. This makes any long-term decisions about deploying a blockchain solution challenging. Some organizations are using design challenges and hackathons as a means of further validating the suitability of blockchain technology and generating ideas about how to apply it within their organizations. The British Columbia Land Titles and Survey Authority, in collaboration with the Digital Identity and Authentication Council of Canada and Identity North, has used a design challenge to deepen its understanding of blockchain technology and generate ideas about how to apply the technology to solve a particular use case (i.e., how digital identity can improve and simplify the process of accessing and distributing electronically delivered state of title certificates [eSTCs]).[56]

Blockchains also work best when multiple stakeholders transact business together. To realize the added value of blockchains, your organization may need to negotiate with multiple business partners (e.g., participants in a supply chain) to encourage them to join a blockchain-based business network if such a network does not already exist. For this reason, many organizations are starting their blockchain transformations with smaller, low-risk pilots that do not radically alter existing business practices or require the involvement of multiple stakeholders right away. The Brazilian land registry office for the Municipality of Pelotas, for example, is experimenting with blockchain technology by creating a mirror of its existing land registry using a blockchain solution.[57] Its approach avoids disrupting existing procedures and technology solutions, while still allowing for experimentation with a new blockchain-based land transaction solution. Some organizations are further along in the process of mainstreaming blockchain technology into their operations. The Swedish land registration authority is now into the third stage of a pilot of blockchain-based land transfer recording using smart contracts across a multi-stakeholder network that includes a digital identity provider, real estate buyers and sellers, banks, and the land title registration authority, and has begun tackling the review and updating of laws, regulations, and procedures needed to support transformation to this new form of recordkeeping.[58]

As organizations seek to determine whether the introduction of blockchain technology is the right move for them, they may discover that there are other, less expensive and complex, means to solve their recordkeeping and business challenges. Observation of current practices reveals that, even if there appears to be a strong business case for the adoption of blockchain technology, organizations still are undertaking a careful review of blockchain's capabilities, applications, shortcomings, and the need for interoperability and integration with existing information systems, infrastructure and operations before moving ahead.[59] At that point, organizations appear to be opting for low-risk pilot studies that, for the most part, do not disrupt existing business operations or technology solutions. Public agencies starting down the path of digital transformation with blockchain technology must remain sensitive to the need to safeguard public trust. Most organizations are far from ready to jump headlong into the use of blockchain technology, but it is clear that adoption of this novel form of recordkeeping is gathering momentum and information governance professionals should be prepared.

NOTES

1. BusinessDictionary.com, s.v. "emerging technologies," accessed October 19, 2017, www.businessdictionary.com/definition/emerging-technologies.html.

2. National Archives and Records Administration (NARA), "NARA Bulletin 2011-02: Guidance on Managing Records in Web 2.0/Social Media Platforms," Record Managers, October 20, 2010, www.archives.gov/records-mgmt/bulletins/2011/2011-02.html.

3. Patricia C. Franks, *How Federal Agencies Can Effectively Manage Records Created Using New Social Media Tool,* (Washington, DC: IBM Center for the Business of Government, 2010).

4. American Council for Technology (ACT) and Industry Advisory Council (IAC), *Best Practices Study of Social Media Records Policies: ACT-IAC Collaboration and Transformation (C&T) Shared Interest Group (SIG)*, March 2011, 11, https://www.actiac.org/system/files/Best%20Practices%200f%20Social%20Media%20Records%20Policies%20-%20CT%20SIG%20-%2003-31-11%20%283%29.pdf.

5. National Archives and Records Administration (NARA), "Federal Agency Records Management 2016 Report," revised October 2, 2017, https://www.archives.gov/files/records-mgmt/resources/2016-federal-agency-records-management-annual-report.pdf.

6. Arian Ravanbakhsh, "Records Management of Social Media and Electronic Records," *The National Archives Records Express*, blog post, January 27, 2017, https://records-express.blogs.archives.gov/2017/01/27/records-management-of-social-media-and-electronic-records/.

7. National Archives and Records Administration (NARA), "NARA Bulletin 2011-02."

8. National Archives and Records Administration (NARA), "NARA Bulletin 2014-02."

9. National Archives and Records Administration (NARA), "NARA Bulletin 2015-02."

10. New York State Archives, "Records Advisory: Preliminary Guidance on Social Media," Managing Records, last modified May 24, 2010, www.archives.nysed.gov/records/mr_social_media.shtml.

11. US National Archives. "Social Media Strategy," page last reviewed December 21, 2016, https://www.archives.gov/social-media/strategies.

12. Lois Evans, Patricia C. Franks, and Hsuanwei Michelle Chen, "Voices in the Cloud: Social Media and Trust in Canadian and U.S. Local Governments." *Records Management Journal* 28 (1).

13. HootSuite, accessed October 21, 2017, https://hootsuite.com/#.

14. "NARA Bulletin 2014-02."

15. Meridith Fiedler Dennes, "How to Start a Blog in 2017 (Step by Step Guide with Images)," July 25, 2017, https://www.linkedin.com/pulse/how-start-blog-2017-step-by-step-guide-images -meridith-fiedler-dennes/.

16. Facebook, "Accessing Your Facebook Data," https://www.facebook.com/ help/405183566203254?helpref=faq_content.

17. LinkedIn, "User Agreement," effective June 7, 2017, https://www.linkedin.com/legal/ user-agreement.

18. Kori Schulman, "The Digital Transition: How the Presidential Transition Works in the Social Media Age," *The White House Blog,* October 31, 2016. https://obamawhitehouse.archives.gov/ blog/2016/10/31/digital-transition-how-presidential-transition-works-social-media-age.

19. Ibid.

20. FINRA, "Social Media Web Sites: Guidance on Blogs and Social Networking Web Sites," Regulatory Notice 10-06, January 2010, www.finra.org/web/groups/industry/@ip/@reg/@notice/documents/ notices/p120779.pdf.

21. SEC Rule 17a-4(f) permits broker-dealers to maintain and preserve these records on "micrographic media" or by means of "electronic storage media," as defined in the rule and subject to a number of conditions.

22. FINRA, "2210. Communications with the Public," *FINRA Manual*, accessed October 22, 2017, http://finra.complinet.com/en/display/display_main.html?rbid=2403&element_id=10648.

23. FINRA, "Communications with the Public," Regulatory Notice 12-29, June 2012, www.finra.org/ sites/default/files/NoticeDocument/p127014.pdf.

24. FINRA, "Communications with the Public: Respective Rule Review Report," December 2014, www.finra.org/sites/default/files/p602011.pdf.

25. FINRA, "Social Media and Digital Communications," Regulatory Notice 17-18, April 2017, www.finra.org/sites/default/files/notice_doc_file_ref/Regulatory-Notice-17-18.pdf.

26. GlobalRelay, accessed October 21, 2017, https://www.globalrelay.com/.

27. IBM, "IBM Social Computing Guidelines," accessed October 22, 2017, www.ibm.com/blogs/zz/en/ guidelines.html.

28. Chris Boudreaux, "Social Media Policy Database," *Social Media Governance.com,* accessed October 22, 2017, http://socialmediagovernance.com/policies/.

29. National Archives, Social Media Strategy 2017–2020, accessed October 22, 2017, http://usnationalarchives.github.io/social-media-strategy/.

30. OpenText Extended ECM for Salesforce, accessed October 22, 2017, https://www.opentext.com/ what-we-do/products/opentext-suite-for-salesforce/opentext-extended-ecm-for-salesforce.

31. CBS News, "3 Emerging Technologies to Go Mainstream in 2011," January 10, 2011, *CBS Money Watch,* video, www.cbsNews.com/video/watch/?id=10495949n?tag=bnetdomain.

32. "About Us," *MIT Technology Review,* Massachusetts Institute of Technology, accessed October 19, 2017, https://www.technologyreview.com/about/.

33. Ibid.

34. Michael Vasilinda, Capital News Service, March 16, 2017, https://policerecordsmanagement.com/ 2017/03/tallahassee-fl-wctv-house-committee-voted-17-0-allow-police-officers-view-footage-body -cameras-submitting-reports-responding-complaints/.

35. IDC, "IDC Sees the Dawn of the DX Economy and the Rise of the Digital-Native Enterprise," November 1, 2016, https://www.idc.com/getdoc.jsp?containerId=prUS41888916.

36. Clayton Christensen, "Disruptive Innovation," accessed October 19, 2017, www.claytonchristensen.com/key-concepts/.

37. IDC. "IDC Sees the Dawn of the DX Economy and the Rise of the Digital-Native Enterprise," November 1, 2016, https://www.idc.com/getdoc.jsp?containerId=prUS41888916.

38. Louis Columbus, "Gartner's Hype Cycle for Emerging Technologies, 2017 Adds 5G and Deep Learning for First Time," *Forbes,* August 15, 2017, https://www.forbes.com/sites/louiscolumbus/2017/08/15/gartners-hype-cycle-for-emerging-technologies-2017-adds-5g-and-deep-learning-for-first-time/#420ad65b5043.

39. Catherine Clifford, "Billionaire Tech Investor: There Will Be a Mark Zuckerberg and Bill Gates of AI," *Forbes*, September 25, 2017, https://www.forbes.com/sites/benkerschberg/2017/09/26/5-best-artificial-intelligence-articles-you-should-read-today-916/#24ac9bcc6d19.

40. Andrew Meola, "What Is the Internet of Things (IoT)? *Business Insider,* December 19, 2016, www.businessinsider.com/what-is-the-internet-of-things-definition-2016-8.

41. Ibid.

42. David Dayen, "Mortgage Companies Seek Time Travelers to Find Missing Documents," *The Intercept,* June 17, 2016, https://theintercept.com/2016/06/17/mortgage-companies-seek-time-travelers-to-find-missing-documents/.

43. Associated Press, "New Foreclosure Defense: Prove I Owe You," NBCNews.com, . February 17, 2009, www.nbcnews.com/id/29242063/ns/business-real_estate/t/new-foreclosure-defense-prove-i-owe-you/#.WgngTIZrxG8.

44. Gideon Greenspan, "The Blockchain Immutability Myth," 2017, https://www.multichain.com/blog/2017/05/blockchain-immutability-myth/.

45. Victoria L. Lemieux, "Blockchain Recordkeeping: A SWOT Analysis," 2017, www.bluetoad.com/publication/?i=454085&ver=htm15&p=22#{"page":22,"issue_id":454085}.

46. Ibid.

47. Nick Szabo, "The Idea of Smart Contracts," 1997, www.fon.hum.uva.nl/rob/Courses/InformationInSpeech/CDROM/Literature/LOTwintersch0012006/szabo.best.vwh.net/idea.html.

48. Victoria L. Lemieux, "A Typology of Blockchain Recordkeeping Solutions and Some Reflections on Their Archival Implications," 2nd *IEEE Big Data Workshop on Computational Archival Science,* 2017.

49. Gideon Greenspan, "Avoiding the Pointless Blockchain Project: How to Determine If You've Found a Real Blockchain Use Case," 2015, https://www.multichain.com/blog/2015/11/avoiding-pointless-blockchain-project/.

50. These questions have been adapted from Greenspan (2015) and the work of colleagues in the W3C's Blockchain Community Group, especially Colleen Kirtland, on identifying the blockchain business case, which the author would like to acknowledge.

51. Scott Nelson, "Looking for a Nail to Hit with My Blockchain Hammer: A Q&A with Adventium Blockchain Expert T.D. Smith," *CIO,* 2017, https://www.cio.com/article/3236559/data-protection/looking-for-nails-to-hit-with-my-blockchain-hammer.html.

52. See, for example, Victoria L. Lemieux, "Trusting Records: Is Blockchain Technology the Answer?" *Records Management Journal* 26, no. 2 (2016): 110–139.

53. Hitoshi Okada, Yamasaki Shigeichiro, and Vanessa Bracamonte, "Proposed Classification of Blockchains Based on Authority and Incentive Dimensions,"IEEE *19th International Conference on Advanced Communication Technology (ICACT).* IEEE; Christian Cachin and Marko Vukolic, "Blockchain Consensus Protocols in the Wild," *Arxiv,* July 17, 2017, https://arxiv.org/pdf/1707.01873.pdf.

54. See *Bitcoin Block Explorer,* https://blockexplorer.com.

55. Greenspan, 2015, en. 7.

56. See Digital Identity and Authentication Council of Canada, "Design Solutions: Using Blockchain for Real Estate Transactions," 2017, https://diacc.ca/design-solutions-using-blockchain-for-real-estate-transactions/.

57. Lemieux, 2017, fn. 5, and Luke Parker, "Brazil Pilots Bitcoin Solution for Real Estate Registration," *Brave Newcoin,* April 9, 2017, https://bravenewcoin.com/news/brazil-pilots-bitcoin-solution-for-real-estate-registration/.

58. Lemieux, 2017, fn. 5, and Lantmäteriet, "Annual Report 2016," www.lantmateriet.se/contentassets/3d550bd6c8104483bac8d1fca69f4a4e/webb_lm.verksamhetsberattelse.eng.2016_170323.pdf.

59. Deloitte, "Six Control Principles for Financial Services Blockchain," 2017, https://www2.deloitte.com/content/dam/Deloitte/ie/Documents/Technology/IE_C_BLOCKCHAINPRINCIPLES.pdf.

CHAPTER 8

Vital (Essential) Records, Disaster Preparedness and Recovery, and Business Continuity

INTRODUCTION

What is a *records disaster?* Simply stated, it is a sudden and unexpected event that results in the loss of records and information essential to an organization's continued operation. Natural or man-made disasters—the terrorist attack that shocked New York City on 9/11, Hurricane Harvey that slammed Texas on August 25, 2017, and the 7.1 magnitude earthquake that shook Mexico City on September 19, 2017—leave devastation in their wake. The loss of life is tragic, and the damage to the local infrastructure can be significant. Long-term recovery efforts are hampered by the interruption of normal economic activity. Even those businesses and public institutions that have disaster preparedness/recovery and business continuity plans in place could find that the effects of these disasters exceed the scope of those plans. Not all records are essential to ongoing operations after a disaster, but those that are must be identified as part of the overall business continuity effort.

BUSINESS RESUMPTION STRATEGIES

By definition, a *business continuity plan* is a "documented plan that defines the resources, actions, tasks, and data required to manage the disaster prevention, emergency preparedness, disaster response and recovery, and business resumption process in the event of a business interruption."[1] Some sources use the terms *business continuity plan* and *disaster recovery plan* interchangeably. Others see the business continuity plan as an umbrella plan that consists of several component plans, among them the disaster preparedness and recovery plan.

ARMA International defines a *disaster recovery plan* as "a written and approved course of action to take after a disaster strikes that details how an organization will restore critical business functions and reclaim damaged or threatened records."[2] A *disaster preparedness and recovery plan* includes not only steps necessary to recover from loss but also steps to take before a disaster or emergency occurs to either avoid or mitigate loss.

The term *vital records* can be used to describe two different types of records:

- Those that record/register life events under a government authority, such as birth and death certificates, marriage licenses, divorce decrees, and adoption.

- Those that are essential for the continuation of an organization during and after an emergency as well as well as those that protect the legal and financial rights of the organization and individuals affected by its activities.

Because of confusion over the two definitions, the term *essential records* is being used more frequently to describe the second category—those necessary to protect the rights and interests of the organization and individuals as well as those necessary for emergency operations.

Unfortunately, the term *essential* has not yet been universally adopted, as evidenced by a 2017 article in *Information Management,* "How to Develop a Vital Records Program Project Plan."[3] In this book, the two terms are used interchangeably, with *vital* most often used when discussing a program or plan and essential when discussing the records themselves. A *vital (essential) records program* is one that consists of the policies, plans, and procedures developed and implemented and the resources needed to identify, use, and protect those records necessary to meet operational responsibilities under emergency or disaster conditions or to protect the rights of the organization or those of its stakeholders. This may be a program element within an emergency management plan.[4]

A *vital records manual* is a communications tool used to document the vital records program. It could be published as a separate document or as part of the overall records management manual, and it would most likely be made available to employees electronically. It is comprised of three elements:

- procedures and objectives
- explanation of the essential records schedule (master list)
- instructions for reconstructing the essential records, including the necessary equipment

Identifying the records essential to the organization's continued operations is the first step toward developing both a disaster recovery plan and a business continuity plan.

VITAL RECORDS PROGRAM

Every organization, large or small, needs a plan to protect essential information from destruction due to earthquakes, floods, terrorism, and other disasters. Large organizations may survive such disasters because they have duplicate records at other sites. Small companies without a vital records program may never be able to reopen due to lost records.

Some companies feel a false sense of security because they have implemented a disaster recovery program. To most companies, this means protecting files on a computer system so that they can get it up and running again. Older records not stored on computer-readable media are not protected under these disaster recovery programs. Nearly three out of four companies responding to a 2014 survey failed from a disaster recovery preparedness standpoint in one or more of the following ways:

- lost one or more of their mission critical software applications
- lost one or more of their virtual machines
- lost critical files
- experienced days of datacenter downtime[5]

Unlike digital records, paper records are rarely backed up off-site. Without medical records, doctors are unable to treat people who need medical attention but whose conditions and medications are unknown. When Hurricane Katrina devastated New Orleans in 2005, only about 25 percent of doctors in the United States reportedly kept electronic medical records.[6] Boxes of paper records were destroyed, and those that were salvaged remained inaccessible, as shown in figure 8.1.

After the disaster, the federal government began a pilot test of KatrinaHealth.org, an electronic health record (EHR) online system, sharing prescription drug information for most of the hurricane evacuees with health care professionals.[7] By the time Hurricane Harvey devastated Texas and roared into Louisiana in 2017, approximately 75 percent of health care providers kept records electronically.[8] That's the good news. The bad news is that patients, first responders, and new healthcare providers had trouble accessing those records when they needed them most: during a disaster. One of the reasons is that medical records remain behind firewalls and in silos—if you have more than one doctor, each will have records they can share with each other only with your permission and usually by fax.

Recognizing this as less than desirable, health officials have been looking for a system that could be used in the event of a national emergency. One pilot project that ran from July 2015 to July 2017 is the *Patient Unified Lookup System for Emergencies* (PULSE), which would allow disaster healthcare volunteers registered and authenticated through California's Emergency System for Advance Registration of Volunteer Health Professionals (ESAR-VHP) to retrieve health information for victims and evacuees from Health Information Exchanges (HIEs), hospital systems, and other sources statewide using national standards.[9]

Although a natural disaster cannot be prevented, the impact of the disaster

FIGURE 8.1 More than five months post-Katrina, salvaged medical records remained inaccessible at Hancock Medical Center, Bay St. Louis, Mississippi.

SOURCE: Electronic Health Association, "HIMSS Katrina Battles Ongoing Hurricane Effects with Health IT Donations," Press Releases, February 13, 2006. Reprinted with permission from HIMSS. Photo by David Collins for HIMSS.

could be mitigated by the development of both a comprehensive disaster preparedness and recovery plan and a business continuity plan. These plans are often designed simultaneously.

Planning a Vital Records Program

A vital records program is necessary to identify and protect those records that specify how an organization will operate during an emergency or disaster, those records necessary to the continued operations of the organization, and those records needed to protect the legal and financial rights of all stakeholders.[10] According to the ANSI/ARMA 2017 technical report, *Vital Records,* a vital records program must be developed in conjunction with those stakeholders responsible for the organization's business continuity, disaster recovery, and/ or emergency management programs. It recommends the following steps:

- identifying vital (essential) records
- classifying records (as vital, important, and useful)
- compiling a vital records schedule
- pretesting the program (e.g., procedures to restore backup files)[11]

The *Vital Records* technical report stresses the importance of reviewing the impact of the loss of essential records on the business itself. The risk management process suggested has two main components: business impact analysis (BIA) and essential records impact analysis. The BIA looks at the loss of essential records through the perspective of the business, including understanding the critical functions of the business in order to prioritize their resumption, identifying potential losses due to disruption, and estimating the time and resources necessary to resume or continue operations. The essential record impact analysis requires understanding the essential records and then linking that back to the business; for example, identify potential disaster-related threats to essential records and determine the cost of protecting them from those threats. This is followed by the development of a vital records loss prevention plan (e.g., reduce, remove, or mitigate risks) and a vital records protection plan (e.g., dispersal and protective storage). Of course, training of staff is necessary—including introduction of the vital records manual.[12]

The Washington State Archives provides advice and resources on Disaster Preparedness, Response and Recovery on their website.[13] Among the resources is a link to the State of Washington's *Essential Records and Disaster Preparedness Manual* (available in both PDF and Microsoft Word formats), which was published to help local agencies within the state protect their essential records from damage, loss, or theft. The manual begins by suggesting the following first steps: defining essential records and protecting them; conducting a risk analysis; reducing the likelihood of damage, loss, or theft; and producing a records disaster recovery plan. It then provides practical advice to follow when a disaster occurs.[14]

When developing the vital records program, the first questions to answer are:

- Who is responsible for a vital records program?
- What is an essential record?
- How do you identify an essential record?

Who Is Responsible for a Vital Records Program?

Clear authority for a vital records program must be established through policies and procedures. A vital records manager must be designated. Often, the organization's records manager fills this role. This person must work with other stakeholders throughout the organization to identify, inventory, protect, store, make accessible, and update as needed the copies of essential records required in an emergency, including records that document legal and financial rights.

The following people should be involved in preparing the vital records inventory:

- **Vital records manager:** to manage the program
- **Records manager (if different from vital records manager):** to work with the vital records manager

- **Department, bureau, and division records liaison officers:** to serve as vital records coordinators and implement the vital records program for their areas, including preparing the inventory and ensuring protection for records within their area
- **Management:** to demonstrate support for the vital records program by making it a priority
- **Information technology (IT) staff:** to ensure electronic systems in their control are regularly backed up and accessible in an emergency
- **All other employees:** to cooperate and assist where and when needed

Under some circumstances, the organization may hire a consultant to speed up the process. This may also help to ensure quality; however, this option will also increase costs.

What is an essential record? Although the type of *essential record* that needs protection may differ slightly between public and private institutions, its value is the same: to re-create the organization's or agency's legal and financial status and to preserve the rights and obligations of stakeholders, including employees, customers, investors, and citizens. The information may be recorded in any format (e.g., paper, digital, electronic, film, or tape). Percentages for categories of records vary depending on source with some estimating as low as 1 percent, but as a rule, not more than 7 percent of an organization's records are considered *essential,* and it is more likely that the figure would be between 3 percent and 5 percent (see figure 8.2).

To continue or resume operations and to meet customer needs, the organization should protect records that identify fixed assets, identify and fulfill existing commitments to customers, rebuild facilities, develop new business, identify the nature and value of inventory, and resume computer system operations and telecommunications. To ensure the rights of employees, the organization should protect records that list salaries and benefits due employees and former employees and document any other corporate commitments to

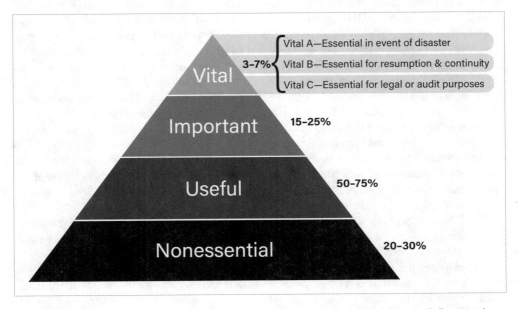

FIGURE 8.2 Records value scale with three classifications of vital (essential) records.

employees, such as union contracts. To safeguard legal, financial, and shareholder interests, the organization should protect records that document receivables, determine liabilities, identify the locations and amounts of cash and securities owned by the company, establish and defend the organization's tax position, identify shareholders and their holdings, meet all legal requirements for establishing the corporate status, and protect intangible assets such as patents and trademarks. Emergency operations records, such as staff contact and assignment information, and the business continuity plan itself, are examples of essential records needed during an emergency.

In many instances, the loss of recorded information can have more devastating consequences for continuation of an organization's operations than the loss of physical space or equipment, which is often replaceable and insured.[15]

The loss of essential records can result in:

- disruption of essential customer services,
- exposure to unplanned expenses of financial settlements or loss of revenue,
- increased vulnerability to litigation, and
- loss of productivity due to gaps in information.

Essential records should not be confused with *permanent records*. Records retain their essential status only if they are necessary to the continued existence of the organization.

How Do You Identify an Essential Record?

Identify the records required to continue functioning during the disaster or to reestablish operations immediately after the event. Too often *vital information* is interpreted as *archival or historical information* preserved for the benefit of researchers and posterity. This is another good reason why the term *essential* makes sense.

Each unit within the organization must analyze its own operations to determine what information is necessary to its continued existence and the attainment of its critical missions. This will feed into the overall vital records inventory for the organization. On the unit level, a committee of senior staff should be convened to undertake this task. It is recommended that the committee meet on a regular basis (e.g., every two weeks) until the records have been identified and a vital records program is in place. The individuals on the committee should be very familiar with their areas and the records in those areas and be willing and able to devote time to the program until it is operational. One person from this committee should assume the role of records liaison to communicate with the vital records program manager.

There are several ways to classify records. Some classification systems do not take into account nonessential records. However, including such a classification makes it easier for employees to understand which records they can immediately disregard when compiling their inventory. The Delaware State Archives classifies records as *vital, important, useful,* or *nonessential* and provides the descriptions of each category (see table 8.1).

The University of Washington also takes into account nonessential records but reduces the categories to three: essential, useful, and nonessential.[16] Regardless of the classification scheme, the committee should begin with the comprehensive records retention schedule. First, eliminate all nonessential records. Then eliminate those records that contain important information but that can be easily reproduced. Identify all situations where information is or can be protected through computer system backups. Finally, reevaluate the remaining records to see if they are essential. To do this, ask two questions:

TABLE 8.1 Classification of records as vital, important, useful, or nonessential.

VITAL RECORDS	These records are essential to the continuity of services during a calamity or the restoration of daily business if it has been interrupted. These records are irreplaceable, and copies do not have the same value as originals.
IMPORTANT RECORDS	This category of records is replaceable only at considerable expense of funds, time, and labor.
USEFUL RECORDS	These records, if lost, might cause some inconvenience but could easily be replaced. Loss of these records does not present any real obstacle to restoring daily business.
NONESSENTIAL RECORDS	Loss of these records presents no obstacle whatsoever to restoring daily business.

SOURCE: Adapted from information at State of Delaware, "The Process of Vital Records Management: Records Classification," Vital Records Management, accessed December 3, 2017, http://archives.delaware.gov/govsvcs/records_policies/vital%20records%20management.shtml.

- What would we be unable to do if this record were destroyed?
- How critical is our inability to do this or what is the impact on our organization?

Increasingly, publications cite the 5 percent of records "you can't live without" but ignore the other 95 percent when providing advice on disaster preparedness/recovery and business continuity.[17] This does not imply that other important records should be ignored. However, it may be easier to set aside a discussion of the other categories to focus on the essential records during the disaster preparedness/recovery planning process.

Vital Records Inventory

The goal of a comprehensive records inventory is to identify records categories, not every record that exists. A physical inventory conducted by properly trained personnel should be conducted. Be sure to inventory not only paper but also computer printouts, microfilm, magnetic media, photographs, slides, engineering drawings, and any other recorded information. Don't forget the digital files stored in enterprise content management systems and with third-party vendors in the cloud.

When a retention schedule is developed, the operational, legal, administrative, and/or historical value of the record is considered. Essential records are appraised in a similar manner with one major difference: the value of the record during and immediately after an emergency is what makes it essential. Essential records are either *rights and interests* records or *emergency operations* records. Rights and interests records can be subcategorized as operational, legal, and fiscal (see table 8.2).

The complete records inventory—which identifies all records, their locations, and the format in which they are maintained—is the basis from which the records retention schedule is created. An essential records inventory can be carried out independently of or at the same time as the comprehensive records inventory introduced in chapter 4. As new records are

TABLE 8.2 Essential Records categories and subcategories.

CATEGORY/SUBCATEGORY	DESCRIPTION
Rights and Interests	
Operational	Any functions necessary to the operation or continuation of your unit or the organization as a whole.
Legal	Any functions that provide proof of the organization's legal status.
Fiscal	Any functions which prove the unit's or the organization's financial status.
Emergency Operations	
Emergency Operations	Any functions needed during an emergency.

created, they should be analyzed to determine their status. A records inventory form should be completed for each records series and include information such as the title of the record, a description, the location, and its format. You've already been introduced to inventory forms for physical and electronic records. Figure 8.3 shows a portion of the Minnesota Historical Society's Records Inventory form, which I find especially useful because it not only asks if the records are vital (essential) but expects the person completing the form to explain why.

Vital Records Analysis

Once the records inventory forms have been completed or gathered, they can be used as the basis for interviews with the organization's management staff. The task is to determine their perception of the value of the records under their jurisdiction and the consequences that would be incurred if those records were lost.

Questions to be asked during the interview could include:

- Who are the stakeholders of the unit or organization?
- What records are produced because of each function (operational, legal, fiscal, emergency management)?
- What is the impact of not providing the records necessary to support each function (i.e., can the work be carried on if the record is gone)?
- How long can you carry out those key functions without the records?
- Which of the records are essential (unique and required in their original form to meet evidential requirements, not easily reproduced, or only reproduced or replaced at a disproportionately high cost)?
- Can these records be replaced from another source?
- Are these records on computer, microfilm, backed up to the cloud, other?
- Are these records duplicated in a different format?
- Is the format easily accessible during or after an emergency?

The records manager should analyze the information gathered from these interviews to determine the protection status of the vital records.

10. RETENTION REQUIREMENTS	YEARS	CITATION	11. RECOMMENDED RETENTION PERIODS
A. Federal Law			A. Agency Office
B. State Law			B. Agency Storage
C. Statute of Limitations			C. State Records Center (State Agencies Only)
D. Audit Period			D. Total Retention (A + B + C)
E. Administrative Needs			

12. A vital record is essential to the continuation or resumption of your operations after a disaster.
Are any documents in this records series considered vital? ☐ Yes ☐ No
If yes, which documents are vital and why?

FIGURE 8.3 Section from the Minnesota Records Inventory Worksheet.

SOURCE: www.mnhs.org/preserve/records/docs_pdfs/recordservices/inventory.pdf.

Vital Records Protection

The goal is to use the simplest, most economical method that fits the circumstances. The two methods of protection, which apply to both physical and electronic records, are duplication and dispersal and protective storage.

Duplication and Dispersal

Records can be protected by making copies and storing them in one or more locations apart from the original records. Methods of dispersal include:

- **Routine dispersal:** This low-cost method is the result of keeping a copy of the record at more than one location as a normal part of business operations. If this method is used, procedures must be put in place so that records can be retrieved easily when necessary.
- **Planned (designed) dispersal:** This method entails duplicating the record for protection purposes rather than as a normal part of the business operation. This involves storing the duplicate off-site with a few exceptions, such as microfilming the records and storing in a vault on-site or creating an extra copy of essential data residing on a computer and transferring that copy to a secure, remote location.
- **Derivative dispersal:** Although this is not a method of dispersal any organization should rely on, it deserves mention when considering the actual life of information. This is a term used to represent information and records intentionally (with or without malice) spread through the use of the Internet, social media, and smart devices. It is a direct by-product of the information age. Information that may or may not be considered records of the organization can be shared virally once made public and have a life of their own beyond that of the useful life determined by the organization. Examples include the documents released through the nonprofit organization WikiLeaks and the tweets now preserved in perpetuity by the Library of Congress.

Protective Storage

Dispersal does not ensure the protection of either the original or the copies. Steps must be taken to provide storage to protect vital assets, for example:

- **On-site storage:** Some organizations, including many local governments, maintain essential records in a vault, fireproof cabinet, or fireproof container on their premises. If this option is elected, the storage equipment must conform to the rating requirements of the National Fire Protection Association (NFPA) standards, which currently require essential records be stored in a vault, or for small volumes, in two-hour records protection equipment in a fire-resistive building.[18]
- **Off-site facility:** A large company may invest in its own off-site storage facility for essential records on a variety of media, including paper, microfilm, tapes, and discs. Others use commercial off-site storage. The facility should be accessible twenty-four hours a day by appropriate officials, have twenty-four-hour climate control with a temperature of approximately 20°C or 68°F and a relative humidity of 30–40 percent, and be located far enough away from the site that the same disaster will not affect records stored at both.
- **Electronically stored information (ESI):** Identify "hot," "warm," and "cold" sites to accommodate electronic records. Consider cloud-based solutions. Be sure systems, applications, and system documentation are stored along with the records. We will address these options in more detail later in this chapter.

Storage Media

When possible, store essential records on a medium that will last as long as the record is needed. Because an essential record may not have permanent retention status, a life span of 500 years for a storage medium is not necessarily required. Compare the expected retention period of the records with the length of life of different media when determining how to store records (see table 8.3).

The actual length of time that storage media remain viable will depend on many factors, including:

- the quality with which the media were manufactured,
- the care with which the media were handled,
- the number of times the media were accessed,

TABLE 8.3 Storage media and length of record life.

MICROFILM	500 years
ACID-FREE PAPER	300 years
REGULAR OFFICE PAPER	20–30 years
ELECTRONIC STORAGE MEDIA	Availability of equipment & software to assess information (review every 3 years)

- the quality of the device used to write to or read from the media, and
- the cleanliness, temperature, and humidity maintained within the storage environment.

In addition to the danger of loss due to longevity of storage media selected, some media will fail. Therefore, essential records must be stored redundantly (backed up on more than one type of media). The media must be tested periodically to ensure that the data are readable and have not been altered.

The Vital Records Schedule

The *vital records schedule* is a listing of an organization's essential records along with an explanation of how each is to be protected from destruction in the event of a disaster. This information is gathered from the records inventory. The easiest way to create this schedule is to create a database. Fields to include in the database will vary; examples include record title, descriptions of records, records media, method of protection, storage location, cycling schedule of records, and critical functions supported by records (see figure 8.4).

Records management software and services can be used to manage both paper and electronic vital records. Applications that comply with *DoD 5015.2-STD: Electronic Records Management Software Applications Design Criteria Standard* will allow for periodic review and cycling of essential records to ensure they are accurate and up-to-date.[19] This involves designating a category or folder as containing essential records and assigning an *essential records review period* (time between reviews) and an *essential records reviewer* (a user or a group of users) to receive email notifications when a review is due. Obsolete copies of essential records would be replaced with copies of current essential records. Once the review is complete, a new *last review date* would be appended. This procedure should be requested for essential records protection even when using software applications that are not DoD 5015.2 certified.

Testing and Updating the Program

Test your disaster recovery and vital records programs by picking a team of employees who would have to reconstruct operations in the event of a disaster. Provide the employees

Vital Records Schedule

Records Series	Original Location: Building, Floor Room, other.	Person Responsible	Vol. in Feet/ Bytes	Media Type	Years Covered	Name of Electronic System, Version Number, and Operating System	Vital Record Security Copy Location	Media Type	VR Contact & Phone	Method of Transporting the Record to Emergency Location (if record is not stored at central off-site facility)	Cycling Schedule

FIGURE 8.4 Vital (essential) records schedule form.

with the list of information needs the organization would have after a disaster. Have them reconstruct the data and provide the information needed using only the protected records. Test the program and revise it annually.

What to Do If a Disaster Does Occur

The need for emergency operations plans is immediate. A copy of the vital records/disaster recovery plan should be stored at or close to the facility and available on a twenty-four-hour basis. In case the immediate area is inaccessible, key employees should also have access to the essential records/disaster recovery program from home either as a print or electronic copy or available online.

In the event of a cataclysmic disaster, communications breakdowns will occur. For example, in 2017, Hurricane Maria decimated the communication, transportation, and utility infrastructure of the island of Puerto Rico. Private residences and businesses were left without power, cable, or landline service, and mobile reception was spotty or nonexistent— not to mention that even if there were cell service, phones would not operate without electricity to recharge them. In a situation like this, the local print copies, if any survive, may be all that are accessible.

DISASTER PREPAREDNESS AND RECOVERY PLANNING

The *disaster recovery plan* is an emergency plan that outlines the steps your organization will take to protect itself from loss due to a disaster and the steps the organization will take if actually impacted by a disaster. The plan coordinates the efforts, staff, and other resources needed to protect the business's information and equipment, as well as its employees and customers.

The disaster preparedness and recovery plan should identify procedures to be implemented to prevent disasters from occurring in the first place and steps that can be taken to mitigate the effect of those disasters that cannot be prevented. Hazards to be evaluated include natural hazards (geological, meteorological, and biological), human-caused events (accidental and intentional), and technologically caused events (accidental and intentional). Any information that may prove useful in preventing disasters, or in being prepared for disasters, should be included in the vital records disaster preparedness and recovery plan.

Pre-disaster Preparedness

Pre-disaster preparedness involves identifying the types of risks most likely to impact your organization, including natural hazards, human-caused events, and technologically caused events.

Natural Hazards

Every business faces some sort of risk from natural hazards, regardless of its geographic location. Some parts of the globe are more likely to be affected by certain types of disasters than others. You should determine the risks presented to the organization based on its geographic location. Figure 8.5 is a map prepared by the Insurance Institute for Business and

Home Safety, a nonprofit initiative of the insurance industry, to help the public identify the natural hazards to which they may be exposed. Through its website, the Institute provides many disaster preparedness/recovery and business continuity resources, including a tool based on this map that allows you to enter your zip code to discover the risks you face in your section of the country.[20]

This type of map is useful when assessing the risks due to natural disasters that may occur within your region in order to best protect your physical and digital assets. It will also come in handy when determining the location for a disaster recovery site. When finding the right spot for a disaster recovery site, you need to select an area that is not likely to be affected by the same type of disaster your primary site faces.

Human-Caused Events

In spite of the attention devoted to loss of information due to major disasters, records damage most often comes from preventable conditions such as equipment failure, arson, terrorism, vandalism, and carelessness. Due to the frequency and sophistication of attacks on data, this topic is addressed in chapter 10.

Damage can also occur due to leaking roofs, burst pipes, and damp conditions in basement storage areas. Although most damage is localized and affects only a small percentage of an organization's vital records, valuable information may still be lost if the recording media is damaged by water, fire, smoke, mold, or chemicals. Salvage and restoration efforts can be expensive if even possible.

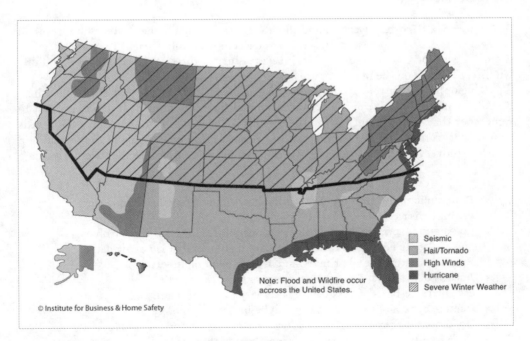

FIGURE 8.5 Natural hazards exposure map.

SOURCE: Insurance Institute for Business and Home Safety, "What Is at Risk?" in *Open for Business: A Disaster Protection and Recovery Planning Toolkit for the Small to Mid-Sized Business,* 2007, 4—now only available as an interactive map at https://disastersafety.org/.

Pre-disaster preparedness efforts require team members to determine if potentially hazardous substances have been used in constructing or equipping offices. If those substances are present in the workplace, essential records should be stored off-site and copies used on a daily basis.

Technologically Caused Events

Events that affect central computers, mainframes, software, or internal and external applications are included in this category. Also included are events that disrupt ancillary support equipment, telecommunications, and sources of energy, power, or utilities, as was experienced on the island of Puerto Rico in 2017.

Increasingly, organizations are entering into agreements to store electronic records in the cloud. The same procedures used to protect records controlled by the organization must be used to protect records stored by service providers. Proof that the service provider has an adequate backup and recovery plan in place is necessary. This information should be included in a terms-of-service agreement (or service contract) negotiated between the organization and the service provider. Periodic tests should be conducted to ensure that the backup recovery systems and processes work as agreed upon. Just as with organization-owned sites, both the service provider's primary site and its own backup site must be geographically located to avoid risk from the same natural disaster.

Disaster Recovery

By October 6, 2017, fifteen weather and climate disaster events in the United States resulted in the deaths of 282 people and caused losses exceeding $1 billion each. They included one drought, two floods, one freezing, seven severe storms, three tropical cyclones, and one wildfire, as shown on the map in figure 8.6.

Developing a disaster recovery plan takes a great deal of time and effort—just how much depends on the size of the organization and the risks identified. It is important to remember that human safety is the first priority. Recovery of information and records comes only after all employees and visitors are safe. Experts disagree on the format of a disaster recovery plan, but when comparisons are made, common elements emerge, such as:

- **Communications strategy:** Determine how you will reach all employees during a disaster.
- **Roles and responsibilities:** Assign responsibilities for everyone involved, and designate backup in case the primary team member is not available. Provide training for all primary and backup team members.
- **Access to systems:** Be sure the primary and backup individuals are assigned role-based access where necessary to perform a recovery.
- **Remote access:** Be sure recovery can be initiated remotely.
- **Document the process:** The disaster recovery procedures should include clear step-by-step instructions for members of the team.
- **Test the plan:** Practice makes perfect. After initial training, at minimum, provide, an annual test of your disaster recovery plan.
- **Evaluate and update your plan.**

A cursory review of disaster recovery plans available on the internet reveals that most tend to emphasize either physical records or digital records. The steps outlined to recover from a disaster may be specific to the medium used to store a majority of the records, but essential records must be protected regardless of the medium.

Recovering Physical Records

Essential records will be listed on your vital records schedule. Depending on the type of organization, those records could include:

- contracts, leases, and license and franchise agreements;
- laboratory notebooks and other research data;
- engineering drawings and blueprints;
- product formulas and production specifications;
- insurance policies;
- articles of incorporation, bylaws, and board minutes;
- patents, trademarks, copyrights; and
- deeds and title to property.

As soon as possible, a *records damage assessment* site survey should be conducted to determine the type of damage that has occurred. Records should be treated based on priorities set previously and the severity of the damage. The site survey would include:

- the name of the surveyor and the date and time of the survey;
- the location (floor, room);

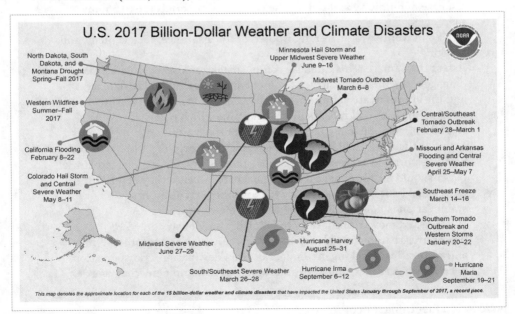

FIGURE 8.6 Natural hazard events result in more than $1 billion each in 2017.

SOURCE: NOAA National Centers for Environmental Information (NCEI) US Billion-Dollar Weather and Climate Disasters (2017). https://www.ncdc.noaa.gov/billions/.

- the type of damage (mold/mildew, mud, water, smoke, fire, sewage, insects, rodents, other);
- the type of media (paper, books, photographs, slides, tapes, microfilm, maps, hard drives, CD-ROMs/DVDs, other); and
- additional information based on type of record.

For essential records, the following information would be recorded: types of records/record series, volume in feet, and dates of records. Figure 8.7 can be used as the basis for your own records damage assessment site survey.

In the event of a disaster affecting your essential records stored on-site in physical formats, you would follow the steps outlined in your own vital records disaster recovery plan. The following steps are provided as one example:

- Stabilize the site and gain access as soon as the building is safe for reentry armed with the vital records schedule and a list of all safe and vault combinations, location of keys to all file cabinets, vaults, or containers that house vital records.
- Restore environmental controls and allow the heating or air-conditioning systems to run 24/7 with the goal of maintaining a temperature below 70°F and a relative humidity below 50 percent.
- Document the damage. The coordinator of the vital records disaster management team is responsible for documenting the damage by taking photographs and videos and/or completing a records damage assessment site survey.
- Toss duplicate records and replaceable or disposable materials to remove a source of humidity and reduce the volume of materials the team must inspect.
- Keep an inventory of material disposed of for insurance, replacement, and tracking.
- Assess the damage. This can be accomplished by analyzing the records damage assessment site survey to determine the extent of the damage and the approximate volume of records affected. Prioritize treatment by handling essential records first. Determine which records are official records on vulnerable media that have not been backed up.
- Stabilize the records. Salvage wet records within forty-eight hours to avoid costly restoration efforts. Photographs, magnetic media, and coated-stock paper should be given highest salvage priority, because they deteriorate more quickly. It may be necessary to move these records off-site if stabilization is not possible in the original environment.
- If necessary, move records off-site following previously agreed-to procedures that include identification of a suitable vendor for handling and restoration, tracking method, relocation destination, transportation, necessary clearances, and personnel assigned to accompany the records.

Recovering Electronic Records

The terrorist attacks of September 11, 2001, sent shock waves around the world. That day Americans realized that natural disasters were no longer the greatest threat to our lives and our economy. Several top financial services firms had offices in the World Trade Center, including Morgan Stanley Dean Witter, Credit Suisse, Commerzbank, and Deutsche Bank. The attacks exposed one area of vulnerability to business continuity: almost no paper records survived the attacks on the World Trade Center (see figure 8.8).

Those businesses with offices in and near the World Trade Center site that had disaster recovery plans in place for electronic data moved to off-site locations and took steps to resume business operations. As a direct result of 9/11, all businesses began to question their own ability to recover from such an event. Whether you develop your own data recovery center or contract with a service provider, keep in mind the following lessons learned:

Records Damage Assessment Site Survey

Surveyor:	Location of Building:
Date:	Floor Number:
Time:	Office Number:

Description of Damaged Materials (check all that apply)

Record Characteristics	Volume in feet:
☐ Vital ☐ Confidential	
☐ Restricted ☐ Important ☐ Useful	Dates of Records:

Type(s) of records/file names:

Type of Damage (check all that apply		Type of Media (check all that apply)	
Debris		Paper	
Mold/Mildew		Books	
Mud		Photographs	
Water, High (dripping wet)		Slides	
Water, Low (damp)		Videos/Audio Tapes	
Smoke		Microfilm/Microfiche	
Fire		Oversized materials (maps,	
Sewage		posters)	
Insects		Glossy paper (magazine stock)	
Rodents		Computer Tapes	
Other		CD-ROMS / DVDs	
		Other	

FIGURE 8.7 Records damage assessment site survey form.

- Don't place backup facilities near each other. One business located in the World Trade Center had a backup facility several blocks away and data was lost at both sites.
- Do regular backups of data residing on desktops and laptops. Synchronize data with the server daily. One data recovery service provider was able to recover 100 percent of the data for their clients—except for data that had not been backed up. Critical works in progress are often neglected when it comes to backing up.
- Don't just back up your data. To restore the data, copies of data catalogs and directories are needed to organize the data and obtain the appropriate permissions to access the data.
- Do avoid incompatibility issues when recovering data by running backup and storage environments like those in daily use.
- Do make sure that backup facilities have the hardware, software, network connectivity, and services needed to run your entire operation.
- Do be prepared to reestablish systems management capabilities quickly, including monitoring, job execution, and security features.
- Do prepare by training internal disaster response teams and identifying the applications and business operations that should be recovered first.[21]

Taking a lesson learned from 9/11, disaster recovery sites should be not only off-site but also in a geographic location that would not be exposed to the same risks from disasters as the original site. The choice must be made between establishing and managing a company-owned site or contracting with a disaster recovery service provider, but a decision on

FIGURE 8.8 Almost no paper survived the 9/11 attacks on the World Trade Center.
SOURCE: Doug Kanter/AFP/Getty Images.

the most appropriate type of site for the organization must be made. Traditional options include:

- **Disaster recovery cold sites:** A cold site is available space without the equipment and data needed to continue business operations. This type of site is attractive for businesses that want to save money and have eighteen or more hours to get up and running. The disadvantage of a cold site is the need to set up your own equipment, load software and data, and make all internet and phone connections.
- **Disaster recovery warm sites:** Warm sites provide not only space but also the equipment you need to continue operations. However, you would need to load or restore your data to the system. This type of site relies on backups for recovery. In the past, the use of tape-based backups meant it might take days to recover from a disaster. When tape-based backup is replaced by electronic vaulting—the transfer of data by electronic means to a backup site—recovery times are near those for hot sites but at a fraction of the cost.
- **Disaster recovery hot sites:** It is essential that financial institutions retain the trust of the public in times of crisis by minimizing disruption to services. Therefore, they use hot sites as the basis for their disaster recovery system. A hot site is a duplicate of the original site, with full computer systems and near-complete backups of user data. This is the most expensive option.

Backup as a Service (BaaS) and Disaster Recovery as a Service (DRaaS)

Cloud-based backup and disaster recovery services are increasingly popular options to meet the need for data protection in a way that reduces the cost of infrastructure, business processes, and other applications.

Backup as a service (BaaS) is "an approach to backing up data that involves purchasing backup and recovery services from an online data backup provider."[22] *Disaster recovery as a service (DRaaS)* is "the replication and hosting of physical or virtual servers by a third party to provide failover in the event of a man-made or natural catastrophe"[23] The two terms are not synonymous. Backup is a copy of your data replicated to another device or location—e.g., a tape drive also on premise or a server at another location. You may have your data, which could be restored if you had your entire system in place. But in the event of a disaster, you'd still have to replace your server, re-install your software and data, and reconfigure the system with your settings and preferences. This could take hours or days.

Cloud-based disaster recovery services began to appear in 2009, and by 2017 DRaaS was a mainstream offering. In 2017, Gartner recognized twenty-four providers that meet the criteria set for DRaaS. Among the leaders were IBM, Sungard Availability Services, Infrascale, Iland, and Recovery Point.[24] Among the critical capabilities evaluated were the provider's industry-related credentials and security features.

As with any third-party service providers, you should select a DRaaS vendor that provides service level agreements that meet your needs at an acceptable risk level. Questions to ask include:

- Will the organization's data be held within the organization's desired geographic boundary?

- Is the data being backed up by the cloud provider to another system for redundancy?
- Is the physical location of the alternate system acceptable?
- Can the data be restored within an acceptable time frame?
- Does the provider meet the organization's security standards and allow for periodic facility audits by the customer?
- Does the service provider's network meet the organization's network requirements related to issues such as compatibility of architecture and bandwidth capabilities?
- Can the service provider offer uninterrupted access to the organization's data?
- How easily and at what cost can you move your data to another cloud provider if you are dissatisfied with its services or a change in its policies?

Although businesses look to cloud-based disaster recovery services to reduce costs that would be incurred with other options, it is essential to understand how the organization will be billed for storage and disaster recovery services. Consideration must be given to the ways in which vital records are handled, for example, stored in a separate location from the organization's other records and the records of other organizations. If the multi-tenant nature of the public cloud poses an unacceptable risk, the organization may want to consider the use of a private cloud.

Integrating Mobile Devices into the Disaster Recovery Plan

Business-critical information may exist on mobile devices. The following steps will help the organization incorporate mobile devices into the disaster recovery plan:

- Inventory the mobile devices. (Where are they? To whom are they assigned? Do employees use personal mobile devices to conduct business?)
- Determine the importance of the mobile device data and applications. (Do they contain business-critical data?)
- Determine how quickly you can recover from a disaster. (What steps can be taken before and after an event to prevent data loss?)

Records managers are responsible for including records that may be stored on mobile devices in their records management programs. IT is responsible for information protection and data recovery. Although most devices will be used to run applications that collect data to be transmitted back to a central server, it is important to plan for cases in which sensitive data does exist on a lost or stolen mobile device.

Several tools are available to protect sensitive data on mobile devices by providing a device lock, enhanced passwords, and a device wipe that can be used by the organization to remotely delete all data on the device and removable storage cards. Recovery will take less time if the organization standardizes mobile devices and has a replacement plan in the event of a wide-scale hardware failure. Upper management will need to be aware of the necessity of standards and support the replacement plan.

Disaster Recovery Policies and Plans

Organizations, both public and private, have a responsibility to employees, partners, customers, and other stakeholders to improve their disaster recovery capabilities. The tactical decisions addressed previously must be performed within an overall disaster recovery policy framework. The governing policy statement should include, at a minimum, the following instructions:

- The organization should have a comprehensive disaster recovery plan.
- A formal risk assessment should be undertaken to determine requirements for the disaster recovery plan.
- The disaster recovery plan should be tested in a simulated environment to ensure it can be implemented in an emergency. Two full tests per year along with several component tests throughout the year are recommended for electronic systems.
- The disaster recovery plan should cover all mission-critical and business-critical activities.
- The disaster plan should be updated as necessary as part of configuration management and change management.
- All staff must be made aware of the disaster recovery plan and their roles in it.

The transition from paper to electronic records means that time can be saved restoring important and useful records. Tape is still considered the dominant backup technology. If stored off-site, information is backed up locally and transported to an off-site facility. However, replication is becoming more popular to protect both mission-critical and business-critical records. After tape backup, synchronous and asynchronous replication methods are favored for critical applications, whereas periodic point-in-time copies and remote backup over a wide area network are used most often for noncritical applications and data.

Disaster recovery is often seen as the organization's ability to recover its IT resources, including infrastructure, databases, and applications. Disaster recovery is just one part of the organization's business continuity strategy.

BUSINESS CONTINUITY PLANNING

The disaster recovery plan, however well designed, does not exist in isolation. It is part of a larger business continuity management (BCM) program that is most effective when grounded in generally accepted standards and built to meet the business's objectives. *Business continuity* (BC) is the strategic and tactical capability of the organization to plan for and respond to incidents and business disruptions to continue business operations at an acceptable predefined level.[25] The Business Continuity Institute provides a broad definition of vital records as any information, documents, or data deemed essential for recovery from a disaster or major incident. The protection and recovery of essential records is a required component of a business continuity plan. The vital records schedule is an important resource for those preparing this plan.

Various standards and legislation relate to business continuity management. The British Standards Institution (BSI) produced a two-part standard, *BS 25999-1:2006 Business*

Continuity Management: Code of Practice and *BS 25999-2:2007: Business Continuity Management: Specification.*[26] In 2010, the American National Standards Institute (ANSI) approved the *ASIS/BSI BCM.01-2010: Business Continuity Management Systems: Requirements with Guidance for Use* standard, a standard that shares the core of BS 25999 while reflecting the differences between the infrastructures, systems, and terminology of the United Kingdom and the United States.[27] In June 2012, *ISO 22313:2012, Societal security—Business continuity management systems—Requirements,* was released. This standard provides a framework for planning, establishing, implementing, operating, monitoring, reviewing, maintaining, and continually improving a business continuity management system (BCMS).[28]

Business Continuity Management Lifecycle

The business continuity management lifecycle depicted in figure 8.9 is comprised of four phases: analysis, solution design, development and implementation, and exercise, maintenance, and review. The cycle should be repeated at predetermined intervals to ensure that it remains current.

Phase 1: Analysis

The *analysis phase* of the business continuity management lifecycle represents a business impact analysis (BIA) designed to prioritize business functions by assessing the potential impacts that might result if an organization were to experience a business interruption. A risk analysis is an essential element of this phase.

Phase 2: Solution Design

The business continuity plan is developed during the *solution design phase.* Alternative business recovery operating strategies for continuation of business within recovery time and/ or according to recovery objectives while maintaining the organization's critical functions are determined. Plans and procedures to communicate with internal stakeholders during incidents are formulated and provision is made for post-incident support and guidance for employees and their families.

Phase 3: Development and Implementation

The *development and implementation phase* includes developing and implementing emergency response procedures in order to stabilize the situation following an incident. Designing, developing, and implementing business continuity and incident management plans that provide continuity within recovery time and/or recovery objectives takes place during this phase.

Phase 4: Exercise, Maintenance, and Review

The *exercise, maintenance, and review phase* includes:

- pre-planning and coordinating the plan through walk-throughs and exercises;

FIGURE 8.9 The business continuity management lifecycle.

- evaluating, updating, improving, and documenting the results of the exercises;
- developing processes to maintain the currency of continuity capabilities, business continuity plans, and incident management plans in accordance with the organization's strategic direction;
- establishing policies and procedures for coordinating incidents, continuity, and restoration activities with external agencies while ensuring compliance with applicable statutes and/or regulations; and
- practical experience in dealing with external agencies.

Many resources exist to help you with your disaster recovery and business continuity plans, including standards documents such as *NFPA 1600: Standard on Disaster/Emergency Management and Business Continuity Programs,* 2016 edition.[29] This standard establishes a common set of criteria for disaster/emergency management and business continuity programs. The 2016 edition was expanded to emphasize the importance of leadership and commitment and includes new requirements for records management. The standard calls for the development of a records management program, as well as policies created, approved, and enforced to address records classification, confidentiality, integrity, retention, storage, archiving, destruction, access control, and document control.

SUMMARY

Vital (essential) records protection, disaster planning, and business continuity management are essential to the survival of an organization impacted by a major disaster. Records and information managers have a key role to play in each of these initiatives.

Essential records contain information required by the organization to re-create its legal and financial status and to preserve the rights and obligations of stakeholders, including employees, customers, investors, and citizens. These critical business records are in most instances irreplaceable, and the organization cannot exist without them. Records managers already responsible for inventorying and appraising records for retention purposes may also be tasked with developing and managing a vital records program.

Disaster planning should be conducted by a committee that includes representatives from all functional areas of the organization, with upper-management support. Because of the volume of digital information produced, IT departments play a major role in developing the disaster plan. A well-devised plan cannot, of course, prevent disaster, but it can serve to mitigate loss through both protection and recovery efforts. Records managers possess the skills and knowledge necessary to assist the organization in developing the sections of the plan related to protection of records in both paper and digital formats and in developing the procedures necessary to recover records affected by a disaster.

Business continuity stresses the importance of *continuing business activities* in spite of interruptions. Some think of business continuity as synonymous with disaster recovery. But although the two may overlap, there are key differences. A disaster plan focuses on preventing or mitigating loss due to a disaster and recovering the essential records and information needed to continue operations after a disaster. Business continuity planning involves developing a process to ensure that critical business processes can continue in spite of any type of interruption, including power failure, vandalism, employee theft, human error, and work stoppages. Records managers can contribute to business continuity planning because of their familiarity not only with essential records but also with essential business operations that require records that must be available during a critical event.

Taking steps to protect essential records and to resume operations after a major disaster is required for an organization's survival. Organizations today recognize the value of data as a business asset that must be protected. One option is to utilize Backup as a Service (BaaS) to store a copy of the organization's data so that it can be restored if necessary. Disaster Recovery as a Service (DRaaS) goes beyond backup by providing an alternative environment to sustain continuing operations.

Business continuity management is necessary to ensure continued operations to meet legal, regulatory, and contractual obligations in the face of any disruption to business, large or small. Records managers have unique knowledge, skills, and perspectives on the business activities of the organization that should be tapped by the organization when developing plans to protect essential records, recover from a disaster, and continue business operations.

Catastrophic disasters do occur that result in changes to daily operations of those organizations that are fortunate enough to resume business. But more often incidents occur that are more local in nature that also require us to respond according to a preapproved plan. Responding to these incidents requires a three-step approach: Activation (of the right plan), Assessment (of the scope of the incident), and Recovery (from the incident).

In her contribution to this chapter, Helen Nelson, Head of Emergency Preparedness for Britain's Wirral University Teaching Hospital National Health Service (NHS) Foundation Trust, shares a case study based on her report of an incident in which electricity was disrupted for the better part of one day and required implementation of their emergency response. Two primary goals were apparent: caring for patients and resuming normal business operations. Note the need for paper-based procedures and future data-entry tasks as a result of IT downtime.

PARADIGM

Wirral University Teaching Hospital NHS Foundation Trust Utility Disruption

Helen Nelson
Head of Emergency Preparedness
Wirral University Teaching Hospital, National Health Service Foundation Trust

What Happened?

On a Thursday morning the hospital suffered a power main failure in its internal electrical supply. Emergency power, supplied by generators, remained, but the hospital was unable to accept elective or emergency patients. Engineers were called to the site and the supply was restored. The power was stabilized in early evening the same day.

Action Taken

The on-call structure was alerted. Command and control was put in place and an initial meeting held. The battle rhythm for the briefing meetings was set for hourly.

The High Voltage (HV) engineers (contractors) had been called to assist the internal HV Authorized Engineers and it was anticipated that a four-hour downtime was required to locate the fault.

All outpatient appointments were cancelled for the day. Patients scheduled for surgery were cancelled. Two patients who had been anaesthetized in operating rooms awoke without having had their procedures. Theatre and endoscopy procedures that were in progress were to be completed, but no new cases were begun. No harm came to any of the patients.

A full ambulance diversion was put in place with patients being diverted to the other local hospitals. The Emergency Department (ED) was also closed to walk-ins. All relevant partners were contacted and informed.

Lessons Identified

A number of lessons were identified:

1. All staff need to be aware which equipment and areas are connected to emergency power supplies. There should be a process for confirming that equipment is appropriately connected and which equipment is connected to the nonessential electrical supply.
2. All staff need an awareness of IT downtime processes and paper-based procedures to be implemented should a power outage occur. Ownership and maintenance of paper-based downtime packs need to be clear.
3. Regular communication with staff (including contractors) is very important and should be maintained as part of the communications strategy, even without electricity. This should include when the end to the incident is declared and business as usual is resumed.

4. Entering data back onto an IT system following downtime must be included in the downtime plan.
5. Communication with external partners is important so that they understand the implications of the incident on the organization's ability to deliver services.
6. Emergency kits that include items such as torches and batteries are useful on wards, but ownership and maintenance need to be clear.
7. A review of what is plugged in and working when only emergency power is available can help to free up plug sockets if some equipment is not needed at any particular point in time.
8. Support from the ambulance service provider is important to manage flow into and from the hospital.
9. Doors, which are usually locked, fail-safe (i.e., remain open) without electricity. Some of these are required to have manned checkpoints established.
10. Those managing the incident need to be relieved of other duties so they can focus on the task in hand. They also need to be appropriately supported in the Incident Control Center (ICC).

Note: Further case studies can be found online (https://www.england.nhs.uk/). All organizations within the National Health Service (NHS) are encouraged to share what they have learned from incidents in order to reduce their impact elsewhere in the NHS and improve service resilience.

NOTES

1. ARMA International, s.v. "business continuity plan," *Glossary of Records and Information Governance Terms,* 5th ed. (Overland, KS: ARMA International, 2016), 7.
2. ARMA International, s.v. "disaster recovery plan," *Glossary,* 16.
3. Amy Van Artsdalen, "How to Develop a Vital Records Program Project Plan," *Information Management* 51, no. 6 (November/December 2017): 33–37.
4. Justia.com, "Management of Vital Records," US Law, 36 CFR ∮ 1236.20 (1995), http://law.justia .com/cfr/title36/36-3.0.10.2.17.html.
5. Willie Mata, "Data Loss Statistics That Will Make You Think Twice About Business Continuity," Center Technologies, May 18, 2015, https://centretechnologies.com/data-loss-statistics-that-will -make-you-think-twice-about-business-continuity/.
6. Megan Molteni, "Harvey Evacuees Leave Their Belongings—and Health Records—Behind," *Wired,* September 1, 2017, https://www.wired.com/story/harvey-evacuees-leave-their-belongings-and -health-records-behind/.
7. Gina Marie Stevens, *Hurricane Katrina: HIPAA Privacy and Electronic Health Records of Evacuees,* Congressional Research Service (CRS) Report for Congress, RS22310, updated January 23, 2007, 1, http://library.ahima.org/xpedio/groups/public/documents/ government/bok1_034961.pdf.
8. Stevens, *Hurricane Katrina;* Molteni, "Harvey Evacuees."
9. HealthIT.gov., "Patient Unified Lookup System for Emergencies (PULSE)," accessed December 2, 2017, https://www.healthit.gov/techlab/ipg/node/4/submission/1801.
10. Justia.com, "Management of Vital Records."
11. ARMA International, *Vital Records,* ANSI/ARMA, TR29-2017 (Overland Park, KS: ARMA International, 2017).
12. Ibid.

13. "Disaster Preparedness, Response and Recovery—Advice and Resources," Washington State Archives, accessed December 3, 2017, https://www.sos.wa.gov/archives/RecordsManagement/ DisasterPreparednessandRecovery.aspx.

14. Ibid.

15. William Saffady, *Records and Information Management: Fundamentals of Professional Practice,* 3rd ed. (Overland Park, KS: ARMA International, 2016), 172.

16. "Vital Records," Records Management Services, University of Washington, accessed December 3, 2017, https://finance.uw.edu/recmgt/vitalrecords.

17. Iron Mountain, "Important Versus Vital Records: The Magic 5% You Can't Live Without," Executive Summary, accessed April 17, 2018, www.ironmountain.com/resources/whitepapers/i/ important-versus-vital-records-the-magic-5-you-cant-live-without.

18. National Fire Protection Association (NFPA), *NFPA 232: Standard for the Protection of Records,* 2017 ed. (Quincy, MA: NFPA, 2017). www.nfpa.org/codes-and-standards/all-codes-and-standards/ list-of-codes-and-standards/detail?code=232.

19. *Electronic Records Management Software Applications Design Criteria Standard,* April 25, 2007, http://jitc.fhu.disa.mil/projects/rma/downloads/p50152stdapr07.pdf.

20. OFB-EZ—Business Continuity Planning, Insurance Institute for Business and Home Safety, accessed December 3, 2017, http://disastersafety.org/ibhs-business-protection/ ofb-ez-business-continuity/.

21. Jan Stafford, "Lessons Learned from 9-11: Disaster Recovery Dos and Don'ts," TechTarget, December 5, 2001, http://searchwindowsserver.techtarget.com/news/784938/Lessons-learned -from-9-11-Disaster-recovery-dos-and-donts.

22. TechTarget, s.v. "backup as a service (BaaS)," accessed December 15, 2017, http://searchdatabackup.techtarget.com/definition/backup-as-a-service-BaaS.

23. TechTarget, s.v. "disaster recovery as a service (DRaaS)," accessed December 3, 2017, http://searchdisasterrecovery.techtarget.com/definition/disaster-recovery-as-a-service-DRaaS.

24. Ron Blair and Mark Thomas Jaggers, "Magic Quadrant for Disaster Recovery as a Service," Gartner, June 19, 2017, www.gartner.com/doc/3746618/magic-quadrant-disaster-recovery-service.

25. Business Continuity Institute, s.v. "business continuity," *Glossary of Business Continuity Terms,* updated April 13, 2017,. https://www.drj.com/downloads/drj_glossary.pdf.

26. British Standards Institution (BSI), *BS 25999-1:2006 Business Continuity Management: Code of Practice* (London: British Standards Institution, 2006).

27. American National Standards Institute (ANSI), *ASIS/BSI BCM.01-2010: Business Continuity Management Systems: Requirements with Guidance for Use* (New York: ANSI, 2010).

28. International Organization for Standardization (ISO), *ISO 22313:2012 Societal Security— Business continuity management systems—Guidance* (Geneva, Switzerland: ISO, 2012).

29. National Fire Protection Association (NFPA), *NFPA 1600: Standard on Disaster/Emergency Management and Business Continuity/Continuity of Operations Programs* (Quincy, MA: NFPA, 2016).

CHAPTER 9

Monitoring, Auditing, and Risk Management

INTRODUCTION

Today's records and information management professionals must know how to monitor the performance of employees as well as the performance of the records management program. They must understand the auditing process and be able to assist with internal and external audits. And they must be in a position to identify and analyze records and information risks—including those posed by new technology, cloud computing, contracts with third parties, e-discovery requests, and Freedom of Information requests—and make recommendations to manage them.

MONITORING THE MANAGEMENT OF RECORDS

In chapter 2, you learned that records management programs are undertaken with specific objectives in mind, including providing effective control, appropriate security, and management of the creation, maintenance, use, and disposition of all records within the organization. *Monitoring* is a process conducted by departmental staff and may involve the internal audit or compliance department to uncover fraud and abuse, measure progress toward goals, and identify the need for an audit. Monitoring includes conducting analyses and making adjustments accordingly. Organizations generally conduct two types of monitoring activities to understand how well the program is performing and to identify areas that need attention: performance monitoring and compliance monitoring.

Performance Monitoring

Performance monitoring is conducted to measure performance and provide ongoing feedback to employees and workgroups on their progress toward reaching their goals. It is a continuous process that involves developing criteria, conducting interviews, and examining documentation to determine whether a process is efficient and effective. In addition to monitoring the performance of individuals, performance monitoring can include monitoring overall performance of the records management program, effectiveness of the records management process, efficiency of records management systems, and strength of the organization's capacity to support records management. The development of a performance monitoring program involves identifying actions to be taken during each stage of the process shown in figure 9.1.

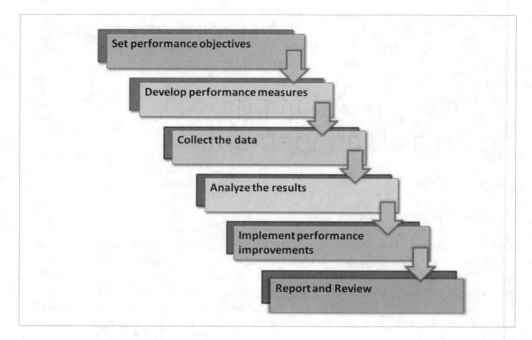

FIGURE 9.1 Steps in the performance monitoring process.

SOURCE: Adapted from Stage Records Authority of New South Wales, "Monitoring Recordkeeping Performance," accessed December 19, 2017, https://www.records.nsw.gov.au/recordkeeping/advice/monitoring/recordkeeping-performance..

Performance measurements are based on predetermined internal or external criteria. Industry benchmarks are often used to compare an organization's performance to that of industry leaders. Individual employees can also be rated based on their performance over time or among other employees. Employee performance plans with accompanying rating systems are used as a basis for pay increases and retrenchment decisions.

Some organizations provide incentives to motivate employees and teams to excel. An employee pay raise is an example of an individual reward. Other rewards can be in the form of an informal or formal thank-you—a pizza party, a bonus, or time off.

Recognizing excellence is an effective way to honor those who have contributed to a superior records management program. In 2016, the Utah State Division of Archives and Records Service presented the Excellence in Information Governance Award to Colleen Mulvey, the city's recorder, for her leadership in developing the city's records management program. Specifically, Mulvey was recognized for:

- implementing a variety of methods to ensure accurate, manageable, and innovative preservation of the city's records
- establishing agency-wide training to educate staff on the importance of proper records management
- actively engaging in professional development and sharing experiences with colleagues[1]

Monitoring is an essential component in measuring employee and organization progress toward goals so that appropriate feedback can be given, corrective action can be taken, and informal and formal rewards can be granted for meeting standards of excellence. Monitoring can also be used to gauge the organization's ability to comply with internal policies and standards as well as external standards, laws, and regulations.

Compliance Monitoring Using Self-Assessments

Compliance monitoring can include targeted assessments of recordkeeping based on the identification of a business issue or problem. One way to measure progress is by conducting an initial evaluation and then using that as a baseline for future studies. In large public and private organizations, self-evaluations may be the most efficient way to gather data. In 2009, the US National Archives and Records Administration (NARA) implemented a mandatory self-assessment process for all federal agencies that required the agencies to complete and return a survey form. The main focus of the 2009 records management self-assessment (RMSA) was email because of the widespread public interest in this topic.[2] Four additional topics were evaluated: program management, records disposition, vital records, and electronic records. Over 90 percent of the federal agencies responded to the self-assessment, and the responses indicated that 79 percent of those agencies were at high to moderate risk of compromising the integrity, authenticity, and reliability of their records.

In 2010, NARA conducted a second RMSA.[3] The report released in May 2011 revealed that 95 percent of the 251 respondents were at high to moderate risk of comprising the integrity, authenticity, and reliability of their records. In 2010, there were fewer agencies considered low risk with regard to their compliance with federal records management regulations and policies than in 2009, possibly because the survey instrument was revised by increasing the nature and number of questions. Therefore, NARA determined the responses to the 2010 survey would be used as the new baseline for future annual self-assessments.

The special topic area in the 2010 survey was training, where the findings indicated:

- a widespread dearth of formal training for staff (and contractors) at all levels;
- training that slights or neglects important records management topics, including vital records; and
- a lack of effective and long-term evaluation mechanisms.

The RMSA was issued separately through 2016. As of 2017, the RMSA report was consolidated with the Senior Agency Officials for Records Management Report and the Federal Email Management Report and published as the "Federal Agency Records Management 2016 Annual Report." The results of the 2016 RMSAs revealed the good news that 45 percent of agencies scored in the low risk category, compared to 5 percent in 2010. The report also revealed that printing and filing email declined from 75 percent in 2013 to 46 percent in 2016.[4]

As with private organizations, it helps when high-level government officials provide support for records management improvements. On November 28, 2011, President Barack Obama took steps to improve the management of federal records by issuing a presidential memorandum directing agencies to move into a digital-based recordkeeping system. Continuing the transformation from physical to digital recordkeeping, the 2018–2022 NARA Strategic Plan includes several relevant objectives, such as:

1. By FY 2024, NARA will digitize 500 million pages of records and make them available online through the National Archives Catalog.
2. By FY 2020, NARA will have policies and processes in place to support Federal agencies' transition to fully electronic recordkeeping.
3. By December 31, 2022, NARA will, to the fullest extent possible, no longer accept transfers of permanent or temporary records in analog formats and will accept records only in electronic format and with appropriate metadata.
4. By FY 2020, NARA will have a career development program in place to support NARA's transition to electronic records.[5]

The federal government is not the only sector facing compliance challenges. Let's turn our attention to issues confronting two other industries.

Compliance Monitoring and Laws and Regulations

Compliance officers are often employed by organizations to ensure that programs are in line with federal and state regulations, as well as industry-specific regulations, such as the Health Insurance Portability and Accountability Act, the Health Information Technology for Economic and Clinical Health Act, the Financial Regulatory Authority, and the Sarbanes-Oxley Act. Organizations may rely on records management personnel to conduct internal reviews, which can help prepare the organization for formal external audits.

Health Insurance Portability and Accountability Act (HIPAA)

One goal of the Health Insurance Portability and Accountability Act (HIPAA) is to protect patients' privacy. The privacy rule of HIPAA protects personally identifiable information (PII) as it moves through the healthcare system. Healthcare organizations, including providers, payers, and clearinghouses, must comply with the privacy rule. HIPAA security standards were developed to help organizations protect PII. The implementation of administrative, physical, and technical safeguards—such as access controls, auditing controls, and workstation security—are necessary to protect PII.

A classic example of the violation of an individual's HIPAA-protected medical information involves a well-known actor, George Clooney. In 2007, he and his girlfriend were riding their motorcycle when a car hit them. They were hospitalized briefly at Palisades Medical Center in North Bergen, New Jersey. According to the Associated Press, as many as twenty-seven hospital employees were not only tempted to look at the actor's medical information but some even tried to sell the records to the tabloids. How do we know? A routine internal records management audit for HIPAA compliance conducted by the hospital's records management personnel uncovered the violation.[6] Those actions resulted in the suspension without pay of dozens of medical personnel. Records managers uncovered lapses in records management practices that resulted in changes to prevent future federal statute violations, and they emerged from this situation as the heroes rather than the scapegoats.

Health Information Technology for Economic and Clinical Health Act (HITECH)

In 2009, the Health Information Technology for Economic and Clinical Health Act (HITECH) provisions of the Economic Stimulus Act expanded HIPAA regulations to include mandatory breach notifications, heightened enforcement, expanded patients' rights, and increased penalties of up to $50,000 for each violation and up to $1.5 million per calendar year.

In January 2017, the Children's Medical Center of Dallas (Children's) was penalized $3.217 million by the US Department of Health and Human Services for its impermissible disclosure of unsecured electronic protected health information (ePHI) and non-compliance with multiple standards of the HIPAA Security Rule. The penalty was based on a 2009 loss of an unencrypted, non-password protected BlackBerry device at the Dallas/Fort Worth International Airport containing data on 3,800 individuals and a loss of a second unencrypted laptop from Children's premises in April 2013 containing data on 2,462 individuals. The issue was the failure of Children's to deploy encryption or an equivalent measure on all company laptops, workstations, mobile devices, and removable storage media.[7]

Today, encryption issues involve not only data stored within the enterprise but also data stored in the cloud and while in transit between the two. An analysis of encryption controls offered by over 12,000 cloud providers revealed that while 81.8 percent of cloud service providers encrypt data in transit from the user to the cloud, only 9.4 percent encrypt data at rest in the cloud. File sharing services account for 39 percent of all company data uploaded to the cloud, and 34 percent of those have uploaded sensitive information including personal health information (PHI).[8] Third-party technologies that encrypt cloud data both at rest and in transit should be employed to enhance security and privacy.

Managing the Compliance Process

The best approach to managing compliance is to establish an intelligent information governance process—one supported by enabling technology. A number of vendors offer software and services to assist organizations with the compliance process.

Some solutions providers take a holistic approach by offering integrated governance, risk, and compliance (GRC) technology. Allgress (https://allgress.com/) is one provider that offers a multimodular, integrated solution for enterprises of all sizes. Allgress' Insight Risk Management platform provides risk oversights in real time and continuous monitoring with actionable insights. The company also offers ComplianceVision, an automated compliance solution within the AWS Cloud.

Some companies offer limited, specific compliance solutions as part of their products and services. For example, Google Vault is a web-based archiving and records management solution that can be purchased on its own for a fee but is included with the GSuite Enterprise or Business or Education edition. Google Vault allows organizations to retain, archive, search, and export email, Hangout chat messages, Google Groups, and Files in Google Drive and Team Drives in response to e-discovery and compliance requests. Retention rules can be used to specify how long data are retained before being deleted from user accounts and Google Systems.[9]

Technology to accomplish your goals will continue to evolve and new solutions will be available to you. In order to select the right product or service, keep in mind the following six critical compliance needs:

- centrally controlled document access management
- document classification policy management
- retention policy management
- destruction and disposition policy management

Risk Culture

Risk culture is a term describing the values, beliefs, knowledge, attitudes, and understanding about risk shared by a group of people with a common purpose. This applies to all organizations—including private companies, public bodies, governments, and not-for-profits.

SOURCE: Institute of Risk Management, accessed December 21, 2017, https://www.theirm.org/knowledge-and-resources/thought-leadership/risk-culture.aspx.

- legal hold management
- metadata generation and management

If you are responsible for records management programs at your organization, you should be familiar with available products and services so you can discuss these options with others involved with compliance issues, such as the information technology (IT) and legal departments. The cost of such products or services can be minor compared to potential losses incurred due to fines, penalties, and loss of reputation related to poor recordkeeping practices.

Thomson Reuters is a firm that offers Compliance Management products and services for firms worldwide. Its *Regulatory Intelligence* solution covers 750 regulatory bodies across the globe and more than 2,500 collections of regulatory and legislative materials. *Regulatory Intelligence Feeds* automate the flow of information extracted from the regulatory database to the organization for immediate review and implementation when changes occur. Technology is essential, but one of the topics we must not ignore when discussing regulatory compliance is the impact of culture (including ethics and integrity) on conduct risk. The

Conduct Risk

A standard definition has yet to be agreed upon, but the following two examples share a common theme—fair treatment to others:

- *Conduct Risk* is the "intentional or negligent actions of employees or agents that may lead to negative outcomes for customers, clients and markets."[*]
- *"Conduct Risk* is the risk that arises as a result of how businesses and employees conduct themselves, particularly in relation to their clients and competitors."[†]

[*] Citi, "Conduct, Culture, and Governance," accessed December 21, 2017, www.citigroup.com/citi/about/citizenship/download/2015/global/2015-citi-global-citizenship-factsheet-conduct-culture-governance-en.pdf.
[†] Risk.net, "Top 10 Operational Risks for 2016," accessed December 21, 2017, https://www.risk.net/risk-management/2441306/top-10-operational-risks-2016.

results of a study conducted by Thompson Reuters revealed that 68 percent of the participating firms had a working definition for "conduct risk," but 87 percent believed that regulatory focus on culture and/or conduct risk would increase personal liability of senior managers.[10]

AUDITING THE RECORDS MANAGEMENT PROGRAM

Auditing is a formal review governed by professional standards that includes:

- completion by professionals independent of the operation under review;
- a structured approach that includes planning, sampling, testing, and validating; and
- formal communication with recommendations, followed by corrective actions and documented follow-up of those corrective actions.

Over time, organizations will be subject to different types of audits, including compliance audits and operational (program) audits.

Records Management Program Audits

Program audits are systematic studies conducted to assess how well a program or operation is working. Similar to performance monitoring but more formal, program audits are used to assess either achievement or progress toward a goal. The audits can be used to monitor an entire program or one portion of it, for example, electronic records management. The audit can evaluate not only practices but also systems, technologies, and facilities.

An audit could be conducted by an internal official of the organization, such as the director of internal audits or chief compliance officer. It could also be conducted by an outside auditor. In either case, the audit results would be formally communicated to the appropriate high-level executive or board of directors. The data gathered must be evaluated in order to identify if and where problems exist. The results should indicate if the records are complete and if security breaches were identified. Policies and procedures should be modified as necessary based upon the findings.

Auditing Procedures

To prepare for an upcoming audit, it is necessary to understand the audit process. Three phases of the audit are planning, conducting, and reporting the findings:

- **Planning the audit:** The *audit plan* is a description of the expected scope and conduct of the audit with sufficient detail to guide the development of the audit program. Auditors meet with management to discuss plans for the audit process and to discover specific risks to the organization to be given special attention by the auditors. To prepare for the meeting, management should uncover areas of concern, such as issues related to email or social media use.

- **Conducting the audit:** Auditors will conduct fieldwork by meeting with employees (including management) responsible for handling sensitive records to ensure they are following standard operating procedures. In order to assure maximum coordination of staff time and availability of records, audit visits should be prepared for as soon as notification is received.
- **Reporting the findings of the audit:** An audit report is completed after the fieldwork has been conducted and the auditors have identified areas of weakness related to government regulations and/or standard operating procedures. The auditors then meet with management to discuss the results and may recommend scheduling a remedial audit in the future to see if the weaknesses have been remedied.

Auditing against a Standard, ISO 15489-1: 2016

An audit must be conducted against some type of measure, and an assessment tool must be acquired or developed. For example, an external audit could be conducted to determine compliance with the ISO *15489-1:2016*.[11]

In addition to a section on principles for managing records, ISO 15489-1:2016 contains five major areas in which an organization could be evaluated:

- records and records systems
- policies and responsibilities
- appraisal
- records controls
- processes for creating, capturing, and managing records

The relevant requirements of ISO *15489-1:2016* could be turned into a series of questions used as a checklist or audit assessment tool. Unlike ISO 15498-1:2001, which had a section on *Regulatory Environment,* the 2016 version subsumes regulations under the section on Appraisal and disperses references to the regulatory environment throughout the standard.

Auditing the Regulatory Environment

To begin our analysis of ISO 15489-1:2016 as related to regulations and the regulatory environment, we find that the fourth of five principles for managing records (Section 4.d.) reads:

> . . . decisions regarding the creation, capture and management of records are based on the analysis and risk assessment of business activities, in their business, legal, regulatory and societal contexts.

That quote indicates that whenever records are created, captured, or managed, the regulatory environment must be considered. Section 4.d. also refers the reader to Clause 7, Appraisal.

Section 5.3.2.3 on compliance for records systems specifies that records systems should be managed in compliance with requirements—including those from the regulatory environment. In addition, compliance with the requirements should be regularly assessed and records of those assessments retained. From Sections 4 and 5 alone, four questions that could be used as a basis for an audit arise:

1. Are regulations considered when making decisions about records creation, capture, and management?
2. Are records managed in compliance with regulatory requirements?
3. Is compliance with the regulatory environment regularly assessed?
4. Are records of such assessments retained?

In addition, Section 6.2 states that policies should define where mandates (including regulations) and best practices affect the creation, capture, or management of records, so a fifth question could be:

5. Does the organization's records management policy include reference to regulations that affect the creation and capture or management of records?

The regulatory environment is not restricted to federal, state, or local regulations. As explained in the first edition of ISO 15489-1, the regulatory environment consists of:

- statute and case laws, and regulations governing the sector-specific and general business environment, including laws and regulations relating specifically to records, archives, access, privacy, evidence, electronic commerce, data protection, and information;
- mandatory standards of practice;
- voluntary codes of best practice;
- voluntary codes of conduct and ethics; and
- identifiable expectations of the community about what is acceptable behavior for the specific sector or organization.[12]

To prepare for an audit on compliance with the regulatory environment, the organization should determine if they are meeting the obligations outlined in the standard. In addition, the audit assessment tool might ask questions about systems, security, metadata, and more.

An auditor would expect to see not only positive responses to the questions but also evidence to support those positive responses. ISO *15489-1* is a general records management standard with requirements that apply across industries. But, as with compliance monitoring, organizations facing compliance audits must understand their industry-specific regulatory obligations.

Industry-Specific Audits: Higher Education

The higher education sector is responsible for complying with a complex legal and regulatory environment relating to privacy and security. Just as in the healthcare industry, higher education institutions must address compliance activities around the HIPAA, including developing policies and procedures and training for handling information about patients and research subjects.

In addition, higher education institutions must address the Family Educational Rights and Privacy Act of 1974 (FERPA).[13] Postsecondary officials must notify students of their FERPA rights, provide tools for students to consent to online and offline sharing of records and to opt out of sharing directory information, and provide training to faculty and staff on the appropriate uses of student records.[14]

A 2017 study revealed that the average cost of each record compromised in US education organizations is $245—$25 higher than the average cost per record for all US organizations. It was found that one of the contributors to the higher cost is that mobile platforms are used more extensively in education. This increases the cost of each comprised record by an average of $6.50.[15] It is important to remember that compliance *does not* equal security. Even fully compliant institutions run the risk of potential data breaches, which can be quite costly.

Industry-Specific Audits: Transportation

SoundTransit plans, builds, and operates express bus, light rail, and commuter train services in the state of Washington. It is one of the most scrutinized public agencies in the state. It is accountable to a fifteen-member volunteer Citizen Oversight Panel, an independent fifteen-member Diversity Oversight Committee, and the US Department of Transportation. SoundTransit defines public records as any information created or received to support its decisions, actions, operations, or business transactions. The 2016 "Internal Audit Report, Records Management Program," conducted by the Washington State Internal Audit Division, revealed the following goals for the records management program: (1) compliance with the Revised Code of Washington (RCW) and (2) management of an ever-increasing amount of digital and physical records and responsiveness to an increasing number of public information requests.[16]

The audit also had two objectives: (1) to determine if departments and divisions had effective document controls to create, use, and store records during the active phase of the records lifecycle and (2) to determine if the Records Management Division had effective controls for retaining and disposing inactive records during the archival phase. This performance audit was conducted in accordance with the Generally Accepted Government Auditing Standards and the International Standards for the Professional Practice of Internal Auditing. The audit process involved data analysis, documentation reviews, site visits, and personnel interviews. Risks identified by the process included inadequate metadata and classification scheme and lack of a records evaluation process. Recommendations were offered to mitigate risks resulting from those deficiencies.

ARMA TR 25-2014, *Auditing for Records and Information Management Program Compliance,* aims to encourage innovation, spur improvement, strengthen information governance efforts, and bolster compliance for all organizations. It provides advice for the implementation of audits that will be useful for assessing an organization's risk exposure and providing opportunities for quality and performance improvement. Now, we'll turn our attention to the topic of risk management.

RISK MANAGEMENT

Organizations face internal and external factors and influences that make it uncertain whether and when they will achieve their objectives. The effect this uncertainty has on an organization's objectives is *risk.* The *level of risk* is determined by multiplying the *probability of the event occurring (likelihood)* times the *level of impact (consequences)* the event would have on the organization if it did occur.

Risk Management Process

ISO 31000:2009 Risk Management—Principles and Guidelines can be used to assess risk for a wide range of activities, including processes, operations, and functions. According to ISO 31000, the risk management process includes:

- communication and consultation with internal and external stakeholders throughout the process;
- establishing the context, including objectives, scope, and risk criteria;
- conducting the risk assessment;
- selecting and implementing the risk treatment to modify risks; and
- monitoring and reviewing the risk management process.[17]

Risk assessment includes risk identification, risk analysis, and risk evaluation as shown in figure 9.2.

ISO 31000 is a general risk management standard. Additional guidance can be obtained from publications developed specifically to evaluate and mitigate risks related to records and information management.[18]

ARMA International's publication *Evaluating and Mitigating Records and Information Risks* categorizes risks into four quadrants: administrative, records control, legal/regulatory, and technology.[19]

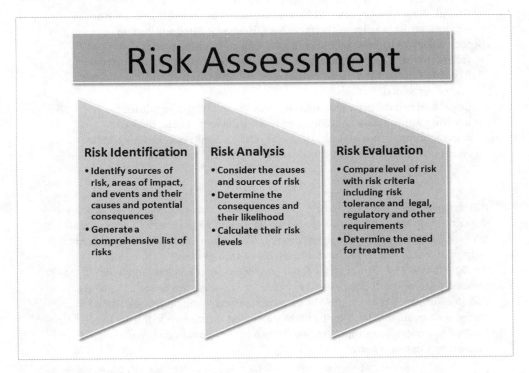

Risk Assessment

Risk Identification
- Identify sources of risk, areas of impact, and events and their causes and potential consequences
- Generate a comprehensive list of risks

Risk Analysis
- Consider the causes and sources of risk
- Determine the consequences and their likelihood
- Calculate their risk levels

Risk Evaluation
- Compare level of risk with risk criteria including risk tolerance and legal, regulatory and other requirements
- Determine the need for treatment

FIGURE 9.2 Risk assessment model.

Risk Identification

The four categories into which ARMA International divides risks can be explained as follows:[20]

- **Administrative risks** are related to the management of the records and information management program, including information governance, change management, and emergency management. As an example, employees may consider records they have been working on *their* records rather than the organization's. Others actually plan to steal confidential data when leaving their jobs, with intellectual property and customer records topping the list. The lack of a policy to secure and/or recover the records of employees in *transition*—due to dismissal, retirement, transfer, or completion of time-bound projects for the firm—could result in the loss of valuable information. According to a 2015 survey, 87 percent of departing employees take records with them; however, only 28 percent admitted to taking data they had not created. The most common methods were saving to a flash or external drive (84 percent), printing hard copies (37 percent), loading to a shared drive (21 percent), or saving to a file synchronizing/sharing service like Dropbox (11 percent).[21]
- **Records control risks** relate to records classification, records retention and disposition, and records storage. As an example, in 2016, nine Canada Revenue Agency (CRA) staff members accessed tax files without authorization in spite of the fact that CRA spent $10.3 million on technology to impose access control. Eight of the nine were fired. The federal privacy commissioner's office issued ten tips to improve situations like this. One of them is to "proactively monitor and/or audit access logs and other oversight tools."[22]
- **Legal and regulatory risks** include risks arising from the failure to institute appropriate controls over mobile devices. These risks can arise from unauthorized physical access, malicious code, device attacks, communication interception, and insider threats. As an example, between

IBM announced a ban on employee use of removable storage devices in all facilities worldwide in May 2018. The reason for the ban, according to Shamla Naidoo, Chief Information Security Officer, was the "possible financial and reputational damage from misplaced, lost or misused removable portable storage devices."

The ban will be disruptive for some employees; however, the firm believes the measures are warranted to prevent massive file leaks like the one in 2013 where hundreds of pages regarding IBM's cloud computing technology were leaked by a former employee. IBM is currently heavily invested in research in the areas of artificial intelligence, quantum computing, and more and this globally enforced policy should help protect its trade secrets.

SOURCE: Parrish, Kevin. "IBM clamps down on leaks, bans works from using external storage," Digital Trends, May 10, 2018.

2013 and 2014, 22,000 smartphones and other electronic devices were left in New York City taxicabs.[23]

- **Technology risks** are associated with information security, electronic communications, and software applications. Records storage in the clouds may be a panacea to some organizations striving to reduce their capital investment in digital infrastructure and software while leveraging the ability the cloud offers to scale up or down depending on the needs of the enterprise. But use of the cloud can magnify the negative impact of a data breach. For example, on April 14, 2016, a US citizen discovered that voter registration records of 93.4 million Mexican citizens—including names, birth dates, home addresses, ID numbers, and more—were visible on the internet. The database was moved out of Mexico and into the United States, contrary to Mexico's data governance laws. The database was made available to the public through Amazon Web Services. Both Mexican and US authorities were notified but it took eight days to remove the database from the public domain. In the words of Lorenzo Cordova Vianello, president of the Mexican National Electoral Institute, "it is not just a criminal offense, it is a national offense."[24]

Risk Assessment Matrix

Once risk has been identified, it must be analyzed and evaluated. Some organizations are in industries that are more heavily regulated than others, and they may have a lower tolerance for certain types of risks. *Risk tolerance* reflects the organization's *attitude* toward risk—how much risk an organization wants or is willing to assume. The amount of risk the organization wants to assume may or may not align with its *risk capacity*—what it needs to assume in order to reach its goals. *Risk capacity* also reflects the amount of loss the organization can incur and still reach its goals.

The organization can develop its own risk assessment matrix to determine the level of risk presented by various events (see figure 9.3). The events that pose risk are slotted into the appropriate categories depending on how likely they are to occur and the severity of the consequences of their occurrence. Action is taken to mitigate risk based on the levels of risk and the organization's tolerance and capacity for risk. For example, events that result in extreme levels of risk require immediate action, whereas those that result in low levels of risk might be ignored. Resources are assigned to mitigate risks that negatively impact the organization and from which it would be difficult to recover.

Risk Mitigation: Cloud Computing, Electronic Discovery, and the Freedom of Information Act (FOIA)

Risk mitigation (i.e., risk reduction) is the systematic reduction in the extent of exposure to a risk and/or the likelihood of its occurrence.[25] A benefit of using the risk assessment matrix is the fact that risks are categorized according to both probability and severity, and those risks can be prioritized for the risk mitigation plan. Once administrative, records control, legal/regulatory, and technology risks are identified and prioritized, mitigation strategies can be identified for each risk that has a high level of adverse impact on the organization in

		Severity of Consequences				
		Insignificant	Minor	Moderate	Major	Catastrophic
Probability of Occurrence	**Almost certainly in most circumstances**	High	High	Extreme	Extreme	Extreme
	Likely and frequently	High	High	High	Extreme	Extreme
	Possible and likely at some point	Significant	High	High	High	High
	Unlikely, but could happen	Moderate	Moderate	Significant	Significant	Significant
	May occur rarely or exceptional circumstances	Low	Low	Moderate	Moderate	Significant
		Levels of Risk				

FIGURE 9.3 Risk assessment matrix.

the event it occurs. The risk mitigation strategies can be incorporated into the risk management plan as procedural guidelines or a code of practice.

Emerging technologies and new or revised laws and regulations will continue to present challenges to the organization. The external environment must be monitored to identify new risks that should be considered when developing the organization's risk management plan. The issues presented next are examples of risks introduced by today's new technologies and the current legal environment.

Risk Mitigation and Cloud Computing

Cloud computing presents both benefits and risks. Fortunately, guidance is available from a number of sources. The National Archives of Australia provides guidance for government agencies about cloud computing and information management that can be useful for public and private organizations as well. When planning to engage a cloud service provider, agencies are expected to consider a number of issues, including:

- **Compliance:** Does the cloud service provider comply with all applicable laws, regulations, standards, and policies governing the government's records?
- **Preservation:** Does the cloud service provider have the ability to preserve the business information stored and managed as long as required?
- **Retention and disposal:** Will the cloud service provider dispose of information, including copies, following instructions from the agency?[26]

In 2016, the *Checklist for Cloud Service Contracts* was released by a committee of the Inter-PARES Trust, a multinational, interdisciplinary research project, that explores issues concerning trust in digital records and data in the online environment.[27] The checklist is available for use under a Creative Commons Attribution. The eight categories are listed below, followed by an example of a relevant question:

- **Agreement:** Is there an explanation of circumstances in which the services could be suspended?
- **Data ownership and use:** Do you retain ownership of the data that you store, transmit, and/or create with the cloud service?
- **Availability, retrieval, and use:** Are the procedures, time, and cost for restoring your data following a service outage clearly stated?
- **Data storage and preservation:** Are there procedures to ensure file integrity during transfer of your data into and out of the system (e.g., checksums)?
- **Data retention and disposition:** Will your data (and all copies, including backups) be destroyed in compliance with your data retention and disposition schedules?
- **Security, confidentiality, and privacy:** Will you be notified in the case of a security breach or system malfunction?
- **Data location and cross-border data flows:** Do you know where metadata are stored and whether they are stored in the same location as your data?
- **End of service—contract termination:** If the contract is terminated, will your data be transferred to you or to another provider of your choice in a usable and interoperable format?[28]

The risks identified could be analyzed, prioritized, and potentially used as questions for a self-study or audit.

Who Audits Third-Party Providers?

If you use public social media or cloud computing services, your organization is working with third-party providers. The provider must also be audited. In the United States, when the social media provider is as large as Facebook or Google, the government takes the responsibility for ensuring that independent audits are conducted not just to protect information from unauthorized access (as with a security audit) but to protect information from both authorized *and* unauthorized access (privacy audit).

In 2011, the Federal Trade Commission (FTC) settled with Google and Facebook after receiving complaints of unfair and deceptive practices in the way they handled their users' personal information. The result? Twenty years of independent audits going forward to be paid for by Google and Facebook. Problems that are uncovered by future audits could result in fines of $16,000 per violation per day if the FTC decides to pursue the issues in court.[29]

There are times when it makes sense to conduct a self-audit and/or contract with an independent firm to conduct an audit for you. In 2017, in response to concerns from advertisers skeptical of the social network's metrics, Facebook Inc. agreed to submit to audits by the Media Rating Council. In this case, Facebook's internal audits revealed some mistakes in reporting to partners and advertisers—which could result in a loss of trust and ad revenue. Audits by an independent organization will go a long way to reestablishing trust among Facebook's corporate customers.[30]

Risk Management and e-Discovery and FOIA Requests

What's the worst that can happen if you can't respond to an e-discovery or Freedom of Information Act (FOIA) request in a timely fashion? Formulating the response to that question is part of the risk management process.

E-discovery and Legal Preparedness

In large firms, corporate counsel or the legal department may manage the discovery process, but the records management team will be involved when requests are made for records and information. *Discovery* is part of the pretrial litigation process during which each party requests relevant information and documents from the other side in an attempt to *discover* pertinent facts. According to the *Federal Rules of Civil Procedure* (FRCP), electronically stored information (ESI) is discoverable. ESI is described as "writings, drawings, graphs, charts, photographs, sound recordings, images, and other data or data compilations—stored in any medium from which information can be obtained either directly or, if necessary, after translation by the responding party into a reasonably usable form."[31]

E-discovery, or *electronic discovery,* refers to the process of locating, securing, and searching ESI with the intent of using it as evidence in a civil or criminal legal case. The pertinent rules in the revised FRCP are 16, 26, 33, 34, 35, 37, and 45.[32] You were introduced to Rules 26 and 37 in chapter 2. The intent of these and additional applicable FRCP rules are shown in table 9.1.

Complying with an e-discovery request can be time-consuming and expensive. In 2007, for example, Microsoft reported spending an average of $20 million for e-discovery *per litigation.* Microsoft's records management analysis manager described e-discovery and records management as two sides of the same coin, adding that the success of a company's e-discovery strategy relies on the strength of its records management function.[33] At the end of 2016, Microsoft's legal department attributed savings of $4.5 million annually to its use of Microsoft Office 365's eDiscovery in the cloud features (including search tools and advanced analytics).[34]

The 2015 amendments to the FRCP modified several FRCP rules, including Rule 26. Rule 26(b)(1) increased the weight given to the scope of discovery and the concept of proportionality in order to rein in the perceived excesses of the discovery process. Rule 37(e) concerning preservation of ESI was also addressed. This issue continues to be fine-tuned because "proper preservation" often depends upon case-specific facts. Courts offer guidance but not prescriptive solutions.[35]

E-discovery software and services are available from a number of vendors. Lawyers working on behalf of the organization must understand how e-discovery software works. In one recent case in Illinois, in a lawsuit subpoena request, a lawyer representing Wells Fargo inadvertently turned over confidential information about thousands of bank clients. In an affidavit, the attorney said she used an e-discovery vendor's software to review what she believed to be a complete set of results and marked some documents as privileged and confidential. She did not realize she was using a view that showed a limited set of documents. Therefore, she turned over documents she had not reviewed for confidentiality and privilege. In addition, she reported having flagging documents for redaction before they were produced, but the documents were not redacted. She explained she misunderstood the role of the vendor and may have miscoded some documents during her review.[36]

TABLE 9.1 Sampling of FRCP rules affecting discovery of electronically stored information.

FRCP RULE	INTENT
16(b)	Allows the court to establish rules around disclosure, privilege, methods and work product prior to electronic discovery commencing.
26(a)	Adds "electronically stored information" (ESI) as a separate category.
26(b) 5	Clarifies procedures when privileged ESI is inadvertently sent over to the requesting party (retrieval of that information).
26(f)	Requires all parties to sit down together before discovery begins to agree on some form of protocol.
33	Includes ESI as part of the business records related to interrogatories.
34(b)	Establishes protocols for how documents are produced to requesting parties.
35	Standardizes discovery agreements (results in an automatic reminder to include ESI).
37(e)	Provides "safe harbor" from sanctions when electronic evidence is lost and unrecoverable as a matter of regular business processes.
37(f)	Allows for sanctions against parties unwilling to participate in the 26(f) discovery conference planning process.
45	45(c) provides protection to a person subject to a subpoena. 45(c)(2)(B) allows such persons who are asked to produce documents, including ESI, to file an objection to production.

During an e-discovery process, the requesting party may wish to see all documents about a specific project or created by a specific individual. He or she will not be concerned with the organization's decision to declare some information a record and other information a non-record. Therefore, the organization's retention policy should include all information. Adding at least one *transitory* record series to the schedule and applying a brief retention period to the category provides a defensible retention category for this information. NARA's "General Records Schedule 5.2: Transitory and Intermediary Records" states that transitory records (those of short-term value—usually less than 180 days) must be destroyed when no longer needed for business use, or according to the agency's predetermined time period or business rule. Intermediary records (those involved in creating a subsequent record) must be destroyed upon verification of successful creation of the final document or file, or when no longer needed for business use, whichever is later.[37]

Although an organization may not be able to control the increasing number of lawsuits, audits, and investigations it faces, it can establish guidelines and policies, employ e-discovery software and services, address e-discovery issues when contracting with third parties, and provide training for employees to mitigate risk to the organization and to the individual.

The Freedom of Information Act

The records of the government belong to the people, and the US Freedom of Information Act (FOIA) ensures public access to US government records. Upon written request, US agencies are required to disclose records requested unless the records can lawfully be withheld under nine specific exemptions in the FOIA.[38] In January 2009, one of the first memoranda President Obama signed was on the subject of FOIA. The fundamental message was that FOIA should be administered with a clear presumption that "in the face of doubt, openness prevails."[39]

The US Department of Justice hosts the FOIA.gov website which provides FOIA data, including requests received, disposition of requests, and backlog. The largest number of requests is for information from the Department of Homeland Security, followed by requests to the Departments of Justice and Defense. The total requests received in 2016 by the Department of Homeland Security alone were 325,780, and a backlog of 64,374 remained by the end of the year (see figure 9.4).

The twenty-day time frame for a response is a challenge for agencies that need to locate and retrieve the documents and then review and redact sensitive information before releasing them. This short time frame, even with one allowed extension under FOIA, makes it difficult for some agencies to meet their obligations. States also have public records laws that provide for a response within a set number of calendar days. Fees for copies of requested documents may be charged.

There are two sides of the public records issue. Access to public information is a right, and the government is obligated to be open and transparent, but the agency responsible to comply with FOIA requests faces challenges, including:

- searching for, retrieving, and duplicating requested information takes time away from activities that relate to the core mission of the agency;

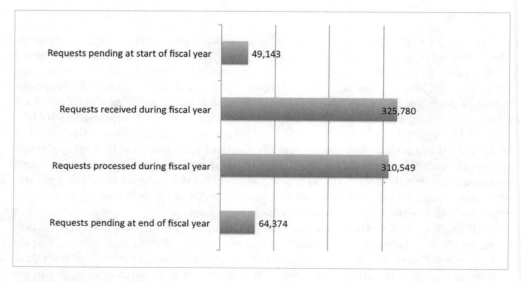

FIGURE 9.4 Department of Homeland Security, FOIA requests received, processed, and pending, fiscal year 2016.

- the current staff may not be sufficient to handle the number of public records requests, so extra staff may be required, resulting in higher payroll costs;
- the charges allowed to be passed along to the requester may not be sufficient to cover the expenses incurred in complying with requests;
- staff training may be needed to ensure that employees gather requested information correctly and redact sensitive information before releasing records to the public; and
- FOIA requests generate new records for agencies that must be managed, including FOIA request logs, copies of forms indicating response (approval/denial), and copies of forms indicating time and cost of information provided.

Most countries have some version of a public records act. For example, Sweden recognized access to information as a constitutional right in 1766, Armenia adopted its Law on Freedom of Information in 2003, Liberia adopted its Freedom of Information Act in 2010, and Yemen's parliament approved its Right to Information Bill in 2012.[40]

What are the consequences for the agency that does not comply with public records requests in a timely manner or at all? Obviously, ill will on the part of the public is one. Organizations such as the Electronic Frontier Foundation (https://www.eff.org/) in the United States exist to champion the public interest and provide the means for citizens to advocate for openness and transparency. This organization often submits its own FOIA requests, including appeals when necessary.

In the United States, if a federal agency denies a request for public information, the requester has the right to appeal the decision to the agency. A nonresponse is treated the same as a denial. If the appeal is not responded to within twenty working days, the requester has the right to file a lawsuit to compel disclosure. This will result in additional work for the agency. If a court finds in favor of the requester, it might allow the requester to recover attorney fees and other reasonable costs incurred in filing the litigation.

SUMMARY

How do you know that you have an effective, efficient, and compliant records management program? One way is to set objectives for your program and then monitor progress toward those objectives. Monitoring can reveal fraud and abuse, provide spot checks on performance, and identify the need for an audit. Performance monitoring is used to monitor the performance of individuals as well as the overall performance of the records management program. Compliance monitoring can determine an organization's adherence to governing regulations, including industry-specific laws and regulations.

Internal compliance officers or records management personnel can conduct internal audits to gather data and to help prepare the organization for formal external audits. A formal audit is a review conducted by professionals independent of the program being audited, using a structured approach and resulting in a formal report with recommendations for improvement.

Auditing is conducted against some type of measure, such as the records management standard ISO *15489-1:2016*, to determine compliance with the regulatory environment, including statute and case laws and regulations governing the sector-specific and general business environment. Industry-specific audits reveal the extent to which the organization complies with laws and regulations affecting that particular industry; for example, higher education institutions must comply with the Family Educational Rights and Privacy Act (FERPA) and SoundTransit of the State of Washington must comply with the state's Revised Code of Washington (RCW).

Organizations must identify sources of risk, analyze risks, and develop action plans to mitigate those risks. A risk assessment matrix can be used to determine the level of risk and provide data that can be used to prioritize risks. New technologies present additional risks that must be considered, as do risks resulting from agreements with third-party providers.

E-discovery and FOIA requests also present challenges to the organization. The cost of complying with e-discovery requests can be high, with fines and other penalties imposed for failure to produce records requested. The inability of government to produce records requested by the public in a timely fashion can result in ill will on the part of citizens. The success of the organization's ability to respond to either e-discovery or public records requests relies on the strength of its records management program.

Risk management involves understanding, analyzing, and addressing risk to make sure organizations achieve their objectives. Risk can arise from an organization's inability to manage its records and information in a legally defensible manner. In her contribution to this chapter, Dr. Lisa Daulby suggests that organizations can combine risk management methodologies with information governance industry principles and maturity models to identify, assess, control, and report on RIM risks.

PARADIGM

Identifying, Assessing, and Controlling Records and Information Management Risks—A Cross-Disciplinary Approach

Lisa Daulby, PhD, CRM, IGP
Faculty, Master of Archives and Records Administration Program
School of Information, San José State University

Introduction to Project

Records and information management (RIM) program decisions must be based on an understanding of risk. Risk management methodologies protect organizations from unacceptable business or reputational events arising from operational, compliance, regulatory, legal, administrative, technological, financial, and other risks while supporting and enabling the organization's overall business strategy. A risk management program identifies, assesses, measures, controls, monitors, and reports on significant risks that face organizations. There are a number of risks associated with the mismanagement of information, including the unauthorized creation, collection, use, over-retention, or disclosure of information. Organizations can accurately and effectively identify, assess, control, and report on RIM risks in a cross disciplinary approach by combining risk management methodologies with established information governance (IG) industry principles and maturity models.

Problem Statement

ARMA International's Information Governance Maturity Model (IG Maturity Model) defines the characteristics of an Information Governance (IG) program for the eight Generally Accepted Recordkeeping Principles (The Principles). The maturity levels are based on the completeness and effectiveness of records/information management competencies and range from Level 1 (Sub-Standard) to Level 5 (Transformational). For those organizations that have an existing, or are establishing, a RIM program within an IG framework, the IG Maturity Model can be employed to advance and grow the program irrespective of the defined level on the maturity spectrum. Although the IG Maturity Model is an excellent instrument for determining RIM program maturity, the measured outcomes can be challenging to communicate internally to senior management, decision-makers, and other stakeholders not familiar with the model. One effective approach in recommending program support is through an integrated risk profile that accurately reflects the potential impact associated with various RIM risks and related vulnerabilities. By combining risk management methodologies with the IG Maturity Model, organizations can accurately identify, assess, control, and report on RIM risks to support enhanced RIM program decision-making and governance (see figure 9.5).

The risk management process is an iterative mechanism that enables stakeholders to collaboratively identify and manage RIM risks. The components of the risk management process include risk identification, risk rating and assessment, risk control, and risk

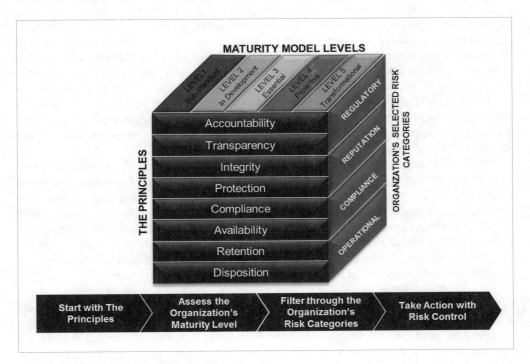

FIGURE 9.5 Intersection of risk management methodologies and the IG Maturity Model.

Courtesy of Lisa Daulby.

monitoring. *Risk identification* describes the process of recognizing risks, whereas *risk assessment* evaluates risks with the goal of providing a foundation on which to construct a response. *Risk controls* are processes or activities designed to offset or mitigate risks, and *risk monitoring* provides insight into the various ways risks are tracked and reported. The risk management process, when framed with the IG Maturity Model, defines a shared discourse that subsequently enriches the value and significance of a RIM program.

Recommended Approach

To begin, an organization must define its RIM risk appetite. Risk appetite is the amount and type of risk that an organization is able and willing to accept in the pursuit of its business objectives. The approach to outlining the RIM risk appetite will vary depending on several factors including IG Maturity Model target levels and the number of principles defined in scope. Organizations may choose to target all eight principles or a defined subset in addition to also selecting the suitable level on the IG Maturity Model scale they wish to attain for each principle. These decisions must be based on an understanding of informed risks. In completing the risk management process, it is important that all stakeholders are engaged to ensure that the risks are appropriately analyzed and ranked so that the results of the assessment are accurate and supported.

Key RIM risks must be identified, validated, and scoped. The IG Maturity Model can be most effectively used during the risk identification phase of the risk management process. The aim of this step is to generate a comprehensive list of all RIM inherent risks and explain them in business terms. The IG Maturity Model can be used as a guide to assist organizations to reliably self-identify RIM risks. For example, by means of the IG Maturity Model, an organization may discover that although it has a retention schedule and policy available, these do not encompass all records and information and the policy is not well-known throughout the organization. This attribute reflects a Level 2 (in development) on the IG Maturity Model scale for the principle of retention. Although this rating may reflect a less-than-ideal situation for most organizations, how can this rating be measured in terms that an organization will understand? From a risk perspective, what does a ranking on the IG Maturity Model mean for organizations?

Organizations understand risk, and the most effective method of communicating IG Maturity Model ratings is through categorizing and rating each level attribute as a quantified risk. The IG Maturity Model encompasses a series of scenarios that can each be rendered or explained as organizational risks. For example, the identified and documented retention principle Level 2 rating could next be assigned a risk category and inherent RIM risk rating. This risk analysis involves consideration of the RIM risk, as well as the impact and likelihood of it adversely affecting one or more of an organization's principle risk categories including operational, compliance, reputational, regulatory, legal, administrative, technological, and financial.

Overall, assessing inherent risk requires using professional judgment supported by a logical, defensible rationale. For example, consider the previously identified RIM risk whereby the retention policies do not encompass all records and information and are not well known around the organization. Furthermore, an additional risk exists if a decision has been made to not purge one or more applications or systems in accordance with criteria established in the retention schedule. This RIM risk results in an exposure to a combination of the organization's principal risks categories including legal, regulatory, reputational, and compliance. If realized, the magnitude of this unmitigated identified risk, when plotted onto a standard risk assessment matrix (see figure 9.3), yields a high risk rating due to the potential risk of privacy or security breaches and service disruptions. This could result in client dissatisfaction, loss of business, regulatory fines, and damaged reputation/brand.

Results

When the outcome of the RIM risks have been measured, an organization must respond to the risks by taking action and implementing controls. Controls can include: (1) putting a process in place to eliminate or minimize the risk, (2) acceptance, whereby no action is taken, (3) sharing or transfer that shifts the risk from one organization to another party, or (4) avoidance by discontinuing the activities or conditions that give rise to risk. This phase of the risk process requires determining whether each risk identified exceeds the organization's risk appetite.

Organizations have several options to deal with risk. Selecting the most appropriate risk control option involves balancing the costs and efforts of implementation against the benefits derived with regard to legal, regulatory, and other requirements. For instance, in response to the second identified failure to purge records that have met their retention requirement, the organization could mitigate the risks by implementing a remediation project to create purge jobs for all noncompliant systems and applications. These actions will reduce the frequency and/or impact of a risk and decrease exposures and adverse effects.

Conclusion

With competing organizational resources and priorities, raising the visibility of and communicating RIM program development with senior management, decision-makers, and other stakeholders can be challenging. Risk management process components are designed to proactively uncover RIM risks dimensions and promote a risk-aware culture. Organizations can make and defend RIM program decisions and judgments based on internal evidence and external risk management criteria. The risk management process, when framed with the IG Maturity Model, accurately reflects the potential impact associated with current and emerging RIM risks. This cross-disciplinary approach enriches stakeholder awareness of identified RIM issues in a way that narrates in defined risk methods. Elevating and embedding RIM program risks into the culture and operations of an organization empowers and clarifies accountability.

NOTES

1. Cedar Hills, Utah, "City Recorder Receives Excellence in Information Governance Award," accessed January 2, 2018, www.cedarhills.org/node/4772.
2. National Archives and Records Administration (NARA), *Records Management Self-Assessment Report 2009*, accessed December 19, 2017, www.archives.gov/records-mgmt/resources/self-assessment.html.
3. National Archives and Records Administration (NARA), *Records Management Self-Assessment Report 2010*, accessed December 19, 2017, www.archives.gov/records-mgmt/resources/self-assessment.html.
4. National Archives and Records Administration (NARA), *Federal Agency Records Management 2016 Annual Report*, October 2, 2017, https://www.archives.gov/files/records-mgmt/resources/2016-federal-agency-records-management-annual-report.pdf.

5. National Archives and Records Administration (NARA), Draft National Archives Strategic Plan, 2017, https://www.archives.gov/about/plans-reports/strategic-plan/draft-strategic-plan.

6. Associated Press, "Hospital Workers Suspended for Allegedly Peeking at Clooney Medical Info," *FoxNews.com*, October 10, 2007, www.foxnews.com/story/0,2933,300648,00.html.

7. "Lack of Timely Action Risks Security and Costs Money," February 1, 2017, HHS.gov., February 1, 2017, https://www.hhs.gov/hipaa/for-professionals/compliance-enforcement/agreements/childrens.

8. Cameron Coles, "Only 9.4% of Cloud Providers Are Encrypting Data at Rest," 2017, https://www.skyhighnetworks.com/cloud-security-blog/only-9-4-of-cloud-providers-are-encrypting-data-at-rest/.

9. "What is Google Vault?" accessed December 21, 2017, https://support.google.com/vault/answer/2462365?hl=en.

10. Stacey English, Susannah Hammond, and Ashley Kovas, "Culture and Conduct Risk 2017," Thomson-Reuters, accessed December 21, 2017, https://risk.thomsonreuters.com/content/dam/openweb/documents/pdf/risk/report/culture-and-conduct-risk-report-2017.pdf.

11. International Organization for Standardization (ISO), *ISO 15489-1:2016 Information and documentation—Records management—Part 1: Concepts and Principles* (Geneva: ISO, 2016).

12. International Organization for Standardization (ISO), *ISO 15489-1:2001: Information and Documentation—Records Management—Part 1: General* (Geneva: ISO, 2001), 4.

13. US Department of Education, Family Educational Rights and Privacy Act (FERPA), accessed December 21, 2017, www2.ed.gov/policy/gen/guid/fpco/ferpa/index.html.

14. US Department of Education, "Protecting Student Privacy by Audience: Postsecondary School Officials, accessed December 21, 2017, https://studentprivacy.ed.gov/audience/school-officials-post-secondary.

15. EAB, "Cost of Data Breaches in Education Hits All-Time High: $245 per Record," July 27, 2017, https://www.eab.com/daily-briefing/2017/07/27/cost-of-data-breaches-in-education-hits-all-time-high-$245-per-record.

16. SoundTransit, "Internal Audit Report: Records Management Program," Report Number 2016-5, December 1, 2017, https://www.soundtransit.org/sites/default/files/Internal%20Audit%20Update-2016%20Records%20Management%20Program.pdf.

17. International Organization for Standardization (ISO), *ISO 31000:2009 Risk Management—Principles and Guidelines* (Geneva: ISO, 2009).

18. Ibid.

19. ARMA International, *Evaluating and Mitigating Records and Information Risks* (Overland Park, KS: ARMA International, 2009).

20. Ibid.

21. Sarah Peters, "Survey: When Leaving Company, Most Insiders Take Data They Created," *Information Week*, December 23, 2015, https://www.darkreading.com/vulnerabilities—-threats/survey-when-leaving-company-most-insiders-take-data-they-created/d/d-id/1323677.

22. Howard Solomon, "Eight Canada Revenue Staffers Fired This Year for Snooping through Records: CBC," *IT World Canada*, December 21, 2016, https://www.itworldcanada.com/article/eight-canada-revenue-staffers-fired-this-year-for-snooping-through-records-cbc/389441.

23. "Mobile Device Security in the Workplace: 6 Key Risks and Challenges," accessed December 21, 2017, https://www.slideshare.net/Forsythe_Technology/mobile-devices-in-the-workplace-5-key-security-risks-11988063/17.

24. Lulu Chang, "The Latest Data Breach Involves the Voting Records of 93.4 Million Mexican Citizens," April 13, 2016, https://www.digitaltrends.com/computing/mexico-voting-breach/.

25. BusinessDictionary.com, s.v. "risk mitigation," accessed December 21, 2017, www.business dictionary.com/definition/risk-mitigation.html.

26. National Archives of Australia, "Cloud Computing and Information Management," accessed December 23, 2017, www.naa.gov.au/information-management/managing-information -and-records/storing/cloud/index.aspx.

27. InterPARES Trust, "Checklist for Cloud Service Contracts: Final Version," last reviewed February 26, 2016, https://interparestrust.org/assets/public/dissemination/NA14_20160226 _CloudServiceProviderContracts_Checklist_Final.pdf.

28. Ibid.

29. Kashmir Hill, "So, What Are These Privacy Audits That Google and Facebook Have to Do for the Next 20 Years?" *Forbes,* November 30, 2011, www.forbes.com/sites/kashmirhill/2011 /11/30/ so-what-are-these-privacy-audits-that-google-and-facebook-have-to-do-for-the-next-20 -years/.

30. Jing Cao, "Facebook Commits to Audit of Its Ad Metrics by Media Watchdog," *Bloomberg Technology,* 2017, February 10, 2017, https://www.bloomberg.com/news/articles/2017-02-10/ facebook-commits-to-audit-of-ad-metrics-by-media-watchdog.

31. The *Federal Rules of Civil Procedure* are accessible at Cornell University School of Law, Legal Information Institute at https://www.law.cornell.edu/rules/frcp.

32. Ibid.

33. Angela Natividad, "Microsoft Calls E-Discovery, Records Management Inseparable Halves," *CMS Wire,* April 30, 2007, https://www.cmswire.com/cms/records-management/microsoft-calls -ediscovery-records-management-inseparable-halves-001238.php.

34. Microsoft, "Office 365 Meets Evolving eDiscovery Challenges in a Cloud-First World," accessed December 24, 2017, https://www.microsoft.com/itshowcase/Article/Content/843/Office -365-meets-evolving-eDiscovery-challenges-in-a-cloudfirst-world.

35. Rhys Dipshan, "FRCP Amendments Dominate 2016 Federal E-Discovery Cases, Report Finds," *Corporate Counsel,* December 14, 2016, https://www.law.com/insidecounsel/2016/12/14/ frcp-amendments-dominate-2016-federal-e-discovery/.

36. Debra Cassens Weiss, "Lawyer's e-Discovery Error Led to Release of Confidential Info on Thousands of Wells Fargo Clients," *ABA Journal,* July 27, 2017, www.abajournal.com/news/article/ lawyers_e_discovery_error_led_to_release_of_confidential_wells_fargo_client.

37. National Archives and Records Administration (NARA), "General Records Schedule 5.2," July 2017, https://www.archives.gov/files/records-mgmt/grs/grs05-2.pdf.

38. US National Archives, The Freedom of Information Act (FOIA) (5 USC § 552), last reviewed February 10, 2017, www.archives.gov/about/laws/foia.html.

39. Barack Obama, "Freedom of Information Act," Memorandum for the Heads of Executive Departments and Agencies, WhiteHouse.gov, accessed December 23, 2017, https://www.sec.gov/foia/president-memo-foia-nov2009.pdf.

40. "List of Countries with Access to Information," accessed December 21, 2017, http://home.broadpark.no/~wkeim/foi-list.htm.

CHAPTER 10

Information Economics, Privacy, and Security

INTRODUCTION

ISO 15489-1:2016, "the" RIM standard, describes records as "assets" without a clear explanation of their value, which leaves the following questions unanswered:

- Do records have economic value?
- If so, how do we determine that value?
- Is the value based, as the value of physical assets can be, upon an appraisal process?

ISO 15489-1:2016 introduces the concept of "appraisal," but it is in terms of an "analysis of business context, business activities and risk to enable decision-making on what records to create and capture, and how to ensure the appropriate management of records over time."[1] The operational words in this statement are: *records* and *creation, capture,* and *management* in relation to *risk*. Missing is the word *use*.

Of course, risk mitigation is extremely important. It is an indirect method of deriving economic benefits from information. We've addressed risk in the previous chapter and will deal with the topic again in the second half of this chapter in relation to privacy and security. For the first half of this chapter, however, we will step through the looking glass into a world where taking care of records and information is NOT the primary goal—accomplishing the core mission of the organization (i.e., making a profit or serving the public) IS. It takes this type of business perspective to understand the direct method of deriving economic benefit from information: the monetization of (earning revenue from) information.

INFORMATION ECONOMICS (INFONOMICS)

In his 2018 work *Infonomics,* Douglas B. Laney of Gartner, Inc. challenges us to consider the economic significance of information. What is its true worth? How do we monetize, manage, and measure it as an actual asset and not merely as a representation of business activities?[2] Laney defines *Infonomics* as "the theory, study, and discipline of asserting economic significance to information."[3]

In a 2012 *Forbes* article, Laney referred to infonomics as "the practice of information economics."[4] Probably the best advice he gave to those of us who profess to hold information as a valuable asset is to go beyond thinking and talking about it and actually value it and treat it as one.[5]

I *nfonomics* is the "emerging discipline of managing and accounting for information with the same or similar rigor and formality as other traditional assets (e.g., financial, physical, intangible, human capital). Infonomics posits that information itself meets all the criteria of formal company assets, and, although not yet recognized by generally accepted accounting practices, increasingly it is incumbent on organizations to behave as if it were to optimize information's ability to generate business value."

SOURCE: Gartner. *Infonomics.* IT Glossary, accessed January 6, 2018, https://www.gartner.com/it-glossary/infonomics.

What Are Business Assets?

Valuing assets is the domain of the finance and accounting profession. If you've taken an introductory accounting course, you know that assets can be tangible (a storefront or a cash register) or intangible (a patent or goodwill). Tangible assets are easily included on a balance sheet, which is a financial statement illustrating a business's net worth by listing assets (what is owned), liabilities (what is owed), and owner's or stockholders' equity (what is left). Figure 10.1 is an example of a simple balance sheet prepared at the end of the fiscal year for a company owned by stockholders. If there were no stockholders, "Owners' Equity" would replace "Stockholders' Equity" to represent the difference between assets and liabilities.

The balance sheet in figure 10.1 includes only tangible assets—current assets such as cash and inventory and fixed assets such as building and equipment.

Intangible Assets

The balance sheet in figure 10.1 does not account for intangible assets (those not physical in nature) such as patents, copyrights, franchises, customer lists, trademarks, trade names, and goodwill (the value of customer relationships). But intangible assets do appear on some balance sheets, as shown in figure 10.2.

Goodwill

Goodwill can be viewed as the amount paid for a company above its *book value* (i.e., tangible assets minus intangible assets and liabilities). Goodwill is reported on the balance sheet along with long-term assets such as land, buildings, and equipment. It is the most common form of intangible asset included on a balance sheet. Goodwill is determined when a company is acquired. In an effort to balance the balance sheet, the difference between the purchase price and the book value of the company is recorded as positive or negative goodwill. Negative goodwill is possible when a company is acquired for less than its book value.

Purchased Intangible Assets

The term *purchased intangible assets* in figure 10.2 covers all other assets not accounted for under tangible assets or goodwill that can be valued. These nonphysical assets have a life greater than one year and are typically recognized, similar to goodwill, when acquired. Intangible assets can also be generated internally.

Examples of intangible assets that may be included on balance sheets include customer lists, patented technology, and computer software. Additional examples include internet domain names, pictures, use rights (drilling for water or oil), and trade secrets (secret formulas and recipes).

Let's look at two examples of intangible assets:

- **Internet domain name:** The most expensive domain name ever sold was Cars.com. It was valued at a staggering $872 million in 2014 by the purchaser Gannett Co., Inc. Don't you wish you had thought of purchasing that domain name years ago? In a filing with the Securities and Exchange Commission, Gannett Co., Inc. explained the valuation of this acquisition in this way: "After the impairment testing date, we completed our acquisition

	Simple Company		
	Balance Sheet		
	December 31, xxxx		
Assets	**$**	**Liabilities**	**$**
Current Assets:		**Current Liabilities:**	
Cash (in Bank)	74,500	Notes Payable	5,000
Petty Cash	400	Accounts Payable	33,400
Accounts Receivable	40,500	Wages Payable	15,000
Inventory	35,000	Utilities	900
Supplies	4,200	Taxes Payable	3,700
Prepaid Insurance	2,500	Unearned revenues	1,500
Total Current Assets	**$157,100**	**Total Current Liabilities**	**$46,000**
Fixed Assets:		**Long-Term Liabilities:**	
Land	250,000	Long-Term Loans	50,000
Buildings	450,000	Mortgage	200,000
Equipment	54,000		
Less: accumulated depreciation	-70,000	**Total Long-Term Liabilities**	250,000
Net Fixed Assets	**$684,000**	**Total Liabilities**	**$296,000**
		Stockholders' Equity	
		Common Stock	225,000
		Retained Earnings	400,000
		Accumulated other comprehensive income	20,100
		Less: Treasury Stock	-100,000
		Total Stockholder's Equity	545,100
Total Assets	**$841,100**	**Total Liabilities & Stockholders' Equity**	**$841,100**

FIGURE 10.1 Balance sheet listing the total of current and fixed tangible assets on the left, "balanced" by the total of liabilities and equity on the right.

of Cars.com and as a result recorded an indefinite-lived trade name valued at $872 million."[6]

- **Trade secrets:** An example of an intangible asset developed internally is the secret recipe for Coca-Cola, which would be classified as a trade secret and included along with other intangible assets. At the end of 2016, Coca-Cola, listed on the Nasdaq as KO, reported the total value of its assets as $87,270,000,000. Intangible assets accounted for 24.2 percent of that total: goodwill of $10,629,000,000 and other intangible assets of $10,499,000,000.[7] The value of the secret recipe is included in this last figure.

Information Assets

By now you are aware that intangible assets have value, and the easiest way to determine their value is upon acquisition. One category of intangible asset that does not appear on the balance sheets of most companies is *information assets,* which are separate from those intangibles recognized by the Generally Accepted Accounting Principles (GAAP) balance sheet item classification system.[8] Definitions of an *information asset* vary—from information systems and solutions to the information itself—as shown in the following definitions:

- Clearwater Compliance defines information asset as a "business application, system or solution that creates, receives, maintains or

CISCO SYSTEMS, INC.
CONDENSED CONSOLIDATED BALANCE SHEETS
(In millions)
(Unaudited)

	July 29, 2017	July 30, 2016
ASSETS		
Current assets:		
Cash and cash equivalents	$ 11,708	$ 7,631
Investments	58,784	58,125
Accounts receivable, net of allowance for doubtful accounts of $211 at July 29, 2017 and $249 at July 30, 2016	5,146	5,847
Inventories	1,616	1,217
Financing receivables, net	4,856	4,272
Other current assets	1,593	1,627
Total current assets	83,703	78,719
Property and equipment, net	3,322	3,506
Financing receivables, net	4,738	4,158
Goodwill	29,766	26,625
Purchased intangible assets, net	2,539	2,501
Deferred tax assets	4,239	4,299
Other assets	1,511	1,844
TOTAL ASSETS	$ 129,818	$ 121,652

FIGURE 10.2 Portion of the 2016–2017 Condensed Consolidated Balance Sheets including goodwill and purchased intangible assets.

transmits sensitive information, such as protected health information (PHI), personally identifiable information (PII), payment card data, company proprietary business plans or financial data, etc., the confidentiality, integrity and availability of which must be safeguarded for the sake of overall business risk management."[9]

- The National Archives of the United Kingdom describes an information asset as "a body of information, defined and managed as a single unit so it can be understood, shared, protected and exploited efficiently. Information assets have recognizable and manageable value, risk, content and lifecycles."[10]

- According to Information Asset Development, Inc., an information asset is "organized information that is valuable and easily accessible to those who need it. Information assets comprise a wide range of corporate product, service and process information."[11]

In the Coca-Cola example, a little more than 20 percent of the balance sheet assets were intangibles, which means almost 80 percent were tangibles. But, according to David Post of the Sustainable Accounting Standards Board (SASB), "intangibles have grown from filling 20% of corporate balance sheets to 80%, due in large part to the expanding nature, and rising importance, of intangibles as represented by intellectual capital vs. bricks-and-mortar, research and development vs. capital spending, services vs. manufacturing, and the list goes on."[12]

Post's reflection on the value of intangibles like intellectual capital, research and development, and services can be quantified in large part based on past and current expenditures. But what of the information assets not measured through traditional accounting methods?

New Business Models

What do Uber, Facebook, Alibaba, and Airbnb have in common?

According to Tom Goodwin, Senior Vice President of Strategy and Innovation, Havas Media, "Uber, the world's largest taxi company, owns no vehicles. Facebook, the world's most popular media owner, creates no content. Alibaba, the most valuable retailer, has no inventory. And Airbnb, the world's largest accommodation provider, owns no real estate. Something interesting is happening."[13] To this we can add BitCoin—the world's largest bank that has no cash.

WORLD'S BIGGEST	ORGANIZATION	BUT . . .
Bank	BitCoin	Has no cash
Taxi Company	Uber	Owns no vehicles
Media Owner	Facebook	Creates no content
Retailer	Alibaba	Has no inventory
Accommodation Provider	Airbnb	Owns no real estate

Let us take one of the five examples, Uber, to see how an *Aggregator Business Model,* also termed *On Demand Delivery Model* or *Uber for X Model,* works. The term a*ggregator* implies the firm will collect and organize different elements to comprise a service and make the service available as a single brand, Uber. The benefits to the customers include: ease of access through the use of an app on their smartphones, a large number of cars on the road resulting in faster service, ability to rate the service they received using the app, and reasonable fares compared to most taxi services (this last may depend on location and other variables).

So how does Uber make money? There are two primary ways: (1) from partnerships with drivers where Uber accepts commissions of between 20 to 25 percent of each fare, and (2) from promotional partnerships with other brands including BMW, Pepsi, and Spotify.[14]

- Uber owns no cabs, so that type of tangible asset is not recorded on the balance sheet. A traditional cab company may own its own fleet and lease cabs on a daily or weekly basis to drivers (such as Black Cabs in London), or they may allow a limited number of drivers to purchase their own branded cabs (such as Yellow Medallions in New York City). The vehicles owned would be included on the cab company's balance sheet. But Uber does things differently:

  - Drivers can use cars they already own or buy for this purpose.
  - Drivers can rent automobiles from Hertz based on an agreement to provide rideshare rentals between Uber and Hertz.
  - Drivers can enter into short-term (three-year) car leases and make weekly payments with car dealerships that have partnered with Uber.
  - Drivers can connect with other owners through HyreCar to use private autos at daily, weekly, and monthly rates.[15]
  - Uber employs no drivers. They are all independent contractors. Therefore Uber's labor costs that appear as an expense on its income statement are lowered—but not nonexistent because other employees are needed to run the operations.
  - Uber utilizes an algorithm to set prices based on distance, weather, traffic congestion, holidays, and more. A downside to the benefits to customers could be the dynamic pricing strategy that results in price surges during peak periods (e.g., rush hour) or specific locations (e.g., airports).

There are other differences based on technology and intelligent management of information assets between traditional cab companies and Uber, as shown in table 10.1.

After reviewing table 10.1, you should begin to understand some of the information assets Uber utilizes to set its fares and serve its customers—some created internally (driver profiles) and some acquired externally (Google Maps). Integration with other systems such as credit card companies is apparent. But there is more to the pricing structure and service model.

Algorithms

Uber benefits from the use of algorithms—both their own and those that enable services they depend upon. For example, Uber takes advantage of the "route finding" algorithm of the traffic and navigation app Waze to get drivers from point A to point B to point C in London. If you've done any programming, you recognize this statement as the basis for a simple

TABLE 10.1 Advantages Uber has over traditional cab companies due to technology and ability to employ knowledge from its information assets.

TAXI	UBER
Driver Anonymity—the client does not know the driver's name or who they are before entering the cab	**No Anonymous Riders**—Uber displays and records the driver's name, photograph, plate number, vehicle and average rating before you get in the car.
Off the Grid—the client does not have a record of the trip if anything goes wrong.	**On the Map**—Uber's GPS technology means there is a record of every trip, and the trip can be shared in real-time with friends and family.
Carrying Cash—cash transactions make drivers a target for fare evasion and robbery. Drivers sometimes claim the card reader is faulty to avoid the credit card charges.	**Cashless Transactions**—transparent fares automatically charged to the client's credit card is possible. Customers should obtain an estimate in-app before riding.
Knowledge base—cab companies often have intensive training for drivers that includes memorizing routes without referring to maps or GPS. In London, for example, cabbies spend 2–4 years learning more than 25,000 streets, mews, and passageways and 20,000 landmarks.	**Knowledge base**—drivers are assisted by GPS navigation systems, their cellphone screens guiding them with Google Maps. In London Uber drivers also employ the Israeli-designed traffic and navigation app Waze.

flowchart depicting a series of steps to be taken. You can insert decision points based on other variables—for example, if traffic between point A and point B is congested, it may be faster to go from point A to point D and then back to point C—skipping B altogether.

Uber uses its own algorithms to set prices, assign drivers, and more. For repeat customers, Uber considers what it learns from previous interactions; for example, their "patience value" is defined as how long the passenger is willing to wait for a car. Drivers are rated according to what proportion of available pickups the driver accepts (they have fifteen seconds to decide) and the average consumer satisfaction rating from passengers. Fees are set based on variables including supply and demand.

Unfortunately, the algorithm can be used in ways that take advantage of both drivers and passengers. Uber is accused of charging different prices for high demand routes and has been accused in the past of displaying a higher fare to the customer than to the driver—with the difference the customer pays going to the company. This last practice resulted in a class action lawsuit filed by drivers in Los Angeles. In a nod toward the caveat "let the buyer beware," Uber released the following statement to the *San Francisco Examiner*: "We price routes differently based on our understanding of riders' choices so we can serve more people in more places at fares they can afford."[16]

In some instances, increasingly savvy drivers have banded together to raise fares by decreasing supply. According to researchers at the University of Warwick, drivers in London and New York manipulate Uber's algorithm by logging out of the app at the same time, making it appear they are busy with other clients. Prices of fares are then increased based on the lower supply of drivers.[17]

Algorithms

In computer science an *algorithm* is a set of steps that must be completed to accomplish a task. Algorithms are used for many purposes and allow massive computational power to be harnessed to solve problems efficiently, including analyzing huge sets of data or selecting intelligently from a number of possible decisions.

Reviewing the two main ways Uber makes a profit—service to passengers and partnerships with other companies—we can understand how Uber is more involved with information assets and their manipulation than with physical plants and equipment.

Valuing Information Assets

So far we've looked at how assets, both tangible and intangible, might appear on a balance sheet. We've learned that for traditional companies (e.g., manufacturing), tangible assets would make up approximately 80 percent of the total assets and intangible assets (e.g., goodwill) the other 20 percent. The Generally Accepted Accounting Principles provide guidance in listing intangible assets on balance sheets. The value of intangibles is usually set because of an acquisition. This can be an outright purchase of a customer list, for example, or the difference between the purchase price of a company less its book value listed as goodwill.

The leading companies of today have turned the traditional business model on its head and tangible assets may only comprise approximately 20 percent of total assets with 80 percent reflected as intangible assets. The Uber example demonstrated how information assets were gathered and leveraged to achieve company goals—making a profit by providing a service more efficiently than competitors and reducing the cost of doing business by avoiding an investment in vehicles and drivers. The example of the use of algorithm-leveraged information assets (e.g., data about drivers and customers) is comprised of two essential components: the algorithm and the information. If an algorithm can be patented, it can be included on the balance sheet as an intangible asset using the cost of development as the basis for value.

In the United States, a pure algorithm is explicitly exempted from being patentable (as are mathematical facts and formulas and ideas), but an application of the algorithm may be patentable. The term *algorithm* began to appear in patent applications in 1979, and by 2016 there were over 18,000 patent applications that included the word in the title, abstract, or description.[18]

Uber owns several patents mainly having to do with its business methods. The patent US 9066206 B2, *System and method for providing dynamic supply positioning for on-demand services,* is one. The background provided in the application illustrates a part of the thought process behind the development and filing of this patent application:

> There are many real-world services that a user can access through a mobile computing device. In some examples, a user can request transportation services or delivery services by operating a mobile computing device. The amount of time the user must wait to be serviced can depend on numerous factors.[19]

The algorithm is an intangible asset with value based on research and development, filing fees, and more. But it must process information to work. How do we value that information?

First, it must be understood that the data or information we are attempting to value is worthy of valuation. A data governance structure should be in place to ensure that data are "quality data" with the following characteristics: validity, completeness, integrity, consistency, uniqueness, precision, timeliness, and accessibility. Subjective data quality metrics that must also be considered include: existence, scarcity, relevancy, usability, interpretability, believability (trustworthiness), and objectivity.[20]

Laney gives us a number of information asset valuation models. I highly recommend reading his book *Infonomics* for details. One method shifts the cost from the income and expense statement to the balance sheet (if accounting regulations allow): the *Cost Value of Information* (CVI) using the formula shown below.

$$CVI = \frac{ProcExp * Attrib * T}{t} \left\{ + \sum_{p=0}^{n} Lost\ Revenue_p \right\}$$

For this method, we must determine the expense incurred to generate, capture, or collect the information. This works best when considering the value of a class of data or information such as customer and driver data in our Uber example (i.e., dataset). The formula takes into account the cost of the process(es) involved in capturing the data, the portion of that expense attributable to information capture, the average lifespan of the data, and the time period over which the process expense is measured.[21] This method can also consider the negative business impact in terms of the cost of reputational or competitive risks if the information is exposed to the public, stolen, or lost due to natural or manmade disasters.

To generate profits, organizations strive to derive income from an information asset that is higher than its acquisition and maintenance costs. A second method of valuing information assets attempts to determine the financial or potential value of information, the *Market Value of Information* (MVI). Organizations could exchange access to the information in return for something else of value.[22] One may engage in bartering, for example, by promising an advanced copy of the results of a survey in exchange for an email list of members of a professional association to whom invitations to participate in the survey could be sent. Organizations could also license access to or use of the information asset (e.g., some of the images in this text were licensed for use from Getty Images). The formula for MVI is shown below.

$$MVI = \frac{Exclusive\ Price * Number\ of\ Licenses}{Premium}$$

The exclusive price is what can be realized from licensing the entire information asset. You might determine it by scanning the external environment to find the licensing fees for comparable information assets. Then, multiply that by the number of licenses estimated to be sold. Finally, divide the results by the premium (amount above the exclusive price) potential customers might pay for rights to access the information. This last amount can be discovered through surveys. At some point, the data will be less valuable and extra licenses may only be desired if provided at a discount. In that case, an inverse premium would be used in place of the premium.

The National Archives (TNA) of the United Kingdom generates income from the sale of digital images through its image library. In the past, the public could view original or copies of photos in person, and more recently, low-resolution versions online. But today TNA allows high-resolution digital images to be downloaded for a per-image "supply" fee—currently £38.75. An additional "reproduction" fee is charged for commercial use and direct reproduction of the images for publication, display, and broadcast in various mediums. Electronic rights can be purchased independently but are included with fees to include images in print materials, including e-books. Discounts are given for multiple images. TNA provides resources on identifying, valuing, and financial reporting of information assets on its website.[23]

The increased value placed on information assets has resulted in an increased concern for the privacy and security of those assets. The remainder of this chapter will explore information asset privacy and security issues.

INFORMATION ASSET PRIVACY AND SECURITY

Privacy and security go hand in hand but they're not the same thing—and definitions of each vary. Privacy generally means an individual's right to be left alone—freedom from interference and intrusion. *Data privacy* is defined by IAPP (a not-for-profit information privacy community) as "the use and governance of personal data—things like putting policies in place to ensure that consumers' personal information is being collected, shared and used in appropriate ways."[24] *Information privacy* is the right to exert some control over personal information that is collected and used by others. In general terms, security can be viewed as the freedom from danger, fear, anxiety, care, and in the case of information, freedom from exposure. According to the SANS Institute (an information security research and education association), *information security* "refers to the processes and methodologies which are designed and implemented to protect print, electronic, or any other form of confidential, private and sensitive information or data from unauthorized access, use, misuse, disclosure, destruction, modification, or disruption."[25]

Privacy

Privacy is focused on the use and governance of personal data, including policies implemented by businesses that govern the collection, sharing, and use of a consumer's personal information. It can be viewed from two perspectives: the right (and expectation) of the individual to privacy and the duty of the entity collecting information to protect that privacy. The following statement appeared in an article entitled "The Right to Privacy," published in the *Harvard Review* in 1890.

Recent inventions and business methods call attention to the next step which must be taken for the protection of the person, and for securing to the individual what Judge Thomas M. Cooley called the right "to be let alone."[26]

Well over a century later we are still struggling with issues of privacy due to recent inventions (e.g., the Internet of Things) and business methods (e.g., the Aggregator Business Model.).

Privacy Legislation—United States

There is no overarching privacy law in the United States at this time. However, the Privacy Act of 1974 establishes a code of fair information practices that governs the collection, maintenance, use, and dissemination of information about individuals that is maintained in systems of records by federal agencies. The agency is required to publish in the *Federal Register* their systems of records (systems from which information can be retrieved by the name of the individual or some identifier assigned to the individual). The agency cannot share information about the individual from the system of record without their consent (unless one of twelve statutory exemptions applies) and must provide a way for the individual to access and seek an amendment of their records.[27]

The E-Government Act of 2002 also deals with personal information contained in government records and systems. Section 208 of the Act requires all federal government agencies to prepare Privacy Impact Statements (PIAs) that develop or procure new information technology or make substantial changes to existing systems that collect, maintain, or disseminate information in identifiable form. The purpose is to demonstrate how privacy protections are incorporated into the lifecycle of the system.[28]

The Constitution and the Courts

Although the term *privacy* is not included in the US Constitution, several amendments allude to personal freedom. The one most often cited in court cases around privacy is the fourth amendment on search and seizure:

> The right of the people to be secure in their persons, houses, papers, and effects, against
> unreasonable searches and seizures, shall not be violated, and no warrants shall issue,
> but upon probable cause, supported by oath or affirmation, and particularly describing
> the place to be searched, and the persons or things to be seized.[29]

This amendment asserts the right of every individual to be protected from unwarranted and unreasonable searches and seizures—but the reasonableness standard changes over time. In The Olmstead Case of 1928, the use of the microphone, telephone, and Dictograph recording device by law enforcement was challenged. The Supreme Court reviewed convictions based on evidence obtained through taps on telephone wires and handed down a five to four ruling that wiretapping was not prohibited by the Fourth Amendment, based on the interpretation of two terms in the amendment: (1) there was no *search* as long as there was no entry into the premises of the individuals involved, and (2) there was no *seizure,* because the evidence was obtained by merely listening to a conversation.[30] Several court cases in the following years used the Olmstead Court case to either uphold or deny the right of the government to access conversations.

In *Goldman v. United States* (1942), Justice Roberts delivered the opinion of the Supreme Court on a case brought by attorneys convicted of conspiring to violate the Bankruptcy Act based on information obtained through the use of a listening device installed with the assistance of the building superintendent in the offices of one of the attorneys. When attempting to listen in on the meeting, the installed device failed. Therefore, the investigators used another device they had with them, a Detectaphone with a receiver that when placed against the wall would pick up sound waves from the office in question and amplify them. In addition to the conversation occurring between those in the office, one side of a telephone conversation was also overheard. In affirming the Appeals Court's ruling, the Chief Justice made the following observations: (1) the use of the Detectaphone was not made illegal by trespass or unlawful entry (the trespass had to do with the listening device that did not work). (2) words spoken in a room in the presence of another into a telephone receiver do not constitute a communication by wire, and (3) the use of the Detectaphone by government agents was not a violation of the Fourth Amendment. The decision was not unanimous. Writing the dissenting opinion, Justice Murphy stated, "For me it is clear that the use of the Detectaphone under the circumstances revealed by this record was an unreasonable search and seizure within the clear intendment of the Fourth Amendment."[31] As part of this case, the petitioners requested the Court to overrule the *Olmstead v. United States* decision. The Court refused to consider the request.

Let us fast forward to the twenty-first century to understand how although the technology has changed, the tension between privacy and security remains the same.

In December 2015, Syed Rizwan Farook and Tashfeen Malik attacked the Inland Regional Center in San Bernardino, California, killing fourteen people before killing themselves in a battle with police. During the investigation, the police came into possession of an iPhone 5c used by Farook but belonging to his employer, San Bernardino County. The FBI obtained a warrant and the County gave permission to allow a search of the phone. But the iPhone was protected by a four-digit code the FBI did not have and a security feature that would render the files inaccessible after ten failed attempts to enter the code. The FBI requested the Apple corporation to bypass the security feature; Apple denied the request. A federal judge ordered Apple to cooperate; Apple again refused. In March 2016, the FBI announced it had successfully retrieved the data from the iPhone with the assistance of a third-party vendor and no longer needed Apple's assistance; the case against Apple was withdrawn. In this complex case, the FBI had a warrant for the device and the permission of the owner of the device but experienced a delay in retrieving data because of the refusal by the manufacturer to assist.[32] Curious as to whether the hack could be used on other Apple devices, three news organizations filed Freedom of Information requests in 2016 to obtain details of the hacking method used. In a decision on one of the requests, a federal court ruled that the FBI does not have to disclose the name of the vendor and the price paid for the solution.[33]

In addition to the conversations transmitted via cellphones, warrants for such devices can reveal other types of information. *Carpenter v. U.S.* stems from a 2011 investigation into robberies in Detroit where law enforcement officials obtained data from cell towers to determine the location of one of the suspects, Timothy Carpenter, without obtaining a warrant. Several large technology companies including Apple, Facebook, Google, and Microsoft urged the Court to set limits on the ways location data can be obtained and used. Other companies including Airbnb, Cisco, Dropbox, and Verizon argued further that there is a need for greater Fourth Amendment safeguards in light of the use of internet technologies and the realistic expectation of individual privacy in this digital age.[34]

In January 2018, a debate over surveillance by the National Security Agency and protections for Americans' privacy rights ensued as Congress took up legislation to extend a program of warrantless spying on the communications of foreigners outside of the United States that was passed in the wake of the September 11, 2001, attacks. Some lawmakers were concerned that US citizens could be caught up in the surveillance under Section 702 of the Foreign Intelligence Surveillance Act (FISA). Regardless of some opposition, both Houses of Congress voted to renew the program and President Donald J. Trump signed the reauthorization.[35]

These examples illustrate concerns of citizens over government surveillance and their own privacy; however, the general attitude of citizens toward the question of security versus privacy fluctuates based on the length of time passed since a serious incident. In 2001, immediately after the 9/11 terrorist attacks and the passage of the Patriot Act, 55 percent of citizens surveyed said it would be necessary to give up some civil liberties and 35 percent said it was not necessary. Ten years later, that figure had almost reversed with 40 percent saying it was necessary for the average citizen to give up some civil liberties to combat terrorism and 54 percent saying it was not.[36]

The federal government also mandates privacy protections based on specific industry sectors such as HIPAA for healthcare or FACTA for the financial sector. See table 10.2 for a sampling of federal laws that include data protection.

Federal law continues to evolve. In the waning months of the Obama administration, the FCC adopted a Privacy Rule for broadband ISPs that established a framework of customer consent required for ISPs to use and share their customers' personal information, which was calibrated to the sensitivity of the information. The rules would have incorporated the controversial inclusion of browsing history and apps usage as sensitive information, requiring opt-in consent. Data security and breach notification requirements were also included. In April 2017, newly elected President Donald J. Trump signed a bill into law repealing those data security and privacy regulations.[37]

Privacy and the States

The courts have determined that privacy rights not granted by the federal government should be left to individual states to protect. As of April 2017, forty-eight states, the District of Columbia, Puerto Rico, and the US Virgin Islands had all enacted notifications of security breaches involving personal information. Only Alabama and South Dakota had not.

The first state to enact a security breach notification law was California in 2002, which became effective on July 1, 2003. The basic tenet is that companies must immediately disclose a data breach to customers, usually in writing. The law, as amended in 2016, took effect in January 2017 and changed the circumstances under which an entity must report a data breach to affected individuals.[38] The previous version required notification of a breach of unencrypted personal information, but the amendment requires notification even if the information is encrypted under some circumstances—such as when an encryption key or security credential may have also been compromised. This means companies may no longer rely on merely the best practice of encryption of data at rest as a defensible position.

California has also enacted an "eraser bill" for children, *Calif. Bus. & Prof. Code §§ 22580-22582, California's Privacy Rights for California Minors in the Digital World Act*. This law permits minors to remove, or to request and obtain removal of, content or information posted on an internet website, online service, online application, or mobile application.[39]

Privacy Legislation outside of the United States

The fragmented array of data protection, privacy, and security laws in the United States is complicated, but that is only part of the picture for companies operating outside of the United States. One uniting factor will be the European Union's (EU) General Data Protection Regulation (GDPR).[40]

The GDPR was approved on April 14, 2016, and took effect May 25, 2018. It is a regulation that replaces the Data Protection Directive 95/46/EC and was designed to harmonize

TABLE 10.2 A sampling of US data protection laws.

THE FEDERAL TRADE COMMISSION ACT (15 U.S.C. §§41-58) (FTC ACT)
This consumer protection law prohibits unfair or deceptive practices and has been applied to off-line and online data privacy and data security policies. The FTC enforces actions against companies who fail to comply with their own posted and privacy policies and for disclosing personal data without authorization.
CHILDREN'S ONLINE PRIVACY PROTECTION ACT (COPPA) (15 U.S.C. §§6501-6506)
The FTC is the primary enforcer of this act, which applies to the online collection of information from children.
THE FINANCIAL SERVICES MODERNIZATION ACT (GRAMM-LEACH-BLILEY ACT [GLB]) (15 U.S.C. §§6801-6827)
This act regulates the collection, use, and disclosure of financial information by financial institutions and other businesses that provide financial services and products. GLB limits disclosure of nonpublic personal information and may require financial institutions to provide notices of their privacy practices and the opportunity for data subjects to opt out of having their information shared. As part of the implementation of GLB, the FTC released several Privacy Rules including the Safeguards Rule (requiring security), the Disposal Rule (requiring protection and proper disposal of consumer report information), and the Red Flags Rule (requiring businesses and other organizations to watch for and respond to indications (red flags) of identity theft.
THE HEALTH INSURANCE PORTABILITY AND ACCOUNTABILITY ACT (HIPAA) (42 U.S.C. §1301 ET SEQ.)
HIPAA regulates medical information by any entities that handle the information, including health care providers, data processors, and pharmacies. Three rules apply: (1) the Privacy Rule, which applies to the collection and use of protected health information (PHI), (2) the Security Rule, which provides standards for protecting medical data, and (3) the Transactions Rule, which applies to electronic transmission of medical data.

[CONTINUED ON FOLLOWING PAGE]

data privacy laws across all twenty-eight EU member states. Its purpose is to protect the personal data and privacy of EU citizens for transactions that occur within EU member states. It also regulates personal data exported outside of the European Union. This regulation takes a broad view of personal identification information; PII extends beyond data like a person's name, address, and social security number to include data like their IP address and cookie data.

Companies can incur penalties for noncompliance with the GDPR of up to 4 percent of their previous year's global annual turnover or twenty million Euros—whichever is higher. Other penalties may include enforcement of corrective measures, compensation to those who have suffered due to an infringement, and reputational damage.

Yaki Faitelson, writing in a 2017 article in *Forbes,* provided practical examples of the ways in which the GDPR might impact companies in the United States.[41] The following comments are based on his article. Companies in countries outside of the European Union must comply with the GDPR if, according to Article 3, they collect personal data (what we call PII in the United States) or behavioral information from data subjects who are in an

TABLE 10.2 [CONTINUED]

THE HIPAA OMNIBUS RULE ALSO REVISED THE SECURITY BREACH NOTIFICATION RULE (45 C.F.R. PART 164)

This rule revised the HIPAA rules from the earlier act and requires covered entities to provide notice of a breach (i.e., acquisition, access, use, or disclosure) of protected health information in a manner not permitted under the Privacy Rule, unless the covered entity or business associate demonstrates that there is a low probability that the PHI has been compromised.

THE FAIR CREDIT REPORTING ACT (15 U.S.C. §1681)
AND THE FAIR AND ACCURATE CREDIT TRANSACTIONS ACT (PUB. L. NO. 108-159)

These acts apply to consumer reporting agencies, both those who use consumer reporting information (e.g., a lender) and those who provide consumer-reporting information (e.g., a credit card company).

THE CONTROLLING THE ASSAULT OF NON-SOLICITED PORNOGRAPHY AND MARKETING ACT (CAN-SPAM ACT) (15 U.S.C. §§7701-7713 AND 18 U.S.C. §1037) AND THE TELEPHONE CONSUMER PROTECTION ACT (47 U.S.C. §227 ET SEQ.)

The first act controls the collection and use of email addresses and the second the collection and use of telephone numbers.

THE ELECTRONIC COMMUNICATIONS PRIVACY ACT (18 U.S.C. §2510)
AND THE COMPUTER FRAUD AND ABUSE ACT (18 U.S.C. §1030)

The first act regulates the interception of electronic communications and the second regulates computer tampering.

JUDICIAL REDRESS ACT (2016)

Through this act, Congress granted citizens of certain ally nations (e.g. EU member states) the right to seek redress in US courts for privacy violations when their personal information is shared with law enforcement.

EU country at the time of data collection. This applies even if the data was not the result of a financial transaction. Because most companies in the United States have a web presence, there is a possibility that some EU citizens may provide personal data on a website created for US citizens. That is not covered by the GDPR. But if the EU data subjects were targets of the US company, the data gathered would be governed by the GDPR and the website would have to be modified to obtain explicit consumer consent. If the data subject signs up for a service or purchases a product, the vendor must obtain explicit permission for each type of processing performed on the personal data (e.g., sharing data with third parties would require one checkbox and registering for email promotions would need a second checkbox). The GDPR also governs protection of the data (e.g., adherence to data security standards such as ISO 27001) and breach notices (e.g., complying with the 72-hour breach notice rule).

Because the GDPR will have an impact on companies in non-EU countries, some countries are working with the EU to harmonize their own data privacy laws with the GDPR. Table 10.3 lists the data protection regulations of five countries and notes related to the GDPR. Japan, for example, is actively cooperating with the EU to ensure smooth transmission of

TABLE 10.3 Privacy laws by country outside of the United States.

ARGENTINA'S PERSONAL DATA PROTECTION ACT

The purpose of this 2000 act is the full protection of personal information recorded in data files, registers, banks, or other technical means of data treatment, either public or private for purposes of providing reports, in order to guarantee the honor and intimacy of persons, as well as the access to the information that may be recorded about such persons, in accordance with the provisions of Section 43, Third Paragraph of the National Constitution. The provisions contained in this act shall also apply, to the relevant extent, to data relating to legal entities. In no case shall journalistic information sources or databases be affected.

NOTE: The Argentina Data Protection Agency proposed a new data protection bill based heavily on the EU General Data Protection Regulation (GDPR). Among other changes, the new law addresses genetic data and biometric data.

AUSTRALIAN PRIVACY PRINCIPLES

The Australian Privacy Principles (2014) comprise thirteen principles (called APPS) in five categories:
Part 1: Consideration of personal information privacy
Part 2: Collection of personal information
Part 3: Dealing with personal information
Part 4: Integrity of personal information
Part 5: Access to, and correction of, personal information. In 2017 the Privacy Amendment (Notifiable Data Breaches) Bill 2016 was passed.

NOTE: The GDPR and the Australian Privacy Act of 1988 have commonalities and differences.

CANADA'S PRIVACY ACT AND PERSONAL INFORMATION PROTECTION AND ELECTRONIC DOCUMENTS ACT (PIPEDA)

The Office of the Privacy Commissioner of Canada oversees compliance with two privacy laws: (1) The Privacy Act, last amended in 2017, covers the personal information-handling practices of federal government departments and agencies. (2) PIPEDA, last amended in 2015, is the federal privacy law for private-sector organizations. It sets out the ground rules for how businesses must handle personal information in the course of commercial activity. It identifies ten responsibilities for organizations: accountability; identifying purposes; consent; limiting collection; limiting use, disclosure, and retention; accuracy; safeguards; openness; individual access; and challenging compliance.

NOTE: Canada has strong privacy laws, but the differences between PIPEDA and the GDPR are sufficient to necessitate work on the part of Canadian companies that wish to avoid potential fines of up to 2 to 4 percent of worldwide turnover.

JAPAN'S ACT ON THE PROTECTION OF PERSONAL INFORMATION (APPI)

The 2003 act required business operators who utilize for their business in Japan a personal information database that consists of more than 5,000 individuals in total identified by personal information on any day in the past six months to protect personal information. The 2015 amendment that went into effect in 2017 applies to businesses in Japan regardless of whether they maintain a database of 5,000 individuals.

NOTE: The Japanese government is cooperating with the EU in light of the GDPR to ensure that each will be able to recognize the other as having adequate protection to allow compliant transfers of personal data without the need for additional legal instruments.

[CONTINUED ON FOLLOWING PAGE]

TABLE 10.3 [CONTINUED]

UNITED KINGDOM DATA PROTECTION BILL (2017)
The Data Protection Bill introduced in 2017 will replace the DPA of 1998 and implements derogations and exemptions from the EU GDPR (General Data Protection Regulation).
NOTE: Since the GDPR took effect on May 25, 2018, and the UK's exit from the EU had not yet occurred, the GDPR is the law in the UK in the interim. After Brexit, the GDPR provisions will be retained in the UK law.

personal data without additional legal steps. Companies in countries that have not harmonized a national data protection law with the GDPR will have to do their own due diligence to avoid costly fines.

Security

Security is focused on the protection of data from access and exploitation by unauthorized entities—this data may or may not expose personal information. Security is necessary to protect data but it alone cannot ensure privacy.

Information Asset Classification

Not all information assets are equal. It's necessary to categorize and prioritize information assets based on potential risks before a decision is made about the information that must be protected and the level of protection necessary. The organization will have to determine the classification system (or a hybrid of two or more) that best suits its needs. First let's consider three specific types of data that we've learned governments and businesses strive to protect from unauthorized access: personally identifiable information, protected health information, and proprietary information. Then we'll review two additional classification systems.

Personally Identifiable Information (PII)

Personally identifiable information (PII) is information by which an individual may be identified. The GDPR terms this *personal data*. According to the National Standards and Technology Institute (NIST), PII is

> any information about an individual that is maintained by an agency, including information that can be used to distinguish or trace an individual's identity, such as name, social security number, date and place of birth, mother's maiden name, or biometric records; and any other information that is linked or linkable to an individual, such as medical, educational, financial, and employment information (based on General Accountability Office and Office of Management and Budget definitions).[42]

In 2017, approximately 143 million social security numbers were compromised when Equifax, a global consumer credit reporting agency, suffered one of the worst data breaches in history. During congressional hearings, the frustration of lawmakers with the current law was expressed, because although there is a requirement to alert those who have been hacked, there is no penalty for not doing so. However, that does not mean Equifax will not suffer due to this breach. In addition to reputational damage, the firm may pay out more than $1 billion, with most of it going, as the result of a class action lawsuit, to the consumers who had their personal data—including birth dates and social security numbers—stolen.[43] In addition, Equifax offered free identity theft protection and credit file monitoring to consumers who had their personal information compromised. The leadership team also suffered, as the Equifax CEO, CIO, and CSO stepped down. The former CEO testified before the House Energy and Commerce Committee that the breach could be blamed on a human error—a single person failed to deploy a patch.[44]

Protected Health Information (PHI)

Protected health information (PHI) is any information on a health condition that can be linked to a specific person. It is a common misconception that only medical care providers, such as hospital and doctors, are required to protect PHI.

Hackers sometimes obtain and reveal PHI to discredit others. In 2016, the World Anti-Doping Agency's (WADA) database was hacked revealing confidential health information of a number of athletes including Serena and Venus Williams. The information was used to expose the fact that they obtained Therapeutic Use Exemptions (TUE) for drugs prohibited by the anti-doping code. Although the International Tennis Federation confirmed that the TUEs released to the public were accurate, WADA said that the athletes had not committed any violation.[45]

Proprietary Information (PI)

We have talked about this already—proprietary information (PI) comprises intangible information assets including copyrights, patents, software programs, source code, and algorithms. Trade secrets are a form of confidential information that companies strive to withhold from the public. If a violation occurs in the United States, though, privacy laws won't protect the company from loss of its trade secrets. But the *Economic Espionage Act* (1996), the *Uniform Trade Secrets Act* (1979), and laws in most states may—as long as the information is unique to the business. To be successful in court, the trade secret must have economic value, provide a competitive advantage, and not be known to the public. Among the protections that can be put in place to protect trade secrets are the following: maintenance of logs of employees with access right to the trade secrets; asking employees to sign nondisclosure agreements; marking papers, photos, and other documents as confidential; attaching electronic sensors to trade secret items; and encrypting electronic files.[46] In 2016, the *Defend Trade Secrets Act* (DISA), which extends the *Economic Espionage Act,* was signed into law. The law allows injured parties to seek compensation for trade secret theft if the trade secret is related to a product or service used in, or intended for use in, interstate or foreign commerce.[47]

In 2017, a Federal Bureau of Investigation complaint filed in US District Court in Newark, NJ, charged a DuPont employee with theft of trade secrets. The employee, who had worked for the company for twenty-seven years, could receive up to ten years in prison and pay a fine of up to $250,000 if convicted. The employee, Anchi Hou, is accused of downloading more than 20,000 files prior to his retirement in 2016 to be used by a consulting firm he had formed and planned to run after he retired.[48]

Types of Data Classifications

In chapter 3, we addressed a number of classification schemes, among them filing systems, the Dewey Decimal Classification Scheme, the Library of Congress Classification System, functional classification schemes, and file plans. Those tools are used to organize, manage, use, and dispose of records and information without prioritization based on importance.

At the Gartner Security and Risk Management Summit in 2017, Gartner's research vice president, Earl Perkins, stated, "You can't protect everything equally . . . we have to find a way to control only what matters."[49] So let's turn our attention to two types of data classifications used to identify information that must be protected: (1) government/military classification and (2) private sector classification. The government/military classifications are shown in figure 10.3.

Private sector classifications may differ among organizations because there is no standard. One example is shown in figure 10.4.

Information assets (data, processing hardware, and storage media) should be inventoried and then prioritized using one of the two data classification systems in order to be managed. Once classified, steps can be taken to secure the sensitive information assets. Become familiar with the ISO 27000 family of standards for information security management systems (ISMS). Updated in 2016, ISO/IEC 27000 provides an overview of information security management systems as well as terms and definitions used in the ISMS family of standards. ISO/IEC 27001:2013 sets out requirements for establishing, implementing, maintaining, and continually improving an ISMS, along with the requirements

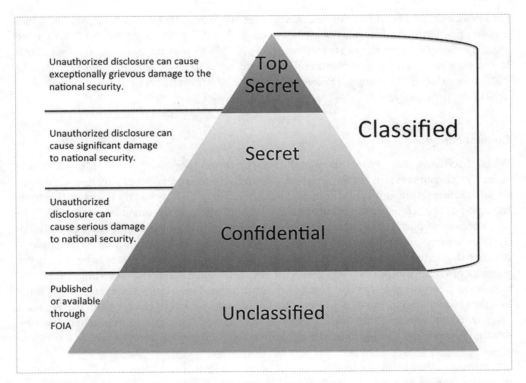

FIGURE 10.3 Government/military security classifications.

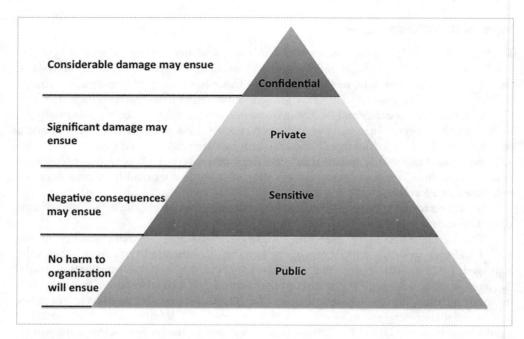

FIGURE 10.4 Example of a private sector classification system.

for assessment and treatment of information security risks. ISO/IEC 27002:2013 provides a code of practice for information security controls taking into account the information security risks faced by the organization. It is possible to become certified for ISO 27001 to reassure customers that recommendations are being followed, but it is not required. In 2016, more than 33,200 organizations became ISO 27001 certified, up from approximately 27,500 the previous year.[50]

Cybersecurity

When discussing security in this digital data, the term *cybersecurity* is often used. Cybersecurity "encompasses a broad range of practices, tools and concepts related closely to those of information and operational technology security. Cybersecurity is distinctive in its inclusion of the offensive use of information technology to attack adversaries."[51]

Because of our technological advances, especially the Internet of Things (IoT), businesses are increasingly likely to be the victims of a cyberattack. Data breaches continue to occur with greater frequency, compromising larger volumes of data than ever before. As the number of compromised records grows, organizations are subjected to stronger financial penalties, greater legislative and regulatory scrutiny, and reputational damage. Steps must be taken to avoid unauthorized access or loss of data. As we know, the best defense is a good offense. Because most companies fall victim to cyberattackers due to unpatched software or human error (e.g., falling victim to phishing emails), education must be part of the cybersecurity strategy.

Symantec has been the leader when it comes to Enterprise Data Loss Prevention for more than ten years, according to Gartner.[52] Symantec offers solutions that allow customers to protect data across data loss channels that present vulnerabilities: cloud apps (e.g., Dropbox, Salesforce, Office 365), endpoints, data repositories, and email and web communications. It employs data detection technologies such as fingerprinting, image analysis, and machine learning to identify sensitive data (e.g., content containing PII, health information, intellectual property) and user behavior analytics to detect malicious activities and threats. It provides an administrative console to manage policies and incidents wherever they occur: on-premises or in a public, private, or hybrid cloud.[53]

In 2009, Symantec provided a six-step process to reduce the risk of data breach, which is valid today:

1. Prevent incursion by targeted attacks.
2. Identify threats.

Common Cyberattacks to Avoid

Advanced Persistent Threats (APT): Social engineering programs or phishing attacks to steal intellectual property such as patent information and confidential project descriptions. One example is *spearphising,* (email to multiple email addresses at once in the hopes one recipient will launch its Trojan virus).

Denial-of-Service (DOS) Attacks: DOS attacks disrupt service to a network by sending high volumes of data or traffic through the network until the network can no longer function due to overload.

Drive-by-Downloads: A small snippet of code is downloaded to a computer when its user visits a site. The snippet of code then reaches out to another computer to get the rest of the code and download the program.

"Main in the Middle" (MITM): Most often the MITM gains access through a non-encrypted wireless access point and obtains information from the end user and the entity with whom he or she is communicating—for example, between you and your bank.

Malvertising: Malvertising compromises a computer with a malicious code downloaded when a user clicks on an infected display ad.

Password Phishing Attacks: Email messages that attempt to trick users out of their login credentials.

Social Media Threats: Rogue application install or friend requests that require a user to give additional access to social media accounts (and the information stored there).

Socially Engineered Malware: A method of attack caused by an end-user tricked into running a Trojan horse program such as data-encrypting ransomware.

Rogue Software: Malware that masquerades as legitimate security software that enters the system when a user clicks on a pop-up window and agrees to terms or updates to their security software.

Unpatched Software: Unpatched software programs have vulnerabilities that are the root cause of the breach.

3. Proactively protect information.
4. Automate security through compliance controls.
5. Prevent data exfiltration.
6. Integrate prevention and response strategies into security operations.[54]

In spite of the steps taken to prevent data loss, the following sentiment prevails: The question is not *if* a data breach will occur but *when*.

Organizations that suffer an incident must be prepared to take steps to secure systems, address vulnerabilities, prevent additional data loss, and notify appropriate parties. The *Data Breach Response Guide for Business* prepared by the Federal Trade Commission provides specific steps you can take in the event of a breach, including a sample letter you can use to notify individuals whose names and social security numbers have been stolen.[55]

In chapter 9, we dealt with disaster preparedness, recovery, and business continuity. Responding to a data breach follows similar procedures—including assembling a team, preparing a recovery plan, and identifying key internal and external stakeholders. Internal stakeholders include the legal department, public relations, CFO, CEO, COO, and information owners. External stakeholders include a forensics firm (identified before a breach occurs), external legal representation, external public relations, customers, the FBI, and specific industry data breach forensics investigators (e.g., in the case of a payment card data breach a payment card industry forensics investigator [PFI] must be employed). The PCI Security Standards Council maintains a list of certified PCI forensic investigators.[56]

An intrusion into Sonic Drive-In's point-of-sale payment system was announced on September 26, 2017. It was believed that up to five million stolen credit and debit card accounts were put up for sale on underground cybercrime stores. Sonic became informed of the issue when its credit card processor noticed unusual activity regarding credit cards that were used at Sonic. Sonic immediately engaged a third-party forensics expert and notified law enforcement. The majority of the 3,600 Sonic locations use this single point-of-sales system, so the impact could be far-reaching. Sonic cautioned customers to closely monitor their credit and debit card payments and report unauthorized or suspicious charges to their financial institutions.[57] Once the incident had been discovered, a preapproved data breach response process similar to the one shown in figure 10.5 was instigated.

The description of the Sonic data breach described discovery (notification by the credit card processor) and forensic investigation: scoping (employment of a third-party provider). What was not described was what came next—containment (stop the incident and preserve the compromised environment); announcement (use of third-party PR firm to inform the public); remediation (repair the damage and prevent future occurrences); employing a PCI forensics investigator (who must be called in to investigate and may repeat much of the work of the initial forensics team); class action law suit and fines (even if the company does everything it should in the first six steps, it will most likely be subjected to fines and a class-action lawsuit).

In an article for which thirty-three cybersecurity experts were asked to provide recommendations on an effective incident response plan, one of the experts, Robert Munnelly from Davis Malm and Dagostine, PC, provided the following recommendations:

1. Assemble an incidence response team.
2. Identify external data security sources.
3. Differentiate (types of) breaches.
4. Create an action item checklist.

5. Track key breach-related rights, obligations, and deadlines.
6. Review and update the response plan regularly.[58]

Ransomware

The economic theory of supply and demand applies not only to products and services (e.g., Uber's price hikes during peak periods) but also to stolen credit card information. Due to the increased volume of personal information hacked (e.g., more than 143 million social security numbers in the Equifax data breach alone), the price for that information is declining. Therefore new forms of cyber crime are emerging. *Ransomware,* also called *cryptoviral* or *cyber extortion,* restricts access to data by encrypting files or locking computer screens. The hacker promises to release the data upon payment of a ransom—until recently most often using the cryptocurrency Bitcoin. In June 2017, South Korean web provider Nayana paid the Bitcoin equivalent of $1 million after a ransomware attack locked up more than 3,400 websites. However, due to the volatility (and scarcity due to increased demand) of Bitcoin, criminals are seeking more stable cryptocurrencies.

Watchguard Technologies recommends three best practices every organization should employ to prevent ransomware attacks:

1. **Education and Awareness.** One recent point-of-sale hack took place because an administrative employee clicked on a link in an email that allowed hackers to move through the administrative system and into the point-of-sale system.
2. **Backup, Backup, Backup.** Infection spreads through connected systems, so include off-line storage of backups as part of your prevention strategy.
3. **Defense in Depth.** The more layers of security in place, the better. Those layers include network protection, visibility into endpoint devices, and connecting the dots between the network and endpoint.[59]

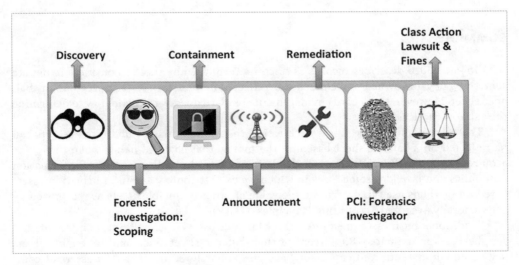

FIGURE 10.5 Example of a data breach response process launched in the event of a recognized incident.

Cyber Extortion Is Not New! The First Known Attack Occurred in 1989.

In 1989, an AIDS researcher, Joseph Popp, PhD, carried out a ransomware attack by distributing 20,000 floppy disks to AIDS researchers in more than ninety countries. Popp claimed the disks contained a questionnaire that could calculate an individual's risk of acquiring AIDS. The disk also contained a malware program that was activated after the computer was powered on ninety times. Once the ninety-start threshold was reached, a message demanding payment of $189 plus $378 for a software lease was displayed. This attack is known as the AIDS Trojan or the PC Cyborg.

SOURCE: Lord, Nate. (2017, December 17). "A History of Ransomware Attacks: The Biggest and Worst Ransomware Attacks of All Time," *Digital Guardian*, https://digitalguardian.com/blog/history-ransomware-attacks-biggest-and-worst-ransomware-attacks-all-time#2.

Organizations do not hesitate to purchase insurance to protect physical assets, and it is not surprising that a class of insurance has emerged to protect information assets—cyber insurance. The goal is to transfer some of the risk of a security breach over to insurance, rather than bear the losses alone. The average cost of a data breach in the United States is $1 million for middle-market companies, and more than 60 percent of small businesses discontinue operations after a cyberattack. Therefore, organizations should consider cyber insurance as part of their business continuity plans.[60] As with any insurance policy, it's necessary to assess potential risks and the organization's risk tolerance, as well as the amount of reimbursement for each breach based on type of attack. For example, a limit of $50,000 for cyber extortion may be adequate for some companies but not for others.

SUMMARY

ISO 15489-1:2016 describes records as *assets*—a term used by those in business to denote something of value owned by a company as reflected in monetary terms on a company balance sheet. However, the records management standard does not explain how to determine the value of those assets.

The value of intangible assets such as internet domain names and trade secrets can be reflected on a balance sheet based on the money that changed hands when they were acquired. In his book *Infonomics*, Douglas B. Laney introduced the concept of information economics and provides some ways in which we can attribute value to information assets based on methods used to determine the value of other intangible assets as recognized by the Generally Accepted Accounting Principles (GAAP).

Traditional businesses most often show tangible assets (e.g., building, equipment, and supplies) as approximately 80 percent of their balance sheet assets and intangible assets (e.g., goodwill, patents, and copyrights) as approximately 20 percent. The assets of companies built upon new business models—such as Uber's Aggregator Business Model—are approximately 20 percent tangible and 80 percent intangible. The new business models base their success not only on the information assets they possess but algorithms that allow massive amounts of data to be analyzed to solve problems efficiently.

The increased value of information has resulted in increased risk. Information assets must be protected against unauthorized access and exposure. There is no overarching privacy law in the United States, so US citizens must seek redress from intrusion into their private information based on a variety of laws—federal, state, and industry-specific. Companies within the United States must understand which data protection laws affect them and how. International regulations also impact US firms that conduct business with or merely collect data from citizens of other countries. The European Union's General Data Protection Regulation (GDPR), which became effective May 25, 2018, is already impacting the data privacy practices of companies in other countries, including those in the United States.

Privacy and security are not the same thing—privacy focuses on the protection of personal data such as PII, PHI, and PI. Security measures must be implemented to safeguard all data from unauthorized access. Data should be classified and prioritized in order to understand the impact of its loss or exposure on the organization. The government/military classifies information according to its potential impact on national security:

1. **Unclassified** (information that may be published during the normal course of business or made available in response to a Freedom of Information request)
2. **Confidential** (unauthorized disclosure that can cause serious damage to national security)
3. **Secret** (unauthorized disclosure that can cause significant damage to national security)
4. **Top secret** (unauthorized disclosure that can cause exceptionally grievous damage)

There is no standard classification system for the private sector but one method could be to consider information as

1. **Public** (no harm to the organization if breached)
2. **Sensitive** (negative consequences may ensue)
3. **Private** (significant damage may ensue)
4. **Confidential** (considerable damage may ensue)

Cybersecurity is closely related to information and operational security but is distinctive for its inclusion of the offensive use of information technology to attack. Just as with disaster recovery plans, all organizations should have data breach response plans that include the formation of an incident response team, the identification of internal and external personnel such as forensic investigators and public relations professionals, and the process to be followed. Organizations should consider purchasing cyber insurance as part of their business continuity plans.

In this chapter, we explored information economics, privacy, and security from a consumer and organizational perspective. In her contribution to this chapter Ilona Koti considers the issues of privacy and security from the perspective of those responsible for recordkeeping and information governance.

PARADIGM

Integrating Information Governance into the Privacy and Security Landscape

Ilona Koti

Principal Consultant, Educator, and ARMA International President 2017–2018

A common industry debate centers on the statement that privacy cannot be had without security, but security can exist without privacy. Regardless, a well-established security or privacy program will typically not be enforceable until an organization's data, records, and information have been identified and classified and its storage locations determined. Not knowing what information is on-hand and where information is stored can leave an organization open to significant risk and liability; therefore, integrating a comprehensive information governance (IG) strategy to manage business data is integral to the success of privacy and security initiatives.

With the advent of the General Data Protection Regulation (GDPR) in 2018, organizations with operations within the European Union or that interact with EU citizens may be mandated to appoint a Data Protection Officer (DPO) to ensure GDPR compliance.[61] With steep fines for GDPR violations ranging up to 4 percent of annual revenue (capped at €20 million), 2 percent of fines may be allocated for improper management of records.[62] New York's Department of Financial Services, also in 2018, mandated that a Chief Information Security Officer (CISO) be appointed to the majority of organizations providing financial services within the state.[63]

Although privacy and virtual security experts have extensive training in their fields, knowing where to find and how to manage information properly throughout the lifecycle of each record and to design the respective information systems to ensure proper classification, retrieval, and defensible disposition strategies is typically not a primary focus for privacy and security officers. Currently, there are over 50,000 local and federal laws and regulations in the United States alone and over 100,000 international laws establishing records retention periods.[64] However, as of this writing, no US law is in place requiring the specific appointment of a Chief Records or Information Governance Officer for non-governmental entities to ensure compliance enforcements.

Regardless of laws and mandates, organizations that are truly interested in managing their data can utilize the Information Governance Reference Model (IGRM) to establish a balance between privacy and security along with records management, technology, legal requirements and general business practices.[65] Beyond security and privacy compliance requirements, proper management of an organization's data can result in increased business process efficiency, competitive intelligence, as well as significant litigation and risk mitigation. ARMA International offers further guidance through its Generally Accepted Recordkeeping Principles maturity model consisting of eight areas against which organizations can benchmark their records compliance.[66]

In conjunction with laws and industry best practices, the equilibrium axis of process, technology, and people management applies the practical aspects of implementing and executing an IG strategy within an organization. The following sections represent enforceable measures to ensure that core components of privacy, security, and IG programs are addressed and interwoven to create an overarching compliance strategy.

Process

Although some risks can be avoided, conducting business generally creates risk, and so organizations evaluate risk mitigation strategies to minimize event impact. In an effort to mitigate privacy and IG risks, the following assessments and evaluations should be conducted, ideally in the order listed below:

- *Records Inventory and Interviews*: To document available data, a physical inventory of both paper and electronic records should be undertaken. Additionally, interviewing staff members who oversee specific records is critical in understanding storage locations and gaining contextual insights.
- *Records Retention Schedules:* Based on the records inventory, records series can be categorized under functional business areas establishing a records retention schedule, which in turn can serve as the basis for a file plan or taxonomy to assist with properly classifying data. Applicable laws and statutes of limitation should be applied to determine appropriate retention periods for each records series. Records should be purged at the end of their lifecycle with the exception of any applicable legal or regulatory holds.
- *Privacy Impact Analysis (PIA):* Establishing an organizational privacy benchmark is critical prior to or in the aftermath of a data breach or litigation. Once PIA results are evaluated, timely remedial actions for any privacy-related gaps should be implemented; subsequent PIAs should be conducted at least annually.
- *Data Maps:* Organizations that are heavily reliant on numerous information systems should identify at a minimum the content, volume, location, and the departmental owner of each system.
- *Workflow Analysis:* A business processes analysis for major tasks can further identify access requirements to enhance security and privacy, as well as identify unnecessary processing steps to increase workflow efficiencies.
- *Policy and Procedure Development:* Numerous policies and procedures should be enacted to ensure that all associates have clearly written guidance to comply with periodic policy audits that should be conducted.
- *Privacy by Design:* A GDPR requirement, Privacy by Design is a best practice that requires system designers, particularly of systems containing PII, to build in privacy triggers so that user-data can easily be purged, thus addressing the Right to Be Forgotten regulation.[67] Ideally, PII should not be collected unless the data are absolutely necessary and then data should only be retained for as long as legally or operationally required and purged in conjunction with the records retention schedule.

Technology

Although technology is integral in providing appropriate access and security parameters, limiting technology or security barriers so that users have unencumbered workflows is essential. Restricting technology budgets to avoid over-purchase of unnecessary features or excessive security settings is also important. Unless organizational security and privacy requirements are high, out-of-box software features will usually suffice. The following concepts can further enhance security components for information and privacy initiatives:

- *Current Events and Technologies:* Keeping current with the latest technologies, data breaches, and malicious hacker-activity is essential. If hackers have compromised similar technology at another organization, strong consideration should be given to either updating, replacing, or supplementing those technologies.
- *Access and Permissions:* Identifying role groups for users and associated permissions is essential. Permissions should be revoked or updated when a user changes roles, transfers to a new department, or leaves the organization.
- *Basic Security Parameters:* Simple security measures, such as locking a computer or file drawer, utilizing a security camera, encrypting emails, or redacting data can prevent or mitigate lower-level data breaches. Technology should be tested regularly to ensure compliance expectations.
- *Align with ISO 27000-1/2:* Although several standards with various security initiatives have been issued, the International Organization of Standardization issued *ISO/IEC 27000: Information Security Management Systems*, a leading standard which can serve as an audit tool for security compliance.[68]

People

The ability to engage staff in corporate initiatives that result in changes to work patterns or potential increased workloads is a complex issue that is the foundation of change management. Information projects often fail not from the lack of technology or careful planning, but as a result of not fully considering the human aspect and failing to obtain support from staff at all organizational levels. Key concepts for successful staff adoption are:

- *Communication Plan:* Establish a communication plan including clearly stated organizational goals outlining staff expectations and involvement. Communicate regularly and provide updates to keep the initiative top of mind.
- *Phased Implementation:* Ideally, phase in initiatives either departmentally or feature-wise, with additional functionality being added over time. Should system errors occur, launching with a controlled number of staff and/or limited functionalities will lower the risk for an affected end-user population versus troubleshooting an enterprise-wide initiative.
- *Training:* Prioritize staff training with an appropriate level of resources allocated to training staff on respective systems and initiatives. As staff learn in different ways, multiple delivery mechanisms for training should be offered whenever possible, for example, computer-based, in-person, online on-demand, or text format.
- *Obtain Buy-In:* Raising awareness and obtaining support from all organizational levels are essential. Senior-level sponsorship is key to enforce compliance; however engaging staff across the enterprise is

just as critical for successful project completion. Holding focus groups or involving staff in user-acceptance testing (UAT) can increase overall adoption rates.

For privacy and security to be executed effectively, an information governance program should be executed concurrently. Proper oversight of data can ensure organizational awareness of where information is being stored, establish exactly what information is on hand, identify what PII or sensitive data are being retained, ascertain necessary security requirements, and establish retention periods and disposition of data in compliance with a comprehensive records retention schedule.

Paradigm Shift

A paradigm shift needs to occur for an information governance program to succeed in the wake of privacy and security initiatives. Senior-level staff focused on information, such as a Chief Information Governance Officer, who are on par with Compliance, Privacy, Security, Technology and Risk Officers will also need to be initially appointed. Until a law specifically mandates the requirement of an individual who is fully trained in information governance and also has privacy, security, technical, and/or legal acumen, there will be significant gaps in the privacy and security initiatives of nongovernmental organizations whose appointed officers are not fully-versed in managing data and records throughout their lifecycle.

NOTES

1. International Organization for Standardization (ISO), *ISO 15489-1:2001: Information and Documentation—Records Management—Part 1: General* (Geneva: ISO, 2001), 4.
2. Douglas B. Laney, *Infonomics: How to Monetize, Manage and Measure Information as an Asset For Competitive Advantage* (New York: Bibliomotion, 2018).
3. Ibid., 9.
4. Douglas B. Laney, "Infonomics: The Practice of Information Economics," *Forbes,* May 22, 2012, https://www.forbes.com/sites/gartnergroup/2012/05/22/infonomics-the-practice-of-information -economics/#111d89ad6ee4.
5. Ibid.
6. US Securities and Exchange Commission. *Commission file number 1-6961, Gannett Co., Inc.*, accessed January 10, 2018, https://www.sec.gov/Archives/edgar/data/39899/000003989915000006/ gci-20141228x10k.htm.
7. Nasdaq, "KO Company Financials," accessed January 10, 2018, www.nasdaq.com/symbol/ko/ financials?query=balance-sheet.
8. "Generally Accepted Accounting Principles (GAAP)," *Investopedia,* accessed January 11, 2018, https://www.investopedia.com/terms/g/gaap.asp.
9. Clearwater Compliance, "The Clearwater Definition of an Information Asset," accessed January 8, 2018, https://clearwatercompliance.com/wp-content/uploads/2015/11/Clearwater-Definition-of -Information-Assets-with-Examples_V8.pdf.
10. The National Archives of the United Kingdom, "What is an Information Asset?" January 2017, www.nationalarchives.gov.uk/documents/information-management/information-assets -factsheet.pdf.
11. Information Asset Development, Inc., "What is an Information Asset?" accessed January 8, 2018, www.informationassetdevelopment.com/what.html.

12. Christopher P. Skroupa, "How Intangible Assets Are Affecting Company Value in the Stock Market," *Forbes,* November 1, 2017, https://www.forbes.com/sites/christopherskroupa/2017/11/01/how-intangible-assets-are-affecting-company-value-in-the-stock-market/#33ba50062b8e.

13. Tom Goodwin, "The Battle Is for the Customer Interface," *TechCrunch,* March 3, 2013, accessed January 9, 2018, https://techcrunch.com/2015/03/03/in-the-age-of-disintermediation-the-battle-is-all-for-the-customer-interface/.

14. Sakshi Singh, "Uber Business Model—How Does Uber Make Money?" *Feeddough.com,* July 19, 2017, accessed January 11, 2018, https://www.feedough.com/uber-business-model/.

15. Nicole Arata, "5 Ways to Get a Car You Need to Drive for Uber or Lyft," *USA Today,* January 8, 2017, https://www.usatoday.com/story/money/personalfinance/2017/01/08/5-ways-get-car-you-need-drive-uber-lyft/96214312/.

16. Joe Kukura, "Uber Admits to Manipulating Fares and Prices," *SFWeekly,* May 22, 2017, www.sfweekly.com/news/uber-admits-manipulating-fares-and-prices/.

17. Cara McGoogan, "Uber Drivers Gang Up to Cause Surge Pricing, Research Says," *The Telegraph,* August 12, 2017, www.telegraph.co.uk/technology/2017/08/02/uber-drivers-gang-cause-surge-pricing-research-says/.

18. Alulive, *Patent Inspiration,* accessed January 12, 2018, https://app.patentinspiration.com/.

19. *System and Method for Providing Dynamic Supply Positioning for On-Demand Services,* US 9066206 B2, accessed January 12, 2018, https://www.google.com/patents/US9066206.

20. Laney, *Infonomics*248–249.

21. Ibid., 256–257.

22. Ibid., 257–258.

23. The National Archives of the United Kingdom, "Information is a Valued Asset," accessed January 12, 2018, www.nationalarchives.gov.uk/information-management/manage-information/planning/information-principles/information-valued-asset/.

24. IAPP, "What Does Privacy Mean?" accessed January 13, 2018, https://iapp.org/about/what-is-privacy/.

25. SANS, "Information Security Resources," accessed January 13, 2018, https://www.sans.org/information-security/.

26. *Cooley on Torts,* 2d ed., p. 29. [p. 195 Note 4 in original]; Warren and Brandeis, "The Right to Privacy," *Harvard Law Review* 4, no. 5 (December 15, 1890) accessed January 13, 2018, http://groups.csail.mit.edu/mac/classes/6.805/articles/privacy/Privacy_brand_warr2.html.

27. US Department of Justice, Privacy Act of 1974, accessed January 16, 2018, https://www.justice.gov/opcl/privacy-act-1974.

28. US Department of Justice, Office of Privacy and Civil Liberties. E-Government Act of 2002, accessed January 16, 2018, https://www.justice.gov/opcl/e-government-act-2002.

29. "Fourth Amendment, US Constitution," Cornell Law School, accessed January 13, 2018, https://www.law.cornell.edu/constitution/fourth_amendment.

30. FindLaw, *Annotation 5—Fourth Amendment: Electronic Surveillance and the Fourth Amendment,* accessed January 13, 2018, http://constitution.findlaw.com/amendment4/annotation05.html#1.

31. *Goldman v. United States,* (1942), No. 962, *FindLaw,* accessed January 13, 2018, http://caselaw.findlaw.com/us-supreme-court/316/129.html#t6.

32. Pierre Thomas and Mike Levine, "How the FBI Cracked the iPhone Encryption and Averted a Legal Showdown with Apple, *ABC News,* March 29, 2016, http://abcnews.go.com/US/fbi-cracked-iphone-encryption-averted-legal-showdown-apple/story?id=38014184.

33. Samantha Masunaga, "FBI Doesn't Have to Say Who Unlocked San Bernadino Shooter's iPhone, Judge Rules," *Los Angeles Times,* October 2, 2017, accessed January 13, 2018, www.latimes.com/business/la-fi-tn-fbi-iphone-20171002-story.html.

34. Lily Hay Newman, "Verizon—Yes, Verizon—Just Stood Up for Your Privacy," *Wired*, accessed January 13, 2018, https://www.wired.com/story/verizon-privacy-location-data-fourth -amendment/.

35. FISA Surveillance Program, "What Is It and Why Is It So Controversial?" January 19, 2018, *FoxNews*, www.foxnews.com/politics/2018/01/19/fisa-surveillance-program-what-is-it-and-why -is-it-so-controversial.html.

36. Lee Rainie and Shiva Maniam, "Americans Feel the Tensions between Privacy and Security Concerns," Pew Research Center, February 19, 2016, 2018, www.pewresearch.org/fact -tank/2016/02/19/americans-feel-the-tensions-between-privacy-and-security-concerns/.

37. David Shepardson, "Trump Signs Repeal of U.S. Broadband Privacy Rules," Reuters, April 3, 2017, https://www.reuters.com/article/us-usa-internet-trump/trump-signs-repeal-of-u-s-broadband -privacy-rules-idUSKBN1752PR.

38. Civil Code 1798.82., *California Legislative Information,* accessed January 13, 2018, http://leginfo .legislature.ca.gov/faces/codes_displaySection.xhtml?lawCode=CIV&sectionNum=1798.82.

39. Business and Professions Code—BPC, Division 8, Chapter 22.1. Privacy Rights for California Minors in the Digital World [22580–22582], accessed January 13, 2018, http://leginfo.legislature .ca.gov/faces/codes_displayText.xhtml?lawCode=BPC&division=8.&chapter=22.1.

40. GDPR Portal, accessed January 15, 2018, https://www.eugdpr.org/.

41. Yaki Faitelson, "Yes, the GDPR Will Affect Your U.S.-Based Business," *Forbes,* December 4, 2017,https://www.forbes.com/sites/forbestechcouncil/2017/12/04/yes-the-gdpr-will-affect-your -u-s-based-business/#23594d536ff2.

42. ITL Bulletin for April 2010, "Guide to Protecting Personally Identifiable Information," accessed January 16, 2018, https://csrc.nist.gov/csrc/media/publications/shared/documents/itl-bulletin/ itlbu12010-04.pdf.

43. Jeff John Roberts, "A Surprise in the Equifax Breach: Victims Likely to Get Paid," *Fortune,* October 10, 2017, http://fortune.com/2017/10/10/equifax-class-action/.

44. Russell Brandom, "Former Equifax CEO Blames Breach on a Single Person Who Failed to Deploy a Patch," *The Verge,* October 3, 2017, https://www.theverge.com/2017/10/3/16410806/equifax-ceo -blame-breach-patch-congress-testimony.

45. Kamakshi Tandon, "In Light of Hack into WADA Database, Venus Williams Defends Her Integrity," *Tennis,* September 15, 2016,. www.tennis.com/pro-game/2016/09/venus-williams-wada-russian -hackers-itf-tues-serena-williams-rio-olympics/61109/.

46. "Don't Let Trade Secrets Leave with Departing Employees," Jux Law Firm, accessed January 16, 2018, https://jux.law/trade-secrets-departing-employees/.

47. Bret A. Cohen, Michael T. Renaud, and Nicholas W. Armington, "Explaining the Defend Trade Secrets Act," *Business Law Today,* September 2016, https://www.americanbar.org/publications/ blt/2016/09/03_cohen.html.

48. Marc S. Reisch, "U.S. Charges Dupont Employee wth Trade Secrets Theft," *C&EN,* April 17, 2017, https://cen.acs.org/articles/95/i16/US-charges-DuPont-employee-trade -secrets-theft.html.

49. Casey Panetta, "5 Trends in Cybersecurity for 2017 and 2018," Gartner, June 14, 2017, https://www.gartner.com/smarterwithgartner/5-trends-in-cybersecurity-for-2017-and-2018/.

50. International Organization for Standardization (ISO), *The ISO Survey of Management System Standard Certification 2016,* accessed January 16, 2018, https://isotc.iso.org/livelink/livelink/ fetch/-8853493/8853511/8853520/18808772/00._Executive_summary_2016_Survey.pdf?nodeid =19208898&vernum=-2.

51. Gartner, s.v. "cybersecurity," accessed January 17, 2018, https://www.gartner.com/doc/2510116/ definition-cybersecurity.

52. Gartner, *Magic Quadrant for Data Loss Prevention,* February 16, 2017, https://www.gartner.com/doc/reprints?aid=elq_&id=1-3TNX4ZE&ct=170216&st=sb&elqTrackId=8d8d38a20614419385976f5b7a11f062&elqaid=3769&elqat=2.

53. Visit the Symantec website at https://www.symantec.com/.

54. Symantec, *6 Steps to Prevent a Data Breach,* 2009, http://eval.symantec.com/mktginfo/enterprise/other_resources/b-6-steps-prevent-data-reach_20049431-1.en-us.pdf.

55. Federal Trade Commission, *Data Breach Response: A Guide for Business,* September 2016, https://www.ftc.gov/system/files/documents/plain-language/pdf-0154_data-breach-response-guide-for-business.pdf.

56. PCI Forensic Investigators (PFIs) database, https://www.pcisecuritystandards.org/assessors_and_solutions/pci_forensic_investigators.

57. Kate Taylor, "Sonic Confirmed That 5 Million Customers May Have Had Their Credit-Card Info Stolen in Data Breach," *Business Insider,* September 27, 2017, www.businessinsider.com/report-sonic-security-breach-could-affect-millions-2017-9.

58. Nate Lord, "Cybersecurity Incident Response Planning: Expert Tips, Steps, Testing & More," *DataInsider,* July 27, 2017. https://digitalguardian.com/blog/incident-response-plan.

59. WatchGuard, "Three Best Practice Tips to Preventing Ransomware Attacks," accessed January 19, 2018, https://www.cdwg.com/content/dam/CDW/resources/brands/watchguard/Ransomware.pdf.

60. Paul King, "The Right Cyber Coverage Can Protect a Business from Financial Ruin," *Insurance Journal,* November 16, 2016, https://www.insurancejournal.com/news/east/2016/11/16/432350.htm.

61. General Data Protection Regulation, www.eugdpr.org/the-regulation.html.

62. Ibid.

63. Pure Point International, "Security in a Changed World: Cybersecurity Officially Meets Physical Security in the NY DFS Regulation," http://the-purepoint.com/security-in-a-changed-world-cybersecurity-officially-meets-physical-security-in-the-ny-dfs-regulation/.

64. Khoste, "Product Overview," http://khoste.com/product-overview/.

65. EDRM, "Information Governance Reference Model (IGRM) ," www.edrm.net/frameworks-and-standards/information-governance-reference-model/using-the-igrm-model/.

66. ARMA International, *Generally Accepted Recordkeeping Principles,* www.arma.org/docs/bookstore/theprinciplesmaturitymodel.pdf.

67. European Commission, "Factsheet on the Right to Be Forgotten Ruling," http://ec.europa.eu/justice/data-protection/files/factsheets/factsheet_data_protection_en.pdf.

68. International Organization for Standardization, *ISO/IEC 27000—Information Security Management Systems,* https://www.iso.org/isoiec-27001-information-security.html.

CHAPTER 11

Inactive Records Management

Records Centers and Archives

INTRODUCTION

Every organization possesses physical and electronic records that are rarely used in daily operations but must be retained to satisfy business needs, legal and regulatory requirements, and community or societal expectations. Paper records stored in file cabinets occupy valuable office space. If the records are referred to infrequently, they should be moved to less expensive storage locations. Digital files can be moved to less expensive online or off-line storage. *Records centers* are designed specifically to retain inactive records until they meet their retention requirements. The majority of records stored in records centers are paper and microfilm, but the growth of digital information has resulted in the addition of media vaults to store digital media such as CDs, DVDs, tapes, and hard drives. Some records centers offer online content management systems and others will even create a digital archive for a particular group of records.

Records with long-term or permanent retention requirements need more stringent storage controls than traditionally provided in a records center. Therefore, they are usually transferred to an *archive*—a repository designed to store and preserve documents that are of value to researchers and historians.

In this chapter, we explore the use of records centers for inactive business records and the role of archives in retaining records and information for research or historical purposes.

INACTIVE RECORDS AND RECORDS CENTERS

An *inactive record* is "no longer needed to conduct current business but preserved until it meets the end of its retention period."[1] Access to inactive records will be infrequent; therefore, separating active records from inactive records yields numerous benefits in the world of physical records, including:

- freeing additional space for active files
- decreasing the chances of misfiling
- improving inactive reference services
- increasing efficiency in records disposition
- avoiding the purchase or use of unnecessary, costly storage equipment (e.g., additional file cabinets)

The definition of inactive records used by the Society of American Archivists (SAA) omits reference to a retention requirement and describes inactive records as "records that are no longer used in the day-to-day course of business, but which may be preserved and occasionally used for legal, historical, or operational purposes."[2] Inactive records can be identified by frequency of access as established by the institution. For example, one institution may classify a record inactive if accessed six or fewer times a year, whereas another may consider a record inactive if used less than once a month.

Some organizations store inactive records in their own records centers, in on-site or off-site facilities located on property that is less expensive per square foot than real estate used for administrative offices. Organizations can maximize the use of their space and potentially reduce costs by offering records storage services to others free of charge or for a fee. Some organizations take advantage of the services of commercial records centers for their inactive records; still others use a combination of the two—in-house and commercial. Once a program is initiated, the outcome should be evaluated periodically to determine if adjustments are necessary. Circumstances attributed to organizational changes, such as acquisitions or mergers, can impact the organization's inactive records management strategy.

Records Center Planning and Design

The term *records center* usually evokes an image of a records center with floor to ceiling shelving units packed with boxes of paper records such as the one shown in figure 11.1.

Records centers may also contain vaults to house vital records and records stored on

different media, including microfilm and computer tapes. Environmental controls vary according to the type of medium on which the record is stored. Smart space planning, including choice of storage equipment, maximizes the volume of records that can be contained in the records center. Staffing depends on the size of the organization, volume of records, and services provided. Environmental, access, and security controls protect the records. Automated processes, such as bar coding and radio frequency identification (RFID), help staff manage physical files so they remain accessible and the company remains compliant. Not every records manager will be responsible for

FIGURE 11.1 Document services supervisor Maggie Turner in the main records vault, City Records Center, Milwaukee. The Records Center is soon to be combined with the Office of Historic Preservation and the Legislative Reference Bureau to form the City Research Center.

SOURCE: Office of the City Clerk, City of Milwaukee. Photo by Andrew Marten.

planning, designing, and managing a records center. But it is important to understand the criteria that must be considered and the resources that are available if the opportunity presents itself.

Estimating Volume and Space Requirements

The information gathered from both the records inventory and the retention and disposition schedule covered in chapter 4 can be used to estimate current and future space needs. The inventory lists records on hand in active and inactive storage locations. The volume of existing inactive records needs to be planned for when designing new or improved space. One rule states that one-third of all records are active and can be found in offices, one-third are inactive and should be stored in a records center, and one-third (or more) have no value and should be destroyed.[3] Before moving to a new or improved records center, dispose of records that have met their retention requirement to reduce the cost of transferring records.

Once you determine the volume of existing inactive records identified through the records inventory, you must consider expansion needs. The estimate for expansion is also one-third, barring unusual circumstances. The volume of inactive records may increase, for example, if a legal hold prevents destruction of records. It is not unusual to have such records retained years past the disposition date while a case or investigation runs its course. The volume of records in inactive storage may decrease over the years, however, if automated processes are implemented that result in an increase in digital information and a decrease in paper records.

The size of space selected or built should be based upon the estimated volume of records to be housed. Floor space and height of ceiling must be considered. Robek, Brown, and Stephens used the formulas in figure 11.2 for estimating space requirements for the stack area of the records center.[4]

A records manager can use these formulas to make preliminary decisions. There are times when the only option is to use space currently available. In that case, the floor area

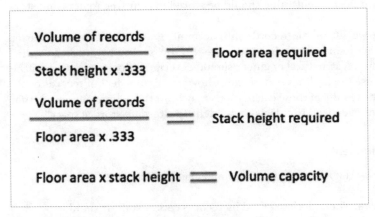

FIGURE 11.2 Formulas used to estimate volume, capacity, and floor area for space planning.

SOURCE: Mary F. Robek, Gerald F. Brown, and David O. Stephens, Information and Records Management: Document-Based Information Systems (New York, Glencoe/McGraw-Hill, 1996), 465.

times the stack height possible (based on structural features such as ceiling height and low-hanging pipes and light fixtures) will reveal the volume of records that can be moved to the inactive storage space. By comparing this figure with the current volume of inactive records plus anticipated growth, one can quickly determine the adequacy of the space for the organization's needs.

Guidance such as "Archives and Records Storage Building" by the National Institute of Building Sciences can help you plan your inactive storage facility and help you determine the shelving best suited to your needs.[5] Steel shelving that is 42 inches high and 32 inches deep is recommended to allow for a row of three standard records center cartons that are 10″ × 12″× 15″. Consultants can help with space planning, and vendors that specialize in shelving and storage systems can provide advice and examples of floor plans.

Storage and Handling

Records centers may restrict the type of storage boxes they will accept. Standard sizes include:

- **Standard records center box:** 10″ × 12″× 15″. They can hold 1 cubic foot of letter-size or legal-size documents (a letter-size file drawer contains 1.5 cubic feet of records and a legal-size file drawer contains 2 cubic feet).
- **Standard storage boxes for CD-ROMs, microfiche, and roll film:** 15″ × 12″ × 5″. These are half the height of a standard records center box.
- **Map, blueprint, and plan boxes:** 12″ × 10″ × 30″.

Space should be left so the lid fits and the box does not bulge. Staff responsible for packing should be instructed to remove metal fasteners, three-ring binders, and binder clips from the materials. Some centers allow staples and paper clips, although these items can rust when stored for long periods.

The primary concern should be access, security, and preservation of records. Records should be stored as part of a records series and remain in file folders when placed in boxes. Records with long-term or permanent value should be stored in acid-free folders and storage boxes.

Be sure to take the weight of the records into account. Each of the standard boxes weighs between 30 and 50 pounds when full and more if water-soaked by overhead sprinklers activated due to a fire. A structural engineer should determine floor strength, and the records manager should use the findings to determine how many cubic feet of records could be stored in the space. The results of these calculations may limit the volume of records that can be stored and perhaps even lead to a decision to identify alternate storage space.

Additional Space Requirements

Areas are needed for use by the records center staff and clients, including:

- **Administrative area:** The office area used by records center staff. It should be close to the stack area, clean, well lit, and air-conditioned. The space required depends on the size of the facility and staff.
- **Reference area:** This area is set aside for visitors or clients to review materials. The equipment needed depends upon the services provided; for

example, a copier and microfilm/microfiche reader/printer. At a minimum, it should include tables arranged to allow staff to observe users and files. Proximity to the administrative area is ideal.

- **Records staging area:** Records are first brought into the records center through the staging area. It should be clean and secure with a doorway wide enough to allow a forklift and pallet to transfer records cartons from the loading dock. Space should be available to house two to three days' worth of records awaiting accessioning.
- **Records processing area:** This area should also be near the loading dock, the stacking area, and the administrative area. It will be utilized for returned files, interfiles (items placed in their proper place within an existing body of materials), and assembling records boxes. It should be furnished with at least one work table, and the doorways and aisles must be wide enough to accommodate records-handling equipment.
- **Records disposal area:** This temporary area stores records awaiting disposal. It should be near the loading dock but separate from the staging area to prevent destruction of the wrong records. If documents are shredded on-site, a commercial shredder and bailer could be housed here, but the space would need an air ventilation/ exchange system and soundproofing. An alternative to shredding in-house is to contract with a commercial shredding or recycling service that will remove your records for shredding or recycling at their facility or provide on-site shredding services using mobile shredding trucks.

Records Protection

The main goal of the records center is to protect the records within its care from damage due to environmental conditions, natural and man-made disasters, theft, sabotage, and vandalism.

Environmental Factors: Temperature, Humidity, Lighting, and Pollution

Storage media can be damaged by fluctuations in temperature and humidity. Modern paper has a life expectancy of only about twenty years due to high levels of acidity in the paper composition and pollution in the atmosphere. Life expectancy can be reduced by exposure to extreme temperatures. Heat causes paper and microforms to become brittle, and humidity promotes the growth of fungus that rots paper and breaks down the composition of microfilm. Table 11.1 presents optimal ranges for paper, film, and electronic media. Avoid temperature fluctuations of more than 5 percent in either direction. When storing mixed media, temperatures between 65 and 70 degrees and relative humidity between 40 and 45 percent are safe for paper, film, and electronic media.

Employ heating, ventilation, and air conditioning (HVAC) controls to maintain fairly consistent temperature and humidity levels. If humidity is difficult to control, fans will keep air circulating in order to prevent mildew. Dehumidifiers may be required in some climates. If used, a drain line should be installed to remove water automatically and checked periodically to be sure it is unobstructed. HVAC systems should be equipped with filters to remove dirt and other harmful particles from the air. Clean or replace filters on a regular schedule.

TABLE 11.1 Optimal temperature and humidity ranges for paper, film, and electronic media.

	TEMPERATURE	RELATIVE HUMIDITY
Paper	65–70° F (+/-20°)	40–50 %
Film	55–68°F (+/-20°)	30–40 %
Electronic Media	68°F (+/-20°)	30–40 %

Ultraviolet (UV) light, strongest in sunlight and fluorescent lighting, can shorten the life of paper and microforms. Light weakens paper fibers, contributes to brittleness, bleaches or yellows paper, and fades print. To protect records from sunlight, attach UV-filtering film to windows and/or use blinds or drapes. If using fluorescent lighting, buy low-UV fluorescent bulbs, install UV-filtering film on the light diffuser panels, and/or use UV-filtering sleeves on the tubes. It's best to run lighting over the aisles parallel to the shelves rather than over the shelves. Locate the light fixtures 14 inches above the highest box or shelf, keep lights off as much as possible, use zone lighting to avoid lighting the entire area, and consider the use of light timers or motion sensors to minimize the use of electricity, to protect records, and to reduce overhead costs.

Pests, including rodents and insects, feed on paper, leather, and pastes found in records storage areas. Inspect records for insects before placing them into storage. Pests can be controlled by chemical means if necessary, but their presence can be discouraged by minimizing the elements essential to their survival, including food and moisture. This can be accomplished through good housekeeping, ongoing monitoring, routine inspection, and staff education.

Natural and Man-Made Disasters: Fire, Water, Theft, Sabotage, and Vandalism

Potential hazards to records include threats caused by fire, water, theft, sabotage, and vandalism.

Fire Prevention

Fire prevention techniques minimize the chance a fire will start and maximize the chance it can be extinguished. Consult the local fire marshal when constructing a new records storage space. Local requirements may impact the floor plan, including height of stacks, width of aisles, and specifications for fire extinguishers, firewalls, fire alarms, and exits. The records spaces should be separated from other portions of the building by firewalls that can withstand fire for a minimum of four hours. An early warning system consisting of fire alarms for heat and smoke detection should be installed. Fire prevention techniques, such as implementing a no smoking policy, keeping records storage areas free of chemicals and cleaning supplies, and keeping records away from sources of heat (e.g., furnace, radiator, heater) will minimize the chance of a fire.

The National Fire Protection Association (NFPA) is the leading authority on fire, electrical, and building safety. One resource that should be a part of a records manager's reference library is *NFPA 232: Standard for the Protection of Records*. This standard provides requirements for records protection equipment and facilities and records-handling techniques that protect records in a variety of media forms, both hard copy (e.g., paper and artwork) and electronic form (e.g., offline storage media including computer tape, magnetic disk drives, optical disks, and flash drives) from the hazards of fire. Table 11.2, adapted from the 2017 standard, illustrates the acceptable storage environment for seven record types based on risk tolerance.[6]

Records may be stored in more protective storage environments than the organization's risk tolerance indicates but are not permitted to be stored in less protective environments. Duplication is an acceptable preventive measure as long as duplicates are stored in a facility away from the same threat of fire as the originals. Electronic records stored in electronic systems must be protected in accordance with *NFPA 75, Standard for the Fire Protection of Information Technology Equipment*. In addition to the types of records described in table 11.2, this document describes a type of record unique to electronic systems, the *master record*. The master record is "an information record on a medium that can be referred to whenever there is a need to rebuild a database."[7]

Several options exist to contain a fire, including waterless fire suppression systems. Dry chemical fire suppression systems can be installed in areas that contain equipment or records that would be damaged by water. Sprinkler systems, once thought to do more harm to records than good, are still popular solutions that can contain a fire near the source and limit the amount of damage to records in adjacent areas.

Water Damage

Water damage is the most likely event to impact records. In addition to sprinkler systems, sources of water damage include leaking roofs or pipes, backed-up plumbing, malfunctioning HVAC equipment, and inclement weather. Preventative measures include keeping records boxes off the floor and away from water pipes. If water damage occurs, a damage assessment tour is required. The problem should be described in broad terms, such as linear feet or number of storage containers, type of materials damaged, and whether they are replaceable. Refer to the inventory of records to classify the records damaged. The extent of damage may include soaked, partially wet, damp, charred, smoke-damaged, and debris-covered records.

TABLE 11.2 Acceptable storage environments for records types based on risk tolerance.

RECORD TYPE	FILE ROOM	RECORDS CENTER	ARCHIVE	VAULT
Vital				X
Archival	X	X	X	X
Important			X	X
Permanent	X	X	X	X
Active	X	X	X	X
Inactive	X	X	X	X
Unscheduled	X	X	X	X

This assessment must be made quickly, efficiently, safely, and without actually handling records when possible.

Water-damaged records can be treated in-house or by contracting with a professional document recovery service. If records can be treated in-house, the first step is to stabilize the environment to inhibit the growth of mold by reducing the temperature to 50°–60°F and reducing the humidity as much as possible to help remove moisture from the records. The choice of treatment depends on the extent of damage incurred and expertise and availability of staff. If records cannot be treated within twenty-four hours, they should be packed for freezing. Records removed from their original location should be inventoried (e.g., name/title of record, dates covered, original location). This information must be kept with the records whether they are sent to a commercial service or spread out to dry on-site.

The options available for treatment of wet records include:

- **Air-drying:** This may be all that is needed. Air-drying should take place in a temperature- and humidity-controlled space at 50°–60°F and 25–35 percent relative humidity. If air-drying does not begin within twenty-four hours, the records should be packed for freezing either in boxes that are lined with plastic garbage bags or in plastic milk crates.
- **Freezing:** If air-drying is not practical, freezing should be used to provide time to determine a course of action. It stabilizes the material so mold does not grow and records do not continue to deteriorate. Freezing also eliminates smoke odor from materials water-damaged due to a fire. Rapid freezing at temperatures below 15°F is recommended to minimize damage from ice crystals when drying out wet materials.
- **Vacuum freeze-drying:** A sublimation process is used to remove water (moisture) from frozen documents in order to maintain their shape and biological structure. The goal is to retain the composition and structure of the material by drying it without applying heat to begin an evaporation process. The freeze-drying process converts water into ice crystals and ice crystals into a gaseous state (vapor), which is removed from the chamber by vacuum pumps. This is the most expensive but most effective process for drying documents.

The recovery process must also include recovery of other types of media, such as computer tapes, microform, and video- or audiotapes. This recovery process should be included in the organization's disaster recovery plan.

Theft, Sabotage, and Vandalism

Physical and logical access controls were covered in detail in chapter 5. In addition to the controls introduced there, the following controls are appropriate for records centers:

- Limit daily access to records center staff.
- Require visitors to sign in and out on a visitor's log and wear a visitor's badge.
- Require all visitors to be accompanied at all times by a records center staff member.
- Utilize windowless spaces when possible. If windows are present,

cover the panes with UV film to protect records from sunlight and bar them to prevent access.

Records Center Management

In addition to space and equipment needs already discussed, well-trained staff is essential to the success of the records center operations.

Records Center Staff

In small organizations, the records manager or a member of the records management staff might manage the in-house records center. In larger organizations, an in-house records center requires dedicated staff to ensure it runs smoothly. The staff should include a manager, administrative staff, and a number of individuals dedicated to tasks related to the services provided. If reference areas are provided, administrative staff must be trained to deliver quality customer service. If the records center provides hard-copy storage, staff will be needed to transport records to and from the facility and to move records within the facility (i.e., from the loading docks to the processing area and stacks). If scanning and microfilm services are offered, staff well-trained in scanning and microfilming is required. A records center that provides storage of computer media and/or remote electronic backup and restore services will need staff with the requisite technical expertise to manage and preserve those records. Job descriptions to fill positions within the records center would not only include a description of duties and knowledge and skill requirements, but also physical requirements as needed.

Records Center Specialist—Physical Requirements

- Perform all physical requirements without assistance.
- Work on your feet all day.
- Lift, load, and move boxes (average weight: 40 pounds).
- Climb stairs, lift up to 70 pounds, and be able to use tools to maneuver materials.

Records Center Operating Procedures

The records center manager is responsible for establishing records control and disposition procedures.

Records Control: Forms and Technology Solutions

Records control involves a number of activities, including coordinating transfer of records to the center, accessioning records, logging storage assignments and storing records, responding to records retrieval requests, performing refiles and interfiles, and disposing of records.

One of the easiest and fastest ways to inform clients of the services of the records center is to develop a website that includes physical location, days and hours of operation, contact information for records center staff, records center forms, and answers to frequently asked questions.

Records forms can be made available for download to be completed and transmitted electronically, sent with the records, or completed online. *Sample Forms for Archival and Records Management Programs,* available from ARMA International and the Society of American Archivists, contains examples of forms for the records center.[8] Forms specific to records center, records control, and records destruction and disposition are listed in table 11.3.

Software solutions are available to manage commercial, corporate, and government records centers. Such products can handle physical and/or electronic records. Software with tracking and inventory control features permit updating, sorting, and reporting.. Some software packages produce bar code or RFID labels that can be used to designate a physical location to cartons so they can be retrieved efficiently. The labels could also be used for check-in, check-out, and a records audit. Internet-based software allows the client to generate requests and access and control account information from anywhere in the world.

Disposition/Destruction of Records

When referring to disposition within the records lifecycle, there are two options: destruction or transfer to an archive. When speaking of disposition in relation to the records center, disposition is synonymous with destruction, and destruction must be irreversible. There are factors that can require extending the disposal date, including pending lawsuits, merger negotiations, audits, and changes in laws and regulations. The requirement that a destruction authorization form be completed before destruction takes place offers the client an opportunity to extend the disposal date by providing a written explanation on the form with the extended disposition date. The client may wish or even be required to send a copy to legal staff for their approval. The legal staff may be aware of litigation about which the client has not yet been informed.

Records destruction should be authorized, appropriate, secure, and confidential, timely, and documented. Document destruction methods include:

- **Disabling:** Often the preliminary step before transferring electronic media to a secure destruction facility, disabling involves rendering the media inoperable so the data cannot be retrieved and read.
- **Dissolution:** Similar to pulping for paper, dissolution is a process to dissolve film-based media (microfiche and microfilm) in a chemical bath.
- **Maceration:** This process involves using chemicals to soften the paper and destroy the writing before pulverizing the documents.
- **Pulping:** This process involves placing paper in a liquid suspension called a slurry that is made of water and chemicals that aid in breaking down the material. The documents are then forced through cutters and screens to reduce the paper to pulp.
- **Recycling:** If records are not confidential, commercial services can be employed to remove and recycle the documents.
- **Shredding:** Shredding can be performed in-house or by employing a records-shredding service. To avoid document reconstruction, the center

TABLE 11.3 Records center/records control and records destruction/disposition forms.

RECORDS CENTER/ RECORDS CONTROL	RECORDS DESTRUCTION/ DISPOSITION
Records transfer/transmittal forms	Records destruction authorization
Records retrieval request form	Certificate of destruction
Records outcards	
Records retrieval authorization form	
Records center box labels	

may opt for shredder models that produce crosscuts (cut paper lengthwise and widthwise) or those that produce rotary cuts (disintegrators) that result in fine particles. Shredders are also available to destroy electronic equipment such as hard drives, cell phones, and tablets.[9]

A bonded service can be engaged to pick up records for destruction. If preferred, a representative of the center can accompany the vendor to witness the destruction of materials. Customers using commercial services will receive a certificate of destruction (COD), which certifies shredding has taken place. However, the service does not certify that the documents on the itemized list presented for destruction were actually in the containers. The COD will contain a unique serial or transaction number, a date and location of destruction of materials, the method of destruction, and a signature of a witness to the destruction (employee of records center, representative of shredding company, and a representative of the client or agency who owns the records if desired).

Commercial Records Centers

Commercial records centers, also known as information management centers because of the increased need for storage of digital media, offer an alternative to an in-house records center. They are designed and equipped to store records in an efficient and economical manner, provide environmentally controlled security for records, and employ procedures that facilitate location, retrieval, and delivery of records when needed.

Services Offered

Records centers manage physical records and often offer additional services, such as:

- web access to data and digital delivery of files
- confidential and secure destruction services
- document-imaging services converting paper and film to an electronic records format
- digital archives
- consulting

- records retention scheduling
- disaster recovery and business continuity services
- archival records storage
- vault storage that provides fireproof and temperature- and humidity-controlled environment for digital data
- electronic vaulting that provides online backup services
- security
- protection against disasters (e.g., fires, earthquakes, floods)
- accessibility

Many of the benefits of managing an in-house records center can be attributed to a commercial records center, such as space cost savings and reduced operating costs. Additional benefits are a climate-controlled environment, authorized and secure destruction, vital records protection, online backups, and enterprise content management and digital archives.

Media Vaults

Digital media will be damaged at temperatures above 125°F and 80 percent relative humidity. Media vaults are designed and built to protect these assets. An option to installing a custom-designed media vault is to contract with a records center that offers this service. Figure 11.3 illustrates the framework of a media vault that provides fire and environmental protection to magnetic media, IT equipment, removable hard drives, micrographic media, optical disks, paper documents of enduring value, and historic artifacts. When selecting commercial storage vendors, the presence of a media vault is a factor that should be considered. However, inclusion of a media vault in an in-house records center is also an increasingly popular option.

Request for Information and Request for Proposal

Initially, when considering the option of using the services of a commercial records storage provider, you may wish to gather information informally. A request for information (RFI) is a document designed to collect information about a prospective vendor. The entire RFI process—from preparation to dissemination to receipt of information—may be accomplished within several weeks.[10]

The RFI may be sufficient for a small, low-budget project, but it may be just the first step for a high-budget project. When considering moving existing records to a commercial records center, it is necessary to determine space and service needs, prepare a request for quotation (RFQ), and then compare vendor proposals. Savings can be considerable in making such a move, but errors in preparing the request and interpreting quotes received can seriously impact the decision made. The development of the request for proposal (RFP), as well as the final contract, should involve the records manager, the records manager's immediate supervisor, procurement/purchasing staff, and the legal department.

Developing the Request for Proposal

In preparing a request for proposal (RFP), William Benedon provides a list of items to be analyzed, including the type of records involved, length of time the contract will cover, cost of the initial move to the storage facility, service and reports requirements, inventory count, safety and security requirements beyond those offered by the vendor, service charges, and termination costs.[11] Another resource, ARMA International's *Guideline for Evaluating Offsite Records Storage Facilities,* provides guidance for developing both the RFI and an RFQ process.[12]

Evaluating Records and Information Storage Options

The Professional Records and Information Services Management (PRISM), the global trade association for information management companies, provides guidance to those selecting an off-site information management company in the form of an online checklist, "Demand the Best."[13]

PRISM suggests the first step is to develop a profile for each alternative by determining its overall mission and how it meets your goals and needs, how long it has been in business, how it differentiates from competitors, if it can provide references, and if it is a member of PRISM. The evaluation process should involve rating factors that are also considered when designing an in-house records center.

When evaluating inactive storage options, there is no substitute for a tour of the physical plant and conversations with current customers.

The following additional resources are available to assist you in determining the best solution for your long-term records storage needs:

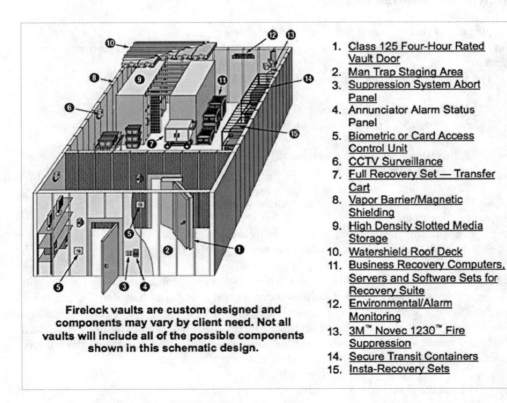

Firelock vaults are custom designed and components may vary by client need. Not all vaults will include all of the possible components shown in this schematic design.

1. Class 125 Four-Hour Rated Vault Door
2. Man Trap Staging Area
3. Suppression System Abort Panel
4. Annunciator Alarm Status Panel
5. Biometric or Card Access Control Unit
6. CCTV Surveillance
7. Full Recovery Set — Transfer Cart
8. Vapor Barrier/Magnetic Shielding
9. High Density Slotted Media Storage
10. Watershield Roof Deck
11. Business Recovery Computers, Servers and Software Sets for Recovery Suite
12. Environmental/Alarm Monitoring
13. 3M™ Novec 1230™ Fire Suppression
14. Secure Transit Containers
15. Insta-Recovery Sets

FIGURE 11.3 Custom-designed media vault.

SOURCE: Firelock, "Media Vault Tour," Vault Design and Engineering. www.firelock.com/media-vault-digital-tour.htm. Courtesy of Firelock.

- ARMA International's technical report *Records Center Operations* (3rd ed.) covers the establishment and operation of a records center under the control of an organization or through the use of a commercial records center.[14] This report also provides guidance on preparing an internal records center budget.
- ARMA's *Understanding Electronic Records Storage Technologies* discusses storage technologies and service offerings for electronic records, including operational issues such as outsourcing considerations and contract-related elements.[15] If records have long-term retention requirements, the record owner must understand the capability of the storage provider to maintain those records, consider the necessity of converting records to a different format in order to comply with long-term retention requirements, and work with the storage provider to develop practices to transition the records to other media over time.

Inactive records can be transferred to a records center or, if they have enduring value, to an archives.

ARCHIVES MANAGEMENT

The purpose of this section is not to cover all archival theory and practice but to introduce some archival concepts to those who are also responsible for records and information management.

The term *archives* has a number of definitions, among them:

1. Materials created or received and preserved because of their enduring value or as evidence of the functions and responsibilities of their creator.
2. The division within an organization responsible for maintaining the organization's records of enduring value.
3. An organization that collects the records of individuals, families, or other organizations.
4. The professional discipline of administering such collections and organizations.
5. The building (or portion thereof) housing archival collections.
6. A published collection of scholarly papers, especially as a periodical.[16]

The Society of American Archivists published "Guidelines for a Graduate Program in Archival Studies" (2016), which describes core archival knowledge that must be mastered by a professional archivist. The core knowledge consists of three facets of archival studies: knowledge of archival material and archival functions, knowledge of the profession, and contextual knowledge. The knowledge of archival material and functions provides a list of topics that describe the elements involved in an archival program:[17]

- the nature of records and archives
- selection, appraisal, and acquisition
- arrangement and description
- preservation

- reference and access
- outreach, instruction, and advocacy
- management and administration
- records and information management
- digital materials management

Archives management (also called archives administration) is "the general oversight of a program to appraise, acquire, arrange and describe, preserve, authenticate, and provide access to permanently valuable records."[18] *Archival science,* the systematic body of archival theory, supports archives management practice.

The views of two influential archivists impact decisions made by archivists today, including the appraisal process: Sir Hilary Jenkinson and Theodore R. Schellenberg. Sir Hilary Jenkinson (1892–1961) held that archives are "documents which formed part of an official transaction and were preserved for official reference."[19] He further argued that the records creator is responsible for determining which records should be transferred to the archives for preservation. Because of his belief that records are evidence of transactions, he did not recognize historical documents as archives, although he did agree collections of personal papers were of value to historians. These collections, he contended, complement archives, and the repositories in which they are stored are called *manuscript repositories*.

Other archivists, especially in the United States, follow the more inclusive view of archival holdings held by Theodore R. Schellenberg (1903–1970). Schellenberg cites primary and secondary values and the need for archivists to appraise records for transfer to archives on the basis of their secondary value (e.g., research, evidential, or informational). Schellenberg's views form the basis for the policy set forth in the "Appraisal Policy of the National Archives and Records Administration."[20]

Appraisal

Two definitions of appraisal illustrate the difference in perspectives between archivists and records managers. Records managers view *appraisal* (also referred to as records appraisal) as defined in *ISO 15489-1:2016, Information and documentation—Records management—Part 1: Concepts and principles,* as the "process of evaluating business activities to determine which records need to be created and captured and how long the records need to be kept." Records are retained as evidence of business activity, and records requirements are derived from business needs, legal and regulatory requirements, and community or societal expectations.[21] Archivists regard appraisal in the "archival context" as the process of determining whether records and other materials have permanent (archival) value. Appraisal decisions are based on a number of factors, including provenance and content, authenticity and reliability, order and completeness, condition and costs to preserve, and intrinsic value (e.g., unique physical format).[22]

Barbara Craig provides a comprehensive definition of archival appraisal in the *Encyclopedia of Archival Science* when she states: "Archival appraisal is a broad term embracing the theory, rationales, policies, and procedures for identifying, acquiring, and selecting institutional or organizational records and personal or private records in all media deemed to have lasting value and worth according to criteria that are articulated and documented."[23]

Criteria will differ depending on the organization and industry. The US National Archives and Records Administration (NARA) has established a high-level framework for the analysis of federal records no longer needed for current business operations. The three broad categories into which permanent records may fall are:

- records documenting the rights of citizens
- records documenting the actions of federal officials
- records documenting the national experience

Additional criteria were established for each of these categories, and general guidelines were provided. Only those records with enduring value can be transferred to the National Archives.

The following set of questions was developed to provide consistent appraisal judgments:

- How significant are the records for research?
- How significant is the source and context of the records?
- Is the information unique?
- How usable are the records?
- Do these records serve as a finding aid to other permanent records?
- Do the records document decisions that set precedents?
- Are the records related to other permanent records?
- Do the files contain non-archival records?
- What are the cost considerations for long-term maintenance of the records?
- What is the volume of records?
- Is sampling an appropriate appraisal tool?

Although most records are born digital and it is possible to digitize physical records, some documentary materials, such as the book shown in figure 11.4, possess qualities and

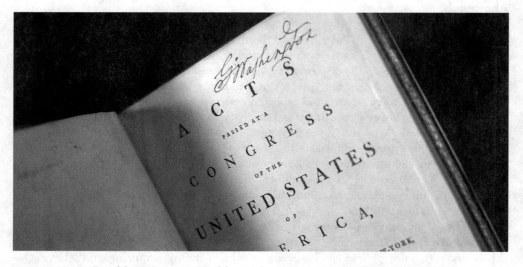

FIGURE 11.4 President George Washington's personal copy of the Acts of Congress, including the US Constitution and a draft of the Bill of Rights with Washington's own signature and handwritten notations.
SOURCE: Win McNamee, Getty Images.

characteristics that make the physical form the only acceptable form for preservation. A book once owned by US President George Washington that contains his annotated copy of the US Constitution and Bill of Rights was sold at auction for $9.8 million dollars in 2012. The 223-year-old book has George Washington's signature on the title page. Washington added brackets and notes within the book highlighting key passages about the responsibility of the president. The Mount Vernon Ladies' Association of the Union purchased the book and returned it to the library at George Washington's Mount Vernon Estate, Museum, and Gardens.[24] The book, which has value because of its contents, was even more valued by collectors because of the signature and annotations made by the first president of the United States.

Acquisition and Accession

The materials received by a repository as a unit are known as an *acquisition*. Acquisitions are guided by an *acquisition policy*, an official statement issued by an archives or manuscript repository identifying the kinds of materials it accepts and the conditions or terms that affect their acquisition. It serves as a document for the guidance of archival staff and organizations and persons interested in donating their records or papers.

If materials meet the criteria established by the archives collection development policy, a decision may be made to accept some or all of the materials. Once the archivist decides to accept a group of records, the following steps must be taken:

- A record of the accession should be created either on paper or using an electronic system.
- A Deed of Gift should be executed to record the transaction between the archives and the donor.
- A preliminary inventory of the materials received should be prepared and attached to the Deed of Gift.

Next, the items must be arranged and described. Archival management software programs, such as the Archivist's Toolkit (www.archiviststoolkit.org/), support accessioning and describing archival materials; establishing names and subjects associated with archival materials, including names of donors; managing locations for the materials; and exporting EAD finding aids.

Arrangement and Description

According to ARMA International, *arrangement* is (1) "the process of organizing materials with respect to their provenance and original order, to protect their context and to achieve physical or intellectual control over the materials," and (2) "the organization and sequence of items within a collection."[25] Archivists strive to arrange materials in the order established by the creator. *Provenance,* also known as *respect des fonds,* requires that every document be traced to its origin and maintained as part of a group having the same origin rather than arranged by subject groups established by the archivist. This principle dictates that records of different origins (provenance) be kept separate to preserve their context.

Archivist Oliver Wendell Holmes, who worked at the US National Archives beginning in 1935, identified five levels of arrangement: repository; collection or record group (subgroups); series; folder (filing unit); and item (document).[26] These levels of arrangement are independent of their containers.

The SAA *Glossary of Archival and Records Terminology* defines *description* as (1) the process of creating a finding aid or other access tools that allow individuals to browse a surrogate of the collection to facilitate access and that improve security by creating a record of the collection and by minimizing the amount of handling of the original materials, and (2) (as applied to records management) a written account of the physical characteristics, informational content, and functional purpose of a records series or system.[27]

Archival description includes information about the content, intellectual, and physical attributes of the material, and context of their creation and use. The SAA Glossary defines *archival description* as (1) the process of analyzing, organizing, and recording details about the formal elements of a record or collection of records, such as creator, title, dates, extent, and contents, to facilitate the work's identification, management, and understanding, and (2) the product of such a process.[28] Archival descriptions will be updated if materials are added to the collection.

Varieties of Archives

If you are considering a career as an archivist, you'll want to explore the environments in which you might work. SAA provides an extensive list of repository types shown in table 11.4.

TABLE 11.4 Repository types.

REPOSITORY TYPE	DESCRIPTION
Colleges and Universities	Preserve materials related to the specific academic institution. May contain a "special collections" division.
Corporate Archives	Manage and preserve the records of a business.
Government Archives	Collect materials related to local, state, or national government entities.
Historical Societies	Preserve and promote the history of a region, a historical period, nongovernment organizations, or a subject.
Museums	Preserve and exhibit items of historical significance (artifacts or artwork rather than books and papers).
Religious Archives	Preserve materials related to traditions or institutions of a major faith, denominations within a faith, or individual places of worship.
Special Collections	Protect materials of individuals, families, and organizations deemed to have significant historical value. Topics vary widely, for example, music, literature, technology, and law.

ADAPTED FROM: Society of American Archivists (SAA), "Types of Archives," Using Archives: A Guide to Effective Research, accessed December 28, 2017, www2.archivists.org/usingarchives/typesofarchives.

There is variation in archival materials collected and maintained even within archives in the same category. For example, the description of one corporate archives states that the goal is to manage and preserve the records of a business. However, physical artifacts are also kept, such as product packaging, advertising signs, toys, and even stories about how the product played a part in customers' lives. Corporate archives exist for the use of members of the organization and are often referred to when gathering information for celebrations and anniversaries or as a basis for marketing efforts. Some corporate archives are open to the general public; others make portions of their collections available online or as exhibits in corporate museums. Archival materials can be housed within facilities designed for visitors, such as the World of Coca-Cola, which is a must-see attraction in Atlanta, Georgia. The vault constructed to house the company's 125-year-old secret formula for Coca-Cola is shown in figure 11.5.

FIGURE 11.5 The Vault of the Secret Formula located in the World of Coca-Cola, Atlanta, Georgia.

SOURCE: World of Coca-Cola, "Vault of the Secret Formula," https://www.worldofcoca-cola.com/explore/explore-inside/explore-vault-secret-formula/. Courtesy of the Coca-Cola Company.

Often, artifacts can be used as the basis for replication of an authentic setting or for costumes used by actors in movies or television. The 2011 television show *Pan Am* attempted to evoke the glamour of the early days of jet air travel. This required replicas of the uniforms worn by flight stewardesses. An image from the Northwest Corporate Archives (shown in figure 11.6) can provide the basis for retro uniforms such as those once worn by air stewardesses of Delta and related airlines, including Northeast, Northwest, Western, and Pan Am.

Two other types of archives you should be familiar with are *dark archives* and *digital archives*.

Dark Archives

A *dark archives* is a collection of materials (not a space) preserved for future use but with no current access. The term *dark archives* is "principally associated with collections of online serial publications and databases that are held by an organization other than the publisher. These materials are kept in escrow for future use in case they are no longer available from the publisher."[29]

Digital Archives

A digital archives is more difficult to describe. In her article "Digital Archives: Democratizing the Doing of History," Cheryl Mason Bolick describes *digital archives* as "collections

FIGURE 11.6 Flight attendants wearing retro uniforms of Delta and related airlines: Northeast, Northwest, Western, and Pan Am.

SOURCE: Marie Force, Archives Director, Delta Flight Museum, https://www.deltamuseum.org/home. Courtesy of Delta Air Lines Corporate Archives.

of numerical data, text, images, maps, videos, and audio files that are available through the Internet."[30] Bolick emphasizes *access* to digital objects. Ludäscher, Marciano, and Moore describe *digital archives* as "dedicated to the long-term preservation of electronic information" and further describe the digital archives mandate as enabling "sustained access despite rapid technology changes."[31] Both *access* and *preservation* are emphasized. Haber and Kamat added another perspective in "A Content Integrity Service for Long-Term Digital Archives." This work describes a content integrity service that has as its goal "to demonstrate that information in the archive is authentic and has not been unintentionally or maliciously altered, even after its bit representation in the archive has undergone one or more transformations."[32] This work brings to the conversation the need to ensure that the *integrity* of the digital objects is being preserved.

Digital materials are not only those that are transformed from analog to digital but also those born digital. In their article "Flexible Processing and Diverse Collections: A Tiered Approach to Delivering Born Digital Archives," Waugh, Roke, and Farr discuss the "need for policies that adapt to born digital collections that vary widely in size, scope, and technical requirements, and that deliver accessible born digital collections arranged and described according to their own significant properties."[33]

Digital archives can also refer to the building that houses the digital repository. The Washington State Digital Archives is an example of a facility designed to blend the latest technologies with traditional archival theory to create a first of its kind repository. It was celebrated as the nation's first archives dedicated to the preservation of electronic records from both state and local agencies that have permanent legal, fiscal, or historical value.[34]

The Washington State Digital Archives includes a research room complete with computer research stations, a high-tech presentation classroom, and a world-class data center. Statistics visible on the homepage of its website informs visitors not only of the number of records preserved and searchable, but also how many were recently added—almost 150,000 in January 2018 alone.[35]

Archives Planning and Design

An archives building or space is designed to house records and artifacts of enduring value. Ownership and control of the records is transferred to the archives. The advice for the planning and design of a records center—including fire protection, security measures, screening of employees, environmental controls, and appropriate storage containers and shelving—also applies to the planning and design of an archives building. However, because the goal of an archivist is to "provide fair, equitable, and timely access to materials for researchers" who may require access at some indeterminate time in the future, archivists strive to preserve holdings for as long as possible.[36] The fact that researchers wish to view and handle (if possible) the original records poses the danger of damage or loss due to access and use.

Storage Conditions: Mixed Media

Keep these pointers in mind if storing paper records in the archive:

- Utilize open steel shelving to allow airflow.
- House records in acid-free folders and boxes to slow deterioration.
- Protect records from fire.
- Reduce ultraviolet light by covering windows and fluorescent lighting with UV-protective film.

More challenging is determining the appropriate temperature and humidity for archival collections that include mixed media that must be preserved as a unit or group. A record group includes all of the records created by an individual, family, organization, government, office, business, or other entity.[37] The objects in the record group may be photographs, sound recordings, letters, and journals. The information may be stored on paper, film, magnetic tape, optical disks, and, more recently, hard drives of computers that are considered part of the collection.

The International Organization for Standardization (ISO) publishes storage standards for individual storage materials based on laboratory studies of records stored on each medium. When possible, it is best to house these materials in the environment most conducive to long-term preservation for each media type. But this desire has to be balanced with the available resources. Realistically, the archivist cannot separate objects in a collection based on media type without destroying the integrity of the collection. Therefore, ISO provides guidance for mixed media in *ISO 18934:2011: Imaging Materials—Multiple Media Archives— Storage Environment.*[38] This standard was last reviewed and confirmed in 2016.

Access: Providing and Controlling

One way to preserve a collection is by controlling access. You were introduced to physical and logical access to active records in chapter 5. Now we'll turn our attention to access controls for archival records.

Controlling Access to Physical Objects

Documents of value to collectors run the risk of damage or loss due to theft, vandalism, or accident. Lessons can be learned from events or actions that result in lost, stolen, or damaged documents. Safeguards to prevent additional similar occurrences must be implemented.

NARA encourages the public to help identify lost or stolen historical US government documents and report them to the NARA Archival Recovery Team. In addition to a website devoted to the topic, a Facebook page is used to educate the public and to enlist the assistance of collectors in recovering lost and stolen artifacts.[39]

In 2009, in response to theft of documents from the New York State Library and Archives, a state and national archival grant was obtained to develop a strategy for the prevention of and response to theft of historical documents. Today numerous resources can be found on the project website.[40]

In addition to access and security controls advised for records centers, it is vital to put in place a system to monitor patrons who use archival materials; some recommendations follow:

- Request identification of researchers.
- Ensure the researcher is in good standing (not banned from facility).
- Require materials to be used only in the assigned archival reading area, adjacent to a staff member who can monitor use.
- Allow only one item to be reviewed at a time—return one before providing another.
- Ensure that materials are not written on, cut, torn, folded, or damaged.
- Institute a copy policy to ensure that fragile documents are not copied.
- Instruct patrons that they will have to hand-copy materials from the archives when necessary.
- Install video cameras in research rooms.
- Limit what researchers can bring into and take out of the research rooms.
- Search bags taken out by both researchers and staff.

The previous tips relate to monitoring the use of archival materials, but artifacts can be stolen from storage areas as well. David Carmichael provides guidance for the control of materials in storage areas, which is the basis for the following recommendations:

- Prevent patrons from entering storage areas.
- Lock all storage areas and keep off limits to all but staff.
- If there is no separate, locked storage area, screen or rope off the storage areas and post staff only signs to define the storage spaces.
- Place valuable items in a closet, file cabinet, or small storage cabinet that can be locked.
- Don't include location information in public finding aids. Use a separate location guide to find specific containers.
- Consider concealing the contents of boxes by using only numbers (not titles) on the boxes.[41]

Long-term preservation of physical records can be accomplished through effective access, control, and storage practices. Long-term preservation of digital objects is more challenging and will be covered in chapter 12.

SUMMARY

Inactive records are those that are no longer needed for current business activities but have not yet met the end of their retention period. In spite of the fact that the digital universe is doubling every two years and most records are now created digitally, legacy paper records remain. Benefits can be derived from moving these inactive records to a less-expensive storage location. Records and information managers may be involved in planning and designing in-house record storage spaces or in identifying and recommending commercial storage services.

Records that have historical or research value are sent to various types of archives for long-term storage, including archives controlled by corporations, universities, and governments. Although it is possible to digitize these valuable objects, which may even be preferable to prevent damage to the originals, the originals—such as the United States Declaration of Independence stored in the National Archives—have intrinsic value that must be protected and preserved. Digital archives are dedicated to the long-term preservation of electronic information that are digitized or, more often, born digital.

Collections are increasingly comprised of information stored on a variety of media types. ISO 18934:2011 sets standards for collections that include mixed media from glass plates to photo prints to magnetic media for CDs. Historical artifacts are in danger of theft, loss, or damage from employees as well as patrons, and controls must be introduced to protect the holdings. The theme of controls appeared throughout this chapter as a method to protect both physical and digital records.

In her contribution to this chapter, Lori Lindberg provides an archivist's view of the relationship between sound records management principles and practices and the archival work involved to create a company archives for the Jelly Belly Candy Company, a firm that had its start in Illinois in 1869.

PARADIGM

Establishing the Jelly Belly Candy Company Archives: A Case Study of a Family-Owned Candy Company's History and Recordkeeping

Lori Lindberg
Archivist and Consultant

Introduction to the Project

The Jelly Belly Candy Company (JBCC) is a great American success story. Gustav Goelitz, an immigrant to the United States from Bavaria, started a confectionery business in 1869 that sold candy corn from a barrel out of the back of a wagon in Illinois. Goelitz candy corn appealed to many, and over the years the Goelitz Confectionery Company grew steadily. Over the next seventy years, three generations of Goelitz family members expanded product lines, sales regions, and manufacturing locales, eventually settling in two main centers of operation in North Chicago, Illinois, and Fairfield, California (by way of Oakland). By the time fifth-generation CEO Herm Rowland took over the business in the 1970s, Goelitz was a significant player in the confectionery industry in the United States, with many distinct candy products. Rowland's fateful discovery of a man in a Santa Monica mall with a cart selling delicious gourmet jelly beans he called "Jelly Bellys" led to a marketing and manufacturing agreement and the eventual Goelitz buyout of the Jelly Belly brand and flavors. With a broader manufacturing, advertising, and distribution base, Jelly Belly jelly beans expanded its flavor assortment and gained a following. One fan was an actor-turned-politician with a sweet tooth for jelly beans who spread word of their goodness far and wide. Eventually, he took his jelly bean habit all the way to the White House. By the 1980s, the popularity of Jelly Belly gourmet jelly beans and their intense unusual flavors, so loved by US President Ronald Reagan, had transformed Goelitz Confectionery Company into a worldwide phenomenon. In 1986, it moved its West Coast offices and manufacturing facility from Oakland to Fairfield, California (near Sacramento). In 2000, it built a new manufacturing and distribution center in Fairfield and in 2001 officially changed the company name to the Jelly Belly Candy Company. The company continues to thrive and has a valuable brand known worldwide for its high-quality candies.

Problem Statement

A JBCC 100th-anniversary candy assortment tin and book provided some of the company history in tangible form. Family and staff had set aside newsletters, packaging samples, limited-edition candy novelties, advertising materials, price lists, candy-making tools and equipment, and more, which formed a rudimentary historical collection. What the company desired was to provide preserved, accessible material that was organized and easily located in one spot in order to provide a sense of historical perspective, serve as evidence of company growth and development, support marketing of the brand, and satisfy the family's goal of eventually creating a museum.

Jelly Belly factory tours are a popular attraction at the Jelly Belly distribution centers in Fairfield, California, and Pleasant Prairie, Wisconsin. Company history displays are located at both locations. Now run by a sixth generation of candy makers, the family is proud of its heritage. Its members have strong political interests and are active in political circles. Mr. Rowland had an extensive collection of Reagan memorabilia and associated Jelly Belly Presidential jelly beans as a part of his personal office collection.

The growth of the Jelly Belly brand presented a brand-new direction and increased scale of operations. There were growing pains. The organization of historic materials was haphazard and inconsistent. Herm Rowland's daughter Lisa Rowland Brasher, JBCC's Vice President at the time, sensed a need to build a consistent collection and provide for its preservation. In 2011, the company initially inquired about working with a student intern from San José State University's School of Information. After discussion with the school, it was determined that a graduate student would be unprepared to direct a project of the desired scope. The university recommended another course of action. JBCC then sought and engaged a consultant to fill the role of project manager/chief archivist.

JBCC's vision was big, but it was not able to conceive how to begin. To get this contract, I had to go way beyond the elevator speech. Preparation, as well as a business case, was key. Not only was there no archives, there was little idea of what constituted archival materials. There was no real records management program to help identify the sources of potential archival records. Much of the recordkeeping was left to independent departments.

JBCC needed someone to take the lead on the project, decide what to do, and plan how to do it, all the while sustaining the family's vision. Gaining Lisa's confidence was the first step, and having a sound business case was instrumental.

Approach Taken

From start to finish, it took a year to establish the JBCC Archives. The crew was comprised of two interns from SJSU and two part-time paid subcontractors, led by the project manager/chief archivist. We were fortunate that the company had an available space for everything—a former training center and office space built into a quiet corner of a distribution center. First, we got to know the company and its history, recording names, dates, places, and products. We began a company organization chart and mapped the manufacturing process from beginning to end. We each read JBCC's 100th anniversary book and interviewed Lisa, her father, and other employees. Next, we studied the industry—its organizations and associations, principal manufacturers, its regulatory context (because it produces an edible product), and its history in the United States. We requested necessary equipment such as a scanner, desktop computers, internet access, and auxiliary digital storage.

Once we were situated in the JBCC context, the approach was straightforward and systematic: We looked everywhere for records and artifacts, taking two full days to walk the campus and record all potential areas where material might be held in four buildings. We encountered a full-sized shipping container of materials, five stacked and shrink-wrapped pallets of boxes near our work space, and even more pallets of boxes in other buildings at the distribution center as well as on shelves in and near the offices that produced them. While recording this information, I discovered from interviews that there were very old records at the manufacturing facility in North Chicago, so I gave my team a work plan to follow during my absence, and off I went to the Midwest. The older records in North Chicago had been organized about twenty years earlier and stored at the factory there. They had been moved to a couple of locations within the factory and finally to the basement of an auxiliary office building located next door. Sometime in the twenty years post-inventory, the records were exposed to a significant amount of water that wicked through the cardboard storage boxes; through folders, binders, and photo album pages; and right into the records. One well-meaning person stored the company's oldest records and paper artifacts in a padded mailing envelope. Water wicked through the sealants, wet the material inside and, due to the plastic bubble padding, kept the material moist for years. When the envelope was opened, mold had destroyed parts of many items and damaged them all. The family spent considerable sums to hire a conservator in Chicago who restored as much as possible. This unfortunate loss underpinned my request to consolidate all historic materials in Fairfield, where the storage facilities would ensure the best protection and the collection would be more complete. Partial processing was done in North Chicago and, after a few hours talking with a hesitant and wistful Bill Kelley, a midwestern member of the family who served as a company vice-president, the records were shipped to California.

A preliminary inventory and appraisal of the records in Fairfield produced a targeted historical collection. Archival supplies were ordered to properly house and preserve the archival materials, detailed descriptions were produced, photographs were digitized as time permitted, and the team advised company department heads on the location, environmental requirements, workflow, storage equipment, and security requirements of the archives facility and infrastructure. An archives information management software package was recommended, acquired, and installed, and initial project staff training on the software was completed. Spreadsheet inventories were transferred to the new software and digital images were uploaded as well. Once most of the records were processed and rehoused, we were able to plan the final layout of the facility space, oversee the installation of shelving, map the space, advise on access profiles for the information management software and its database, roll out, and train selected staff on searching the database, provide reference services, and begin internal marketing efforts. Access to the database contents is currently not available to the general public.

Results

After initial doubts and fears, and surprise at the somewhat slow, deliberate pace of archival work, in twelve months the Jelly Belly Candy Company had a functioning archives. One of the initial subcontractors was retained as a part-time archivist. As employees seeking information became aware of the archives and the information infrastructure, database utilization increased and a reference workflow was established. Departments were encouraged to consult with the archivist concerning the records they produce, and the beginnings of a records retention schedule was established to identify archival materials and facilitate the steady transfer of records to the archives. An opening reception encouraged employees to visit the archives and learn what it holds. As a result, employees now take an active interest in the materials held there. The archives continues to grow and further refine its policies and processes today. Although its role in the development of a future museum is yet to be realized, the archives' value as a location of important historic material and information continues to increase.

Lessons Learned

With privately held, family-based companies, take the time to build their confidence in you and establish a strong professional relationship. In these types of contexts, it is important to be sympathetic to the family's personal attachments to records. Don't speak in professional jargon and expect them to understand it. Communicate regularly and consistently. Create scheduled progress reports. Encourage staff to visit the archives and see the work in action. Create a welcoming research space. Respond to information requests promptly. Remind your client of the incremental pace of the work. Have your team distributed across different processing activities so that progress on specific priorities is visible. Think outside the box regarding what constitutes a record. (Yes, a sample bag containing an assortment of twenty-four flavors can be a record!) Consider unconventional formats (in this case candy jars and novelty packaging), as useful sources of evidence and information. When making your case for retention or disposal decisions stay firmly grounded in archival principles and apply them with confident compassion. Most of all, never lose your enthusiasm!

NOTES

1. ARMA International, s.v. "inactive record," *Glossary of Records Management and Information Governance Terms*, 5th ed. (Overland Park, KS: ARMA International, 2016).
2. Richard Pearce-Moses, s.v. "inactive record," *Glossary of Archival and Records Terminology*, Society of American Archivists, accessed May 22, 2017, www2.archivists.org/glossary/terms/i/inactive-records.

3. Mary F. Robek, Gerald F. Brown, and David O. Stephens, *Information and Records Management: Document-Based Information Systems* (New York: Glencoe/McGraw-Hill, 1996), 463.

4. Ibid., 465.

5. Edward Acker, "Archives and Records Storage Building," National Institute of Building Sciences, updated March 21, 2017, https://www.wbdg.org/building-types/archives-record-storage-building.

6. National Fire Protection Association (NFPA), *NFPA 232: Standard for the Protection of Records,* 2017 ed., (Quincy, MA: NFPA, 2017), http://catalog.nfpa.org/NFPA-232-Standard-for-the-Protection-of-Records-P1243.aspx.

7. National Fire Protection Association (NFPA), *NFPA 75: Standard for the Fire Protection of Information Technology Equipment,* 2017 ed. (Quincy, MA: NFPA, 2017), http://catalog.nfpa.org/NFPA-75-Standard-for-the-Fire-Protection-of-Information-Technology-Equipment-P1200.aspx?icid=D538.

8. ARMA International and Society of American Archivists, *Sample Forms for Archival and Records Management Programs* (Lenexa, KS: ARMA International, 2002).

9. New York State Archives, "Administration of Inactive Records," New York State Archives Technical Information Series 49, 1996, www.archives.nysed.gov/a/records/mr_pub49_accessible.html#introduction; Robert J. Johnson, *Information Disposition: A Practical Guide to the Secure, Compliant Disposal of Records, Media and IT Assets* (Phoenix, AZ: NAID, 2017), 125–32.

10. Denise Brandenberg, "Request for Information vs. Request for Proposal," eHow, updated December 26, 2017, www.ehow.com/about_6462623_request-information-vs-request-proposal .html.

11. William Benedon, "Outsourcing: The Right Decision?" *Information Management Journal,* January 2000, 34–41.

12. ARMA International, *Guideline for Evaluating Offsite Records Storage Facilities,* (Lenexa, KS: ARMA International, 2007).

13. PRISM International, Demand the Best, accessed December 28, 2017, www.prismintl.org/Buy-From-a-PRISM-Member/Free-Resources/demand-the-best.html.

14. ARMA International Standards Development Program Workgroup, *Records Center Operations,* 3rd ed., ANSI/ARMA TR01–2011 (Overland Park, KS: ARMA International, 2011).

15. ARMA International, *Understanding Electronic Records Storage Technologies,* ARMA TR26–2014 (Overland Park, KS: ARMA International, 2014).

16. Pearce-Moses, s.v. "archives," www2.archivists.org/glossary/terms/a/archives.

17. Society of American Archivists, "Guidelines for a Graduate Program in Archival Studies" (2016), accessed May 22, 2017, www2.archivists.org/prof-education/graduate/gpas.

18. Pearce-Moses, s.v. "archives management," *Glossary of Archival and Records Terminology.*

19. Pearce-Moses, s.v. "archives," *Glossary of Archival and Records Terminology,* www2.archivists.org/glossary/terms/a/archives.

20. National Archives and Records Administration (NARA), "Appraisal Policy of the National Archives and Records Administration," 2007, https://www.archives.gov/records-mgmt/publications/appraisal-policy.pdf.

21. International Organization for Standardization (ISO), *ISO 15489-1:2016, Information and documentation—Records management—Part 1: Concepts and principles* (Geneva: ISO, 2016).

22. Pearce-Moses, s.v. "appraisal," *Glossary of Archival and Records Terminology,* www2.archivists.org/glossary/terms/a/appraisal.

23. Barbara Craig, "Appraisal." In *Encyclopedia of Archival Science,* edited by Luciana Duranti and Patricia C. Franks (Lanham, MD: Rowan & Littlefield, 2015).

24. CBS/Associated Press, "George Washington's copy of Constitution on display at Mount Vernon estate," *CBS News,* September 17, 2012, www.cbsnews.com/news/george-washingtons-copy-of-constitution-on-display-at-mount-vernon-estate/.

25. ARMA International, s.v. "arrangement," *Glossary.*

26. Oliver W. Holmes, "Archival Arrangement—Five Different Operations at Five Different Levels," National Archives and Records Administration (NARA), 1964, accessed May 22, 2017, www.archives.gov/research/alic/reference/archives-resources/archival-arrangement.html.

27. Pearce-Moses, s.v. "description," *Glossary of Archival and Records Terminology,* www2.archivists.org/glossary/terms/d/description.

28. Pearce-Moses, s.v. "archival description," *Glossary of Archival and Records Terminology,* www2.archivists.org/glossary/terms/a/archival-description.

29. Pearce-Moses, s.v. "dark archives," *Glossary of Archival and Records Terminology,* www2.archivists.org/glossary/terms/d/dark-archives.

30. Cheryl Mason Bolick, "Digital Archives: Democratizing the Doing of History," *International Journal of Social Education* 21, no. 1 (Spring-Summer 2006), 122, http://eric.ed.gov/PDFS/EJ782136.pdf.

31. Bertram Ludäscher, Richard Marciano, and Reagan Moore, "Preservation of Digital Data with Self-Validating, Self-Instantiating Knowledge-Based Archives," *ACM SIGMOD Record,* September 2001, 54-63, 10.1145/603867.603876.

32. Stuart Haber and Pandurang Kamat, "A Content Integrity Service for Long-Term Digital Archives" (presented at the IS&T Archiving 2006 Conference, Ottawa, Canada, May 23-26, 2006), www.hpl.hp.com/techreports/2006/HPL-2006-54.pdf.

33. Dorothy Waugh, Elizabeth Russey Roke, and Erica Farr, "Flexible Processing and Diverse Collections: A Tiered Approach to Born Digital Archives," *Archives and Record,* 37, no. 1, (2016), 3-19.

34. Washington State Archives, "Digital Archives Background," accessed May 22, 2017, www.digitalarchives.wa.gov/StaticContent/background.

35. To search the Washington State Digital Archives, visit the digital archives homepage at www.digitalarchives.wa.gov/Home.

36. Attributed to SAA President Anne Kenney in testimony in 1993 US Senate Hearings. Quote taken from secondary source: Randall Jimerson, "Responding to the Call of Justice," Tidsskriftet Arkive, under no. 6, accessed May 22, 2017, https://journals.hioa.no/index.php/arkiv/article/view/923.

37. David W. Carmichael, *Organizing Archival Records: A Practical Method of Arrangement and Description of Small Archives* (Walnut Creek, CA: AltaMira Press, 2004), 6.

38. International Organization for Standardization (ISO), *ISO 18934:2011: Imaging Materials—Multiple Media Archives—Storage Environment* (Geneva: ISO, 2011).

39. You can view these websites at www.archives.gov/research/recover/ and https://www.facebook.com/archivalrecoveryprogram/?fref=nf.

40. New York State Archives, "Historical Records Theft: Strategies for Prevention and Response," accessed May 22, 2017, www.archives.nysed.gov/records/security.

41. David W. Carmichael, *Organizing Archival Records: A Practical Method of Arrangement and Description of Small Archives* (Walnut Creek, CA: AltaMira Press, 2004), 6.

CHAPTER 12

Long-Term Digital Preservation and Trusted Digital Repositories

INTRODUCTION

The fact that the digital universe is doubling in size every two years is not only due to the increasing number of people communicating, collaborating, and conducting business online but also to the number of smart devices connected to the internet. Of course, not everything must be stored. In fact, research shows that by 2020, if storage capacity remains constant, only 15 percent of the digital universe *could* be stored.[1] Progress is being made to increase storage capacity. However, in light of the limited resources individual entities have available to invest in capturing, managing, and preserving information for current and future use, a strategic approach must be taken to determine what should be retained and for how long. This requires an understanding of the value of information when determining what should be preserved, as well as the systems that can be employed to enable preservation and use for the long-term.

LONG-TERM DIGITAL PRESERVATION

A December 2011 headline announced, "Today's Digital Documents Are Tomorrow's Dinosaurs."[2] This was a reflection on President Barack Obama's order to federal agencies to "improve the management of federal records" and embrace a "digital-based records-keeping system."[3] Digital documents are either born digital (have never existed in another form) or have been digitized (converted from analog form to digital form). A broad term used to describe digital objects is *digital materials*. Converting documents from analog form to digital form shifts the focus from analog storage to digital preservation.

When speaking of preservation of *permanent records*, we use the term *long-term preservation*. To some that means more than ten years; to others it means more than fifty. Some consider "long term" to mean *indefinitely*. The Digital Preservation Coalition (DPC) defines *digital preservation* as "a series of managed activities necessary to ensure continued access to digital materials for *as long as necessary*."[4]

A pioneer in the move to digital documents (both digitized and born digital) is the Finnish government, which has announced a two-prong approach to cutting archival costs and improving data availability. By 2030, according to Mikko Erakaski, development director at the National Archives of Finland, all original documents will be destroyed after they have been digitized, and the National Archives will accept only digital formats in the future. However, exceptions will be made on cultural, historical, or juridical grounds.[5] This approach requires a trusted long-term digital preservation solution.

Digitization and Digital Preservation

The point of preservation is to provide access to the content of the materials preserved. Although some materials warrant preservation in their physical form, the majority of new materials are born digital and many others can be converted to digital form. Digital technologies are used to convert text, images, sound, and video to digital materials. Text and images (e.g., maps) can be digitized through the use of a scanner, which captures the image and converts it to an image file, such as a bitmap. If access involves text searching, an optical character recognition program is used to convert each character (alphabetic letter or numeric digit) into ASCII code. Metadata considerations must be addressed. Many institutions, such as the Smithsonian Institution Archives, have experience digitizing objects and share their standards online.

JPEG 2000 (saved with a .JP2 extension) is the preferred format for digitization of objects transferred to The National Archives (TNA) of the United Kingdom, which now digitizes approximately eight million pages of archival material each year. If scanning software does not produce .jp2 images natively, the images are converted and the original images retained until quality assurance is completed and TNA confirms destruction can take place. Various tools are used for validation of scanned images and metadata. The requirements for digitizing analog records are explained in detail in the 2016 publication "Digitization at the National Archives").[6] Figure 12.1 provides an overview of the complex digitization process employed.

Digitization of sound and video is accomplished through the use of an analog-to-digital conversion process that changes a continuously variable (analog) signal, without altering its content, into a multilevel (digital) signal.[7] The US National Archives and Records Administration provides practical advice about the digitization of various archival formats including audio, video, and motion picture film.[8]

Audio

Advice for those charged with digitizing and preserving audio begins by identifying audio formats that include magnetic media, digital audiotape (DAT), grooved recordings, and optical media. Identifying a vendor to copy audio records is often the best option, because specialized hardware and software are expensive, large data throughput requires more robust computers than found in most offices, deterioration of records may make playback complicated, and equipment needed for playback may be old or obsolete. Along with the technical requirements comes the issue of ownership; permission to preserve and provide access is necessary. For example, the Library of Congress shares more than 10,000 sound records made by the Victor Talking Machine Company between 1901 and 1925 with the public through its National Jukebox. The original record labels are now owned by Sony Music Entertainment, which has granted a gratis license to stream digitized acoustical recordings.[9]

Video

Video guidance addresses identifying video formats available commercially since 1956, which include 2-inch open reel tapes stored in specialized containers, flash cards, videocassettes, and optical discs. The same reasons to seek the services of a trained professional to digitize audio files apply to video files.

Motion Picture Film

Motion picture film guidance begins with a caution to avoid interchanging the terms *film* and *video*. Film is usually stored in a flat roll, most often in a plastic or metal can; it has small holes on one or both sides; and it can be read by the naked eye when held up to the light.

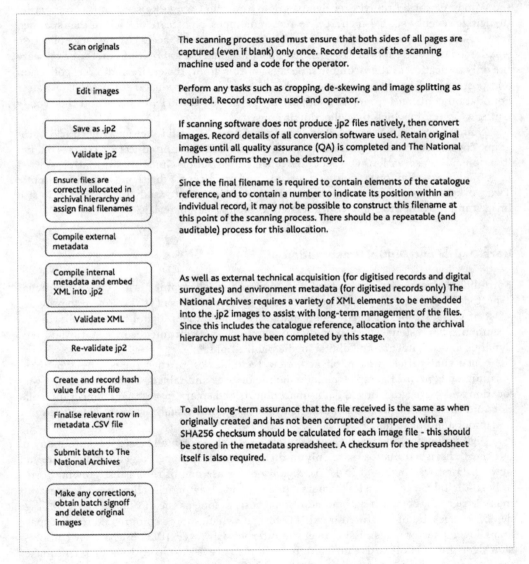

FIGURE 12.1 Overview of National Archives of the United Kingdom's digitization process.

Among the formats of motion picture film are 35-mm black-and-white negative, 16-mm color reversal, and 16-mm color print (with soundtrack). Digitization of motion picture film requires specialized equipment and expertise. The original should always be retained, because it may very well last longer than copies if stored properly.

Once the digitization activity occurs, attention must be turned to sustaining the digital audio, video, and motion picture film surrogates by migrating the data from one file format to another as formats improve or evolve.

Public and private grants may provide funding for digitization. For example, in 2010, the Woody Guthrie Archives received a grant from the George Kaiser Family Foundation to digitize seventy-six 1/4-inch, reel-to-reel audiotapes, a postcard collection that spanned from 1940 to 1960, and additional materials. Before the grant, access to the tape collection was denied to researchers due to their fragile nature, and the annotations on the boxes were the only indication of their contents. Because of this grant, the entire audio reel collection and postcard collection are now accessible to researchers in digital format.[10] The Kaiser Foundation continues to provide support to the Woody Guthrie Archives and the Woody Guthrie Center, in which the collection is housed.

Numerous resources are available to assist those who wish to set up a digitization program. The Society of American Archivists (SAA) offers continuing education courses on digitization and preservation. The Federal Agencies Digitization Guidelines Initiative, started in 2007, defines common guidelines, methods, and practices for digitizing historic content.[11] Two workgroups were formed as part of this initiative—one to study issues related to still images and the other to study issues related to audiovisual materials.

Born Digital and Digital Preservation

Born-digital documents are created and managed in electronic form. They were never expected to have an analog equivalent. An essay by Ricky Erway of OCLC Research provides a list of various types of born-digital materials, among them digital photographs, digital documents, harvested web content, digital manuscripts, electronic records, static data sets, dynamic data, digital art, and digital media publications.[12]

Since that article was published, new technologies further fueled the growth of born-digital content. Examples include mobile devices and tablets, cloud computing, geolocation and geotagging, linked data, smart objects and smart spaces that connect information and the physical world, games as learning tools, and visualizations to bring meaning and understanding to data.[13]

Digital photographs provide an example to which we can all relate, because many of our most cherished photos exist only in digital format. Although digital cameras are not new (the first was invented in 1975), digital photos are one of the fastest-growing forms of born-digital content. Digital cameras, tablets, and smartphones allow users to create as many images as they wish without additional cost, as long as they fit on the active storage device. Images are often stored in a JPEG format, which can be compressed to save space and allow for faster transmission over the internet. However, JPEG uses a lossy compression algorithm that discards information the human eye is least likely to notice. This makes the format popular for sharing but unacceptable for preservation purposes.

Preservation of digital images begins by moving files from the device to a durable storage media in an archival format. Unlike the JPEG format, the JPEG 2000 standard is an archival format. JPEG 2000, the international standard for image compression (ISO/IEC

15444-1:2016), is the successor to the familiar JPEG format written by the ISO Joint Photographic Experts Group (JPEG). Among the advantages to JPEG 2000 are higher compression without compromising quality, lossy (small file size but loss of quality) and lossless compression (larger file size but no loss of quality) options, and the fact that the JP2 (JPEG 2000) file format (.JP2) is XML-based metadata.[14]

Those who are responsible for providing access to images in the present and preserving them for future generations may use different file formats for different purposes; for example, they might elect to use the JP2 file format with lossy compression as service images but retain masters in the JP2 format with lossless compression or as uncompressed bitmaps in the Tagged Image File Format (TIFF). Institutions charged with digital preservation publish guidance for recommend formats. For example, the *Recommended Formats Statement* produced by the Library of Congress for internal professionals and external creators, vendors, and archivists encourages creation and maintenance of images in a file format that lends itself to preservation. The *2016–2017 Recommended Formats Statement* cites TIFF, JPEG2000, and PNG among its preferred formats whereas it lists Photoshop and widely used proprietary Camera Raw formats as merely acceptable.[15]

Digital Preservation Approaches and Media

Approaches to digital preservation can be classified as *passive* and *active*. *Passive preservation* ensures continuing integrity of and controlled access to digital objects along with their associated metadata. The original digital objects are kept intact without changing the technologies used to store or process them. *Active preservation* seeks to ensure the continued accessibility of electronic records over time by actively intervening in how records are stored and managed.[16] Examples of passive preservation are refreshing data, replication, and emulation. Migration is the most often used method of active preservation.

Microfilm

We're all familiar with the benefits of microfilm, including longevity (it has a 500-year life expectancy), sustainability, and fixity. Innovations in archive writers and scanning equipment make it possible to convert from digital format to microfilm and back again. The benefits of computer output to microfilm (COM) include reduction of paper, cost reduction, and electronic record retention and archiving. The US National Archives and Records Administration continues to microfilm records, because, in their words, "microfilm is a low-cost, reliable, long-term, standardized image storage medium. The equipment needed to view microfilm is simple, consisting of light and magnification."[17] However, not everyone feels the same way (see the Somerset County insert).

Hard Disks and Tapes

When searching for reliable solutions to long-term storage, the Library of Congress (LC) comes to mind. Its mission is "to provide Congress, and then the federal government, and the American people with a rich, diverse, and enduring source of knowledge that can be relied upon to inform, inspire, and engage them, and support their intellectual and creative endeavors."[18] To ensure that the source of knowledge—collections held in a myriad of

Somerset County Switches from Microfilm to PDF/A Files for Long-Term Preservation

In spring 2017, the Pennsylvania Historical and Museum Commission approved the preservation of government documents in the PDF/A format. The Somerset County microfilm department conducted a cost-benefit analysis of switching from microfilm to PDF/A for long-term preservation and concluded it could save $30,000 a year on microfilm writing alone. In January 2018, Director Jeff Kimmel announced the switch from microfilm to the PDF archival format to preserve government documents going forward.

SOURCE: Ellich, Judy D.J. (2018, January 24), "Changing of the guard: County Microfilm department going digital," *Courier Express*, accessed January 30, 2018, www.thecourierexpress.com/news/state/changing-of-the-guard-county-microfilm-department-going-digital/article_7951da66-ea95-596a-adb5-25bc105ab03b.html.

formats—is *enduring*, LC employs state-of-the-art preservation techniques and invests in cutting-edge research and development.

LC uses a tiered storage, including both disk and tape storage, which allows for the use of different types of storage media for different categories of data based on how often it is accessed. According to Jane Mandelbaum, special projects manager for the information technology services directorate, the LC manages multiple petabytes of digital content in four data centers.[19] LC's policy of redundancy and diversity requires two to three copies of material stored in different locations and on different kinds of hardware running different kinds of software.

M-DISC

An innovation suitable for individuals and small businesses is the M-DISC, a "write once read forever" (WORF) medium that cannot be overwritten, erased, or corrupted by natural processes. The files are laser-engraved on a natural stone-like substance (the M-DISC itself) using an M-READY writer drive. The M-DISC is compatible with any DVD player. One estimate is that data engraved on an M-DISC will be reliable for at least 1,000 years. The storage capacity of one M-DISC is equivalent to 100,000 documents, 1,200 photos, or three hours of video. The Naval Air Warfare Center at China Lake, California, tested the M-DISC under conditions based on 185°F/85 percent relative humidity with full-spectrum sunlight. The results revealed that the M-DISC suffered no data loss. These discs run as low as $3 each, depending upon storage capacity, and come with a lifetime warranty. The challenge in 1,000 years will be to find a DVD or Blu-ray player that can read the M-DISC.[20]

Chemical Solution to Shrink Digital Data Storage

In addition to proven technology, we should look to projects currently in the testing phase and consider implications for digital preservation in the future. Case Western Reserve University researchers demonstrated that "commonly used polymer films containing two dyes can optically store data in quaternary (four-symbol) code, potentially requiring about half as much space."[21] In addition to the saving space, the film appears to be extremely durable for disaster recovery and preservation purposes, because the code remained legible after the film had been rolled, bent, written on with permanent marker, submersed in boiling water, and even rubbed with sandpaper. It's not certain this research project will result in practical applications, but if it does, it could result in a shift away from the use of binary code to write computer programs.

Cloud Storage

Due to the advantages the cloud offers (resource pooling, elasticity, measured service, and convenience, to name a few), inexpensive online storage services such as Amazon's Glacier, Blackblaze, Google Drive, and One Drive are attractive options. Cloud storage services rely on technology under the control of a third-party provider, but information stored within the cloud must still be monitored to ensure what is stored is accessible and usable for the long term. One should not confuse cloud storage, even services that offer a ten- or twenty-year preservation period, with long-term digital preservation in the cloud, a topic that will be explored later in this chapter.

Building a Business Case for Digital Preservation

There is a growing concern over digital rot. This doesn't mean the digital bits die but that the media and file formats holding them fail to remain viable. Data dies because hard drives crash, tapes are stored in poor environmental conditions, CDs fail, and objects are pulled from the internet before they can be captured. A preservation plan is necessary to ensure long-term viability of digital information. But preservation entails a cost that not every organization is willing to pay. Business cases are frequently used to justify spending money on large or small purchases. The same approach can be used to justify funds needed for preservation of digital material.

A business case is essentially a proposal that states a problem, offers a solution, explains how much it would cost to implement the solution, and describes the value to stakeholders, including return on investment (ROI) or cost avoidance (CA), that could be realized if the solution were implemented. When building a business case, include the following elements at a minimum:

- executive summary
- current situation
- proposal
- value of the information objects (including financial proof in terms of ROI and CA)
- conclusion
- supporting materials

In 2010, the National Digital Information Infrastructure and Preservation Program (NDIIPP) of the Library of Congress prepared a report, "Strategies for Sustainable Preservation of Born Digital Public Television," that examines the requirements for long-term preservation of born-digital video files created for viewing on public television.[22] The goal is to promote the notion that a sustainable preservation approach is necessary to preserve these files for future use. This approach is built on the premise that digital preservation is not an additional optional expense but can be incorporated into production budgets as a necessary requirement for ongoing usability of the materials. It is an example of the beginnings of a business case for digital public television that could be applied to digital materials generated in other industries.

The Scottish Government's *ScotlandsPeople* website, the official government site for searching government records and archives, provides valuable services for a fee.[23] Searches can be performed on people, places, or images. Fees are imposed based on type of order placed. For example, at the time of this writing, digital images of statutory registers of births, deaths, and marriages can be downloaded for a fee of £1.50; one statutory birth certificate can be ordered for £12; and one high-quality tiff image (such as the first official recorded message of tartan within clothing accounts for King James V in 1538) can be purchased for £30. The Crown copyright images can be used in the following ways: (1) book, journal, magazine, newspaper, publication, broadcast, (2) online use (limited to twenty images per website), and (3) display, exhibition, talk, presentation. As a satisfied customer, I can personally attest to the reasonable cost, convenience, and ease of use of the *ScotlandsPeople* website (see figure 12.2).

In 2014, Preservica, a world leader in digital preservation technology, released *A Guide to Making the Business Case for Digital Preservation*, which includes a business case template and enumerates expected benefits to the corporation aligned with organizational priorities and

FIGURE 12.2 The Declaration of Arbroath, 1320. Letter from the barons, freeholders, and the whole community of the kingdom of Scotland to Pope John XXII.

SOURCE: National Records Scotland.

policies.[24] Among the benefits are financial savings, increased operational efficiency, and meeting statutory and legal requirements. However, additional benefits cited include better decision-making, as well as the potential for income generation and new service models. Because management is concerned with the bottom line—making a profit—the problem and potential benefits are best stated in business terms. Records and archives management programs are considered cost centers rather than profit centers, but a case might be made that they can be either.

DIGITAL CURATION AND STEWARDSHIP

According to the Digital Curation Centre (DCC) of the United Kingdom, *digital curation* is "maintaining and adding value to a trusted body of digital research data for current and future use; it encompasses the active management of data throughout the research lifecycle."[25] "Digital curation involves organizing and preserving digital information so it will be available for future use."[26] The digital curation lifecycle includes preservation and much more (see figure 12.3).

Institutions that generate research data must put a data preservation plan in place to ensure that digital research data, as well as digital media content and information acquired from third parties, remains authentic, reliable, and usable while maintaining integrity. The DCC website is a valuable resource for custodians of digital research data.

Digital stewardship is a concept that brings together digital curation and digital preservation that embraces the idea of holding digital resources in trust for future generations. Digital stewardship merges the digital curation lifecycle model with research in digital libraries and electronic records archiving while ensuring that digital preservation remains as a core component.

In 2007, Kevin Bradley clarified the difference between digital curation and digital stewardship when he defined stewardship as addressing the "cultural, public policy, and ethical questions about how and what we remember and forget," and curation as "maintaining and adding value to a trusted body of digital information for current and future use."[27] In 2010, a consortium of organizations committed to the long-term preservation of digital

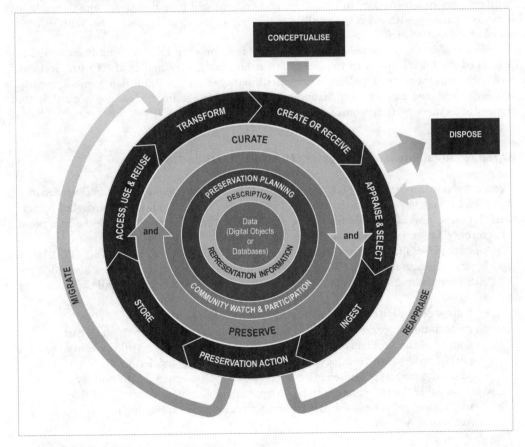

FIGURE 12.3 Digital curation lifecycle.

SOURCE: "Digital Curation Centre, University of Edinburgh," www.dcc.ac.uk/resources/curation-lifecycle-model.

information formed the National Digital Stewardship Alliance (NDSA) as an initiative of the Digital Information Infrastructure and Preservation program of the Library of Congress. In 2016, the NDSA moved to the Digital Library Federation (DLF) at the Council on Library and Information Resources (CLIR). Unlike the DCC, which focuses on preserving digital content for future use, the NDSA is concerned first with assessing and selecting content categories worthy of preservation. Currently the seven content areas are government; geospatial; news, media, and journalism; science, mathematics, technology and medicine; social sciences; cultural heritage; and arts and humanities.[28]

BUILDING A TRUSTED DIGITAL REPOSITORY

In 2000, the Research Libraries Group (RLG) and the Online Computer Library Center (OCLC) recognized the development of national and, increasingly, international systems of digital repositories that are or will be responsible for the long-term access to the world's social, economic, cultural, and intellectual heritage in digital form. This working group emphasized that to encourage contributions to this system of digital repositories, content creators, owners of information, and current and potential users must be able to trust repositories with the responsibility to provide access to and preserve content. What is needed are *trusted digital repositories*.[29]

The mission of a trusted digital repository is to provide reliable, long-term access to managed digital resources to its designated community, now and in the future. As with other systems mentioned earlier for document management, content management, records management, and information management, standards are necessary to ensure that the repositories meet certain requirements.

Open Archival Information System (OAIS) Reference Model

Before standards were developed, a framework called a *Reference Model for an Open Archival Information System* was designed that could be used to describe and analyze digital preservation issues, provide a basis for future standards-building activity, and serve as a point of reference for vendors interested in building digital preservation products and services. The *Open Archival Information System* (OAIS) was published as a standard, ISO 14721:2003, and later revised as ISO 14721:2012. Among the mandatory responsibilities identified for an OAIS-type archive are two that illustrate the different parties served and their needs:

- Follow documented policies and procedures that ensure that the information is preserved against all reasonable contingencies, including the demise of the Archive, ensuring that it is never deleted unless allowed as part of an approved strategy. There should be no ad-hoc deletions.
- Make the preserved information available to the Designated Community and enable the information to be disseminated as copies of, or as traceable to, the original submitted data objects with evidence supporting its Authenticity.[30]

The framework developed for trusted digital repositories is shown in figure 12.4. The process involves ingesting digital files from producers and then storing, managing, and preserving those objects for the purpose of providing long-term access to consumers. Beyond providing basic functionality, the trustworthy digital repository must be able to understand and defend against threats to and risks within the system. This requires monitoring, planning, and maintenance, as well as all of the actions necessary to carry out the mission of preservation.

Producer-Archive Interface Methodology Abstract Standard (PAIMAS)

The first step in the OAIS reference model is the Ingest action where the producer submits a Submission Information Package (SIP) into the system. What is not explained are the interactions (relationships, obligations, responsibilities) that occur between the producer and the archive until the information objects are received and validated by the archive. This is where the *Producer-Archive Interface Methodology Abstract Standard* (PAIMAS), ISO 20652:2006, is invaluable.

PAIMAS defines and provides structure to the relationships and interactions between an information producer and an archive. It covers the first stage of the ingest process as defined in the OAIS reference model and describes parts of the functional entities for administration and ingest (negotiate submission agreement, receive submission, and quality assurance).[31] This standard was last reviewed and confirmed in 2014.

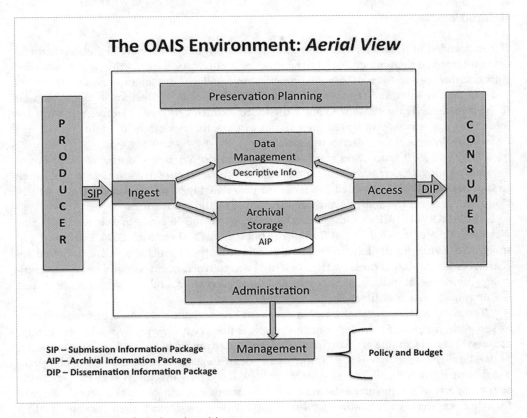

FIGURE 12.4 OAIS functional entities.

ISO 16363 Standard for Trusted Digital Repositories

The international community is making good progress toward developing international standards to provide the infrastructure for ISO certification of trustworthy digital repositories.

In 2005, a joint task force comprised of members of the RLG and NARA published *Trustworthy Repositories Audit and Certification: Criteria and Checklist* (TRAC). This documented was updated in 2011 and incorporated into an international standard, *ISO 16363:2012 Space Data and Information Transfer Systems—Audit and Certification of Trustworthy Digital Repositories,* released in February 2012.

ISO 16363:2012 defines a recommended practice for assessing the trustworthiness of digital repositories and is applicable to a wide range of digital repositories. It can be used as the basis for certification.[32]

In 2017, the Primary Trustworthy Digital Repository Authorization Body Ltd. (PTAB), Dorset, the United Kingdom, was the first organization in the world to receive accreditation to perform audit and certification. PTAB is registered as TD 001 on the Register of Certification Bodies of National Accreditation Board for Certification Bodies (NABCB). In addition to the certification audit, PTAB can perform re-certification audits for repositories who wish to maintain ISO 16363 certification.[33]

Related Works

Recommended practices for the audit and certification of trustworthy digital repositories were released in September 2011 in the form of a publication called the *Magenta Book*.[34] This document defines recommended practice on which to base an audit and certification process for assessing the trustworthiness of digital repositories. Although the document is meant primarily for those who audit digital repositories or seek objective measures for evaluating the trustworthiness of their repository, the metrics can be used during a design or redesign processes for a digital repository.

ISO/DIS 16919 Space Data and Information Transfer Systems—Requirements for Bodies Providing Audit and Certification of Candidate Trustworthy Digital Repositories was published in October 2014 and is intended primarily for those setting up and managing the organizations that perform the auditing and certification of digital repositories.[35]

The APARSEN (Alliance for Permanent Access to the Records of Science in Europe Network) Project, funded by the European Union from 2011 through 2014, combined and integrated European digital preservation efforts with the intent of creating a virtual research center for digital preservation. One goal was to reach common agreement on terminology, evidence, standards, services needed for preservation, and access and reuse of data holdings over the whole lifecycle.[36]

The APARSEN integrated a vision for digital preservation within a business process as shown in figure 12.5. The focus of this model is preservation. However, objects that are preserved but not usable are worthless; therefore, steps must be taken to ensure users can understand the digitally encoded information. Such steps involve transforming objects to a different format. As addressed earlier in this chapter, organizations respond positively to the opportunity to leverage the value of their assets, including digital objects preserved for other reasons (e.g., regulations and research), to help them reach their strategic goals. A business case, for example, may be made that intellectual property rights associated with specific digital objects will result in additional revenue. The business case relates directly to the business model. How will the additional revenue be generated? At the same time, costs will be incurred to create and preserve the digital objects. How will those be addressed? Preservation is not a stand-alone project. It must be considered as part of the larger business process.

Supporting Standards

A number of technical standards mentioned throughout this book are also applicable to a digital preservation program. Some relate to metadata and file formats, including:

- **EAD (Encoded Archival Description)** is a nonproprietary de facto standard for the encoding of finding aids for use in a networked (online) environment. First released in 2002, the most recent version, EAD3, was adopted by the Society of American Archivists in 2015.[37]
- **PREMIS (PREservation Metadata: Implementation Strategies)** is hosted by the Library of Congress. The PREMIS Data Dictionary for Preservation Metadata is the international standard for metadata to support the

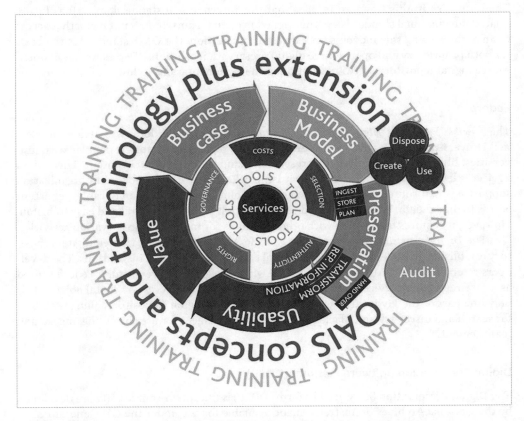

FIGURE 12.5 Integrated vision for digital preservation in a business process.

SOURCE: APARSEN, www.alliancepermanentaccess.org/index.php/community/common-vision/.

preservation of digital objects and ensure their long-term usability. PREMIS version 3 was updated November 2015.[38]

- **METS (Metadata Encoding and Transmission Standard)** is an XML encoding standard maintained by the Library of Congress. This enables digital materials to be packaged with archival metadata. METS Schema Revision 1.11 was released January 7, 2015. On May 21, 2015, the University of North Texas Libraries made a new METS profile available for use that describes rules and requirements for using METS as an Archival Information Package (AIP).[39]

Aside from standards specific to digital objects and systems, general standards must be considered, such as the ISO/IEC 27000 family of standards to keep information assets secure and the ISO 9000 family of international standards on quality management and quality assurance.

Trusted Digital Repository Software Solutions

The OAIS Reference Model described earlier is an *open archival information system* model. The term *open* in this standard implies that this international standard, as well as future related international standards, was developed in open forums. It does not mean that access to an archive using this model is unrestricted. In addition, the OAIS standard is the basis for both proprietary and open-source digital preservation solutions. Two examples of open-source digital repository software solutions and implementations follow:

Fedora

The *Flexible Extensible Digital Object Repository Architecture* (Fedora) was created at Cornell University in 1997. This open-source, modular repository system is popular with universities, libraries, and archives for preservation and access of digital content. The Fedora Project is led by a group under the stewardship of DuraSpace, a not-for-profit organization supporting open-source technology projects and solutions that focus on durable, persistent access to digital data. Fedora is a stand-alone tool that is format neutral and easy to install. However, it requires integration with other products for ingest and preservation activities.

The *Digital Repository of Ireland* (www.dri.ie/) is an interactive, trusted digital repository established in 2011 for social and cultural content held by Irish institutions. The developers referred to the OAIS Reference Model when designing the repository. Fedora is used as a core repository service for the storage, management, and access of digital objects. It is only one part of the Hydra framework selected for the Digital Repository, along with Solr for search and discovery and Blacklight to provide interfaces for user browsing, ingest, and management.[40]

Digital Preservation Software Platform (DPSP)

The Digital Preservation Software Platform (DPSP) is free, open-source software developed by the National Archives of Australia, made available for use under the GU General Public License version 3 (the GPLv3). Several applications comprise the software suite: *Xena* (Xml Electronic Normalizing for Archives) to convert proprietary file formats to preservation formats; *Manifest Maker,* which prepares a list of digital records being transferred to the archive to verify the integrity of digital records and tracks them when they are being processed; *Digital Preservation Recorder,* which manages the processing of records into the archive (including workflows, conversion to preservation formats, storage, and access); and *Checksum Checker,* which monitors the archive for data loss or corruption.[41]

The National Archives of Australia is charged with preserving the Commonwealth's records and making them accessible in the future. Visitors to the National Archives of Australia website can perform a records search online. SODA (Stream of Digital Archives) is a feature that allows visitors to view newly scanned records from the Archives, including photographs and physical records (e.g., Outgoing Passenger Cards and Inspection Reports by Lighthouse Engineers)[42]

CLOUD DIGITAL PRESERVATION AS A SERVICE

Cloud computing services, such as cloud storage, offer advantages in terms of convenience and cost. Cloud storage, also called archive storage (e.g., email archives and image archives), is designed to secure, retain, and protect digital information for extended periods of time, but not for the long term. Cloud digital preservation services go beyond cloud archive services by adding management and curation functions in order to accomplish digital preservation goals, including migration and long-term preservation.

Barriers to adoption of cloud digital preservation services are similar to those for any cloud service (e.g., handing over sensitive data to a third party, threat of data breach or loss, uptime/business continuity, and financial strength of the cloud computing provider). Two examples of cloud preservation service providers follow.

ArchivesDirect

Archivematica's (http://archivesdirect.org/) OAIS-based digital preservation workflows are combined with archival cloud storage and preservation services from DuraSpace to offer an open-standards, hosted solution to preserve all types of digital resources. Key features include assigning permanent identifiers and checksums, virus checking, file format identification and validation, technical metadata extraction, transforming files upon ingest to preservation formats, and generating PREMIS and METS metadata for inter-repository data exchange.

Preservica

Preservica (http://preservica.com/) is a commercial long-term digital preservation and access software based on OAIS. It is also the name of the company that provides digital preservation technology, consulting services, and research products. In addition to providing compliant workflows for ingest, data management, storage, access, administration, and preservation, Preservica provides a Universal Access module that allows content to be shared with the public. A feature added to benefit the records management field is functionality for retention and disposition, because long-term digital preservation actions may need to be taken on documents with a lifespan as brief as ten years due to technology refresh cycle acceleration. The retention and disposition feature brings up the need for consideration of a related issue—a *legal hold* or "freeze" on disposition.

DIGITAL PRESERVATION RESEARCH

Digital preservation research is ongoing. An IMLS-grant funded project, POWRR (*Preserving* digital *Objects With Restricted Resources*), resulted in the digital POWRR Grid based on the intersection of the Digital Curation Lifecycle and the OAIS Reference Model that can be used to evaluate tools and services (see figure 12.6).

Of the six technologies tested using the POWRR grid illustrated in figure 12.6—Archivematica, Curator's Workbench, DuraCloud, Internet Archive, MetaArchive, and Preservica—both Preservica and the combination of Archivematica + DuraCloud (now known as ArchivesDirect) provided all of the functional requirements investigated.[43] The POWRR Tool Grid v2 is available on the Community Owned digital Preservation Tool Registry (COPTR) wiki, which is part of the Digipres Commons.[44]

Another project that deserves special attention is Preservation as a Service for Trust (PaaST), an InterPARES Trust Research Project lead by Kenneth Thibodeau, formerly of the US National Archives and Records Administration (NARA) and currently a guest researcher at the National Institute of Standards and Technology. PaaST identifies functional and data requirements for digital preservation for all information (not just records), flexible enough to support different policies and objectives, under various in-house and contractual agreements, including the Cloud. PaaST has partnered with the Object Management Group to develop a standard for digital preservation.

The PaaST model revolves around the Intellectual Entity—an object intended to convey information, such as a document, map, software, book, photograph, simulation, GIS system, and device driver. The intent of the project is to facilitate verifiable preservation that requires three types of permanent features: uniqueness (preservation target must be different from all others), instantiation (must faithfully reproduce the original), and composition integrity (objects that comprise the preservation target must remain intact with interrelationships maintained). Ideally, the ultimate goal of the project is to ensure the survival of authentic digital records over time and changes in technology. Practically, the desired outcome is the optimal use of automated methods to enable continuing access to digital records.[45]

In 2015, Chief Internet Evangelist at Google and "Father of the Internet," Vint Cerf, explained his concern about digital content in this way, "what can happen over time is that

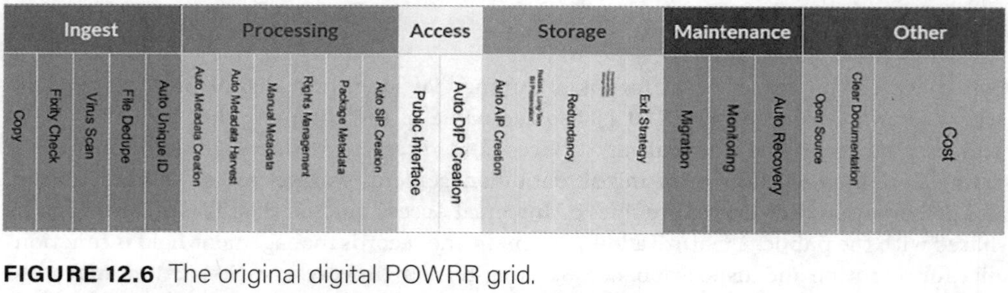

FIGURE 12.6 The original digital POWRR grid.
SOURCE: Digital POWRR, http://digitalpowrr.niu.edu/digital-preservation-101/tool-grid/.

even if we accumulate vast archives of digital content, we may not actually know what it is." His idea is to take an xray snapshot of the content (including metadata), application, and operating system together with a description of the machine it runs on and retain that for the long term. He refers to this xray as "digital vellum."[46]

Digital preservation depends upon the integration of preservation requirements built into systems used at every stage of the digital lifecycle. There is both good news and bad news to report. First, the bad news—the information provided in this chapter will surely change even by the time you read this book. Second, the good news—the information provided in this chapter will surely change even by the time you read this book. Change will bring about improvements to systems that will allow us to ensure the integrity and authenticity of archived content.

SUMMARY

Records that have historical or research value are sent to various types of archives for long-term storage, including archives controlled by corporations, universities, and governments. Digital archives are dedicated to the long-term preservation of electronic information.

Scanners can be used to convert text and photographs into digital images that will save space (presuming the originals are discarded) and enhance access to collections. Optical character recognition software can be used to enable full-text searching. Standards have been established that facilitate long-term retention. The JPEG 2000 compression standard, for example, reduces file size and produces high-quality images that provide an acceptable alternative to the traditional TIFF format for digital preservation.

Born-digital objects are created and managed in a digital form. Examples include digital photographs, digital documents, harvested web content, digital manuscripts, electronic records, static data sets, dynamic data, digital art, and digital media publications.

Preservation comes at a cost. An archivist or records manager should be able to develop a business case that includes return on investment (ROI) and/or cost avoidance (CA) figures that would be realized if a recommended solution were accepted.

Digital curation involves maintaining and adding value to a trusted body of digital research data for current and future use. The Digital Curation Centre (DCC) of the United Kingdom is a valuable source of information on digital curation and long-term preservation. Producers and consumers of digital research data must be able to trust the systems that store and provide access to that data. International efforts related to trusted digital repositories is ongoing. *ISO 16363 Space Data and Information Transfer Systems—Audit and Certification of Trustworthy Digital Repositories* was released in 2012, and *ISO/DIS 16919 Space Data and Information Transfer Systems—Requirements for Bodies Providing Audit and Certification of Candidate Trustworthy Digital Repositories* was released in 2014.

A number of digital preservation approaches exist, including refreshing data, replication, emulation, and migration. Research continues to find better storage solutions. Microfilm, because of its 500-year life and ability to be read by the naked eye, is still regarded as the most effective option.

Cloud digital preservation service is a natural progression from cloud storage and archiving services. But preservation services must include management and curation functions that will accomplish digital preservation goals, including long-term preservation. The tool grid produced by the POWRR project was useful in testing early archival preservation products and services. Work continues on version two of this grid as it is shared through the

COPTR (Community Owned digital Preservation Tool Registry wiki. An InterPARES Trust research project that specifically addresses preservation of authentic records in the cloud is Preservation as a Service for Trust (PaaST).

The key to digital preservation may be the integration of preservation requirements built into systems at every stage of the digital lifecycle. Archivists and records and information managers must constantly scan the environment for new technologies and approaches to inactive records and information management and preservation.

There is no one-size-fits-all solution for long-term digital storage and preservation. Each organization must determine the technology solution that best supports its unique situation. In their contribution to this chapter, Lori Ashley and Patricia Morris introduce us to the approach taken to use a popular commercial service to establish an eArchive for Pharmaceutical pre-Clinical Research Study Information. That is followed by a second case documenting a practical open-source solution for institutions with limited financial resources contributed by Amber D'Ambrosio, Processing Archivist and Records Manager, Willamette University Archives and Special Collections.

PARADIGM 12.1

Use Case—eArchive for Pharmaceutical Pre-Clinical Research Study Information

Patricia Morris
President and Chief Process Consultant,
eArchive Science, LLC

Lori Ashley
Principal,
Tournesol Consulting, LLC

Introduction

Pharmaceutical and biotechnology companies have numerous compelling use cases for long-term digital archiving and preservation capabilities for their scientific records. Research, development, and manufacturing processes that bring medical products and devices to market are complex, decades in duration, and subject to health authority regulatory and industry standards. With only minor exceptions, information and records generated during drug development are now managed exclusively in digitally encoded format. A significant portion of these electronic business records requires long-term retention in excess of fifty years.

Problem Statement

This paradigm is a description of the process used by a pharmaceutical company (the Company) to establish a digital archive for electronic study records and data generated during the Pre-Clinical Research phase of drug development. These records are created in-house and at multiple external Contract Research Organizations (CROs).

The digital information identified for preservation and storage in the Company eArchive is subject to regulations issued by health authorities, as well as relevant laws pertaining to electronic recordkeeping. Strict compliance to these laws and regulations is essential to Company operations and is routinely audited for assurance. In this instance, compliance to a specific set of regulations from the United States Food and Drug Administration (US FDA Code of Federal Regulations) that define archiving practices for records created according to Good Laboratory Practice (GLP) was the primary driver for the development of the GLP eArchive. These essential business records have significant value to the Company in terms of scientific evidence.

Approach

The scope of the GLP eArchive project was to determine a technology solution to support long-term preservation and management of electronic Pre-Clinical GLP records and data sets. This effort was undertaken with the understanding that the business processes, roles and responsibilities, workflows, and technology must work in concert to cover the entire spectrum of required capabilities and life span controls defined by future users of the solution. To that end, a cross-functional team was convened which included Pre-Clinical scientists, Quality Managers, and Information Technologists. External consultants, who were experts in delivering long-term digital preservation and pharmaceutical electronic archiving solutions, supported the team. This collaboration resulted in the development of a formal set of user requirements and technical specifications for the GLP eArchive.

A select set of commercial digital archiving solutions was identified by the project consultants on the basis of a preliminary analysis of content to be ingested into the GLP eArchive. Initially, there was an emphasis on finding a solution for the long-term preservation of structured and proprietary data sets to be transferred from the external Contract Research Organizations (CROs). Demonstrations of six solutions were conducted to stimulate project team discussion and ensure that user requirements for the GLP eArchive were sufficiently robust to meet future operational and compliance demands. The solutions reviewed ranged from full-blown enterprise records and content management solutions to database archiving to long-term digital preservation systems. As a result of the demonstrations and an additional review of the full requirements (beyond the initial scope) it was determined that more than one technology solution may ultimately be required to address the full spectrum of content types (structured, semi-structured and unstructured information) and the access/use requirements of the Pre-Clinical Research function to assure compliance.

A deeper analysis of the inventory of records to be ingested was then conducted. Project team members confirmed that some of the Pre-Clinical study raw data files created by CROs were in proprietary file formats. There was significant content in unstructured file formats to be ingested as well. Hence, the initial narrow scope of the team's assignment shifted over the course of this phase of the project towards integrated solutions capable of ingesting unstructured study records that required long-term retention (50+ years) and providing long-term digital preservation services to ensure access and integrity of these precious records of scientific evidence over time. It was determined that the structured data in proprietary file formats could be maintained by the CROs until a future solution could be implemented to archive them at the Company.

Also during this phase of the project, the external consultants developed an initial eArchive Operating Model so the project team could envision how records would be appraised, ingested, and archived. The basis of this model was the approach defined in *ISO 14721:2012 Space data and information transfer systems—Open archival information system (OAIS)—Reference model* with customizations based on internal process demands. The model showed the records moving from production systems, through appraisal and preparation for ingest, long-term management and storage in the eArchive (including file format transformations when necessary), subsequent search and retrieval, and potential disposition. At this point, the project team produced the final set of user requirements for the solution.

As a result of this newly confirmed focus and adjustment to the project scope and user requirements, a formal request for proposal (RFP) was issued from the Company to the two long-term digital preservation system vendors who had demonstrated the highest degree of capability for the required ingest and lifespan management capabilities for the Pre-Clinical GLP eArchive.

The outcome of the RFP process was that Preservica was the best-fitting solution to fulfill project requirements. A three-month Proof of Concept (POC) project was completed using the Preservica Cloud Edition and the results confirmed the suitability of the solution.

Results

During the POC, several other business units expressed interest in the digital preservation solution. The categories of records considered eligible for ingestion were expanded to include other research and development records as well as long-term general business records.

Following the POC and based on the expanded technical and legal requirements of establishing a repository for multiple tenants, the Company selected the Preservica Enterprise Edition for their final solution. Preservica Enterprise Edition is a modular on-premise preservation platform that will be configured and customized to meet Company needs. The Company's central IT will manage the repository and the archival content storage will be based on the Company's Amazon S3 account. The logical architecture is a standard three-tier web-application architecture. The presentation tier (access interface) is primarily a web interface serving a combination of static and dynamic HTML pages. The application tier is a series of Java-based applications, using J2EE standards. The relational database will be based on MS SQL and hosted internally.

Following issuance of a purchase order for the software, the Company launched the next phase of the project to implement Preservica Enterprise Edition as their eArchive technology. It was understood that in order to maintain compliance to applicable external regulations, the solution would need to be fully validated against the approved user requirements and technical specifications (as well as internal IT standards), so effort was put towards finalizing those documents. Work was undertaken in parallel to revise and update records transfer and archiving processes and the associated roles and responsibilities within the record-creating units. The end result delivers their new way of preserving essential electronic drug development records for the long-term with the expectation that compliance requirements will be met.

Next Steps

The final goal of the project is to implement a validated eArchive Service for records requiring long-term digital preservation using Preservica as the technical platform along with defined operating and governance models. Multiple tenant capability within the Preservica repository will provide distinct boundaries between records sets and user groups while leveraging common preservation administration, planning, and management. Common, as well as GLP-specific, Metadata Standards will be developed to help assure consistency and enhance accessibility for future search and retrieval, as well as lifespan management activities (including disposition).

This eArchive Service will be hosted/managed by a central group within the Company's Quality Management group with a designated Electronic Archivist (eArchivist) to oversee day-to-day operations and assure the integrity and trustworthiness of the process and system. Preservation services will be offered to other business units with records that are eligible for ingestion (inactive records with a retention of 7+ years), with priority given to records generated during the drug development life cycle.

Lessons Learned

The project may have benefited from defining the process more fully before starting to investigate what technology was available. This might have reduced the amount of time creating, editing, and honing the final requirements for the solution. As well, a better and more detailed understanding earlier in the project of what was to be ingested might have improved the efficiency of the outcomes overall.

The project team kept an open mind with regard to what it envisioned the original project would deliver and how the final solution was defined. The detailed records inventory and description was essential to honing the requirements of the solution. The technology review and demonstration exercise were invaluable for exploring options and refining the user requirements. The team was adept at baselining and then integrating new concepts as the project progressed. It was important for the team to vision beyond the traditional paradigm of paper archiving and utilizing CRO archiving services. Even though many of the core principles of their current processes applied to the project, the project team was able to envision new ways of working that could effectively serve current and future users.

PARADIGM 12.2

Archivematica to ArchivesDirect:
A Practical Solution for Limited Staff Resources

Amber D'Ambrosio
Processing Archivist and Records Manager
Willamette University Archives and Special Collections

Introduction to Project

As with many institutions, Willamette University's Archives and Special Collections recognized the need for some method of digitally preserving and archiving materials received on a variety of volatile media. This included university records stored on hard drives and shared drives that the records manager wanted to transfer according to the retention schedules for preservation, as well as emails from a departed president. Among the other media in the various collections were thumb drives of emails from an artist's papers; CDs and DVDs of records, photographs, and videos; VHS tapes and audio cassettes of university events; and floppy disks from university offices and a politician's papers.

Problem Statement

Willamette University Archives and Special Collections had no workflow or processing procedures in place to handle digital records of any kind. Preservation of digital objects created by digitizing analog materials was handled by the digital asset management librarian using local backups and Amazon's Glacier, but this method was intended solely for publicly presented (online) digital objects. This digital preservation method did not seem sufficient or appropriate for batches of digital records that needed to be restricted in some fashion due to deed of gift requirements or university policy. The problem was how to handle the processing and preservation of digital records accessioned by Archives and Special Collections that were not intended for public online availability.

Approach Taken

In order to help address this problem, Ashley Toutain (then processing archivist and records manager) attended several Digital Archiving Specialist (DAS) courses offered by the Society of American Archivists (SAA) for a week in 2014. During the courses, software used by digital archivists was discussed. The instructor mentioned Archivematica as a tool for digital archiving because it was open-source and accomplished many of the requirements for digital records processing relatively seamlessly. Ashley had limited knowledge of digital records preservation and processing prior to attending the DAS courses, and, although she learned a great deal, there was still much to grasp. Archivematica seemed to be almost a catch-all for processing and preserving digital records without having to expend a lot of hands-on time. Of the programs covered in the DAS courses, Archivematica was the one that she perceived to do the most work without the need for multiple software applications, appeared to be the easiest to understand, and seemed like it would fit the Archives' digital processing needs.

She discussed Archivematica with the University Archivist and the Hatfield Library systems team, and everyone agreed to go ahead with a trial of a self-hosted instance of Archivematica. Ashley developed workflow and processing instructions, and for several months the self-hosted instance of Archivematica was tested and digital records were ingested into the system. However, the processing archivist and systems team encountered enough difficulty with ingesting into the system to feel that the self-hosted version of Archivematica was causing more trouble than they had the time and energy to address without the assistance of Artefactual's team of specialists. At that stage, the decision was made to contract with Artefactual to use its hosted and supported version of Archivematica, called ArchivesDirect.

It was in the middle of this process that I was hired as processing archivist and records manager after my predecessor had moved out of state. I also had limited knowledge of digital records processing and preservation coming into the position, but I started taking DAS courses as they were offered in Oregon, and I attended Skyped tutorials on how ArchivesDirect works and read all of the documentation provided by Artefactual. I also started reading blogs about digital archiving, which I found helpful to obtain a perspective on the overall state of the still-emerging process. Based on the knowledge I gained, I revised the workflow and processing instructions, which has been revised several times since as I learn more and as we incorporate additional best practices into the workflow.

Results

Although we do have to pay an annual fee for ArchivesDirect, we receive valuable support from Artefactual. As a digital archiving team (consisting of a digital asset management librarian and myself), we have discovered that the problems encountered in the self-hosted Archivematica instance haven't vanished with ArchivesDirect, but we can now turn to Artefactual for support in resolving these issues or determining what needs to be adjusted in our approach to work around difficulties. One significant problem that I have the impression is the case regardless of the system or systems used for digital processing is the issue of scale. Any batch of digital records beyond a certain size can essentially clog ArchivesDirect, and the ingest process will never complete. Artefactual is aware of this problem, but the service model they have adopted requires that an issue of this scale involve a partner who will fund or develop the code to address the issue with Artefactual. As our institution is not in a position to become such a partner, we have to wait patiently for Artefactual to cultivate a partner. Until then, we have to determine how we want to handle the processing of that batch of records. We can either work around the problem by breaking the ingest into smaller batches of digital records, or we can wait until a solution is developed for ArchivesDirect.

Overall, having now worked with BitCurator in a DAS course, and having seen a demonstration of Preservica at the 2017 SAA Annual Meeting, I feel confident we have the best system for our needs and resources. For all of the limitations mentioned above, ArchivesDirect makes my work significantly easier. My responsibilities include processing physical collections; overseeing the records management program for the university; training and supervising student interns and workers; archiving our website with Archive-It; managing access to our finding aids using a combination of ArchivesSpace, CONTENTdm, and ArchivesWest; serving on library committees; and a variety of other tasks as needed. More simply put, I don't have time to spend going through a variety of systems strung together by a workflow to process our digital records, even with the aid of something like BitCurator.

ArchivesDirect allows me to go through a few initial steps with command line to capture a directory inventory and checksums, and then I simply transfer and ingest into ArchivesDirect. If I encounter any errors, I can assess them using the documentation and contact support if I don't see a way to resolve the errors. All that's left is to document the ingest and UUID (universally unique identifier) in ArchivesSpace. In the future, there's also promise that ArchivesDirect and ArchivesSpace will link up smoothly and allow me to transfer the information about the ingest directly into ArchivesSpace without extra steps. Although the link does currently exist, it's not configured in such a way that it supports our batch digital record processing workflow. The current configuration is intended more to document individual digital files in ArchivesSpace, which would be cumbersome and unnecessary for the majority of digital records we ingest into ArchivesDirect.

Lessons Learned

Prior to implementing an open-source system it's important to gauge the amount of time, effort, and skills required to successfully implement and troubleshoot the system. Our systems team has successfully implemented and modified a number of open-source systems to suit our needs, but the specialized nature of Archivematica and its errors drained too many resources from the team. Because Archivematica processes a wide variety of variables (file sizes, file types, transfer permissions, etc.) and is always in development, the scales tipped in favor of a hosted version for our purposes. ArchivesDirect works well for our needs, allowing us the advantages of Archivematica without spending time and effort troubleshooting when one of the many variables causes an error. We are now more keenly aware of the balance between our available resources and the monetary cost and advantages when considering a locally hosted open-source system versus a third-party hosted open-source system.

Conclusion

Implementing an open-source system like Archivematica at a small institution can be challenging, especially when its development is a work in progress. For our purposes, the amount of specialized knowledge required to troubleshoot the self-hosted version caused more problems than the system solved for our digital archiving workflow. Subscribing to ArchivesDirect has provided us the advantages of Archivematica without requiring the extra resources.

NOTES

1. IDC, "Data Growth, Business Opportunities, and the IT Imperatives," April 2014, https://www.emc.com/leadership/digital-universe/2014iview/executive-summary.htm.
2. Rob Hummel and Jimmy Kemp, "Today's Digital Documents Are Tomorrow's Dinosaurs," *Washington Times,* December 22, 2011, www.washingtontimes.com/news/2011/dec/22/todays-digital-documents-are-morrows-dinosaurs/.
3. Ibid.
4. Digital Preservation Coalition, (DPC), "Digital Preservation," Introduction—Definitions and Concepts, accessed June 12, 2017, http://dpconline.org/handbook.
5. E. Haaramo, Finnish government scraps paper and digitizes archives, *ComputerWeekly.com,* June 28, 2017, www.computerweekly.com/news/450421553/Finnish-government-scraps-paper-and-digitises-archives.
6. The National Archives, United Kingdom, "Digitization at the National Archives," August 2016, http://nationalarchives.gov.uk/documents/information-management/digitisation-at-the-national-archives.pdf.
7. WhatIs.com, s.v., "digitization," last modified April 2007, http://whatis.techtarget.com/definition/digitization.
8. National Archives, Archival Formats, accessed June 12, 2017, https://www.archives.gov/preservation/formats#audio-video-motion-pictures.
9. Library of Congress "About the National Jukebox," accessed June 13, 2017, www.loc.gov/jukebox/about.
10. PRNewswire, "George Kaiser Family Foundation to Bring Woody Guthrie Archives to Oklahoma," December 28, 2011, accessed June 12, 2017, www.prnewswire.com/news-releases/george-kaiser-family-foundation-to-bring-woody-guthrie-archives-to-oklahoma-136316763.html.
11. Federal Agencies Digitization Guidelines Initiative, accessed June 12, 2017, www.digitizationguidelines.gov/.
12. Ricky Erway, "Defining 'Born Digital,'" OCLC Online Computer Library Center, accessed June 12, 2017, www.oclc.org/content/dam/research/activities/hiddencollections/borndigital.pdf?urlm=161291.

13. James G. Neal, "Preserving the Born-Digital Record," *American Libraries,* May 5, 2015, https://americanlibrariesmagazine.org/2015/05/28/preserving-the-born-digital-record/.

14. International Organization for Standardization (ISO), *ISO 15444-1:2016 Information Technology— JPG 2000 image coding system: Core coding system,* accessed June 22, 2017, https://www.iso.org/standard/70018.html.

15. Library of Congress, "Library of Congress Recommended Formats Statement," 2016–2017, accessed June 12, 2017, https://www.loc.gov/preservation/resources/rfs/RFS%202016-2017.pdf.

16. International Records Management Trust, "Training in Electronic Records Management—Module 4: Preserving Electronic Records," Laura Millar, ed., 2009, http://irmt.org/documents/educ_training/term%20modules/IRMT%20TERM%20Module%204.pdf.

17. NARA, "Microfilm" (2015), https://www.archives.gov/preservation/formats/microfilming.html.

18. Library of Congress, "Library of Congress Strategic Plan FY2016 through FY2020: Serving Congress and the Nation," accessed June 13, 2017, https://www.loc.gov/portals/static/about/documents/library_congress_stratplan_2016-2020.pdf.

19. John Hilliard, "The King of All Backup Jobs: Backing Up the Library of Congress," *TechTarget,* 2013, accessed June 22, 2017, http://searchdatabackup.techtarget.com/feature/The-king-of-all-backup-jobs-Backing-up-the-Library-of-Congress.

20. Millenniata, M-DISC, accessed June 13, 2017, www.mdisc.com/corporate/.

21. Phys.org. "Researchers Find a Chemical Solution to Shrink Digital Data Storage," June 21, 2017, https://phys.org/news/2017-06-chemical-solution-digital-storage.html.

22. Yvonne Ng, Nan Rubin, and Kara Van Malssen, "Strategies for Sustainable Preservation of Born Digital Public Television," accessed June 13, 2017, www.thirteen.org/ptvdigitalarchive/files/2009/10/PDPTV_SustainabilityStrategies.pdf.

23. National Records of Scotland. *ScotlandsPeople,* accessed June 23, 2017, https://www.scotlandspeople.gov.uk/.

24. Preservica, "A Guide to Making the Business Case for Digital Preservation," 2014, http://preservica.com/files/2014/04/A-Guide-to-Making-the-Business-Case-for-Digital-Preservation-2014.pdf.

25. Digital Curation Centre (DCC), "What Is Digital Curation? DCC Charter and Statement of Principles," accessed June 13, 2017, www.dcc.ac.uk/about-us/dcc-charter.

26. Ibid.

27. Kevin Bradley, "Defining Digital Sustainability," *Library Trends* 56, no. 1 (2007), 148–163, http://hdl.handle.net/2142/3772.

28. NDSA, Case Studies, http://ndsa.org/activities/case-studies/.

29. Research Libraries Group (RLG), Trusted Digital Repositories: Attributes and Responsibilities, An RLG-OCLC Report, May 2002, www.oclc.org/programs/ourwork/past/trustedrep/repositories.pdf.

30. The Consultative Committee for Space Data Systems (CCSDS), Reference Model for an Open Archival Information System (OAIS): Recommendation for Space Data System Practices, June 2012, http://public.ccsds.org/publications/archive/650x0m2.pdf.

31. https://www.iso.org/standard/39577.html.

32. International Organization for Standardization (ISO), *ISO 16363:2012 Space Data and Information Transfer Systems—Audit and Certification of Trustworthy Digital Repositories* [abstract], accessed January 23, 2013, www.iso.org/iso/iso_catalogue/catalogue_tc/catalogue_detail.htm?csnumber=56510.

33. PTAB—Primary Trustworthy Digital Repository Authorization Body Ltd, 2017, "PTAB First in the World to Be Accredited to Perform ISO 16363 Audit and Certification," accessed July 2, 2017, www.iso16363.org/.

34. Consultative Committee for Space Data Systems (CCSDS), *Recommendation for Space Data System Practices: Audit and Certification of Trustworthy Digital Repositories—Recommended Practice* (Magenta Book), CCSDS 652.0-M-1, CCSDS Secretariat, September 2011, http://public.ccsds.org/publications/archive/652x0m1.pdf.

35. *ISO 16919:2014: Space data and information transfer systems—Requirements for bodies providing audit and certification of candidate trustworthy digital repositories,* https://www.iso.org/standard/57950.html www.iso.org/iso/catalogue_detail.htm?csnumber=57950.

36. APARSEN, "About Digital Preservation," accessed April 29, 2018, www.alliancepermanentaccess.org/.

37. Library of Congress, "Encoded Archival Description," accessed April 29, 2018, www.loc.gov/ead/index.html.

38. Library of Congress, "Preservation Metadata Maintenance Activity," accessed April 29, 2018, www.loc.gov/standards/premis/.

39. Library of Congress, "Metadata Encoding and Transmission Standard," accessed April 29, 2018, www.loc.gov/standards/mets/.

40. DRI, "Building the Digital Repository of Ireland Infrastructure," 2015. Accessed June 21, 2017, https://repository.dri.ie/catalog/qr474f68n.

41. National Archives of Australia, "Digital Preservation Software Platform (DPSP)," 2013, accessed June 21, 2017, http://dpsp.sourceforge.net/.

42. National Archives of Australia, "SODA: Newly Scanned Records from the Archives," accessed June 21, 2017, http://soda.naa.gov.au/.

43. IMLS, "From Theory to Action: 'Good Enough' Digital Preservation Solutions for Under-Resourced Cultural Heritage Institutions. [Whitepaper], Institute of Museum and Library Services, 2015, https://commons.lib.niu.edu/bitstream/handle/10843/13610/FromTheoryToAction_POWRR_WhitePaper.pdf?sequence=1&isAllowed=y.

44. Digipress Commons, "About the POWRR Tool Grid," accessed June 22, 2017, www.digipres.org/tools/about/.

45. K. Thibodeau, "Preservation as a Service for Trust" (PaaST) (unpublished presentation), June 2017, InterPARES Trust.

46. P. Ghosh, "Google's Vint Cerf Warns of 'Digital Dark Age,'" *BBC News*, February 13, 2015, www.bbc.com/news/science-environment-31450389; V. Cerf, "Digital Vellum and Archives," *NITRD—The Networking and Information Technology Research and Development Program,* August 12, 2016, https://www.nitrd.gov/nitrdgroups/index.php?title=DigitalVellumAndArchives.

CHAPTER 13

Lifelong Learning

Education, Training, and Professional Development

INTRODUCTION

Thriving in today's world marked by the unprecedented growth of information and technological change depends upon the ability of the individual to adapt and evolve. The organization can play a part in providing training and guidance for employees, but gone is the day that an employee will spend her or his life working for one (patriarchal) organization. Employees must invest in themselves through professional development, which includes education, training (including that provided by the employer), and lifelong learning. This, of course, does not negate the employer's responsibility to provide training and guidance to enable employees to better carry out their responsibilities.

Records and information management is perceived as a program for which a few dedicated employees are responsible. *Managing records and information,* on the other hand, is the responsibility of every employee who creates or maintains them, whether in the form of paper, microfilm, voicemail, email, social media posts, or computer data (e.g., letters, electronic calendar, database, etc.). This distinction means that organizations must consider two different types of individuals: records and information professionals and *everyone else.* Although the organization does have an obligation to ensure that employees understand their records and information management responsibilities, those wishing to pursue a career in records and information management (and associated fields) must ensure their own professional development.

If records and information management is to be considered a profession, it must possess certain characteristics, including theory-based education, professional organizations, professional literature, and codes of ethics. A formal educational program at the master's level will introduce the learner to the theory and principles underpinning professional practice. Conversely, training programs, which are shorter in duration, provide participants with a discrete set of skills and knowledge. Training can be used for a variety of purposes, including orientation, policy updates, and the use of new software or hardware. Additional means of continuous learning include what first comes to mind when most of us hear the words "professional development": attending conferences, reading professional publications, networking with experts in the field, and more.

Today's records and information management professional must be a specialist when it comes to records and information management but a generalist when it comes to understanding the core business responsibilities of the organization and possessing the skills and abilities to interact with professionals from other domains, including legal, compliance, business, information technology, information governance, and security and risk management.

In this chapter, we'll explore the options available to individuals who wish to prepare for positions in records and information management, and we'll suggest ways in which those individuals can develop and implement enterprise-specific records management training for others.

PREPARATION FOR RECORDS MANAGEMENT PROFESSIONALS

In the United States, the records management profession can credit its existence to archivists employed to help the United States federal government manage its records. In 1949, Emmett J. Leahy, a founding member of the Society of American Archivists (SAA), called for *records engineers* to serve the needs of management in identifying records to be destroyed, leaving only those of value for preservation by the US federal government.[1] These records engineers were archivists who assumed records management responsibilities.

More than sixty years later, in March of 2015, the US Office of Personnel Management, recognizing that records management involves administrative functions, announced a new classification for the records and information management workforce, *Records and Information Management Series, 0308.* The title for the series is *Records and Information Management Specialist,* and the general description reads:

> Records and Information Management (RIM) work involves the creation, dissemination, research, storage, and disposition of federal records. Records and Information Management (RIM) Specialists formulate policy, perform strategic analysis and planning, conduct program outreach, coordinate training, develop metrics, and ensure that sound information governance and accountability measures are in place. RIM Specialists ensure compliance with Federal laws, regulations, and guidance and advise managers on any issues in this area. Additionally, RIM Specialists are familiar with agency goals, objectives, and priorities, and ensure that the RIM program supports the organization's mission and needs.[2]

Records manager is not listed in the *Occupational Outlook Handbook (OOH)* as a distinct occupation. The description of *Administrative Service Manager* includes the following reference to recordkeeping: "Their specific responsibilities vary, but administrative service managers typically maintain facilities and supervise activities that include recordkeeping, mail distribution, and office upkeep."[3]

In spite of the recent recognition by the federal government of the administrative duties carried out by records and information management professionals and the still mislabeled title and narrow scope of the OOH position title, many records and information managers assume positions of responsibility equivalent to their peers in other functional areas of their organizations, including finance, human resources, and marketing. Others rise even higher within their organizations to assume responsibilities as chief records officers.

Records management skills and knowledge can be acquired through experience, certification, formal education, and professional development (see figure 13.1). Over the course of their careers, records professionals will probably take advantage of all four avenues to improve their employment prospects.

Experience

"Experience is the best teacher" is an often-quoted proverb that aptly describes the value of professional experience to the records manager. There is no substitute for the opportunity to learn from other records management professionals, especially when it comes to accepted practices and technical skills. A recent advertisement (shown in figure 13.2) seeks a person to fill a position, the criteria for which are based on the applicant's previous experience and not specific records management education—notice the bonus points for in-house and start-up experience.

The responsibilities for this position (which are not shown in the figure) are varied but include establishing company-wide policies with respect to information retention, management, and disposal; fostering adherence to applicable records management standards and laws; conducting inventories of physical and electronic records across all company locations; assessing the team's compliance with their information management obligations; partnering with IT and security architects to ensure compliance with data security and privacy mandates; spotting and anticipating issues; recommending solutions to the legal department; and incorporating e-discovery considerations and preparation into information management systems and processes.

The exciting part of this position is the opportunity to work in one of the emerging markets mentioned in chapter 7: this is a driverless car company building autonomous vehicles. They expect "novel and complex" legal issues to arise and want someone who can help solve them. The need for a broad view of the organization is expressed in the statement: "The ideal candidate is an empowered problem solver, with excellent attention to detail, who can win over and provide practical legal/regulatory/business advice to [the company's] diverse engineering and operational teams."[4]

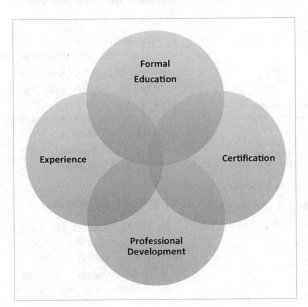

Certification

When seeking a position in response to an advertisement, an applicant will be asked to provide evidence to support his or her claims. The applicant would, of course, provide documentation, such as letters of recommendation. Because letters of recommendation are subjective, the prospective employer may also seek an objective means to evaluate applicants, perhaps requiring

FIGURE 13.1 Records and information management lifelong learning.

certification of skills and knowledge. The position announcement shown in figure 13.2 also cites certification—CRM, CRA or IGP—as highly desirable.

Certified Records Manager (CRM)

The Institute of Certified Records Managers (ICRM) is an international certifying body for professional records and information professionals and members of the Nuclear Information and Records Management Association (NIRMA). The ICRM was incorporated in 1975 to establish a standard by which persons involved in records and information management could be measured, accredited, and recognized according to criteria identified by their peers. The primary mission of the ICRM is to develop and administer relevant examinations and certification maintenance programs. Applicants who meet the requirements set by ICRM for education and experience will be approved to take the first five parts of the examination. Those who pass all five parts are eligible to sit for the sixth part. The six parts are as follows:

- **Part 1:** Management Principles and the Records and Information Management Professional
- **Part 2:** Records and Information: Creation and Use
- **Part 3:** Records Systems, Storage, and Retrieval
- **Part 4:** Records Appraisal, Retention, Protection, and Disposition
- **Part 5:** Technology
- **Part 6:** Business Cases

Certified Reference Managers (CRMs) must pay an annual membership fee and maintain certification by earning credit for participation in professional development activities.[5]

Records & Information Lifecycle Manager

Cruise ★★★★☆ 25 reviews - San Francisco, CA

View or apply to job

Requirements:

- Bachelor's Degree
- 3+ Years Records and Information Management experience
- Experience defining requirements and implementing processes
- Experience working in tech, especially for a large or scaling organization
- Knowledge of Records/Content Management Systems and tools
- Strong presentation and communication skills, and ability to win over and work with diverse teams
- Understanding management of structured and unstructured data content
- Strong ability in MS Excel, PowerPoint, Word
- Attention to detail

Bonus Points:

- In-house experience
- Start-up experience
- CRM, CRA or IGP Certification

Certified Records Analyst (CRA)

Professionals who wish certification before complying with all six parts of the CRM may obtain the Certified Records Analyst (CRA) designation based on educational background, professional experience, and successful completion of Parts 2, 3, and 4.[6]

CRM/Federal Specialist

The CRM/Federal Specialist is a post-certification specialty designation for CRMs working in records and information management programs of

FIGURE 13.2 Job posting for records and information lifecycle manager.

the U.S. Government, whether as a Federal government employee, uniformed military personnel, consultant, or contractor. The body of knowledge tested is comprised of three categories: management and organizational structure; policy, standards and governance; and RIM program operations.[7]

Nuclear Specialist (CRM/NS)

The Institute of Certified Records Managers (ICRM) offers a specialty certification on behalf of the Nuclear Information Records Management Association (NIRMA). Candidates for this designation must pass the core CRM exam before sitting for an additional exam section related to nuclear information records management. The successful candidate receives the CRM/NS designation.[8]

Certified Archivist (CA)

The traditional records management lifecycle ends when records are destroyed or transferred to an archive. However, archivists may become involved with records of enduring value at any stage of the records lifecycle. They understand the importance of records within an

Graduates of San José State University's MARA Degree Program Offered Fast Track to CRM/CRA Certification

There are benefits to combining both education and certification. A strategic partnership between the San José State University's School of Information and the Institute of Certified Records Managers allows graduates of the Master of Archives and Records Administration (MARA) degree program, who have completed their course work and have met established qualifications for ICRM candidacy, to apply for credit for Parts 1 through 5 of the ICRM exams. The benefits of this partnership extend to graduates applying to become a Certified Records Analyst (which requires credit for Parts 2, 3, and 4 of the exam) or to sit for Part 6 of the CRM exam to become a Certified Records Manager (which requires prior credit for parts 1 through 5).

Ossie Thomas, a 2016 MARA graduate, was the first to obtain her CRA through this partnership. The combination of degree and certification allowed her to assume additional responsibilities at her current place of employment. Thomas has some words of advice for those seeking advancement or recognition in their career field:

> "Don't be afraid to step out of your comfort zone," she says. "Look for opportunities that will cause you to stretch yourself to new possibilities and be open to new ideas and experiences."*

Thomas also suggests looking towards professional organizations like ARMA International and AIIM for networking and professional development purposes.

* Ossie Thomas, email message to author, January 1, 2018.

organization as evidence of transactions and events, but they also appreciate the potential historical and research value of the same records for future generations. The same could be said of records managers, who often—especially when employed in local, state, and federal government positions—must deal with both active use and preservation of records. It is becoming more common to see records professionals who are not only certified records managers (CRMs) but also certified archivists (CAs).

A CA is an individual who has met the Academy of Certified Archivists' (ACA) requirements for education, experience, and knowledge. The ACA is a not-for-profit accrediting agency developed through the efforts of SAA to improve educational opportunities and establish credentials for the archival field. The examinations test the applicant's mastery of a body of knowledge categorized into seven domains:

- **Domain 1:** Selection, Appraisal, and Acquisition
- **Domain 2:** Arrangement and Description
- **Domain 3:** Reference Services and Access
- **Domain 4:** Preservation and Protection
- **Domain 5:** Outreach, Advocacy, and Promotion
- **Domain 6:** Managing Archival Programs
- **Domain 7:** Professional, Ethical, and Legal Responsibilities

Examinations are administered at various locations around the United States each August. Recertification is required every five years either by retaking the examination or by petition (listing activities that earn at least 100 points during the previous five years).[9]

Additional Professional Certifications

Additional certifications can demonstrate mastery of knowledge related to a specific industry or related knowledge domains.

Project Management Professional (PMP)

Sooner or later, every records manager will be involved in a project that calls for project management skills, whether serving as team leader or a contributing member of the team. The PMP designation, certified by the Project Management Institute (PMI), provides evidence that the individual has the experience, education, and competency to successfully lead and direct projects. Applicants who meet the education and experience requirements are eligible to sit for a 200-question multiple choice exam covering the following project management domains:

- Initiating
- Planning
- Executing
- Monitoring and Controlling
- Closing[10]

Certified Information Privacy Professional (CIPP/United States)

The growth and volume of electronic records, including emerging technology, present unprecedented privacy and data protection challenges for the enterprise. The CIPP designation is one of three offered by the International Association of Privacy Professionals. The other two are the Certified Information Privacy Manager and the Certified Information Privacy Technologist. Candidates for the CIPP/US must first pass an exam currently comprised of ninety objective questions on five topics:

- Introduction to the US Privacy Environment
- Limits on Private-Sector Collection and Use of Data
- Government and Court Access to Private-Sector Information
- Workplace Privacy
- State Privacy Laws[11]

Certified Information Professional (CIP)

In 2011, AIIM introduced the certified information professional (CIP) designation for those who wish to demonstrate they can meet information management challenges both on-premises and in the cloud, and can bridge the gap between enterprise information technology and business executives. The 100-question objective test, administered at test centers around the world, covers six domains:

- Creating and Capturing Information
- Organizing and Categorizing Information
- Governing Information
- Automating Information-Intensive Processes
- Managing the Information Lifecycle
- Implementing an Information Management Solution

The most recent Certified Information Professional Outline, CIP Study Guide, and additional resources are available through AIIM.[12]

Formal Education

Formal education for archivists and records managers exists most often at the graduate level. Curriculum for these programs in often influenced by guidance published by professional associations such as SAA and ARMA International.

Guiding Principles and Core Competencies

SAA maintains a directory listing of archival education that can be searched by program delivery method (on campus, online, a hybrid delivered both on campus and online) and by degrees or certificates offered (certificate, associate, bachelor, graduate certificate, master, and PhD). Currently, the list includes programs from twenty US states and two Canadian provinces. Many of these programs are offered through library and information science schools or information and computer science departments.

SAA does not endorse any programs, but it does provide guidelines for developing a graduate program in archival studies to prepare students for careers in archives and records management, including digital archives management and historical records preservation. According to SAA, the graduate-level program should be comprised of both core archival knowledge and complementary knowledge from other disciplines, including economics, history, information studies, law, management, and technology as they relate to archival work.

ARMA International also provides guidance for institutions developing records management programs and courses. ARMA identifies core competencies that define the knowledge, skills, characteristics, and traits that contribute to performing successfully in the records and information management (RIM) profession. RIM professionals can use *Records and Information Management Core Competencies,* 2nd edition, to identify their level of proficiency in six defined domains:

- Business Functions
- RIM Practices
- Risk Management
- Communications and Marketing
- Information Technology
- Leadership[13]

The core competencies can also be used by those designing records and information management educational offerings or training programs.

Credit Courses and Programs

Records and information are created and must be managed in all organizations and at all levels. Accordingly, employees can find themselves interacting with records and information regardless of their position within the organization. The type of education most useful to individuals depends on their previous knowledge, skills, and experiences; their current position within the organization; and their career goals. The hierarchy of credit-bearing educational programs is illustrated in figure 13.3, with certificate programs that are often nine to twelve months in duration at the base and doctoral programs, which generally take an additional five to seven years beyond a master's, at the top.

Certificate Programs

Individuals employed as or interested in positions as records and document-imaging analysts, records technicians, and office or administrative personnel may benefit from completing a technical certificate in records and information management, such as the Office Administration Certificate in Records Management offered through Vancouver Community College, Vancouver, BC, Canada. This certificate introduces students to the systematic control of all office records from creation or receipt, through processing, distribution, organization, and retrieval, to their final disposition.[14]

Associate's Degree Programs

Associate's degree programs are often related to technical preparation programs offered through community colleges, such as the Associate in Applied Science (AAS) degree in Records Management offered through San Antonio College, San Antonio, Texas.[15] Courses in this degree program, in addition to records and information management, include business math, business English, introduction to spreadsheets, and database applications. This type of degree would be useful to a student preparing to enter the workforce.

Bachelor's Degree Programs

Very few colleges and universities offer bachelor's degrees in records management. Students interested in archives and records and information management often major in history, business, or information science at this stage of their educations. However, those specializing in a particular industry, such as healthcare, may find programs to fit their needs, such as the online Bachelor of Science in Information Technology with a Health Information Management Specialization through Capella University.[16]

Master's Degree Programs

A number of programs exist on this level for archives, records, and information management. These programs honor the term *management* by preparing individuals to assume administrative positions related to archives and records/information management. Graduate programs include both theory and practice and encourage research that contributes to the profession.

Records management courses are included in archival studies programs and can be found within many of the programs listed in the SAA's Directory of Archival Education.[17] Among those listed as specializations within an MLIS degree is one offered through the University of Pittsburgh's School of Computing and Information. This option provides students with several career pathways, including "Information Culture and Data Stewardship." This pathway contains courses in records and recordkeeping systems; digital preservation, curation, and stewardship; and legal and ethical issues.[18]

FIGURE 13.3 Increasing levels of formal education can prepare a records professional for increasing levels of responsibility and authority.

Recognition of the value of records management and the need to educate records professionals in both archival studies and records and information management for positions in public and private organizations have resulted in new degree titles, such as the Master of Archives and Records Administration (MARA) degree through the School of Information at San José State University.[19] This unique program, delivered 100 percent online, was founded on the core competencies identified by ARMA International and the five knowledge domains that comprise the Certified Records Manager examination, as well as guidance for graduate programs in archival studies from the SAA and the seven domains that comprise the Certified Archivist examination. It was further enhanced to provide students with the skills and knowledge necessary to move into information governance positions.

Advanced Certificates

Advanced certificates in archives and records management are available to those pursuing a degree in another field or as a post-master's option. Long Island University, for example, offers an advanced certificate in archives and records management that can be earned concurrently with the library science master's degree or by students who hold a previously completed master's degree in any discipline.[20]

Some advanced certificate programs have specific course prerequisites. For example, students pursuing the Archives and Records Management Certificate Program at Western Washington University must either possess a master's degree in history or take at least one history course in addition to the courses required in the certificate program.[21]

Doctoral Studies

Doctoral programs in archives and records management prepare students to investigate and develop professional methodologies, models, frameworks, and standards. The Archives and Records Management PhD at the University of Liverpool in England explores topics related to ethics and professional practice; user needs; roles and responsibilities; legal, compliance, and governance issues; metadata; data integrity and exchange; and preservation management.[22]

Options abound for those who wish to advance their education through formal channels, but there also are countless opportunities to acquire new skills and knowledge through the less formal channels often labeled as professional development.

Professional Development

Professional development can be defined as "the process of obtaining the skills, qualifications, and experience that allow you to make progress in your career, often through continuing education."[23] Continuing education is also a condition that certifying bodies impose in order to retain certification. Professional development experiences that count toward maintenance credit for the CRM, for example, range from attendance at workshops and conferences to publishing articles and teaching courses. Certified archivists must recertify every five years either by retaking the examination or submitting a petition for recertification based on participation in activities and events including full-time professional archival employment, courses taken in any of the archival domains, attendance at professional archival meetings, participation in conferences as panelists, delivering a paper, and teaching a semester course in an accredited college or university on topics in the archival domain.[24]

Professional associations offer continuing education opportunities either as stand-alone courses or certificate programs (which are not to be confused with certification). In addition to a newsletter, professional journal, and standards, ARMA International offers both online courses for a fee and web seminars that are free to members. A learning management system allows ARMA members to track the courses they've taken and credits earned. Courses can be sorted to see which apply toward the CRA, CRM, or IGP certifications.[25] AIIM offers a variety of training programs in such topics as enterprise content management, electronic records management, business process management, and SharePoint.[26] SAA offers online on-demand courses in the form of archived audiovisual recordings of live presentations, as well as live courses, seminars, and webinars on topics such as style sheets for encoded archival description (EAD), digital curation, and project management for archivists.[27] SAA offers two certificate programs: The Digital Archives Specialist (DAS) Certificate and the Arrangement and Description (A&D) Certificate.[28]

RECORDS MANAGEMENT TRAINING PROGRAMS

At some point, records professionals might be expected to design a training program for other records professionals and/or for all employees who create or manage records during the course of daily operations. Some even earn recognition for the Records and Information Management or Information Governance programs they manage.

Recognition for Meeting Records Management Program Requirements

In 2017, Farmers Insurance was the recipient of the ARMA International Award of Excellence for an Organization. The Award recognizes the achievement of one organization that has implemented or enhanced its records and information management or information governance program based on the total points earned for each of the eight Principles: Accountability, Availability, Compliance, Disposition, Integrity, Protection, Retention, and Transparency and the maturity level of the program based on the ARMA International Information Governance Maturity Model.[29] The necessity of a training program is reflected in several of the Principles; for example, to achieve the highest level (transformational) for the Principle of Accountability, the organization would, among other criteria, meet the following requirement: "There is an organized training and continuous improvement program across the organization."[30]

An introduction to the records lifecycle and specific topics such as retention schedules, information access, and search and retrieval methods will help the individual understand her or his role in the entire process. A good first step is orientation to the records management policy and procedures manual.

Records Management Policies and Procedures Manuals

The term *manual* evokes the image of a physical book of instructions. At one time, records management policies were distributed exclusively in physical format, often as pages in a three-ring binder that could be updated by removing pages that contain information no longer valid and inserting new pages. Today most businesses post policies and procedures manuals on their intranet or within a collaborative workspace such as SharePoint, while many government agencies, in the spirit of openness and transparency, publish policies and procedures on their public websites.

For example, the *Records Management Policy* of the Department of Cultural Affairs and Sport, Western Cape Government, Republic of South Africa, is available on the Web. The introduction to the policy underscores the value of information (both physical and digital) as "a significant economic, political, and cultural activity."[31] The policy upholds the Records Continuum Model (RCM) because it supports the concept that archival principles must be applied throughout the life of a record. Five policy statements comprise the Records Management Policy document: creation or receipt; records classification; retention/disposal; maintenance and use; and training. Roles and responsibilities and monitoring and review of the policy are also addressed.[32]

Sending hard or electronic files or posting digital versions of records management policies online isn't enough, however. The policy manual must be written clearly, and employees must acknowledge they received or accessed the policy, have read it, and understand it. As stated previously, all new employees should be introduced to the records management policy as part of the new employee orientation. At that time, employees could be required to acknowledge receipt of the manual and initial training. In addition, all current employees should receive periodic reminders of their responsibilities, including updates to current policies and procedures. If notification is made using an electronic distribution list, a copy of the names on the distribution list must be retained for compliance purposes.

Records management policy manuals and training programs will differ depending on the industry in which the organization conducts business and its governing laws and regulations.

Developing a Records Management Training Program

Regardless of the content of the training, the steps listed in table 13.1 can be used to develop the training program.

Basic RIM Training Topics

The following topics should be included in a basic records management training workshop:

- definition of records management
- key records management laws and regulations
- definition and example of electronic records
- electronic records management (ERM)
- steps to safeguard records
- personal papers versus corporate records
- recordkeeping responsibilities
- records retention
- records schedules
- identifying and managing essential records
- managing web records
- ethics and behavioral norms

Specific topics should be added as new technologies and practices emerge, such as those dealing with social media, cloud computing, and the use of mobile devices. Both training

TABLE 13.1 Steps to design and develop a records management training program.

1. IDENTIFY PURPOSE; SET GOALS AND OBJECTIVES
What do you want the training to accomplish? Identify both short- and long-term goals.
What do you want learners to know and be able to do? Define learning objectives that are concrete, measurable, and attainable. Differentiate training according to staff responsibilities.
2. CHOOSE A TRAINING METHOD AND TOOLS
Classroom training (lectures, case studies, simulations, hands-on software instruction, role play, behavioral modeling)
Distance learning (books, videos, web-based instruction such as e-learning, and computer-based instruction)
On-the-job training (job rotation, apprenticeship, coaching, mentoring, and performance appraisal)
3. DETERMINE DELIVERY METHOD
Who will conduct the training? (in-house trainers, external trainers, local universities)
Where will it be held? (on-site, off-site, virtual)
How long should it last? (1–2 hours, half day, full day, several days?)
What adjustments must be made for the audience based on size, demographics, ability, and readiness (level of content, amount of discussion, types of technology, types of exercises)
4. MOTIVATE EMPLOYEES
To attend training (required, voluntary)
To perform well in training (incentives such as job security, money, advancement)
To use their training on the job (opportunity to use newly acquired skills, recognition for performance improvement)
5. INSTITUTE REVIEW AND REPORTING MECHANISMS
Maintain records of individuals and of the programs offered
Evaluate the results of training (track success of individuals and of all employees)
Revise and update the training program as necessary
Develop a method to ensure ongoing training for all employees

and tracking can be automated using learning management systems, training tracking software, and solutions that combine both.

Automating the Regulatory Training Process

Industry-specific training, such as compliance training, can be added to the basic RIM training topics, especially for organizations in heavily regulated industries. Rather than develop training programs and courses in-house, it is possible to take advantage of commercial, web-based services that automate the regulatory training process, including regulations emanating from the following departments and agencies:

- **Department of Health and Human Services (HHS):** health information privacy and security
- **Department of Labor (DOL):** human resources and labor law compliance training
- **Department of Justice (DOJ):** corporate ethics, compliance, and risk management training
- **Occupational Safety and Health Administration (OSHA) and Environmental Protection Agency (EPA):** health and safety compliance training
- **Securities and Exchange Commission (SEC):** financial services and banking compliance training

Thomson Reuters provides compliance training courses based on its tracking of over 800 regulators and exchanges globally. Three of the seven topic areas covered are privacy, confidentiality, and information security; employee conduct and business ethics; and risk management. Course titles include Business Continuity Management, Electronic Communications, FERPA, the General Data Protection Regulation (GDPR), and HIPAA Privacy and Security.[33]

If using commercial training services, look for solutions that can also manage workflow (capturing employee and supervisor or manager e-signatures), automatically notify employees of recertification requirements, and assign appropriate training.

Automating the Records Management Training Program

The irony of developing training programs for employees and contractors to help them manage records is that the training programs themselves produce records that must be managed. Many commercial solutions will include an administrative function (similar to ARMA International's dashboard) to automate some elements of the training program.

Training management software is also available dedicated only to keeping track of training. This responsibility may be a part of the human resources function or of a training manager and not specifically the records manager, but it is important to understand what is available to manage training records and ensure employees are compliant with training requirements. Common features of a training records database include the ability to assign required training by individual, job function, or group; the ability to record attendance, training completion, and cancellations; and the ability to print status reports to demonstrate compliance on a companywide basis or for a specific individual.

Records Management Training Programs for Records Management Staff

A modular approach to training for records management works well, because it is important to provide training geared to the individual's level of involvement with records management activities. Training for records management staff will be more complex than that for all other employees and will depend upon the size and configuration of the records management function, which in turn depends on the magnitude and structure of the organization.

Individuals hired to fill recordkeeping positions are expected to possess the skills required to conduct the duties specified in their job descriptions. However, an introduction to the organization and the department in which they will work should be planned as part of the new employee orientation. In addition, there may be systems and procedures specific to the department that will need to be introduced. This can occur during a workshop at the start of employment or by learning on the job with the guidance of more experienced staff members.

Take advantage of the training and resources provided by hardware and software vendors when appropriate, such as Microsoft Ignite, which provides on-demand sessions on topics such as "Automate records management in Office 365 and keep high-value data securely in-place," and "Governance and compliance with Office 365 Groups."[34]

Records Management Training Programs for All Employees

Because all employees who create or manage records have recordkeeping responsibilities, training should be provided to help them carry out those responsibilities and reduce both individual and organizational risk. NARA provides a training model that can be used as the basis for records management training in large organizations.

The NARA Training Model

In keeping with the concept that all federal government employees have federal records management responsibilities, NARA makes training and resources available to all employees and contractors who create and manage records and information. A website dedicated to information about records management serves as a hub to records management-related resources. In addition to links to records management publications, resources, and NARA's YouTube Channel, information about the National Records Management Training Program is provided.[35] Registered users of the system have access to a portal that allows them to check and change classes they're enrolled in, view their learning progress (including courses completed and exams passed), and print out certificates for classes completed.

The NARA model employs a modular approach to training that takes into account the training needs and time constraints of participants and covers a variety of topics, comprised of one optional knowledge area (Records Management Overview) and the five knowledge areas shown below that can result in a Certificate of Federal Records Management Training:

- **Knowledge Area 2:** Creating and Maintaining Agency Business Information
- **Knowledge Area 3:** Records Scheduling
- **Knowledge Area 4:** Records Schedule Implementation
- **Knowledge Area 5:** Asset and Risk Management
- **Knowledge Area 6:** Records Management Program Development[36]

Candidates for this certification must complete each training course in person and then take and pass a test administered online. If they do not pass the test, candidates have the option of retaking it without repeating the course. Once all tests are successfully completed, the applicant will receive a certificate in the mail. This certification does not result in a CRM designation as established by the ICRM. NARA's Certificate of Federal Records Management Training was designed to focus only on the policies and procedures unique to the federal government. In addition to required courses, courses on emergency planning and response and specialty classes, such as vital business information and electronic records management, are offered.[37]

SUMMARY

Formal education introduces the learner to the theory and practice of a discipline, and training programs introduce participants to new skills they can apply directly to their work.

Records professionals can acquire skills and knowledge through experience, certification, formal education, and professional development (including training programs). Experience can be earned through employment, internships, and even volunteer work.

Certification provides a standard by which professionals can be measured, accredited, and recognized according to criteria established by their peers. The certifying organization for records professionals is the Institute of Certified Records Managers (ICRM), and the successful candidate is designated a certified records manager (CRM) or a certified records analyst (CRA). ARMA International oversees the Information Governance Professional (IGP) certification program, and archivists can earn the certified archivist (CA) designation from the Academy of Certified Archivists (ACA).

Records managers who wish to assume additional responsibilities may expand their skills and knowledge into other domains and seek certification to demonstrate those competencies. Related certifications include nuclear specialist (CRM/NS), CRM/Federal Specialist, project management professional (PMP), certified information privacy professional (CIPP), and certified information professional (CIP).

Formal education is valued for records professionals throughout the world. In the United States, archives and records management programs are taught in community colleges, colleges, and universities. Master's degree programs and professional certificates are becoming more common.

Professional associations offer continuing education opportunities in a variety of formats, including annual conferences, webinars, publications, and even courses or certificate programs. The primary records management association in the United States and Canada is ARMA International. In the United States, records professionals often also belong to SAA and AIIM. And those who work in records management positions in local, state, and the federal government benefit from membership in NAGARA—the National Association of Government Archives and Records Administrators.[38]

Records managers can be expected to develop and conduct records management training programs for other records professionals and for all employees. The type of training varies depending upon the purpose, goals, objectives, and target audience.

Training may be as short as a few hours or as long as several days. Instruction can take place in face-to-face classes or web-based courses. An introduction to the organization and the records management program should be included in every new employee orientation. The records management policies and procedures manual is usually introduced at that time. Components of the manual can be the focus of more intense training; for example, email management and business continuity.

Curriculum can be developed in-house or acquired through commercial training providers. It is advisable to investigate external providers for complex topics such as regulatory compliance for specific industries. Records management training programs generate records that must also be managed. Training management software can keep track of training and generate reports that can be used as evidence of compliance.

In the United States, there is an obvious divide between Archives and Records and Information Management when it comes to professional associations and certification. But a closer look at the curriculum contained within educational programs for both fields may surprise you. In recognizing the value that archival studies programs offer the records and information management profession, the ARMA International Education Foundation (AIEF) presented the first Award for Excellence in Education to the Master of Archival Studies program at the University of British Columbia, Canada. In her contribution to this chapter, Dr. Luciana Duranti will describe the program that has benefitted more than 700 graduates since its inception.

PARADIGM

Graduate Archival Education—The Master of Archival Studies at the University of British Columbia

Luciana Duranti
Professor, School of Library, Archival and Information Studies
The University of British Columbia, Vancouver, British Columbia, Canada

Introduction

In September 1981, an inaugural class of ten students enrolled in the Master of Archival Studies (MAS) Program at the then-named School of Library Studies at the University of British Columbia (UBC). That class, which graduated in 1983, was the first ever in Canada to study archival science and prepare for professional archival work in an independent program granting a degree in Archival Studies. Since then, more than seven hundred professional archivists have graduated with an MAS degree from the School of Library, Archival and Information Studies, a name that was changed by the UBC Senate in 1982 to emphasize the presence in the School of separate, autonomous MAS and MLIS degrees.

The Master of Archival Studies (MAS) is a two-year graduate program for records professionals (e.g., records managers, archivists, digital records preservers, designers of recordkeeping systems, manuscripts curators, legal documentary evidence experts, cultural heritage experts, and Freedom of Information and privacy officers). The core of the program is constituted of the theory, methods, and practices of archival science, as well as archival history and scholarship. This knowledge is delivered through classes, internships, and other forms of experiential learning, and active participation in international research projects. As records derive their meaning from the administrative, juridical, procedural, documentary, and technological contexts in which they are created, maintained, used, and preserved, the program also delivers education in administrative, juridical, and legal systems, in documentary analysis or diplomatics, and in record-making, recordkeeping, and record preservation technologies. Thus, the program is highly interdisciplinary, in that it brings the knowledge of complementary disciplines to bear on archival methods and practices.

Problem Statement

Half a century ago, Sir Hilary Jenkinson wrote: "I become more and more convinced that the apparent complexity of our jack-of-all-trades profession . . . can be resolved quite simply if we attach ourselves firmly to a few primary and unchanging essentials."[39] He was echoing the words of Italian educator Giovanni Vittani, who, in 1913, had written: "An archival school must not have the pretense of creating the complete archivist, but must make the student able to continue his education while working in any kind of archives. This is obtainable by reducing the curricula to those components that are really essential."[40] And in 1928, another Italian educator, Eugenio Casanova, had reinforced this point by stating: "There is always the risk of demanding and doing too little or presenting exaggerated pretensions."[41] Vittani definitely thought that little was better. He continued: "To include too much in a curriculum makes it superficial and provides students with a superficial attitude towards their work. If students understand principles and methods, when dealing with different materials in different institutions, they are supported by the analogy of various situations. A graduate from a professional school must be armed to deal with problems, to compare situations with what he has learned, and to solve them."[42]

Approach Taken

The MAS at UBC is a program of professional education rather than training: its goal is to form the archival professional mind-set and draw out the students' intellect to see the whole of the ideas that form the theoretical foundation of the profession and to engage in their development. For this reason, the MAS program delivers in the first term of the first year a common core of archival knowledge that provides the students with their unique professional identity, that is, with what is central, enduring, and distinctive about their profession. The content delivered is selected on the basis of the recognition that archivists, on the one hand, have to deal with a universal body of theory and with a practice directed towards the development and implementation of international standards; on the other, they are immediately concerned with the specific, local, and unique aspects of the material they handle. Thus, the curriculum is designed to harmonize the universal and the specific by providing knowledge of archival science as it is understood in Canada and abroad, as well as delivering methodological instruction on how to discover the characteristics of specific or local records and their context.

The structure of the curriculum and of the individual courses is based on awareness of the scholarly and practical nature of archival work. The main purpose of the curriculum is to give future archivists theoretical and methodological knowledge in class. The offering of practica provides structured opportunities to apply in-class learning and test theoretical and methodological knowledge in the professional arena.

Research is a critical component of the MAS program because it is an expression of the intellectual nature of the archival discipline, the scholarly substance of the work that record professionals do, and the academic status of archival studies in the university. Several courses enable students to engage in scholarly enquiry. In addition, the program has an outstanding record of expanding the opportunities for research by involving students in grant-funded faculty research: these research projects enable students to acquire research skills while contributing to the advancement of their disciplinary knowledge and interacting with a local, national, and international archival community of scholars and practitioners.

The MAS curriculum is based on the belief that a strong disciplinary knowledge is the necessary presupposition of strong interdisciplinary and multidisciplinary professional and scholarly activities, which are needed in an archival world made increasingly complex by the use of continuously developing digital technology and the growing legal implications of such use, nationally and internationally.

Finally, the MAS curriculum content and structure reflect the view that the archival field encompasses the entire records lifecycle, that the records management function requires archival education, and that the MAS graduates must be scholars and professionals of all records, in every media, of every age and origin, and at any stage in the records lifecycle, from creation to permanent preservation.

Curriculum

The MAS degree is awarded on completion of forty-eight credits of course work and such noncredit courses and activities (e.g., field visits) as required. Following completion of the first term, a student may take up to fifteen credit hours per term during the Winter Session without special permission, although the recommended course load is twelve credits per term. Very few courses are offered during the Summer Session. The minimum completion time is therefore two consecutive Winter Sessions. The program must begin in Term 1 of a Winter Session (that is, in September).

During the first term of the Winter Session, students must take four required courses, which constitute the MAS core: ARST 510, Archival Diplomatics; ARST 515, Arrangement and Description of Archival Documents; ARST 516, Management of Current Records; and ARST 573, The Archival System in the Profession.[43]

In the second term of the first year, they must take one required course, ARST 520, Selection and Acquisition of Archival Documents, and three electives.

In addition to the twelve credits from core courses, during the following eighteen months, students must earn thirty-six additional units of credit. Of the total forty-eight units, fifteen credits are from required courses and thirty-three credits from elective courses—twelve of which may be the thesis, and three of which may be the Internship. Students who opt to take the elective Internship course devote twelve weeks between the two Winter Sessions to it. This course consists of practical experience in all archival functions under the supervision of a qualified records manager or archivist, and the observation of the professional work of others. It takes place in a recognized program or repository in Canada or abroad. Another form of experiential learning is the Professional Experience, which can be taken after successful completion of twenty-four credits of MAS courses during any of the subsequent terms. This course consists of a definable project, most often proposed by an archives, an institution, or an organization, and approved by the School as being appropriate for three credits.

The other MAS elective courses are designed to build upon the knowledge acquired in the core courses, as follows:

Building on ARST 510 Archival Diplomatics
ARST 556H, Digital Diplomatics and Digital Records Forensics

Building on ARST 515 Arrangement and Description of Archival Documents
ARST 545, Advanced Arrangement and Description of Archival Documents

Building on ARST 516 Management of Current Records
ARST 560, Records and Information Governance
ARST 575J, IT Security, Information Assurance, and Risk Management
ARST 565, Administering Records under Freedom of Information and
    Protection of Privacy Legislation

ARST 517, History of Record Keeping
ARST 556E, Records Systems in the Digital Environment

Building on ARST 520 Selection and Acquisition of Archival Documents
ARST 575K, Personal Archives

Building on the whole core
ARST 540, Archival Public Services
ARST 550, Management of Audio-Visual and Non-Textual Archives
ARST 555, The Preservation of Digital Records
ARST 580, Records, Archives, and the Law
ARST 587, Preservation (of all media)
ARST 575H, Information Visualization and Visual Analytics
ARST 500, Information Technology and Archives
ARST 570, Management of Archives
ARST 554, Database Design
ARST 556K, Research Data Management for Information Professionals

All MAS courses involve research and writing its results in formal essays. However, there are two elective courses completely dedicated to research, the Directed Research Project and the Directed Study. A twelve-credit thesis is optional. In addition, all students are invited to participate as Graduate Research Assistants (GRAs) in the research projects in which MAS professors are involved as principal investigators. All MAS students contribute to the initiatives of the Centre for the International Study of Contemporary Records and Archives (www.ciscra.org).

Every year, UBC's Student Chapter of the Association of Canadian Archivists (ACA) organizes an International Seminar and Symposium: this involves developing the program; extending invitations; fund-raising and marketing; planning breaks and meals; assisting eight to ten guest speakers with travel, accommodation, orientation at UBC and in the city; running the conference; and creating a website of the event.[44]

Successes

In 1998, the MAS program received the Society of American Archivists' Distinguished Service Award. In 2012, it was granted the ARMA International Educational Foundation's highest recognition, the Academic Excellence Award, because, as the text of the citation read, it had

> contributed significantly to the growth of education in Records and Information Management at an international level and its graduates have given voice at the highest levels in local, regional, and international public and private organisations with regard to the administration and management of records, archives, and information and have brought distinction to the profession. The School of Library, Archival and Information Studies is therefore deserving of the first ARMA International Educational Foundation's Award for Academic Excellence in the combined areas of outstanding teaching, outstanding research accomplishments and outstanding contribution to the university and college communities, governments, the private sector and the global citizenry as a whole.

MAS students have received ARMA International Educational Foundation scholarships in large numbers.

The UBC MAS graduates have found employment within a few months of graduation. Several of them occupy positions that require knowledge of different systems, theories, and methods; familiarity with international and multicultural environments; and understanding of the entire lifecycle of records (e.g., at the World Health Organization, the International Atomic Energy Agency, and UNESCO).

Conclusion

The MAS program is designed to nurture a distinctive disciplinary and professional identity while fostering alliances with other disciplines, partnerships with other departments and faculties at home and in other universities worldwide, and collaboration with other professions. The prestige it has acquired over the years has proven the validity of such an approach.

NOTES

1. Emmett J. Leahy, "Modern Records Management," *American Archivist* 12, no. 3 (July 1949): 239, http://archivists.metapress.com/content/52344260u1064020/fulltext.pdf.

2. US Office of Personnel Management, Position Classification Flysheet for *Records and Information Management Series, 0308*, March 2015, p. 5, https://www.opm.gov/policy-data-oversight/classification-qualifications/classifying-general-schedule-positions/standards/0300/gs0308.pdf.

3. Bureau of Labor Statistics, US Department of Labor, *Occupational Outlook Handbook*, Administrative Services Managers, accessed December 31, 2017, https://www.bls.gov/ooh/management/administrative-services-managers.htm.

4. Indeed, "Records & Information Lifecycle Manager," accessed December 31, 2017, https://www.indeed.com/q-Records-Manager-jobs.html?vjk=2bb7f425ca652cc7.

5. Details about the CRM designation and examination can be found at the ICRM website at www.icrm.org/taking-the-exams/.

6. Ibid.

7. ICRM, "The Institute of Certified Records Managers (ICRM) announces the CRM/Federal Specialist, a Post-Certification Specialty Designation," September 6, 2017, https://www.icrm.org/crm-federal-specialist.

8. Details about the Nuclear Information and Records Specialist (NS) Advanced Designation can be found on the IRM website at https://www.icrm.org/nirma/.

9. Details about the Academy of Certified Archivists and the CA designation can be found at the ACA website at www.certifiedarchivists.org/.

10. Details about the Project Management Professional (PMP) certification are located on the Project Management Institute website at https://www.pmi.org/certifications/types/project-management-pmp.

11. Details on the exams administered by the IAPP can be found at https://iapp.org/certify/cipp/.

12. Details about the Certified Information Professional designation can be found at www.aiim.org/Education-Section/CIP.

13. ARMA International. *Records and Information Management Core Competencies*, 2nd ed. (Overland Park, Kansas, 2017).

14. Vancouver Community College, "Office Administrative Certificate—Records Management Skills," accessed December 31, 2017, www.vcc.ca/programscourses/program-areas/business/office-administration-certificate---records-management-skills/.

15. San Antonio College, "Records Management (Tech Prep Program) A.A.S.," Archived Catalog, accessed December 31, 2017, http://mysaccatalog.alamo.edu/preview_program.php?catoid =72&poid=3685&returnto=1997.

16. Capella University, "Health Information Management Specialization, Bachelor of Science in Information Technology," accessed December 31, 2017, https://www.capella.edu/online-degrees/ bachelors-it-health-information-management/.

17. The SAA directory can be viewed at https://www2.archivists.org/dae.

18. University of Pittsburgh, School of Computing and Information. "Information Culture and Data Stewardship," accessed December 31, 2017, www.icds.pitt.edu/degree-programs/master-of-library -and-information-science-mlis/archives-and-information-science-pathway/.

19. School of Information, San José State University, "Master of Archives and Records Administration," accessed December 31, 2017, http://ischool.sjsu.edu/programs/master-archives -records-administration-mara.

20. The certificate information can be viewed at www.liu.edu/CWPost/Academics/Schools/CEIS/ PSLIS/Graduate-Programs/AC-ARM.aspx.

21. Western Washington University, "Archives and Records Management Certificate Program," accessed December 31, 2017, https://catalog.wwu.edu/preview_program. php?catoid=7&poid=2787&returnto=1031

22. Details of the Archives and Records Management PhD at the University of Liverpool can be found at https://www.thecompleteuniversityguide.co.uk/courses/details/10379302.

23. *Macmillan Dictionary*, s.v. "professional development," accessed December 30, 2017, https://www.macmillandictionary.com/dictionary/british/professional-development.

24. You can view the requirements at www.certifiedarchivists.org/members-area/certification -maintenance.html#petition.

25. ARMA International, Dashboard, accessed January 2, 2018, http://education.arma.org/diweb/ dashboard.

26. Details about AIIM Training are available at www.aiim.org/Education-Section/ Education-Landing-Page.

27. SAA Continuing Education webpage, https://www2.archivists.org/prof-education/ continuing-education.

28. SAA Certificate Programs, https://www2.archivists.org/prof-education/ certificate-programs.

29. ARMA International, "ARMA Recognizes Farmers Insurance with Coveted Award of Excellence," November 9, 2017, www.arma.org/news/377159/.

30. ARMA International Information Governance Maturity Model, accessed January 1, 2018, https://www.lva.virginia.gov/agencies/records/psrc/documents/Principles.pdf.

31. Western Cape Government, "Archives: Records Management Policy of WC Governmental Bodies 2017," accessed January 1, 2018, https://www.westerncape.gov.za/general-publication/ archives-records-management-policy-wc-governmental-bodies-2017.

32. Western Cape Government, "Records Management Policy of Western Cape Governmental Bodies 2017," accessed January 1, 2018, https://www.westerncape.gov.za/assets/departments/ cultural-affairs-sport/wc_records_management_policy_2017.pdf.

33. Thomson Reuters, "Compliance Learning Course Catalog," accessed January 1, 2018, https://risk.thomsonreuters.com/en/compliance-training-courses.html.

34. Microsoft, "On Demand Sessions," accessed January 1, 2018, https://myignite.microsoft.com/ videos?q=records%2520management#ignite-html-anchor.

35. National Archives and Records Administration (NARA), "Records Management Training," accessed January 1, 2018, www.archives.gov/records-mgmt/.

36. National Archives, Records Managers, "Certificate of Federal Records Management Training," accessed January 1, 2018, https://www.archives.gov/records-mgmt/training/certification.html.

37. NARA Learning Center, accessed January 1, 2018, https://nara.csod.com/LMS/BrowseTraining/BrowseTraining.aspx?tab_page_id=-6#f=1&s=588&o=1.

38. NAGARA website, https://www.thecompleteuniversityguide.co.uk/courses/details/10379302.

39. Sir Hilary Jenkinson, "Roots," *Selected Writings of Sir Hilary Jenkinson*, edited by Roger Ellis and Peter Walne (Gloucester: Alan Sutton, 1980), 372.

40. Giovanni Vittani, "La formazione dell'archivista," *Annuario del R. Archivio di Stato di Milano* 1913, reprinted in Giovanni Vittani, *Scritti di diplomatica e archivistica* (Milano: Cisalpino-Goliardica, 1974), 154.

41. Eugenio Casanova, *Archivistica* (Siena: Lazzeri, 1928), 468.

42. Giovanni Vittani, "La formazione dell'archivista," 154.

43. The description of the core courses as well as the electives mentioned later on can be found on the SLAIS website at http://slais.ubc.ca/programs/courses/course-list/.

44. Examples can be seen at http://acasymposium.slais.ubc.ca/; http://acasymposium2015.sites.olt.ubc.ca/; and http://acasymposium2016.sites.olt.ubc.ca/.

CHAPTER 14

From Records Management to Information Governance

An Evolution

INTRODUCTION

In today's world, records managers accustomed to focusing on details like completing an inventory or developing a records retention schedule are beginning to take a holistic approach to managing the records and information of their organizations. This chapter builds upon the previous thirteen chapters by illustrating how records managers can use their skills and knowledge to develop a strategic records management plan and an efficient and legally defensible records management program.

The increased awareness of the value of enterprise-wide information governance provides an opportunity for records and information managers to use their expertise and expand their sphere of influence by becoming invaluable members of the information governance team. Therefore, this chapter also provides guidance for those involved in developing and implementing an information governance strategy.

In 2009, ARMA International identified eight Generally Accepted Recordkeeping Principles (see figure 14.1) that can be used as a best-practice framework to develop both a records management program and an information governance strategy. A year later the ARMA International Maturity Model for Information Governance was devised to define the eight principles at differing levels of maturity, completeness, and effectiveness.

Diane K. Carlisle, ARMA International, will provide her perspectives on Information Governance and managing information assets based on the Principles and the Maturity Model at the end of this chapter. But first, let's turn our attention to the primary role of records management—developing an effective and legally defensible records management program.

DEVELOPING A RECORDS MANAGEMENT PROGRAM

A records management program is a governance structure that assesses risks and compliance needs to manage records and information assets across the organization. It is one component of the information governance structure and incorporates records retention schedules, disaster recovery and business continuity, training, change management, monitoring and auditing, and continuous improvement.

Whether the intent is to implement a records management program where none exists or to improve an existing program, the work involves developing a records management strategy, records management policies and procedures, and a strategic records and information management plan as shown in figure 14.2.

Records Management Strategy

A *records management strategy* is defined in a publication issued by the Public Records Office of the State of Victoria as "a high level document that provides an overview of the records management environment of an agency."[1] Their strategy is comprised of two documents:

- the records management strategy itself
- the action or implementation plan[2]

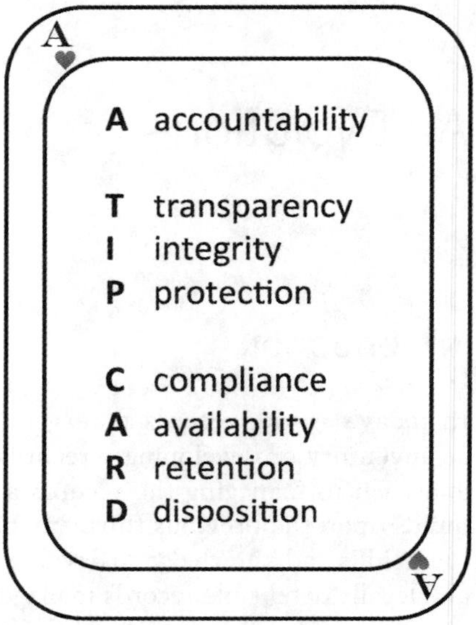

The records management strategy aligns the purpose of records management with the strategic direction of the organization and contributes to the organization's information governance strategy, if one exists. It provides a framework for all records management activities. Typical contents of a records management strategy document include an introduction, scope, aims (goals), key elements (e.g., responsibility, accountability, management, security, access, audit, training), and implementation (reference to the records management policy and plan).

FIGURE 14.1 The Mnemonic "A TIP CARD" listing the Eight Principles.

SOURCE: Adapted from ARMA TR30-2017, Implementing the Generally Accepted Recordkeeping Principles, Overland Park: Kansas, 2017.

Records Management Policies and Procedures

The records management policy provides high-level direction in the form of goals for managing records across the organization throughout their lifecycle and assigns implementation responsibilities. In writing the policy document, keep the target audience in mind. The document must be clearly written, and consequences for noncompliance should be specified. Although policies are often written in response to legal and regulatory requirements, their value to the organization lies in the guidance they provide to ensure that the work of the organization is carried out efficiently and effectively, while reducing risk and ensuring compliance.

The records management policy document may contain records management procedures in the form of guidance to units within the organization that are developing their own internal plans. These procedures can help the organization identify and organize records into specific categories (e.g., administrative records, business unit records, fiscal records, and reference documents) and subcategories (e.g., current, inactive, temporary, permanent, confidential, essential [vital] and archival) of records.

Additional topics found in a policy include high-level direction on records creation, maintenance and use, storage, disposition, disaster recovery, and training. The contents of the records management policy will depend upon the policy framework of the organization. Table 14.1 provides an outline of a records management policy (by omitting sections 7 through 12) or a records management policy and procedures document (by including sections 7 through 12).

Although some policy and procedures documents contain recommendations for the implementation of improvement plans, those recommendations are better included in the strategic plan. The strategic plan should include short-term and long-term goals that can be evaluated and updated as necessary.

Developing the Records and Information Management Strategic Plan

The strategic plan is used to develop a records management program that meets current and future needs. A needs assessment and business process analysis will provide the basis for formulating the strategic plan to improve recordkeeping practices. The plan typically covers a three- to five-year period and answers the following questions:

- What is the current state of the organization's records and information management program?
- What is the desired state?
- What steps should be taken to bridge the gap between the two?

The strategic plan provides a blueprint for constructing or improving a records and information management program, a plan to effectively manage the lifecycle of records and

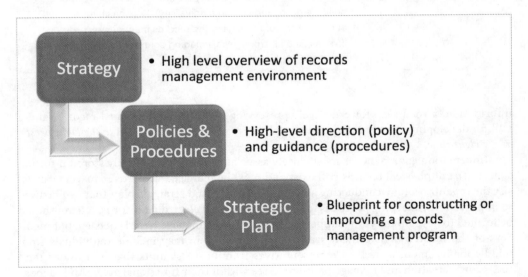

FIGURE 14.2 Essential elements of a records management program.

TABLE 14.1 Example of outline for records management policy.

Section/Title	Description
1. Purpose	The *purpose* section provides the rationale of the records management, policies, and procedures (e.g., support the core functions, comply with legal and regulatory obligations, and contribute to management effectiveness).
2. Policy Statement	The *policy statement* explains the guiding principles on which the records management practices have been established (e.g., ARMA's Generally Accepted Recordkeeping Principles).
3. Relationship with Other Policies	The *other policies* section identifies related policies for which the records manager is responsible (e.g., electronic records management policy, e-mail policy, document imaging policy, content management policy). This section also provides examples of related policies (e.g., information security policy managed by the security manager, internet usage policy managed by the IT manager, social media policy managed by the corporate communications manager).
4. Scope and Target Audience	The *scope and intended* audience section identifies the intended audience of the policy by providing a description of the work practices that are impacted by the policy (e.g., all employees involved in records creation and access).
5. Regulatory Framework	The *regulatory framework* section identifies regulations that must be complied with (e.g., U.S. 21 CFR Part 11 Electronic Records; Electronic Signatures)
6. Roles and Responsibilities	The *responsibility* section defines the title of the senior executive who has ultimate responsibility for the records management policy (e.g., the registrar in a university). Responsibility for additional senior managers, the records manager, records liaisons, and all employees including contractors and volunteers should be explained.

[CONTINUED ON FOLLOWING PAGE]

information, a road map for effectively preserving historical and archival records, and a tool for developing a system that ensures *delivery of the right information to the right person at the right time.*

Information governance is most closely associated with electronically stored information (ESI), but physical records still exist and must be managed. Records managers can assist the organization by conducting a needs assessment and strategic plan that can be used to improve recordkeeping practices for both physical and electronic records. A team should be formed to develop the plan. Support from upper-level management is needed, but members of the records management strategic planning group may include individuals from middle management as well as representatives from business units that best understand the records creation and management processes within their functional areas. An independent consultant or consulting firm may be employed to work with the team to conduct the

TABLE 14.1 [CONTINUED]

Section/Title	Description
7. Records Classification Systems and Related Storage Areas	Tip: Keep the policy short!
	Sections 7–12 can be included to create a policy and procedures document. However, the policy could instead refer the reader to a list of resources on these and related topics, perhaps available from the records manager, so that the policy is shorter and easier to update.
8. Disposal of Records	
9. Storage and Custody	
10. Access and Security	
11. Legal Admissibility and Evidential Weight (both paper and electronic)	The guidance could cover:
	1. Records creation
	2. Business classification (for filing schemes)
	3. Records Retention Schedule
12. Training	4. Records storage
	5. Records destruction
	6. Archival records selection and management
	7. External codes of practice and relevant legislation
13. Monitor and Review	The policy should assign responsibility (specific person/role) to *monitor compliance* with the policy and prepare reports.
14. Definitions	Provide *definitions* of terms that have technical meaning within the policy.
15. References	Provide all *resources* referenced in the policy or that confirm the policy.
16. Authorization (name/date)	*Authorization* is provided in a statement such as "this policy was approved by (Chief Executive Officer or Head of Governmental Body) on (date)."

needs assessment and prepare the resulting strategic plan. The program of work for the records management team, including consultants if any, includes the steps identified in figure 14.3. Each of the steps required to develop a strategic records management plan merits further explanation.

Understanding the Corporate Culture

Corporate culture can determine the success or failure of any new initiative. It is important to understand the formal structure of the organization—an organizational chart can provide this information. But it is even more important to understand the factors not included on an organizational chart such as tolerance for risk, resistance to change, relationship between performance and rewards, and individual autonomy. Records management programs are successful when records management is integrated into the corporate culture by including representatives of business units in planning meetings, soliciting support of leaders

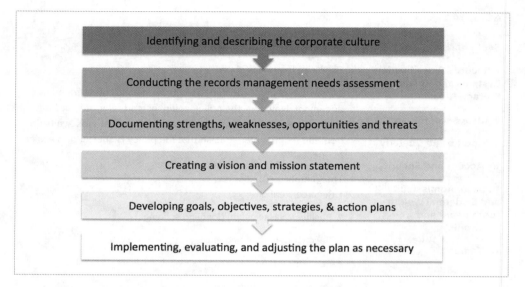

FIGURE 14.3 Developing a strategic records management plan.

to promote the program, and developing employee awareness and training programs that underscore the benefits of the proposed changes to individual employees as well as to the organization. Often the most progressive individuals (i.e., early adopters) will be easy to identify. They should be included if conducting a pilot program before implementing massive changes organization-wide. Success stories will help promote the program beyond the individuals/units involved in the pilot program.

Conducting a Needs Assessment

A needs assessment is a systematic process for determining the gap (or needs) between the current state of an organization and its desired state (wants) before developing solutions or programming. Upon completion of the needs assessment, a plan must be developed to close the gap. Because a primary goal of records management is to mitigate risks to the organization, the desired state is one in which the organization experiences a low level of risk. It is also one in which information needed to support the core mission of the organization can be located and used in a timely manner.

Needs Assessment Goals and Methodology

A needs assessment can be completed by an internal team (e.g., records management staff) or an external consulting firm. Once the team is assembled, the following actions should be taken. The first task in performing the needs assessment is defining goals, including but not limited to the following:

- Gain a thorough understanding of the current records situation across the organization (or in specified departments).
- Provide information regarding serious risks related to the current records, including the existence and location of duplicate records.

- Provide recommendations for potential areas of improvement in the existing records management program.

The second task is determining how information will be gathered. An inventory of existing records and information assets is necessary and can be conducted by a member of the team, gathered though the use of a survey, or via a combination of the two. The physical inventory and/or survey will provide statistical data related to records types and locations throughout the organization. If a survey is used, one employee from each department or functional area should complete the survey on behalf of the work unit. Someone from the records management team or consulting firm conducting the survey should be available to assist those completing it. In rare instances, it may be necessary for a team member to conduct the inventory with the department contact.

Keep in mind that employees may not provide accurate information due to their inability to accurately complete the survey or their unwillingness to highlight deficiencies in their approach to records storage. Therefore, the results of the survey should be verified by:

- physically reviewing and confirming record types, volumes, and conditions at each location;
- inspecting and reviewing the data and questioning those who completed the form about responses markedly different from the norm; and
- comparing the data across departments for consistency.

The survey of electronic assets can start with an existing *systems data map* introduced in chapter 4. The IT department should be able to provide this. A layer of data assets residing outside of the enterprise—including information residing in social media, mobile devices, and cloud storage—must be added if this has not already been done. If no data map exists, work with the IT department to develop an accurate and complete understanding of the sources and types of electronic records generated, received, and used within the organization. It's also important "to include any records retention policies, or policies focused on the purging and deletion of ESI, in your data map."[3] The system data map can be used to minimize risk presented by pending litigation by creating a defensible and repeatable discovery process for identifying potentially relevant ESI. The organization's legal department can use it to meet the minimum requirements specified in the *Federal Rules of Civil Procedure* (FRCP).[4] In addition, the data map can be used to identify records/information custodians and to locate ESI for immediate preservation in response to an e-discovery request.

As an alternative or in addition to the data provided by the IT department, vendors can assist the organization in creating a data map of an organization's ESI. One product, the Exterro E-Discovery Data Mapping application, not only enables the legal team to build and maintain an up-to-date directory of electronic files mirroring the organization's data source inventory but also provides automated maintenance of the data map through configurable process workflows. An interactive dashboard displays key information regarding data sources in a single view.[5]

The third task is conducting on-site interviews with representatives from each department or functional area to assess the organization's records management processes, needs, and facilities. During this process:

- evidence will be gathered about current records management practices,
- key business functions that involve records will be documented,

- the overall condition of each department's or functional area's records management practices will be revealed, and
- risks related to the existing records management business processes will be identified.

The fourth task involves analyzing the information gathered to:

- identify the benefits of recommended improvements and prioritize the list of recommendations, and
- prepare a records management policy and an actionable strategic plan.

Documenting Strengths, Weaknesses, Opportunities, and Threats

A SWOT analysis is a tool that can be used to identify the organization's (or unit's) strengths and weaknesses (internal factors), as well as opportunities and threats (external factors). Developed in the 1960s from research conducted at the Stanford Research Institute (SRI), it is still a useful tool that can help the records management team or consultant(s) determine what actions must be taken to mitigate weaknesses and risks and to take advantage of strengths and opportunities (see figure 14.4).[6]

Information gathered from the analysis of the internal and external environment related to records and information management can reveal the types of strengths, weaknesses, opportunities, and threats shown in table 14.2. Internally, the following types of factors should be analyzed:

- recordkeeping systems
- recordkeeping accountability

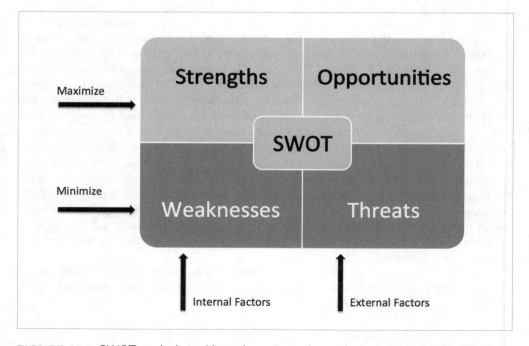

FIGURE 14.4 SWOT analysis tool based on research conducted at SRI International.

- recordkeeping culture
- recordkeeping processes

Externally, the following types of events should be monitored:

- emerging technologies
- proposed laws and regulations
- court rulings related to records and information management

Not all of these factors will present the same level of risks for every organization. Refer to the risk assessment matrix in (figure 9.3) for guidance in determining the level of risk presented to the organization by each factor identified.

Creating Records Management Vision and Mission Statements

Vision statements are common to all organizations, and entities below the top tier often develop their own vision statements as well. If so, these must fit under the overarching organizational vision statement, but their main purpose is to describe the entity's commitment to improved records management and the broad objective to be achieved. The vision statement will describe how the records management program will look. It can be used to provide direction for strategic and operational decision-making. The vision statement of the Office of Records Management at Florida Golf Coast University, for example, reads:

> The Office of Records Management will assist FGCU departments to comply with University, state and federal records management practices.[7]

TABLE 14.2 Factors that may be discovered as a result of a SWOT analysis.

INTERNAL FACTORS	EXTERNAL FACTORS
Strengths - Well-educated and –trained records management staff - Well-managed organization-run records center for paper records - Corporate interest in having a sound records management program to support business operations as well as to meet legal and regulatory obligations	**Opportunities** - Impetus of related legislation (e.g., FOIA, SOX, in the US and the EU's GDPR) can drive awareness and standards for records management. - Cloud computing options (e.g., Gmail) can relieve burden on in-house technical support. - Information governance initiatives put records management in the spotlight.
Weaknesses - Resistance by operations staff to managing electronic records - Lack of integration between electronic and paper records management - Inadequate funding to implement electronic records solutions	**Threats** - Use of emerging technologies and mobile devices adds a layer of complexity to records creation and capture. - Changes in terms of service agreements by social media providers make it more challenging to control records posted to external sites. - Use of collaborative worksites can create silos of information that must be managed.

Mission statements identify the mission within the context of realistic goals. The records management mission statement of the Office of Records Management at FGCU is specific to the core mission of the department:

> The mission of the Office of Records Management is to develop, evaluate, and implement a records management program that promotes university-wide participation and accountability, in efforts to achieve compliance with Florida State Statutes, University Regulations and Policies, and contribute to the preservation and advancement of Florida Gulf Coast University.[8]

The records management program of FGCU is comprehensive in that it is responsible for inventory, content management, filing and storage, retention, public records requests, destruction, discovery/litigation, and vital (essential) records.[9]

Developing Strategies, Goals, Objectives, and Action Plans

A *strategy* is designed to help you achieve your vision and mission. It is developed after the needs assessment, including SWOT analysis, has been completed. The strategic plan may have several strategies, all supporting the vision and mission of the records management program. The *goals* provide additional details about what must be accomplished in order to achieve the vision, mission, and strategy identified. The factors revealed by conducting the SWOT analysis can be the basis for developing *SMART* (specific, measurable, achievable, relevant, and time-bound) *objectives*.[10] The objectives should focus on the strategic and not the operational level. The strategies should aim to exploit strengths and opportunities, minimize or neutralize threats, and avoid or remove weaknesses. Once the strategic plan has been completed, develop an *operational* or *action plan* to identify the tasks that will help the organization achieve the goals specified in the strategic plan. Two types of action plans are needed:

- A high-level action plan to show how each goal will be achieved. You may include this as part of the *strategic plan*.
- Individual action plans for each service the program delivers (e.g., scanning, records center, electronic records management). The action plan on this level is often referred to as the individual unit's *operational plan*. It must designate the task, responsible party, expected results, and completion date.

An alternative to the SWOT analysis proposed by some is SOAR: strengths, opportunities, aspirations and results.[11] This forward-looking approach is suggested as a means to inspire innovation. Aspirational questions are asked, such as "Who do we want to be? What does our desired future look like?" The results component involves asking, "What measurable results do we want to achieve?" However, rather than dismissing the notion of identifying weaknesses and threats, I recommend using both tools. The SWOT analysis will provide a realistic view for the organization at this point in time, and the SOAR tool will provide an aspirational view for the future.

Implementing, Evaluating, and Adjusting the Strategic Plan

Organizations that wish to establish a records management program where none exists should start with the appointment of a records manager charged with the authority and responsibility for establishing and maintaining the records management program. The procedures for establishing the entire program involve conducting all of the activities covered in earlier chapters, including:

- developing policies and procedures,
- conducting a records inventory,
- creating a records retention and disposition schedule,
- preparing a records classification schedule, and
- developing an inactive records program.

Organizations that wish to improve an existing records management program can begin by relying on the expertise of a records manager and/or records consultant to conduct a needs assessment and develop a strategic plan. Depending on the scope of the goals and strategic initiatives and the culture of the organization, implementation may take place enterprise-wide (e.g., moving all email to a cloud email provider) or within one or more functional areas, adding users after success is demonstrated on a smaller scale (e.g., SharePoint implementation). The SMART goals identified for the strategic plan can be used to evaluate progress by comparing them with the results of the tasks listed in the action plan.

When the terms *monitoring* and *evaluating* are used in this context, they refer to monitoring and evaluating the *planning activities* and the *implementation of the plan,* not the records and information management program. The purpose of monitoring and evaluating is to ensure that the plan is being followed or that deviations from the plan are based on sound rationale. The plan must be updated to reflect the new direction that results from deviations from the initial plan.

As you learned in chapter 9, monitoring and evaluating is a matter of answering questions related to the plan being implemented. Questions might include:

- Are the goals and objectives being achieved? If not, are they still realistic?
- Are they being achieved on time? If not, should the schedule be changed?
- Are adequate resources (e.g., people, money, training, equipment) allocated to achieve the goals?

The strategic plan must identify the party responsible for implementation, as well as the parties responsible for each goal and objective. Someone must also be identified to monitor the status of the implementation, including progress toward each strategic goal. Status reports should include trends regarding the progress toward goals and objectives as well as answers to questions similar to those listed previously.

The reporting structure must be in place—from the bottom up. Those with the responsibility to carry out tasks within the action plan will report to those responsible for the high-level action plan, who in turn will report to those responsible for each of the strategic initiatives (goals and objectives assigned to them). These individuals might be expected to submit a report to the chief executive in charge of implementation.

Because a records management program provides an overarching governance structure designed to manage records and information assets across the organization, some contend that records management has always been responsible for information governance. But others will argue that records management is one subset of information governance. Both statements are correct. Recordkeepers intimately familiar with developing records management programs can play an important role in their organization's information governance initiatives.

The next section provides an overview of the steps to be taken to formulate an information governance strategy. As you review the material, identify with one or more of the stakeholders to understand how this role fits within the overarching information governance structure.

IMPLEMENTING AN INFORMATION GOVERNANCE STRATEGY

Information governance is a high-level, strategic function that involves stakeholders from across the organization, each with their own expertise and responsibilities. The realization that an information governance strategy is necessary is often the result of the dramatic changes that have taken place due to the growth of electronic records, especially unstructured records; an increased emphasis on e-discovery; and the lack of sufficient controls over all electronically stored information (ESI). As shown in figure 14.5, information governance must address a number of issues, only one of which is records lifecycle management. With the implementation of information governance, two main goals of a records management program—legal compliance and defensible disposal—become a shared responsibility with stakeholders from across the organization. Before an information governance strategy can be developed, it is necessary to understand how the responsibilities of the stakeholders are intertwined.

Information Governance Reference Model

To understand the dependencies of various stakeholders, we can look to the Information Governance Reference Model (IGRM) developed to provide a point of reference to promote cross-functional dialogue and collaboration.[12] The model shown in figure 14.6 is different from other models we've studied so far in that it is a *responsibility model* and not a lifecycle model. The stakeholders identified in this model (i.e., *Business, Privacy/Security, IT, RIM,* and *Legal*) may not match those assuming key roles in your information governance strategy. For example, *Privacy and Security* may be a part of *IT*, and *Compliance* and *Risk Management* may be additional segments apart from *Legal*.

A good place to start when using this model is with the information at its center, then branch out to see which stakeholders are involved. Each segment of figure 14.6—*Business, Privacy and Security, Information Technology, Records and Information Management,* and *Legal*—could be explained as follows:

- Information has value to business units that, in the private sector, strive to make a profit. Information is created and used as part of normal business operations.
- Business units look to IT to help them manage their information assets. Efficiency is the goal of IT.
- Privacy and Security is a new segment in version 3.0 of the IGRM model. The model still recognizes that assets must be "stored" and "secured." However, because of the concern over privacy and security issues, privacy and security are now included on the model as an additional stakeholder along with Business, Legal, RIM, and IT.

- Records and information management is responsible for ensuring that regulatory obligations for information are met. Records management can assist both business units and IT with guidance related to retention, disposition, and preservation requirements in order to reduce risk.
- Legal also plays a role in mitigating risk. Legal notifies both Records Management and IT in the event of a potential lawsuit, defines what to put on hold and collect for e-discovery, and informs Records management and IT when a hold should be lifted.

This reference model illustrates a unified governance approach built on cooperation, collaboration, and transparency among the parties involved in creating and managing information. This reference model should be referred to when formulating the information governance strategy.

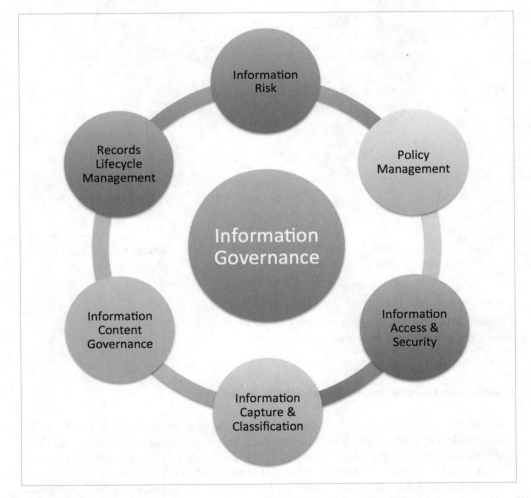

FIGURE 14.5 Information governance components based on the Information Governance Maturity Model matrix by EMC[2].

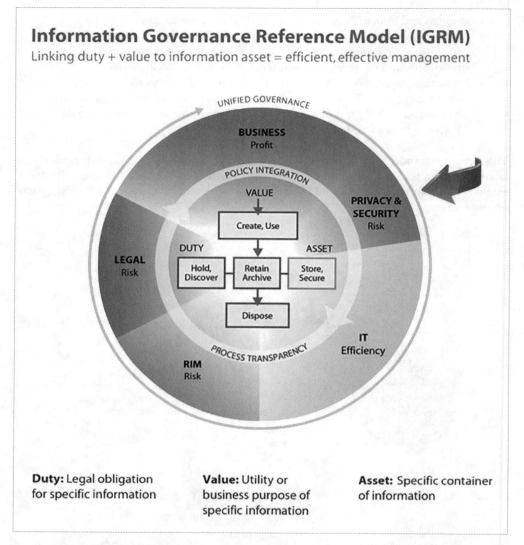

FIGURE 14.6 Information Governance Reference Model.

SOURCE: "EDRM (Electronic Discovery Reference Model," Duke Law,
www.edrm.net/wp-content/uploads/2012/10/IGRM_v3.0.png.

Information Governance Roles and Responsibilities

The Information Governance Reference Model helps us understand what can be called "functional stakeholders" and their information management responsibilities: IT, Business Units, Privacy and Security, Records Management, and Legal. But they are not the only individuals with information governance roles and responsibilities. The number of individuals involved in information governance and the roles and responsibilities they assume depends on the size and type of organization. The corporate governance structure, for example, differs from the government governance structure.

Corporate Governance

Corporate governance is the responsibility of the firm's board of directors, which has a myriad of duties including hiring, supervising, and replacing the chief executive officer; approving major strategic decisions; making decisions about mergers and acquisitions; and overseeing financial reporting and audits. The members of the board of directors are elected by the shareholders and, as a consequence of the Sarbanes-Oxley Act of 2002 (SOX), have a primary fiduciary duty to the shareholders and a secondary duty to the corporation.[13] SOX has made it riskier for members of the board to serve, and therefore costlier for the organization to compensate board members.[14]

Government Governance

Governance in the public sector focuses on a budget that reflects policy decisions and proposals. Just as corporations are required to release financial reports, governments are expected to provide an account of their actions to their primary stakeholders, the public. Accountability is vital and must be supported by adequate management, supervision, and control. This *government governance* premise is the basis for transparency and openness initiatives at all levels of government in order to promote accountability and an informed citizenry.

In reflecting on the descriptions of corporate and government governance, it is apparent that records and information are the assets that, when shared with stakeholders, demonstrate accountability. Members of the organization at all levels carry out their responsibilities within the environment created at the top level of public or private organizations. Individuals holding positions at the top level of the management hierarchy are often referred to as C-level managers.

Governance and C-level Management

C-level is an adjective used to describe high-ranking executive titles within an organization. Within this context, *C* stands for *chief.* Records management departments and responsibilities may be placed under the purview of any one of several C-level managers (e.g., chief information officer, chief knowledge officer, or chief compliance officer). But the 2010 appointment of Paul M. Wester Jr. as the National Archives and Records Administration's first chief records officer brought attention to the growing trend of recognizing records management as a C-level function. This ensures that records management responsibilities are considered when making strategic decisions that involve all levels and functional areas of the organization.

In his 2018 book *Infonomics,* Douglas B. Laney of Gartner Inc. makes the case for an emerging C-level position that deserves serious attention: *Chief Data Officer* (CDO). The CDO is responsible for improving the efficient and value-generating capacity of their organization's information ecosystem (the data—not the technology). This includes the following type of data:

- **Operational Data:** Examples include log data, smart meters, security camera feeds.
- **Dark Data:** Examples include information collected during the course of business but not accessible or structured for analysis, such as emails, multimedia, and intellectual property.

- **Commercial Data:** Examples include data gathered by data aggregators such as Equifax, which can include credit ratings, real estate holdings, and contact information.
- **Public Data:** Examples include census data and economic data.
- **Social Media Data:** Examples include tweets gathered by the US Center for Disease Control.
- **Web Content:** Examples include content scraped from the websites of competitors or partners.[15]

Information Governance Steering Committee

Regardless of the number and variety of C-level positions, a board of directors will benefit from the formation of an information governance steering committee to develop a strategic information governance plan and to provide:

- advice on the organization's information management strategy with regard to quality and integrity, safety and security, and appropriate access and use of records and information assets; and
- assurance in relation to processes for creating, collecting, storing, disseminating, sharing, using, and disposing of information.

Assurance includes the practice of managing information-related risks known as *information assurance* (IA). IA strives to protect and defend information systems by ensuring confidentiality, integrity, authentication, availability, and nonrepudiation, whether the information is in storage, processing, or transit. The charge of some information governance steering committees also includes prioritizing the deployment of resources supporting information management. The information governance steering committee provides a vehicle to bring together representatives from legal, compliance, IT, information security, records management, business units, and other functional areas to create strategies, policies, and procedures related to the distribution of information both inside and outside of the organization.

An organization may appoint an information governance manager to perform such duties as developing and implementing information governance initiatives (legal and regulatory compliance, security, and data integrity and quality), producing the annual improvement plan, providing operational support, and preparing routine performance reports. Committee members fill specific roles for which they are accountable. An example of possible roles and responsibilities is shown in table 14.3.

Formulating an Information Governance Strategy

A review of a number of information governance strategy documents reveals a structure that includes at a minimum an introduction, scope statement, and conclusion; however, the sections illustrated in table 14.4 are the most common. Notice that the purpose statement shown provides the context for the information governance plan, and the scope statement refers to the information governance policy, needs assessment, and annual action (improvement) plan.

TABLE 14.3 Partial example of information governance committee membership.

ROLE	RESPONSIBILITY OF	RESPONSIBLE FOR
Accountable officer	Chief executive officer	Information governance across the organization
Information governance lead	Information governance manager	Accessing, monitoring, and reporting compliance with information governance
Information security officer	Senior IT security specialist	Ensuring compliance with information security standards (ISO/IEC 27000 family of standards)
Data protection and freedom of information lead	Information governance manager	Accessing and monitoring compliance with data protection and freedom of information legislative requirements
Records management lead	Chief records officer	Providing advice on and monitoring compliance with laws, regulations, and best practices in records management

Information Governance Plan

The IG plan is a required component of the IG strategy that should be brief but concise. It provides the actions to be taken and could be in the form of a list with dates each task is accomplished; such tasks include:

- Assign information governance roles and responsibilities and identify an information governance lead.
- Approve information governance policy or policies. Information governance policies can include not only the IG policy and strategy itself but also a records management policy and strategy, information security policy, and confidentiality policy. It may also refer to additional governing policies, such as the email and internet policy, mobile computing procedures, and risk management strategy.
- Approve an information governance improvement plan. The plan may address new business processes that reflect policies, performance measurements, change management, lifecycle management, legal issues, physical records, and access control.

Information Governance Strategic Policy

The second important component of the information governance strategy is the information governance policy. The policy will provide further details that were not included in the plan. The outline of the IG policy may resemble the one presented in table 14.5. The IG policy includes sections that provide guidance for those implementing the IG plan, including foundational principles, governing legislation, and best practices.

TABLE 14.4 Information governance strategy: One example.

Section/Title	Description
1. Introduction	An *introduction* asserts the value of information as a vital asset and the importance of ensuring that it is efficiently managed. Information governance is established in the introduction as the framework for information management.
2. Purpose Statement	A *purpose statement* provides the context for the information governance plan in relation to other organizational strategies, such as risk management service planning and business management.
3. Scope Statement	The *scope statement* clearly states the components of the strategy, such as an information governance policy and an annual action (improvement) plan derived from comparing the needs assessment against standards set for the information governance program.
4. Goals Section	A *goals section* explains the overarching goals of information governance and the goal of the strategic plan, which is to ensure effective information governance. Methods to achieve effective information governance are provided, such as complying with all legislation and minimizing inappropriate uses of personal data.
5. Strategic Objectives	*Strategic objectives* for a specific period of time (e.g., 2018–2022) are included in the goals section or immediately following it. The objectives would provide the requirements and plan of action, monitoring and assessment methods, identification of lead (position within organization, not an individual's name), and target date for completion.
6. Key Strategic Areas	A *key strategic areas* section explains the role of the Information Governance Steering Committee and any sub-groups, such as information governance project teams.
7. Responsibilities	A *responsibilities section* clarifies individual responsibilities, such as for the Information Governance Manager, senior managers, line managers, and all employees.
8. Conclusion	A *conclusion* reinforces the importance of the information governance strategy, information governance policy, and information governance action plans to ensure that information is managed effectively and risk is reduced.

Technology Strategy

For effective unified governance, an information governance strategy must include a technology strategy. The technology strategy will be broad, because it will cover centralized IT services (e.g., email, storage) as well as business unit-specific software solutions (e.g.,

TABLE 14.5 Information governance strategic policy: One example.

Section/Component	Description
1. Introduction	The *introduction* provides the rationale for the policy, including the place of information governance within the overall governance structure, the information governance initiatives in place (e.g., confidentiality and data protection assurance, information governance management, corporate information assurance), and the benefits of information governance (IG) to the organization, its employees, and its clients.
2. Policy Statement	The *policy statement* outlines the objectives of the IG strategic policy (e.g., confidentiality, integrity, availability, and quality), and the aims (goals) of the policy.
3. Principles	The information governance policy is predicated on *foundational principles* that are then reflected in the information governance initiatives (e.g., openness, information security assurance, information management, confidentiality and data protection assurance, corporate information insurance).
4. Legislation	Organizations are required to comply with the *governing legislation* of the countries and industries in which they operate. Examples of legislation from the United States are the Federal Rules of Civil Procedure; Freedom of Information Act; Sarbanes-Oxley Act; and Health Information Portability and Accountability Act. Examples from the United Kingdom include the Data Protection Act; the Copyright, Designs and Patents Act; the Health and Social Care Act; and the Freedom of Information Act. The far-reaching EU standard is the General Data Protection Regulation.
5. Best Practices	*Best practices* for information governance can be identified by industry (e.g., healthcare), job function (e.g., records management), across industries (e.g., maturity assessments and business cases), and based on specific applications and software tools that facilitate information governance (e.g., SharePoint). Best practices are also found in published standards; for example, the use of the ISO 27000 family of standards is considered an international best practice for information security management systems. Internal best practices can be identified by collecting and analyzing data across the enterprise and then establishing a baseline for performance (e.g., time to locate records in response to an e-Discovery or FOIA request).

[CONTINUED ON FOLLOWING PAGE]

purchasing, payroll). It will cover in-house systems as well as systems residing in the cloud, both corporate-owned and provided by third parties. Enabling technology should include:

- Machine learning or artificial intelligence to classify content, separate active versus inactive content, and take action on content such as disposition of expired content;

TABLE 14.5 [CONTINUED]

Section/Component	Description
6. Improvement Plan and Assessment	The success of the information governance initiatives must be assessed in order to identify areas needing improvement. An *annual assessment* should be conducted and an *action plan* developed to address areas of concern during the upcoming year. This information would be presented to the Information Governance Steering Committee, which would then prepare a report for the Information Governance Board.
7. Auditing and Monitoring Criteria	The policy would describe the *auditing and monitoring requirements* (e.g., compliance with the information governance policy), explain the method (e.g., annual assessments and action plan), and assign responsibility (e.g., the Information Governance Steering Committee).
8. Implementation and Dissemination	This section would state how the policy document is *disseminated*. *Implementation strategy* would be shared. For example, the policy could be posted to the internet or intranet or a collaborative workspace (e.g., SharePoint). The effective date for implementation would be specified.
9. Responsibility for Document	*Overall responsibility* for the document would rest with the Information Governance Steering Committee
10. Attachments/ Appendices	A variety of *attachments and appendices* might be included; for example, a list of related policies and procedures such as a data protection policy, email policy, mobile computing policy, social media policy, and records retention policy.

- Backup technology for recovery from system failure and data loss, and archiving technology to manage inactive content no longer used in daily operations—including web-based and social media content;
- Records management capabilities that help manage high volume content, allow storage outside of the production system, and impose event-based and time-based retention on content, including litigation holds; and
- Legal case management and e-discovery features that allow the creation of processes for responding to e-discovery and other legal searches across a number of repositories.

Another component of the IG policy is an annual assessment to identify areas needing improvement and an improvement plan to make the necessary changes.

Assessment Tools and Services

Tools and services are available to help the information governance steering committee identify areas for improvement. These tools measure the level with which the organization complies with established norms for information governance. They may be general in nature and applicable to any industry or industry-specific.

Information Governance Assessment, ARMA International: An Example

Many organizations adhere to ARMA International's eight Principles and strive to improve their records management and information governance programs using the Information Governance Maturity Model. They can take the next step and assess their program's maturity level using ARMA International's Information Governance Assessment software platform, which will help them identify risks, measure severity, track deficiencies, monitor progress, and assess the sufficiency.[16]

Information Governance Self-Assessment Tool, Health Information, and Quality Authority: An Example

The Health Information and Quality Authority is an independent authority to improve healthcare and social services in Ireland. It provides a number of self-assessment tools for this industry including the Information Governance Self-Assessment Tool that is designed to identify areas where immediate action or improvement is needed.[17] Two levels of assessment can be conducted: (1) minimum/basic requirements primarily based on governing legislation, and (2) more advanced requirements all organizations should strive to meet. The goal for the organization is to eventually answer "yes" to all questions in both sections. Examples of questions in each section are provided in table 14.6.

An increasing number of large enterprises and government agencies are investing in information governance programs. Smaller organizations may not have the capacity to develop a full-blown information governance program as outlined in this chapter. However, they must also take steps to manage their records and information in a way that supports the core mission of the business and complies with existing laws and regulations.

Certified Information Governance Professional

Continuous learning is expected of individuals involved in any profession, and the recordkeeping profession is no exception. As illustrated in figure 14.7, over the years records professionals have transitioned from managing only physical records to managing both physical and electronic records to serving as vital members of the team responsible for managing all the information of the organization.

In 2013, ARMA International introduced the Information Governance Professional (IGP) certification, which recognizes the efforts of professionals who possess the knowledge, skills, and abilities to perform competently as an IG professional.[18] This certification was developed according to *ISO/IEC 17024:2012 Conformity Assessment—General Requirements for Bodies Operating Certification of Persons* and complements the CRM. Individuals who meet the eligibility requirements for education and experience must pass a 140-question, multiple-choice exam to earn the IGP certification. Check the ARMA International website at arma.org for details.

TABLE 14.6 Examples of questions from the Health Information and Quality Authority Information Governance Self-Assessment Tool.

SELF-ASSESSMENT LEVEL 1, BASIC	
	Is there an overarching information governance framework/policy for the organization?
	Does a confidentiality agreement form part of all contracts of employment including third-party contracts?
	Is access to personal health information restricted to those who need to access it?
	Are all portable electronic devices that are capable of handling or displaying personal health information and databases password protected and encrypted?
SELF-ASSESSMENT LEVEL 2, ADVANCED	
	Is information governance a standard agenda item for discussion at senior management meetings?
	Is compliance with information governance policies/procedures monitored or audited regularly?
	Are records audited for quality and accuracy?
	Is there an information governance breach management action plan in place?
	Is there ongoing/refresher training provided to staff?
	Is information governance a standard agenda item for discussion at senior management meetings?

SOURCE: https://www.hiqa.ie/sites/default/files/2017-01/IG-Self-Assessment-Form.pdf.

SUMMARY

In this chapter, you learned how the information covered in previous chapters could be used to design both a records management program and an information governance strategy.

According to ISO 15489-1:2016, *records management* is the "field of management responsible for the efficient and systematic control of the creation, receipt, maintenance, use, and disposition of records, including processes for capturing and maintaining evidence of and information about business activities and transactions in the form of records."[19]

The emphasis is on control of information that is considered to be records. To records managers, records are media neutral, and records no longer of use to the organization must be disposed of.

Information management, according to AIIM, includes both physical and electronic information that must be managed throughout the information lifecycle for delivery through multiple channels. AIIM further explains that information is resident in line of business applications such as the following: enterprise content management (ECM), electronic records management (ERM), business process management (BPM), taxonomy and metadata, knowledge management (KM), web content management (WCM), document management (DM) and social media governance technology solutions and best practices.[20] But the value comes from the *use* of information (which can be the domain of the CDO) rather than the control of information (traditionally the domain of the CTO). Employees are accountable to "capture, manage, store, share, preserve and deliver information."[21]

A few of the benefits of Information governance are:

- reduced risk;
- improved e-discovery preparedness;
- increased transparency, trust, and reputation; and
- reduced product and information cycle times as the result of improved information flows.

The emphasis is on actions to be taken to bring about a desired state. Information governance focuses on both *control and use* of information considered a valuable asset to the organization.

Information governance does not replace either records or information management but recognizes the value of both for the benefit of the organization. In 2009, ARMA International brought attention to the principles of recordkeeping that form the basis for effective records management programs by publishing eight Generally Accepted Recordkeeping Principles that identify the critical hallmarks of information governance. Shortly afterward, the Information Governance Maturity Model was released to paint a more complete picture of what information governance looks like. For each of the eight principles, various characteristics were identified and used to rank the status of current recordkeeping programs.[22]

As promised earlier, Diane Carlisle, CRM, Director of Professional Development for ARMA International, will provide her perspective on information governance and managing information assets.

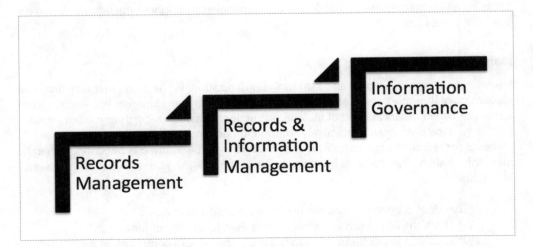

FIGURE 14.7 The evolution from records management to information governance.

Perspectives on Information Governance and Managing Information Assets

Diane K. Carlisle
CRM, Information Governance Program Advisor, ARMA International

Introduction

Information assets are the lifeblood of an organization's business activity. It is only through the information an organization records in the normal course of business that it can know what it has done and effectively plan for the future. Few would argue that organizations are *not* dependent on their information.

However, the past several years have seen some significant shifts in how organizations create, organize, secure, use, and maintain their information assets. We have seen an upward trajectory in volumes of information to be managed, complexity in the laws, statutes, and regulations that mandate specific requirements for information, and rapidly changing technology. Despite these changes, organizational information must still be governed in ways that effectively support the organization's activities, including:

1. Facilitating and sustaining day-to-day operations
2. Supporting predictive activities such as budgeting and planning
3. Assisting in answering questions about past decisions and activities
4. Demonstrating and documenting compliance with applicable laws, regulations, and standards

Shifting Requirements, Tools, and Perspectives

Shifts in requirements have resulted in new perspectives throughout the information management profession.

Manage Information Assets

Information is now viewed as an asset to the organization, in the same that way financial resources, real property, and employee talent are assets. Therefore, we see a shift to the term *information assets* instead of making distinctions between records and information.

To manage such assets effectively, information governance professionals must compete for resources and support in the management hierarchy. It is becoming easier to meet this challenge as we have better answers to the following questions than we've had in the past.

- What does a good information governance program look like?
- What are the key information issues and risks facing my organization?
- What solutions will bring value to the organization and contribute to its overall success?

- What level of resources is required to implement the solution?
- What benchmarks and measures will demonstrate the impact of my program on the organization?
- How can I ensure that my records management program is sustainable over time?

Information professionals are becoming more intentional about fitting their professional knowledge into the context of the organizations they serve. The goals have broadened to use information assets to facilitate the organization's success in its core mission, in addition to ensuring compliance with external and internal requirements.

Information Governance Requires Collaboration

The term *information governance* is quite common, but the definitions are many and varied. ARMA International emphasizes the cross-disciplinary nature of information governance in its *Glossary of Records and Information Management Terms*, 5th ed., 2016 (TR22–2016):

> A strategic, cross-disciplinary framework composed of standards, processes, roles, and metrics that hold organizations and individuals accountable for the proper handling of records and information. The framework helps organizations achieve business objectives, facilitates compliance with external requirements, and minimizes risk posed by sub-standard information-handling practices. [Note: Records and information management (RIM) is an essential building block of an information governance program. RIM policies and procedures are operational enablers that lead to effective information governance.]

To achieve effective information governance, the requirements from a broad range of laws, regulations, litigation needs, privacy requirements, business operating requirements, and protecting information integrity must be viewed from a strategic perspective. Many of these requirements will be at odds with one another and resolving them requires input from all the affected stakeholder groups.

These relationships are represented in figure 14.8. At the center are the records and information management standards and principles that information professionals have espoused for years. These standards and principles are still relevant today. The large gears around the perimeter show the various segments in the organization that create or use information and have a vested interest in how it is handled. Their key contribution is listed inside the gear (e.g., "Business Units—Define use of information assets"). The outermost tier represents the value or outputs the segment is primarily involved with. Although each of the larger gears has professionals who can do a deep dive into that segment, the Information Governance Professional (IGP) is critical to ensure that the overall governance of the information is coordinated and strategic. This coordination maximizes the value of the information assets and mitigates risks that arise from poorly managed information.

A Framework for Information Governance

In 2009, ARMA International released a comprehensive and authoritative resource for information professionals to use in creating effective and efficient information governance programs. The resource has two key elements: The Generally Accepted Recordkeeping

Principles (the Principles) and the Information Governance Maturity Model. These resources were updated in 2016 and combined into an ANSI/ARMA Technical Report available through the ARMA online bookstore (www.arma.org/bookstore).

The Principles

The eight principles (see sidebar) identify the critical hallmarks of effective information governance. They form the framework within which records professionals can design processes and roles, use existing standards and guidelines to ensure that processes are efficient, and create and monitor metrics to ensure the program is an effective contributor to organizational goals.

The principles set forth the characteristics of an effective information governance program, while allowing flexibility based upon the unique circumstances of an organization's size, sophistication, legal environment, or resources. Applying the principles should yield a responsive, effective, and legally compliant recordkeeping system.

FIGURE 14.8 Core Concepts of Information Governance.

SOURCE: ARMA International, 2017.

Generally Accepted Recordkeeping Principles

Principle of Accountability

A senior executive (or a person of comparable authority) shall oversee the information governance program and delegate responsibility for information management to appropriate individuals.

Principle of Integrity

An information governance program shall be constructed so the information assets generated by or managed for the organization have a reasonable guarantee of authenticity and reliability.

Principle of Protection

An information governance program shall be constructed to ensure an appropriate level of protection to information assets that are private, confidential, privileged, secret, classified, essential to business continuity, or that otherwise require protection.

Principle of Compliance

An information governance program shall be constructed to comply with applicable laws, other binding authorities, and the organization's policies.

Principle of Availability

An organization shall maintain its information assets in a manner that ensures their timely, efficient, and accurate retrieval.

Principle of Retention

An organization shall maintain its information assets for an appropriate time, taking into account its legal, regulatory, fiscal, operational, and historical requirements.

Principle of Disposition

An organization shall provide secure and appropriate disposition for information assets no longer required to be maintained, in compliance with applicable laws and the organization's policies.

Principle of Transparency

An organization's business processes and activities, including its information governance program, shall be documented in an open and verifiable manner, and that documentation shall be available to all personnel and appropriate, interested parties.

The complementary Information Governance Maturity Model (Maturity Model) provides metrics by which the effectiveness of and compliance with the records and information management program can be measured.

The Maturity Model

The Information Governance Maturity Model (Maturity Model) paints a more complete picture of what effective information governance looks like. See excerpt in figure 14.9.

The complete Maturity Model defines characteristics for each of the five levels in the model:

- *Level 1 (Substandard):* This level describes an environment where recordkeeping concerns are either not addressed at all, are addressed minimally, or are addressed in a sporadic manner. These organizations should be concerned that their programs will not meet legal or regulatory requirements and may not effectively serve their business needs.
- *Level 2 (In Development):* This level describes an environment where there is a developing recognition that information governance has an impact on the organization, and that the organization may benefit from a more defined information governance program. The organization is still vulnerable to legal or regulatory scrutiny because practices are ill-defined, incomplete, nascent, or marginally effective.
- *Level 3 (Essential):* This level describes the essential or minimum requirements that must be addressed in order to meet the organization's

THE PRINCIPLE	LEVEL 1 (Substandard)	LEVEL 2 (In Development)
Accountability **A senior executive (or a person of comparable authority) shall oversee the information governance program and delegate responsibility for information management to appropriate individuals.**	No senior executive (or person of comparable authority) is aware of the need to manage records and other information assets. The information manager role is largely nonexistent, or it is an administrative or clerical role distributed among general staff. Employees are not made aware of their responsibilities for managing the information assets they create or receive. Information assets are managed inconsistently or not at all.	A senior executive (or person of comparable authority) is aware of the need to manage information assets but is not actively engaged in coordinating with individual departments. The information manager role is recognized, but the person in that role is responsible only for tactical operation of the information management program, which is concerned primarily with managing specific records rather than all information assets. The information management program primarily covers only paper records. The information technology function or department is the *de facto* lead for storing electronic information, and the information manager is not involved in discussions about electronic systems; information assets are not stored in a systematic fashion. Only those employees with direct information management program responsibilities receive training about managing information assets, but that training is limited to their program responsibilities.

FIGURE 14.9 Excerpt from *Information Governance Maturity Model.*

SOURCE: ARMA International, 2017.

legal, regulatory, and business requirements. Level 3 is characterized by defined policies and procedures, and more specific decisions taken to improve information governance.

- *Level 4 (Proactive):* This level describes an organization-wide, proactive information governance program with mechanisms for continuous improvement. Information governance issues and considerations are routinized and integrated into business decisions.
- *Level 5 (Transformational):* This level describes an organization that has integrated information governance into its infrastructure and business processes such that compliance with the program requirements is routine. These organizations have recognized that effective information governance plays a critical role in cost containment, competitive advantage, and client service.

The most comprehensive versions of both the Principles and the Information Governance Maturity Model are combined in the publication Implementing the Generally Accepted Recordkeeping Principles (ARMA International TR 30-2017), newly available from ARMA International's online bookstore (https://www.arma.org/store/ViewProduct.aspx?id=1048 2978).

Information Governance Professional Qualifications

Figure 14.8 refers to an information governance professional who is key to coordinating the various business needs and conflicting requirements from a strategic perspective. The Information Governance Professional (IGP) Certification provides a means for information professionals to demonstrate they have the skills necessary to coordinate with all of the interest areas and understand each segment sufficiently to resolve conflicts between them. A person holding the IGP credential may come from any of the critical segments of information governance and will rely on professionals in each segment to implement the program throughout an organization.

Why should information professionals consider this certification? As stated by an ARMA International Board member:

> Information governance is more important and more complex than ever. By earning the IGP credential, information professionals demonstrate that they have the fundamental knowledge and skills to lead their organization in adopting and implementing IG.

This certification will set you apart as one who has the strategic perspective and skills required to enhance the value of the organization's information assets, to minimize the risk posed by poorly managed information, and to do so in a cost-effective manner.

More information about IGP Certification is available at www.arma.org/page/Certifi cations.

Summary

Effective information governance serves the interests of the organization's management, legislators and regulators, and information professionals. They, along with the Maturity Model and a variety of assessment tools available from ARMA International, will help records professionals establish the need for and develop programs that serve their organization's business, compliance, and operational needs.

These tools provide a variety of types of support—from diagnosing an organization's challenges and risk areas to prioritizing its improvement initiatives, gathering support and resources from various other interested internal stakeholders, and ensuring that routine measurements of programs contribute to the long-term sustainability of its information governance program.

NOTES

1. Public Record Office of Victoria, State of Victoria, *Guideline: Records Management Strategy, Version Number 2.0*, July 19, 2015, 6, https://www.prov.vic.gov.au/sites/default/files/2017-01/PROS1010-G5-v2.0.pdf.
2. Ibid.
3. Special Council, "ESI Data Mapping Basics for eDiscovery," *D4*, accessed January 4, 2018, http://d4discovery.com/discover-more/esi-data-mapping-basics-for-ediscovery#sthash.CcCrZ7in.dpbs.
4. The *Federal Rules of Civil Procedure* are accessible at Cornell University School of Law, Legal Information Institute at https://www.law.cornell.edu/rules/frcp.
5. Exterror, "Data Mapping Policy Brief 2016," accessed January 4, 2018, https://www.exterro.com/resources/data-mapping/
6. Albert S. Humphrey, "SWOT Analysis for Management Consulting," *SRI Alumni Association Newsletter* (SRI International), December 2005, 7–8, https://www.sri.com/sites/default/files/brochures/dec-05.pdf.
7. Florida Gulf Coast University. "Records Management." Accessed January 4, 2018, https://www2.fgcu.edu/recordsmanagement/.
8. Ibid.
9. Ibid.
10. David Ortega, "Strategic Planning Using SMART, SWOT and SOAR Analysis, *ToughNickel*, April 16, 2018, https://toughnickel.com/business/Strategic-Planning-Using-SOAR-and-SWOT-and-SMART-Objectives.
11. G. T. Doran, "There's a S.M.A.R.T. Way to Write Management's Goals and Objectives," *Management Review* 70, no. 11 (AMA Forum), 35–36.
12. Duke Law, "EDRM," accessed January 5, 2018, https://www.edrm.net/frameworks-and-standards/information-governance-reference-model/white-paper/.
13. Sarbanes-Oxley Act 2002, "A Guide to the Sarbanes-Oxley Act," accessed January 5, 2018, www.soxlaw.com/.
14. Michael Cohn, "As Sarbanes-Oxley Nears 15-Year Anniversary, Ethics Fall Short," *Accounting Today*, July 24, 2017, https://www.accountingtoday.com/news/as-sarbanes-oxley-nears-15-year-anniversary-ethics-fall-short.
15. Douglas B. Laney, *Infonomics* (New York: Gartner Inc., 2018): 61–66.
16. Details about the Information Governance Assessment tool can be requested at http://nextlevel.arma.org/.
17. The tool can be downloaded from www.hiqa.ie.
18. Details about the IGP examination are available at https://www.arma.org/default.asp?page=IGP_Future.
19. *ISO 15489-1:2016. Information and documentation—Records management—Part 1: Concepts and Principles*, 3.
20. AIIM, *What is Information Management?* accessed January 6, 2018, www.aiim.org/Resources/Glossary/Information-Management#.
21. Ibid.
22. ARMA International, "ARMA International Maturity Model for Information Governance," accessed January 6, 2018, https://www.lva.virginia.gov/agencies/records/psrc/documents/Principles.pdf.

APPENDIX

A Sampling of Records Management Laws and Regulations Outside of the United States

EUROPEAN UNION

The EU General Data Protections Regulation (GDPR). Effective May 25, 2018

This Act is considered the most important data privacy regulation in 20 years, designed to harmonize data privacy laws across Europe. It replaces Data Protection Directive 95/46/EC. Although its goal is to protect the privacy rights and freedoms of individuals residing in the EU, it will have an impact on corporations outside of the EU that offer goods or services to, or monitor the behavior of, EU data subjects. It applies to all companies processing and holding the personal data of data subjects residing in the European Union, regardless of the company's location.[1]

AUSTRALIA

Archives Act of 1983

This act established the National Archives of Australia, the organization mandated with providing records management standards and advice for government agencies. Each of the states in the Commonwealth has records management regulations that define how records should be managed. Records administration is the responsibility of each of the states.

Corporations Act of 2001

This act governs corporate law in Australia. It covers who can be a company director or secretary, the responsibilities of a company director, company records, takeovers, and fundraising.

Freedom of Information Act of 1982

The regulation gives members of the public rights of access to official documents about themselves or other documents of the Government of the Commonwealth and of its agencies, including ministers, departments, and public authorities of the Commonwealth (unless exempt from such requests). Individuals may request amendment or annotation of their personal records. Part II of the act establishes an information publication scheme (IPS) for agencies. Agencies are required to publish a plan detailing the information they propose to publish, how, and to whom.

Privacy Act of 1988

The Privacy Act regulates the handling of personal information about individuals. It includes thirteen Australian Privacy Principles (APPs), which apply to some private sector organizations as well as most government agencies. The APPs set out standards, rights, and obligations for the handling, holding, use, accessing, and correction of personal information (including sensitive information).

Each of the above Acts has been amended over time. For the current, amended versions, visit the Australian Government's Federal Register of legislation at https://www.legislation.gov.au/Home.

CANADA

Access to Information Act (1985)
The purpose of this act is to extend the present laws of Canada to provide a right of access to information in records under the control of a government institution in accordance with the principles that government information should be available to the public, that necessary exceptions to the right of access should be limited and specific, and that decisions on the disclosure of government information should be reviewed independently of government.

National Archives of Canada Act (R.S.C., 1985, c. 1 (3rd Supp.))
This act provides a definition of a record, assigns responsibilities for the preservation of records to the National Archives of Canada, establishes the governance structure for the National Archives, defines the scope of acquisition to acquire both public and private records, covers transfer of records to the archivist, and further defines the responsibilities of the archivist.

Personal Information Protection and Electronic Documents Act (PIPEDA)
This is the federal privacy law for private-sector organizations. It sets out the ground rules for how businesses must handle personal information in the course of commercial activity based on ten fair information principles: (1) accountability, (2) identifying purposes, (3) consent, (4) limiting collection, (5) limiting use, disclosure, and retention, (6) accuracy, (7) safeguards, (8) openness, (9) individual access, and (10) challenging compliance.

Privacy Act (1985)
The purpose of this act is to extend the present laws of Canada that protect the privacy of individuals with respect to personal information about themselves held by a government institution and that provide individuals with a right of access to that information.

Each of the above Acts has been amended over time. For the current, amended versions, visit Government of Canada's Justice Laws Website at http://laws-lois.justice.gc.ca/eng/.

FRANCE

Délibération n° 2009-474
Issued on August 9, 2009, by the French Data Protection Authority (CNIL), this statute details the legal requirements for French/US data transfers in discovery activities related to litigation or for US investigations.

Freedom of Information Act (Loi n° 78-753)
This law on Free Access to Public Documents was passed in 1978, closely mirroring US law. The Directorate of the Archives of France is mandated with providing useful standards for electronic records, including long-term preservation. Title I addresses freedom of access to administrative documents and the reuse of public information. The act defines the right of everyone

to information as defined and guaranteed by the provisions of chapters I, III, and IV of this title regarding freedom of access to government documents, including records, reports, studies, statistics, directives, instructions, circulars, notes and ministerial responses, correspondence, opinions, forecasts, and decisions.

French Data Protection Act (DPA)

The purpose of the DPA is to ensure that any use of information technology does not violate human identity, human rights, privacy, or individual or public liberties. It applies to both public and private sectors. On December 13, 2017, the French Ministry of Justice published a draft law to accompany the General Data Protection Regulation 2016/679 (GDPR) and Directive 2016/680 governing handling of data in law enforcement situations. The goal is to approve this new law by May 25, 2018, when the GDPR comes into effect.

Ordinance 2004–178 (National Patrimony)

This legislation provides for official definition of records and archives as governed by French records management, data protection, and archival laws. According to French records and archival laws, records are the whole of documents—regardless of date, form, and physical support—created or received by any physical or juridical person and by every public or private agency or organization in the course of their activities.

For access to laws and decrees published in the "Journal officiel," visit Legifrance.gouv.fr.

GERMANY

DOMEA (German Ministry of Interior)

DOMEA stands for "Document Management and Electronic Archiving in Electronic Business" and is also known as the "Paperless Office Concept." This initiative of Germany's Department of Interior defines records management policies for government electronic records. DOMEA is intended to support the creation of a government-wide IT system that supports records management, the creation of electronic records, and cooperative business processes.

Federal Data Protection Act (Bundesdatenschutzgesetz, BDSG)

The BDSG requires that personal data (i.e., data referring to an individual [natural person]) may only be stored or processed if either the person agrees in writing or the law allows the storage/processing. On April 27, 2017, Germany passed a new BDSG to replace the original BDSG in order to comply with the EU GDPR effective May 24, 2018. Companies operating in Germany are now governed by the BDSG of 2017.

German Corporate Governance Code

The German Corporate Governance Code presents essential statutory regulations for the management and supervision of German-listed companies and contains internationally and nationally recognized standards for good and responsible governance. The current code, dated April 24, 2017, is available at www.dcgk.de/en/home.html.

Network Enforcement Act (Netzwerkdurchsetzungsgesetz or NetzDG)

This law became effective January 1, 2018, and requires social networks, regardless of size, to remove posts considered hate speech within twenty-four hours (or seven days, if the content is difficult to evaluate). Those that fail to comply may be fined up to 50 million euros ($58 million) by the country's Ministry of Justice. Companies like Facebook, Twitter, and YouTube were considered the initial targets but others may be targeted as well.

Telecommunications Data Retention Law

For years, a struggle has been waged between lawmakers and telecommunications service providers about the length of time certain metadata (e.g., number of the calling and called party and date and time of conversation) should be retained in order to fight crime. The latest effort, in 2017, to retain data for ten weeks was temporarily suspended by a Higher Administrative Court. The issues surrounding this law have not yet been resolved.

Federal Ministry of Justice and Consumer Protection provides nearly all current federal law for free at www.gesetze-im-internet.de/beurkg/.

UNITED KINGDOM

Data Protection Act 1998

This act regulates the use of "personal data" and applies to most personnel records (paper, microform, or computerized format). The Data Protection Bill introduced in 2017 replaces the DPA of 1998 and implements derogations and exemptions from the EU GDPR (General Data Protection Regulation).

Electronic Communications Act 2000

Regulations apply to communications data that is generated or processed in the United Kingdom by public communications providers in the process of supplying the communications services concerned.

Freedom of Information Act 2000

This act of Parliament creates a public "right of access" to information held by public authorities. It does not impose any obligation on public authorities or their agents to retain documents for a certain period. However, it does make it a criminal offense to destroy documents after a request for information (a "subject access request") has been made, if the destruction was with the intention of preventing disclosure.

Public Records Act of 1958 (and The National Archives 2002)

The Public Records Act of 1958 is an act of Parliament that forms the main legislation governing public records. It applies to the United Kingdom Central Government, including Executive Agencies and Non-Departmental Public Bodies. The act with all changes made before January 31, 2018, can be viewed at legislation.gov.uk. TNA 2002 defines functional requirements for electronic documents and records management (taking into account the obligations defined by the Freedom of Information Act, *ISO 15489, MoReq,* e-government interoperability framework of the United Kingdom, and Data Protection Act of 1988).

For the current, amended versions, visit legislation.gov.uk.

NOTE

1. EUGDRP.org. (n.d.) "GDPR Portal: Site Overview," accessed April 29, 2018, https://www.eugdpr.org/.

GLOSSARY

access control: The process by which users are identified and granted certain privileges to information, systems, or resources; can allow or deny access to a physical environment or an electronic environment. (DISA, *Access Control in Support of Information Systems*)

accession: Process of accepting legal and physical control of materials, documenting information about them in a register, database, or log, and establishing parameters for their use. *Note:* May also include acceptance of legal custody. (Excerpted from *Glossary of Records Management and Information Governance Terms*, 5th ed., ©ARMA International, www.arma.org/, used with permission)

acquisition: Process of adding to the holdings of a records center or archives by transfer under an established and legally based procedure, by deposit, purchase, gift, or bequest. (Excerpted from *Glossary of Records Management and Information Governance Terms*, 5th ed., ©ARMA International, www.arma.org/, used with permission)

acquisition policy: An official statement issued by an archives or manuscript repository identifying the kinds of materials it accepts and the conditions or terms that affect their acquisition. It serves as a basic document for the guidance of archival staff and organizations and persons interested in donating their records or papers. (Pearce-Moses, *Glossary of Archival and Records Terminology,* ©SAA, www2.archivists.org/glossary, used with permission)

action plan: A sequence of steps that must be taken, or activities that must be performed well, for a strategy to succeed. Also known as *operational plan*. (BusinessDictionary.com)

active preservation: An approach to digital preservation that seeks to ensure the continued accessibility of electronic records over time by actively intervening in how records are stored and managed (e.g., migration). (IRMT, *Training in Electronic Records Management*)

active record: A readily accessible record related to current, ongoing, or in-process activities and referred to on a regular basis to respond to day-to-day operational requirements. Also known as *current record*. (Excerpted from *Glossary of Records Management and Information Governance Terms*, 5th ed., ©ARMA International, www.arma.org/, used with permission)

administrative access controls: Access controls that result from administrative action that includes developing policies and procedures, providing education and training, and monitoring and evaluating use. (DISA, *Access Control in Support of Information Systems*)

administrative metadata: Data that is necessary to manage and use information resources and that is typically external to informational content of resources. (Pearce-Moses, *Glossary of Archival and Records Terminology,* ©SAA, www2.archivists.org/glossary, used with permission)

administrative record: A record that is related to budget, personnel, supply, audit, accounting, or similar support operations common to all organizations; the official record of decisions, proceedings, or process. Also known as *operational record*. (Excerpted from *Glossary of Records Management and Information Governance Terms*, 5th ed., ©ARMA International, www.arma .org/, used with permission)

administrative risks: Risks related to the management of the records and information management program, including information governance, change management, and emergency management. (ARMA International, *Evaluating and Mitigating Records and Information Risks*)

aggregator business model: A networked model where a firm collects the information about a particular good or service provider(s), makes the providers their partners, and sells the goods or services under their own brand. Examples are taxis (Uber) and travel (Make My Trip).

algorithm: A step-by-step procedure for solving a problem or accomplishing some end, especially by a computer. (*Merriam-Webster Online*)

alphabetic filing system: A system in which files and documents are arranged in alphabetic order from A to Z. (Excerpted from *Glossary of Records Management and Information Governance Terms*, 5th ed., ©ARMA International, www.arma.org/, used with permission)

appraisal: 1. The evaluation of a records series or an individual record's value for retention or archival purposes, based upon its current or predicted use(s) for administrative, legal, regulatory, fiscal, research, evidentiary, or historical purposes. Also referred to as records appraisal. (Excerpted from *Glossary of Records Management and Information Governance Terms*, 5th ed., ©ARMA International, www.arma.org/, used with permission) **2.** Analysis of the business context, business activities and risk to enable decision-making on what records to create and capture, and how to ensure the appropriate management of records over time. (*ISO 15489-1:2016*)

archival authority: Agency or program responsible for selecting and preserving archives, making them available, and approving destruction of other records. (Excerpted from *Glossary of Records Management and Information Governance Terms*, 5th ed., ©ARMA International, www.arma.org/, used with permission)

archival description: The process of analyzing, organizing, and recording details about the formal elements of a record or collection of records, such as creator, title, dates, extent, and contents, to facilitate the work's identification, management, and understanding; the product of such a process. (Pearce-Moses, *Glossary of Archival and Records Terminology,* ©SAA, www2.archivists.org/glossary, used with permission)

archives: The noncurrent records created or received and accumulated by a person or organization in the course of the conduct of affairs and preserved because of their continuing or enduring value; an institution or a division within an institution responsible for collecting, organizing, preserving, and providing access to records of enduring value. (Excerpted from *Glossary of Records Management and Information Governance Terms*, 5th ed., ©ARMA International, www.arma.org/, used with permission)

archives management: The general oversight of a program to appraise, acquire, arrange, describe, preserve, authenticate, and provide access to permanently valuable records. Also known as *archives administration.* (Pearce-Moses, *Glossary of Archival and Records Terminology,* ©SAA, www2.archivists.org/glossary, used with permission)

archivist: An individual responsible for appraising, acquiring, arranging, describing, preserving, and providing access to records of enduring value, according to the principles of provenance, original order, and collective control to protect the materials' authenticity and context. (Excerpted from *Glossary of Records Management and Information Governance Terms*, 5th ed., ©ARMA International, www.arma.org/, used with permission)

arrangement: Process of organizing materials to reflect their provenance and original order in order to protect their context and to achieve physical or intellectual control over the materials; the organization and sequence of items within a collection. (Excerpted from *Glossary of Records Management and Information Governance Terms*, 5th ed., ©ARMA International, www.arma.org/, used with permission)

attribute: A characteristic of an element or data that defines its nature and provides additional information. (Excerpted from *Glossary of Records Management and Information Governance Terms*, 5th ed., ©ARMA International, www.arma.org/, used with permission)

audit: A review of information-related activities to ensure that sufficient policies, procedures, and controls are in place and complied with to meet all operational, legal, and regulatory obligations and to identify where and how improvements should be made. (Excerpted from *Glossary of Records Management and Information Governance Terms*, 5th ed., ©ARMA International, www.arma.org/, used with permission)

audit plan: A description of the expected scope and conduct of the audit with sufficient detail to guide the development of the audit program; this includes a set of instructions and a means to control and record the proper execution of the work. (State Records of South Australia, *Records Management Audit Guideline*)

audit trail: Information in records that tracks a transaction from beginning to end, making it possible to review whether it was done according to relevant policies and standards. (Pearce-Moses, *Glossary of Archival and Records Terminology*, ©SAA, www2.archivists.org/ glossary, used with permission)

augmented reality (AR): A type of virtual reality that aims to duplicate the world's environment in a computer. An augmented reality system generates a composite view for the user that is the combination of the real scene viewed by the user and a virtual scene generated by the computer that augments the scene with additional information. (*Webopedia*)

authenticity: Sum of the qualities of a record that establishes the origin, reliability, trustworthiness, and correctness of its content. (Excerpted from *Glossary of Records Management and Information Governance Terms*, 5th ed., ©ARMA International, www.arma.org/, used with permission)

bar code: A predetermined pattern of vertical lines that, when read by an optical reader, can be converted to machine-readable language. (Excerpted from *Glossary of Records Management and Information Governance Terms*, 5th ed., ©ARMA International, www.arma.org/, used with permission)

big bucket schedule: A type of flexible records schedule that applies disposition instructions against a large body of records grouped at a level of aggregation greater than the traditional file series or electronic system and that can be along a specific program area, functional line, or business process. Also known as *large aggregation schedule*. (NARA, "NARA Bulletin 2008-04")

Big Data: Data so large that it is difficult to process with traditional database and software techniques. (*Webopedia*)

blog: An online journal with regular chronological entries written by one or more individuals that may provide readers with the ability to comment on postings. Derived from the phrase "web log." (ARMA International, *Implications of Web-Based, Collaborative Technologies in Records Management*)

Boolean logic search: Method of searching electronic information systems that uses specific terms and symbols to refine a search and improve the chances of obtaining successful search results. (Excerpted from *Glossary of Records Management and Information Governance Terms*, 5th ed., ©ARMA International, www.arma.org/, used with permission)

born digital: Information created in electronic format. (Pearce-Moses, *Glossary of Archival and Records Terminology*, ©SAA, www2.archivists.org/glossary, used with permission)

built-in (designed) dispersal: Regular distribution of records (especially vital records) to additional locations as a method of protection. (Excerpted from *Glossary of Records Management and Information Governance Terms*, 5th ed., ©ARMA International, www.arma.org/, used with permission)

business case: A type of decision-making tool used to determine the effects a particular decision will have on profitability. (BusinessDictionary.com)

business classification scheme: Tools for linking records to the context of their creation. (ISO, *ISO 15489-1:2016*)

business continuity: An organization's ability to continue to operate during as well as after a disaster or disruption.

business continuity plan: The documented plan that defines the resources, actions, tasks, and data required to manage the disaster prevention, emergency preparedness, disaster response and recovery, and business resumption process in the event of a business interruption. (Excerpted from *Glossary of Records Management and Information Governance Terms*, 5th ed., ©ARMA International, www.arma.org/, used with permission)

business process: Related activities, sequential or parallel, that have been systematically implemented to produce a specific service or product. (Pearce-Moses, *Glossary of Archival and Records Terminology*, ©SAA, www2.archivists.org/glossary, used with permission)

business process analysis: The activity of reviewing and changing existing business practices in order to fit new and improved automated processes.

business process improvement (BPI): Improving quality, productivity, and response time of a business process, by removing non-value-adding activities and costs through incremental enhancements. Also known as *functional process improvement*. (BusinessDictionary.com)

business process mapping: Assigning variables to given work tasks and plotting how work moves from one department to the next and from one employee to the next. (Drive Your Success, "Understanding Business Process Mapping and Workflow Diagrams")

business process model (BPM): A sequential representation of all functions associated with a specific business activity. For example, a BPM diagram that depicts how an order is fulfilled will show the customer request, order entry, communication with shipping, inventory picking, ship scheduling, and delivery. (BusinessDictionary.com)

business resumption: Process of restoring the interrupted operations of a firm in the immediate aftermath of an accident, disaster, emergency, and/or threat. (BusinessDictionary.com)

business system: Organized collection of hardware, software, supplies, policies, procedures, and people that stores, processes, and provides access to an organization's business information. (ISO, ISO *23081-2:2009*)

BYOD (bring your own device): A phrase that has become widely adopted to refer to employees who bring their own computing devices—such as smartphones, laptops, and PDAs—to the workplace for use and connectivity on the corporate network. (*Webopedia*)

certified archivist (CA): An archivist who has successfully met all criteria for membership in the Academy of Certified Archivists (ACA). (Excerpted from *Glossary of Records Management and Information Governance Terms*, 5th ed., ©ARMA International, www.arma.org/, used with permission)

certified information governance professional (IGP): The IGP will recognize the efforts of those professionals who are most accomplished with respect to the implementation of the Generally Accepted Recordkeeping Principles. (ARMA International, "Certified Information Governance Professional")

certified information privacy professional (CIPP): An individual who has achieved any one of the five IAPP (International Association of Privacy Professionals) credentials. All CIPPs have demonstrated knowledge of both broad global and specific regional or sectorial concepts of privacy and data protection law and practice. (IAPP)

certified information professional (CIP): An information professional who has taken and passed a 100-question examination to demonstrate competence in six domain areas across content and information management. (AIIM)

certified records manager (CRM): Professional records manager who has satisfactorily passed the certified records manager examination administered by the Institute of Certified Records Managers and who remains a member in good standing. (Excerpted from *Glossary of Records Management and Information Governance Terms*, 5th ed., ©ARMA International, www.arma.org/, used with permission)

chief records officer (CRO): A high-ranking executive within an organization who is responsible for the organization's records management program and who interacts with other C-level officers when strategic decisions are made that involve all levels and functional areas of the organization.

chronological filing system: A filing system set up by date and used to organize business records such as invoices, purchase orders, and bills of lading.

classification: System identification and/or arrangement of business activities and/or records into categories according to logically structured conventions, methods, and procedural rules. (ISO, ISO *15489-1:2016*)

C-level management: C-level is an adjective used to describe high-ranking executive titles within an organization (e.g., CEO, chief executive officer; CFO, chief financial officer; and CRO, chief records officer).

cloud computing: Cloud computing is a model for enabling ubiquitous, convenient, on-demand network access to a shared pool of configurable computing resources (e.g., networks, servers, storage, applications, and services) that can be rapidly provisioned and released with minimal management effort or service provider interaction. (Mell and Grance, *The NIST Definition of Cloud Computing*)

cloud digital preservation: A service providing digital preservation of information and data. (LTDP, "Cloud Digital Archive and Digital Preservation Service Requirements")

cloud storage: The storage of data online in the cloud wherein a company's data are stored in and accessible from multiple distributed and connected resources that comprise a cloud. (*Webopedia*)

cold site: An alternative computing facility used as a backup site for disaster recovery in which the vendor provides the office space, but the customer provides and installs all the necessary equipment and software. In some cases, the customer may maintain office space, equipment, and software. (Excerpted from *Glossary of Records Management and Information Governance Terms*, 5th ed., ©ARMA International, www.arma.org/, used with permission)

commercial records center: A facility that stores the records of other organizations and provides services on a for-profit, fee basis. (Excerpted from *Glossary of Records Management and Information Governance Terms*, 5th ed., ©ARMA International, www.arma.org/, used with permission)

compliance: Certification or confirmation that the doer of an action (such as the writer of an audit report) or the manufacturer or supplier of a product meets the requirements of accepted practices, legislation, prescribed rules and regulations, specified standards, or the terms of a contract. (BusinessDictionary.com)

compliance monitoring: Activities undertaken to establish whether a process or procedure is carried out in conformance with relevant external requirements, whether set through legislation, regulations, or directions. (NSW Government, "Monitoring Records Management")

computer: An electronic device that accepts data as input which is then analyzed or manipulated according to specific instructions, with the resulting data stored for future use, output in human-readable form, or used as input to another process or to control another device; one who counts or adds numbers. (Pearce-Moses, *Glossary of Archival and Records Terminology*, ©SAA, www2.archivists.org/glossary, used with permission)

conceptual analysis: A term that can be applied to all examinations of message content; a category of content analysis.

conceptual model: Data model that represents an abstract view of the real world. (ISO, *ISO 23081-2:2009*)

content analysis: A research tool used to determine the presence of certain words or concepts within texts and sets of texts.

content management: Techniques to set policies and supervise the creation, organization, access, and use of large quantities of information, especially in different formats and applications throughout an organization. (Pearce-Moses, *Glossary of Archival and Records Terminology,* ©SAA, www2.archivists.org/glossary, used with permission)

content standard: A set of formal rules that specify the content, order, and syntax of information to promote consistency. (Pearce-Moses, *Glossary of Archival and Records Terminology,* ©SAA, www2.archivists.org/glossary, used with permission)

controlled language: *See* **controlled vocabulary.**

controlled vocabulary: A limited set of terms and phrases used as headings in indexes and as access points in catalogs. (Pearce-Moses, *Glossary of Archival and Records Terminology,* ©SAA, http:// www2.archivists.org/glossary, used with permission)

conversion: Process of changing records from one record to another. *See also* **migration.** (ISO, *ISO 15489-1:2016*)

CRM/Federal Specialist: A post-certification specialty designation for CRM's working in records and information management programs of the U.S. Government, whether as a Federal government employee, uniformed military personnel, consultant, or contractor. (ICRM)

crowdsourcing: A slang term used to describe the practice of using both the skills and time of underpaid—or unpaid—amateurs to create content or solutions for established businesses. Basically, crowdsourcing means to "use the talents of the crowd," and is a play on the word *outsourcing.* (*Webopedia*)

cybersecurity: Measures taken to protect a computer or computer system (as on the Internet) from unauthorized access or attack. (*Merriam-Webster Online*)

dark archives: A collection of materials preserved for future use but with no current access. (Pearce-Moses, *Glossary of Archival and Records Terminology,* ©SAA, www2.archivists.org/glossary, used with permission)

data governance: The overall management of the availability, usability, integrity, and security of data used in an enterprise. A sound data governance program includes a governing body or council, a defined set of procedures and a plan to executive those procedures. (TechTarget)

data lake: A collection of storage instances of various data assets additional to the originating data sources stored in a near-exact, or even exact, copy of the source format. The purpose is to present an unrefined view of data to only the most highly skilled analysts, to help them explore their data refinement and analysis techniques independent of any system-of-record in a traditional analytic data store (such as a data mart or data warehouse). (Gartner IT Glossary)

data map: A comprehensive and defensible description of each IT system, which includes its media (online and offline), the business unit(s) it services, its responsible data stewards and custodians, a business unit contact, the policies that govern access to the system, and the associated retention policies and procedures. (Excerpted from *Glossary of Records Management and Information Governance Terms,* 5th ed., ©ARMA International, www.arma.org/, used with permission)

data mart: A specific, subject-oriented repository of data gathered from operational data and other sources and designed to serve the needs of a particular community of knowledge workers. (Anupindi, "Inmon vs. Kimball")

data privacy: The use and governance of personal data—things like putting policies in place to ensure that consumers' personal information is being collected, shared and used in appropriate ways.

data security: The protection of data from access and exploitation by unauthorized entities. (IAPP)

data warehouse: A central aggregation of data (that can be distributed physically) that starts from an analysis of what data already exists and how it can be collected and later used. (Anupindi, "Inmon vs. Kimball")

de facto standard: A consistent manner of doing something that has been established by practice. (Pearce-Moses, *Glossary of Archival and Records Terminology,* ©SAA, www2.archivists.org/glossary, used with permission)

de jure standard: A consistent manner of doing something established by a deliberate process. (Pearce-Moses, *Glossary of Archival and Records Terminology,* ©SAA, www2.archivists.org/glossary, used with permission)

derivative dispersal: A term used to represent information and records intentionally (with or without malice) spread through the use of the internet and Web 2.0 technologies.

description: The process of creating a finding aid or other access tools that allow individuals to browse a surrogate of the collection to facilitate access and that improve security by creating a record of the collection and by minimizing the amount of handling of the original materials. (Pearce-Moses, *Glossary of Archival and Records Terminology,* ©SAA, www2.archivists.org/glossary, used with permission)

descriptive metadata: Information that refers to the intellectual content of material and aids discovery of such materials. (Pearce-Moses, *Glossary of Archival and Records Terminology,* ©SAA, www2.archivists.org/glossary, used with permission) (Excerpted from *Glossary of Records Management and Information Governance Terms,* 5th ed., ©ARMA International, www.arma.org/, used with permission)

destruction: Process of eliminating or deleting a record, beyond any possible reconstruction. (ISO, *ISO 15489-1:2016*)

destruction hold: A hold placed on the scheduled destruction of records due to foreseeable or pending litigation, governmental investigation, audit, or special organizational requirements. (ARMA glossary) Also known as *legal hold.*

diffusion of innovation: Theory that every market has groups of customers who differ in their readiness and willingness to adopt a new product, and that an innovative product spreads (diffuses) through a market not in one straight course but in successive, overlapping waves. Most populations show the following pattern in the adoption of new consumer goods: innovators (2 percent of population), early adopters (14 percent), early majority (34 percent), late majority (34 percent), and laggards (16 percent). (BusinessDictionary.com)

digital archives: A specialized storage repository and service with supporting data and storage services used to secure, retain, and protect digital information and data usually for extended periods of time, but not including long-term. (LTDP, "Cloud Digital Archive and Digital Preservation Service Requirements")

digital preservation: A digital object is preserved when information consumers can access, examine, reuse, and interpret digital information and verify it as authentic over any period of time including long-term. The goals of digital preservation are to keep any designated digital object accessible, interpretable, secure, reliable, and authentic over time. (LTDP, "Cloud Digital Archive and Digital Preservation Service Requirements")

digital rot: A colloquial computing term used to describe either a gradual decay of storage media or the degradation of a software program over time. Also known as *bit rot, bit decay, data rot,* or *data decay.* (StackExchange.com)

digitized: Converted (as data or an image) to digital form. (*Merriam-Webster Online*)

disaster preparedness and recovery plan: *See* **disaster recovery plan**.

disaster recovery plan: A written and approved course of action to take after a disaster strikes that details how an organization will restore critical business functions and reclaim damaged or threatened records. (Excerpted from *Glossary of Records Management and Information Governance Terms,* 5th ed., ©ARMA International, www.arma.org/, used with permission)

discovery: The process of identifying, locating, securing, reviewing, and protecting information and materials that are potentially relevant to specific litigation and may need to be produced to other parties. (Excerpted from *Glossary of Records Management and Information Governance Terms,* 5th ed., ©ARMA International, www.arma.org/, used with permission)

dispersal: Transfer of duplicate copies of vital records to locations beyond those where the originals are housed. (Excerpted from *Glossary of Records Management and Information Governance Terms,* 5th ed., ©ARMA International, www.arma.org/, used with permission)

disposition: Range of processes associated with implementing records retention, destruction, or transfer decisions that are documented in disposition authorities or other instruments. (ISO, *ISO 15489-1:2016*)

disruptive innovation: The process of developing new products or services to replace existing technologies and gain a competitive advantage. For example, in a typical innovative high-technology business, disruptive innovation tends to shake up a market when it is introduced externally, and it typically requires a more creative internal attitude toward the product development and promotion process. (BusinessDictionary.com)

document: Information or data fixed in some media, but which is not part of the official record; a non-record. (Pearce-Moses, *Glossary of Archival and Records Terminology,* ©SAA, www2.archivists.org/glossary, used with permission)

document management: Techniques used to regulate the creation, use, and maintenance of documents according to established policies and procedures. (Excerpted from *Glossary of Records Management and Information Governance Terms,* 5th ed., ©ARMA International, www.arma.org/, used with permission)

document management system(s) (DMS): The use of a computer system and software to store, manage, and track electronic documents and electronic images of paper-based information captured through the use of a document scanner. (AIIM)

document type definition (DTD): A set of rules that specify the structure of a document and the tags used to define that structure and that can be used to validate whether a document is well formed. (Pearce-Moses, *Glossary of Archival and Records Terminology,* ©SAA, www2.archivists.org/glossary, used with permission)

duplex numeric system: A filing system using numbers with two or more parts separated by a dash, space, or comma. (Excerpted from *Glossary of Records Management and Information Governance Terms,* 5th ed., ©ARMA International, www.arma.org/, used with permission)

dynamic web page: *A web page* that delivers custom content and is generated in response to a user request, drawing content from a database and displaying the content in a predetermined format. (ARMA International, *Website Records Management*)

dynamic website: A website that can use a single URL to generate a webpage with content that changes based on a number of factors. (Pearce-Moses, *Glossary of Archival and Records Terminology,* ©SAA, www2.archivists.org/glossary, used with permission)

electronic discovery (e-discovery): The required production of information to an opposing party during the pretrial phase of litigation or a government investigation. (ARMA International, "What Is Electronic Discovery?")

electronic document management system(s) (EDMS): A system consisting of software, hardware, policies, and processes to automate the preparation, organization, tracking, and distribution of electronic documents. (Excerpted from *Glossary of Records Management and Information Governance Terms,* 5th ed., ©ARMA International, www.arma.org/, used with permission)

electronic document records management system(s) (EDRMS): A system designed to manage electronic content, documents, and records and support four key functions: input (creation and capture); management (content, documents, records); collaboration/process management; and output/delivery. (JISC InfoNet, "infoKits")

electronic record: Data or information that has been captured and fixed for storage and manipulation in an automated system and that requires the use of the system to render it intelligible by a person. (Pearce-Moses, *Glossary of Archival and Records Terminology,* ©SAA, www2 .archivists.org/glossary, used with permission)

electronic records management (ERM): The application of records management principles to electronic records; the management of records using electronic systems to apply records management principles. (Excerpted from *Glossary of Records Management and Information Governance Terms,* 5th ed., ©ARMA International, www.arma.org/, used with permission)

electronic records management system(s) (ERMS): A system consisting of software, hardware, policies, and processes to automate the preparation, organization, tracking, distribution and disposition of records regardless of media. (Excerpted from *Glossary of Records Management and Information Governance Terms,* 5th ed., ©ARMA International, www.arma .org/, used with permission)

electronic signature: An electronic symbol or process attached to or logically associated with an electronic record and executed or adopted with the intent to authenticate the record. Also known as *digital signature.* (Excerpted from *Glossary of Records Management and Information Governance Terms,* 5th ed., ©ARMA International, www.arma.org/, used with permission)

emulation: The use of one system to reproduce the functions and results of another system. (ARMA International, *The Digital Records Conversion Process*)

encoding scheme: Controlled list of all the acceptable values in natural language and/or as a syntax-encoded text string designed for machine processing. (ISO *23081-1:2017*)

enterprise content management (ECM): The strategies, methods, and tools used to capture, manage, store, preserve, and deliver content and documents related to organizational processes. (AIIM)

enterprise content management system(s) (ECMS): This term encompasses the technologies, tools, and methods used to capture, manage, store, preserve, and deliver content across an enterprise. Content examples are contracts, files, email, and so on. (AIIM)

enterprise information system(s) (EIS): An EIS integrates the key business processes into a single software system that enables information to flow seamlessly throughout the organization.

entity: Any concrete or abstract thing that exists, did exist, or might exist, including associations among those things. (ISO, *ISO 23081-1:2017*)

ESI (electronically stored information): As referenced in the US *Federal Rules of Civil Procedure,* information that is stored electronically, regardless of the media or whether it is in the original format in which it was created, as opposed to stored in hard copy (i.e., on paper). (Sedona Conference, *The Sedona Conference Glossary*)

Essential Records (see vital record).

Ethernet: A computer network architecture consisting of various specified local area network protocols, devices, and connection methods; first-known use 1976. (*Merriam-Webster Online*)

evaluation: The process of assessing the value of records, especially regarding their destruction. (Pearce-Moses, *Glossary of Archival and Records Terminology,* ©SAA, www2.archivists.org/ glossary, used with permission)

Extensible Markup Language (XML): A standard developed by the World Wide Web Consortium (W3C) that defines a format for representing and sharing information between people and computers. (Excerpted from *Glossary of Records Management and Information Governance Terms,* 5th ed., ©ARMA International, www.arma.org/, used with permission)

faceted classification: A system for organizing materials into categories based on a systematic combination of mutually exclusive and collectively exhaustive characteristics of the materials (facets) and displaying the characteristics in a manner that shows their relationships. (Pearce-Moses, *Glossary of Archival and Records Terminology,* ©SAA, www2.archivists.org/ glossary, used with permission)

faceted search: A type of navigation model that leverages metadata fields and values to provide users with visible options for clarifying and refining queries. Also known as *guided navigation.*

field search: A search for a term or number within a particular data field of a document or database.

file format (examples: PDF, TXT, TIF, HTML, ASCII): A format for encoding information in a file. Each different type of file has a different file format. The file format specifies first whether the file is a binary or ASCII file, and second, how the information is organized. (*Webopedia*)

file plan: A classification scheme that describes and identifies all files, including indexing and storage of the files, and referencing the disposition schedule for each file. (Excerpted from *Glossary of Records Management and Information Governance Terms,* 5th ed., ©ARMA International, www.arma.org/, used with permission)

flexible scheduling: A technique to apply disposition instructions to different types of information or categories of records. *See also* **big bucket schedule**. (Pearce-Moses, *Glossary of Archival and Records Terminology,* ©SAA, www2.archivists.org/glossary, used with permission)

floppy disk: A thin, plastic magnetic medium for portable data storage, encased in plastic, and available in various sizes, including 3.5, 5.25, and 8 inches. (Excerpted from *Glossary of Records Management and Information Governance Terms,* 5th ed., ©ARMA International, www.arma.org/, used with permission)

folksonomy: A collaborative effort by users to create and manage their own tags for the classification and categorization of online content. (ARMA International, *Implications of Web-Based, Collaborative Technologies in Records Management*)

full-text search: The capability of a system to provide search and retrieval of documents based on a search of the complete text within the documents, not just on keywords. (Excerpted from *Glossary of Records Management and Information Governance Terms,* 5th ed., ©ARMA International, www.arma.org/, used with permission)

functional classification system: A system for organizing materials on the basis of the function, activity, or task performed by an organization to fulfill its mandate, instead of by department, name, or subject. (Excerpted from *Glossary of Records Management and Information Governance Terms,* 5th ed., ©ARMA International, www.arma.org/, used with permission)

functions thesaurus: A classification tool built from the business classification scheme listing the terms in alphabetical order.

gap analysis: A technique for determining the steps to be taken in moving from a current state to a desired future state. Also known as *need-gap analysis, needs analysis, and needs assessment.* (BusinessDictionary.com)

Generally Accepted Recordkeeping Principles: A framework of definitive principles for governing an organization's information as a strategic asset. These information governance principles support organizational goals, facilitate compliance with regulatory, legislative, and information management requirements, and limit risks. (Excerpted from *Glossary of Records Management and Information Governance Terms,* 5th ed., ©ARMA International, www.arma.org/, used with permission)

geographic filing system: The classification of records, usually arranged by numeric code or in alphabetic order, by geographic location such as country, region, state, province, county, city, or other geographic identifier. (Excerpted from *Glossary of Records Management and Information Governance Terms,* 5th ed., ©ARMA International, www.arma.org/, used with permission)

geographic information system(s) (GIS): A combination of hardware, software, and rules that supports complex analysis of geospatial and temporal information and that often uses static or dynamic maps for reports. (Pearce-Moses, *Glossary of Archival and Records Terminology,* ©SAA, www2.archivists.org/glossary, used with permission)

glossary: An alphabetical list of terms in a particular domain of knowledge with definitions for those terms. Also known as *vocabulary. (Wikipedia)*

goal: An observable and measurable end result having one or more objectives to be achieved within a more or less fixed time frame. (BusinessDictionary.com)

governance: System, structures, tone, and behaviors by which the organization is directed and controlled and accountability clearly defined. (BSI, *BS 31100:2011*)

hard disks: A magnetic storage device designed to provide rapid access to large quantities of data. Also known as *hard drive.* (Pearce-Moses, *Glossary of Archival and Records Terminology,* ©SAA, www2.archivists.org/glossary, used with permission)

hot site: An alternate computing facility that has the equipment and resources to immediately recover the business functions affected by the occurrence of a disaster. (Excerpted from *Glossary of Records Management and Information Governance Terms,* 5th ed., ©ARMA International, www.arma.org/, used with permission)

Hypertext Markup Language (HTML): The publishing language of the Web used to provide structure that tells the Web browser how to present the webpage.

inactive record: A record no longer needed to conduct current business but preserved until it meets the end of its retention period. (Excerpted from *Glossary of Records Management and Information Governance Terms,* 5th ed., ©ARMA International, www.arma.org/, used with permission)

index: An ordered list of controlled language terms that points to the location of information related to each term. (ARMA International, *Controlled Language in Records and Information Management)*

indexing: The act of specifying the predetermined topic, name, number, or caption under which a document is to be filed.. (Excerpted from *Glossary of Records Management and Information Governance Terms,* 5th ed., ©ARMA International, www.arma.org/, used with permission)

Infonomics: The theory, study, and discipline of asserting economic significance to information. (Laney, *Infonomics)*

information: Data that has been given value through analysis, interpretation, or compilation in a meaningful form. (Excerpted from *Glossary of Records Management and Information Governance Terms,* 5th ed., ©ARMA International, www.arma.org/, used with permission)

information age: A period beginning about 1975 and characterized by the gathering and almost instantaneous transmission of vast amounts of information and by the rise of information-based industries. (Dictionary.com)

information governance: The specification of decision rights and an accountability framework to encourage desirable behavior in the valuation, creation, storage, use, archiving, and deletion of information. It includes the processes, roles, standards, and metrics that ensure the effective and efficient use of information in enabling an organization to achieve its goals. (Gartner, *IT Glossary*)

information governance maturity model: The IG maturity model defines characteristics of five levels of recordkeeping programs based on the eight principles as well as a foundation of standards, best practices, and legal/regulatory requirements. (ARMA International, "Information Governance Maturity Model, Metrics")

information governance professional (IGP): An individual who has the strategic perspective, knowledge, and skills to lead an organization's information governance initiatives, leverage information for maximum value, reduce costs, and mitigate risks associated with using and governing information assets. (Excerpted from *Glossary of Records Management and Information Governance Terms,* 5th ed., ©ARMA International, www.arma.org/, used with permission)

information management: Principles and techniques to process, store, retrieve, manipulate, and control access to information so that users can find information they need. (Pearce-Moses, *Glossary of Archival and Records Terminology,* ©SAA, www2.archivists.org/glossary, used with permission)

information technology: The use of hardware and software, especially digital computers, to capture, process, store, and disseminate complex data in many forms, including audio, images, and text. (Pearce-Moses, *Glossary of Archival and Records Terminology,* ©SAA, www2.archivists.org/glossary, used with permission)

information technology governance (IT governance): The process that ensures effective and efficient use of information in enabling an organization to achieve its goals. (Logan, "What Is Information Governance?")

infrastructure as a service (IaaS): Infrastructure as a service is the delivery of computer infrastructure, generally virtualized platform environments, as a service.

intangible asset: A nonphysical asset, such as patents, copyrights, franchises, customer lists, trademarks, trade names, and goodwill.

integrity (of a record): The quality of a record that is complete and unaltered from the time of creation throughout its life. (Excerpted from *Glossary of Records Management and Information Governance Terms,* 5th ed., ©ARMA International, www.arma.org/, used with permission)

Kaizen: An action plan that involves organizing events focused on improving specific areas within the company. A philosophy that espouses building a corporate culture where all employees are actively engaged in suggesting and implementing improvements.

keyword search: A type of search that looks for matching documents that contain one or more words specified by the user.

LAN: *See* **local area network.**

law: The whole of statutes, administrative regulations, judicial precedents, and legal principles that define socially accepted limits and obligations on human behavior; a statute. (Pearce-Moses, *Glossary of Archival and Records Terminology,* ©SAA, www2.archivists.org/glossary, used with permission)

lean: A tool used by business to streamline the manufacturing and production processes by eliminating unnecessary and wasteful steps that do not add value to the finished product.

legal and regulatory risks: Risks related to compliance and arising from litigation. (ARMA International, *Evaluating and Mitigating Records and Information Risks*)

legal hold: *See* **destruction hold.**

local area network (LAN): A collection of computers, printers, storage devices, and other devices connected to allow resource sharing. (Pearce-Moses, *Glossary of Archival and Records Terminology*, ©SAA, www2.archivists.org/glossary, used with permission)

logical access control: Logical access controls are found in databases, applications, servers, and even in transit. Access to critical data is determined by a person's role, and the need for access is reviewed regularly. (DISA, *Access Control in Support of Information Systems*)

long-term digital preservation: A series of managed activities necessary to ensure continued access to digital materials for as long as necessary. (DPC, "Introduction—Definitions and Concepts")

long-term record: A record with a retention period of between 10 years and permanent. (Excerpted from *Glossary of Records Management and Information Governance Terms,* 5th ed., ©ARMA International, www.arma.org/, used with permission)

mashups: In the Web environment, a combination of information, media, or tools from two or more sources that previously had no relation to each other, which results in new content or a new service. (ARMA International, *Implications of Web-Based, Collaborative Technologies in Records Management*)

M-DISC: A natural stone-like substance used as a "write once read forever" (WORF) medium on which files are laser-engraved and cannot be overwritten, erased, or corrupted by natural processes. (Millenniata, "M-DISC")

media vault: A vault designed and built to protect digital media from temperatures above 125°F and 80 percent relative humidity.

Metadata: The structured information that describes, explains, locates, or otherwise makes it easier to retrieve, use, or manage information resources. (Excerpted from *Glossary of Records Management and Information Governance Terms,* 5th ed., ©ARMA International, www.arma .org/, used with permission)

Metadata Encoding and Transmission Standard (METS): An Extensible Markup Language (XML) schema used to package digital objects, along with descriptive, administrative, and structural metadata. (Pearce-Moses, *Glossary of Archival and Records Terminology,* ©SAA, www2.archivists.org/glossary, used with permission)

metadata for records: Structured or semistructured information that enables creation, management, and use of records through time and within and across domains. (ISO, *ISO 23081-1:2017*)

metadata framework: A high-level set of instruments to establish and implement metadata specifications consistently across systems and organizations. (ISO, *ISO 23081-1:2006*)

metadata schema: A logical plan showing the relationships between metadata elements, normally through establishing rules for the use and management of metadata specifically as regards the semantics, the syntax and the optionality *(obligation level)* of values. (ISO, *ISO 23081-1:2017*)

METS: *See* **Metadata Encoding and Transmission Standard.**

microblog: An internet service that delivers and stores limited text messages. Unlike email, which is generally a "push" service, these messages can be "pulled" through user subscription to a particular author or topic. The character length limitation makes it ideal for using with mobile devices, such as smartphones. (ARMA International, *Implications of Web-Based, Collaborative Technologies in Records Management*)

microfilm: A high-resolution film in roll form containing or mounted onto aperture cards containing microimages; the action of recording microimages on film. (Excerpted from *Glossary of Records Management and Information Governance Terms,* 5th ed., ©ARMA International, www.arma.org/, used with permission)

migration: Process of moving records from one hardware or software configuration to another without changing the format. *See also* **conversion.** (ISO, *ISO 15489-1:2016*)

mission statement: A written declaration of an organization's core purpose and focus that normally remains unchanged over time. Properly crafted mission statements (1) serve as filters to separate what is important from what is not, (2) clearly state which markets will be served and how, and (3) communicate a sense of intended direction to the entire organization. (BusinessDictionary .com)

monitoring: Supervising activities in progress to ensure they are on-course and on-schedule in meeting the objectives and performance targets. (BusinessDictionary.com)

needs assessment: *See* gap analysis.

nuclear specialist (CRM/NS): Designation that indicates a certified records manager has passed an additional exam section related to nuclear information records management. (NIRMA)

numeric filing system: Any classification system designed to arrange records based on numbers that are assigned or taken directly from a record, such as a purchase order.

ontology: A working model of entities and interactions in some particular domain of knowledge or practice, such as transportation. (Gruber, "Ontology")

operational plan: *See* action plan.

operational value: The usefulness or significance of records to support ancillary operations and management of an organization. *Principally Canadian:* The usefulness or significance of records related to the mandate, role, or mission of an organization by documenting the duties, responsibilities, functions, activities, and services performed. (Pearce-Moses, *Glossary of Archival and Records Terminology,* ©SAA, www2.archivists.org/glossary, used with permission)

passive preservation: An approach to digital preservation that ensures continuing integrity of and controlled access to digital objects along with their associated metadata. The original digital objects are kept intact without changing the technologies used to store or process them (e.g., refreshing data, replication, and emulation.) (IRMT, *Training in Electronic Records Management*)

performance monitoring: Method to continually measure performance and provide ongoing feedback to employees and workgroups on their progress toward reaching their goals. Performance monitoring can also monitor the overall performance of programs, processes, and systems.

Personally identifiable information (PII): Information by which an individual may be identified, including an individual's name, social security number, date or place of birth, financial history, and employment information.

physical access controls: Physical access controls limit access to physical and electronic assets through the use of strategies (e.g., human screeners) and tools (e.g., ID cards, safes, vaults, and biometric systems based on fingerprints or the patterns visible within the iris of an eye). (DISA, *Access Control in Support of Information Systems*)

platform as a service (PaaS): A common reference to the layer of cloud technology architecture that contains all application infrastructure services, which are also known as *middleware* in other contexts. (Gartner, *IT Glossary*)

policy-based data preservation: A set of elements—purpose, properties, policies, procedures, state information, assessment criteria, and federation—that are integrated into the preservation system as actionable rules and executable computer procedures. (Moore et al., *NARA Transcontinental Persistent Archive Prototype*)

preservation: The process and operation involved in ensuring the technical and intellectual survival of authentic records through time. (Excerpted from *Glossary of Records Management and Information Governance Terms,* 5th ed., ©ARMA International, www.arma.org/, used with permission)

Preservation Metadata: Implementation Strategies (PREMIS): The name of an international working group sponsored by OCLC and RLG from 2003–2005. When referring to PREMIS, most people mean the PREMIS Data Dictionary, but occasionally they may be referring to the XML schema, the working group, or the entire effort, including the maintenance activity carried out by the Library of Congress. (Caplan, *Understanding PREMIS*)

primary value (of records): The value of records derived from the original use that caused them to be created. (Pearce-Moses, *Glossary of Archival and Records Terminology,* ©SAA, www2 .archivists.org/glossary, used with permission)

professional development: Process of improving and increasing capabilities of staff through access to education and training opportunities in the workplace, through outside organizations, or through watching others perform the job. (BusinessDictionary.com)

program audits: Systematic studies conducted to assess how well a program or operation is working.

project management professional (PMP): The PMP designation, certified by the Project Management Institute, provides evidence that the PMP has the experience, education, and competency to successfully lead and direct projects. (Project Management Institute)

proprietary information (PI): Intangible information assets including copyrights, patents, software programs, source code, and algorithms.

protected health information (PHI): Any information on a health condition that can be linked to a specific person.

provenance (n.; provenancial, adj.): The origin or source of something. Information regarding the origins, custody, and ownership of an item or collection.

radio frequency identification (RFID): A technology that uses radio frequencies and a data tag to identify, track, locate, and manage items. (Excerpted from *Glossary of Records Management and Information Governance Terms,* 5th ed., ©ARMA International, www.arma.org/, used with permission)

really simple syndication (RSS): Form of web coding that allows information from a site to be displayed on a computer or other webpage as a continuous stream of information. Individuals are able to subscribe to particular feeds and are notified each time the content is updated or changed. Any content including text, music, and pictures files can be converted and transmitted in an RSS form. This type of service is beneficial to users who want to view in one place information from many various sources. (BusinessDictionary.com) Also known as *rich site summary or rich site syndication.*

record: Any recorded information, regardless of medium or characteristics, made or received by an organization in pursuance of legal obligations or in the transaction of business. (Excerpted from *Glossary of Records Management and Information Governance Terms,* 5th ed., ©ARMA International, www.arma.org/, used with permission)

record group (archives): A collection of records that share the same provenance and are of a convenient size for administration. Also known as *archive group.* (Pearce-Moses, *Glossary of Archival and Records Terminology,* ©SAA, www2.archivists.org/glossary, used with permission)

records: Information created, received, and maintained as evidence and as an asset by an organization or person, in pursuance of legal obligations or in the transaction of business. (ISO, *ISO 15489-1:2016*)

records and information management (RIM): Field of management responsible for establishing and implementing policies, systems, and procedures to capture, create, access, distribute, use, store, secure, retrieve, and ensure disposition of an organization's records and information. Also known as *records management.* (Excerpted from *Glossary of Records*

Management and Information Governance Terms, 5th ed., ©ARMA International, www.arma
.org/, used with permission)

records appraisal: *See* appraisal.

records capture: Ensuring that a record (e.g., a receipt, contract, or directive) becomes fixed
so that it cannot be altered or deleted and that it is stored in a location where it can be
retrieved, accessed, preserved, and managed.

records center: 1. (digital records) A storage device with lower operating costs, which may be
online or off-line depending on the speed and frequency of access required for the records.
2. (paper records) An area for lower-cost storage, maintenance, and reference use of semi-active records pending their ultimate disposition. (Excerpted from *Glossary of Records Management and Information Governance Terms,* 5th ed., ©ARMA International, www.arma
.org/, used without permission)

records classification: The process followed to categorize or group records into retrieval units.

records classification scheme: A tool used to classify records and other business information
based on the business activities that generate records. Also known as *file plan.*

records continuum: A model of archival science that emphasizes overlapping characteristics of
recordkeeping, evidence, transaction, and the identity of the creator. (Pearce-Moses, *Glossary of Archival and Records Terminology,* ©SAA, www2.archivists.org/glossary, used with
permission)

records control risks: Risks related to records classification, records retention and disposition,
and records storage. (ARMA International, *Evaluating and Mitigating Records and Information Risks*)

records disaster: A sudden and unexpected event, which results in the loss of records and information essential to an organization's continued operation.

records inventory: A detailed listing that includes the types, locations, dates, volumes, equipment, classification systems, and usage data of an organization's records. (Excerpted from
Glossary of Records Management and Information Governance Terms, 5th ed., ©ARMA International, www.arma.org/, used with permission)

records lifecycle: The span of time of a record from its creation or receipt, through its useful
life, to its final disposition, whether that disposition is destruction or retention as a historical record. (ARMA International, *Requirements for Managing Electronic Messages as Records*)

records management (RM): Field of management responsible for the efficient and systematic control of the creation, receipt, maintenance, use, and disposition of records, including
processes for capturing and maintaining evidence of and information about business activities and transactions in the form of records. (ISO, *ISO 15489-1:2016*)

records management application (RMA): Software that aids the management of records,
especially electronic records, including the use of a file plan for classifying records and of a
records schedule for identifying records that are due for disposition. (Pearce-Moses, *Glossary of Archival and Records Terminology,* ©SAA, www2.archivists.org/glossary, used with
permission)

records management policy: Mandated guidelines for managing records within an organization. (Excerpted from *Glossary of Records Management and Information Governance Terms,*
5th ed., ©ARMA International, www.arma.org/, used with permission)

records management procedures: Records management procedures are a set of steps, instructions, and/or other methodologies to follow in order to complete records management
tasks in a predictable and orderly way.

records management strategic plan: A blueprint for constructing or improving a records and
information management program, a plan to effectively manage the lifecycle of records and

information, a road map for effectively preserving historical and archival records, and a tool for developing a system that ensures delivery of the right information to the right person at the right time.

records manager: Individual within an organization who is responsible for systematically managing the recorded information generated and received by the organization. (Excerpted from *Glossary of Records Management and Information Governance Terms,* 5th ed., ©ARMA International, www.arma.org/, used with permission)

records retention and disposition schedule: *See* records retention schedule.

records retention schedule (RSS): A comprehensive list of records series titles, indicating for each series the length of time it is to be maintained. Also known as *records retention and disposition schedule.* (Excerpted from *Glossary of Records Management and Information Governance Terms,* 5th ed., ©ARMA International, www.arma.org/, used with permission)

records series: A group of related records filed/used together as a unit and evaluated as a unit for retention purposes (e.g., a personnel file consisting of an application, reference letters, benefit forms, etc.). (Excerpted from *Glossary of Records Management and Information Governance Terms,* 5th ed., ©ARMA International, www.arma.org/, used with permission)

regulation: The process of controlling something through rule or procedure; a rule that is issued by an authorized government agency and that has the force of law. (Pearce-Moses, *Glossary of Archival and Records Terminology,* ©SAA, www2.archivists.org/glossary, used with permission)

relational content analysis: A method of content analysis that goes beyond determining the presence of concepts to looking for meaningful (semantic) relationships between those concepts. Also known as *semantic analysis.* (Palmquist, Carley, and Dale, "Applications of Computer-Aided Text Analysis")

relational database: Information that has been organized, structured, and stored into tables of rows and columns (flat files) so that related data elements from different tables can be manipulated and extracted for various purposes. (Pearce-Moses, *Glossary of Archival and Records Terminology,* ©SAA, www2.archivists.org/glossary, used with permission)

relational database management system(s) (RDBMS): A type of database management system (DBMS) that stores data in the form of related tables. (*Webopedia*)

reliability: The quality of being trustworthy over time. (Excerpted from *Glossary of Records Management and Information Governance Terms,* 5th ed., ©ARMA International, www.arma .org/, used with permission)

repository: A place where things can be stored and maintained; a storehouse. (Pearce-Moses, *Glossary of Archival and Records Terminology,* ©SAA, www2.archivists.org/glossary, used with permission)

request for information (RFI): Request made typically during the project planning phase where a buyer cannot clearly identify product requirements, specifications, and purchase options. RFIs clearly indicate that award of a contract will not automatically follow. (BusinessDiction ary.com)

request for proposal (RFP): Document used in sealed-bid procurement procedures through which a purchaser advises the potential suppliers of (1) statement and scope of work, (2) specifications, (3) schedules or time lines, (4) contract type, (5) data requirements, (6) terms and conditions, (7) description of goods and/or services to be procured, (8) general criteria used in evaluation procedure, (9) special contractual requirements, (10) technical goals, (11) instructions for preparation of technical, management, and/or cost proposals. RFPs are publicly advertised and suppliers respond with a detailed proposal, not just with a price quotation. (BusinessDictionary.com)

request for quotation (RFQ): Document used in soliciting price and delivery quotations that meet minimum quality specifications for a specific quantity of specific goods and/or services. (BusinessDictionary.com)

respect des fonds: This archival principle dictates that records of different origins (provenance) be kept separate to preserve their context. *See also* **provenance**.

reverse index search: The reverse index tells you what documents contain the word you are searching for.

rights management: A system that identifies intellectual property rights relevant to particular works and that can provide individuals with access to those works on the basis of permissions to the individuals. (Pearce-Moses, *Glossary of Archival and Records Terminology,* ©SAA, www2.archivists.org/glossary, used with permission)

RIM: *See* **records and information management.**

risk analysis: Process to comprehend the nature of risk and to determine the level of risk. (BSI, *BS 31100:2011*)

risk appetite: Amount and type of risk that an organization is willing to pursue or retain. (BSI, *BS 31100:2011*)

risk assessment: Overall process of risk identification, risk analysis, and risk evaluation. (BSI, *BS 31100:2011*)

risk capacity: The amount and type of risk an organization is able to support in pursuit of its business objectives. (Ernst and Young, "Risk Appetite")

risk level: Magnitude of a risk or combination of risks, expressed in terms of the combination of consequences and their likelihood. (BSI, *BS 31100:2011*)

risk management: The identification, assessment, and prioritization of risks (defined as the effect of uncertainty on objectives, whether positive or negative) followed by coordinated and economical application of resources to minimize, monitor, and control the probability and/or impact of undesired events. (Excerpted from *Glossary of Records Management and Information Governance Terms,* 5th ed., ©ARMA International, www.arma.org/, used with permission)

risk mitigation: A systematic reduction in the extent of exposure to a risk and/or the likelihood of its occurrence. Also called risk reduction. (BusinessDictionary.com)

risk tolerance: Organization's or stakeholder's readiness to bear the risk after treatment in order to achieve its objectives. (BSI, *BS 31100:2011*)

RMA: *See* **records management application.**

RSS: *See* **really simple syndication.**

schema: A formal description of a data structure. (Pearce-Moses, *Glossary of Archival and Records Terminology,* ©SAA, www2.archivists.org/glossary, used with permission)

secondary value (of records): The usefulness or significance of records based on purposes other than that for which they were originally created. (Pearce-Moses, *Glossary of Archival and Records Terminology,* ©SAA, www2.archivists.org/glossary, used with permission)

semantic analysis: Semantic analysis goes beyond determining the presence of concepts to looking for meaningful (semantic) relationships between those concepts. Also known as *relational content analysis.* (Palmquist, Carley, and Dale, "Applications of Computer-Aided Text Analysis")

semantic search: A semantic search will search and discover the meaning of words and not just their occurrence.

Semantic Web: An extension of the current World Wide Web that catalogs information on a webpage and reprocesses it so that other machines including computers can understand the information. (BusinessDictionary.com)

semantics: Semantics refers to the meaning of words.

semi-structured data: Unstructured data that has been organized and/or has metadata attached that describes its content, for example, SharePoint lists and document libraries.

service level agreement (SLA): A contract between an application service provider (ASP) and the end user that stipulates and commits the ASP to a required level of service. An SLA should contain a specified level of service, support options, enforcement, or penalty provisions for services not provided, a guaranteed level of system performance as relates to downtime or uptime, a specified level of customer support, and what software or hardware will be provided and for what fee. *See also* **terms of service (TOS) agreement.** (*Webopedia*)

SMART objectives: A set of goals that are characterized by being specific, measurable, available at an acceptable cost, relevant, and time-bound. SMART objectives are typically used in a business context by project managers when initially evaluating and setting goals for a project. (Business Dictionary.com)

social bookmarking: A method for storing and managing bookmarks of webpages with individually chosen keywords; also the sharing of this data. (Dictionary.com)

social media: Tools and platforms, usually on the internet, specifically designed for participatory interaction such as publishing, conversing, and sharing content, including multimedia. The tools include but are not limited to blogs, wikis, photo or video sharing, microblogging, and social networking sites. (ARMA International, *Implications of Web-Based, Collaborative Technologies in Records Management*)

social media policy: A social media policy (also called a social networking policy) is a corporate code of conduct that provides guidelines for employees who post content on the internet either as part of their job or as a private person. (SearchCompliance, "Social Media Policy")

social media record: Social media content, regardless of physical form or characteristics, which meets the organization's criteria for a record. The term is used in this text to represent all records posted to, created through, or residing in social media technologies.

social networking: A special type of social media that uses web and internet technology to enable interactions between people through the use of such features as personal profiles, blogs, content sharing, and messaging surrounded by an enabling framework of file storage, navigation, searching, and access controls. (ARMA International, *Implications of Web-Based, Collaborative Technologies in Records Management*)

social networking site: A website that provides a virtual community for people to share their daily activities with family and friends, or to share their interest in a particular topic, or to increase their circle of acquaintances. (PCMag.com, *Encyclopedia*)

software as a service (SaaS): Delivery of software over the internet, eliminating the need to install the software on the organization's own computers.

static website: A website that uses Uniform Resource Locators (URLs) to point to fixed content. (Pearce-Moses, *Glossary of Archival and Records Terminology,* ©SAA, www2.archivists.org/glossary, used with permission)

strategic plan: A broadly defined plan aimed at creating a desired future. (BusinessDictionary.com)

strategy: A method or plan chosen to bring about a desired future, such as achievement of a goal or solution to a problem; the art and science of planning and marshaling resources for their most efficient and effective use. (BusinessDictionary.com)

structural metadata: Information about the relationship between the parts that make up a compound object. (Pearce-Moses, *Glossary of Archival and Records Terminology,* ©SAA, www2.archivists.org/glossary, used with permission)

structured data: Data organized in a way that makes it identifiable, such as a database structured in the form of columns and rows.

structured search: Structured search is a method of using the structure of a document to help users find the right documents in a large collection of documents. (McCreary, "Structured Search")

subject filing system: A file system in which each document relates to a specific subject matter and is arranged in alphabetic order by subject. (Excerpted from *Glossary of Records Management and Information Governance Terms,* 5th ed., ©ARMA International, www.arma .org/, used with permission)

SWOT analysis: Situation analysis in which internal strengths and weaknesses of an organization, and external opportunities and threats faced by it are closely examined to chart a strategy. (BusinessDictionary.com)

system of engagement: A type of system characterized by interactions, immediacy, and accessibility, collaboration, and conversations. Examples are web conferences and microblogs. Also known as *social business systems.* (Moore, *A Sea Change in Enterprise IT*)

system of record: A type of system characterized by transactions, accuracy, and completeness, authored content, and documents (text and graphics). Examples are systems to manage human resources, order processing, customer relationships, and supply chain management. (Moore, *A Sea Change in Enterprise IT*)

tagging: A specific piece of metadata—keyword term or phrase—that is assigned to a content object for use in browsing or searching. The process of tagging generally refers to the ability of users to collaboratively add their own descriptive tags to information. (ARMA International, *Implications of Web-Based, Collaborative Technologies in Records Management*)

tangible asset: An asset having a physical form, such as buildings, machinery, and inventory.

taxonomy: A collection of controlled vocabulary terms used to describe an organization's information components. The taxonomy may or may not have a hierarchical structure. (Excerpted from *Glossary of Records Management and Information Governance Terms,* 5th ed., ©ARMA International, www.arma.org/, used with permission)

technology risks: Risks associated with information security, electronic communications, and software applications. (ARMA International, *Evaluating and Mitigating Records and Information Risks*)

telecommuting: Substitution of telecommunications for transportation in a decentralized and flexible work arrangement that allows part-time or full-time employees to work at home via a computer attached to the employer's data network. (BusinessDictionary.com)

telework: European term for *telecommuting.* (BusinessDictionary.com)

terms of service (TOS) agreement: Rules one must agree to and abide by in order to use a service. Also known as *Terms of Use or Terms and Conditions. See also* service level agreement (SLA).

text content analysis tools: Tools that provide statistics about the text (written content)—such as word count, number of sentences, and reading ease—to help users improve their writing.

thesaurus: A controlled vocabulary of terms arranged in a structured order and with relationships between terms indicated with standardized designations; used to aid document indexing and searching. (Excerpted from *Glossary of Records Management and Information Governance Terms,* 5th ed., ©ARMA International, www.arma.org/, used with permission)

topic map: A set of topics and associations. The user can freely define any relationship, and it is possible to link subjects to a related information resource. (Topic Maps Lab)

Topic Maps: Topic Maps is an international industry standard (*ISO 13250*) for technology that enables information management and interchange. (Topic Maps Lab)

transfer (custody): The change of custody, ownership, and/or responsibility for records. (Excerpted from *Glossary of Records Management and Information Governance Terms,* 5th ed., ©ARMA International, www.arma.org/, used with permission)

transient data: Data created within an application session that passes quickly into and out of existence producing results beyond itself; at the end of the session, it is discarded or reset back to its default and not stored in a database (PCMag.com, *Encyclopedia*)

transitory records: Records needed for a short time that can be acted upon and then destroyed. (Archives of Ontario, *Transitory Records*)

trend spotting: The process of systematically monitoring and assessing both the internal and external environments to identify changes taking place over the short or long term, analyzing their implications for the organization, and interpreting their impact on professional practice.

trusted digital repository: One whose mission is to provide reliable, long-term access to managed digital resources to its designated community, now and in the future. (RLG, *Trusted Digital Repositories*)

trustworthiness: The quality of being dependable and reliable; in the context of electronic records, trustworthiness often implies that the system is dependable and produces consistent results based on well-established procedures. (Pearce-Moses, *A Glossary of Archival and Records Terminology*, ©SAA, www2.archivists.org/glossary, used with permission)

unstructured data: A generic label for describing any corporate information that is not in a database. (SearchBusinessAnalytics, "What Is Unstructured Data?")

usability: Qualities of a record that allow it to be accessed, processed, and understood over time. (Excerpted from *Glossary of Records Management and Information Governance Terms*, 5th ed., ©ARMA International, www.arma.org/, used with permission)

vector search model: The vector search model considers a search query a vector in keyword space and then scores the items located based on the distance from your query, calculated by counting the number of times keywords appeared in each document, the size of the document, and the density of the keywords in the document. Also known as the *vector space search model*.

virtual office applications: Software applications that enable staff to access web-based tools (e.g., email, calendar, word processing, spreadsheets, and web conferencing) remotely.

virtual world: A virtual world is an interactive simulated environment accessed by multiple users through an online interface. Also known as *digital world, simulated world,* or, in some cases, *immersive environment.* (VWR, "What Is a Virtual World?")

vision statement: An aspirational description of what an organization would like to achieve or accomplish in the mid-term or long-term future. It is intended to serve as a clear guide for choosing current and future courses of action. *See also* **mission statement**. (BusinessDictionary .com)

vital record: A record that is fundamental to the functioning of an organization and necessary to the continuance of operations. (Excerpted from *Glossary of Records Management and Information Governance Terms,* 5th ed., ©ARMA International, www.arma.org/, used with permission)

vital records manual: A communications tool used to document the vital records program either published separately or as part of a records management manual.

vital records program: Policies, plans, and procedures developed and implemented and the resources needed to identify, use, and protect the essential records needed to meet operational responsibilities under emergency or disaster conditions or to protect the organization's rights or those of its stakeholders. (Environmental Protection Agency, "Glossary of Terms")

vital records schedule: A listing of an organization's vital records along with an explanation of how each is to be protected from destruction in the event of a disaster. The information can be gathered from the records inventory.

vital statistics: Public records required by law that document significant life events, such as births, deaths, marriages, divorces, and public health events, and that are kept by city, county, state, or other governmental bodies. (Pearce-Moses, *Glossary of Archival and Records Terminology,* ©SAA, www2.archivists.org/glossary, used with permission)

vocabulary: The set of terms used in an index or in the headings of a catalog. *Computing:* The set of labels used in an Extensible Markup Language (XML) document. (Pearce-Moses, *Glossary of Archival and Records Terminology,* ©SAA, www2.archivists.org/glossary, used with permission)

warm site: An alternative computing facility that has the equipment and resources available to recover business functions in the event of a disaster and is regularly synchronized with the main site. (Excerpted from *Glossary of Records Management and Information Governance Terms,* 5th ed., ©ARMA International, www.arma.org/, used with permission)

Web 2.0: The name given to the second generation of the World Wide Web that utilizes social media and other collaborative services. (ARMA International, *Implications of Web-Based, Collaborative Technologies in Records Management*)

Web 3.0: A term also used interchangeably with the *Semantic Web* by some experts. Web 3.0, a phrase coined by John Markoff of the New York Times in 2006, refers to a supposed third generation of internet-based services that collectively comprise what might be called "the intelligent web"—such as those using Semantic Web, microformats, natural language search, data-mining, machine learning, recommendation agents, and artificial intelligence technologies—and that emphasize machine-facilitated understanding of information in order to provide a more productive and intuitive user experience. (Spivack, "Timeline and Definition")

web archiving: Saving the pages from websites as they change over time for historical purposes. Using spiders similar to the ones search engines routinely deploy, there are services that archive the pages of a company's own website or pages from selected websites across the internet. (PCMag.com, *Encyclopedia*)

web content management system(s) (WCMS): Allows a number of people to maintain a website using a simple web-browser-based interface (instead of manually authoring webpages). Most use a database to store and control a dynamic collection of web material.

web publishing: Creating a website and placing it on the web server. (PCMag.com, *Encyclopedia*)

web services: A standardized way of integrating web-based applications using the XML, SOAP, WSDL, and UDDI open standards over an internet protocol backbone. (*Webopedia*)

wide area network (WAN): Data and voice communication network that extends beyond the geographical limitations of a local area network (LAN). (BusinessDictionary.com)

wiki: A webpage or series of webpages hosted on the internet or an intranet that allow those with access and permissions to easily edit, contribute, and publish content. (ARMA International, *Using Social Media in Organizations*)

word processing: The process of creating, formatting, and editing documents with the assistance of computers. (Pearce-Moses, *Glossary of Archival and Records Terminology,* ©SAA, www2.archivists.org/glossary, used with permission)

word processor: 1. A type of software that displays characters based on a user's input on an external or internal keyboard. The software allows the user to edit, modify, and format documents based on display preferences. The most common word processors are Microsoft Word and WordPerfect. **2.** A machine similar to a typewriter that prints text as a user strokes keys on a keyboard. These machines have mostly been replaced with personal computers. (BusinessDictionary.com)

workflow: A series of tasks defined within an organization to produce a final outcome. (Excerpted from *Glossary of Records Management and Information Governance Terms,* 5th ed., ©ARMA International, www.arma.org/, used with permission)

workflow diagram (WFD): Graphical depiction of steps taken, time spent, distance traveled, and other aspects of the way a particular piece of work is done. (BusinessDictionary.com)

World Wide Web (WWW): The massive collection of information and services accessible over the internet through the hypertext transfer protocol (HTTP); the servers and network infrastructure used to store and deliver web-based information and services. (Pearce-Moses, *Glossary of Archival and Records Terminology,* ©SAA, www2.archivists.org/glossary, used with permission)

"write once read forever" (WORF): A WORF medium cannot be overwritten, erased, or corrupted by natural processes. (Millenniata, "M-DISC") *See also* M-DISC.

XML: *See* Extensible Markup Language.

XML schema: Documents defining the legal building blocks of an XML document.

BIBLIOGRAPHY

Acker, Edward, AIA. "Archives and Records Storage Buildings." National Institute of Building Sciences, updated March 21, 2017.

AIIM. Training. www.aiim.org/Education-Section/Education-Landing-Page.

_____. "What is Enterprise Content Management (ECM)?" Glossary. Accessed September 1, 2017. www.aiim.org/What-is-ECM-Enterprise-Content-Management#.

_____. *ANSI/AIIM/ARMA TR48-2006 Revised Framework for Integration of Electronic Document Management Systems and Electronic Records Management Systems.* Silver Spring, MD: AIIM International, 2006.

_____. "What is Information Management?" Accessed January 6, 2018. www.aiim.org/Resources/Glossary/Information-Management#.

Alulive. "Patent Inspiration." Accessed January 12, 2018. https://app.patentinspiration.com/.

American Council for Technology (ACT) and Industry Advisory Council (IAC). Best Practices Study of Social Media Records Policies: ACT-IAC Collaboration and Transformation (C&T) Shared Interest Group (SIG), March 2011, 11. https://www.actiac.org/system/files/Best%20Practices%20of%20Social%20Media%20Records%20Policies%20-%20CT%20SIG%20-%2003-31-11%20%283%29.pdf.

American National Standards Institute (ANSI), *ASIS/BSI BCM.01-2010: Business Continuity Management Systems: Requirements with Guidance for Use.* New York: ANSI, 2010.

AncientScripts.com. "Cuneiform." Accessed August 13, 2017. www.ancientscripts.com/cuneiform.html.

Apache Solr. The Apache Software Foundation. Accessed September 24, 2017. http://lucene.apache.org/solr/.

Arata, Nicole. "5 Ways to Get a Car You Need to Drive for Uber or Lyft." *USA Today.* January 8, 2017. https://www.usatoday.com/story/money/personalfinance/2017/01/08/5-ways-get-car-you-need-drive-uber-lyft/96214312/.

ARMA International. "ARMA International Maturity Model for Information Governance." Accessed January 6, 2018. https://www.lva.virginia.gov/agencies/records/psrc/documents/Principles.pdf.

_____. "ARMA Recognizes Farmers Insurance with Coveted Award of Excellence." November 9, 2017. www.arma.org/news/377159/.

_____. *Controlled Language in Records and Information Management.* Lenexa, KS: ARMA International, 2008.

_____. *Dashboard.* Accessed January 2, 2018. http://education.arma.org/diweb/dashboard.

_____. *Evaluating and Mitigating Records and Information Risks.* Overland Park, KS: ARMA International, 2009.

_____. *Generally Accepted Recordkeeping Principles.* www.arma.org/docs/bookstore/theprinciplesmaturitymodel.pdf.

_____. *Glossary of Records Management and Information Governance Terms.* 5th edition. Overland Park, KS: ARMA International, 2016.

_____. *Guideline for Evaluating Offsite Records Storage Facilities.* Lenexa, KS: ARMA International, 2007.

_____. *Implementing the Generally Accepted Recordkeeping Principles,* TR 30-2017. Overland Park, KS: ARMA International, 2017.

_____. *Information Governance Maturity Model.* Accessed January 1, 2018. https://www.lva.virginia.gov/agencies/records/psrc/documents/Principles.pdf.

_____. *Records Center Operations,* 3rd Edition. Overland Park: Kansas, 2011.

_____. *Records and Information Management Core Competencies,* 2nd Edition. Overland Park: Kansas, 2017.

_____. *Standards Development Program Workgroup, Records Center Operations,* 3rd ed., ANSI/ARMA TR01-2011. Overland Park, KS: ARMA International, 2011.

_____. *Understanding Electronic Records Storage Technologies.* ARMA TR26-2014. Overland Park, KS: ARMA International, 2014.

_____. *Using DoD 5015.02-STD outside the Federal Government Sector.* ARMA TR 04-2009. Lenexa, KS: ARMA International, 2009.

_____. *Vital Records,* ANSI/ARMA, TR29-2017. Overland Park, KS: ARMA International, 2017.

_____. *Website Records Management: An ARMA International Guide.* Overland Park, KS: ARMA International, 2009.

Associated Press. "Hospital Workers Suspended for Allegedly Peeking at Clooney Medical Info." *FoxNews.com.* October 10, 2007. www.foxnews.com/story/0,2933,300648,00.html.

_____. "New Foreclosure Defense: Prove I Owe You." *NBCNews.com.* February 17, 2009. www.nbcnews.com/id/29242063/ns/business-real_estate/t/new-foreclosure-defense-prove-i-owe-you/#.WgngTIZrxG8.

Atkinson, Edward. "Data Warehousing—A Boat Records Managers Should Not Miss." *Records Management Journal* 11, no. 1, 35–43.

AWS. "What is a Data Warehouse?" https://aws.amazon.com/data-warehouse/.

Bailey, Kyle O., James S. Okolica, and Gilbert L. Peterson. "User Identification and Authentication Using Multi-Modal Behavioral Biometrics." *Computers & Security* 43, 77–89.

Bailey, Steve. *Managing the Crowd: Rethinking Records Management for the Web 2.0 World.* London: Facet Publishing, 2008.

Bellis, Mary. "History of Email & Ray Tomlinson." About.com Guide. Accessed August 13, 2017. http://inventors.about.com/od/estartinventions/a/email.htm.

Belsie, Laurent. "Wal-Mart: World's Largest Company." *The Christian Science Monitor.* February 19, 2002. www.csmonitor.com/2002/0219/p01s04-usec.html.

Benedon, William. "Outsourcing: The Right Decision?" *Information Management Journal,* January 2000, 34–41.

Bentley, Michael. "Fighting Amazon's Supply Chain Takeover," *Logistics Management,* January 31, 2017. www.logisticsmgmt.com/article/fighting_amazons_supply_chain_takeover.

BISG. *Complete Subject Headings List, 2016 Edition.* Accessed September 8, 2017. http://bisg.org/page/BISACEdition.

Blair, Ron, and Mark Thomas Jaggers. "Magic Quadrant for Disaster Recovery as a Service." Gartner. June 19, 2017. https://www.gartner.com/doc/3746618/magic-quadrant-disaster-recovery-service.

Bolick, Cheryl Mason. "Digital Archives: Democratizing the Doing of History." *International Journal of Social Education* 21, no. 1 (Spring-Summer 2006), 122. http://eric.ed.gov/PDFS/EJ782136.pdf.

Boudreaux, Chris. "Social Media Policy Database." Social Media Governance.com. Accessed October 22, 2017. http://socialmediagovernance.com/policies/.

Bradley, Kevin. "Defining Digital Sustainability." *Library Trends* 56, no. 1 (2007), 148–163. http://hdl.handle.net/2142/3772.

Brandenberg, Denise. "Request for Information vs. Request for Proposal." *eHow.* Updated December 26, 2017. www.ehow.com/about_6462623_request-information-vs-request-proposal .html.

Brewer, Laurence. Memorandum to Federal Senior Agency Officials for Records Management and Agency Records Officers: Federal Agency Records Management Report. September 28, 2017. https://www.archives.gov/records-mgmt/memos/ac39-2017.

British Standards Institution (BSI). *Business Continuity Management: Code of Practice.* BS 25999-1, 2006. London: British Standards Institution.

Broadridge Financial Solutions. "Welcome Disney Shareholders." Accessed October 7, 2017. http://shareholder.broadridge.com/disneyinvestor/#navTabs4.

Brooks, Chad. "Document Management Systems: A Buyers Guide." *Business News Daily.* January 19, 2017. www.businessnewsdaily.com/8026-choosing-a-document-management-system.html.

Business and Professions Code—BPC, Division 8, Chapter 22.1. Privacy Rights for California Minors in the Digital World [22580–22582]. Accessed January 13, 2018. http://leginfo.legislature.ca.gov/faces/codes_displayText.xhtml?lawCode=BPC&division=8.&chapter=22.1.

Business Continuity Institute. "Business Continuity," *Glossary of Business Continuity Terms.* Accessed December 3, 2017. https://www.drj.com/downloads/drj_glossary.pdf.

BusinessDictionary.com. Accessed December 21, 2017. www.business diction-ary.com/definition/risk-mitigation.html.

Business Insider. "Messaging Apps Are Now Bigger Than Social Networks." September 20, 2016. www.businessinsider.com/the-messaging-app-report-2015-11.

Cachin, Christian, and Marko Vukolic. "Blockchain Consensus Protocols in the Wild" *Arxiv.* July 17, 2017. https://arxiv.org/pdf/1707.01873.pdf.

Cao, Jing. "Facebook Commits to Audit of Its Ad Metrics by Media Watchdog," Bloomberg Technology. Accessed December 23, 2017. https://www.bloomberg.com/news/articles/2017-02-10/facebook-commits-to-audit-of-ad-metrics-by-media-watchdog.

Capella University. "Health Information Management Specialization, Bachelor of Science in Information Technology." Accessed December 31, 2017. https://www.capella.edu/online-degrees/bachelors-it-health-information-management/.

Capterra. "Top Live Chat Software Products." Accessed August 13, 2017. www.capterra.com/live-chat-software/.

Carthy, Mike. "10 Things You Need to Know about the GDPR," *Information and Records Management Bulletin,* March 2017, 196.

Carmichael, David W. *Organizing Archival Records: A Practical Method of Arrangement and Description of Small Archives.* Walnut Creek, CA: AltaMira Press, 2004.

Casanova, Eugenio. *Archivistica.* Siena: Lazzeri, 1928.

Castro, Arielle. "E-Signature Market Update: What to Expect in 2017," *RPost,* December 19, 2016. www.rpost.com/blog/e-signature-market-update-expect-2017/.

CBS News. "3 Emerging Technologies to Go Mainstream in 2011," January 10, 2011. *CBS Money Watch.* (video). www.cbsnews.com/video/watch/?id=10495949n?tag=bnetdomain.

CBS/Associated Press. "George Washington's Copy of Constitution on Display at Mount Vernon Estate." *CBS News.* September 17, 2012. www.cbsnews.com/news/george-washingtons-copy-of-constitution-on-display-at-mount-vernon-estate/.

Cedar Hills. "City Recorder Receives Excellence in Information Governance Award." Accessed January 2, 2018. www.cedarhills.org/node/4772.

Cerf, V. Digital Vellum and Archives. NITRD—The Networking and Information Technology Research and Development Program. August 12, 2016. https://www.nitrd.gov/nitrdgroups/index.php?title=DigitalVellumAndArchives.

Chang, Lulu. "The Latest Data Breach Involves the Voting Records of 93.4 Million Mexican Citizens." April 13, 2016. https://www.digitaltrends.com/computing/mexico-voting-breach/.

Christensen, Clayton. (n. d.). "Disruptive Innovation." Accessed October 19, 2017. www.claytonchristensen.com/key-concepts/.

Christensen, Jen, and Elizabeth Cohen. "Medical Errors May Be Third Leading Cause of Death in the U.S," *CNN.* May 4, 2016. http://edition.cnn.com/2016/05/03/health/medical-error-a-leading-cause-of-death/.

Cisco, Susan. "How to Win the Compliance Battle Using 'Big Buckets.'" *Information Management.* July-August 2008. http://content.arma.org/IMM/JulyAug2008/How_to_win_the_compliance_battle.aspx.

Civil Code 1798.82. California Legislative Information. Accessed January 13, 2018. http://leginfo.legislature
.ca.gov/faces/codes_displaySection.xhtml?lawCode=CIV&sectionNum=1798.82.

Clearwater Compliance. "The Clearwater Definition of an Information Asset." Accessed January 8, 2018.
https://clearwatercompliance.com/wp-content/uploads/2015/11/Clearwater-Definition-of
-Information-Assets-with-Examples_V8.pdf.

Clifford, Catherine. "Billionaire Tech Investor: There Will Be a Mark Zuckerberg and Bill Gates of AI,"
Forbes. September, 25, 2017. https://www.forbes.com/sites/benkerschberg/2017/09/26/5-best
-artificial-intelligence-articles-you-should-read-today-916/#24ac9bcc6d19.

Cohen, Bret A., Michael T. Renaud, and Nicholas W. Armington. "Explaining the Defend Trade Secrets Act."
Business Law Today. September 2016. https://www.americanbar.org/publications/blt/2016/09/03
_cohen.html.

Cohen, David. "New Look for Pinterest Business Profiles," November 30, 2016. www.adweek.com/digital/
pinterest-business-profiles-update/.

Cohn, Michael. "As Sarbanes-Oxley Nears 15-Year Anniversary, Ethics Fall Short," *Accounting Today*,
July 24, 2017. https://www.accountingtoday.com/news/as-sarbanes-oxley-nears-15-year-anniversary
-ethics-fall-short.

Coles, Cameron. "Only 9.4% of Cloud Providers Are Encrypting Data at Rest." Accessed December 19, 2017.
https://www.skyhighnetworks.com/cloud-security-blog/only-9-4-of-cloud-providers-are-encrypting
-data-at-rest/.

Columbus, Louis. "Gartner's Hype Cycle for Emerging Technologies, 2017 Adds 5G and Deep Learning
for First Time," *Forbes*. August 15, 2017. https://www.forbes.com/sites/louiscolumbus/2017/08/15/
gartners-hype-cycle-for-emerging-technologies-2017-adds-5g-and-deep-learning-for-first-time/
#420ad65b5043.

Constine, Josh. "Facebook Now Has 2 Billion Users . . . And Responsibility." *TechCrunch*. June 27, 2017.
https://techcrunch.com/2017/06/27/facebook-2-billion-users/.

Consultative Committee for Space Data Systems (CCSDS). *Reference Model for an Open Archival Information
System (OAIS): Recommendation for Space Data System Practices*. June 2012. http://public.ccsds.org/
publications/archive/650x0m2.pdf.

———. *Recommendation for Space Data System Practices: Audit and Certification of Trustworthy Digital
Repositories—Recommended Practice (Magenta Book)*, CCSDS 652.0-M-1, CCSDS Secretariat, September
2011. http://public.ccsds.org/publications/archive/652x0m1.pdf.

Cornell University Law School. "Electronic Signatures in Global and National Commerce." 15 USC § 96.
Legal Information Institute. Accessed September 1, 2017. www.law.cornell.edu/uscode/15/usc
_sup_01_15_10_96.html.

———. "Federal Records Act of 1950, 44 USC § 2901 et seq." Legal Information Institute. Accessed
September 1, 2017. www.law.cornell.edu/uscode/html/uscode44/usc_sup_01_44_10_29.html.

———. "Fourth Amendment, US Constitution." Accessed January 13, 2018. https://www.law.cornell.edu/
constitution/fourth_amendment.

Cover pages. "W3C Director Tim Berners-Lee Awarded Millennium Technology Prize." Accessed August 13,
2017. http://xml.coverpages.org/ni2004-04-23-b.html.

Cox, Richard J. *Closing an Era: Historical Perspectives on Modern Archives and Records Management*.
Westport, CT: Greenwood Press.

Craig, Barbara. "Appraisal." In *Encyclopedia of Archival Science*, edited by Luciana Duranti and
Patricia C. Franks. Rowan and Littlefield, 2015.

Davis, Jessica. "7 Largest Data Breaches of 2015." *Healthcare IT News*. December 11, 2015.
www.healthcareitnews.com/news/7-largest-data-breaches-2015.

Dayen, David. "Mortgage Companies Seek Time Travelers to Find Missing Documents." *The Intercept*.
June 17, 2016. https://theintercept.com/2016/06/17/mortgage-companies-seek-time-travelers-to-find
-missing-documents/.

DealBook. "AOL to Sell ICQ Service to D.S.T. for $187.5 Million." *The New York Times,* April 28, 2004. 2017. https://dealbook.nytimes.com/2010/04/28/aol-to-sell-icq-service-to-d-s-t-for-187-5-million/.

DELL-Stephanie N. "@DellOutlet Surpasses $2 Million on Twitter." *Direct2Dell: The Official Dell Corporate Blog,* June 2009. http://en.community.dell.com/dell-blogs/direct2dell/b/direct2dell/archive/2009/06/11/delloutlet-surpasses-2-million-on-twitter.aspx.

Deloitte. "Six Control Principles for Financial Services Blockchain." 2017. https://www2.deloitte.com/content/dam/Deloitte/ie/Documents/Technology/IE_C_BLOCKCHAINPRINCIPLES.pdf.

Dennes, Meridith Fiedler. "How to Start a Blog in 2017 (Step by Step Guide with Images)." July 25, 2017. https://www.linkedin.com/pulse/how-start-blog-2017-step-by-step-guide-images-meridith-fiedler-dennes/.

Department of Defense. *DoD 5015.02-STD: Electronic Records Management Software Applications Design Criteria Standard.* Washington, DC: United States Department of Defense, April 25, 2007. www.dtic.mil/whs/directives/corres/pdf/501502std.pdf.

_____. Instruction, Number 5015.02, Incorporating Change 1. August 17, 2017. www.esd.whs.mil/Portals/54/Documents/DD/issuances/dodi/501502p.pdf?ver=2017-08-17-142503-963.

Dictionary.com. http://dictionary.reference.com.

Digipress Commons. (n. d.) "About the POWRR Tool Grid." Accessed June 22, 2017. www.digipres.org/tools/about/.

Digital Curation Centre (DCC). "What Is Digital Curation? DCC Charter and Statement of Principles." Accessed June 13, 2017. www.dcc.ac.uk/about-us/dcc-charter.

Digital Identity and Authentication Council of Canada. "Design Solutions: Using Blockchain for Real Estate Transactions." 2017. https://diacc.ca/design-solutions-using-blockchain-for-real-estate-transactions/.

Digital Preservation Coalition. (DPC). "Digital Preservation." Introduction—Definitions and Concepts." Accessed June 12, 2017. http://dpconline.org/handbook.

"Disaster Preparedness, Response and Recovery—Advice and Resources." Washington State Archives. Accessed December 3, 2017. https://www.sos.wa.gov/archives/RecordsManagement/DisasterPreparednessandRecovery.aspx.

DLM Forum Foundation. *MoReq2010: Modular Requirements for Records Systems.* Accessed October 7, 2017. http://MoReq.info/.

"Don't Let Trade Secrets Leave with Departing Employees." Jux Law Firm. Accessed January 16, 2018. https://jux.law/trade-secrets-departing-employees/.

Doran, G. T. "There's a S.M.A.R.T. Way to Write Management's Goals and Objectives." *Management Review* 70, no. 11 (AMA Forum), 35–36.

Dreyfuss, Emily. "American Spies Now Have Their Very Own Smartphone App." *Wired.* April 4, 2017. https://www.wired.com/2017/04/american-spies-now-smartphone-app/.

_____. "The Wikipedia for Spies—And Where It Goes From Here." *Wired.* March 10, 2017. https://www.wired.com/2017/03/intellipedia-wikipedia-spies-much/.

DRI. "Building the Digital Repository of Ireland Infrastructure." 2015. Achttps://repository.dri.ie/catalog/qr474f68n.

Duke Law. "EDRM." Accessed January 5, 2018. https://www.edrm.net/frameworks-and-standards/information-governance-reference-model/white-paper/.

Dunwoodie, Brice. "Vignette a Leader in ECM Magic Quadrant," October, 25, 2004. www.cmswire.com/cms/enterprise-cms/vignette-a-leader-in-ecm-magic-quadrant-000459.php.

EAB. "Cost of Data Breaches in Education Hits All-Time High: $245 per Record." July 27, 2017. https://www.eab.com/daily-briefing/2017/07/27/cost-of-data-breaches-in-education-hits-all-time-high-$245-per-record.

eBay. "Open for Business." Accessed July 24, 2017. https://www.ebayinc.com/stories/podcast/.

eBizMBA Guide. "Top 15 Most Popular Blogs, July 2017." Accessed August 13, 2017. www.ebizmba.com/articles/blogs.

EDRM. "Information Governance Reference Model (IGRM)." www.edrm.net/frameworks-and-standards/information-governance-reference-model/using-the-igrm-model/.

Engage Digital. "IBM Saves $320,000 with Second Life." Accessed August 13, 2017. www.engagedigital.com/blog/2009/02/27/ibm-saves-320000-with-second-life-meeting/.

English, Stacey, Susannah Hammond, and Ashley Kovas. "Culture and Conduct Risk 2017." Accessed December 21, 2017. https://risk.thomsonreuters.com/content/dam/openweb/documents/pdf/risk/report/culture-and-conduct-risk-report-2017.pdf.

Ennis, Sharon R., Merarys Ríos-Vargas, and Nora G. Albert. *The Hispanic Population: 2010. 2010 Census Briefs.* May 2011. www.census.gov/prod/cen2010/briefs/c2010br-04.pdf.

Enterprise Search. "Lucidworks 3 Released!" January 25, 2017. Accessed September 24, 2017, www.enterprisesearchblog.com/open-source/.

Environmental Protection Agency. Office of Environmental Information. *EPA Information Procedures: Vital Records Procedures.* June 8, 2009. www.epa.gov/irmpoli8/policies/CI02155P010.pdf.

Erway, Ricky. *Defining "Born Digital."* OCLC Online Computer Library Center, Inc. November 2010. www.oclc.org/research/activities/hiddencollections/borndigital.pdf.

Etherington, Suzanne, and Ann Marie Przybyla. *Inventory and Planning: The First Steps in Records Management.* Archives Technical Information Series, 76 (2003). www.archives.nysed.gov/a/records/mr_pub76_accessible.html.

Europa. "Protection of Personal Data." Last modified January 2, 2011. http://europa.eu/legislation_summaries/information_society/data_protection/114012_en.htm.

Executive Office of the President. Memorandum for the Heads of Executive Departments and Agencies and Independent Agencies. August 24, 2012. https://www.archives.gov/files/records-mgmt/m-12-18.pdf.

ExpertGlossary. "Electronic Record." Accessed December 1, 2012. www.expertglossary.com/definition/electronic-record#.

Facebook. "Accessing Your Facebook Data." https://www.facebook.com/elp/405183566203254?helpref=faq_content.

Faitelson, Yaki. "Yes, the GDPR Will Affect Your U.S.-Based Business." *Forbes.* December 4, 2017. https://www.forbes.com/sites/forbestechcouncil/2017/12/04/yes-the-gdpr-will-affect-your-u-s-based-business/#23594d536ff2.

Federal Agencies Digitization Guidelines Initiative. Accessed June 12, 2017. www.digitizationguidelines.gov/.

Federal Trade Commission. "Data Breach Response: A Guide for Business." September 2016. https://www.ftc.gov/system/files/documents/plain-language/pdf-0154_data-breach-response-guide-for-business.pdf.

Ferriero, David S. "Criteria for Managing Email Records in Compliance with the Managing Government Records Directive (M-12-18)." April 6, 2106. https://www.archives.gov/files/records-mgmt/email-management/2016-email-mgmt-success-criteria.pdf.

Financial Industry Regulatory Authority (FINRA), "Regulatory Notice 17-18—Social Media and Digital Communications: Guidance on social networking websites and business communications," April 2017. https://www.finra.org/sites/default/files/notice_doc_file_ref/Regulatory-Notice-17-18.pdf.

FindLaw. Annotation 5—Fourth Amendment: Electronic Surveillance and the Fourth Amendment. Accessed January 13, 2018. http://constitution.findlaw.com/amendment4/annotation05.html#1.

———. "Time Limits for Filing Product Liability Cases: State-by-State." Accessed September 14, 2017. http://injury.findlaw.com/defective-dangerous-products/defective-dangerous-products-law/state-time-limits-for-filing-product-liability-cases.html.

FINRA, "2210. Communications with the Public," *FINRA Manual.* Accessed October 22, 2017. http://finra.complinet.com/en/display/display_main.html?rbid=2403&element_id=10648.

———. "Communications with the Public." Regulatory Notice 12-29, June 2012. www.finra.org/sites/default/files/NoticeDocument/p127014.pdf.

_____. "Communications with the Public: Respective Rule Review Report." December 2014. www.finra.org/sites/default/files/p602011.pdf.

_____. "Social Media and Digital Communications." Regulatory Notice 17-18, April 2017. www.finra.org/sites/default/files/notice_doc_file_ref/Regulatory-Notice-17-18.pdf.

_____. "Social Media Web Sites: Guidance on Blogs and Social Networking Web Sites." Regulatory Notice 10-06, January 2010. www.finra.org/web/groups/industry/@ip/@reg/@notice/documents/notices/p120779.pdf.

Fister, Barbara. "The Dewey Dilemma." _Library Journal._ May 2010. http://lj.libraryjournal.com/2010/05/public-services/the-dewey-dilemma/.

Florida Department of State. "General Records Schedule GS4 for Pubic Hospitals, Health Care Facilities, and Medical Providers," State Library and Archives of Florida, December 1997. (Technical updates May 2007). https://www.unf.edu/uploadedFiles/anf/controllers/records_management/GS04_Retention_Schedule_for_Health_Care_Facilities.pdf.

Florida Gulf Coast University. "Records Management." Accessed January 4, 2018. https://www2.fgcu.edu/recordsmanagement/.

Foote, Keith D. "Data Governance and Information Governance: Contemporary Solutions," DATAVERSITY. September 13, 2013. www.dataversity.net/data-governance-information-governance-contemporary-solutions/.

FoxNews. "FISA Surveillance Program: What Is It and Why Is It So Controversial?" January 19, 2018. www.foxnews.com/politics/2018/01/19/fisa-surveillance-program-what-is-it-and-why-is-it-so-controversial.html.

Franks, Patricia C. _How Federal Agencies Can Effectively Manage Records Created Using New Social Media Tools._ Washington, DC: IBM Center for the Business of Government, 2010.

Franks, Patricia C., et. al. "Retention and Disposition in a Cloud Environment, Final Report." May 17, 2016. InterPARES Trust. https://interparestrust.org/assets/public/dissemination/NA06_20160902_RetentionDispositionInCloud_FinalReport_Final.pdf.

G2 Crowd. "Best Video Hosting Software." Accessed August 14, 2017. https://www.g2crowd.com/categories/video-hosting.

_____. "Best Web Content Management Systems." Accessed October 7, 2017. https://www.g2crowd.com/categories/web-content-management.

GDPR Portal. Accessed January 15, 2018. https://www.eugdpr.org/.

Gareth, Morgan. "Leading Vendors Collaborate for Records Management Scheme." _Computing.co.uk._ July 14, 2011. www.computing.co.uk/ctg/news/2094155/leading-vendors-collaborate-records-management-scheme.

Gartner. "Cybersecurity." Accessed January 17, 2018. https://www.gartner.com/doc/2510116/definition-cybersecurity.

_____. "Magic Quadrant for Data Loss Prevention." February 16, 2107. https://www.gartner.com/doc/reprints?aid=elq_&id=1-3TNX4ZE&ct=170216&st=sb&elqTrackId=8d8d38a20614419385976f5b7a11f062&elqaid=3769&elqat=2.

_____. "Magic Quadrant for Enterprise Integration Platform as a Service." March 30, 2017. https://www.gartner.com/doc/reprints?id=1-3X0Y452&ct=170403&st=sb.

_____. "Magic Quadrant for Web Conferencing." November 10, 2106. https://www.gartner.com/doc/reprints?id=1-3LPJBEI&ct=161110&st=sb.

_____. "What Is Enterprise Content Management (ECM) Software?" _Gartner Peer Insights._ Accessed September 1, 2017. https://www.gartner.com/reviews/market/enterprise-content-management.

General Data Protection Regulation. www.eugdpr.org/the-regulation.html.

Gerroll, Olivia. "Rule 1, 16, 26, 34, 37: FRCP Amendments Pertaining to eDiscovery. "March 9, 2106. http://d4discovery.com/discover-more/2016/3/the-2015-amendments-to-the-frcp-that-pertain-to-ediscovery#sthash.ppDeMjR1.dpbs.

Getty Research Institute. "Categories for the Description of Works of Art," J. Paul Getty Trust,. Last modified October 6, 2015. www.getty.edu/research/publications/electronic_publications/cdwa/index.html.

Ghosh, P. "Google's Vint Cerf Warns of 'Digital Dark Age.'" *BBC News.* February 13, 2105. www.bbc.com/news/science-environment-31450389GlobalRelay. https://www.globalrelay.com/.

Ghosh, Sudipto. "Content Management Systems with Web Analytics & Social Media Integrations Key to Industry." *Market Technology Insights.* March 2017. http://martechseries.com/content-marketing/content-management/content-management-systems-with-web-analytics-social-media-integrations-key-to-industry/.

Goldman vs. United States (1942). No. 962. FindLaw. Accessed January 13, 2018. http://caselaw.findlaw.com/us-supreme-court/316/129.html#t6.

Golliher, Sean. "SemTech 2011 Coverage: PayPal Discusses Social Commerce and the Semantic Web, DATAVERSITY. June 13, 2011. www.dataversity.net/semtech-2011-coverage-paypal-discusses-social-commerce-and-the-semantic-web/.

Goodwin, Tom. "The Battle Is for the Customer Interface." *TechCrunch.* March 3, 2105. https://techcrunch.com/2015/03/03/in-the-age-of-disintermediation-the-battle-is-all-for-the-customer-interface/.

Gordon, C. H. *Forgotten Scripts: Their Ongoing Discovery and Decipherment.* New York: Basic Books, 1982.

Grand, P. M. *Prehistoric Art: Paleolithic Painting and Sculpture.* Greenwich: New York Graphic Society, 1967.

Great Britain Patent Office. *Patents for Inventions: Abridgments of Specifications Relating to Printing, Including Therein the Production of Copies on All Kinds of Materials.* London: George E. Eyre and William Spottiswoode, 1859.

Greenspan, Gideon. "Avoiding the Pointless Blockchain Project: How to Determine If You've Found a Real Blockchain Use Case." Blog post, November 2015. https://www.multichain.com/blog/2015/11/avoiding-pointless-blockchain-project/.

———. "The Blockchain Immutability Myth." Blog post, May 2107. https://www.multichain.com/blog/2017/05/blockchain-immutability-myth/.

Greenwell, Matthew. *Defense-in-Policy Begets Defense-in-Depth.* SANS Institute. March 26, 2015. https://www.sans.org/reading-room/whitepapers/leadership/defense-in-policy-begets-defense-in-depth-35882.

Gruber, Thomas R. "Toward Principles for the Design of Ontologies Used for Knowledge Sharing" (Technical Report KSL 93-04, Knowledge Systems Laboratory, Stanford University), paper presented at the International Workshop on Formal Oncology, Padova, Italy, March 1993. www-ksl.stanford.edu/KSL_Abstracts/KSL-93-04.html.

Haaramo, E. "Finnish Government Scraps Paper and Digitizes Archives." *ComputerWeekly.* June 28, 2107. www.computerweekly.com/news/450421553/Finnish-government-scraps-paper-and-digitises-archives.

Haber, Stuart, and Pandurang Kamat. "A Content Integrity Service for Long-Term Digital Archives." (published in and presented at the IS&T Archiving 2006 Conference, Ottawa, Canada, May 23–26, 2006). www.hpl.hp.com/techreports/2006/HPL-2006-54.pdf.

Headwaters Group. "Your Unstructured Data is Sex—You just Don't Know It." May 23, 2017. http://content.theheadwatersgroup.com/blog/your-unstructured-data-is-sexy-see-how.

HealthIT.gov. "Patient Unified Lookup System for Emergencies (PULSE)." 2017. Accessed December 2, 2017. https://www.healthit.gov/techlab/ipg/node/4/submission/1801.

Heritrix. Accessed October 20, 2017. https://webarchive.jira.com/wiki/spaces/Heritrix/overview.

HHS.gov. "Lack of Timely Action Risks Security and Costs Money." February 1, 2017. https://www.hhs.gov/hipaa/for-professionals/compliance-enforcement/agreements/childrens.

Hill, Kashmir. "So, What Are These Privacy Audits That Google and Facebook Have to Do for the Next 20 Years?" *Forbes.* November 30, 2011. www.forbes.com/sites/kashmirhill/2011 /11/30/so-what-are-these-privacy-audits-that-google-and-facebook-have-to-do-for-the-next-20 -years/.

Hilliard, John. "The King of All Backup Jobs: Backing up the Library of Congress." *TechTarget.* 2013. http://searchdatabackup.techtarget.com/feature/The-king-of-all-backup-jobs-Backing-up-the -Library-of-Congress.

HIPPA Journal. "Major 2016 Healthcare Data Breaches: Mid-Year Summary." July 11, 2016. https://www.hipaajournal.com/major-2016-healthcare-data-breaches-mid-year-summary-3499/.

"The History of European Archival Literature." *The American Archivist* 2, no. 2 (April 1939), 69–70. http://americanarchivist.org/doi/pdf/10.17723/aarc.2.2.d7821153t468kr64?code=same-site.

Hobert, Karen A., Gavin Tay, and Joe Mariano. "Magic Quadrant for Enterprise Content Management." Gartner. October 26, 2016. https://www.gartner.com/doc/reprints?id=1-3KZPGDB&ct=161031&st=sb.

Hobert, Karen A., Michael Woodbridge, Joe Mariano, and Gavin Tay. "Magic Quadrant for Content Services Platforms." Gartner. October 5, 2017. https://www.m-files.com/en/Gartner-Magic-Quadrant-CSP -2017.

Holmes, Oliver W. "Archival Arrangement—Five Different Operations at Five Different Levels." National Archives and Records Administration (NARA). 1964. www.archives.gov/research/alic/reference/ archives-resources/archival-arrangement.html.

HootSuite. Accessed October 21, 2017. https://hootsuite.com/#.

HQ PaperMaker. "All about Paper." Accessed August 13, 2017. www.hqpapermaker.com/paper-history/.

Hummel, Rob, and Jimmy Kemp. "Today's Digital Documents Are Tomorrow's Dinosaurs," *Washington Times.* December 22, 2011. www.washingtontimes.com/news/2011/dec/22/todays-digital-documents -are-morrows-dinosaurs/.

Humphrey, Albert S. "SWOT Analysis for Management Consulting." *SRI Alumni Association Newsletter* (SRI International), December 2005, 7–8. https://www.sri.com/sites/default/files/brochures/dec-05.pdf.

IA. "What is Information Governance?" *Information Architecture Inc.* (Blog). Accessed August 29, 2017. www.informationarchitected.com/blog/what-is-information-governance/.

IAPP. "What Does Privacy Mean?" accessed January 13, 2018. https://iapp.org/about/what-is-privacy/.

IBM. "IBM Sametime." Accessed August 13, 2017. https://www-03.ibm.com/software/products/en/ ibmsame.

———. "IBM Sets New Record for Magnetic Tape Storage; Makes Tape Competitive for Cloud Storage," August 2, 2017. www-03.ibm.com/press/us/en/pressrelease/52904.wss.

———. "IBM Social Computing Guidelines." Accessed October 22, 2017. www.ibm.com/blogs/zz/en/ guidelines.html.

IDC. "Data Growth, Business Opportunities, and the IT Imperatives." April 2014. https://www.emc.com/ leadership/digital-universe/2014iview/executive-summary.htm.

———. "IDC Sees the Dawn of the DX Economy and the Rise of the Digital-Native Enterprise." November 1, 2016. https://www.idc.com/getdoc.jsp?containerId=prUS41888916.

Idpf. EPUB 3.1, latest version January 5, 2017. www.idpf.org/epub/31/spec/epub-spec.html#sec-epub-specs.

IMLS. "From Theory to Action: 'Good Enough' Digital Preservation Solutions for Under-Resourced Cultural Heritage Institutions." 2014. (Whitepaper). *Institute of Museum and Library Services.* Accessed June 22, 2017. https://commons.lib.niu.edu/bitstream/handle/10843/13610/FromTheoryToAction _POWRR_WhitePaper.pdf?sequence=1&isAllowed=y.

Indeed. "Records & Information Lifecycle Manager." Accessed December 31, 2017. https://www.indeed.com/q-Records-Manager-jobs.html?vjk=2bb7f425ca652cc7.

InetSoft. "Enterprise Data Mashups." 2017. Accessed August 12, 2017. https://www.inetsoft.com/solutions/ enterprise_data_mashup/.

Influence Health. "Content Management System (CMS) by Influence Health." 2017. Accessed October 7, 2017. https://www.influencehealth.com/consumer-experience-platform/content-management-system.

Information Asset Development, Inc. "What is an Information Asset?" Accessed January 8, 2018. www.informationassetdevelopment.com/what.html.

Information Governance and Society of American Archivists. *Sample Forms for Archival and Records Management Programs.* Lenexa, KS: ARMA International, 2002.

Inmon, Bill. "A Tale of Two Architectures." Corporate Information Factory. Accessed September 27, 2017. www.inmoncif.com/products/A%20TALE%200F%20TWO%20ARCHITECTURES.pdf.

InsideBigData. "The Exponential Growth of Big Data." February 16, 2017. https://insidebigdata .com/2017/02/16/the-exponential-growth-of-data/.

Internal Revenue Service (IRS). "How Far Back Can the IRS Go to Audit My Return?" IRS Audit FAQs, last modified September 11, 2017. https://www.irs.gov/businesses/small-businesses-self-employed/ irs-audits#far-backs.

International Organization for Standardization (ISO). *ISO 15444-1:2016 Informationt technology— JPG 2000 image coding system: Core coding system.* Accessed June 22, 2017, https://www.iso.org/ standard/70018.html.

_____. *ISO 15489-1:2016 Information and documentation—Records management—Part 1: Concepts and principles.* Geneva: ISO, 2016.

_____. *ISO 15489-1:2001: Information and documentation—Records management—Part 1: General.* Geneva: ISO, 2001.

_____. *ISO 15836:2009 Information and documentation—The Dublin Core Metadata Element Set.* Geneva: ISO, 2009.

_____. *ISO 16175-1:2010 Information and documentation—Principles and functional requirements for records in electronic office environments—Part 1: Overview and statement of principles.* Geneva: ISO, 2010.

_____. *ISO 16363:2012: Space data and information transfer systems—Audit and certification of trustworthy digital repositories* (abstract). Accessed January 23, 2013. www.iso.org/iso/iso_catalogue/catalogue_tc/ catalogue_detail.htm?csnumber=56510.

_____. *ISO 18934:2011: Imaging materials—Multiple media archives—Storage environment.* Geneva: ISO, 2011.

_____. *ISO 23081-1:2017 Information and documentation—Records management processes—Metadata for records—Part 1: Principles.* Geneva: ISO, 2017.

_____. *ISO 23081-2:2009 Information and documentation—Managing metadata for records—Part 2: Conceptual and implementation issues.* Geneva: ISO, 2009.

_____. *ISO 22313:2012 Societal security—Business continuity management systems—Guidance.* Geneva, Switzerland: ISO, 2012.

_____. *ISO/IEC 27000 Information security management systems.* https://www.iso.org/isoiec-27001 -information-security.html.

_____. *ISO 31000:2009 Risk management—Principles and Guidelines.* Geneva: ISO, 2009.

_____. "ISO Survey of Management System Standard Certification 2016. September 2017." Accessed January 16, 2018. https://isotc.iso.org/livelink/livelink/fetch/-8853493/8853511/8853520/18808772/00 ._Executive_summary_2016_Survey.pdf?nodeid=19208898&vernum=-2.

InterPARES Trust. "Checklist for Cloud Service Contracts: Final Version," last reviewed February 26, 2016. https://interparestrust.org/assets/public/dissemination/NA14_20160226_CloudServiceProvider Contracts_Checklist_Final.pdf.

Investopedia. "Generally Accepted Accounting Principles (GAAP)." Accessed January 11, 2018. https://www.investopedia.com/terms/g/gaap.asp.

Iron Mountain. "The IG Initiative Definition of Information Governance." 2017. Accessed August 28, 2017. www.ironmountain.com/Knowledge-Center/Reference-Library/View-by-Document-Type/General -Articles/T/The-IG-Initiative-Definition-of-Information-Governance.aspx.

_____. (n. d.). "Important Versus Vital Records: The Magic 5% You Can't Live Without." Executive Summary. www.ironmountain.com/resources/whitepapers/i/important-versus-vital-records-the-magic-5-you -cant-live-without.

ITL Bulletin for April 2010. "Guide to Protecting Personally Identifiable Information." Accessed January 16, 2018. https://csrc.nist.gov/csrc/media/publications/shared/documents/itl-bulletin/itlbu12010-04.pdf.

JDSUPRA. "Court Approves Defendant's Proposed Sampling Production Plan: eDiscovery Case Law. May 5, 2017. www.jdsupra.com/legalnews/court-approves-defendant-s-proposed-42450/.

Jenkinson, Sir Hilary. *"Roots," Selected Writings of Sir Hilary Jenkinson.* Eds. Roger Ellis and Peter Walne. Gloucester: Alan Sutton, 1980.

Johnson, Laurie. "Major Brands Are Betting Big on Podcasts and It Seems to Be Paying Off." August 28, 2016. www.adweek.com/digital/major-brands-are-betting-big-on-podcasts-and-it-seems-be-paying-173035/.

Johnson, Robert J. *Information Disposition: A Practical Guide to the Secure, Compliant Disposal of Records. Media and IT Assets,* Phoenix, AZ: NAID, 2017.

Joint Interoperability Test Command (JITC). "RMA Product Register." Accessed September 1, 2017. http://jitc.fhu.disa.mil/projects/rma/reg.aspx.

Justia.com. "Management of Vital Records." US Law, 36 CFR § 1236.20 (1995). http://law.justia.com/cfr/title36/36-3.0.10.2.17.html.

Kennedy, Jay and Cherryl Schauder. *Records Management: A Guide to Corporate Recordkeeping.* 2nd Ed. Melbourne: Longmans, 1998.

Kerry, Cameron F. "Lessons from the New Threat Environment from SONY, Anthem and ISIS." March 26, 2015. Brookings. https://www.brookings.edu/blog/techtank/2015/03/26/lessons-from-the-new-threat-environment-from-sony-anthem-and-isis/.

Khan, Kamran. "Here's Why Insight Engines Are the Next Big Thing." *CMS Wire,* August 8, 2017. www.cmswire.com/digital-workplace/heres-why-insight-engines-are-the-next-big-thing/.

Kharpal, Arjun. "Amazon Wins Patent for a Flying Warehouse That Will Deploy Drones to Deliver Parcels in Minutes." *CNBC.* December 30, 2016.

Khoste. "Product Overview." http://khoste.com/product-overview/.

King, Paul. "The Right Cyber Coverage Can Protect a Business from Financial Ruin." *Insurance Journal.* November 16, 2016. https://www.insurancejournal.com/news/east/2016/11/16/432350.htm.

Kong, Weize. "Extending Faceted Search to Open-Domain Web." June 2016. *ACM SIGIR Forum.* (Newsletter), 60, no 1., 90–91.

Krizanic, Sarah. "Mobile Devices and Applications are Transforming Clinical Practice." *California Healthcare News.* August 8, 2017. www.cahcnews.com/articles/08-2017/ca-skrizanic-0817.php.

Kukura, Joe. "Uber Admits to Manipulating Fares and Prices." *SFWeekly.* May 22, 2017. www.sfweekly.com/news/uber-admits-manipulating-fares-and-prices/.

Laney, Douglas B. *Infonomics: How to Monetize, Manage and Measure Information as an Asset for Competitive Advantage.* New York: Bibliomotion, 2018.

_____. "Infonomics: The Practice of Information Economics." *Forbes.* May 22, 2012. https://www.forbes.com/sites/gartnergroup/2012/05/22/infonomics-the-practice-of-information-economics/#111d89ad6ee4.

Lantmäteriet. "Annual Report." 2016. www.lantmateriet.se/contentassets/3d550bd6c8104483bac8d1fca69f4a4e/webb_lm.verksamhetsberattelse.eng.2016_170323.pdf.

Leahy, Emmett J. "Modern Records Management." *American Archivist* 12, no. 3 (July 1949). http://archivists.metapress.com/content/52344260u1064020/fulltext.pdf.

Legal-Explanations.com. "Bill of Lading." www.legal-explanations.com/definitions/bill-of-lading.htm.

Lemieux, Victoria L. "Blockchain Recordkeeping: A SWOT Analysis." www.bluetoad.com/publication/?i=454085&ver=htm15&p=22#{"page":22,"issue_id":454085}.

_____. "Trusting Records: Is Blockchain Technology the Answer?" *Records Management Journal* 26 no. 2, 2016.

_____. "A Typology of Blockchain Recordkeeping Solutions and Some Reflections on Their Archival Implications." 2nd IEEE Big Data Workshop on Computational Archival Science: IEEE, 2017.

Lemieux, Victoria Louise, Brianna Gormly, and Lyse Rowledge. "Meeting Big Data Challenges with Visual Analytics," *Records Management Journal,* July 2014.

LexisNexis. "Search Basics." Lexis Advance Support and Training. Accessed September 24, 2017.
    https://www.lexisnexis.com/en-us/support/lexis-advance/search-basics.page.

Library and Archives Canada. Government of Canada Records Management Standard.
    February 7, 2006.

Library of Congress. Classification Web. Accessed September 8, 2017. www.loc.gov/cds/classweb/.

———. "About the National Jukebox." Accessed June 13, 2017. www.loc.gov/jukebox/about.

———. "Library of Congress Recommended Formats Statement." 2016–2017. Accessed June 12, 2017.
    https://www.loc.gov/preservation/resources/rfs/RFS%202016-2017.pdf.

———. "Library of Congress Strategic Plan FY2016 through FY2020: Serving Congress and the Nation."
    Accessed June 13, 2017. https://www.loc.gov/portals/static/about/documents/library_congress
    _stratplan_2016-2020.pdf.

———. "Metadata Encoding and Transmission Standard (METS)," Standards, last modified August 18, 2017.
    www.loc.gov/standards/mets/.

———. "METS: An Overview & Tutorial." Standards, last modified March 30, 2017. https://www.loc.gov/
    standards/mets/METSOverview.v2.html.

———. "MIX: NISO Metadata for Images in XML Schema." Standards, last modified November 23, 2015.
    www.loc.gov/standards/mix/.

Lifewire. "Everything You Need to Know about SMS & MMS." Accessed August 13, 2017.
    https://www.lifewire.com/what-is-sms-mms-iphone-2000247.

———. "What Happened to AIM Chat Rooms?" Accessed August 13, 2017. https://www.lifewire.com/
    what-happened-to-aim-chat-rooms-3969418.

LinkedIn. "The Top 100 CEOs on Social Media." March 17, 2016. https://www.linkedin.com/pulse/
    top-100-ceos-social-media-steve-tappin.

———. "User Agreement." Effective June 7, 2017. https://www.linkedin.com/legal/user-agreement.

Lord, Nate. "Cybersecurity Incident Response Planning: Expert Tips, Steps, Testing & More." *DataInsider*.
    July 27, 2017. https://digitalguardian.com/blog/incident-response-plan.

Ludäscher, Bertram, Richard Marciano, and Reagan Moore. "Preservation of Digital Data with Self-
    Validating, Self-Instantiating Knowledge-Based Archives." *ACM SIGMOD Record*. September 2001.
    doi.10.1145/603867.603876.

Lundy, James, Kenneth Chin, and Karen M. Shegda. "Start Planning for Enterprise Content Management."
    Gartner. November 16, 2017. https://www.gartner.com/doc/461344/start-planning-enterprise
    -content-management.

Lupton, Deborah. "The Quantified Self Movement: Some Sociological Perspectives." November 4, 2012.
    https://simplysociology.wordpress.com/2012/11/04/the-quantitative-self-movement-some
    -sociological-perspectives/.

MacMillan Dictionary. "Professional Development." Accessed December 30, 2017.
    https://www.macmillandictionary.com/dictionary/british/professional-development.

Mancini, John. "The Next Wave: Moving from ECM to Intelligent Information Management." *AIIM*. 2017.
    Accessed August 27, 2017. www.aiim.org.

Manning, Patricia. "Competency Statement E. (e-Portfolio Prepared in Partial Fulfillment of MARA
    Degree)." Unpublished essay, 2011.

MARA. School of Information, San José State University. Accessed December 31, 2017.
    http://ischool.sjsu.edu/programs/master-archives-records-administration-mara.

Massachusetts Society of Certified Public Accountants, Inc., *The Record Retention Guide, 2004*.
    www.cpa.net/resources/retengde.pdf.

Masunaga, Samantha. "FBI Doesn't Have to Say Who Unlocked San Bernardino Shooter's iPhone, Judge
    Rules." October 2, 2017. *Los Angeles Times*. www.latimes.com/business/la-fi-tn-fbi-iphone-20171002
    -story.html.

Mata, Willie. "Data Loss Statistics That Will Make You Think Twice About Business Continuity." Center Technologies. May 18, 2015. https://centretechnologies.com/data-loss-statistics-that-will-make-you -think-twice-about-business-continuity/.

Matney, Lucas. "YouTube Has 1.5 Billion Logged-In Monthly Users Watching a Ton of Mobile Video." *TechCrunch.* June 22, 2017. https://techcrunch.com/2017/06/22/youtube-has-1-5-billion-logged-in -monthly-users-watching-a-ton-of-mobile-video/.

McGoogan, Cara. "Uber Drivers Gang Up to Cause Surge Pricing, Research Says." *The Telegraph.* August 12, 2017. www.telegraph.co.uk/technology/2017/08/02/uber-drivers-gang-cause-surge-pricing-research -says/.

McLellan, Charles. "IT Budgets 2016: Surveys, Software and Services." *ZDNet.* October 1, 2015. Retrieved from www.zdnet.com/article/it-budgets-2016-surveys-software-and-services/.

Meola, Andrew. "What Is the Internet of Things (IoT)? *Business Insider.* December 19, 2016. www.businessinsider.com/what-is-the-internet-of-things-definition-2016-8.

Merriam-Webster Online. http://unabridged.merriam-webster.com/unabridged/information.

Metz, Cade. "Web 3.0." *PC Magazine.* March 14, 2017. https://www.pcmag.com/article2/0,2817,2102852,00.asp.

Metz, Rachel. "Second Life Is Back for a Third Life, This Time in Virtual Reality." *MIT Technology Review.* January 27, 2017. https://www.technologyreview.com/s/603422/second-life-is-back-for-a-third-life -this-time-in-virtual-reality/.

Microsoft. "Office 365 Meets Evolving eDiscovery Challenges in a Cloud-First World." December 19, 2016. Accessed December 24, 2017. https://www.microsoft.com/itshowcase/Article/Content/843/Office -365-meets-evolving-eDiscovery-challenges-in-a-cloudfirst-world.

———. "On Demand Sessions." Accessed January 1, 2018. https://myignite.microsoft.com/videos?q=records %2520management#ignite-html-anchor.

Microsoft Office. Accessed October 12, 2017. https://products.office.com/en-us/business/get-office-365-for -your-business-with-latest-2016-apps?&WT.srch=1&wt.mc_id=AID623587_SEM_udcTpKDH.

Millenniata. *M-DISC.* Accessed June 13, 2017. www.mdisc.com/corporate/.

Ministry of Education, Culture, and Sport. "History of the General Archive of Simancas," General Archive of Simancas. Accessed on August 13, 2017. www.mecd.gob.es/cultura-mecd/en/areas-cultura/archivos/ mc/archivos/ags/presentacion/historia.html.

MIT Technology Review. "About Us." Massachusetts Institute of Technology. Accessed October 19, 2017. https://www.technologyreview.com/about/.

Moar, James. "Wearables—The Heartbeat on Your Sleeve." *Juniper Research.* November 2015.

———. "Fitness Wearables—Time to Step Up." *Juniper Research.* January 2016.

"Mobile Device Security in the Workplace: 6 Key Risks and Challenges." Accessed December 21, 2017. https://www.slideshare.net/Forsythe_Technology/mobile-devices-in-the-workplace-5-key-security -risks-11988063/17.

Modeling Cross-Domain Task Force. "Appendix 16: Overview of the Records Continuum Concept" [electronic version], in International Research on Permanent Authentic Records in Electronic Systems (InterPARES) 2: Experiential, Interactive and Dynamic Records, Luciana Duranti and Randy Preston, eds. (Padova, Italy: Associazione Nazionale Archivistica Italiana, 2008). www.interpares.org/display _file.cfm?doc=ip2_book_appendix_16.pdf.

Molteni, Megan. "Harvey Evacuees Leave Their Belongings—and Health Records Behind." *Wired.* September 1, 2017. https://www.wired.com/story/harvey-evacuees-leave-their-belongings-and-health -records-behind/.

MoReq. *MoReq2010.* Accessed September 1, 2017. www.MoReq.info/.

Munro, Dan. "U.S. Healthcare Ranked Dead Last Compared to 10 Other Countries." *Forbes/Pharma & Healthcare.* June 16, 2014. https://www.forbes.com/sites/danmunro/2014/06/16/u-s-healthcare -ranked-dead-last-compared-to-10-other-countries/#89ab65a576fd.

Murray, Athol L. "The Lord Clerk Register." *The Scottish Historical Review* 53, no. 156. Edinburgh, Scotland: Edinburgh University Press. October 1974. www.jstor.org/stable/25529087.

NAGARA. https://www.thecompleteuniversityguide.co.uk/courses/details/10379302.

Nasdaq. "KO Company Financials." Accessed January 10, 2018. www.nasdaq.com/symbol/ko/financials?query=balance-sheet.

The National Archives of the United Kingdom. "Digitization at the National Archives." August 2016. http://nationalarchives.gov.uk/documents/information-management/digitisation-at-the-national-archives.pdf.

——. "Information is a Valued Asset." Accessed January 12, 2018. www.nationalarchives.gov.uk/information-management/manage-information/planning/information-principles/information-valued-asset/.

——. "What is an Information Asset? "Accessed January 8, 2018. www.nationalarchives.gov.uk/documents/information-management/information-assets-factsheet.pdf.

National Archives of Australia. "Cloud Computing and Information Management." Accessed December 23, 2017. www.naa.gov.au/information-management/managing-information-and-records/storing/cloud/index.aspx.

——. "Digital Preservation Software Platform (DPSP)." 2013. Accessed June 21, 2017. http://dpsp.sourceforge.net/.

——. "Digital Records," National Archives of Australia. Accessed September 27, 2017. www.naa.gov.au/information-management/digital-transition-and-digital-continuity/digital-transition-policy/digital-transition/index.aspx.

——. "Everyone Working for Government." National Archives of Australia. Accessed September 2, 2017. www.naa.gov.au/information-management/getting-started/for-everyone-who-works-for-government/index.aspx.

——. "SODA: Newly Scanned Records from the Archives." Accessed June 21, 2017. http://soda.naa.gov.au/.

National Archives and Records Administration (NARA). "Appraisal Policy of the National Archives and Records Administration." 2007. https://www.archives.gov/records-mgmt/publications/appraisal-policy.pdf.

——. "Archival Formats." Accessed June 12, 2017. https://www.archives.gov/preservation/formats#audio-video-motion-pictures.

——. "Certificate of Federal Records Management Training." Accessed January 1, 2018. https://www.archives.gov/records-mgmt/training/certification.html.

——. "Context for Electronic Records Management (ERM)," Records Managers, last reviewed May 10, 2017. www.archives.gov/records-mgmt/initiatives/context-for-erm.html.

——. "Draft National Archives Strategic Plan." Accessed December 20, 2017. https://www.archives.gov/about/plans-reports/strategic-plan/draft-strategic-plan.

——. "Fast Track Products." Accessed September 1, 2017. www.archives.gov/records-mgmt/policy/prod6a.html.

——. "Federal Agency Records Management 2016 Annual Report." revised October 2, 2017. https://www.archives.gov/files/records-mgmt/resources/2016-federal-agency-records-management-annual-report.pdf.

——. Freedom of Information Act (FOIA) (5 USC § 552), last reviewed February 10, 2017. Accessed December 23, 2017. www.archives.gov/about/laws/foia.html.

——. "General Records Schedule 5.2." Accessed December 24, 2017. https://www.archives.gov/files/records-mgmt/grs/grs05-2.pdf.

——. "NARA Bulletin 2010-03: Flexible Scheduling." Records Managers, May 3, 2010. https://www.archives.gov/records-mgmt/bulletins/2010/2010-03.html.

——. "NARA Bulletin 2011-02: Guidance on Managing Records in Web 2.0/Social Media Platforms." Records Managers. October 20, 2010. www.archives.gov/records-mgmt/bulletins/2011/2011-02.html.

_____. "NARA Bulletin 2014-02."

_____. NARA Learning Center. Accessed January 1, 2018. https://nara.csod.com/LMS/BrowseTraining/BrowseTraining.aspx?tab_page_id=-6#f=1&s=588&o=1.

_____. Presidential Libraries: Archived Presidential White House Websites. Last reviewed January 18, 2017. https://www.archives.gov/presidential-libraries/archived-websites.

_____. "Records Management Self-Assessment Report 2009." Accessed December 19, 2017. www.archives.gov/records-mgmt/resources/self-assessment.html.

_____. "Records Management Training." Accessed January 1, 2018. www.archives.gov/records-mgmt/.

_____. "Social Media Strategy," page last reviewed December 21, 2016. https://www.archives.gov/social-media/strategies.

National Fire Protection Association (NFPA). *NFPA 1600: Standard on Disaster/Emergency Management and Business Continuity/Continuity of Operations Programs.* Quincy, MA: NFPA, 2016.

_____. *NFPA 75: Standard for the Fire Protection of Information Technology Equipment,* 2017 ed., (Quincy, MA: NFPA, 2017). http://catalog.nfpa.org/NFPA-75-Standard-for-the-Fire-Protection-of-Information-Technology-Equipment-P1200.aspx?icid=D538.

_____. *NFPA 232: Standard for the Protection of Records,* 2017 ed. Quincy, MA: NFPA, 2017. www.nfpa.org/codes-and-standards/all-codes-and-standards/list-of-codes-and-standards/detail?code=232.

National Records of Scotland. *Scotland's People.* Accessed June 23, 2017. https://www.scotlandspeople.gov.uk/.

Natividad, Angela. "Microsoft Calls E-Discovery, Records Management Inseparable Halves." *CMS Wire.* April 30, 2017. https://www.cmswire.com/cms/records-management/microsoft-calls-ediscovery-records-management-inseparable-halves-001238.php.

Neal, James G. "Preserving the Born-Digital Record." *American Libraries.* Accessed June 12, 2017. https://americanlibrariesmagazine.org/2015/05/28/preserving-the-born-digital-record/.

Nelson, Scott. "Looking for a Nail to Hit with my Blockchain Hammer: A Q&A with Adventium Blockchain Expert T.D. Smith." *CIO.* 2017. https://www.cio.com/article/3236559/data-protection/looking-for-nails-to-hit-with-my-blockchain-hammer.html.

New York State Archives. "Administration of Inactive Records, New York State Archives Technical Information Series 49, 1996. www.archives.nysed.gov/a/records/mr_pub49_accessible.html#introduction.

_____. "Historical Records Theft: Strategies for Prevention and Response." Accessed May 22, 2017. www.archives.nysed.gov/records/security.

_____. "Records Advisory: Preliminary Guidance on Social Media," Managing Records. Last modified May 24, 2010. www.archives.nysed.gov/records/mr_social_media.shtml.

Newman, Lily Hay. "Verizon—Yes, Verizon—Just Stood Up for Your Privacy." *Wired.* Accessed January 13, 2018. https://www.wired.com/story/verizon-privacy-location-data-fourth-amendment/.

Ng, Yvonne, Nan Rubin, and Kara Van Malssen. "Strategies for Sustainable Preservation of Born Digital Public Television." 2010. Accessed June 13, 2017. www.thirteen.org/ptvdigitalarchive/files/2009/10/PDPTV_SustainabilityStrategies.pdf.

NIST. "The NIST Definition of Cloud Computing." September 2011. Accessed August 13, 2017. http://nvlpubs.nist.gov/nistpubs/Legacy/SP/nistspecialpublication800-145.pdf.

Obama, Barack. "Freedom of Information Act." Memorandum for the Heads of Executive Departments and Agencies. WhiteHouse.gov. Accessed December 23, 2017. https://www.sec.gov/foia/president-memo-foia-nov2009.pdf.

_____. "Presidential Memorandum—Managing Government Records," The White House, November 28, 2011. www.whitehouse.gov/the-press-office/2011/11/28/presidential-memorandum-managing-government-records.

OFB-EZ—Business Continuity Planning. Insurance Institute for Business and Home Safety. Accessed December 3, 2017. http://disastersafety.org/ibhs-business-protection/ofb-ez-business-continuity/.

Oh, Justin. "Vodcast Brings the Twitch Community Experience to Uploads." May 31, 2017. https://blog.twitch.tv/vodcast-brings-the-twitch-community-experience-to-uploads-54098498715.

Okada, Hitoshi, Yamasaki Shigeichiro, and Vanessa Bracamonte. "Proposed Classification of Blockchains Based on Authority and Incentive Dimensions." *IEEE 19th International Conference on Advanced Communication Technology.*

"OpenText Extended ECM for Salesforce." Accessed October 22, 2017. https://www.opentext.com/what-we-do/products/opentext-suite-for-salesforce/opentext-extended-ecm-for-salesforce.

Oxford Dictionaries Online. https://en.oxforddictionaries.com.

Palmquist, Michael E., Kathleen M. Carley, and Thomas A. Dale. "Applications of Computer-Aided Text Analysis: Analyzing Literary and Nonliterary Texts." In *Text Analysis for the Social Sciences: Methods for Drawing Statistical Inferences from Texts and Transcripts,* ed. Carl W. Roberts. Mahwah, NJ: Lawrence Erlbaum Associates, 1997.

Panetta, Casey. "5 Trends in Cybersecurity for 2017 and 2018." Gartner. June 14, 2017. https://www.gartner.com/smarterwithgartner/5-trends-in-cybersecurity-for-2017-and-2018/.

Parker, Luke. "Brazil Pilots Bitcoin Solution for Real Estate Registration." 2017. *Brave Newcoin.* April 9. https://bravenewcoin.com/news/brazil-pilots-bitcoin-solution-for-real-estate-registration/.

PC Encyclopedia. Accessed August 13, 2017. https://www.pcmag.com/encyclopedia/term/54834/word-processing-machine.

PCI Forensic Investigators (PFIs) Database. https://www.pcisecuritystandards.org/assessors_and_solutions/pci_forensic_investigator.

Pearce-Moses, Richard. *A Glossary of Archival and Records Terminology.* Society of American Archivists. www2.archivists.org/glossary/terms/i/inactive-records.

Peter, Ian. "The History of Email." *Net History.* Accessed August 13, 2017. www.nethistory.info/History%20Of%20the%20Internet/email.html.

Peters, Isabella. *Folksonomies: Indexing and Retrieval in Web 2.0.* Berlin: Walter de Gruyter GmbH, 2009.

Peters, Sarah. "Survey: When Leaving Company, Most Insiders Take Data They Created," *Information Week,* December 23, 2015. https://www.darkreading.com/vulnerabilities—-threats/survey-when-leaving-company-most-insiders-take-data-they-created/d/d-id/1323677.

Pew Research Center. "Social Media Fact Sheet." Accessed July 9, 2017. www.pewinternet.org/fact-sheet/social-media/.

Phys.org. "Researchers Find a Chemical Solution to Shrink Digital Data Storage." Accessed June 26, 2017. https://phys.org/news/2017-06-chemical-solution-digital-storage.html.

Pinterest. "Success Stories." Accessed August 13, 2017. https://business.pinterest.com/en/success-stories.

PREMIS Editorial Committee. PREMIS Data Dictionary for Preservation Metadata, Version 3, *Library of Congress.* June 18, 2016. www.loc.gov/standards/premis/index.html.

PRISM International, "Demand the Best." Accessed December 28, 2017. www.prismintl.org/Buy-From-a-PRISM-Member/Free-Resources/demand-the-best.html.

PRNewswire. "George Kaiser Family Foundation to Bring Woody Guthrie Archives to Oklahoma." December 28, 2011. www.prnewswire.com/news-releases/george-kaiser-family-foundation-to-bring-woody-guthrie-archives-to-oklahoma-136316763.html.

PTAB—Primary Trustworthy Digital Repository Authorization Body Ltd. "PTAB First in the World to Be Accredited to Perform ISO 16363 Audit and Certification." 2017. Accessed July 2, 2017. www.iso16363.org/.

Public Record Office of Victoria, State of Victoria, Guideline: Records Management Strategy, Version Number 2.0. July 19, 2015. https://www.prov.vic.gov.au/sites/default/files/2017-01/PROS1010-G5-v2.0.pdf.

Pure Point International. "Security in a Changed World: Cybersecurity Officially Meets Physical Security in the NY DFS Regulation." http://the-purepoint.com/security-in-a-changed-world-cybersecurity -officially-meets-physical-security-in-the-ny-dfs-regulation/.

Radicati Group, Inc. "Email Statistics Report, 2017–2021." London, United Kingdom. Accessed August 13, 2017. www.radicati.com/wp/wp-content/uploads/2017/01/Email-Statistics-Report-2017-2021 -Executive-Summary.pdf.

Raheem, Faufu Oluwatoyin. "Human Workflow Task for ONE-Admin of Mediator for the Interaction of Internet Protocol Network and Transport Network Management System." *The IUP Journal of Knowledge Management* 14 no. 3., 23–43.

Rainie, Lee, and Shiva Maniam. "Americans Feel the Tensions between Privacy and Security Concerns." Pew Research Center. February 19, 2016. Accessed January 13, 2018. www.pewresearch.org/ fact-tank/2016/02/19/americans-feel-the-tensions-between-privacy-and-security-concerns/.

Randolph C. Watson Library, Kilgore College, "Library of Congress vs. Dewey Decimal." Accessed September 8, 2017. http://library.kilgore.edu/library/lc_dewey.htm.

Ravanbakhsh, Arian. "Records Management of Social Media and Electronic Records." *The National Archives Records Express.* (Blog). January 27, 2017. https://records-express.blogs.archives.gov/2017/01/27/ records-management-of-social-media-and-electronic-records/.

RecordLion. "Records Management Software." 2017. Accessed September 14, 2017. www.recordlion.com/ solutions/objective/records-management/.

"Register House: The Adams Building." *The Scottish Historical Review* 53, no. 156, 117. Edinburgh, Scotland: Edinburgh University Press, October 1974. www.jstor.org/stable/25529087.

Reinsel, David, John Gantz, and John Rydning. "Data Age 2025: The Evolution of Data to Life-Critical." *IDC White Paper.* April 2017. www.idc.com.

Reisch, Marc S. "U.S. Charges DuPont Employee with Trade Secrets Theft." *C&EN.* April 17, 2017. https://cen.acs.org/articles/95/i16/US-charges-DuPont-employee-trade-secrets-theft.html.

Research Libraries Group (RLG), "Trusted Digital Repositories: Attributes and Responsibilities, An RLG-OCLC Report, May 2002. www.oclc.org/programs/ourwork/past/trustedrep/repositories.pdf.

Rhys, Dipshan. "FRCP Amendments Dominate 2016 Federal E-Discovery Cases, Report Finds." Corporate Counsel. December 14, 2016. https://www.law.com/insidecounsel/2016/12/14/frcp-amendments -dominate-2016-federal-e-discovery/.

Robek, Mary F., Gerald F. Brown, and David O. Stephens, *Information and Records Management: Document-Based Information Systems.* New York: Glencoe/McGraw-Hill, 1996.

Roberts, C. W. "Content Analysis." In *International Encyclopedia of the Social and Behavioral Sciences.* Accessed September 8, 2017. http://dx.doi.org/10.1016/B0-08-043076-7/00707-5.

Roberts, Jeff John. "A Surprise in the Equifax Breach: Victims Likely to Get Paid." *Fortune.* October 10, 2017. http://fortune.com/2017/10/10/equifax-class-action/.

RSOE—Emergency and Disaster Information Service Alert Map. Accessed August 13, 2017. http://hisz.rsoe.hu/alertmap/index2.php.

Russell, Brandon. "Former Equifax CEO Blames Breach on a Single Person Who Failed to Deploy a Patch," *The Verge,* October 3, 2017. https://www.theverge.com/2017/10/3/16410806/equifax-ceo-blame -breach-patch-congress-testimony.

Russell Working. "6 Lessons from Dell's 'Social Media University.'" Accessed August 13, 2017. https://www.ragan.com/Main/Articles/6_lessons_from_Dells_Social_Media_University _52028.aspx.

SANS. "Information Security Resources." Accessed January 13, 2018. https://www.sans.org/information -security/.

Saffady, William. *Records and Information Management: Fundamentals of Professional Practic.e* 3rd Edition. Overland Park, KS: ARMA International, 2016.

San Antonio College, "Records Management (Tech Prep Program) A.A.S.," Archived Catalog. Accessed December 31, 2017. http://mysaccatalog.alamo.edu/preview_program.php?catoid=72&poid=3685 &returnto=1997.

Sarbanes-Oxley Act 2002, "A Guide to the Sarbanes-Oxley Act." Accessed January 5, 2018. www.soxlaw.com/.

Schulman, Kori. "The Digital Transition: How the Presidential Transition Works in the Social Media Age." *The White House* (Blog). October 23, 2016. https://obamawhitehouse.archives.gov/blog/2016/10/31/ digital-transition-how-presidential-transition-works-social-media-age.

SearchCIO. "Sarbanes-Oxley Act (SOX)." Accessed September 1, 2017. http://searchcio.tech target.com/ definition/Sarbanes-Oxley-Act.

SearchDataManagement. "Business Intelligence (BI)." Accessed September 27, 2017. http://searchdatamanagement.techtarget.com/definition/business-intelligence.

SearchStorage. "Information Life Cycle Management." Last modified September 2005. http://search storage.techtarget.com/definition/information-life-cycle-management.

SearchStorage.co.UK, U.K. Data Protection Act 1998 (DPA 1998). Last modified January 2008. http://searchstorage.techtarget.co.uk/definition/Data-Protection-Act-1998.

Securities and Exchange Commission. (SEC). Commission file number 1-6961, Gannett Co., Inc. Accessed January 10, 2018. https://www.sec.gov/Archives/edgar/data/39899/000003989915000006/ gci-20141228x10k.htm.

_____. "SEC Adopts Rules on Retention of Records Relevant to Audits and Reviews." Accessed September 14, 2017. https://www.sec.gov/news/press/2003-11.htm.

Sedona Conference. "The Sedona Conference Commentary on Proportionality in Electronic Discovery," May 2017. *The Sedona Conference Journal* 18, 141-76.

Shakespeare, William. *The Tempest.* In the Complete Pelican Shakespeare, ed. Alfred Harbage New York: Penguin Group, 1969.

Sharpe, Reginald R. D.C.L., editor. *Calendar of Letter Books Preserved Among the Archives of the Corporation of the City of London, Introduction.* [ebook] London: John Edward Francis, BreaiM's Buildings, E.C., 1912. www.archive.org/details/cu31924103071134.

Shegda, Karen M., and Gavin Tay. "Critical Capabilities for Enterprise Content Management." *Gartner Report.* November 29, 2016. www.project-consult.de/files/Gartner_ECM_Critical_Capabilities _2017_Jan2017.pdf.

Shell, Adam. "Wall Street Traders Mine Tweets to Gain a Trading Edge." *USA Today.* May 4, 2011. www.usatoday.com/money/perfi/stocks/2011-05-03-wall-street-traders-mine-tweets_n.htm.

Shepardson, David. "Trump Signs Repeal of U.S. Broadband Privacy Rules." Reuters. April 2017. https://www.reuters.com/article/us-usa-internet-trump/trump-signs-repeal-of-u-s-broadband -privacy-rules-idUSKBN1752PR.

Singh, Sakshi. "Uber Business Model—How Does Uber Make Money?" *Feeddough.com.* July 19, 2017. https://www.feedough.com/uber-business-model/.

Skroupa, Christopher P. "How Intangible Assets Are Affecting Company Value in the Stock Market." *Forbes.* November 1, 2017. https://www.forbes.com/sites/christopherskroupa/2017/11/01/how-intangible -assets-are-affecting-company-value-in-the-stock-market/#33ba50062b8e.

Smarsh. "Point West Credit Union Uses Smarsh Web Archiving for Compliance Peace of Mind." Accessed October 20, 2017. www.smarsh.com/case-studies/point-west-credit-union.

SmartDraw. (n. d.). "Business Process Mapping." Accessed September 27, 2017. https://www.smartdraw .com/business-process-mapping/.

_____. "Easy and Powerful Business Process Management Software." Accessed August 13, 2017. https://www.smartdraw.com/business-process-mapping/business-process-management-software .htm?id=62200.

Smith, Craig. "42 Amazing Wordpress Statistics and Facts." April 2017. http://expandedramblings.com/index.php/wordpress-statistics/.

Society of American Archivists. "Guidelines for a Graduate Program in Archival Studies." 2016. Accessed May 22, 2017. www2.archivists.org/prof-education/graduate/gpas.

Solomon, Howard. "Eight Canada Revenue Staffers Fired This Year for Snooping through Records: CBC." *IT World Canada,* December 21, 2016. https://www.itworldcanada.com/article/eight-canada-revenue-staffers-fired-this-year-for-snooping-through-records-cbc/389441.

SoundTransit. (2016, December 1). "Internal Audit Report: Records Management Program," Report Number 2016-5. Accessed December 21, 2017. https://www.soundtransit.org/sites/default/files/Internal%20Audit%20Update-2016%20Records%20Management%20Program.pdf.

Special Council. "ESI Data Mapping Basics for eDiscovery," D4, April 5, 2017. http://d4discovery.com/discover-more/esi-data-mapping-basics-for-ediscovery#sthash.CcCrZ7in.dpbs.

Spivack, Nova. "AI, BI, and the Necessity of Automating the Analyst—It's Time to Automate the Analyst." September 8, 2016. www.novaspivack.com/science/ai-bi-and-the-necessity-of-automating-the-analyst.

Stafford, Jan. "Lessons Learned from 9-11: Disaster Recovery Dos and Don'ts," *TechTarget,* December 5, 2001. http://searchwindowsserver.techtarget.com/news/784938/Lessons-learned-from-9-11-Disaster-recovery-dos-and-donts.

The State Records Authority of New South Wales. "Effectively Manage the Migration of Your Digital Records (Guideline 22)." Revised February 2015. https://www.records.nsw.gov.au/recordkeeping/advice/effectively-manage-digital-records-migration.

Statica. "Cumulative Total Number of Tumblr Blogs from May 2011 to July 2017." Accessed August 13, 2017. https://www.statista.com/statistics/256235/total-cumulative-number-of-tumblr-blogs/.

Statista. "Most Popular Mobile Messaging Apps Worldwide as of January 2017, based on number of monthly active users (in millions)." Accessed August 13, 2017. https://www.statista.com/statistics/258749/most-popular-global-mobile-messenger-apps/.

Statistics Canada. "Geographic Classifications (SGC) 2016—Volume I, The Classification." Last modified May 16, 2016. www.statcan.gc.ca/eng/subjects/standard/sgc/2016/index.

Stevens, Gina Marie. Hurricane Katrina: HIPAA Privacy and Electronic Health Records of Evacuees, Congressional Research Service (CRS) Report for Congress, RS22310, updated January 23, 2007, 1. http://library.ahima.org/xpedio/groups/public/documents/government/bok1_034961.pdf.

Sweet, Ken. "Getting Up to Speed on the Equifax Data Breach Scandal." *ABC News.* September 11, 2017. http://abcnews.go.com/Technology/wireStory/speed-equifax-data-breach-scandal-49771561.

Symantec. "6 Steps to Prevent a Data Breach." 2009. Accessed January 17, 2018. http://eval.symantec.com/mktginfo/enterprise/other_resources/b-6-steps-prevent-data-reach_20049431-1.en-us.pdf.

System and Method for Providing Dynamic Supply Positioning for On-Demand Services, US 9066206 B2. Accessed January 12, 2018. https://www.google.com/patents/US9066206.

Szabo, Nick. "The Idea of Smart Contracts." 1997. www.fon.hum.uva.nl/rob/Courses/InformationInSpeech/CDROM/Literature/LOTwintersch0012006/szabo.best.vwh.net/idea.html.

Tamturk, Venus. "Hyland Completes Acquisition of Lexmark's Perceptive Business." CMS Connected. July 12, 2017. www.cms-connected.com/News-Archive/July-2017/Hyland-Completes-Acquisition-of-Lexmark-s-Enterprise-Content-Management-Unit-Perceptive.

Tandon, Kamakshi. "In Light of Hack into WADA Database, Venus Williams Defends Her Integrity." *Tennis.* September 15, 2016. www.tennis.com/pro-game/2016/09/venus-williams-wada-russian-hackers-itf-tues-serena-williams-rio-olympics/61109/.

Tapscott, Don. "Macrowikinomics: New Solutions for a Connected Planet." Accessed January 27, 2013. http://dontapscott.com/books/macrowikinomics/.

Taylor, Christine. "Structured vs. Unstructured Data." *Datamation.* August 3, 2017. www.datamation.com/big-data/structured-vs-unstructured-data.html.

Taylor, Kate. "Sonic Confirmed That 5 Million Customers May Have Had Their Credit-Card Info Stolen in Data Breach." *Business Insider.* September 27, 2017. www.businessinsider.com/report-sonic-security-breach-could-affect-millions-2017-9.

TechCrunch. "Instagram Stories Is Stealing Snapchat Users." January 30, 2017. https://techcrunch.com/2017/01/30/attack-of-the-clone/.

TechTarget. "Backup as a Service." http://searchdatabackup.techtarget.com/definition/backup-as-a-service-BaaS.

Texas Department of State Health Services. "State of Texas Records Retention Schedule." May 1, 2016. www.dshs.state.tx.us/Records/MentalHealthHospitals.pdf.

Thibodeau, K. "Preservation as a Service for Trust (PaaST)." (unpublished presentation). June 2017. InterPARES Trust.

Thomas, Pierre, and Mike Levine. "How the FBI Cracked the iPhone Encryption and Averted a Legal Showdown with Apple. *ABC News.* March 29, 2016. http://abcnews.go.com/US/fbi-cracked-iphone-encryption-averted-legal-showdown-apple/story?id=38014184.

Thomson Reuters. "Compliance Learning Course Catalog." Accessed January 1, 2018. https://risk.thomsonreuters.com/en/compliance-training-courses.html.

Treasury Inspector General for Tax Administration. "Additional Efforts Are Needed to Ensure the Enterprise E-Mail Records Management Solution Meets All Requirements Before Deployment, Ref. No. 2017-20-039." August 7, 2017. https://www.treasury.gov/tigta/auditreports/2017reports/201720039fr.pdf.

Twitter. "About." Accessed August 13, 2017. https://about.twitter.com/en_us/company.html.

Twitter Counter. "Twitter Top 100 Most Followers." Accessed August 13, 2017. https://twittercounter.com/pages/100.

US Department of Education. Family Educational Rights and Privacy Act (FERPA). Accessed December 21, 2017. www2.ed.gov/policy/gen/guid/fpco/ferpa/index.html.

_____. "Protecting Student Privacy by Audience: Postsecondary School Officials." Accessed December 21, 2017. https://studentprivacy.ed.gov/audience/school-officials-post-secondary.

US Department of the Interior, "What is a Records Series?" Records Management Questions. Accessed September 14, 2017. https://www.doi.gov/ocio/policy-mgmt-support/information-and-records-management/records-management-questions.

US Department of Justice, Office of Privacy and Civil Liberties. E-Government Act of 2002. Accessed January 16, 2018. https://www.justice.gov/opcl/e-government-act-2002.

_____. Privacy Act of 1974. Accessed January 16, 2018. https://www.justice.gov/opcl/privacy-act-1974.

US Department of Labor, Bureau of Labor Statistics. *Occupational Outlook Handbook,* Administrative Services Managers. Accessed December 31, 2017. https://www.bls.gov/ooh/management/administrative-services-managers.htm.

US Government Printing Office. Health Insurance Portability and Accountability Act of 1996, H.R. 104-191, 104th Cong. (1996). Accessed September 1, 2017. www.gpo.gov/fdsys/pkg/PLAW-104publ191/content-detail.html.

US Office of Personnel Management. Position Classification Flysheet for Records and Information Management Series, 0308. March 2015. https://www.opm.gov/policy-data-oversight/classification-qualifications/classifying-general-schedule-positions/standards/0300/gs0308.pdf UPS, "Defining Logistics, How it Relates to Your Supply Chain—And Why It's Crucial for Your Company." Accessed October 7, 2017. https://www.ups.com/us/en/services/resource-center/Logistics-Definition.page.

University of Alabama. "Mission/Vision Statement." Procurement Services. Accessed September 23, 2017. www.missiontexas.us/city-departments/purchasing-department.

University of California. "Records Disposition Schedules Manual." Accessed September 14, 2017. www.ucop.edu/recordsretention/.

University of Pennsylvania, University Archives and Records Center, "University of Pennsylvania Records Retention Schedule: Academic/Student Records," University Records Center, last modified June 17, 2011. www.archives.upenn.edu/urc/recrdret/studtacad.html.

University of Pittsburgh, School of Computing and Information. "Information Culture and Data Stewardship." Accessed December 31, 2017. www.icds.pitt.edu/degree-programs/master-of-library -and-information-science-mlis/archives-and-information-science-pathway/.

Van Artsdalen, Amy. "How to Develop a Vital Records Program Project Plan." November/December 2017. *Information Management* 51 no. 6, 33–37.

Vancouver Community College, Office Administrative Certificate—Records Management Skills. Accessed December 31, 2017. www.vcc.ca/programscourses/program-areas/business/office-administration -certificate—-records-management-skills/.

Vasilinda, Michael. Capital News Service. March 16, 2017. https://policerecordsmanagement.com/2017/03/ tallahassee-fl-wctv-house-committee-voted-17-0-allow-police-officers-view-footage-body-cameras -submitting-reports-responding-complaints/.

Vednere, Ganesh. "The Quest for eDiscovery: Creating a Data Map." *Infonomics* 23, no. 6, 28–33.

"Vital Records." Records Management Services, University of Washington. Accessed December 3, 2017. https://finance.uw.edu/recmgt/vitalrecords.

Vittani, Giovanni. "La formazione dell'archivista." Annuario del R. Archivio di Stato di Milano 1913, re-printed in Giovanni Vittani, *Scritti di diplomatica e archivistica* (Milano: Cisalpino-Goliardica, 1974), 154.

W3C, "W3C Semantic Web Frequently Asked Questions." Accessed August 13, 2017. www.w3.org/RDF/FAQ.

Warland, Andrew. "How Office 365 Challenges Traditional Records Management Practices." Blog post, September 27, 2016. https://andrewwarland.wordpress.com/2016/09/27/how-office-365-challenges -traditional-records-management-practices/.

Warren, Samuel D., and Louis D. Brandeis. "The Right to Privacy," *Harvard Law Review* 4 no. 5. December 15, 1890. http://groups.csail.mit.edu/mac/classes/6.805/articles/privacy/Privacy_brand_warr2.htm.

Washington State Archives. "Digital Archives Background." Accessed May 22, 2017. www.digitalarchives .wa.gov/StaticContent/background.

WatchGuard. "Three Best Practice Tips to Preventing Ransomware Attacks," 2017. Accessed January 19, 2018. https://www.cdwg.com/content/dam/CDW/resources/brands/watchguard/Ransomware.pdf.

Waugh, Dorothy, Elizabeth Russey Roke, and Erica Farr. "Flexible Processing and Diverse Collections: A Tiered Approach to Born Digital Archives." *Archives and Records* 37, no.1, 3–19, 2016.

Webopedia. www.webopedia.com/TERM/B/big_data.html.

Weiss, Debra Cassens. "Lawyer's e-Discovery Error Led to Release of Confidential Info on Thousands of Wells Fargo Clients." *ABA Journal*. July 27, 2017. www.abajournal.com/news/article/lawyers_e _discovery_error_led_to_release_of_confidential_wells_fargo_client.

Western Cape Government, Archives: Records Management Policy of WC Governmental Bodies 2017. https://www.westerncape.gov.za/general-publication/archives-records-management-policy-wc -governmental-bodies-2017.

Western Washington University. "Archives and Records Management Certificate Program." Accessed December 31, 2017. https://catalog.wwu.edu/preview_program. php?catoid=7&poid=2787&returnto=1031

"What is Google Vault?" Accessed December 21, 2017. https://support.google.com/vault/ answer/2462365?hl=en.

Whatman, Patrick. "Apple Event: What We Learned from 500,000+ Social Mentions. September 13, 2017. www.business2community.com/mobile-apps/apple-event-learned-500000-social-mentions -01917637#0iBSSd885887Wih0.97.

WhiteHouse.gov. "Privacy Policy." Accessed October 20, 2017. https://www.whitehouse.gov/privacy#section-340861.

Whiting, Rick. "M-Files Adding AI Capabilities to Its Content Management System with Acquisition." August 29, 2017. www.crn.com/news/applications-os/300091296/m-files-adding-ai-capabilities-to-its-content-management-system-with-acquisition.htm.

Wong, Wayne. "Managing Your Way to Data Compliance with a Data Atlas." *Information Management.* (January/February 2012), 21–25.

Woodbridge, Michael. "The Death of ECM and Birth of Content Services." *Gartner Blog Network.* January 5, 2017. http://blogs.gartner.com/michael-woodbridge/the-death-of-ecm-and-birth-of-content-services/.

World Wide Web Consortium (W3C). "Semantic Web." Accessed September 24, 2017. https://www.w3.org/standards/semanticweb/.

YourDictionary. http://computer.yourdictionary.com/crowdsourcing.

Yu, Eileen. "Oracle Looks to Clear Air on Big Data." *ZDNet.* October 4, 2012. www.zdnet.com/oracle-looks-to-clear-air-on-big-data-7000005211/.

Yurieff, Kayla. "Amazon Patent Reveals Drone Delivery 'Beehives,'" June 23, 2017. http://money.cnn.com/2017/06/23/technology/amazon-drone-beehives/index.html.

Zaino, Jennifer. "2017 Trends for Semantic Web and Semantic Technologies," DATAVERSITY. November 29, 2016. www.dataversity.net/2017-predictions-semantic-web-semantic-technologies.

ABOUT THE AUTHOR
AND CONTRIBUTORS

Patricia C. Franks, PhD, CA, CRM, IGP, FAI, is professor in the School of Information at San José State University, where she serves as coordinator of the Master of Archives and Records Administration (MARA) degree program. She develops and teaches courses related to archives, records management, digital preservation, and information governance. She is an active member of ARMA International and was inducted into the ARMA Company of Fellows in 2014 for her many contributions, which included serving as Consensus Group Leader for the ANSI/ARMA standard *Implications of Web-Based Collaborative Technologies*. Dr. Franks has written and presented widely on the topics of social media, cloud computing, knowledge management, digital preservation and information governance. She was co-editor of the *Encyclopedia of Archival Science* published in 2015. Her current projects include editing the *International Directory of National Archives* to be published 2018 and co-editing the *Encyclopedia of Archival Writers (1500–2015)* to be released in 2019.

■■■

Stephen Aaronson, Director and Head of IT Legal, Shire Pharmaceuticals

Stephen Aaronson leads a corporate IT function that has partnered with Legal to deliver a multi-year RIM program technology strategy. Stephen has a diverse background in leadership, management, solution delivery, and consulting. In Stephen's eighteen-year career in IT within the pharmaceutical industry, he spent significant amounts of time working on challenges related to IG and ESI. Stephen holds a BS from Temple University and several certifications in IT management-related disciplines.

Paradigm: The Art and Science of ERMS Deployment, co-author

Lori Ashley, Principal Consultant, Tournesol Consulting, LLC

Lori Ashley is an advisor and educator dedicated to helping public and private sector organizations improve their record management and digital preservation practices. An experienced business strategist, she developed numerous cross-functional approaches to jump-start and sustain collaboration among stakeholders who share accountability for effective and efficient lifecycle controls over valued records and information assets. Lori co-developed the Digital Preservation Capability Maturity Model (DPCMM) with Dr. Charles Dollar, and manages the companion www.DigitalOK.org self-assessment survey site.

Paradigm: Use Case—eArchive for Pharmaceutical Pre-Clinical Research Study Information, co-author

Barclay T. Blair, Founder and Executive Director, Information Governance Institute

Barclay T. Blair is an advisor to Fortune 500 companies, technology providers, and government institutions across the globe, and is a speaker, author, and internationally recognized authority on Information Governance. Barclay has led several high-profile consulting engagements at the world's leading institutions to help them globally transform the way they manage information. He is the president and founder of the advisory firm ViaLumina and Executive Director and Founder of the Information Governance Initiative, a think tank and community of information professionals.

Perspective: Information Governance: We Are Finally Asking the Right Questions

Diane K. Carlisle, Director of Professional Development, ARMA International

Diane K. Carlisle, IGP, CRM is the director of Professional Development for ARMA International. She provides direction for the development of ARMA's educational offerings, oversees the Information Governance Professional credentialing program, and represents the association in various professional venues. In addition, she works with executive leadership in executing ARMA International's strategic plans. Diane has over thirty years' experience in the areas of information governance strategy and policy development, litigation support and information governance.

Perspective: Perspectives on Information Governance and Managing Information Assets

Susan Cisco, Information Governance Subject Matter Expert and Educator

Susan Cisco has more than thirty years' experience in the RIM profession as a practitioner, educator, and consultant. Cisco's seminal work in the application of Big Bucket theory to the classification and retention of records has simplified ECM deployment strategies and optimized user adoption for organizations around the world. She holds a MLS degree and a PhD in Library and Information Science from the University of Texas at Austin, is a CRM, and is an ARMA Fellow.

Paradigm: Leveraging a New Retention Schedule to Launch an Information Governance Program

Charlene Cunniffe, Associate Director, Information and Records Management, Sanofi

Charlene Cunniffe, MS, CRM, CIP, IGP, is an experienced information and records management professional and project manager, with degrees from Harvard University and Simmons College, as well as years of experience in law, engineering, government, biotech/pharma, and academia. She is associate director, Governance and Operational Support in Information and Records Management, as well as a Lean Leader and Continuous Improvement Coach in Shared Business Services at Sanofi. Charlene facilitates transversal and departmental process improvement.

Paradigm: Introduction of Continuous Improvement in Records Management Programs and Processes Using Lean Practices.

Amber J. D'Ambrosio, Processing Archivist and Records Manager, Willamette University

Amber J. D'Ambrosio earned her Master of Science in Information Science in 2012 from the University at Albany to complement her Master of Arts in English Renaissance Literature. Since then she has filled a variety of roles, including information literacy librarian, special collections librarian, archivist, and records manager. Her role as digital archivist is incidental to her current position, and she continues to improve her knowledge and application of best practices to digital processing.

Paradigm: Archivematica to ArchivesDirect: A Practical Solution
for Limited Staff Resources

Lisa Daulby, Faculty, Master of Archives and Records Administration,
School of Information, San José State University

Dr. Lisa Daulby is a lecturer at the School of Information, San José State University. Lisa holds a PhD in Information Technology and is a Certified Records Manager (CRM) and Information Governance Professional (IGP). Lisa teaches on a variety of subjects, which include emerging technology trends and their effect on the management and governance of records and information.

Paradigm: Identifying, Assessing, and Controlling Records and Information Management Risks:
A Cross-Disciplinary Approach

Luciana Duranti, Professor, University of British Columbia

Luciana Duranti teaches archival science and diplomatics at the master's and doctoral levels. Her research focuses on the application of archival and diplomatics theories to the creation, management, use, and preservation of digital records. Among the research projects she has developed and directed are InterPARES (1998–2018), Records in The Cloud (2012–2016), Digital Records Forensics (2008–2011), and the Preservation of the Integrity of Electronic Records, known as the MAS project (1994–1997). She developed the discipline of archival diplomatics.

Paradigm: Graduate Archival Education—The Master of Archival Studies at the University of
British Columbia

Peg Eusch, University Records Officer, University of Wisconsin–Madison

Peg Eusch is a Certified Records Manager and the UW–Madison Records Officer. She has responsibility for managing and directing the UW–Madison Records Management Program. Peg has over thirty-five years of diverse records management experience in manufacturing, corporate, legal, and healthcare. She holds master's degree in Library and Information Science (MLIS) from University of Wisconsin–Milwaukee and received her professional certification as a Certified Records Manager from the Institute of Certified Records Managers in 2010.

Paradigm: University Records Management File Plans

Morgan King, Director and Head of Records and Information Management,
Shire Pharmaceuticals

Morgan is an innovative and results-oriented IG professional within the pharmaceutical industry. In partnership with IT, she is accountable for her organization's award-winning Electronic Records Management System. Morgan holds her master's in Archives and Records Administration from the School of Library and Information Science of San José State University and her master's in Psychology from Boston College. She serves on the Board of Directors for PRIMO (http://pharma-rim.org/) and chairs her organization's Information Governance Council.

Paradigm: The Art and Science of ERMS Deployment, co-author

Ilona Koti, Principal Consultant, ARK-IGC

Ilona Koti is a former diplomat and information governance subject matter expert. Her certifications include: Certified Records Manager, Certified Project Manager, Certified Document and Image Architect; she holds two master's from Syracuse University: Master of Library Science and Master of Science, Information Management. Ilona is a director for the Institute of Information Management Africa, a teaching fellow at the University of Dundee—Scotland, a past California Historical Records Advisory Board Director, and 2017–2018 president of ARMA International.

Paradigm: Integrating Information Governance into the Privacy and Security Landscape

Victoria L. Lemieux, Associate Professor, Archival Science,
The University of British Columbia

Victoria L. Lemieux, PhD, CISSP, is associate professor of Archival Science at the University of British Columbia. Her research focuses on risk to the availability of trustworthy records. She is the winner of a number of awards, including the 2015 Emmett Leahy Award and a 2016 Emerald Literati Award for her research on blockchain technology. She also leads the development of standardized terminology for the International Standards Organization's Technical Committee on Blockchain and Distributed Ledger Technologies.

Paradigm: Blockchain Technology and Recordkeeping

Lori Lindberg, Archivist, Consultant, Lecturer, Lori Lindberg, Archivist (private consultancy), San José State University School of Information

Lori Lindberg, MLIS, CA, is an archives consultant with numerous public and private clients. She has also taught courses in digital preservation, digital repositories and archival science for major universities, as well as lectures and workshops for professional organizations and associations. Lori is a participating member of both regional and national archives and records associations, most actively in the Society of American Archivists. Lori has been a panel presenter and moderator at meetings, conferences, and organizational gatherings.

Paradigm: Establishing the Jelly Belly Candy Company Archives: A Case Study of a Family-Owned Candy Company's History and Recordkeeping

Patricia M. Morris, President and Chief Process Consultant, eArchive Science, LLC

Patti Morris is a subject matter expert on records and information management with twenty-two years' experience at several global pharmaceutical companies. Her work has supported all areas of the business, with a focus on records and information to be archived in all formats (paper/electronic) generated during drug development. In her current consulting practice, Patti delivers solutions for managing business records in any format through their entire lifespan to clients in the United States and European Union.

Paradigm: Use Case–eArchive for Pharmaceutical Pre-Clinical Research Study Information, co-author

Helen Nelson, Head of Emergency Preparedness, Wirral University Teaching Hospital Foundation Trust

Helen has worked for more than twenty-five years in the United Kingdom's National Health Service, predominantly in risk management and more recently in emergency preparedness.

She is responsible for ensuring that the hospital complies with the NHS England "Emergency Preparedness, Resilience & Response" Framework. During the last couple of years, Helen has supported two major incidents resulting in live testing of their Major Incident plans. Helen has completed the Emergency Planning College/Cabinet Office Training-Civil Contingency Act/ Business Continuity.

Paradigm: Wirral University Teaching Hospital NHS Foundation Trust Utility Disruption

Robert F. Smallwood, Founding Partner IMERGE Consulting, Head of the Institute for Information Governance

Robert F. Smallwood, MBA, IGP is the world's leading IG author and trainer, with seven published books on information governance topics, including his latest, *Information Governance for Healthcare Professionals: A Practical Approach* (Taylor and Francis, 2018). He has over twenty-five years' experience in the information technology industry and holds an MBA from Loyola University of New Orleans.

Paradigm: The Information Governance Imperative in Healthcare

INDEX